D1368782

BEACHAM'S ENCYCLOPEDIA OF
POPULAR FICTION

Volume 14

GALE GROUP

Detroit
New York
San Francisco
London
Boston
Woodbridge, CT

Mark W. Scott, *Publisher, Literature Product*

Scot Peacock, *Managing Editor, Literature Product*

Katy Balcer, Sara Constantakis, Kristen A. Dorsch, Lisa Kumar, Marie Lazzari, Thomas McMahon, Colleen Tavor, *Editors*; Shayla Hawkins, Motoko Fujishiro Huthwaite, Arlene M. Johnson, Thomas Wiloch, *Associate Editors*; Alana Foster, Jennifer Kilian, Michelle Poole, Judith Pyko, *Assistant Editors*; Joshua Kondek, *Technical Training Specialist*

Susan M. Trosky, *Content Director*

Alan Hedblad, *Managing Editor*

Library of Congress Catalog Card Number 89–18048

ISBN 0–7876–5150–8
ISSN 1530–1028

Printed in the United States of America
10 9 8 7 6 5 4 3 2 1

INTRODUCTION

———————————◆———————————

Beacham's Encyclopedia of Popular Fiction is one of the few reference sources published that provides students, teachers, and general readers alike with signed critical analyses of works of popular literature. From its inception in 1986 as *Popular Fiction in America*, the series has been received by the reading public, students and teachers, librarians, professors of literature, critics, and some of the authors themselves with praise and appreciation for its essential premise: to explain rather than to judge. The current volume—Volume 14 of the Analyses series of the encyclopedia—continues with the practice of the preceding volumes in examining both the works of contemporary popular writers, such as Louise Erdrich, Dick Francis, and Toni Morrison, and "popular" classics from such authors as Sir Walter Scott, Jane Austen, and Ernest Hemingway.

In compiling *Beacham's Encyclopedia of Popular Fiction*, the editors have attempted to identify writers and works of fiction that readers have taken seriously, either by virtue of attracting a large audience or by the amount of critical attention they have received. We have cast no moral or even critical judgment about social redemption versus sensationalism. The underlying thesis of the series is that fiction that becomes enormously popular contains elements that touch on deep-rooted social attitudes, concerns, fears, or desires, and is often a barometer of social or psychological change. Fiction can be viewed as pieces of data that the perceptive investigator can use as clues to unravel social history, human psychology, and the imagination. Along the way, fiction incorporates history, mythology, theology, linguistics, science, law, and most intellectual pursuits of modern times. The writers here have observed and recorded voluminous social data that reveals much about American society.

Beacham's Encyclopedia of Popular Fiction is designed to serve several equally important functions. One is to record the history of popular fiction, and in that regard the initial twelve volumes provide only a skeleton for adding many more authors and works. The series includes authors and books that may never be read again except by students of the genre. Gene Stratton Porter, Booth Tarkington, Erskine Caldwell, and others were the most widely-read authors of their time—Porter's novels were made into twenty-seven motion pictures; Tarkington won two Pulitzer Prizes; and Caldwell had more copies of books in print in 1943 than any other author in the world. Today, if they are read at all, Stratton is relegated to the genre of "girls' fiction," Tarkington as creator of the bad boy Penrod, and Caldwell as a perverse painter of degenerate Southern poverty. But these writers, and many others who have fallen into obscurity, must be included in any serious review of American literature or society. Others, who have not been widely read for decades, may reappear as contemporary spokespersons. Who would have thought that three of Jane Austen's novels of manners would have been made into high profile, mega-budget films in the same year of 1996? The series also includes some writers, such as S. J. Perelman, Garrison Keillor, and Hunter S. Thompson, whose works are not strictly regarded as fiction but whose techniques have been widely influential in the development of the genre.

A second function of the *Encyclopedia of Popular Fiction* is to provide criticism for some popular novelists who have received no critical attention other than book reviews in the popular press. We were surprised by how many best-selling authors have been ignored by the critics, especially in the genres of science fiction and fantasy, but also with mainstream bestselling writers, such as Pat Conroy, Judith Krantz, and Scott Turow. For some of the writers included in the series, such as Sidney Sheldon, this is the only critical study of their work, while with others, such as Patricia Cornwell, it is the most extensive. Generally, though not by editorial design, the length of the articles reflects the current interest in the writer or the complexity of his/her work. Margaret Atwood, for example, receives in-depth analysis because her work is so diverse and rich, and because she is regarded by many readers and critics as one of the most important voices in contemporary literature.

A third function of the series is to recognize the importance and influence of other countries and cultures on our own. Although the first complete form of the modern novel appeared in England in the eighteenth century, the genre owes its roots to other European art forms. Quickly after the modern form of the novel was established in England, it spread to Europe where it was shaped to reflect the social and intellectual fabric of vastly different countries. By the turn of the twentieth century, American novelists were being increasingly influenced by the ideas coming from Europe, and the complexion of American fiction was altered because of them. Beginning with Henry James, William Dean Howells, Edith Wharton and their circles, extending through Virginia Woolf, Marcel Proust, James Joyce and their circles, and continuing through the American expatriates in Paris after World War I, American writers have reflected European concerns in their fiction. *Beacham's Encyclopedia of Popular Fiction* includes analyses of some of the influential European works, and will add more to the continuing series.

As the western hemisphere began to consolidate after 1950, it became clear to a few critics and scholars that the most innovative fiction was being written, but not exported, from Mexico and Latin America. Supported by grants during the affluent 1960s, academics began to translate and find publishers for some of the most exciting modern novelists, including Carlos Fuentes, Gabriel García Márquez, Julio Cortázar, and Jorge Luis Borges. Since the discovery of these writers, other Latin American novelists, such as Laura Esquivel, have received a wide American audience. While the Latin American novelists were experimenting with form, language, myth and cultural history, emerging Africans, such as Alan Paton and Chinua Achebe, wrote of the social horrors that resulted from one culture attempting to suppress another. The Latin American and African writers included in the series are but a beginning to the ones we will add in subsequent volumes.

A fourth function of *Beacham's Encyclopedia* is to provide a research mechanism for students who want to write about popular fiction. Increasingly, works of popular, contemporary writers, such as Toni Morrison, Amy Tan, and others, have found their way on to the English reading lists in high school classes and undergraduate programs. Also, students in language arts courses have more opportunity to read and write on popular works of their own choosing, including the more popular genres of science fiction, fantasy, mystery, and romance. Most writing topics for fiction are related to a writer's life, the ideas contained in the work, the historical or social climate in which the work was produced, the location and period of the story, or the literary form or techniques. The entries contained in *Beacham's Encyclopedia of Popular Fiction* are designed to support research and analysis of all of these points.

Finally, some notes about the organization and scope of this series. *Beacham's Encyclopedia of Popular Fiction* actually consists of two separate series. One series (Volumes 1–3) is labelled Biography and Resources and includes biographical and critical commentary on the life and works of specific authors. Each entry in the Biography and Resources volumes contains the following elements:

- Full name of the author, including birth and death dates (when appropriate)

- Chronological listing of Major Works of the author

- About the Author, which includes a brief biographical sketch of the author's life and career

- Publishing History, Critical Reception, Honors, and Popularity, which provides a survey of both popular and critical reception of the author's works and notes those works that won any major awards

- Resources, which includes a bibliography for further study that is divided into two sections—one listing biography, autobiography, interviews, and correspondence of the author, the other listing criticism, bibliographies, manuscripts, and reviews.

The second and more extensive series in *Beacham's Encyclopedia* is the Analyses set (Volumes 1–14, including the current volume). Entries in the Analyses volumes focus on individual works written by popular writers. It is here where the reader should turn for in-depth analyses and commentary on the leading novels and stories written by popular authors. Each entry in the Analyses volumes contains the following elements:

- Name of the literary work, genre (e.g., novel, short story, nonfiction, etc.), and year of first English-language publication

- Full name of the author

- Social Concerns, including discussion of the essential topics or issues that inform the plot and actions of the principal characters

- Themes, which identifies the central themes of the work and examines how the author develops those themes through various literary techniques, such as plot, character, language, and so on

- A section on Characters focuses on the behavior and motivations of the principal characters in the story and how these advance the themes and social concerns of the author

- Techniques, which provides insight into various literary devices—such as symbolism, foreshadowing, narrative point of view, and so on—that the author uses to create mood, define his or her characters, and build the story

- Literary Precedents attempts to place the work in the context of a specific literary tradition or school of writing

- Related Titles, which identifies and discusses similarities between the work and other titles by the same author

- Adaptations, when applicable, briefly discusses adaptations of the work into other media, such as film, theater, or audio recordings
- Ideas for Group Discussion is a unique feature that offers a series of essential questions about the work that readers can use to facilitate group discussion and students can use to develop topics for research papers; book clubs and readers' groups will find these questions invaluable for generating discussion and achieving a deeper appreciation of the author and his or her works

The current volume (Volume 14 in the Analyses series) also includes an appendix and two essential indexes. The Appendix of Titles Grouped by Social Concerns and Themes includes more than 500 standardized literary topics or themes and alphabetically lists the works treated in Volume 14 beneath the themes that are important to that work. The Appendix serves as a quick guide to the themes and topics covered in the volume and helps readers, especially teachers and students, locate works that deal substantially with certain social issues and literary themes. There is also a Cumulative Index to Authors with Analyzed Titles and a Cumulative Master Index in the volume. The former provides an alphabetical listing of the authors and titles covered in the series to date: beneath each author entry is a listing of all of his or her works treated in the encyclopedia. The Cumulative Master Index provides a straight alphabetical listing of all of the authors and individual works discussed in the series. Both indexes include the volume number and page reference where either the biographical entry—in the case of the Biography and Resources series—or the entry on an individual work—in the case of the Analyses series— can be found. Entries in bold type in the Master Index indicate the authors and/or works discussed in Volume 14.

The editors would like to thank our many contributors for their excellent work on this series; their insights and love of popular fiction have made the encyclopedia possible. We also want to thank the many librarians who have expressed such enthusiastic appreciation for the series, and for its companion series on young adult literature—*Beacham's Guide to Literature for Young Adults*. We welcome inquiries and suggestions from our readers. Write to Gale Group, Publisher of Literature Product, 27500 Drake Road, Farmington Hills, MI, 48331–3535.

CONTRIBUTORS

◆

Without the expertise and generosity of the hundreds of contributors to this series, the depth of criticism now available to readers would not have been possible. To all of our contributors, past, present, and future, we gratefully acknowledge your contributions.

Contributors whose analyses appear in this volume are:

Kara L. Andersen
Northeastern University

Samuel I. Bellman, Professor, Emeritus
California State Polytechnic University-Pomona

Scott Bunyan
University of Sussex

Rhonda Cawthorn
American Literature/Southern Literature, University

Colette Colligan
Queen's University, Canada

David Dougherty
Loyola College in Maryland

Brian Forsyth

Kelly Fuller
Claremont Graduate University

Jessica Horn
Pennsylvania State University

Theodore C. Humphrey
California State Polytechnic University-Pomona

Barbara Jaindl

Marlon Kuzmick
Cornell University

Martha Smith Lane

Andrew Macdonald

Gina Macdonald
Nicholls State University, Thibodaux, LA

Nancy McCabe
Presbyterian College

Grace Moore
University of Exeter

Heidi R. Moore
Northern Virginia Community College

Lisa K. Perdigao
Northeastern University

Julie Scanlon
University of Sheffield, England

Ann Barton Sciba
Wharton High School Library

David Slater
University of Minnesota

H. R. Stoneback
State University of New York at New Paltz

Peter Swirski
Comparative Literature, University of Alberta

Jack Turner
Wesley College, Dover,
Delaware

Harriett S. Williams
University of South Carolina

Jennifer Williams
University of Texas at Austin

CONTENTS

◆

ASHES TO ASHES

Novel

1999

Author: Tami Hoag

◆

◆ SOCIAL CONCERNS ◆

T ami Hoag begins to voice her novel's most explicit—though not necessarily most significant—social concern as early as the acknowledgments. By thanking a series of FBI agents, members of the CASKU (Child Abduction Serial Killer Unit), officers of various victim services groups, and, of course, members of the police department, Hoag signals the central importance of law enforcement for this crime fiction mystery in which a serial killer is preying upon prostitutes.

Hoag's research into the practices of the police and FBI have given her special insight into the problems faced by law enforcement officers. These problems include both those of a personal nature and those more strictly related to fighting crime.

The unwritten presumption of Hoag's novel is that the "cops" and FBI agents themselves (as opposed to their various superiors) are the only ones who really care about solving crimes, cleaning up the streets, and protecting civilians. Certain characters in the novel (Kovac, Quinn, Kate Conlan) represent "the good ones," to use Kate's own words: "They did a hard job for little credit and not enough pay for the plain old-fashioned reason that they believed in the

necessity of it." Kovac in particular represents the novel's ideal of the good cop: "he was the best investigator in the PD, a straight-up good guy who lived the job and hated the politics of it." The "politics" of the job involve coping with superiors (the mayor, the county attorney, the chief of police), who are simultaneously incompetent and demanding. They require immediate results for their own political reasons (i.e., achieving re-election), but in their push to get these results they inevitably sabotage the investigation, creating the very failure for which they blame the "good cops."

According to the novel's core group of officers, the entire justice system is compromised by corruption at nearly every level. Not only are their immediate superiors in thrall to political power, but the court system itself depends on lawyers and "expert witnesses" who supposedly care more about money and prestige than punishing criminals. The cops routinely complain about the "scum lawyers," even referring to the public defender as "Worm Boy."

Perhaps the most telling vignette occurs late in the novel when the reader encounters Dr. Lucas Brandt, a psychotherapist who knows something about the case but refuses to give any information because it would be a breach of his professional ethics. Kovac suspects that Brandt is withholding the information for personal reasons, because, as it turns out, Kovac has a "history" with Brandt. Kovac had worked on a case involving a man who had killed his girlfriend. Brandt was the expert witness at the trial and argued that the killer was abused as a child, was temporarily insane at the time of the killing, and was, thus, not a danger to society. The killer is charged with manslaughter rather than murder. He serves very little time in prison, and, once released, he rapes a woman in his neighborhood and "beats her head in with a claw hammer." This scenario is, of course, one of the great cliches of contemporary crime fiction. Nevertheless, it is a moment that cannot be ignored, because it is the fantasy of "wronged-ness" that constitutes the foundation of the novel's politics. The key issue at stake here is the power held by a sophisticated, wealthy, educated elite—and the way in which this elite sector of the population is out of touch with the "reality" that the cops "face on the streets" every day.

Though the issues faced by police officers and FBI agents may seem restricted in their possible appeal, it quickly becomes clear that the problems faced by these characters are particular instances of more general problems faced by members of many other sectors of society. By making her good cops resentful of authority and elitism, Hoag is tapping into a growing populist movement in contemporary American political life. It is sometimes difficult to locate this movement on the traditional political spectrum because it does not seem tied to the left or right as they currently are constituted (by the Democrats and Republicans, respectively). For instance, there is strong anti-corporate sentiment (traditionally a position held by the left), but also strong anti-liberal sentiment (clearly a right-wing position). In the novel, the wealthy businessman, Peter Bondurant, is attacked for being detached from normal human emotions,

for being enclosed in his own unfeeling corporate empire. Yet, at the same time, the novel's feminist activist, Toni Urskine, is criticized for being a "bleeding heart liberal," out of touch with the real-life experiences of the prostitutes she wants to help.

The anti-elitist strand runs throughout the novel, although it sometimes appears in subtler ways. When female officer Nikki Liska interviews a possible suspect in a coffeehouse, we are treated to an implicit critique of coffeehouse culture from the populist position outlined above: "Two older men—one tall and slender with a silver goatee, one shorter and wider with a black beret—sipped their espressos and argued the merits of the National Endowment for the Arts. A younger blond man with bug-eye gargoyle sunglasses and a black turtleneck nursed a 'grande' something-or-other." This "something-or-other" lets us know that these fashionable, European coffees are alien to Liska's experience, and furthermore, she probably does not care. This passage provides a catalogue of things (the university set, the arts, lattes and cappuccinos) that are opposed to the novel's model of authenticity—the good cop. Another example which should not be ignored is the Mapplethorpe book that Kovac accidentally (or purposefully, we are not told) flips off the end of Dr. Lucas Brandt's coffee table. Again, this is a moment that is liable to slip by unnoticed, but it is absolutely crucial as a sign of what the novel wants us to see as elitist moral decadence. Mapplethorpe's nude men represent not only the world of art, but also the possibility of gay desire—a possibility that most cop novels are anxious to disavow (serial killing itself has, notoriously, been aligned with sexual deviance in popular culture—see *Psycho, The Silence of the Lambs,* etc.).

The novel's many moments of social commentary serve as much to provide a comfortable site for reader identification as they do to provide politically committed social critique. In fact, committed social critique is itself criticized in this novel under many headings: the "bleeding heart liberals," the "PC Nazis," the "Worm Boy" public defender, and so on. Thus, when we hear that Quinn, Conlan, Liska, and Kovac "live the job and hate the politics of it," we must understand this formulation as a reference to a political position that wants to be *outside* of politics as defined by "PC Nazis" and inept, meddling public officials. This anti-authoritarian, anti-elite strain has been a factor in American politics since before the United States of America actually existed; indeed, the contemporary populist movement often sees itself as more in touch with the founding fathers of the constitution than either of the current political parties. And though the political efficacy of such an apolitical movement must itself be questioned, what cannot be questioned is the movement's marketability in popular culture—particularly in contemporary fiction and contemporary radio (innumerable political talk shows adopt these political views because they seem to appeal to the widest variety of listeners).

It is thus both ironic and fitting that the novel is set in Minneapolis, the largest city in the state that first elected one of the neo-populists (former wrestler Jesse Ventura). But the importance of the Midwestern setting surely exceeds this coincidence.

The threat posed by this wealthy, sophisticated, amoral elite supposedly is aimed squarely at the family. Nearly every one of the police officers is divorced; in their eyes it simply "comes with the job." Again, we cannot interpret this as exclusively pertaining to real-world officers; it clearly is meant to resonate with all readers who feel their marriages/families threatened by workplace stress, government regulations (i.e. the current uproar over the marriage tax), and a perceived decay in public moral standards.

The novel casts the serial killer himself—along with the runaways, drug addicts, and prostitutes of the novel—as a symptom of this decay of the family and family values, of the general fragmentation of the purity of domesticity.

Given that the main character of *Ashes to Ashes* is a female in a predominantly male world, and given that she works with teenaged girls driven to prostitution, one would expect the problems faced by women in contemporary society to be a major concern of the novel. When faced with problems such as prostitution and self-mutilation (Angie DiMarco, like an increasing number of young American girls, cuts herself with razors in an attempt to relieve anxiety), the novel cannot help but present us with implicitly feminist positions. However, the novel's feminist moments are, interestingly, rather intermittent to say the least. The reasons for this are complex. As is the case with most popular novels about crime and punishment, this text wants to hold the villain absolutely responsible for his actions. Thus the importance of his childhood abuse, for instance, must be played down. By denying the causal importance of "victimization," the novel forecloses many possible feminist arguments. Women like characters Toni Urskine (who runs a shelter for prostitutes) and Michelle Fine (who writes feminist folk songs with a friend), and even Alanis Morissette (satirized on at least two occasions in this novel) are criticized for "whining" about their problems. The novel argues that the "correct" response to "victimization" involves moving on with one's life.

◆ THEMES ◆

As with any novel about manifestly social issues, the themes of *Ashes to Ashes* are not at all separate from its social concerns. Thus, the primary importance of "family, marriage, and motherhood" in this novel is not at all separate from the issues discussed above.

The very fact that the reader is invited to empathize with Kate Conlan over her divorce and the loss of her child indicates that the novel's implicit world view values marriage and motherhood while at the same time experiencing anxiety over their tenuousness. Kate's past complicates her relationship with Angie DiMarco, the teenaged prostitute for whom she is an advocate. Although Angie is not Kate's own daughter, their interactions take on many of the qualities of mother-daughter relations. Implicitly, Angie becomes a surrogate daughter for Kate. Kate remarks that Angie is the same age that her own daughter would have been had she lived, and when Angie disappears, Kate feels exactly the same guilt and anxiety she experienced when her own daughter died. She blames herself for both her daughter's death and Angie's disappearance; these parallel traumas constitute the emotional problem that the novel must ultimately resolve to achieve its "happy ending."

Kate's inability to connect on an emotional level with Angie is a displaced manifestation of maternal anxiety concerning the difficulties presented by teenaged children. That Hoag's implied reader is a parent rather than a child is evident from the fact that most passages are focalized through a maternal gaze. The narrative voice (inflected by Kate's presence at this moment) jokes: "The girl made the snotty shrug that had driven parents of teenagers from the time of Adam to consider the pros and cons of killing their young." Later, once Kate has "lost" her second daughter, Angie returns as the killer's accomplice; this is, again, an extreme manifestation of the parents' fear that they are losing touch with their teenaged child. Ironically, when her rebellious independence causes her to turn on the killer

himself, Angie's teenaged disobedient streak is what saves her.

Kate's melancholic memories of her daughter open onto the second major theme of the novel: trauma and memory. Hoag presents a number of characters who are troubled by mysterious, secret pasts. Each character's past is a mystery-within-the-mystery, and a great deal of the reader's pleasure comes from slow revelations of past events. Once their pasts are presented, the reader is faced with a number of characters who are haunted by memories. Quinn, for instance, is haunted by images of the murder victims he has seen: "There had been too many bodies in the last few years. Their names scrolled through his mind at night when he tried to sleep. Counting corpses, he called it. Not the kind of thing that inspired sweet dreams."

Kate's reflections on Angie's trauma bring us to the third key theme: victims and victimization. Kate knows that Angie, like herself, like Quinn, is also haunted by the past: "There was a story there somewhere." Kate suspects alcoholic parents, perhaps a cycle of abuse:

> Virtually every kid on the street had lived a variation of that story. So had every man in prison. Family was a fertile breeding ground for the kind of psychological bacteria that warped minds and devoured hope. Conversely, she knew plenty of people in law enforcement and social work who came from that same set of circumstances, people who had come to that same fork in the road and turned one way instead of the other.

As Kate suggests later, "Everyone was a victim of something." This statement, repeated a handful of times in the text, becomes a mantra of sorts. The novel's moral center surely lies here—in the assertion that what really counts (since everyone is a victim) is how you react to your own victimization. At the very conclusion of the novel, Kate comes to believe that "The test was whether a person could rise above it [being a victim], push past it, grow beyond the experience."

This brings us, finally, to the novel's key metaphor: the phoenix rising from the ashes. Images of fire, ashes, and rebirth abound. Clearly the title, with its reference to the killer's methods of setting fire to his victims, is one good example. Burning is the novel's symbol for negativity of all sorts: the loss of life, the loss of family, the loss of self-respect. In view of this metaphorical system, and especially in view of the obvious fact that the killer burns his victims, it would not be a stretch to suggest that burning is actually symbolically equivalent to victimization in this novel. If the novel's moral center is concerned with proper reactions to victimization, and if burning represents the novel's most consistent metaphor for victimization, we should not be surprised to find the image of the phoenix rising at the end of *Ashes to Ashes*. By naming the halfway house for prostitutes the Phoenix, Hoag already has hinted that the "right" way to respond to victimization involves rising from one's own ashes. In the novel's final moments, Kate looks at her burning home, looks at John Quinn, and thinks "of all things, of the phoenix rising from the ashes. The events that had brought them to this place in this time may have been devastating, but here was their chance for a new beginning. Together." This redemptive, rather maudlin conclusion creates a new domestic space for Kate, recreating the possibility of family in the face of the various threats articulated in the novel.

♦ CHARACTERS ♦

Hoag's characters are often somewhat stock cliches, yet one must keep in mind the fact that the genre itself depends on certain stereotypes in order to attain its desired effects. As is often the case with stock characters, Hoag's characters are usually either good or bad. The good characters serve as sites for identification and mouthpieces for the novel's ideas, while the bad characters serve as objects of scorn and critique.

As the novel's main character, Kate Conlan is the major position for reader identification. Novels of this genre often have females as main characters, and one senses that Kate's character owes at least a little bit to Thomas Harris's Clarice Starling and Patricia Cornwell's Kay Scarpetta. As the novel opens, Kate is trying to start a new life in Minneapolis after losing her child, her husband, and her job with the FBI. Her travails make her an immediately sympathetic character, for although most readers cannot identify with an FBI agent, they can identify with a divorced, grieving mother.

Once they have identified with Kate, readers are able to gain a certain amount of pleasure from her ability to "read" the world. As a former FBI agent she clearly has the ability to interpret both clues and people, and much of Hoag's prose is devoted to articulating Kate's precise insights. This ability to "read" things is shared by the novel's "good" cops: John Quinn, Sam Kovac, and Nikki Liska.

To Kate's remarkable interpretive abilities, Quinn adds an impressive array of "people skills." In fact, he is so capable of adjusting his behavior to suit a given situation that he loses touch with his own identity: "Midwesterners tended to be reserved and didn't quite trust people who weren't. In the Northeast he would have given more of the steel. On the West Coast he would have turned up the charm, would have been Mr. Affable, Mr. Spirit of Cooperation. Different horses for different courses, his old man used to say. And which one was the real John Quinn—even he didn't know anymore." If Kate is searching for a new family to replace the one she lost, Quinn is searching for a domestic space that will guarantee a stable identity. He is haunted by memories of past death, and compassion and reassurance are "emotions he had stopped giving out in full measure long ago because it took too much from him and there was no one around to help him refill the well." If Kate finds her "home" with Quinn (as she says on the novel's last page), Quinn uses Kate to "refill the well."

Sam Kovac shares much with Quinn. Like Quinn, he has an "emotionally dead" quality that recalls the stereotypical "hard-boiled" detective that one would find in a Raymond Chandler novel. Like Quinn, he loves the job but does not enjoy the politics. Unlike Quinn, he is completely incapable of being diplomatic. Between the two of them, Quinn and Kovac represent the two possible ways of dealing with the "inhumanity of the system."

If Kovac provides a foil for Quinn, Nikki Liska provides a foil for Kate. Liska is a peculiarly masculine woman. Described as "Tinkerbell on steroids," she often seems to be "one of the guys." She "talks tough," she too has no time for the job's politics, and she takes a self-assured, almost brazen attitude toward sexual matters. Her sexual openness allows her to say things about Quinn's appearance, for instance, that the reader is supposed to know, but that Kate does not say because she is too restrained.

One of the novel's key relationships clearly arrives with the uncomfortable pairing of the independent, strong-willed Kate and the witness whose case she takes. Angie DiMarco is a homeless teenaged runaway forced into prostitution for mysterious reasons. One of Hoag's subplots involves Kate's attempts to understand her enigmatic charge. Angie is one of the novel's key "victims," and the major question is whether or not she will be able to overcome that status.

Ted Sabin and Rob Marshall embody the incompetent, demanding authority figures that the novel wants to critique. Sabin de-

mands results without knowing how to get them, and he further offends the reader by making sexual advances toward Kate. Marshall is awkward, ugly, and ineffective, and the fact that he is simultaneously Kate's boss *and* the serial killer is surely evidence of narrative wish-fulfillment. As the serial killer, Marshall constantly is seeking power and control; clearly Hoag wants us to view this as merely an extension of the petty power-hungriness of low-level managerial staff everywhere.

Peter Bondurant, Jillian Bondurant, Grace Noble, Edwyn Noble, and Dr. Lucas Brandt should be dealt with as a group, because the primary point Hoag is making with this collection of characters involves the sort of incestuous networking that constitutes political and economic power. As a wealthy businessman, Bondurant obviously has a great deal of power in Minneapolis, but this economic power becomes political power through his ties to the mayor. Bondurant's lawyer is Edwyn Noble, Mayor Grace Noble's husband. Not only does the novel explicitly tie political networking to criminal networking, but it also literalizes the incestuous nature of this network by hinting at a possible sexual relationship between Jillian Bondurant, the murder victim at the center of the novel, and her father. To make matters worse, the presence or absence of the literal incest is hidden by Dr. Brandt, who is both Jillian's therapist and her father's lackey.

Finally, any discussion of the novel's characters would be incomplete without a reference to Toni Urskine, the woman who runs the halfway house for prostitutes. We learn that Kate (and thus the implied reader) does not like Urskine. "Urskine worked around the clock to keep her indignation cooking at a slow burn. If she or her ideals or 'her victims,' as she called the women at the Phoenix, hadn't been slighted outright, she would find some way of perceiving an insult so she could climb up on her soapbox and shriek at anyone within hearing distance." Urskine's sixties-style political activism rubs Kate the wrong way, and because of this, Kate thinks that Urskine is one of the "bleeding-heart liberals who spent too much time bad-mouthing the police." Thus, though Urskine would seem to be the sort of empowered woman that a person in Kate's position would admire, Hoag makes her an object of criticism.

◆ TECHNIQUES ◆

Hoag offers more than the standard "who-done-it" mystery in *Ashes to Ashes*. There are a number of subplots that constitute mysteries-within-the-mystery. Readers are forced to ask a number of questions. Who is Angie? Who is the body? What do Quinn and Kate have to do with one another? Was there an incestuous relationship? By weaving these multiple mysteries together, Hoag attempts to create a richer text.

Like other authors writing in the crime genre, Hoag puts a great deal of emphasis on precision and detail when it comes to describing life in law enforcement. Readers who are devoted to crime fiction derive pleasure from these details; the ability to interpret clues along with the investigators offers the reader a chance to be an "insider."

Hoag's major technique for bringing readers into the minds of "insiders" is what narratologists refer to as "free indirect discourse," in which a character's thoughts or utterances are presented without "tag clauses" like "she thought" or "he said." When Hoag writes "Kate waited patiently, keenly aware of the girl's rising tension. Even to a streetwise kid like Angie, seeing what she had seen had to be an unimaginable shock," the second sentence actually represents Kate's thoughts, in spite of the omission of a tag clause (i.e., "Kate thought"). There are six characters whose thoughts we "see" in

this way: the four "good" cops (Kate, Quinn, Kovac, and Liska), Angie, and the killer. Thus, while the novel seems to be narrated in the third person by an "omniscient narrator," this does not tell us all we need to know about the style of the narration. Hoag takes us into the minds of selected characters for important reasons: to allow us to participate in the intellectual feats of the officers, to help us identify with a character's emotions, or even to scare us by bringing us a little too close to the perverse thoughts of a killer.

However, it would be difficult to argue that Hoag's—or, for that matter, the reader's interest—in the serial killer comes from a pervasive desire to offer a complete etiology of this particular form of illness. The immense detail with which Hoag describes the killing scenes is a good indication that the serial killer is most appealing as an object for the reader's voyeurism. Indeed, some of Hoag's most baroque prose is lavished on the killing scenes themselves:

> He recalls the tremor in her voice as she pleaded for her life, the unique pitch and quality of each cry as he tortured her. The exquisite music of life and death. For one fine moment he allows himself to admire the drama of the tableau. He allows himself to feel the heat of the flames caress his face like tongues of desire. He closes his eyes and listens to the sizzle and hiss, breathes deep the smell of roasting flesh.

As is the case with any psychosexual thriller, many of this novel's aesthetic effects are gained through representations of intense—often misogynistic—violence. And it is an open question whether or not the supposed critique of this violence makes up for the apparent thrills the author and implied reader take in the nearly gratuitous description.

Finally, one tendency in Hoag's writing which may seem out of place is the prevalence of "romance novel" language. When Kate and Quinn finally kiss, make love and so on, the reader is likely to feel as though he has been thrown into a Harlequin romance: "Her hands traveled over his body. Ridges and planes of muscle and bone. Smooth, hot skin. The valley of his spine. His erection straining against her, as hard as marble, as soft as velvet." While romantic suspense is, indeed, a popular genre in its own right, the serial killer genre does not seem well suited to romance.

◆ LITERARY PRECEDENTS ◆

While Hoag's work inevitably is compared to that of Patricia Cornwell (*Postmortem, Body of Evidence, All That Remains,* and many others), the most relevant literary precedent for *Ashes to Ashes* is the work of Thomas Harris. Cornwell's work often involves a similar mix of romance and mystery, and her main character, Dr. Kay Scarpetta, is in some ways similar to Hoag's Kate Conlan (both are single women associated with the legal system). However, when it comes to novels about serial killers, Harris's novels have been unimaginably successful and, thus, influential.

Harris's trilogy—*The Red Dragon, The Silence of the Lambs,* and *Hannibal*—makes use of the serial killer as an awesome spectacle for the viewer. The pleasure of these books is in observing the sublime intellect of the killer—and the sublime violence of his acts. The FBI profilers are involved in a battle of wits with Lecter, who is himself fully aware of their actions. Like Lecter, Hoag's killer toys with his enemies (police, FBI, victims). Though less superhuman, he too seems to have certain intellectual capabilities that surpass those of all but the main investigator (Quinn in this case). When he shows up in an interrogation room to help question the very witness who can incriminate him, Hoag's killer performs the sort of act that indicates that he, like Lecter, takes a pleasure in the "aesthetics" of killing.

◆ RELATED TITLES ◆

Some of the peculiarities of *Ashes to Ashes* can be understood if one takes into account Hoag's development as a novelist. Her first novels, *Magic* (1990), *Sarah's Sin* (1992), and *Lucky's Lady* (1992), were more typical romances—they involved a degree of suspense, but nowhere near as much death as her later work. As her career has progressed (*Cry Wolf* [1993], *Dark Paradise* [1994], *Night Sins* [1995], *Guilty as Sin* [1996], *A Thin Dark Line* [1997]), Hoag's novels generally have oscillated between romance and suspense, but they also have become increasingly gory and violent. *Ashes to Ashes* is perhaps her most extreme novel yet, but it is interesting to note that it retains a few passages of prose that are very much in keeping with the romance genre.

Hoag has also just published a sequel to *Ashes to Ashes*—appropriately titled *Dust to Dust*—that continues to chronicle life in the Minneapolis Police Department. Two of the earlier novel's minor characters, Nikki Liska and Sam Kovac, take center stage in another psychosexual murder mystery.

◆ IDEAS FOR GROUP DISCUSSIONS ◆

In *Ashes to Ashes* one must read closely to discover the novel's explicit and implicit arguments, but one must also question the validity of these arguments, their ideological blind spots, and their political implications.

1. How does Hoag differentiate "good" cops from "bad" city officials, businessmen, and lawyers? What techniques does Hoag use to give certain characters authority? How do we know that Kovac and Quinn are "right" in Hoag's eyes? What sort of political stance does the novel take?

2. Why did Hoag choose Minneapolis for the novel's setting? Does the Midwest's position in America's collective consciousness explain its relevance as a setting for the novel? Does the novel's generally populist political position help us understand the choice of setting?

3. Not only is *Ashes to Ashes* full of victims, it is also concerned with debates over what it *means* to be a victim. Most members of the police and FBI in the book insist that victimization does not preclude responsibility. Does the book's narrative challenge or prove this point? Are even the police forced into certain forms of behavior given their relatively disadvantaged social and economic position (i.e., their economic "victimization")? As far as the novel is concerned, how *should* we react to victimization?

4. While Kate Conlan seems to be a relatively "empowered" woman, other strong women in the novel are criticized on multiple occasions. The mayor is too power hungry; Toni Urskine is too liberal; Michelle Fine is too bohemian— even Alanis Morissette is attacked on two separate occasions for "whining" (most would be more likely to view her as the voice of a strong, youthful feminist). Why? What possibilities does the novel leave open for women? If the novel's key crusader for women's rights (Toni Urskine—not to mention Alanis) is attacked on supposedly personal grounds, where does this leave the cause she is furthering? Is the ending of the novel—when Kate gets to be Quinn's "something beautiful and warm," resting on his chest which for her is "home"— conservative or even reactionary?

5. Why does Hoag choose to present her subplots as mysteries in themselves? Why, for instance, does she delay revealing crucial information about Kate's relationship with Quinn? How do these various "mini-mysteries" contribute to the main narrative? Do some of them simply get in the way of the central mystery? Do some of them (such as the question concerning Jillian Bondurant's possible incestuous relations with her stepfather) actually become more interesting than the "who-done-it" puzzle?

6. Every reader will quickly notice passages depicting graphic, and often sexual, violence in this novel. What does Hoag accomplish by including such moments? Is she just trying to shock us? Is the reader meant to derive pleasure from such passages? How? Does the "pleasure of detail" extend to scenes of violence as well?

7. Hoag began her career as a romance novelist. Thus, it is not surprising that love scenes typical of romance novels appear in this text. Do they fit with the dominant tenor of the narrative? Are they out of place? What do they add to the novel? Why did Hoag choose to include them?

8. Who is Hoag's implied reader? Does the book anticipate a male reader or a female one? What is the implied reader's age? Class? What clues do we find in *Ashes to Ashes* that answer these questions? Does the novel challenge the reader's expectations and beliefs? Does it reinforce the implied reader's prejudices?

Marlon Kuzmick
Cornell University

BACK ROADS

Novel

2000

Author: Tawni O'Dell

◆──────────────◆──────────────

◆ SOCIAL CONCERNS ◆

In this classic yet contemporary bildungsroman (coming-of-age novel), Tawni O'Dell implicitly includes a great deal of social commentary in a novel that seems, on the surface, to be the poetic, sarcastic, and often comic musings and rantings of a boy becoming a man amid the pressure, tension, and fatigue forced on him by the fact that his mother is serving a life sentence for the murder of his father. The protagonist is nineteen-year-old Harley Altmyer, who is trying to take care of his three younger sisters, and O'Dell's choice to write from the point of view of this emotionally disturbed teenager offers her opportunities to deepen the effect of her fiction by using all the forms of irony, especially dramatic irony, wherein the audience knows what the character does not know. Thus, Harley, even with all his faults, becomes a sympathetic character with whom the audience can relate and for whom they can feel pity and empathy. Readers are taken into the mind of a young man who is being taken in by most of the other characters. Though he is mentally unbalanced, sexually adventurous, occasionally selfish, and recklessly impulsive, he is still the moral center of the novel, and he becomes the spokesperson for all those who are striving to do what they think is right while surrounded by what can sometimes seem a venal, corrupt, and nonsensical society that focuses on the quotidian and sensual at the expense of the eternal and spiritual.

Tempestuous, poignant oppositions abound throughout the novel and have broad, important social implications: youth versus adult; truth versus dishonesty; passion versus love; self versus family; duty versus desire; sanity versus insanity; justice versus the law; the poor versus the rich; parent versus parent; sibling versus sibling, and history versus the future, to name only the most obvious ones. O'Dell subtly explores each of these conflicts as they threaten to tear apart the mind and life of Harley, who learns, as most readers already have, that life is not fair and that ultimately the best one can do is try to value and protect one's self and one's family, even when those entities may be at war with one another.

The adults in Harley's life tend to push him around (his bosses and the legal authorities), seduce him (Callie), or attempt to pigeonhole him (his counselors). They often think he is kidding when he says what is on his mind, and he constantly has to tell them and the reader that he is serious. Yet his sardonic sense of humor is one of his greatest strengths, even though it is more internal than external. Like Holden Caulfield in J. D. Salinger's *The Catcher in the Rye* (1951), Harley *readily can* see the phoniness and the selfishness in the adults around him, and he never hesitates to skewer them, at least in his mind. Even so, their power over him is sometimes frightening and is always real because it is built into the social structure. Moreover, adults tend to devalue or undervalue the thoughts and feelings of younger people, as clearly can be seen in *Back Roads*.

Throughout the novel, Harley wrestles with the concepts of love, desire, and duty, tries to square his definitions with those of society, and finds that these concepts and conflicts can intermingle into horrific knots of destructive power, strangleholds that threaten his very existence. For example, he is torn between his love for his sister Amber and his instinctive drive to protect her. As she pulls away and rebels from him, he is drawn closer to her, and eventually this closeness proves unhealthy and disastrous for both of them.

Harley's methods of coping with poverty and the unusual burden brought about by his suddenly becoming the head of the Altmyer household are ingenious and industrious: he juggles two full-time jobs while effectively caring for his sisters and sensitively looking after even the emotional needs of his dog, Elvis. When Harley gets into trouble with the law, he wants to use his only phone call to comfort his youngest sister, Jody, and he is worried that Elvis will think of himself as a "bad dog" who has been rightfully deserted. Even though Harley is brutalized and manipulated by the police, he cares more about his family and his dog than he does about himself. Thus, no matter what readers may think of his nontraditional sense of morality, they must eventually see that this protagonist is a hero in the full sense of the word, not just in the literary sense. He represents the oppressed as well as the young.

The system seems to be against him. In order not to lose his sisters to Social Services and foster homes, he must constantly prove to a psychologist that he is sane, while he sees the counselor's questions and probing during his regular visits as usually irritating and occasionally ridiculous. Even so, the reader can understand why Harley needs such counseling and can see how the past is threatening to overwhelm his future. Therefore, the practice of psychology is both ridiculed and shown to be valuable, though flawed, and history is presented as not so much a guiding light but a blinding fire that can consume the future if not understood and held in check.

The strikingly appropriate symbol of Harley's tragic family history is the jagged pipe left over from his father's ripped-out TV satellite system. Harley is obsessed with the cutting down and covering up of that danger, with protecting his sisters from hurting themselves on the rusted metal, so he thinks of various ways to deal with it, the pipe being anchored in a large mound of buried concrete. Temporarily he covers it up with an old couch, but symbolically the brutal reality of his father's abuse of the family is always lurking below the surface, ready to tear into anyone who recalls it fully, just as the rough-edged pipe would lacerate anyone's feet and legs should they stumble across it.

The most important social concern of the novel centers on such abuse and the need to face its reality and come to terms with its consequences, with the ripples in the social pond that occur when child and spousal abuse explode and blow apart the placid surface. The abuse in Harley's past will damage many generations to come unless he and others can find effective ways to prevent such damage, which often takes the form of more abuse, causing a vicious cycle that tears away at the core of civilization.

◆ THEMES ◆

The social conflicts that Harley Altmyer endures and attempts to understand are inextricably woven into the themes of *Back Roads,* so that it is impossible to separate them neatly, and Harley bemoans those English teachers who take the pleasure out of books by "breaking them down into themes and sentence structure." However, the best novels do have important themes, and this one is so well written that its pleasures are indestructible. By definition, the most vital theme of any bildungsroman is the process of, and the necessity for, maturity. Harley's progress can be summed up by two especially riveting scenes: the one in which he seeks and accepts the help of Betty, his first counselor, and the one in which he confronts the authorities after he is arrested. No longer does he fantasize that he is capable of complete independence; he allows his counselor to take him into her home and comfort him because he knows he needs her and that she is good at her job. At the jail, when the sheriff makes a snide remark about Callie, Harley yells for him to shut up, knowing that this outburst will bring even more physical abuse from the deputies. A bit earlier when Harley is talking to his uncle Mike on the phone from jail and Mike asks incredulously if Harley is sure that he wants to use his only phone call to talk to his sister Jody, a six-year-old girl, Harley simply and assertively says, "Right." He has grown up a lot, not completely, not without scars, and not without severe damage, but by the end of the novel, he is very nearly an adult, and he can accept both help and responsibility.

He is also no longer a teenager. At the conclusion of the story, Harley is twenty years old, having "celebrated" his birthday by having a few beers and hiding his uncle's rifle. Harley has come to realize that the rifle, which was used to kill his father, is more of a danger to the family than an instrument of protection.

Another important theme is the pull of family, the primeval drive to react emotionally to one's parents and siblings, even when those reactions can be tremendously, irreversibly destructive, as in the case of incest, which figures prominently in *Back Roads.* A subtheme here is parental responsibility versus the selfish, id-driven desire for pure pleasure and the need to vent one's anger. Harley's father has abused his family, and this abuse has led to his murder. Harley feels compelled to provide for and to protect his family, yet he also has the strong and often self-centered sexual desires of any normal adolescent, desires that pull him away from his family and into the adult world of sensuality. Callie, who has an affair with him, feels both a strong obligation to her family and the powerful desire to satisfy her sexual needs with a younger, more virile man. These contending forces lead to ecstatic pleasure and shocking violence.

Perhaps the largest, most overarching theme is the self against society. The young feel injustice more strongly because it is new to them; adults must become somewhat jaded in order to survive and be happy. Harley is stung by every arrow of misfortune, and there is usually someone, often an adult authority figure, to blame. Of course, what he is beginning to realize as the novel closes is that he himself has made the choices that have led him to where he is, and that he is the one who can provide the hope that he needs to become whole again. No one is perfect, least of all those in Harley's deeply dysfunctional family, and no one is always honest, but everyone is human and is individual. This humanity and uniqueness is occasionally at odds with a society that seems determined to preserve order even at the cost of justice. When Harley protests to various legal authorities that he knows his mother is innocent, they simply tell him that, innocent or not, she has been convicted, and the case is closed.

By the end of the story, Harley has come a long way toward accepting society the way it is: "This place is not so bad," he says, specifically referring to the institution in which he resides but generally perhaps speaking of the world. His illusions that happiness is simply a matter of taking care of your family and being in control, and that good sex is virtually the same thing as love are replaced by the realities that hardly anyone is completely in control, that no one always pleases his or her family, and that the passion involved in sex can veer suddenly into hatred and death just as easily as it can lead to love and fulfillment. Thus, one sees that the common theme of illusion versus reality is also prevalent, as is natural when the protagonist is youthful and has a vibrant imagination. Harley is often stunned by the wide variance between what he expects and what actually happens, and between what he perceives and what really exists.

◆ CHARACTERS ◆

O'Dell develops Harley so completely that readers can begin to anticipate what his reactions are going to be, but there is little physical description of him. We know that he is a poor boy from the backwoods of Pennsylvania, that he is tall and in good shape, that he wears a baseball-style cap, tee shirts, and blue jeans; but that is about it. The lack of physical details allows O'Dell to present Harley as more of an Everyman, and readers can envision themselves or someone they know engaging in essentially the same actions that Harley does, based on his rough-and-tumble personality, his hand-

to-mouth existence, and his violence-plagued childhood. He is a fully realized, sympathetic character who inspires empathy and understanding, rather than simply some guy in a tragic news story.

O'Dell succeeds in giving readers a richly detailed glimpse into the mind of a troubled youth, and that glimpse is both horrifying and fascinating. Harley is not a harlequin but a "real" person. While he occasionally resembles such forerunners as Holden Caulfield in looking askance at adult behavior, there never has been anyone quite like him. Harley is an original creation, and more than anything else, his persona drives the events of the novel and the echoing effects of O'Dell's art, while ironically he often seems to be tossed by winds of circumstance that would knock anyone down. His ultimate strength, though, is based on his own brand of individuality, which is by nature indomitable, persuasive, and entertaining, though at the same time fragile, prone to mistakes, and sometimes irritatingly shrill. Harley's humanity wins the battle against the dehumanizing effects of the cherished sameness of an orderly society, and O'Dell's message of tolerance shines through his eyes.

As is the case with most of the other characters, Harley's name is both fitting and ironic. He has the physical strength of a motorcycle but is also dangerous to himself and others; he tries to be macho but does not succeed enough to fit his name. He cries several times, and when confronted with heartbreaking, gut-wrenching events, he throws up and nearly falls apart emotionally. Thus, he is both like a motorcycle and very unlike a mechanized creation.

His sister Amber's name matches the color of a caution light, yet the character is anything but cautious. Harley is occasionally impulsive, but Amber makes him look like a Boy Scout with her wild, provocative rebelliousness, which is somewhat normal for a sixteen-year-old attractive girl, but Amber goes well beyond the bounds of normal by the time the story reaches its climax. Like the rest of her family, she has been seriously damaged by the physical, emotional, and verbal abuse that her father inflicted.

Perhaps no one feels that damage as deeply as Misty, the middle sister, who is on the verge of her teenage years but is much too old inside. Like her name, she is vague and dimly outlined. O'Dell spends comparatively little time on describing Misty, but this character proves to be the most important in the unraveling of the plot, which includes more shock and more revulsion than most readers could possibly anticipate. Events and revelations spring up like unimagined monsters, and Misty holds some of this harsh reality within her young, impressionable, twisted mind, though she appears to be the most normal and calm of all the characters throughout most of the novel. Like Harley, she works to bring in money, and she sometimes chides him when he fails to keep the family foremost in his thoughts and actions.

The youngest sister, Jody, is the most emotionally compelling character in *Back Roads,* for she likely will be the one who feels the most pain from the events of the story, and she probably will feel it for the longest time. With an androgynous name, she represents all children. Jody is too young to have much of a detailed memory of her father's abuse, but her meticulous writing of her daily "to-do" lists is a powerfully effective indication of her need to control her future and deny her past, as is her kicking, screaming aversion to emotional therapy. Jody also has a need to understand things, as most six-year-olds do, so Harley feels a corresponding need to explain them to her. His love for her is one of the most touching aspects of this tumultuous, unflinchingly realistic story. To any reader who would condemn the novel for its occasional obscenity and somewhat graphic (though not pornographic) sex scenes, the relationship between Harley and Jody, as well as the one between him and his dog, tends to balance out the uglier facets of the book, in which O'Dell is after all describing the way people really are, not the way one would like them to be.

Callie, for example, is a wonderful mother and a dutiful wife, but she is also (appropriately for her name) callously selfish and irresponsible in her seduction of Harley. He and she share an appreciation for impressionist art, and the novel itself is impressionistic, especially when O'Dell is describing the passion between this woman in her mid-thirties and her teenage lover. Callie and Harley initially make love at a creek outside her home after he has discovered a horrible truth, has begun to weep uncontrollably, and has ended up at her house more or less by accident. Their relationship is not simply a tabloid affair, and its ending is one of the most memorable in American fiction. Their conversations best show O'Dell's deft ear for dialogue and include one of Harley's funniest lines. In the year and a half that his mother has been in prison, he has only been to see her two times, and Callie asks him how often he goes to visit her. "Twice every life sentence," he replies deadpan.

The secondary characters are effectively drawn, and O'Dell avoids presenting only stock characters to play the bit parts. The sheriff, though he allows his deputies to be brutal and though he is correctly seen by Harley as a conniving small-town politician, does show intelligence and compassion. Harley's mother is presented as fairly simple, although her motives and her mental life turn out to be much more complicated than first meets the eye. In that sense, she is symbolic of the story itself, which has a smooth, almost pleasant surface but has whirling currents underneath, and which begins in a deceptively simple fashion but develops into an emotional tornado.

Betty, Harley's Behavioral Health Services counselor, tries to help him deal with the events and emotions that threaten to destroy him, and she is an interesting, though secondary, character. Although she relies too heavily on theory she has learned by rote (what Harley calls "her textbooks") and the comfort of distance, she is also humane and effective in her professional relationship with Harley. He notes that her house is expensive and that she must not financially need the government job she is doing, and she is honest with him when she says that she does need the job, but not financially.

Brad, Callie's husband, who is at first perceived by Harley as a typical well-to-do banker, eventually says that he hates bankers and that he wanted to be a teacher, and Harley is forced to admit to himself that this rival for Callie's affection is really a pretty nice fellow. Like Brad, the other secondary characters also show quirks that lift them out of any easy stereotypes that readers might have formed.

◆ TECHNIQUES ◆

O'Dell effectively uses the first-person point of view and retroactive development to draw the reader into the novel. One can readily identify with Harley's humanity— his frailties, temptations, failures, and successes (the "I" becomes our eye)—and can easily enjoy his sense of humor. By thrusting the reader immediately into the story at an emotional and violent point, O'Dell creates interest and suspense, then fills in what screenwriters call "the backstory" by means of an extended flashback. The novel begins and ends in the present tense; in between, Harley narrates his story appropriately in the past tense.

Playing against what appears to be an almost stereotypical, melodramatic, soap-opera plot, O'Dell uses impressionism, realism, and shocking plot twists to create something original. In an early conversation with Callie, Harley accidentally provides a good definition of impressionistic art when he says that it represents not what is there but what the effect of the scene is on the viewer, and often throughout the novel, he describes only bits and pieces of what he sees, just enough to create a vivid impression for the reader. For example, when Harley is hiding his uncle's rifle, he is interrupted by Amber, who has walked barefoot across the muddy yard to the shed. He describes her painted toenails in the black mud as looking like "grape jelly beans," and readers are not only visually drawn into the scene but also presented with a picture that embraces both the grotesque and the beautiful almost equally, as in the art of Vincent van Gogh, among others. At one point, Harley focuses on the sunflowers at the prison where his mother is incarcerated, and O'Dell's allusion to one of van Gogh's most well-known paintings is clear.

At the same time, O'Dell's realistic portrayal of Harley's world is unflinching and engrossing. Nothing is too vague; nothing is unduly distorted. When Harley discovers the body in the old mine office, O'Dell gives almost a photographic view of what he sees, so that when he gets violently ill, we can readily understand why. Throughout the book, O'Dell clearly is presenting the facts and setting the scenes but also using poetic, evocative language to do so, and such an approach is traditional in the best literary novels.

Another effective technique in *Back Roads* is irony, and all three forms are used: dramatic, whereby we understand or anticipate what the character does not; verbal, in which the speaker says one thing but means another; and situational, wherein the characters are placed in a situation that is especially fitting or telling, or may reveal a contrast between expectation and fulfillment or between appearance and reality. Dramatic irony is usually rife in a first-person novel, especially a bildungsroman, where the main character is not as mature as the average reader. For example, we can see that Callie, who is often scantily dressed, is attracted to Harley and is open to having an affair with him long before he catches on. "Harley," she says early on, laughing and touching his shoulder, "You're great." "I didn't know what that meant," Harley writes, but the readers are well aware.

Verbal irony is used most often when Harley is disgusted with something and is being sarcastic. When Amber announces that she is going to move in with one of her boyfriends, Harley says, "Oh, great. That's just great," but of course what he means is that such a move would be unwise and irrational, especially since this particular boyfriend wants her to live with him and two other guys in a trailer.

Perhaps the best example of situational irony is the main setting itself, a small, impoverished former mining town called Laurel Falls in the mountains of western Pennsylvania, the region where O'Dell herself was raised. On the dust jacket of the novel, she refers to the area as "a beautifully ruined place where the rolling hills are pitted with dead-gray mining towns like cigarette burns on a green carpet." Ostensibly the town is named after a nearby waterfall, but symbolically the name is deeply ironic. Laurel wreathes were bestowed on heroes, poets, and athletic champions in ancient times, and the inhabitants of Laurel Falls seem defeated and resigned to their fate, as if their laurels have fallen and they have no prospect of recapturing such success, if indeed they ever had it or even the possibility of it. The exception is Harley, whom readers come to know as poetic and heroic but whom most people would probably overlook as simply an awkward young man working in menial jobs in the middle of nowhere. Thus, the title of the novel is symbolic: Harley lives among the back roads, even though he has qualities of greatness. O'Dell is calling attention to the plight of the ignored and the undervalued by placing her vividly realized and intensely human characters in a backwater town that is almost invisible to the outside world. Look, she seems to say, there are real people living inside those "cigarette burns," people as worthy of our attention as those who live in Hollywood or Washington, D.C.

◆ LITERARY PRECEDENTS ◆

Similar novels include *The Catcher in the Rye* (mentioned earlier), S. E. Hinton's *The Outsiders* (1967), John Irving's *The Cider House Rules* (1985), Mark Twain's *Huckleberry Finn* (1884), Stephen Crane's *The Red Badge of Courage* (1895), Henry James's *What Maisie Knew* (1897), and other such novels that present impressionable young characters facing adult situations and often being horrified and deeply changed by what they see. Especially relevant comparisons can be made between *Back Roads* and *The Catcher in the Rye* because both protagonists are presented very effectively via the first-person point of view and tell their stories in extended flashbacks, both are often sarcastic regarding adults, both have a strong emotional bond with a younger sister, both are in psychiatric care at novel's end, and both go through a process of maturation.

However, there are important differences: Harley is lower middle class at best, Holden is upper middle class; Harley has important responsibilities, Holden has few responsibilities; and perhaps because of Harley's obligations to his family, he exhibits more selflessness and has more ties to the community than does Holden, who seems isolated, selfish, and contemptuous of society in general. The major exception to this stance is his openness and genuine affection for his sister, Phoebe. Their relationship is comparable to Harley and Jody's, except that Phoebe sometimes seems to be more mature than Holden, seems to take care of him, rather than vice versa, notwithstanding his altruistic fantasy of being the "catcher" who saves children from falling off an imaginary cliff into the corruption of adulthood.

Holden's and Harley's styles of expression are also quite different. Although both show signs of high intelligence, Harley's manner of speaking and writing is more poetic and sensitive, whereas Holden's often seems bitter and cynical, even though he attempts to appear breezy and cool. Humor is important in both novels, though, and both protagonists find strength in it.

◆ ADAPTATIONS ◆

An abridged audio cassette recording of the novel, narrated by Dylan Baker, was released in 2000 by Harper Audio.

◆ IDEAS FOR GROUP DISCUSSIONS ◆

Tensions between youths and adults and between children and parents are common because young people naturally rebel while going through the formation of their personalities. There have to be some differences between youths and adults because, given the nature of individuality, children cannot become exactly like their parents or other authority figures, even if they wanted to, which most of them do not. Another reason for this emotional battleground is that the mores of the older generation have been tempered by experience and usually tend to be more conservative than those of the younger generation, whose ideas are more influenced by current trends and by peer pressure. Harley Altmyer is forced to play the role of an adult because he is thrust into being a surrogate parent to his sisters, but his social role does not fit his emotional maturity. Therefore, normal adolescent tensions become virtually overwhelming for him when amplified by the pressures caused by his present and his past. Ultimately, though reluctantly, he seeks and receives professional help from his counselor, Betty, but by then the events surrounding him have spun well beyond his control. When he finally phones her in desperation, she asks who is calling, and he shakily says, "I don't know," thereby showing the importance of personality formation in the process of mental growth and also indicating that he has become wise enough to know that he does not know. He has taken the most important step toward self-knowledge and maturity by admitting that he is not independent or omniscient.

Just as important as the theme of maturation is that of the primacy of the family in the life of the individual. Implicitly, O'Dell shows that families are the glue that holds society together but that family history is like gravity and just as hard to fight. Though Harley's father is dead, his influence on the family is enormous, and the events surrounding his death will continue to scar the family well into the future, just as his abuse of his children will emotionally scar them for life. Rising above the negativity, though, are the huge, life-changing sacrifices that Harley and his mother make for their family.

1. To what extent does Harley's family get in the way of his process of maturation and self-discovery? How does the family help him on that journey?

2. On one hand, Harley attempts to rid himself of the awful legacy of his father by hacksawing down the pipe that held his father's TV satellite, yet on the other

hand, Harley often wears his father's camouflage hunting jacket. What are some of the characteristics he shares with his father? How is he clearly unlike him?

3. As Harley explores his individuality and becomes more comfortable with his personality, he seems at odds with the conformity that he sees around him in Laurel Falls. Is this conflict always necessary in personality development? How does Harley's case differ from those of other youths who are going through the same difficult years in their lives? How is it similar? Compare and contrast Harley with other young characters you have experienced in your reading or in movies.

4. O'Dell's use of the first-person point of view may strike some readers as odd, courageous, or both, because she is writing from the viewpoint of a young man. William Styron was criticized when he wrote from the point of view of a slave in *The Confessions of Nat Turner;* some African-American readers were upset that a white man would think that he could understand and fully empathize with the plight of a black man enduring the horrific conditions of slavery. Could O'Dell be criticized in the same way, in the sense that she could never really imagine what it is like to be a young man? Do you find her account of Harley's actions and feelings accurate and believable? Why or why not?

5. The profanity and the sex scenes in this novel will offend some readers. What would have been the effect on the impact of the novel had O'Dell left out such scenes and such language? What would have been the effect on your impression of Harley's character?

6. Identify and discuss examples of irony not covered in the essay above. For example, the old mine office is the setting for several scenes. How are they related in terms of situational irony?

7. Tawni O'Dell's college degree (from Northwestern) is in journalism. How does her writing in *Back Roads* show her training as a reporter? How does it go against and grow beyond any stereotypes you may have of newswriting?

Jack Turner, Ph.D.
Wesley College, Dover, Delaware

BASTARD OUT OF CAROLINA

Novel

1992

Author: Dorothy Allison

◆

Abuse and poverty play roles in the development of many children in America, having consequences that affect adulthood. In the semiautobiographical *Bastard out of Carolina*, Dorothy Allison is writing to help heal the wounds from her childhood. Whether the circle of abuse can be broken rather than passed to the next generation is Allison's greatest concern. Efforts to combat abuse and poverty from outside the family have met with limited success. Parents sometimes are unable to provide the safe, loving environment that is the ideal situation in which a child can grow, not because they do not desire to, but because circumstances do not allow them to. Society is not always sympathetic to the plight of the poor or to the unequal treatment of women in the workplace. Neither is society always helpful when child abuse is discovered. As the tendency toward violence in everyday life continues to escalate, it becomes more necessary for parents to recognize and deal with abuse to their children, should it occur.

Ruth Anne Boatwright, nicknamed "Bone" by her family because she was born prematurely after a car accident and was "small as a knucklebone," is the illegitimate daughter of fifteen-year-old Anney, whose choices as a single mother in 1950s South Carolina are limited to finding a husband or living with her mother for the rest of her life. Her only support system consists of her mother and sisters, all of whom are caught in the same circle of poverty. None of the Boatwright sisters has a husband who is willing to put the responsibility for the family before his desires.

The Boatwright brothers are known for their hard-drinking, hard-fighting, hard-living ways. Having been in jail is a source of pride rather than shame. Writing in *The Nation*, Randall Kenan describes the Boatwright men as "the stereotype of poor white trash: liquored-up, malevolent, unemployed, undereducated, country-music-listening, oversexed, foul-tempered men" and their women as "long-suffering, quickly aging, overly fertile, too-young-marrying, hard-headed women." All these things are true. For Anney this type of family member is normal.

The men are not good husbands and fathers, or good providers, being unable to sustain the effort. They are dedicated to having fun. When they are moved to protect family members, the action taken is violent. Of these brothers, Uncle Earle figures most prominently.

Anney marries Glen, who was abused and continues to be abused by his father. As "Daddy Glen" he fails at one job after another, unable to support the family, and begins to take out his anger and frustration on Bone. Once he begins to use Bone as that outlet, he cannot stop, and Bone suffers from the physical and mental hunger and humiliation poverty brings, coupled with the beatings from her stepfather. He tries to keep the abuse secret, and when Anney finds out he is beating Bone, she is paralyzed by indecision, willing to believe Glen's explanation for his discipline. Eventually Aunt Raylene discovers that Daddy Glen is abusing Bone and tells the brothers. They will not tolerate the abuse, inflicting a beating on Glen, thinking he will take this as a warning and leave Bone alone.

That Bone is able to continue to do well in school is her first step toward breaking the pattern of abuse that is handed down to her. College and the outside world give Allison a framework to deal with her childhood.

◆ THEMES ◆

The overarching theme of *Bastard out of Carolina* is the part child abuse and poverty play in forming the character of Bone. Within that theme, the helplessness of the women and children in the family and the losses of family members to death and incarceration erode the process of growing up for Bone and her sister and cousins. Writing for the *New York Times Book Review*, Allison says, "We are the ones they make fiction of—we gay and disenfranchised and female—and we have the right to demand our full, nasty, complicated lives." She has done that in *Bastard out of Carolina*.

Mental and physical abuses by Bone's stepfather destroy her self-esteem. She feels she is worthless, at fault, and bad to the core, and she is unable to tell anyone as she

then will become worthless in that person's eyes. After the first beating, she hears Glen lie to her mother; Bone knows her mother will not believe her so she does not try to tell her what really happened. From then on, Glen looks for excuses to "discipline" Bone, knowing Anney is incapable of stopping him. As Anney comforts Bone after a beating, she asks what *Bone* did to cause the beating, further destroying Bone's self-esteem. Anney is in the middle of a contest as Glen competes with Bone for her attention and affection.

Some psychologists equate the beginnings of the curiosity about the differences in the sexes as a desire to know a secret. Deborah Horvitz, writing in *Contemporary Literature*, says that in the case of Bone, "she attempts to transform her nightmare into narrative as a means of coping with what she considers to be her 'damaged' and 'ruined' body, but that proves impossible since her stories themselves, along with her desires, wishes, and passions, are entrenched in sadomasochism." Bone says that her "fantasies got more violent and more complicated as Daddy Glen continued to beat me. . . . I was ashamed of myself for the things I thought about when I put my hands between my legs."

Horvitz feels that *Bastard out of Carolina* "represents oppressed female sexuality formed on and from violence. A powerful indictment of men, marriage, and heterosexuality, this text yokes male-female intimacy with the potential denial/destruction of women." Bone fantasizes various tortures while masturbating, confusing sex with the violence of which she is victim. Gospel music becomes an escape. Although she cannot sing, Bone dreams of becoming a gospel singer—a way to escape her tormentor and find a release. A link to God might be the salvation she needs and craves.

Bone feels responsible for what is happening to her—that she must be completely bad simply because she is there: "I lived in a world of shame. I hid my bruises as if they were evidence of crimes I had committed. I knew I was a sick disgusting person." When Aunt Raylene discovers the welts on her legs, Bone tries to keep her from telling anyone. Bone feels a shock go through her: "Suddenly I was terrified, unreasonably, horribly terrified." Aunt Raylene goes directly to her brothers with the discovery. When Anney is asked if Glen would hurt her, she says, "He'd never raise a hand to me," and hangs her head. In spite of her self-loathing at her inability to protect Bone, Anney tries to excuse Glen and herself by saying that she loves him and that he loves all of them. Bone tries to exonerate her mother by saying "I made him mad. I did."

The place of the poor within the community and within the smaller community of the family is another theme. Allison, in an interview with Minnie Bruce Pratt for the *Progressive,* describes her place in the community: "The community I saw myself in— at the edge of the world—hated me. The white Southerner hates with a passion everybody different from them—there's no way around it." Anney understands this. This is her motivation for wanting a clear birth certificate—one without "illegitimate" stamped on it in red ink—for Bone. Within the family community, Allison knew as a teenager that she had more in common with the black community and the civil rights movement than with her stepfather, especially since he was abusing her. She realized that she was an outlaw because she felt she was evil among "that whole nation of the invisible, the dead, and the damned." Allison imbues Bone with these characteristics, showing her pain when she finds herself on the fringe of the community. Bone dreams of a different community, one made up of gospel music and gospel singers.

Bone's friendship with Shannon, an albino considered so physically unattractive

that she is shunned by most people in the community, is another sign that Bone feels herself outside the community in which she lives. For a time she uses the friendship in an attempt to distance herself from her family. She tries to break off the friendship but is drawn to Shannon. When Shannon is accidentally killed, her death haunts Bone, magnifying other small events in the family. Reese, Bone's stepsister, decides to be best friends with Patsy Ruth, a cousin. Bone is sent home from school for wearing jeans. Girls in the 1950s do not wear jeans to school, only dresses or skirts and blouses. Money is scarce. The people who might help out are out of work or in jail. Bone becomes concerned with her physical appearance and what others see in her. Anney tries to protect her from Glen by sending her to Aunt Alma's after school for a few days. Bone begins to recognize her anger at Daddy Glen. The death of Aunt Ruth, who has been a refuge, provides another shock, followed by the death of Aunt Alma's baby girl. This death, though expected, is shocking enough to Aunt Alma to cause her to destroy her home and try to kill her husband. Bone witnesses the aftermath of Aunt Alma's breakdown when she goes with Anney to try to calm her. Bone knows that everything in her world is uncertain.

◆ CHARACTERS ◆

Ruth Anne Boatwright is about six years old when the story opens and nearly thirteen when it ends. Glen's abuse begins soon after his marriage to her mother while Anney is in the hospital giving birth to his son, who dies. Even worse, she can have no more children. Bone, typical of a child her age, does not tell anyone what has happened to her because she does not understand what happened. Daddy Glen makes sure she feels it is her fault. She is a deprived child; deprived of enough to eat and a safe place to live in a home with people she can trust. Since she has had safety and love in the past, it is difficult for her to be sure she is not misreading Daddy Glen's intentions. She is angry with Glen and her mother but is too young to understand and verbalize her anger. From the beginning of her life, Bone is in an unusual position in the family because she is illegitimate. As she grows older, events put her farther and farther from the core of the family, adding to her feelings of anger and rejection. When her mother stands by and allows Glen to beat her and then continues to accept Glen after he rapes Bone, her ostracism from the family is complete. By age thirteen she is able to recognize her anger and reject the mother she knows she cannot change.

For Anney, having the red stamp on Bone's birth certificate declaring her to be illegitimate is more than she can bear. She tries each year to get a birth certificate without the stamp, unsuccessfully. The stamp symbolizes everything she hates about what people think of her, and yet she is unable to change her patterns of behavior. The clerks at the courthouse are visibly amused at her efforts to obtain a birth certificate without the stamp. This is so important to her that she consults an attorney, who also is amused. After giving half her money back, he advises her to wait until the ordinance is repealed. To her amusement, the courthouse burns down first. Anney thinks the most precious gift she could give Bone would be a birth certificate without the red "illegitimate" stamp. Anney is caught in a trap of her own making, powerless to make choices that will help Bone. Poor and a woman, she has little education and no job skills. She marries, only to be widowed by a freak automobile accident, leaving her with two small children, worse off than before. When she chooses to marry the "somewhat sinister Glen," himself a victim of child abuse, she closes the circle, locking herself and Bone into a situation

with terrifying consequences. She cannot see the evil in Glen. Anney loves her daughters, and her desire is to have a home where they are well cared for. The reality is a home where Glen acts out the abuse he has suffered, passing it on to Bone. Anney makes excuses for Glen and his inability to provide for the family. Bone refuses to acknowledge Glen as her father, telling him "I'd rather die than go back to living with you." Her refusal to accept his last punishment is the final insult to Glen, the first time she has had the courage to fight back. Even after Glen rapes Bone, Anney finds it impossible to break with him. All she can do for Bone is give her the unmarked birth certificate.

Glen Waddell understands completely that he cannot physically harm Anney in any way. Earle Boatwright and Glen are "workmates" when Glen first sees Anney and remarks on her looks, not knowing Earle is her brother. Earle's face gives him warning that he is to treat Anney with respect. Glen has suffered mental abuse from his father and been laughed at by his brothers for "his hot temper, bad memory, and general uselessness" his whole life. Earle is his ideal, the man he wants to be, whose approval he now craves with Anney his ticket into the Boatwright mystic. He decides he will "shame daddy and shock his brothers" by marrying Anney, since to the Waddells, the Boatwright family is "poor white trash." Bone and Reese experience his family's prejudice against them, and Bone retaliates by stripping the rosebuds from the bushes in the Waddell garden. Glen's marriage to Anney becomes a competition with Bone for Anney's attention and affection, and Bone's refusal to acknowledge him makes him furious. He must then act out the rage, abusing her.

Uncle Earle, among Anney's brothers, is the most strongly defined. He is Bone's favorite uncle, visiting Anney and the girls many evenings between the death of Lyle, Reese's father and Anney's first husband, and Anney's marriage to Glen. After the marriage, Earle's visits become fewer and fewer. Bone regrets this, since Uncle Earle "made them laugh." Bone then has no one who might stop the beatings. Raylene takes Bone to visit Earle at the county farm. From Uncle Earle, Bone gains a small measure of self-assurance when he shows her a small blade he has been able to steal from the leather shop. This upwelling of pride and strength leads to the break-in at Woolworth's, the only way Bone can think of to get even with all the people who are making her life unbearable. It is Earle who initiates Glen's punishment when Aunt Raylene discovers that Bone is being beaten.

Aunt Raylene is "different." She lives alone, by the river, supporting herself by selling produce she raises and jams and jellies she makes. The bend in the river at the foot of her property gives up treasures that can be cleaned, repaired, and sold for additional income. As a girl, Raylene had a love affair with another woman who could not leave her husband and small child. The affair marks both their lives, leaving Raylene to continue hers alone.

◆ TECHNIQUES ◆

Allison uses language and dialect to depict the world of the poor people of the South of this period. In the interview with Pratt, Allison explains some of the reasons for her uses of language and dialect. The speech of poor white working-class people is often thought to be a worthless language. Much of the natural flow of the speech patterns has been lost with the advent of television and a more universal dialect in the United States. Allison says that the "language rhythms of the people I am writing about come entirely from gospel music, country music, and the church . . . the peo-

ple whose voices I am using are very smart people. They are simply uneducated." She goes on to say that she had to "argue for my spelling of two words in particular. One was 'mama.' And one was 'an't'—as in 'I an't having any.'" Word repetition is another use of language that allows the reader into the novel's setting. Phrases such as "black, black hair" show these rhythms.

Allison admits that *Bastard out of Carolina* is somewhat autobiographical. Her mother, to whom the book is dedicated, gave birth to her at age fifteen. Allison's stepfather sexually abused her from about age seven until she told an aunt, who told her mother. Her mother put a stop to the abuse, but it scarred Allison. She uses storytelling as a way of dealing with her feelings about the past.

Telling the story from the viewpoint of the child, beginning at age six, before she is able to understand or express her feelings about the events she is caught up in, sets up a tension more terrifying than a horror movie. Bone's survival is at stake from the beginning. Allison explains the difficulties of living in poverty, showing how Bone becomes more and more aware of her place—or lack of place—in the community as she grows older. Bone's growing resentment against anyone she perceives to have slighted her or her family is told in a matter-of-fact way that warns of the ease with which any child can be ostracized within a community.

◆ LITERARY PRECEDENTS ◆

Hailed by George Garrett in the *New York Times Book Review* as "a major new talent," Allison's *Bastard out of Carolina* can be compared to the work of several authors. In *Contemporary Literature*, Horvitz compares it to Gayl Jones's *Corregidora*. Horvitz focuses on "the complex, commingled relationships between sexual trauma, its repression, and its potential healing through narration/narrative" present in both texts. Comparing Bone and Ursa, saying that both are in slavery, Horvitz continues, "both novels emphasize the crucial need to understand and integrate one's past, especially when that story derives from and is embedded in sexual/violent trauma."

According to Patricia Gulian in *Library Journal*, the character Sister in Janice Daugharty's *Like a Sister* is reminiscent of Bone, since both are living in poverty, are abused and abandoned, and feel the discomfort of being an outsider. Bone will escape but not Sister.

tions based on friends, family, and acquaintances." The memoir includes photographs of family members, and Allison says, "The bottom line is I'm writing to save the dead."

Cavedweller was published in 1999. The story is about a rock singer, Delia Byrd, who returns to her hometown in Georgia after a ten-year absence. She is searching for her daughters, whom she abandoned when she fled an abusive husband. A review in *Christian Century* calls it "a narrative about an entire community." The theme is redemption: how Delia can make amends to her daughters, her husband, and the community.

◆ RELATED TITLES ◆

Allison's collections of poems and short stories, *The Women Who Hate Me* and *Trash*, gained recognition for her writing ability in the 1980s. Writing for *DISCovering Authors*, Annmarie Pinarski says that the poems in *The Women Who Hate Me* "explore love, sexual desire, betrayal, and bitterness . . . weaving memory and metaphor together with specific experience." *Trash*, a collection of short stories that draw on childhood experiences, physical violence, poverty, class politics, and lesbian sexuality, won two Lambda Book Awards for lesbian fiction.

Nonfiction by Allison includes *Skin: Talking about Sex, Class, and Literature*, a collection of essays, performance pieces, and autobiographical narratives, an expression of Allison's ongoing commitment to her overarching theme, feminism. According to Pinarski, another tribute to the women in Allison's life is *Two or Three Things I Know for Sure*, a multimedia piece that was first performed in San Francisco in 1991. Revised and rewritten for publication in 1995, the book is dedicated to Allison's sisters. She says, however, that the characters are "crea-

◆ ADAPTATIONS ◆

Aired on Showtime on December 15, 1996, Anjelica Huston's adaptation of *Bastard out of Carolina* is a "blunt, at times shockingly graphic approach" to the book, says Lisa Schwarzbaum in *Entertainment Weekly*. Originally made for TNT, Ted Turner refused to air the film, calling it "too disturbing." Starring eleven-year-old Jena Malone as Ruth Anne, Jennifer Jason Leigh as Anney, and Ron Eldard as Daddy Glen, the film focuses on Ruth Anne's "misery and her growing resolve to fight back." Having to watch the violence makes the viewer ashamed, but it is the creation of "a sense of blood ties and love, even among family members as beaten down as the Boatwrights" that is Huston's accomplishment with the film, Schwarzbaum says.

Dorothy Allison reads on a sound recording produced in 1993. Consisting of two cassettes, the audio version is 180 minutes in all. *Publishers Weekly* calls the reading "persuasive in its eerie emotional tenor," adding that Allison's voice conveys the "ominous flat stillness of a calm before a storm."

The fact that Allison is able to overcome the abuse and poverty of her childhood shows that the effects need not be permanent. However, research shows she is the exception rather than the rule. Many children reared in poverty cannot break out because they can see no way to change their lives. Allison gives Bone the drive to learn, to do well in school in spite of her home life, a drive that served Allison so well in her own escape from poverty.

1. Federal and local governments have programs to assist low-income families. Find out what is available in your community.

2. Recognizing that being self-supporting builds self-confidence, suggest ways to improve a person's ability to earn a living.

3. Suggest ways your local schools can help to ensure that all students graduate with the skills needed to make a living.

4. Should the community encourage unwed mothers to complete their education?

5. Discuss alternatives that may be open to an unwed, teenage mother.

6. Look for information about the effects of giving up a baby for adoption on the later life of the mother.

7. How does Allison express her ideas about feminism in *Bastard out of Carolina?*

8. What does research tell us about the effects of an open adoption on the child? On the birth mother? On the adoptive family?

9. Do research into the causes of death in infants in your area.

10. Compare the job outlook for a woman today with the job outlook for a woman in the 1950s.

Ann Barton Sciba
Wharton High School Library

BEFORE I SAY GOOD-BYE

Novel

2000

Author: Mary Higgins Clark

◆

◆ SOCIAL CONCERNS ◆

Mary Higgins Clark owes her enormous popular success as the "Queen of Suspense" to her penchant for the news. All of her novels have drawn from American current affairs, whether child abduction, capital punishment, or health maintenance organizations. In *Before I Say Good-bye,* Clark again buttresses her murder mystery with two newsworthy topics: corruption in the construction industry and fraud in the burgeoning field of psychic communication. The mystery revolves around a cabin cruiser that was purposely blown up in New York Harbor, apparently killing four business associates, but the answer to the mystery lies in the criminal activities of New York's construction and psychic industries. Drawing from articles in the *New York Times* on the graft and fraud in the construction industry, Clark fictionalizes the bid-rigging and bribery among architectural firms, building contractors, and real-estate developers as a springboard for murder. ESP is also at the heart of this murder mystery. Having read in the news about how New York welfare recipients were being trained as psychics, Clark became interested in psychic phenomena and the industry that has built up around it. After Nell MacDermott learns about her husband's accident on the

boat, she attempts to correspond with him through a psychic, Bonnie Wilson, who can communicate with the dead. The novel balances belief in ESP with skepticism, juxtaposing the "phonies" in the industry against real psychic experience. While it authenticates Nell's psychic contact with her parents after their death in a plane accident, it repudiates the industry that capitalizes on people's grief and naivete.

Another consistent, if understated, social concern in *Before I Say Good-bye* is its feminism. Here, as in all of her fiction, Clark focuses on a strong female character in duress who is capable of coping with adversity with grace and intelligence. Nell is a well-educated, financially independent, ambitious woman who writes a newspaper column for the *New York Journal* and has a brilliant career ahead of her in New York congressional politics. Her political career, however, is hampered by resistance from her husband, Adam Cauliff, who himself has what looks like an auspicious career as an architect. For years, he reproaches Nell for her political ambitions, but it is not until after his accident that she begins to question his opposition to her career choices and reconsider the soundness of their marriage. As she realizes that her marriage was a pretense, she also discovers that her husband is guilty of corruption and also responsible for the bombing. Adam blows up the boat in order to feign death and disappear with the cache he has amassed from bribes in the construction industry. Before the boat explodes, he makes a daring escape, but forgets the safety deposit key that he needs to collect his stash. In order to retrieve the key, he persuades Bonnie to con Nell into believing that he is contacting her from the dead, but he proves unsuccessful. In the final climactic scene, Adam discloses himself and his ruse to Nell; he attempts to murder her for interfering with his plans, but ultimately plummets to his own death in the process. Nell is just one among many of Clark's female heroines who is victimized by the men in her life. Yet, like Clark's other heroines under siege, Nell eventually prevails over her husband. Mitigating the novel's feminism, however, is the introduction of an alternative love interest for Nell, Dr. Dan Minor. When Dan finally rescues Nell from her husband's brutality, the novel succumbs to a stock narrative convention that assumes women's fragility and establishes them as victims who require male protection. Clark's novel endorses a conservative rather than combative feminism, one that allows for women's financial and professional independence, but suggests that their emotional needs must be met by a male counterpart. *Before I Say Good-bye* may insist on women's full participation in society, finally revealing Nell as the winner of the congressional seat her grandfather had occupied for many years and establishing Dan as her most ardent supporter, but the novel does not challenge the heterosexual ideal or essentialist notions about femininity. The novel has the makings of a feminist murder mystery, with Nell as an amateur female detective at the helm, but it resorts to romantic platitudes that shift the focus away from female heroism and agency onto male heroism. Once Dan rescues Nell from the fire, Nell's char-

acterization as an independent career woman/amateur sleuth becomes moot: in terms of plot development, she is simply the beautiful lady in distress.

The novel's social conservativeness manifests itself not only in its brand of feminism, but also in its focus on the professional classes. It is not the lives of the poor or even the middle class in which this novel is interested, but rather those of the privileged. While there are a bevy of indigents and social misfits who appear in the novel (like the petty criminal Jed Kaplan and the besotted street ladies Quinny and Karen Renfrew), they occupy a minor role, their history and psychology nowhere nearly as complete as their more affluent and successful counterparts. Nell, with her trust money and Upper East Side Manhattan apartment, Adam with his new forty-foot cabin cruiser, and Cornelius MacDermott (Mac) with his longtime Manhattan congressional seat, are the characters on which the novel dwells. Clark shows a materialist preoccupation with the glamour and luxury of their lives, noting Nell's "green silk Escada pants suit," the family dinner at the Four Seasons, and the precious Chivas Regal that Adam consumes. *Before I Say Good-bye* ultimately concerns itself then with admiring the lifestyle of Manhattan's elite and providing its largely middle-class readers a glimpse into a life about which they can only fantasize.

◆ THEMES ◆

Invasion is Clark's primary thematic focus in *Before I Say Good-bye*. As she reveals in an interview with Claire E. White, "I write about very nice people whose lives are invaded. They're not screeching at each other at the breakfast table. Something happens that cuts across their lives. They have to respond to it and solve the problem. . . . It's not *American Beauty*; it's not that kind of relationship at all. I choose to write about people whose trouble comes from the outside, not the inside." In other words, it is not psychological, but social disruption that intrigues Clark. As the novel describes the attack on Nell's life by her husband, it correlates this abuse to larger social problems: women's victimization by men and the threat to the professional classes by the refractory rabble. *Before I Say Good-bye* presents us with an insular world of privilege, where a woman may be able to take over the patriarch's place as its head representative, but where other kinds of social mobility are thwarted. Adam attempts to enter this world of privilege by marrying Nell and exploiting her high-profile connections to find himself a position at a renowned architectural firm; however, he remains a perpetual outsider. Nell's grandfather, Mac, disapproves of him from the beginning. Although he never clearly outlines his grounds for disapproval, he reveals a prejudice against his lowly background when he notes the incongruity between Adam's appearance and reality: "You're from a one-horse town in North Dakota, but you look and sound like a preppie from Yale." Alluding continually to Adam's disadvantaged socioeconomic background in order to justify its ultimate assessment of him as a sociopath, the novel implicitly suggests that Adam's upbringing in a hick town and a "broken home" explains how he becomes a threat both to women and the professional classes. As his past employer explains about him, "Adam Cauliff believed absolutely that he had a right to anything he wanted, be it a woman or a simple possession . . . [he] has a serious personality disorder and is probably a full-fleged sociopath. . . . He appears to have a complete disregard for, and to be in conflict with, the normal social code by which most people conduct their lives." Once Adam is killed, Dan conveniently assumes Adam's former role as Nell's love interest. A more suitable match for

Nell, in terms of both background and pedigree, his character symbolizes the reinstatement of the social order as the novel defines it: one where women can succeed as well as men while still maintaining the trappings of femininity and one where politicians marry doctors, not small-town hicks.

Linked to this fear of invasion is the desire to retain power. Informing the two key power struggles in the novel are the social divisions of class, gender, and age. The first contest of power is between Adam and Mac. Adam's incursion into Manhattan's professional elite threatens class boundaries. Mac repudiates him on the grounds of social inferiority, while Adam resents his prejudice, observing to Nell, "I was never good enough for you, never good enough to mix with your precious grandfather's cronies." Siding with Mac, the novel condemns Adam as a sociopath and kills him off in the end; it apparently supports the class distinctions that Mac fights to uphold. The second, and more complex, contest of power occurs between Mac and Nell. Nell's attempt to enter the political sphere that her grandfather once dominated is fraught with tension.

Reluctant to lose his position as Manhattan's reigning patriarch, he proves to be a domineering, though benevolent, mentor to Nell. "They fight constantly," Clark reveals in her interview with White, "but they are crazy about each other." After he retires, he encourages Nell to campaign for his old congressional seat, but he monitors her passage at every step: he advises her when to seek election, how to campaign, and how to avoid scandal. Adam aptly observes that Mac is unwilling to relinquish his dynasty:

> Nell simply refused to acknowledge the fact that Mac wanted her to run for his former seat for only one reason: he intended to make her his puppet. All that pious mouthing about retiring at eighty rather than be the oldest member of the

House was a lot of baloney. The truth was that the guy the Democrats were putting up against him at the time was strong and might have staged an upset. Mac didn't want to retire; he just didn't want to go out a loser.

Albeit an unreliable observer, who assumes Mac's political vulnerability when there is no other evidence to support his claim, he does recognize Mac's ambivalence about abdicating his authority. The contest between Mac and Nell is both generational and gendered: Mac is not altogether prepared to embrace his old age or accept the social changes that have increased women's political opportunities. The transition of power from Mac to Nell, however, is far more successful than that between Mac and Adam. Nell eventually wins her seat, a victory proving that, in this novel, class difference is a more inflexible social barrier than either age or gender.

◆ CHARACTERS ◆

Before I Say Good-bye continually alternates point of view, introducing more than a dozen characters with a broad scope of psychological profiles. Fascinated by human psychology, Clark designs detailed character biographies for all of her characters, though she focuses on some more than others. This novel focuses predominantly on the community surrounding Nell, who, as the novel's central character, is the most psychologically rich. An independent and intelligent woman with political prospects, she is also vulnerable. Orphaned as a young girl, she is a lonely woman. Although she was raised with love by her grandfather Mac and Aunt Gert, they are her only family. Throughout the novel, she noticeably lacks a female community of friends. Eventually we learn that she had married Adam after a whirlwind romance in order to fill this void in her life. Mac and Gert, who are

exact psychological opposites, influence Nell differently, though equally significantly. Like Mac, Nell is aggressively rational and pragmatic, but like Gert, she shares a belief in the supernatural. Adam, the other most significant person in Nell's life, unfortunately turns out to be a sociopath. When writing about a disturbed personality, Clark reveals to CNN Book Chat that she carefully researches it: "I've taken many psychology courses and I always check with friends who are psychologists or psychiatrists to be sure I'm on target when I write about the psychopathic personality." Adam, as a result of this research, comes across as a textbook sociopath with his charming persona but ruthless indifference. Dan, the last person in Nell's immediate circle, promises to fill the emotional vacuum that Adam cannot. Yet, at least in terms of the novel's feminist sympathies, more promising than Dan's love is perhaps the friendship of Lisa Ryan. Lisa, the wife of one of the victims of the boat explosion, shows friendship to Nell by the end of the novel by supporting her election campaign. While the novel yields to convention by introducing a new love interest to combat Nell's loneliness, it also finally acknowledges the importance of a community of women.

Besides Nell's circle, there is a throng of minor characters. One of the most interesting of these is Winifred Johnson. Believed to have the "gumption of a wallflower," she proves to be deceptively cunning. Yet, Clark depicts her sympathetically. "Her background was very harsh, and as a result she has a very vivid fantasy life," Clark explains in the interview with White, "and she harbors a great deal of resentment which has to come out somewhere." A plain old maid ruled by her mother, Winifred finds herself susceptible to Adam's charm and professed affection. Having worked as a secretary in a prominent architecture firm for years, she discloses the industry's covert and illegal activities to Adam in order to help him gain financially from this knowledge. Jimmy and Lisa Ryan are also among the more fully developed characters. Jimmy is one of the victims of the boat explosion. When Lisa discovers fifty thousand dollars in his workshop after his death, she is surprised and puzzled to learn that he accepted a bribe. A few years back, he had quit his job as a construction worker on ethical grounds, exposing the use of substandard materials in construction. Lisa, left to discover the secret of his depression the months leading up to his death, unravels the mystery. Unemployed and in debt for years, Jimmy was grateful to Adam for finding him a job, but subsequently felt helpless to resist pressure from Adam to burn a landmark building on a site that he hoped to develop. In return for his act of arson, he accepted the bribe, but discovered to his horror that he had killed a street lady trapped in the building—a woman who proves to be Quinny, the long lost mother Dan attempts to locate throughout the novel. Other noteworthy characters are those who function to heighten the suspense: Ben Tucker, a boy who witnesses the accident and has nightmares about a man who escapes from the boat as it explodes; Peter Lang, a hot-shot real estate developer, who should have been on the boat, but has a timely car accident that prevents him from getting on it; and Jed Kaplan, a thief who hates Adam Cauliff for buying property that he sees as his due inheritance.

One of the more interesting aspects of characterization in this novel is that it is organized on both psychological and thematic levels. While all of the characters have independent identities, they also are grouped in social units. Clark employs her understanding that identity is not formed in isolation, but rather in community, for literary and thematic effect. Gender is key to characterization in this novel and connects to its overarching assumption that women are victims of male violence and control. Although the female characters are individually distinct, they all are burdened by the men in their lives. Nell, Winifred, and Bonnie are all victims of Adam's manipulation and brutality, while Lisa suffers from her husband's secret guilt. The novel explores the different ways in which the characters respond to the same problem; Winifred's submissiveness, for instance, functioning as a foil to Nell's aggressiveness. If characters are organized into gendered thematic clusters, they also are organized into familial ones. As the novel explores the issue of contested authority, it introduces four characters whose lives are affected problematically, if differently, by parental authority. Nell struggles with Mac's domineering tendencies; Winifred is psychologically hampered by the continuous complaints and demands of her ailing mother; and Jed feels frustrated with his mother, who is far too savvy to allow him to control the purse strings. Connected to the issue of parental authority is parental abandonment. The characters of both Nell and Dan are formed by the loss of their parents to death and alcohol respectively. As the novel shows how identity is formed in relationships, it explores how people differently respond to similar social environments to become unique human beings, a literary feat that makes *Before I Say Good-bye* more psychologically sophisticated than the standard murder mystery.

◆ TECHNIQUES ◆

Before I Say Good-bye is a murder mystery, a tautly plotted novel that relies on continuous suspense and intrigue for its success. As Clark insists in her interview with CNN Book Chat, "I want to keep the reader guessing until virtually the last page." In order to prolong the suspense, Clark relies on a series of literary ploys that are the hallmark of the genre. Multiple suspects, red herrings, cliffhangers, and missing information are all the tricks of the trade that Clark exploits as a means to conceal the secret around which the mystery revolves. As in most murder mysteries, the murder happens within the first few chapters. Almost immediately, the novel begins its investigation by casting suspicion and uncovering motive, introducing multiple suspects in the process. The ensuing investigation uncovers Jed's experience with explosives, Peter's frustration with Adam for impeding his lucrative, but precarious, real-estate project, Jimmy's fifty thousand dollar hush money, and Winifred's mysterious source of income. All of these false clues function as red herrings, their purpose to obfuscate and mislead readers so that they do not guess too far in advance that Adam is the true criminal. In order to provide multiple suspects and construct red herrings, the novel is selective about the information it reveals. One of the functions of the shifting narrative perspectives is to present false or misleading information to readers, thus placing them in the same position as the investigator whose knowledge is incomplete. For instance, early in the novel, one chapter is devoted to Adam's point of view, but Clark is chary about revealing too much information about him. She never intimates Adam's plans to blow up the boat, but rather encourages readers to sympathize with him for being the underappreciated son-in-law of the congressman. By so doing, Clark ensures that readers do not include Adam among the lists of suspects too soon.

In addition to these literary ploys, the novel follows other literary conventions of the murder mystery, particularly its narrative structure. Like most fiction of its kind, it begins with a murder, proceeds with an investigation, introduces a final and unexpected twist at the end (when Adam reappears from the dead), concludes with a full disclosure of the crime, follows with a climactic final conflict, and then finishes with a resolution. The narrative structure of the murder mystery reveals the fundamental conservativism of the genre; novels like Clark's depend on the thrill of danger, suspense, and crime for their success, but also carefully regulate and suppress this kind of social disruption in their conclusion. As a literary genre, the murder mystery is highly regulated and formulaic; as a social text, it is equally conservative.

◆ LITERARY PRECEDENTS ◆

Clark's novel follows in a long tradition. Wilkie Collins popularized the mystery novel in Victorian times with his publication of *The Woman in White* (1860) and *The Moonstone* (1868). Clark does not cite Collins as an influence, but she does acknowledge a literary debt to later turn-of-the-century and early twentieth-century mystery writers such as Sir Arthur Conan Doyle and Agatha Christie. While she does not mention any contemporary influences or favorites (with the exception of her daughter Carol Higgins Clark, herself a fledgling mystery writer), a part of her success is owing to the flourishing interest in the thriller—whether the murder mystery, spy novel, crime novel, legal and medical thriller, police procedural, or horror story. Not only the book industry, but also the film and television industries have fueled and capitalized on the audience's desire for a thrill. Often the same story is adapted to different media, and in some cases, a story presented in one medium will influence a work created in another. *Before I Say Good-bye*, for example, recalls Jerry Zucker's film *Ghost* (1990), a psychological suspense that involves a husband who communicates with his wife from the dead in order to catch his killer. The difference with Clark's novel is that the psychic communication is an elaborate ruse perpetrated by a husband who is not dead, but in fact the killer.

Clark's novel shares many similarities with the contemporary mystery novel, particularly in its attention to the professional classes. Professionalism is a key feature in recent mysteries, perhaps because many of the authors themselves have lucrative careers and identify with the lifestyle and concerns of the affluent and successful. *Before I Say Good-bye* is different from other contemporary mysteries, however, because of its lack of sex and violence. As Clark says in an interview with David Weich, "I don't use explicit sex or violence so I wind up on the reading list for the seventh grade. And it's not that I'm a prude; I've always just preferred the idea of implied violence. The Hitchcock way. How many ways can you shoot people up? I think footsteps—that can be scarier." Clark's novel is also distinctive for its increased focus on women and domesticity. While the novel chooses a professional woman as its protagonist, it describes her frequently in private settings where it freely explores both the architecture of her home and her mind. Many recent mystery writers, such as Sue Grafton, Patricia Cornwell, and Nora Roberts, choose female protagonists, but Clark is special because she has done so consistently during her twenty-five years as an author.

◆ RELATED TITLES ◆

This novel is consistent with much of Clark's earlier fiction. Outside of her fictional biography of George Washington, *Aspire to the Heavens* (1968), Clark has written a total of twenty-two mystery novels. All of her novels concentrate on a topical issue in the news, and typically, they feature a female protagonist who, out of exigency, adopts the role of amateur sleuth. The theme of female victimization also appears frequently in her fiction. In *Let Me Call You Sweetheart* (1995), a beautiful woman is murdered by her male lover, and in *You*

Belong to Me (1998), a ruthless and deranged man hunts lonely women on cruise ships. Clark's novels also typically focus on the professional classes. *We'll Meet Again* (1999) bases its story on a female journalist and a doctor's wife. *The Lottery Winner: Alvirah and Willy Stories* (1994) is a notable exception to this spotlight on the professional classes. Alvirah, the wily protagonist of these stories, is a housekeeper who is only catapulted to the life of luxury—and crime—after she wins the lottery. In short, Clark's novels differ little from one another in terms of their thematic concerns and narrative structure. What makes them distinct is the specific topical issues that they explore.

◆ ADAPTATIONS ◆

In 2000, *Before I Say Good-bye* was published in hardcover and on-line as an electronic text. Both abridged and unabridged versions of the novel have been recorded on audiocassette and compact disc, read by Jan Maxwell.

◆ IDEAS FOR GROUP DISCUSSIONS ◆

Before I Say Good-bye draws attention to women's interests and the professional classes, but neither its feminism nor its professionalism is clearly defined. While it focuses on female independence and intelligence, it also assumes female vulnerability. Similarly, while it spotlights the professional classes, it conveys the point of view of social misfits like Jed Kaplan and Karen Renfrew. Insofar as the novel furnishes an array of voices from the social spectrum, it may have more egalitarian sympathies than its concentration on the lives of the privileged initially suggests. The social concerns, themes, and characters that Clark introduces address these two issues, working both with and against each other to complicate the novel's stance. Her novel both creates and reflects the complexity with which the issues of feminism and elitism have been debated within American society itself.

1. To what extent is this novel a feminist murder mystery? Is its feminism consistent? Does its focus on female psychology, its assumption of female victimization, and its insertion of romance into the action preclude a male readership?

2. Is this novel elitist because it concentrates on the lives of the successful and affluent? Many contemporary mystery novels focus on the professional classes; is the genre itself an elitist one?

3. Is this novel an example of pulp fiction or high literature? To what extent does Clark's focus on topical issues from the news make her work more trendy than durable? What is the basis of the distinction between popular and literary novels?

4. Clark researches the psychological profiles of her characters. She consults psychologists about psychopathic personalities and, as she mentions to CNN Book Chat, consulted a psychologist about her character little Ben Tucker, the boy who witnessed the explosion of the boat. Does her research make her characterization more vivid and accurate, or does it make it more stiff and academic? Consider in particular the characterization of Adam, Winifred, and Ben.

5. This novel combines elements of the murder mystery, the romance, and the ghost story. In an interview with Claire E. White, Clark admits that the most challenging aspect of writing this book "was the balancing of the psychic elements with the suspense elements." Is the novel successful at combining these multiple genres, or do the aims of these genres conflict too readily to be joined?

6. Carol Higgins Clark likes to refer to her mother as "scary Mary." Yet, Clark's novels avoid gratuitous violence and instead rely on implied violence for their effects. Does Clark's avoidance of explicit violence diminish the "scariness" of the novel or heighten it? Consider what induces more terror: a chainsaw or a shadow.

7. Are feminism and professionalism, the two key social issues in *Before I Say Good-bye*, still of contemporary relevance? Or are these concerns now resolved and superannuated?

Colette Colligan
Queen's University, Canada

THE BIRDS

Short Story

1952

Author: Daphne du Maurier

◆ SOCIAL CONCERNS ◆

Since du Maurier's short story "The Birds" never fully resolves itself and since it contains no explanation for the birds' attack on people, one must rely on individual interpretations of the story's action to find du Maurier's social concerns. The author merely suggests that social concerns are at the heart of the bizarre, supernatural events related in "The Birds." These concerns include a lack of respect for nature, a self-destructive impulse, and a deep-seated suspicion peculiar to the Cold War.

Perhaps the simplest explanation for the uncanny events related in "The Birds" involves the notion of revenge. Humans have slaughtered birds for thousands of years; could their attack simply constitute a turning of the tables? One must read between the lines to find support for this explanation in the text, but it is there. For example, the story takes place on a coastal farm. Students must keep in mind that authors who write in a medium as tight and closely controlled as a short story rarely leave anything to chance; the most minute detail often carries a great deal of significance. The farm represents mankind's most exacting control over nature. Fields, plants, and animals are carefully organized and the

food they provide systematically collected. Farming, though essential to human survival, signifies mastery over rather than cohabitation with the natural order. Since du Maurier starts the birds' attack on the site of such human dominance, the reader might infer that mankind's control over nature causes the author some degree of anxiety. Yes, we are a dominant species capable of keeping the natural world under our collective thumb. But is this a true dominance, or merely an illusion? "The Birds" functions in part as a warning against the hubris inherent in assumptions of mankind's dominance over nature. Should nature turn against us, we human would surely be on the losing side.

Even without nature turning against mankind, the species is to some degree doomed by its own penchant for self-destruction. Again, du Maurier's plot appears secondary to the truths of human nature revealed under extraordinary circumstances. The anxiety and fear prompted by the birds' attack draws too many parallels to war for a merely coincidental connection. When the crisis first strikes, the first impulse of Nat's wife is to have the authorities call out the army: "'what they ought to do,' she said, 'is to call the army out and shoot the birds. That would soon scare them off.'" Clearly, this suggestion has no rational basis; no army could put down an attack by billions of birds. That, however, is exactly du Maurier's point. Warfare never works as a rational explanation for the resolution of conflict. To instigate the slaughter of thousands of countrymen and foreigners is never a rational thing to do. The solution appears no less absurd when proposed for the resolution of a conflict between birds and humans.

Not only the suggestions for dealing with the birds seem absurd, however. Throughout the story, individuals attempt to rationalize the birds' behavior by linking it to the Soviet Union. In this way du Maurier introduces another social concern: the paranoia that struck the western world during the years of the Cold War. Beginning after World War II and continuing until at least the collapse of the Berlin Wall in 1989, the activities of the Soviet Bloc remained largely unknown to the public citizens of Western Europe and the United States. That their actions were unseen does not mean people did not imagine or guess at what they were doing. Because both the Soviet Union and its western counterpart, the United States, amassed nuclear weapons, people constantly feared political tensions would explode into a war that would bring about an end to humankind. Not surprisingly, this situation inspired a good deal of paranoia. In the United States this paranoia manifested itself in the persecution of well-placed individuals suspected of having ties to the communist party. The so-called McCarthy witch hunts (led by Wisconsin Senator Joe McCarthy) destroyed dozens of careers and reputations. The fears which fueled the trials were, of course, unfounded.

Implicitly, du Maurier critiques this mood of paranoia by having a few of her characters blame the Soviet government for the birds' bizarre behavior. Early in the story, before the birds' behavior turns deadly,

Nat has a conversation about the birds with a local farmer:

> "Well, what do you make of it? They're saying in town the Russians have done it. The Russians have poisoned the birds."
>
> "How could they do that?" asked Nat.
>
> "Don't ask me. You know how stories get around."

Stories simply get around, inspired by the public's irrational fear of the Soviet Union's power to destroy the western way of life. When faced with an unexplainable situation, the Soviet Bloc always made a convenient scapegoat during the Cold War.

Du Maurier criticizes more than the irrational fear of the Soviet Union, however. Set in Great Britain, "The Birds" gives du Maurier an opportunity to descry England's unreasonable reliance on American military strength. After her country's own efforts have apparently failed, Nat's wife says in desperation: "'Won't America do something . . . they've always been our allies, haven't they? Surely America will do something?'" This confidence in America's ability to extricate them from a crisis clearly caused by some supernatural force appears no less misguided than the assertion that Soviet scheming lies behind the crisis. Unfortunately for the characters in "The Birds," there are some forces beyond the control of the superpowers.

◆ THEMES ◆

Du Maurier clearly shows a stronger interest in psychological issues than social concerns in "The Birds." Three major themes garner as much of du Maurier's attention as the relatively simple plot. All these themes relate to the ways in which people deal with highly stressful situations.

The first of these themes is the hubris of mankind. When placed in an incomprehensible situation, du Maurier's characters continue to use their experience to exert some measure of control over the situation around them. People simply have too much pride, du Maurier suggests, to concede defeat or to admit that events such as the mass slaughter of people by birds are beyond their ken. Nat, for example, explains the birds' behavior away with references to natural habits. When the first, solitary bird attacks Nat he can explain it naturally: "frightened, he supposed, and bewildered, the bird, seeking shelter, had stabbed at him in the darkness. Once more he settled himself to sleep." Nat can sleep soundly after settling his mind with an explanation that seems reasonable. Birds act erratically when frightened, so the erratic behavior of this bird must be the result of fear.

Even when such rational explanations become absurd, du Maurier's characters continue to make them. Apparently, people can delude themselves a great deal when faced with untenable circumstances. As mentioned above, some characters turn to the evil machinations of the Soviet Union as a social explanation for the supernatural phenomenon. Clearly, though, such explanations are indicative of nothing more or less than the absurd way in which people assert their capacity for understanding even the most inexplicable situations.

Once the characters give up on trying to explain the crisis in which they find themselves, they give over to the mood swings that accompany a highly stressful situation. Nat's family is variously hysterical, meditative, and desperate in the face of the birds' attack. Having endured the thuds of the birds on their roofs and windows for a day and a night, Nat's children relieve their anxiety by laughing at the situation: "This was the way to face up to it. This was the spirit. If they could keep up like this, hang on like this until seven, when the first news bulletin came through, they would not have done too badly."

The morning light and the familiar sound of the news coming over the radio can replace the emotional relief provided by laughter. In fact, a variety of small comforts can, du Maurier asserts, lessen the anxiety caused by imminent danger. Nat understands this, so he puts his wife and children to small, more or less meaningless tasks in the hope that these chores will make them feel as if a degree of normalcy remains. Nat believes that this is as important for his wife as it is for his children: "It kept his wife occupied, undressing the children before the fire, seeing to the bedding, one thing and another, while he went round the cottage again, making sure that nothing had worked loose." Domestic habit ameliorates the feeling of dread as much as hysterical laughter. Anything, it seems, that distracts du Maurier's characters from the danger outside their cottage's walls aid them in coping with their fear.

Eventually, though, a dangerous situation will break those who do everything in their power to endure the anxiety it causes. This happens in the final pages when, enjoying a temporary break in the birds' attack, Nat prepares to leave in order to gather supplies. Having relied on his steady calm through the night of terror, his wife gives into despair: "'Take us with you,' she begged, 'we can't stay here alone. I'd rather die than stay here alone.'" Du Maurier's characters thus run the whole gamut of psychological states. They cope with small familiarities or laughter. After sustaining their tension for so long, however, du Maurier finally narrates the breaking of their spirit, their resignation to their fate.

◆ CHARACTERS ◆

Du Maurier tells "The Birds" in the third person. Nevertheless, the events related are filtered through the consciousness of one character, Nat. This solitary man lives on the English coast with his small family in a humble farming cottage. His resourcefulness and cautious habits preserve his and his family's lives long enough to make a compelling story. He also contributes to du Maurier's thematic interest in the psychological responses of people in extraordinary circumstances.

Having coexisted with nature for his entire life, Nat feels as if he understands the patterns of life quite well. When he first sees birds massing in unusual ways, he has a plethora of natural explanations. He thus demonstrates a very human trait; he relies on his personal experience to rationalize and contain unfamiliar experience. This reaction is especially understandable given the precariousness of his situation. When faced with danger, Nat tries to deflate that danger by making it more familiar and understandable.

In addition to demonstrating the human tendency to explain away all disagreeable appearances, Nat shows a large capacity for crowd control. He understands how the stress affects his wife and children, so Nat takes pains to deflect their anxiety through productive channels. In a sense, Nat is the surrogate author, standing back from the crisis and evaluating it objectively. He remains calm and collected throughout, commenting on the folly of his neighbors and the rising fear of his wife and children.

The Trigg family works as a foil to Nat's family. They are near neighbors with the same background as Nat and his kin. The Triggs, however, betray a failure to accept the extremity of a crisis beyond their experience. They have lived their entire lives dominating the birds, so when the tables are turned, they do not accept the fact. When the birds begin swarming overhead, Mr. Trigg responds by grabbing his shotgun and heading out for a shooting party. He does not think to take cover as Nat does. The Triggs, then, represent the hubris or excessive pride of humanity. They are either unwilling or unable to imagine a world in which they do not dominate every other species.

◆ TECHNIQUES ◆

Obviously, du Maurier's story of supernatural events and almost unbearable suspense relies most heavily on its author's great talent for creating and maintaining tension. She very carefully constructs every portion of the story to maintain a constant feeling of foreboding in her reader. The story opens with an eerie indication that the world is about to be thrown into disarray, that chaos is about to be unleashed: "On December the third the wind changed overnight and it was winter." Du Maurier taps into her readers' primal sense of the weather as a harbinger of good and bad tidings. The sudden cooling of the earth prompts the reader's instinctive fear of the cold and the dark. By situating a seemingly innocuous image of the coming winter in her story's first sentence, du Maurier sets the tone with an appeal to her reader's deepest feelings.

The tension created by this first phrase never slackens. Throughout the story's thirty-eight pages the reader remains anxious about what might happen to Nat and his family. One way readers are kept thus on edge involves du Maurier's tendency to deny both her characters and her readers a clear view of the horror massing against them. Holed up in their small cottage, Nat's family cannot see the attacking birds, but the sounds they make indicate that danger lurks just beyond their sight. The sounds are foreboding to say the least: "Now and again came a thud, a crash, as some bird dived and fell." Nat and his family know they are in danger, but, since they cannot see the birds, they cannot guess the nature or extent of the threat. The suspense created by sound becomes more powerful when the birds of prey make an appearance at the cottage. Though he never sees the hawks and vultures that scratch at the window, Nat is sure that the crisis has become more intense when he hears the sound of talons ripping at his fortifications.

Du Maurier constantly ups the ante in other respects. The story builds in a steady crescendo. The massing of gulls at sea appears first as a curiosity. Soon, however, the mood becomes more ominous as a single bird swoops and strikes at Nat. Opening a window in the night, Nat felt that "something brushed his hand, jabbing at his knuckles, grazing at the skin. Then he saw the flutter of the wings and it was gone, over the roof, beyond the cottage." The story would contain much less emotional impact if the first bird attack produced a fatality. The intensity of attacks slowly builds until Nat knows he and his family are in real danger. Once holed up in their cottage, the intensity of the attack continues to build as the size of the birds' increases. The story is an excellent example of the power of du Maurier's technique of introducing, then steadily increasing, tension.

◆ LITERARY PRECEDENTS ◆

Du Maurier's clearest American predecessor is poet and short story writer Edgar Allen Poe. Like du Maurier, his stories narrate supernatural events that remain largely unexplained. "The Fall of the House of Usher" (1840), for example, relates events surrounding the accidental burial of a young woman, her re-emergence, and the destruction of the house in which all the events occur. Though this narrative sequence of events seems mysterious and remains largely unexplained, these attributes of the story are secondary to Poe's primary focus, the atmosphere created within the story and the psychological reactions the events provoke in the characters.

Poe was the first literary critic to theorize the short story at great length. He asserted that a great short story must do two things: first, it must remain short enough to read in a single sitting; second, it must create a single mood. In "The Fall of the House of Usher," the mood created is one of foreboding and unfocused dread. Du Maurier creates a similarly unified mood in "The Birds." Like Poe's tales, the plot remains somewhat secondary to atmospheric and psychological considerations.

In its reliance on animals as a vehicle for social and psychological commentary, "The Birds" recalls George Orwell's novel *Animal Farm* (1945). This classic text tells the story of a group of farm animals who organize against the farmers who oppress them and create their own utopian society. This society eventually devolves into a fascist regime with a pig named Napoleon at its head. Though stylistically similar, thematically the stories are quite different. du Maurier implies that constant suspicion of the Communist regime in the Soviet Union is irrational. Orwell, on the other hand, argues that all socialist societies necessarily disintegrate into oppressive, tyrannical, and manipulative communities.

◆ RELATED TITLES ◆

The other stories in the collection in which "The Birds" appears explore similar themes related to nature's power to confound. The title story, "The Apple Tree" for example, tells of an apple tree's supernatural power over a man. The tree sprouts up shortly after the death of his wife, and the man becomes convinced that the tree represents her. Unfortunately, he never loved his wife, so he endeavors to destroy the tree. It shows supernatural resilience, however, and only succumbs to the axe and saw. Even with the tree gone, though, the man cannot escape it. In the end, he trips over a root and falls in the snow. The story, like "The Birds," does not assign specific moral or even rational explanations to the events. The reader must decide if the occurrence is motivated by the man's psychological state or if the tree truly does enact revenge from beyond the grave. Other stories in the collection have similarly implausible plots. "Kiss Me Again, Stranger" for instance tells the impossible story of a man who falls in love with a strange woman, then realizes that she is a murderess. It, like "The Birds" relies much more heavily on the atmosphere created than the plot points related.

One of du Maurier's later stories, "Don't Look Now" (1971) repeats "The Birds" atmospheric intensity. The plot of the tale is almost absurdly simple, but the density of the story's atmosphere is overwhelming. The events related take place in Venice. John, the protagonist, is so affected by the city's brooding darkness that he eventually follows a girl that seems uncannily familiar down an alley. Unfortunately, the girl is actually a misshapen, murderous woman who turns on him and plunges a knife in his throat. When retold in this vein, the story seems absurd. Du Maurier's talent, displayed in "Don't Look Now" and "The Birds," is to invest an otherwise mediocre plot with psychological intensity.

◆ ADAPTATIONS ◆

Alfred Hitchcock adapted "The Birds" to film in 1963. The film worked from a screenplay written by Evan Hunter that made substantial departures from du Maurier's text. Hunter wove a love story into du Maurier's relatively simple tale of suspense. Additionally, Hitchcock's film transports the story from its setting on the coast of England to a small resort town in northern California.

The movie version of "The Birds" opens in San Francisco where Melanie Daniels, played by "Tippi" Hedren, meets the dashing Mitch Brenner (Rod Taylor). What ensues is a somewhat convoluted love story involving Mitch and Melanie as well as Mitch's mother (Jessica Tandy) and his former lover, Annie (Suzanne Pleshette). Melanie follows Mitch to his home in Bodega Bay, a small resort town north of the city. There the bird attacks ensue and Melanie is forced to hole up in Mitch's home. Eventually, the group heads out of town during a lull in the birds' attack.

The twists and turns of this plot make for more compelling cinema, but they also detract from du Maurier's tight, suspenseful production. Unlike du Maurier's depiction of worldwide apocalypse, Hitchcock's film suggests that the bird attack is in isolated incident. Furthermore, the film ends on a much more hopeful note for the main characters. Though battered, they seem, as the scene fades for the last time, to be headed for safety. Du Maurier's story ends on a more ambiguous note. Nat has stored his home with provisions and blocked every entryway, but larger birds seem to come every night, threatening even his most stalwart preventative measures.

Du Maurier hated Hitchcock's adaptation of her story. "The Birds" remained one of her favorite stories until her death. Its power, she thought, lay in its simplicity, its reliance on atmosphere and tension rather than plot. She never understood why Hitchcock took such liberties with her ideas. Clearly, her complaints were justified. Hitchcock's movie is a masterpiece in its own right; nevertheless, it is a perversion of du Maurier's masterpiece.

What Hitchcock's film does provide, however, is a powerful series of visual images. Though the special effects employed in the film seem antiquated in today's era of computer generated graphics, they did represent cutting edge technology when first presented to the public. Even du Maurier's vivid descriptions fail to capture the eeriness of seeing a field or playground heavily laden with birds as well as Hitchcock's haunting visuals.

◆ IDEAS FOR GROUP DISCUSSIONS ◆

"The Birds" is a disturbing story of suspense that never provides its readers with a resolution. Generic suspense tales bring tidy conclusions to their events. Du Maurier, however, frustrates her readers by failing to answer two important questions: Why do the birds attack? Will Nat and his family survive? Though at first frustrating, this lack of resolution makes the story great. Perhaps it is best to consider du Maurier's unresolved suspense liberating rather than frustrating. Readers can draw their own conclusions about the events. Thus, du Maurier allows for a degree of imagination most writers deny to their readers. Rather than simply imagining the scene, du Maurier's reader can imagine the end.

Du Maurier's story also gives important insights into the psychological dynamics of stress. Isolated and afraid, Nat and his family undergo a wide range of emotions while listening to the thud of birds on their walls and windows. Though tied to a fantastic event, du Maurier's psychological insights could apply in nearly any tense situation. Readers and writers alike might apply the coping mechanisms of du Maurier's characters to characters in other traumatic situations, from war to natural disaster.

1. Perhaps the easiest question to ask but most difficult to answer is, simply, Why do the birds attack?

2. Why does Nat make more efficient preparations for the birds' attack than his neighbors? What aspects of his character make him a more cautious man?

3. What chances do you think Nat and his family have for survival? Does the story itself give you any indication of whether they will live or succumb to the birds' attack?

4. The story often makes reference to war. Nat remembers the war; at one point the British government calls out warplanes in an effort to stop the birds. What parallels might one draw between war and the events related in du Maurier's story?

5. Compare and contrast du Maurier's story with Alfred Hitchcock's film version. Why does Hitchcock take such enormous liberties with du Maurier's tightly controlled story? Are du Maurier's descriptions or Hitchcock's special effects more powerful?

6. Why is Nat's wife unwilling to remain behind when he leaves for supplies in the story's final pages? Why might she willingly place herself and her children in danger rather than stay in the relative safety of the cottage?

David Slater
University of Minnesota

BLACK NOTICE

Novel

1999

Author: Patricia Cornwell

◆

◆ SOCIAL CONCERNS ◆

Patricia Cornwell's *Black Notice* tackles a number of social concerns. These include officials whose ambition, greed, and personal jealousies lead them to betray the public trust; wealthy families whose power and influence hide the depravity of black-sheep family members; administrators of justice who ignore or block the findings of forensic scientists and coroners for political reasons; and government agencies who reject competent employees because of their gender orientation, their old-fashioned lifestyles, or other private life choices. In sum, Cornwell attacks those who abuse their positions of authority, wealth, and power for private benefit or to further private visions of political reality.

Deputy Chief Diane Bray is the prototype of the corrupt official who has schemed her way into high position through political and sexual maneuvering, and whose actions interfere with the work of true professionals. She ferrets out the weaknesses of her opponents to undermine and defeat them. She resorts to gossip, innuendo, misdirection, and underhanded tricks (like putting a spy in Dr. Scarpetta's office to promote disharmony through petty theft and vandalism). She abuses her power, creating situations to justify getting rid of competent underlings like Police Captain Pete Marino with the excuse of insubordination or failure to implement orders, and replacing them with the less competent who owe their position and authority solely to her. She puts Marino back in uniform (an insult to a detective captain); she reprimands him in public and tries to kill his spirit because she cannot control him. She has contempt for her minions, but forgives the sloth, arrogance, incompetence, and even criminality of such subordinates in return for their loyalty and their willingness to forward her schemes to undercut the opposition and promote her causes. Her rush to power results from her need for personal aggrandizement, not concern for the public weal.

Deputy Chief Bray has big plans and is willing to resort to any means to achieve them. At the scene of one murder, Bray and Scarpetta clash over who is in charge, with Scarpetta pointing to the state law that gives the chief medical investigator jurisdiction over the victim's body until her collection of evidence is complete; yet Bray's underlings, with her permission, repeatedly contaminate crime scenes through amateurish bungling. Throughout the novel, Scarpetta's refrain is that too many people wander into the crime scene before her investigation is complete. Scarpetta's longtime associate, Captain Marino, attacks Bray for playing power games for sound bites over the bodies of the dead and thereby compromising evidence, making it questionable in court if a perpetrator is caught. Greed and ambition drive her to commit crimes and to shift blame for her mistakes and misdeeds. In previous works in the Scarpetta series, such overly ambitious, power-hungry characters were males who institutionalized sexism and directed it against Scarpetta, but in *Black Notice* Bray is a lesbian who directs her sexist attacks against straight males like Captain Marino while at the same time scheming to use the lesbianism of Scarpetta's niece Lucy Farinelli against Scarpetta. Bray employs her sexuality as a weapon to tempt males and seduce females. Only when she dies at the hands of the serial killer whose capture she has made more difficult do her superiors begin to ask where she got the money to support the high-level lifestyle she flaunted. Hand in hand with Bray is the tyrannical chief of police, Rodney Harris, an aggressive political animal who puts personal benefit over public need. He is the one who raised Bray to her position of authority and delegated power to her without caring about the havoc she might wreak. At the end, he seeks to shift responsibility for her misdeeds away from his office and can be manipulated into doing the right thing because it serves his interest. Cornwell blames his politically motivated choices for the near breakdown of the official investigative machine.

Another establishment villain is summed up by the Chandonne family. This powerful family has lived in one of the oldest, wealthiest parts of Paris, France (on the Ile Saint-Louis), since the seventeenth century. They hide behind their aristocratic facade, their highly publicized philanthropy, and their highly placed political connections while running "one of the biggest, bloodiest organized crime cartels in the world."

Furthermore, they have concealed and protected a psychopathic elder son, nicknamed Loup-Garou because of his hairy body and his pattern of biting, slashing, and beating his victims as he butchers them. Knowing the hideous murders he commits, they continue to protect him, even when he kills his brother, Thomas, the dead body discovered at the beginning of the novel.

Interpol brings Scarpetta and Marino to talk to Parisian coroner Dr. Stvan, whose vital forensic evidence has been blocked by the French judicial system. In France, forensic pathologists lack investigative power, asserts Cornwell, and are commissioned only to determine cause of death. Thus, the police and the magistrates may disregard their evidence with impunity. The fact that such magistrates may be in the pocket of the wealthy and powerful means justice thwarted. Cornwell, like her fictive creation Scarpetta, believes that this lack of investigative power obviates a thorough investigation, one removed from politics and human prejudice, and her criticism of the French system warns of the pitfalls and dangers of limiting the power of the American coroner.

◆ THEMES ◆

In addition to the themes of social justice and betrayal of the public welfare, Cornwell explores the nature and effects of grief. At the close of the previous novel in this series, *Point of Origin* (1998), Benton Wesley, Dr. Kay Scarpetta's lover, fiance, and friend, was tortured, mutilated, and slaughtered by a maniacal serial killer who literally stole the faces of his victims as trophies that confirmed his power (twenty-seven faces were found at his residence). *Black Notice* explores the different ways in which characters deal with their grief for Benton. Scarpetta, as the chief medical examiner for Virginia, buries herself in her duties, working long hours and driving herself to exhaustion. The novel begins with a missive from the dead, a letter Benton wrote Scarpetta and left with a friend (Senator Frank Lord) to be delivered a year from his death (during the Christmas holidays). Therein, Benton describes behavior that Scarpetta's associates confirm later in the novel: her rejection of the usual consolations of family and friends, and instead her half-life existence as a workaholic, racing to crime scenes, doing more autopsies than ever, being consumed by her duties to the court, by lecturing, running an institute, and with whatever else she can fill her days and nights. Benton writes that he knows she will avoid the well-meant solicitude of her neighbors, worry about her niece Lucy, get irritated with Marino, and in general opt out of life. Benton's postmortem advice is for her to stop dodging the pain, to take comfort from her memories of their life together, and, in a more practical vein, to invite Marino and Lucy to dinner and to talk openly about their shared loss, a topic they have avoided since Benton's death. Following Benton's targeted advice leads Scarpetta to the discoveries on which the novel turns: unknown associates have been using her grief to their advantage—to taint her public and private image and to undercut the credibility of her office.

Her niece Lucy has blamed herself for Benton's death because the murderer had once been her lesbian lover, and Scarpetta must help her understand that Lucy herself was the targeted prey from the very start of the relationship and that she was in no way to blame for the nightmare acts of a very clever but insane killer. Lucy expresses her grief by a disturbing disdain for her own life and a fascination with guns and other weapons of destruction; she volunteers for dangerous missions (the most recent against the crime organization run by the Chandonne family) and employs deadly force that endangers her life and career and the life of her partner. At the novel's close she must decide whether to ruin her prospects by an unnecessary kill or revel in the self-destructive violence that reflects her sense of personal responsibility for Benton's death.

Marino handles his grief in yet another way, with tough-guy cynicism that seeks conspiracies, including the possibility that Benton is still alive, on a secret mission, and using his death as misdirection to prevent detection. He is irritable and antagonistic, and takes pride in pushing his image as an out-of-date dinosaur. In France, when he realizes Scarpetta has spent the night with their Interpol contact, he explodes in anger, attacking Scarpetta for betraying Benton's memory. He starts a brawl in the hotel lobby, trying to punch out everyone within arm's length until Scarpetta helps him see that he is doing exactly what Lucy was doing—using violent confrontation as a way of striking out against the universe for the unfair death of the man who was Scarpetta's lover and friend, Lucy's father figure, and Marino's best buddy.

Cornwell also uses her medical examiner sleuth to comment on the spread of violence in America, the growing need for international connections between law enforcement officers as killers move rapidly from state to state and country to country, and the superiority of the American investigatory system's reliance on forensic evidence. In *Black Notice,* the first victim shows up in a cargo container shipped from Europe, and the evidence ties in the psychopathic son of the rich and influential Parisian family Lucy has been investigating indirectly through a Florida sting operation against their crime organization. The French system has been unable or unwilling to identify their serial murderer, and now his violence spills over into Richmond, Virginia, Scarpetta's hometown.

The Internet proves a major tool for criminals in Cornwell's novels. Here, someone has broken into Scarpetta's e-mail system and has rudely or insidiously answered messages she knew nothing about—messages from friends, associates, superiors, and fellow investigators—rejecting invitations, turning down opportunities to comfort the families of victims, alienating all, and creating the illusion of nervous exhaustion. Someone has also set up an online chat room that features expert medical commentary mixed with inept, uncaring advice, both in Scarpetta's name, an embarrassing fraud that suggests she is on the verge of a nervous breakdown. Those who know her (like her long-time secretary, Rose) assume her unwillingness to deal with problems and her supposed extreme statements online are a measure of her grief, and they try even harder to protect her from herself. But when Scarpetta finds out, she realizes someone is out to undermine her authority, to reduce the power of her investigative office, and to injure those closest to her as well. Memos marked private and confidential have never arrived, and Scarpetta begins to realize that a nasty scenario is at work: someone wants her out of her office so it will be vulnerable to takeover by Public Safety, the division that Bray has her eye on for her next step up the political rungs.

Through Scarpetta, Cornwell asserts the rights of the dead and the respect due them; her detailed descriptions of autopsy results, of what the medical evidence reveals about the suffering of the victims and of the effects of violent assault, and of the nature and acts of the murderer speak eloquently for the dead and for the need for official retribution. Her descriptions of the meticulous steps taken by the coroner's office to protect forensic evidence; to find trace elements, fingerprints, chemicals, and fibers; to do DNA testing and profiling; and to provide the police a modus operandi for identifying the criminal confirms the importance of this office in any fair investigation. In addition to the physical evidence recovery kit (PERK), the Halliburton aluminum scene case, lasers, Luma-Lite (which uses fiber optics to detect body fluids, drugs, fingerprints, and trace evidence not evident to the naked eye), and the support of criminalists, forensic psychiatrists, forensic pathologists, and computer programs for accessing police, FBI, and Interpol files, Cornwell makes clear that Scarpetta must also bring to her investigation and analysis personal experience and an almost paranoid awareness of the political ramifications of her medico-legal investigation of death. This combination of disciplined scientific techniques and intuitive analysis of the results and their personal, political, and judicial ramifications brings to life a profession normally dismissed as morbid by the general population.

Furthermore, Cornwell captures, to some extent, the convoluted dynamics of psychopaths, though she is less interested in the psychopath in this novel than in the political conflicts. In the Scarpetta series, her villains are frequently murderous deviants who kill again and again in hideous ways, like those depicted by Thomas Harris in *Manhunter* (1981) and *Silence of the Lambs* (1988). They are clever, inventive, and demented. They stalk their prey using the Internet, police radios, or whatever tools they can acquire. They revel in blood and slaughter. Benton, whose presence is inescapable in this novel despite his death, was a criminal profiler whose psychological training enabled him to interpret forensic evidence and predict the patterns and psychoses of serial killers. With his death, Scarpetta is missing an essential part of her detection team and has greater difficulty intuiting where the killer she seeks will strike next. Perhaps this is one reason her Chandonne "werewolf" killer never comes to life as a malignant personality and seems as much offended against as offending, a twisted, pathetic freak of nature.

◆ CHARACTERS ◆

Dr. Kay Scarpetta, the series's heroine, is, of course, the central character around whom the action turns. She is brilliant and distinguished, experienced, practical, creative, scientific, and intuitive. Yet, she fears a loss of control, and she has problems dealing with people. She loses herself in her work and fails to take the minimal actions necessary to maintain relationships, especially since Benton's death. Her loss has so traumatized her that she is blind to the barriers she has constructed between her family and friends and the obsession with work that her employees and associates can too easily misinterpret. In this vulnerable stage in her life, she is easy game for the predatory Deputy Chief Bray, who sees demolishing Scarpetta's public image as the pathway to higher office for herself. However, Scarpetta's true values are always quite clear. When her niece and her niece's girlfriend Jo brag about going undercover against the One-Sixty-Fivers, a French organized crime unit, and the two young women jokingly describe watching an autopsy, Scarpetta responds with horror. She asserts that they should always imagine that the dead are listening, so that when the living speak, they speak with respect, not cold indifference. She asks them to imagine someone they love on the autopsy table being mocked by tough-sounding youths showing off for their friends and laughing about the size of his penis, the stench, or the manner of death. This humane understanding of the psychology of death and this desire to be an advocate for the victims of the depraved and the indifferent makes Scarpetta more than an efficient technician and a competent medical examiner. Along with respect for the dead, her sense of justice and right drives her to seek accurate explanations and solutions to criminal violence.

Benton, though dead, figures prominently throughout the book for a number of reasons. First, the woman who masterminded his death and who almost destroyed both Scarpetta and her niece Lucy still affects Lucy's choices and actions. Second, Benton's letter from the grave and his advice awaken Scarpetta to her surroundings, to how much she has alienated her friends, relatives, and associates, and to the plot that threatens to destroy her career as well as the careers of Marino and Lucy. Finally, Benton's profiling keeps Scarpetta on target in her investigation, and his love gives her the courage to endure and, with time, find renewal in a new love relationship.

Scarpetta's niece Lucy is a complex character, a mixture of competence, immaturity, and self-destruction. She despises her feminine and selfish mother as much as her mother despises Scarpetta for stealing her daughter's affection and accepting her lesbianism rather than ranting against it. She is bright, a quick learner, a computer whiz. Encouraged by Marino to consider law enforcement as a career choice, she has excelled in the FBI program at Quantico, trained to be an astronaut for NASA, then signed on as a helicopter pilot for the Bureau of Alcohol, Tobacco and Firearms, and later as an undercover agent. Physically tough, she is trained in assault techniques and assault weapons. However, having had her first lesbian affair with a psychopath has tainted her self-image. She blames herself for Benton's death and seeks punishment by making herself the target of heavy fire when carrying out her missions. In doing so, she also endangers her new love, Jo Sanders, whose Drug Enforcement Agency position has led her to interagency undercover work. When Lucy's spiteful mother tells Jo's Southern Baptist parents that their daughters share a lesbian relationship, Lucy finds herself banned from Jo's hospital room and very much on her own. Despite her unquestionable skills, Lucy is psychologically on edge: Scarpetta's joy and her bane.

Marino is a throwback to the old-fashioned police style. Politically incorrect, he is nonetheless very good at what he does. He recently has finalized a divorce and has celebrated by trading in his Mustang for a red Corvette. He is estranged from his only child, Rocky, and will not say why. He is a mass of contradictions. He is a bodybuilder who drinks too much; a big-bellied Marlboro man, he carries a Sig-Sauer nine-millimeter pistol and calls women who offend him "babe." Yet, he is a tender, loyal friend who considers two competent women the most important people in his life. A conservative who disapproves of homosexuality, he has nonetheless taken Lucy under his wing, accepted her lesbian relationships, and treated her like the daughter he wishes he had. Scarpetta finds him a painful irritant and an irreplaceable friend and associate; he has worked alongside her on case after case, and she has come to depend on his instincts and his watchfulness. He has a nose for trouble, and the respect of the cops who work under him. He is insolent and insubordinate but a good person to have around in troubled times. A corrupt female detective calls him a "used-up, washed-up, redneck loser," but he is still around long after she has been kicked off the force. Scarpetta, in contrast, calls him "the most experienced, decent homicide detective" she has ever known.

A minor character who comes in near the end of the book is Jay Talley, an ATF agent acting as liaison for Interpol. Marino considers him a snotty, egotistical playboy and threatens to punch him out for having sex with Scarpetta. However, Talley is a talented agent. Barely thirty, he is strikingly handsome, with penetrating hazel eyes, dark good looks, broad shoulders, a Roman profile, full lips, and an aristocratic pedigree of wealth and privilege that he has rebelled against through his chosen career. The end of *Black Notice* suggests that he will play a significant role in Scarpetta's life in future novels in the series.

Basically, Cornwell likes to employ contrasting characters. She sets off the methodical and humane professional Scarpetta, who has worked her way to the top of her profession, against the selfish and ambitious amateur Bray, who has slept, cajoled, and blackmailed her way to the top, run roughshod over all in her way, and betrayed the values for which she is supposed to stand. Cornwell also sets the competent, though old-fashioned, former Deputy Chief Al Carson, head of investigations, against the modern, eminently fashionable new head, Deputy Chief Bray. Bray's choice of leading subordinate, Deputy Rene Anderson, a sloppy, gum-chewing amateur with an attitude, contrasts directly with the careful professionalism of Captain Marino. While Anderson looks hip and modern, she is lazy and uncaring, proud of her high connections and unwilling to learn from those more knowledgeable and experienced than she. Marino, in contrast, is impatient and rude because he knows how things should be done and is horrified when his authority is undermined by neophytes with no idea about how to handle a crime scene so that the evidence will stand up in court. Rose, Scarpetta's loyal, competent, and unquestionably honest secretary, is played off against the lazy, irresponsible, disloyal Chuck Ruffin. While Rose protects Scarpetta and the integrity of the office, Ruffin steals drugs he is supposed to destroy. Scarpetta, a nurturing woman but not a mother, is contrasted with her sister, Lucy's mother, Dorothy. Personal appearance and numerous affairs are the most important part of Dorothy's life; yet her need to control her daughter and twist her into an image of herself makes Dorothy spitefully jealous. "I want her [Lucy] to adore me, too!" she asserts; to which Scarpetta replies, "you're the most selfish person I've ever known." Finally, Benton's maturity is contrasted with

Talley's youth, his studious care with Talley's impetuosity, his forgiving love for Scarpetta with Talley's needy love for her. Such character contrasts provide an underlying structure and unity.

◆ TECHNIQUES ◆

Cornwell employs the standard techniques of the detective genre—a series of murders, a set of clues, an investigator with knowledgeable (and not so knowledgeable) assistants, suspense, and shifting suspects. To these she adds a surprise assault on the sleuth and an unusual resolution to two types of crimes and criminals. That resolution not only explains the criminal activities of Deputy Chief Bray and the capture of the Loup-Garou, but also resolves the political conflicts involved (Scarpetta's power over the crime scene reconfirmed; Marino's authority and position as Captain reasserted) and resolves grief, with Lucy coming to terms with her violence, Marino facing his grief-driven desire to smash and injure, and Scarpetta opening her heart to the possibility of a new love.

The novel's crime subgenre is that of the forensic sleuth, with scientific scene-of-the-crime discoveries and autopsy results essential to the progress of the plot. Cornwell details the scene-of-the-crime procedure, the tools Scarpetta and her staff employ, and the physical signs of violence and rage (the severity of the lacerations, the pattern of round and linear wounds, the bits of bones and broken teeth, the knuckle bruises, and striated abrasions). She explains, for example, the process of "stringing," a tedious, methodical technique involving protractors and trigonometry to track the individual trajectory of each droplet of blood from the wound to a target surface in order to determine velocity, distance traveled, and angles. Cornwell's enumeration of the gory details of the initial investigation of the victim's body and of the autopsy which follows is tempered with explanations of how this knowledge furthers the criminal investigation and the identification of the criminal. Fine blonde hairs and an animal smell at the crime scene, for example, lead to a killer suffering from hypertrichosis, a disease in which hairiness progressively increases until almost the entire body is covered; the face is asymmetrical, the teeth pointed, the genitalia stunted, and the number of fingers and toes larger than normal. Occasional metaphorical diction dramatizes the clinical details: "It was as if a wild animal had dragged her dying body off to its lair and mauled it."

Structurally, the private details of Scarpetta's love life frame the public duties and concerns of the body of the novel. The story begins with a lost love, introduces a new love interest at midpoint only to drop him, and then ends with that new love being confirmed. Cornwell sets her novel in two locations, Richmond, Virginia, and Paris, France. The crime that begins in Virginia leads Scarpetta to Interpol and Paris; then, once the serial killer is identified, the plot returns to Virginia for its denouement. At the same time, local politics threaten the efficiency of Scarpetta's office, and she must detect and counter a troublemaker within her own department in order to defeat the schemes set in motion by Diane Bray. The Bray subplot seems far more developed than the serial murderer plot because it takes place on home territory and involves internal politics and direct competition between different branches of the same system. It allows Cornwell to explore varying degrees of culpability, to demonstrate the destructive effects of politics in an investigation, and to contrast a model public official with her negative counterpart. In contrast, the serial murderer of the main plot never clearly comes into focus; readers never share his thoughts or motives; he is clearly genetically defective and, at the end, almost pathetic.

◆ LITERARY PRECEDENTS ◆

Cornwell's Kay Scarpetta novels are set firmly in the detective fiction subgenre of forensic pathology. Scarpetta is a pathologist who also actively detects. While the role of coroner or forensics expert has recurred in detective fiction from its earliest days—for example, R. Austin Freeman's Dr. Thorndyke, a forensic pathologist and forensic scientist (early 1900s), H. C. Bailey's crusading Reggie Fortune, critic of police bungling of evidence (1920s), C. St. John Sprigg's Sir Colin Vansteen, consultant pathologist to His Majesty's Home Office (1930s), and George Harmon Coxe's Dr. Paul Standish, medical examiner of Union City, Connecticut—the early fictional forensic experts were short on biochemical expertise, asserting knowledge about the victim and crime that, from a modern perspective, seems highly dubious, though their detection may well hold up in other areas. In contrast, the modern coroner or forensic pathologist as detective is unquestionably a medical authority, whose expertise in matters of tissue, blood samples, blood spatter patterns, rigor mortis, and so on is stunningly impressive and horrifying. Modern forensic novels take readers through detailed autopsies, with technical descriptions of wounds, stomach contents, cell trauma, etc.

Lawrence G. Blockman's Daniel Webster Coffee, the pathologist at Pasteur Hospital, Northback, plies his trade competently though, perhaps, tediously in *Diagnosis: Homicide* (1950) and in *Clues for Dr. Coffee* (1964), both of which are introduced by real and distinguished medical examiners. John Feegel's *Death Sails the Bay* (1978), along with the other books in Feegel's series, made autopsy procedures an exciting search for scientifically discovered clues unavailable

any other way. Michael Butterworth, writing as Sarah Kemp, introduced Dr. Tina May in the 1980s, but her forays into forensic psychiatry on the basis of pathological evidence made her seem more stylish than wise. Noreen Ayres's Smokey Brandon is another 1980s investigating pathologist in *Carcass Trade* and *A World the Color of Salt*.

Patricia Cornwell's Scarpetta novels carry this tradition a step further. As fictional chief medical examiner for the Commonwealth of Virginia, Scarpetta applies the latest technology of forensic science to criminal investigation. She draws on experts in forensic pathology, forensic psychiatry, criminalistics, profiling, and so on, and as a result of the concrete factual information she has at her command, she can direct the police investigation and even run her own investigation, oftentimes in cooperation with outside agencies like the ATF, FBI, and Interpol.

◆ RELATED TITLES ◆

Recent fictive forensic detectives include Clare Rayner's Dr. George Barnabas, Nigel McCrery's Dr. Samantha Ryan, Kathy Reichs's Dr. Temperance Brennan, and Leonard S. Goldberg's Joanna Blalock. Clare Rayner's novels like *Flanders: The Poppy Chronicles* feature historical settings, whereas the other two writers focus on the present. In McCrery's *Silent Witness* (1998), the police fix on an unsavory club owner as perpetrator in a pair of ritual killings in Cambridge's fen country (garroting, mutilation, and placement on consecrated ground), but Dr. Samantha Ryan, the Home Office pathologist, finds compelling forensic evidence that Bird has been framed. In *The Spider's Web* (1999), Ryan is called in for a second opinion on the autopsy of what seems like an accident victim only to discover forensic evidence of foul play that neither the police forensic expert nor the police superintendent accept until her investigation, assisted by forensic scientist Marcia Evans, unravels a bizarre series of related murders. Kathy Reichs's *Deadly Decisions* (2000), like *Deja Dead* (1998) and *Death du Jour* (1999), features Temperance Brennan, a fictional forensic anthropologist with a very long commute between jobs in North Carolina and Montreal. She links a skull in Montreal, the partial skeleton of a North Carolina teenager who has been dead since 1984, and a nine-year-old girl who is the shooting victim of a Canadian outlaw motorcycle gang war. In Leonard S. Goldberg's *Deadly Exposure* (1998) forensic pathologist Blalock's discovery of cholera in a dead Chinese infant in Los Angeles leads to a floating laboratory off the coast of Alaska and an iceberg that seems to be releasing a deadly, 65,000,000-year-old toxin. Other titles in the Blalock series include *Deadly Medicine, A Deadly Practice, Deadly Harvest,* and *Lethal Measures.*

These titles build on the formulas and conventions established and popularized by Patricia Cornwell throughout her Kay Scarpetta forensic series. Cornwell's *Postmortem* (1990), *Body of Evidence* (1991), and *Point of Origin* (1998) all feature serial killers.

◆ IDEAS FOR GROUP DISCUSSIONS ◆

This novel is about learning to cope with grief and about carrying on with life and responsibility. In this case, responsibility means unmasking serial killers, despite interference from the very officials and agencies commissioned to assist in such cases. Cornwell depends on contrasts to establish character, carry theme, and assert social concerns.

1. What is the significance of the title? Who in the book receives a Black Notice? Why?

2. Cornwell captures the debilitating effects of grief. Why is Kay Scarpetta grieving? What form does her grief take? How do her enemies use her grief against her?

3. What series of events or realizations help her finally come to terms with her grief?

4. Scarpetta's niece Lucy and her associate Marino also are grieving, but their grief takes a very different form. Explain.

5. Scarpetta sees conspiracies everywhere. How many conspiracies does she suspect? Which prove genuine? Which false?

6. What early clues prepare readers for the unusual nature of the serial killer? Is he credible? Why or why not? Ultimately, which figure seems more evil, Deputy Chief Diane Bray or the werewolf serial killer? Why?

7. Cornwell carefully contrasts two successful professional women who have risen in the ranks through very different means. What do Chief Bray and Dr. Scarpetta have in common? How are they different? How significant are these differences? Explain.

8. What role does Lucy play in the story? How does she help humanize Dr. Scarpetta?

Gina Macdonald
Nicholls State University, Thibodaux, LA

BLOOD AND CHOCOLATE

Novel

1997

Author: Annette Curtis Klause

◆

◆ SOCIAL CONCERNS ◆

Like the novels which Klause has written which precede *Blood and Chocolate*, especially *The Silver Kiss*, *Blood and Chocolate* is almost an allegory for the coming-of-age of young adults who live in a world today that can be as frightening and as thrilling as the experience of reading a horror novel itself. Klause's teenagers face many frightening experiences which have little to do with wolves, witches, ghosts, or demons—there are the temptations to succumb to other darknesses within as well. Kids grow up fast in the world Klause depicts for us. Sex is a given for young adults. Drugs and alcohol are a temptation. Vivian attends parties where marijuana smoke is thick in the air and liquor is present everywhere. Vivian lacks few role models as far as this temptation is concerned. Her mother is often hung over as are many of the pack, the group of young male werewolves that Vivian is now trying to distance herself from.

Families too are a concern with Klause, and she depicts both Vivian's and her love interest Aiden's family problems with great detail. Aiden's mother is more old-fashioned and protective that Vivian's bar-hopping mother who has a different man in her bed almost every night of the week (no wonder Vivian seems so sexually liberated for a girl of only sixteen!), but Klause hints at problems within even the "normal" Aiden's family. Her most obvious indication of cracks beneath the veneer of Aiden's parents' relationship is when Aiden's father makes sexual advances toward Vivian.

Klause's depiction of awakening adolescent sexuality is a vicious one—none of her adolescents are sexually innocent. Vivian and Aiden would have sexually consummated their relationship had Vivian not decided to share with Aiden her secret— and metamorphosed into a wolf in front of him (choosing, unfortunately, the night that Aiden has filled a room with flickering candles to celebrate their first lovemaking). Vivian, like her mother, is depicted as a character very hungry for sex. She is no virgin. As she changes into her wolf-self soon after meeting Aiden, she thinks to herself, "*I will howl for you, human boy . . . I will hunt you in my girl skin but I'll celebrate as wolf.*" Aiden seems to move a little more slowly than Vivian, and Vivian is frustrated by this. She longs for him to bite her, scratch her, and wants their physical encounters to be more violently charged. Often during their sexual encounters, Vivian will begin to metamorphose into her wolf-self, and her nails will lengthen, though Aiden never seems to notice. Although we can attribute some of Vivian's sexual hunger to her bestial essence, we can see Klause making feminist suggestions (perhaps implying that female desire is just as powerful as male desire?). We can also see her as making suggestions that perhaps teens today move so quickly into sexual relationships that they often cannot control their (animal) impulses. Perhaps this is why Klause depicts even the normal characters as leading lives that are spinning out of control into dangerous areas. The popular, self-controlled Aiden, for example, has a taste for witchcraft, Satanism, and black magic.

◆ THEMES ◆

Klause explores many themes through the character of Vivian. One of the chief themes is the importance of honesty and the dangers of dishonesty. The tension throughout the novel results mainly from the reader's wondering when she will reveal her identity as a werewolf to Aiden. Because Vivian is dishonest about this fact from the beginning, she is forced to pay a price for it. She not only loses Aiden as a romantic partner, she also brings on the very real threat of his death. Once she does reveal to him that she is a werewolf, the pack has to decide if they should kill him to prevent being discovered by the other townspeople. In this way, Klause complicates the theme of honesty in the novel. We might wonder, momentarily, if Vivian should have remained dishonest with Aiden. We quickly realize, though, that such dishonesty would have been impossible for Vivian to maintain. Klause underscores this important detail with Vivian's near metamorphoses throughout the novel, whenever she and Aiden begin expressing their attraction physically. Sooner or later, we know, Aiden would have witnessed one of these changes and would have been, as he eventually is,

scared by them. Klause also draws our attention to the fact that had Vivian responsibly avoided a relationship with a human, the question of honesty never would have arisen.

Another theme in this novel is that of the complexity of human relationships. None of the relationships in this book are typical. Vivian's relationship with her mother and her relationship with Aiden are relations we could hardly call normal. Vivian talks to her mother as if she were her friend rather than her mother. Vivian's mother, Esme, encourages this kind of openness—but this relationship is not idealized. Klause shows us what is sacrificed when a parent eschews the responsibilities of parenthood. Alone in her adolescence with the loss of her father and her mother's abandonment of the motherly role, Vivian begins to make a series of decisions that could endanger both herself and her pack. She also becomes the victim of a setup that could result in the loss of her life or her position within the pack, as Astrid's son, Ulf, begins planting stray human body parts in Vivian's room to convince everyone that she (instead of his mother) is indeed the wolf-murderer of the "meat-people" in the town.

This theme of the complexity of human relationships is closely related to Klause's idea of the importance of home in this novel. Vivian longs for a normal home, which she sees represented in Aiden's family life. This is one of the reasons she so frequently argues with her mother. Klause underscores the emphasis on home throughout this novel by the issue of the wolves' wanderings from West Virginia to Maryland—they have to keep moving to avoid being found out by the humans in the world. They can never really enjoy a stable home life like other human beings. Klause writes,

> Vivian had thought that by this time they would have made plans for the future, but

now the whole pack seemed to be crazy, her mother included. With more than half of them dead, no one knew his or her place anymore. There was constant squabbling. Survival depended on their blending in while they organized and decided where they would move and settle for good, but at any moment the pack was likely to explode into a ball of flying fur.

Hence, the wolves' existence is complicated by yearnings they can never satisfy. Denied the pleasures of a traditional life, the wolves seem to carry an anger with them that can explode at any moment in rage at humans or other members of their pack.

This theme is related to Vivian's overall longing for normalcy throughout the novel and Klause's theme of the importance of belonging and being accepted. One of the major sources of Vivian's distress is that she is not accepted by the other kids at school. Being accepted into the "in crowd" is a common concern among teens, but even this kind of typical acceptance is denied Vivian, since the more human friends she acquires, the more risk there is that her true wolf nature will be discovered. This longing is magnified because now Vivian desperately wants to fit in with someone besides the Five, since she partially blames them for her father's death. We might wonder, though, at Esme's decision to send Vivian to a public school despite the risks of being found out by other teens when, inevitably, something happens to make them aware a werewolf is in their midst.

The other major theme is the transformative power of puberty. Just as Vivian's body defies her against her will, causing her to metamorphose into a wolf even when she does not want to, Vivian's body is changing in other ways as well as she matures into a woman. Hence, she must accept the dangers and responsibilities that womanhood implies, especially for a young she-wolf who is desperately longed for by all the males. Klause suggests that coming of age for a young adult in today's world can be dangerous and risky for a woman. Vivian is surrounded by men who lust for her, some of them willing to commit violence, even murder, just to sleep with her. Perhaps Klause is using the metaphor of transforming into a wolf to portray a coming-of-age experience that is both animalistic and violent in the twentieth century.

The other major theme in this novel is one of loss. Klause never lets us forget throughout the course of the novel that we are dealing with a pair of characters in Vivian and Esme who have suffered the loss of a very great man. Vivian is alone in her loss as well—she cannot tell the human Aiden about the loss of her wolf-father, the late leader of the wolf clan. Klause draws our attention to how this loss isolates Vivian from others throughout the novel. At one moment in the book, Aiden complains about how much he hated being forced to go on hunting trips with his father:

> "I hated it. There should be more to being with your father than going out and killing something together."
>
> Vivian didn't speak. She'd give anything to be able to go out and kill something with her father again.

Through the flaws in both Vivian's and Esme's characters, Vivian's reckless rebellion and Esme's effort to forget her husband through a parade of other men, Klause reminds us that great pain can often lead people to become confused and act out in ways that are not familiar to their characters. We realize at the end of the novel that Vivian has transcended her loss when she stops rebelling against nature and takes the wolf Gabriel for her mate as a gift to her deceased father, giving into the traditions that he abided by. *"Like my father,"* she thought to herself, *"This is what I owe him. This is how I make it up to him."*

Vivian Gandillon is Klause's heroine, her most carefully depicted character, and her most contradictory one as well. Vivian seems confident, self-possessed, strong, and naturally smart—yet, she does not recognize the impossibility of her relationship with a human, nor does she consider the harm that she could bring him in all kinds of senses. Not only might the jealous members of the pack kill Aiden just because Vivian rejects all of them as suitors, but he will have to be killed if Vivian reveals her secret to him. Despite the fact that Vivian has been forced to grow up before her time—not only because of her father's death but because of having to assume a kind of responsibility and foresight because of her duty to her werewolf clan—she seems to lack foresight where Aiden is concerned. She seems blind to the fact that Aiden is only immaturely flirting with the unknown and will, naturally, be scared out of his wits when Vivian metamorphoses in front of him. Another important facet of Vivian's character is her blindness to the consequences of telling Aiden the truth. We might wonder at this blindness since her father was killed in a fire created by suspecting neighbors. Does Vivian not realize, we might wonder, based on her own personal losses, the consequences of such honesty with a human? Perhaps Klause is underscoring a theme of the blindness that can result in immature love relationships and the consequences of such blindness.

Klause also emphasizes Vivian's anger and recklessness. The book begins with an allusion to Vivian's father's death. Klause could be trying to illustrate, through Vivian's character, a young woman breaking under the great pressures of extreme grief and sorrow while trying to also deal with the very anxiety-creating dilemma of trying to fit in, even further complicated by her awakening sexuality. Her most obvious source of anger is her mother, who is no role model for the young Vivian morally, leaving Vivian virtually to raise herself.

In the character of Esme, Klause creates a very paradoxical portrait of a mother. Esme not only hangs out at bars and brings a different man home every night, she also encourages her daughter to become sexually active, in her efforts to steer her away from the human, Aiden, and toward the other young wolves in the clan. Klause hints, though, that Esme's behavior is connected to her husband's death, just as Vivian's behavior can be explained by the loss of her father.

> [Vivian] thought of her father and the aching emptiness that still gnawed at her. Her parents had seemed so happy together. She'd thought her mother shared that ache, but now Esme was acting like a stupid fourteen-year-old.
>
> "Didn't you love Dad?" she finally said.
>
> Esme looked startled at this question out of the blue. "Yes, I loved him."
>
> "Then why are you out running around?"
>
> "A year's a long time, Vivian. I'm tired of crying. I'm lonely. Sometimes I want a man in my bed."

Esme is frequently dressed in short, tight dresses throughout the novel, drawing attention to her very sexual nature.

Aiden Teague is the object of Vivian's affections and he is a complex character as well. From the beginning of his entrance into the novel, Klause emphasizes his handsomeness, his intelligence, and his talent—which is what attracts Vivian to him in the first place—in the form of the beautiful poem he wrote, significantly titled "Wolf Change" which draws Vivian to him in curiosity of what he might know. When she reads these lines in his poem, she feels as if Aiden has embedded a special message within them solely for her:

Blood and Chocolate

A pentagram is burning
in your eyes
and soft, pale twists
of wolfbane
squeeze your heart.
A grinding pain
is writhing in your thighs
the crunch of bones
proclaims the change's start.

How could Vivian resist?, we wonder, since every time she changes throughout the novel, what Klause emphasizes most is this "crunch[ing] of bone" that announces the final step of the transformation from human into wolf. Vivian is doomed to feel a kinship to Aiden, we feel, and so our sympathies are with her from the beginning. When we read this poem, we become as intrigued with his character as Vivian is. In this way, Klause draws our hearts into the novel and places our empathy with Vivian.

Aiden is an interesting character, and Klause makes it difficult for us not to like him from the moment Vivian meets him. He is handsome, mysterious, smart, and romantic. At one point, early in their relationship, the unsuspecting Aiden (who has no idea that Vivian is avoiding him because the moon is full and she is afraid she might change in front of him) brings Vivian a moonlight supper of wine and cheese. At another moment, he tells her she is the most beautiful woman in the world and swears that he has found his soul mate. Aiden makes it impossible for either Vivian or the reader to resist his charms.

Aiden, however, is not the courageous rebel that Vivian thinks he is. Although he likes dabbling in the "black arts" and has an interest in witchcraft and the supernatural, Vivian is mistaken when she assumes that the actually conventional Aiden will be able to handle her transformation into a wolf right in front of him. Aiden turns ghastly white and throws a mug at Vivian's head when she begins to change in front of him. Vivian is, of course, crushed, since she thought the very postmodern Aiden would think her wolf-self beautiful.

◆ TECHNIQUES ◆

One of the most pleasing aspects of *Blood and Chocolate* is Klause's writing style which is lyrical, atmospheric, and highly imaged. The first sentence of the novel immediately pulls us into the book with its seductive language: "Flames shot high, turning the night lurid with carnival light." Throughout the novel, everything we see and are told is filtered through the consciousness of Klause's protagonist Vivian. However, Klause is not limited visually by this first person point of view, as she not only enables us to experience Vivian's journey with her but to *see* Vivian, the other characters, and the world about them as well. She describes their hair, clothing, facial expressions, movements, and the atmosphere with great detail. We know that Rafe, one of the Five, sports "a goatee and mustache" and that he has "thick, long brown hair." Klause draws our attention to Vivian's beauty at many moments throughout the novel: "She was tall and leggy ... with full breasts, small waist, and slim hips that curved enough to show she was female. Her skin was gently golden ... and her tawny hair was thick and long and wild." In the same vivid detail, Klause describes the metamorphosis of Vivian and the rest of the clan of loups-garoux into their wolf selves. This is Klause's first description of Vivian's metamorphosis into a wolf:

> The flesh of her arms bubbled and her legs buckled to a new shape ... then grimaced as her teeth sharpened and her jaw extended. She felt the momentary pain of the spine's crunch and then the sweet release.
>
> She was a creature much larger and stronger than any natural wolf. Her toes and legs

were too long, her ears too big, and her eyes held fire.

Although stylistically beautiful in its prose, Klause never lets us forget that she is telling us a horror story. However, in terms of genre, this novel could also be classified as a work of feminist fiction, as Vivian's journey is one of self-empowerment; fantastic fiction, for its unrealistic and horrifying qualities; or even a work of gothic romance, in its brooding terror and its focus upon the thwarted relationship between Vivian and Aiden. Most of all, despite its horrific elements, Vivian's repression of and final acceptance of her undeniable wolf essence, creates parallels with the tradition of the coming-of-age novel.

In all three of her novels, *Alien Secrets*, *Blood and Chocolate*, and *The Silver Kiss*, Klause uses creatures of the night (ghosts, werewolves, vampires) to symbolize the plight of a young woman coming of age in a world which has become terrifying for young people growing up, as terrifying as the horror novel we are reading. Klause drives this point home in *Blood and Chocolate* by showing us the chinks in the armor of the allegedly "normal" characters' lives. Although Aiden's family is much more protective and structured than Vivian's, Aiden is not protected from a hankering for dabbling in the dangerous world of the black arts. He listens to satanic music, flirts with witchcraft, and gives Vivian a necklace with a pentagram charm on it, signifying devil worship and witchcraft. He seems to be reaching out for dark comforts in an effort to distract himself from the pains of adolescence. Aiden is not a completely innocent character in *Blood and Chocolate* as are none of the popular crowd at school that Vivian so desperately wants to be accepted by. Likewise, when Vivian breaks into the house of a girl whom she has seen kissing Aiden soon after he has ended their relationship because she showed him her wolf-self, Vivian describes Kelly's room as one "of a little

girl gone bad. Beneath the haphazard pictures full of naked chests, flannel, and tattoos, she could see pink, flowered wallpaper." Klause depicts the world for adolescents today as one that is fraught with dangers: too-early sexual experience, drugs, black magic, and violence. Her portraits of teens today are of young people who seem to know too much too early for their own good.

Klause relies mainly on suspense throughout this novel, much as Stephen King relies on suspense to keep us turning the pages of his novel, by ending each chapter with an unanswered question. Chapter one, for instance, in which Vivian has finally approached Aiden, the human meat-boy that she is overwhelmingly attracted to, and winked at him, ends with the following lines: "'Do I know you?' he asked. He waited expectantly, with a bemused look on his face." Klause leaves us waiting expectantly at the end of most of her chapters as well, leaving us just on the brink of discovery of one of the major mysteries of the novel. Who is killing the humans? Has Vivian severed the hand she has found in her room from a human body? Why can she remember nothing about the previous night's events? Just as Vivian has convinced herself of her own guilt, chapter twenty-four ends with "She gazed out the dining room window in time to see two police officers coming up the front path." Clearly Klause's goals are not only to keep us reading her novels until their often fiery ends, she also wants to intensify the experience of the reader. She succeeds quite effectively at helping us to enter the minds of her characters. Hence, we experience Vivian's triumphs and trials with her, feeling them as she does.

Klause also draws our attention to the moon's importance to both the characters' and the plot's development in the novel by breaking up the chapters of the novel with divisions which remind us of the months in the year and the cycles of the moon. For example "May: Ghost Moon" is the title of the prologue chapter which presents us with the story of Vivian's father's death. He is the important "ghost" who hovers over this novel, since, in order to understand both Vivian and her mother's behavior, we must keep in mind that they are grieving the loss of him. "September: Harvest Moon" titles the chapters which conclude the novel: Vivian's recovery of her ability to metamorphose into a wolf again and her decision to become sexually involved with the older and fellow werewolf, Gabriel.

◆ LITERARY PRECEDENTS ◆

Blood and Chocolate is one of many books in a field of literary interest for young adults that has literally exploded in the last decade, especially the late 1990s: the genre of romance horror for young adults. Two authors in particular both precede and continue to publish similar books alongside Annette Curtis Klause: Vivian Vande Velde and Lisa Jane Smith. Vande Velde's *Companions of the Night* (1995) has become a classic for teens interested in this genre, and it was awarded the ALA Best Book for Young Adults Award upon its publication. *Companions,* like *Blood and Chocolate,* achieves its primary tensions (as with many books in this genre) through a central love affair between a human and not-so-human being. Kerry, a non-vampire girl, is in love with the seductive vampire boy Ethan. Smith's *Huntress* (1997) in particular, shares very similar themes and a similar plot to *Blood and Chocolate.* In *Huntress,* a half-vampire/half vampire hunter has to rejoin her gang of bloodthirsty vampires in order to save the human boy that she loves. Klause has broken ground with her atypical focus on werewolves, since the genre typically favors vampires and witches. Another important literary precedent is Patricia Windsor's *The Blooding* (1996). This novel is another book about werewolves in the romantic horror fiction for young adults genre. It is the story of another group of werewolves who take the roles of ordinary humans by day and centers around the problem of a werewolf, Derek, falling in love with a human, Maris.

◆ RELATED TITLES ◆

There are many books one can find today that share similar themes and characters to Klause's *Blood and Chocolate.* It seems that Klause's work has only further inspired more authors to contribute to the already booming genre of juvenile horror fiction. Matthew T. Anderson's *Thirsty* (1997), published around the same time as *Blood and Chocolate,* focuses upon a teenage vampire living in Massachusetts. *Demon in My View* (2000), by Amelia Atwater-Rhodes, focuses on a young author who writes novels about vampires and then is actually confronted with one of the characters of her books at her high school. A book very similar in theme and character depiction to Klause's *Blood and Chocolate* is Vivian Vande Velde's *The Changeling Prince* (1998), which focuses upon a sixteen-year-old werewolf named Welland, who like Vivian, is growing tired of the tensions between his daytime and nighttime worlds.

◆ ADAPTATIONS ◆

A project for a movie based on *Blood and Chocolate* was announced in 1997, and was rumored to star Jennifer Love Hewitt. However, production has been delayed by the death of the original director, Leslie Libman. Po-Chih Leong (director of *The Wisdom of Crocodiles*) has now taken over the project. Interestingly, the screenwriter who is adapting *Blood and Chocolate* for movie format is Christopher Landon, the son of "Little House on the Prairie'''s Michael Landon who starred in the movie *I Was a Teenage Werewolf*. The movie's tentative release date is sometime in 2001.

In *Blood and Chocolate* Klause has produced a book which has social relevance for teens in what it says about the importance of family, friends, a self-concept, and the inner strength to face the growing temptations for teens in today's rapidly changing world. Most teens feel isolated, lack confidence, and want desperately to join in "a pack" that will make them feel loved and accepted. Klause intensifies this struggle for Vivian and draws our attentions to the pain of growing up for teens by making Vivian significantly different not only from other teens at her school, but different from human beings altogether.

1. What is the significance of Klause's title?

2. Is Vivian a rational character? For instance, how clearly does she think about the consequences of her relationship with a *Homo sapien*?

3. Is Vivian being honest with herself throughout the course of the book? For example, could the relationship between Aiden and Vivian have *ever* worked out?

4. How does Vivian differ from the other members of the pack, especially "the Five"?

5. How do you feel about the character of Aiden? How does he compare to Klause's characterization of Gabriel? Who is the more noble character, do you think?

6. What about this curious figure of a mother that Klause paints in her character of Esme? How are Vivian's problems as an adolescent magnified by the behavior she sees her mother exhibiting every day?

7. What comparisons can you see Klause making with adolescent sexual awakening and the metamorphoses into wolf?

8. What comparisons does Klause seem to be making between desire and bestiality? (Keep in mind what Gabriel says about the animal in everyone.)

9. If you have read Klause's *The Silver Kiss,* compare Klause's themes in this novel to *Blood and Chocolate*.

10. How does the forest become symbolic throughout the course of the novel?

11. What does the mural Vivian paints represent in the book? What about her dream?

12. Do you think Vivian has experienced an epiphany by the end of the book? In other words, has she experienced a revelation about herself that will help her to embrace life in a healthier manner from here on out? Has she come of age?

Rhonda Cawthorn
American Literature/Southern Literature,
University of South Carolina

THE BLOOD LATITUDES

Novel

2000

Author: William Harrison

◆

*T*he *Blood Latitudes* explores the nature andconsequenceofpower—of"power in the blood" as they say—the power of ethnic and tribal relationships and history, and the power of European and American colonial exploitation of Africa for slaves at first, then for rubber, diamonds, oil, and other natural resources, and for strategic bases. It explores the nature of "the other" and the ferocious and terrible consequences of "othering" whether of one tribe to another or of son for father. It asserts, finally, that

> All the world is Africa, barbaric and primeval, and what's in the blood is more savage than we can know or possibly understand, and it comes for us like a marauder, it comes through the streets for us, it finds its way into our veins and moves toward our hearts. We refine and insulate ourselves, but our cultivations rupture, our yearnings betray us, and we want cobras in our gardens.

It is serious work, indeed, and appropriate work for Harrison's artistically crafted fictions to embody these disconcerting and at times terrifying themes and social issues. They are the work of a thirty-plus year career as a serious writer as well as teacher

of the craft. *The Blood Latitudes* is the culmination of that career to this point.

The questions Harrison invites us to ask of *Blood Latitudes* as well as of each of his four other "African" novels (*Africana* [1977], *Savannah Blue* [1981], *Burton and Speke* [1982], and *Three Hunters* [1989]) include What is the nature of power?, Who has it?, What are the consequences of its presence or absence?, Who or what is the marauder that comes for us?, and Why do we want cobras in our gardens? *The Blood Latitudes* explores the power of our social institutions such as marriage, the press, religion, education, and the fundamentals of sex, ethnicity, and racial hatred. Finally, in this novel as in all of his fictions there is enacted that essential conflict between barbarism and civilization, between the natural man and the civilized man, between Adam before and Adam after the Fall, around which the arguments and the actions of Harrison's fictional defining moments gather.

For instance, in *Africana* (1977), the first of his five African novels, one finds a passage suggesting that these fundamental conflicts and incongruities are part of the land itself, that its contrasts and mysteries mark every aspect of life:

> The bush, the forest, the savannah, the veldt, the highlands. Nothing was ever

explained out there, nothing was ever understood; dreams were inexplicable like the patterns of leaves; beauty was accidental like the orchid set in rot; death smothered everything, yet that was irrational and bloody wondrous, for life always came back, green, moving the last seasons of decay aside . . . both the slavers and the missionaries failed. Every exploit, every philosophy, each cause or movement became as fragile and as transient as the jungle's smallest fern.

True as they are, these are also the thoughts of the dominant madman in *Africana*, the soldier-philosopher Leo. His counterpart in *The Blood Latitudes* is Papa Ngiza, the well-spoken, well-read, well-educated leader of a band of Hutu militia. *Ngiza* means "darkness," the name given Lake Turkana by the native tribes who wandered its shores for thousands of years. Hence Papa Ngiza may be read as signifying the father of darkness. His band of militia has as its mission murdering and mutilating Tutsi men, women, and children—using pruning nippers to amputate the limbs of their victims, "cutting them down to size," Papa Ngiza, one of the "short" Hutus, explains.

Harrison examines the complex causes of this bloody tribal warfare in his African fictions, especially *The Blood Latitudes, Africana,* and *Savannah Blue*. Christian mythology portrays Satan, synonymous with evil, as darkness, the absence of light resulting from an absolute distance from the Godhead. Here, in *The Blood Latitudes*, Harrison gives the powers of darkness the body and purposes of a modern, civilized Hutu tribesman, well educated in the West, articulate, charismatic, and totally ruthless. Two somewhat similar characters appear in earlier novels and represent different ethnic and political forces from those ostensibly enacted by Papa Ngiza. Leo is a bloodthirsty Welsh mercenary in *Africana* (1977), and establishes his reputation fighting in the internal wars of Kenya and later Biafra in the 1960s; Quentin Clare is a brilliant, driven, and arguably psychotic mixed-blood assassin in *Savannah Blue* (1981), who strikes out at Western, especially American, exploiters of the post-colonial period in Africa. Each of the three is in his own right a fanatic, fantastic figure, an appalling and frightening human being who emerges from the nightmarish confusion of postmodern Africa, symbolic of all that is wrong with twentieth-century politics, philosophy, and technology. Each dies violently but only after committing bloody rampages across his particular section of Africa. Each is a brilliant creation that demonstrates just how serious (and effective) William Harrison is in dealing seriously with a fundamental issue of humanity, the problem of evil itself and its effects on each of us. As he writes suggestively (and pessimistically) at the end of *The Blood Latitudes*, "all the world is Africa, barbaric and primeval."

The Blood Latitudes and *Africana* give the problem of evil an all-too-human face of catastrophic tribal wars that provide the context and background for these novels. Enabled, encouraged, and abetted by European and American arms manufacturers and dealers, the rebellion by Biafra in Nigeria and the genocide in Rwanda are only two in the long train of conflicts nurtured by mercenaries and colonialists and exploiters of every sort. These slaughters are, Harrison argues, the continuing consequence of European and American exploitation of Africa and Africans.

Harrison structures *The Blood Latitudes* with a series of powerful thematic contrasts. The novel opens with Will Hobbs, a U.S. journalist, recently retired and now living in the civilized comfort of London, where modern homes, civility, decadence, and old money contrast with the desperate fear, poverty, brutality, and blood savagery of Eastern Africa in the last third of the twentieth century. Harrison contrasts Hobbs' memories of the old days of Kenya as a huge sportsman's preserve, of leisurely afternoons for privileged whites at the Long Bar, and of other parts of East Africa as they never quite were with the brutal reality of today, a nightmarish and flickering landscape of warfare, deprivation, and death. Into this landscape comes Will's son, Buck, whose youth, inexperience, rashness, and ignorance contrast with the age, wisdom, experience, discipline, and wisdom of Will. East Africa has changed fundamentally from the old days of Hemingway. Will tries unsuccessfully to educate Buck about the complexities of the new Africa, an Africa that has been lost because of overpopulation, the spread of AIDS and other diseases, mindless European and American exploitation, the legacy of such nineteenth-century colonialists as King Leopold of Belgium, and other causes too mind-numbing to enumerate. Yet today, the West consistently ignores Africa, especially sub-Saharan Africa, and incessant tribal warfare exacerbated by four centuries of colonial exploitation is now waged with heavy artillery and automatic weapons (supplied by the West) rather than spears and pangas. The outbreak of ferocious ethnic warfare between the ruling Tutsi minority and the Hutu in Rwanda triggers the novel's action and continues Harrison's fictional analysis of a variety of social issues including the international arms trade and its role in stimulating and supporting the war.

Yet another and complementary social theme is the nature of civilization as portrayed by Will's life in London, his big, comfortable house (provided by his late wife's fortune), the comfortable life of late dinners and fine wines, of books and conversation. This civilization, however, is illustrated not only by Will's life in retirement; it is also defined by contrast with the wild, the jungle. More tellingly, perhaps, it is revealed as hollow and decadent as seen in contrast with the savagery of modern man whether tribal or colonial, African or European.

Harrison characterizes Will consistently as a man not without temptations and failings, but a man whose actions are guided by principle and a moral code. He is a "rare civilized sort." Consequently, when back in Africa searching for his son, he refuses to kill his captors when, in several instances, he could have done so, saves both himself and perhaps others, and escapes. Still, he feels like an impostor, as someone who has taken on his English wife's money, friends, family, and culture as his own but who has been found out. He is forced to reflect on the nature of culture and who may possess it by a series of significant challenges to his moral center that test his conduct in the face of several profound provocations: the loss of his son, his sexual attraction to his daughter-in-law, and the dangers he faces while a captive of the Hutu militia.

Harrison's book argues then that a serious and complex relationship exists between personal sexual morality and cultural and national morality, that if "everybody's screwing everybody" then "everybody's killing everybody," although he does not put it quite that specifically. But Will's refusal to surrender to the powerful attraction between him and his daughter-in-law and his determination to do everything he can to find his son testify to his fundamental and powerful moral center, and it contrasts sharply and tellingly with the apocalyptic and brutal mass maiming and murder he witnesses as he descends into "the heart of darkness" in his search.

Will's failure as a father is represented in his having never been around at home for the little events of Buck's childhood, of his being father (and husband) in absentia, on assignment in Nairobi, and thus modeling, as all fathers model in one way or another, the role of father for his son. Buck, it is clear, even as an adult resents his father's absence from his childhood. With the birth of Willie, Buck and Key's son, "Buck had Will's fierce affection," but even that is not enough to overcome Buck's resentment or his sense that he is engaged in a fierce competition with his father and therefore must take risks and ignore his father's advice and help. Buck's pride and anger demand his fatal disobedience.

◆ THEMES ◆

A number of important themes resonate throughout the novel, many of which are connected with the social issues present in the novel and discussed above. But a number have a kind of universality that Harrison acknowledges, especially the idea that cultural misunderstanding is a "human universal." Some scholars of post-colonialism argue that while cultural difference is real enough, there are also traits all human beings have in common, and thus appear to echo the position taken by Sir Thomas Hobbes who believed that people share many of the same thoughts and passions. Africa is a land of extraordinary beauty and extraordinary sorrow. The great herds of wild animals, the powerful and compelling landscape of plain, mountain, and jungles as well as the farms and villages carved out by native peoples and colonial invaders which testify to a fundamental human drive for survival. The tribal warfare between Tutsi and Hutu testify to the intractability of human nature. The miscommunication and misunderstanding between father and son testify to a fundamental theme of the son's desire to supplant the father. In *The Blood Latitudes* the Oedipal conflict is ironically reversed as Buck, the son, meets his death apparently and mysteriously at a "crossroads" in Rwanda, and leaves his wife and his father to wrestle with the temptations and dangers of a possible sexual liaison. Another theme of this complex novel examines the nature of love in a marriage. It is the best thing that ever happened. It is a "deep thing of the heart." It is not immune to temptation or absence or destruction. But it is powerful, and for Will Hobbs, his love for Rennie has given him a center, a focus that helps to guide him even in her absence.

But finally, the basic theme in this novel is the old, old question of identity: "What is man? Who are we? Who am I?" While Harrison's examination of these questions centers on the experiences of Will Hobbs as he searches for his son in the terrifying chaos of fratricidal war in Rwanda (and elsewhere in Africa), the novel clearly expands the question to cover all of humankind. This theme intersects with the social issues of violence, overpopulation, tribal prejudice, and internecine strife; of the consequences of centuries of exploitation of native populations by colonial powers; and of the destabilization of post-colonial governments. Harrison explores the complex theme of social responsibility at various levels of the human community, from the relationship of the senior Alpha male and the females of his family to the assault on children in the mindless wars of the late twentieth century, especially tribal wars which seem to enact the biological imperative of lower animals to kill and mutilate the offspring of the competition.

But the theme is given an interesting twist through Will's attraction to his daughter-in-law, an attraction that makes him feel, he muses, "like a leftover Victorian gentleman in heat," a complex allusion since the present-day problems of Africa stem in large measure from nineteenth-century imperialism, a connection Harrison makes in a number of ways. What is the responsibility of the individual for his own morality, for his family, for his tribe, for his community, indeed, for civilization itself? Responsibility for Will Hobbs has in the past been mainly a matter of telling the story, of covering his African news desk accurately and competently, of writing well. Now that his son has been assigned to his old desk and heads for Nairobi when the Tutsi-Hutu War breaks out, Hobbs attempts to give his son useful advice, but Buck is in a total competitive mode with his father and refuses to hear his father's advice. Thus Will Hobbs later makes it his quest to find his lost son and avoid a sexual entanglement with his son's wife. And at the end of the story after his adventures and after his failure to save his son, he is left with the feeling that "words were like dry leaves . . . whirling across the bare floors of vacant houses." This image contrasts with Will's prayer, said silently as he gazes out into the lights blinking in London darkness: "Don't let the dark see or touch us . . . don't let it gather us in. Let us be gifted with language and speak the words that wake us up and set us free," a prayer that will be answered in Will's struggles against Papa Ngiza.

Harrison's argument is that the gift of language offered by writers as something that can assuage the pain and move back the dark is finally impotent and unable to stop the madness that is Africa and, by extension, all the world. Words cannot, finally, save the victims of genocide, nor can they heal rifts in a family, or save the son, or heal the pain.

◆ CHARACTERS ◆

The central figure of this novel is Will Hobbs, in his late fifties, a retired American journalist living alone in London in the quiet comfort of his big house in Queen's Gate, his wife Rennie having died two years earlier. Harrison develops him as intelligent, capable, competent in his profession as a journalist, sociable, sensitive, caring. He is also a chef, a culinary expert who can and does prepare feasts throughout the

novel, sometimes in the most unlikely situations. Harrison's characterization of Hobbs in this particular reveals him to be a nurturing, caring man. By cooking he gives and sustains life; by refusing to kill his captors when he has a reasonable opportunity to do so, he enacts a belief in the sanctity of life, a rare quality amidst the insanity of the intertribal warfare in Rwanda. This warfare serves as both background and foreground of Will's search for his son, Buck, who is also a journalist, and tests and toughens him.

Will's culinary skills set him apart from his journalistic colleagues and his family, even including his late wife, Rennie, his cultured British wife who had carried on an affair with an old friend for years, and Buck, their son who is married to Key and the father of a three-year-old son, Willie. Buck has been assigned to Will's former job, the Nairobi desk, and outwardly Will is glad, but he knows that Buck is still immature, impetuous, and extremely competitive because he wants to convince his father that he is, finally, a man equal to his father. Will is also smitten with a lust for Key, his daughter-in-law. Civilized and responsible man that he is, he keeps the "wild jealousy and resentment [of Buck that] he had no right to feel" at bay. Harrison introduces the father-son conflict early in the novel, establishing it as one caused in part by Will's extensive absences on assignment while Buck was growing up. It is not something that Will can fix at this point either by cooking or by giving advice to Buck. As he tries to tell his son shortly before Buck takes up his new post in Nairobi, the one that had been Will's, "Africa's lost, that's the first thing to see," but Buck will have none of it, determined as an idealist and as his own man to carve out his own reputation as a journalist, whatever it takes.

Key, Buck's wife and the mother of Willie, is developed as a beautiful, seductive, intelligent, and courageous young woman without education but very much able to use all of her considerable skills to create security for herself and her son. She is perhaps more attracted to Will than to Buck, and at one point she indicates that she fell in love with Will from listening to the stories that Buck told about him. Her character is, indeed, in many ways a key to understanding Will Hobbs for it is in resisting her seductiveness that he proves himself a man of high principles.

The other most important character is Papa Ngiza, Father Darkness, a self-proclaimed theologian educated in the West and the leader of a Hutu militia band, "five men dressed for a circus of mayhem," who are scouring their district and attempting to exterminate all Tutsis. Ngiza explains to Hobbs the nature and history of the conflict between Hutus and Tutsis, his explanations revealing the fundamental insanity and horror of the civil war as well as something of their history. He is a mystic with anger in his heart and thus the symbol of all religious fanatics who kill in the name of their beliefs, and he loves riddles. Clever and ruthless, he nevertheless functions as a kind of moral mirror to Hobbs who comes to understand his relationship to both his son and his daughter-in-law more clearly as a result of his involuntary association with Ngiza.

◆ TECHNIQUES ◆

Harrison's techniques are sound and traditional ones put cleverly into play. Drop a "good guy" (and Will is a good guy) plausibly into one of the more common testing grounds of one's moral center—sexual temptation, on the one hand, and into some sort of extreme situation created by the human race on the other—and see how he behaves. How does the hero act in such extreme situations? What will his being thrust into

these twin crucibles reveal about Will's character? What will his experiences teach us?

Harrison names his central figure Will Hobbs by which we are perhaps to understand the philosophic conflicts between free will and materialistic determinism. In his first name we find an allusion to "will" as in "free will" or "agency," the power to recognize and make moral choices. Perhaps in his surname we find an allusion to the ideas of Sir Thomas Hobbes, the English materialistic philosopher of the seventeenth century (although Harrison claims no recollection of having ever read him) who wrote, "*Nosce teipsum*, Read thyself: [an instruction] which was ... meant ... to teach us ... the similitude of the thoughts and passions of one man, to the thoughts and passions of another." This powerful and effective moral advice would appear to lie at the heart of Will Hobbs' journey and search. *The Blood Latitudes*, set in Africa in the last third of the twentieth century, certainly functions as a moral *exemplum*, a fiction that teaches important lessons. As Sir Thomas Hobbes outlines his treatise in his book *Leviathan*, he articulates his topics—man, government, and evil—and distinguishes between a Christian commonwealth and the Kingdom of Darkness. Hobbes says that man is both the created and the creator of government and he works to clarify how government is made, the rights and power or just power of a sovereign, and what preserves or dissolves it. Harrison's powerful novel offers his own contrast between the two kingdoms in his figuring of the decadent Christian commonwealth of contemporary England and the Kingdom of Darkness figured in central Africa. Harrison explicitly connects the political and the sexual contexts, the public and the private worlds of moral choice and civilized action in the first chapter of *The Blood Latitudes* when his daughter-in-law Key exposes her "dark pubic triangle" to Will in his hot tub on the first night after Buck, Willie, and Key arrive in London. Furthermore, Thomas Hobbes also assures us that wisdom comes not "by reading of books, but of men," which is exactly the skill that Will Hobbs has and by which he has made his living as a journalist and by which he will save his own life later on. But he is not certain how to read his daughter-in-law, nor is he certain at the beginning of the novel of the accuracy of his self-knowledge. But he knows how necessary it is that one knows one's self. He has made his living as a journalist by reading men and their actions and by examining his own life with some care.

Harrison structures *The Blood Latitudes* as a heroic quest novel, presented in a specific and realistic historical and geographical context, the genocidal conflict between Hutus and Tutsis in Rwanda of the early 1990s. The basic plot line follows the archetypal quest of the hero, a useful analysis of which is Joseph Campbell's *The Hero with a Thousand Faces* (1949). As a man of mature middle age, Will Hobbs must seek to find his lost son and his own obscured moral center. For these purposes he sets off on a traditional mythic journey, a journey into "the heart of darkness" to come to knowledge of himself, to find himself if not his son. He separates himself from his comfortable home in Queens Gate, London, a home that Rennie had bought with her money, crosses numerous borders, discovers a source of power within himself by descending into the belly of the whale (the lorry being used by Papa Ngiza and his militia), and has a series of defining and informing adventures. He is opposed by the forces of darkness in the person of Papa Ngiza, whose name means "the father of darkness," the leader of a band of Hutu militia with whom Hobbs travels unwillingly after they capture him. They allow him to live because Hobbs hides his identity as a veteran journalist (Ngiza does not like journalists and has killed several, perhaps even Buck Hobbs) and assumes the nurturing identity of a chef. In

that character he cooks for his captors. Ngiza and his band patrol their sector, killing, looting, and maiming Tutsis. Hobbs and Ngiza have numerous philosophical discussions, Hobbs agreeing with Ngiza that the crimes against humanity occurring in East Africa have ample historical precedent, and his insight here helps Will to see the correct moral choices he must make in the matter of his daughter-in-law. He is also witness to several atrocities, is unable to escape, and confesses his attraction for Key to his captor. Ngiza celebrates Will's passion then invites him to compare what the Hutus are doing to the great historical catalog of Western atrocities. Will agrees with him and concludes that the world "at best was in a barbaric twilight." The land through which they travel is blighted, the land cursed, the people "just warring factions, each trying to be more brutal than the other." In the process they come across a coffee plantation and are greeted by a blind old man who gives them honey wine, and they are stalked by the mysterious Ragman, a magical figure who kills the members of Ngiza's band one by one. Ngiza and Will discuss the great question, "What is Man?" Is he only the sum of what he does? Or does he have a true essence? At last, they come to a red-brick church, built by the Belgians years ago. Inside are a band of Tutsi children and a dying Swedish literacy worker. Hobbs gets into the church with the children, and they formulate a plan to overcome Ngiza and what is left of his band. Will cooks for the children and for the dying literacy worker, suggesting Christ's assertion that inasmuch as one serves his fellow man, he serves Christ. "I was hungered and ye fed me." Hobbs, attempting to protect the Swede, kills Cutter, the one who has cut off the feet of children with his tree lopper. He and the children then capture Ngiza, the children killing him by inches with shots to the leg and panga cuts in retribution for the pain he has inflicted on them and other

Tutsis. After the battle Hobbs and the children get into the lorry and, after other difficulties, finally make it back across the border into Kenya, returning in accordance with the archetypal heroic journey, to the village, to civilization. Will bears the boon of self-knowledge as well as a conviction that his son is dead and that he himself, a representative of the West, is no longer one of the innocent. Will Hobbs re-enters the world, knowing on an emotional as well as intellectual level how evil man can be, seeing a spreading "ring of darkness" to the northwest as he flies back into Nairobi.

Harrison's characterization of Hobbs, his conversations, the response of other characters to him, and most specifically his actions are all classic techniques. The depth of his characterization is such that Hobbs emerges in the novel as a convincing and compelling figure, fully realized and credible.

◆ LITERARY PRECEDENTS ◆

Harrison alludes to Joseph Conrad's *Heart of Darkness*, the quintessential Western examination of the horrors engendered by European discovery and exploitation of Africa. Conrad was once Harrison's favorite author, and he also admires Karen Blixen's *Out of Africa* as a nearly perfect prose meditation. But for a writer and a teacher of writing in a university context, it seems clear that many writers, all writers, have influenced him. *The Blood Latitudes* alludes to many writers and texts from Ernest Hemingway to George Adamson. It is clear that Harrison knows the history and the brutal realities of European colonialism, of the WWI realignment of colonial properties, and the post-WWII independence movements that revealed how much the indigenous peoples had learned from their colonial masters. However, he says that "Africa itself has always been the greater intoxicant. I think I need to go back again."

◆ RELATED TITLES ◆

Africana, Savannah Blue, Burton and Speke, and *The Three Hunters* are all novels by William Harrison that have Africa as their setting and theme. Each is a different kind of fiction. *The Three Hunters* he conceived as a comedy about a dysfunctional family and the youngest son's search for love in all the wrong places. It parodies the hunting stories of Hemingway and others. *Savannah Blue,* Harrison's best-selling novel, is a mystery set partly in Africa, partly in Washington, D.C., fascinating for its characterization of Quentin Clare as a clever and dedicated killer and its deft handling of a large cast of characters and a complicated plot. *Burton and Speke* is a fictionalized treatment of the relationship of John Hanning Speke and Richard Francis Burton, their attempts to discover the headwaters of the Nile, and the consequences of those efforts, deeply researched and convincingly presented. *Africana* is a story about the role of mercenaries in the civil wars of Biafra, Katanga, and Kenya. *The Blood Latitudes* is the last and most satisfying of the five African novels and shows Harrison at the top of his form.

◆ IDEAS FOR GROUP DISCUSSIONS ◆

The discussion between Papa Ngiza and Will Hobbs about the nature of tribal warfare and the relationship of the present bloodshed to a number of historical antecedents should stimulate thinking about the individual's responsibility in the face of social and cultural atrocities. The relationship between one's personal morality and the larger social and political contexts in which individuals operate is always a useful area for discussion.

1. The relationship between Will Hobbs and his son Buck is difficult and problematic. Does it make a difference that

Will Hobbs is sexually attracted to his daughter-in-law, Key? Is she really in love with Will or is she merely opportunistic and seeking security for herself and Willie? What is the relationship between sexual fidelity and the other arenas of moral choice represented in the novel?

2. Why does Will not take action to overcome his captors and escape earlier than he does? Is the delay merely a function of Harrison's plotting or is it a function of his characterization of Hobbs? Is it simple fear that motivates Will's failure to act or is it something else?

3. Will is a great cook. Considering the occasions of his preparing food, the nature of the food, the implications of this performance and considering mythic, theological, and political implications, what does Harrison want his readers to do with this aspect of Will's behavior? How does it fit (or not) with the other aspects of his character as revealed in his actions?

4. What is the relation between the characterization of Will Hobbs and the themes of the novel?

5. Considering the representations of Africa and Africans, Europeans and Americans, what does the novel argue about what Africa means for the rest of the world? What is the meaning of Will's thoughts at the end of the novel, that "all the world is Africa, barbaric and primeval . . . and we want cobras in our gardens."

6. What does Harrison mean when he writes that "words were like dry leaves blowing through old windows left open, whirling across the bare floors of vacant houses, across gray meadows, across history. All intelligent men lived at the edge of depression"? Is Harrison

arguing ironically that only actions make a difference, that words and the work of writers, including journalists as well as poets, make no difference? Consider among other aspects of the novel the discussions between Will and Papa Ngiza and the actions that Will takes.

7. Considering all the evidence, for example, the personal and familial relationships examined in the novel, argue whether *The Blood Latitudes* presents a pessimistic or an optimistic view of life.

8. Compare and contrast the Rwandan conflicts that form the historical background of this novel and cost perhaps 800,000 lives with those of other "intratribal" wars such as WWI, WWII, and the American Civil War. Can one make a convincing argument that Hobbs is right, that "all the world is Africa, barbaric and primeval, and what's in the blood is more savage than we can know or possibly understand"? What do you think he means? What other writers have you read who express a similar idea? What are we to do with that knowledge?

9. Compare Harrison's treatment of the warrior in his other African stories. What do you think Harrison is saying about the condition of the post-WWII world? Is colonialism really dead or has it merely assumed other forms?

10. Compare Harrison's African novels with those by William Boyd, Chinua Achebe, Isak Dinesen, and Joseph Conrad.

Theodore C. Humphrey
California State Polytechnic University,
Pomona

THE BRETHREN

Novel

2000

Author: John Grisham

◆

◆ SOCIAL CONCERNS ◆

A t its heart, *The Brethren* is full of warnings for our society. The novel displays a frightening distrust of American officials and government. The three blackmailers are former judges of varying levels from different states, suggesting widespread corruption among our justice system officials. Not only are they all guilty of crimes to begin with, showing great fallibility in those most trusted to safeguard justice, but they have dedicated themselves to full-time crime in prison. While all were caught by the system, the sense conveyed is that they are not exceptional but typical, and any confidence the legal system regains by the fact that they were caught and convicted is lost when we see the innocent Buster in prison because of the poor judgment of a prosecutor and yet another judge.

The novel includes lawyers in its indictment of legal professionals with its portrayal of the immoral lawyer Trevor Carson. Grisham makes his characters seem very realistic, almost too much so. They have drinking and smoking addictions, marriage problems, gambling interests, exercise habits. Grisham appears intent on showing us that the legal system is full of individuals who are not above corruption and criminal activity.

Despite his indictment of the legal system, Grisham embeds the majority of his warnings in his second plot thread, pointing out the dangers of trusting the behind-the-scenes machinations of those in the intelligence community. First, he paints a frightening picture of how dangerous the most powerful people in government on the intelligence front charged with safeguarding the United States can be. The CIA director, Teddy Maynard, is willing to subvert the entire democratic election process, to sacrifice innocent lives and to break any law in order to launch his plan to protect the country against certain future military challenges he predicts. Regardless of whether the threats Maynard sees are real, there is little doubt that his work to save the United States threatens everything worth saving in the country.

As Grisham puts Maynard into action, he has Maynard winnow down all the possible U.S. officials to the cleanest, most honest one, Aaron Lake, and then shows that this clean-cut type who does not even eat sugar has a dark secret. Worse for the reader's faith in government than the revelation of Lake's secret sexual preference is that this rare, honest politician does not hesitate to participate in the plan to break every major election law and illegally manipulate the entire election process in order to become president. All politicians are simple to entrap, Maynard declares at one point, wishing his international enemies were so easy. In numerous ways, the novel casts doubt on government officials of every level, in all branches of government.

The method by which the CIA director pursues his election scheme proclaims Grisham's next social concern. Grisham highlights the importance of money in government elections, showing that elections can essentially be bought. First, money can be used to assemble and coordinate all the staff and equipment one needs to run and to pay for spectacular events, then Congressional endorsements can be purchased, and finally the all-important commercials and air time can be paid for. Grisham even shows, with eerily convincing realism, how by backing an issue which would generate enormous government spending within a given industry, a candidate could garner the full financial support of all the companies within that industry for his or her campaign. Grisham's cynical reading of the election process coincides with the negative views in this novel of the judicial system and intelligence communities to create a vision of an entirely corrupt government.

◆ THEMES ◆

By focusing on flawed characters, Grisham appears intent on commenting on the universal nature of corruption. In his novel, corruption certainly is present in all arms of the United States government. However, he also shows the unofficial prison court, run by unscrupulous men, ironically fulfilling a beneficial role in the prison. Without the ad-hoc court to decide disagreements, there would doubtless be more conflict and even violence in the minimum-security prison. Therefore, Grisham shows some faith in the idea of justice and a court system even while repeatedly reinforcing the theme that all humans are flawed and subject to moral and ethical failings.

Accompanying the theme of corruption is that of greed, for it is greed which drives the brethren in their illicit behavior. It is even greed, greed for power, which leads the congressman Lake to fall. Only the CIA director's corruption is not related to greed; his fall appears more related to the old maxim that power corrupts.

With the actions of the CIA director, Grisham explores the question of when the ends justify the means. If a government leader believes his country to be in peril, does that justify any action on his part in its defense? If so, what exactly is he defending? What defines a "country"? These are some of the philosophical questions Grisham explores. After building a compelling motivational case to justify drastic action, Grisham does a masterful job of arguing through the text that the ends do not justify the means.

◆ CHARACTERS ◆

The interesting thing about *The Brethren* is that none of the characters qualify as protagonists. The "brethren" of the title are obviously loathsome men. The three ex-judges have their own habits, hobbies, and failings, but they are united in being unsympathetic criminals, greedy and uncaring for others. Their co-conspirator and lawyer, Trevor Carson, is equally despicable. He does not even have the level of dignity of the judges, being a small-time, small-town crook. The director of the CIA is no better. Teddy Maynard is still working hard to serve his country even though he is in pain and confined to a wheelchair. He sees a great danger looming and wants to save the United States. However, he is also a power-happy manipulative tyrant with little regard for democracy or ordinary citizens' lives. Maynard is interesting as a Macchiavellian mastermind, but he is not a sympathetic character or a true protagonist. He may believe that the end of saving his country justifies the means he employs to achieve that goal, but Grisham demonstrates the fallacy underlying Maynard's reasoning.

The moment Aaron Lake agrees to allow the CIA to manipulate the election for him, he also loses the reader's sympathy. He is not as powerful as the other main characters in the book in the sense that he is not initiating or guiding the action, but he is culpable of collaborating with Maynard. Not only is Lake willing to let the CIA break numerous election laws, but he maintains complicitous silence even when he learns that Maynard is arranging heinous, murderous acts to help Lake's campaign.

There are some minor characters in the novel who are not immoral; however, they lack enough importance to count as full protagonists. It is also unusual that not only are there no protagonists, but the main antagonists all accomplish their goals: the bad guys win. Grisham's decision not to include any sympathetic heroes or heroines is an unusual move for a mainstream bestseller. Apparently, he wanted the readers to focus on what the antagonists' corruption represents in the scope of the book or in our society.

◆ TECHNIQUES ◆

Grisham opens *The Brethren* with a false court presided over by the imprisoned judges and a character who performs the duties of a bailiff but thinks of himself as the "court jester." This mockery of justice neatly foreshadows the opinion Grisham offers in this novel of the real court system, showing that it and the rest of government are not what they are supposed to be. And

yet, in prison, the three ex-judges appear to pass fair decisions and help keep the peace, so Grisham shows us the positive aspects of a justice system even at its lowest. This does not, however, redeem the ex-judges.

Two main story lines intersect in this novel. The first is the squalid tale of the ex-judges running their blackmail scam, and the second is the election plot, tied into an epic tale of an impending third world war. This thread seems like a classic spy thriller, except that it is only a sketch of a plot. Grisham zooms in on the first storyline, the tale of the fallen judges in mimesis, full close-up mode with extensive dialogue and description, while offering the secondary plot in diegesis, or summary-style story telling with indirect dialogue and exposition. When the characters from the secondary plot, Lake and Maynard, intersect with the first plot, then they are given scenes full of detailed description as they happen, especially with Maynard's agents, but this mimesis is in context of the first storyline, the blackmailing scam, and the second story-line always remains in the background.

The point of view in *The Brethren* is third-person omniscient, as the view follows all the action from a neutral, removed perspective. Characters' thoughts are rarely given, at least not in depth, and yet the amount of descriptive detail given makes the characters appear very realistic. Grisham's use of detail is one of his most conspicuous traits. The novel creates a believable sense of group life for the three judges through its use of concrete details. We see what they wear, what prison jobs they have, how much they get paid for those jobs, where they spend most of their time; we witness them ironing out the details of their scam, reviewing minor details, and drafting extortion letters. We see the good and bad habits of each, learn about their past and present marital statuses, and study their attitudes toward prison. The reality of minimum-security life and the reality of the blackmailing ring are both depicted in fine clarity. As a matter of fact, we not only see the brethren running their scam in regards to the main victim, Lake, but we see numerous examples of how it plays out with lesser victims. And then we watch as the CIA exhaustively pieces together the scam bit by bit. This level of detail creates an aura of authenticity around the fiction. Readers may not have any protagonists to cheer for, but they do have fully-rendered situations to study.

◆ LITERARY PRECEDENTS ◆

Tom Clancy novels are obvious contemporary models for the world military/political intrigue plot in *The Brethren*. This subplot is also reminiscent of older spy thrillers such as the classic La Carre novels. The view of society as corrupt has roots in hard-boiled detective novels such as Raymond Chandler's, Dashiell Hammett's, or Ross MacDonald's.

◆ RELATED TITLES ◆

After rising to fame with adventure/chase novels in *The Firm* and *The Pelican Brief*, John Grisham has been experimenting with different narrative forms within the legal fiction subgenre. He is a legal expert, and his novels go into great detail on aspects of the legal profession such as ambulance chasing, jury deliberation, and inheritance law in *The Rainmaker*, *The Runaway Jury*, and *The Testament*, respectively. In *The Chamber*, Grisham focuses on the death penalty and its execution. With *The Brethren*, Grisham continues to focus on the legal system by having his main antagonists be ex-judges in prison, partnered with a crooked lawyer. However, Grisham continues to attempt to develop his range in this novel, not only staying far from any real courtroom action but including a full-fledged spy plot for the first time.

◆ IDEAS FOR GROUP DISCUSSIONS ◆

In many ways, Grisham's novel emphasizes milieu and theme over character and plot. Using thorough description, Grisham carefully paints a world inside a prison where a small group of men are doing something abhorrent. Readers gain a strong feel for the fictional workings of this prison scam as well as other aspects of the prison and justice system. Carefully intertwined with this environment is a secondary plot concentrating on theories about the function of our government and our election system. Thus, Grisham highlights many topics of importance in our society today.

1. In the CIA subplot, Teddy Maynard is willing to break laws and sacrifice individuals for the good of the nation. Does the fact that, unlike the other characters, he is not breaking laws for his own benefit justify his actions to any degree?

2. Does the lack of female characters affect your involvement in the novel?

3. What are the advantages to not including any protagonists?

4. Does reading a novel which weaves such a realistic web of details around its characters affect how you view similar real life figures such as judges and politicians at all?

5. Much of the body of the novel is dialogue. Does the dialogue sound realistic to you? What criteria can you use to tell if dialogue between character types you may never have met such as judges or CIA directors is in fact realistic? What effect does this have on your perception of the novel?

6. When Grisham makes money the key to any election, it implies a pervasive negative influence. How important is money in your life? Do people you know who have more money seem to have an advantage in many different areas?

Brian Forsyth

THE BRIDE COMES TO YELLOW SKY

Short Story

1898

Author: Stephen Crane

◆ SOCIAL CONCERNS ◆

Stephen Crane's story of the Texas frontier town's marshal, Jack Potter, who goes to San Antonio to meet and marry a girl of questionable background (for him), is stricken by a guilty conscience, then returns with her only to find the town badman gunning for him, is justifiably considered one of his best short fictions. It also remains one of his most enduring stories. A number of interesting and cogent reasons for this might be advanced, to say nothing of individual reasons from appreciative readers over the past hundred years and more who have found in it a particular narrow feature of special appeal. First off, there are a number of strange, provocative, seemingly out-of-place references and overstatements scattered throughout the narrative—aside from Crane's stilted and pretentious expressions that he might have picked up from reading popular (or pulp) Westerns.

As the train approaches Yellow Sky, Potter is fully aware that his marriage is so important a thing to the town that it can "only be exceeded by the burning of the new hotel." After Potter and his unnamed bride arrive in Yellow Sky, they come face to face with the town menace, the drink-crazed Scratchy Wilson. The two of them have had a number of familiar encounters over the barrel of a gun, and while the townsfolk are accustomed to these confrontations, there is no telling how deadly any one of them in the future might turn out to be. Now, on this auspicious occasion, when Scratchy puts the marshal in his line of fire, the bride is described oddly. Her face goes "as yellow as old cloth" and she is "a slave to hideous rites, gazing at the apparitional snake." But Potter makes two announcements about himself to Scratchy: he is not carrying a gun, and he has just gotten married. These revelations blow Scratchy's mind. Stunned by the momentous news, which he can barely deal with, Scratchy yells "No!" and then, Crane writes, he is "like a creature allowed a glimpse of another world." Finally he manages to pose a kind of question to Potter. He supposes that now "it's all off." Potter replies that it is up to Scratchy to decide, since he (Potter) was not the one that started the trouble. Scratchy, after getting the message about Potter's new status and new attitude, decides that it *is* all off, and leaves the scene.

Aside from Crane's enigmatic wording, there is an array of social concerns that reveal the story's broad scope, and may help to explain its genuine appeal to a wide range of readers. First, there is the matter of

---

one going "headlong over all the social hedges," i.e., violating society's tacitly understood behavior code, which includes the selection of appropriate associates, particularly a domestic partner. A number of tantalizing remarks by Crane reveal Potter's deliberate nonconformity in the matter of his choice of a life partner, and the trouble that his reckless behavior gets him into. The girl's common, "underclass" facial expression, as well as the impression she gives (on the train to Yellow Sky) of dutifully expecting to continue cooking, gives the impression that she is far from being the town marshal's social equal. Crane offers the reader enough of Potter's unhappy situation to fill in the supportive details and dispel the mystery of his dark mood and guilt over having "committed an extraordinary crime." Potter is stricken apparently by the realization that he married down, so to speak, allying himself with someone clearly beneath him: a choice that will not sit well with the townsfolk of Yellow Sky, who might somehow feel embarrassed by her. This is not to say that Potter regrets his action, wishes (however faintly) that he could undo it, or fantasizes about a more suitable lady he might have chosen. He simply must face the consequences of his action in taking this particular woman for his wife, and the prospect of facing them is not a pleasant one.

Now, going "headlong over all the social hedges" may or may not mean a serious breach of the social code, but Crane's heavy emphasis, amounting to gross exaggeration, on Potter's impropriety suggests something deeper than the mere social risk, or misjudgment, of marrying down. He feels "heinous" for having committed that crime, and moreover, "His friends could not forgive him." This may relate to the statement given above, to the effect that his marriage was such an important thing in Yellow Sky, "it could only be exceeded by the burning of the new hotel." The reason for this odd comparison seems close at hand: the burning of that hotel would leave the town at a very big disadvantage, for where else would travelers or visitors stay during their stopover, and where else could newcomers count on lodging until they got properly settled? Moreover, if an important business establishment like the hotel were to burn, that would mean a considerable loss of revenue for the town. But the marshal's marriage, which would require the town' approval, might (in the event of a bad rating, as with a wife who would not fit in at all) oblige Potter to leave the town, while also causing Yellow Sky to be vulnerable to bad men and other disturbers of the peace. Hence, one may assume, this is the reason for Crane's curious revelations about the workings of the bridegroom's mind; as the train made its way to Yellow Sky, "Jack Potter was beginning to find the shadow of a deed weigh upon him like a leaden slab."

Closely related to the social concern about someone going "headlong over all the social hedges" is a social concern that, like the first, adds considerably to the story's suggestive, possibly disturbing, quality. This second concern involves the array of social and psychological hazards that one incurs by marrying in haste, regardless of whether the chosen partner will be socially acceptable within one's group. However in this case the bride's possible unacceptability is clearly a cause for worry by her husband. "Face to face with this girl in San Antonio, and spurred by his sharp impulses, he had gone headlong over all the social hedges." Since he had not consulted Yellow Sky first, about any aspect of his intention to wed, Potter "was now bringing his bride before an innocent and unsuspecting community." Thus, there is no telling how the townsfolk will treat his wife on a personal level, or how she will react to them, and there is no telling how he himself will be treated, by the townsfolk or by his wife. While the story does not echo the familiar adage,

"Marry in haste, repent at leisure," Potter's precipitate action proves very troubling to him nevertheless.

There are two reasons why these closely linked social concerns have a special significance in Crane's story, giving it a suggestive quality—perhaps even a disturbing quality—that is hard to pin down. One reason, obvious enough to many readers, is that so little information is given about the bride, notwithstanding the narrator's superficial descriptions and the bride's individual responses; clearly something important is left out of the story. As a result, there will be lively speculation about what the author was up to in the first place. The second reason is that there are elements in the story line that may be related, one way or another, to Crane's own life. This gives "The Bride Comes to Yellow Sky" that very special literary feature, "the quality of felt experience"—even if a disguise of sorts may be detected in the text.

A number of commentators and critics have pointed out a connection of sorts between Jack Potter's taking his bride and Crane's taking his own domestic consort. But that insight, which needs to be examined more closely, is only one important key to the inner meaning of the story hidden within Crane's very frequently anthologized good vs. evil thriller, which was at the same time his spoof of wild West pop fiction, and his too-tender romance.

Though Crane does not directly suggest that the morals or the conduct of Jack Potter's bride could stand improvement, or that Potter is a raffish person accustomed to associating with low, vulgar characters, Crane himself by the time he wrote "The Bride Comes to Yellow Sky"—near the end of his life—had long shown that he was a determined dropout from polite society. For whatever psychological reasons, Crane's lifestyle proved markedly different from that of his parents and other relatives in a fairly prestigious family background. The last of an enormous brood, Crane was born to a prominent Methodist minister who occupied various pulpits in New York and New Jersey until his death in 1880, and to his wife, the daughter of a Methodist clergyman and the niece of a Methodist bishop. His parents were active in the temperance movement. Crane's "Revolutionary War namesake," Stanley Wertheim and Paul Sorrentino point out in their documentary biography *The Crane Log* (1994), was a two-term "delegate from New Jersey to the Continental Congress in Philadelphia." An indifferent and restless student, within a three-year period, 1888-91, Stephen Crane attended or rather spent some time at Claverack College (New York), Lafayette College (Pennsylvania), and Syracuse University (New York). Though college courses in general were not to his liking, baseball was, along with expressing himself on paper: writing sketches and stories, and trying his hand at news reporting. But Crane was not to be the familiar college-dropout figure lacking focus and self-knowledge.

Crane's maverick tendency was already evident during his brief sojourn at Claverack College. Some of his classmates there remembered Crane "as a contradictory personality," according to Linda H. Davis's *Badge of Courage: The Life of Stephen Crane* (1998). One considered Crane self-deprecatory and arrogant, while another felt he was a bit of a rebel, with very irregular habits: "a law unto himself." The wild streak of uninhibited willfulness in his character, tinged with a suggestion of cautionary restraint, would apparently help shape a number of his story plots, for example what one finds in "The Bride Comes to Yellow Sky." Crane sought action and adventure—as a reporter, war correspondent, and fiction writer—in the Bowery, the wild West, Mexico, Cuba, Greece. He drank, no matter the temperance culture of his parents. As a young journalist he experimented briefly with living as a vagrant, "going forth to eat as the wanderer may eat, and sleep as the homeless sleep," surviving on and off the mean streets of New York, which yielded "An Experiment in Misery," printed in the *New York Press* in 1894. Though Crane was "far from sympathetic to the opium habit," his biographer Linda H. Davis writes, his newspaper sketch "Opium's Varied Dreams" for the McClure Syndicate "was evocative and precisely detailed, clearly suggesting that the writer had tried the drug."

Prone to taking risks in his personal relations with others, in fact living on the edge, he happened to show an affinity for certain individuals who might have caused great offense to his parents or certain other family members, had the facts been revealed. That is, women living a bohemian or even shadier existence—performing on the stage, indulging in transitory liaisons, or being involved in prostitution. In familiarizing himself with, and consorting with, females of easy virtue, Crane displayed a particular sympathy toward their precarious existence. Evidence of this may be seen in his groundbreaking novelette *Maggie: A Girl of the Streets* (1893) and in his contending (at considerable personal risk) with a hostile police officer bent on charging a possibly innocent chorus girl with solicitation of men.

What capped Crane's fairly brief but perfervid life as an amorist (he died at the age of twenty-eight) was his bonding relationship with a colorful, sexually uninhibited woman of the world who was some years older than he. A divorcee estranged from her second husband (an English aristocrat's son), she was Cora Taylor, "born into a respectable Boston family . . . related on her mother's Quaker side to the poet John Greenleaf Whittier" (according to Christopher Benfey's biography *The Double Life of Stephen Crane*). When she and Crane

(about six years her junior) met and they took to each other, in Jacksonville, Florida, at the end of 1896, she was the proprietor of a flourishing house of assignation—or, according to Davis's *Badge of Courage,* Jacksonville's "finest bawdy house"—called Hotel de Dream. Before she was twenty, according to Davis, she lived with a lover and was employed as a hostess in a New York Tenderloin district gambling house. After that and until she began her relationship with Crane, Cora entered into two marriages and a string of adulterous affairs.

For the remainder of his short life, Cora remained loyal to him, representing herself as Mrs. Crane, and even, like him, traveling to Greece as a war correspondent so that they might cover the Greco-Turkish War together. Almost all of their remaining time as a domestic couple was spent in England, where they socialized with such prominent authors as Joseph Conrad, H. G. Wells, and Henry James. A year or so after Crane's death in June of 1900, according to Wertheim and Sorrentino's *The Crane Log,* Cora operated a house of prostitution and an annex to it in the Jacksonville area. But five years after Crane's death, Cora entered into a bigamous marriage with Hammond McNeil, who in 1907 shot to death a man he thought was her lover, following which Cora "fled to England to avoid testifying at the trial."

Benfey's comparison of the Crane-Cora Taylor union with that of Yellow Sky's marshal Jack Potter and the woman he brought home from San Antonio, while not entirely convincing, nevertheless contains enough of a challenge to appeal to Crane aficionados seeking connections between fiction and autobiography. In Benfey's view it "mirrors the disorientation of Crane and Cora, passing for man and wife, in England." He considers the town's name as a quite plausible one "for gas-lit, coal-clouded London. The bride is . . . nameless, as Cora must remain in Crane's family and to his

New York friends." But "disorientation" seems a curious word to describe the pair's mental condition, in their leased estate in Sussex. Linda H. Davis in her Crane biography *Badge of Courage* expresses the feeling that although Cora "was not the woman Stephen's friends would have chosen for him" she did not detract from the pleasure of his company. The pair's "English acquaintances generally accepted her as Stephen's wife"—some were unaware of their true relationship—"and appreciated her devotion to him and her kindness to them."

Given the importance of the twin social concerns of leaping over the social hedges and marrying in haste, in regard to Crane's tale of the bride's coming to Yellow Sky, a few additional remarks may be desirable. Commentators disagree on whether or not Crane's description of the bride's features in the story match Cora's own features. But the nameless woman is portrayed as a reticent, submissive, mousey creature, whereas Cora, who had, like Crane, a prominent and quite respectable family background, yet had also gone "headlong over all the social hedges," was willful and extravagant: anything but meek and docile. Davis in *Badge of Courage* mentions, in regard to their brief (English) sojourn at Brede Place in Sussex, that their landlord's daughter considered Cora "the worst type of bossing American woman," even using the word "terror" to describe her. Still, there is something bothersome about Jack Potter's bride, neither pretty nor very young, with her "plain, underclass countenance . . . drawn in placid, almost emotionless lines," and wearing a blue cashmere dress adorned "with small reservations of velvet" and abounding with steel buttons . . . this woman embarrassed by her stiff, straight, and high puff sleeves, accustomed to cooking and dutifully expecting to continue cooking.

What is bothersome about the bride has been touched on above, but bears being repeated for further consideration. It is Jack Potter's feeling heinous, unforgivable, like a "traitor to the feelings of Yellow Sky," guilty of having "committed an extraordinary crime"—by going to San Antonio to meet and propose to "a girl he believed he loved," and by his intending to foist her on an innocent and unsuspecting community. And the marshal's feeling that way is bothersome because a girl merely plain, a bit aged, and underclass, would not be likely to induce such pronounced guilt feelings in him, even if he did the proposing "like a man hidden in the dark," with a knife easy in his hand "to sever any friendly duty, any form," as Crane puts it. The bride just may be a woman with a checkered past, or a woman of easy virtue, simply marrying out of her lower class state, determined to put her past forever behind her, and fearing she will not really fit in or be able to make it in Yellow Sky.

Two points may be mentioned here, to bolster the argument that there well may be something irregular, very far out in fact, about the new domestic relationship that is the essence of Crane's story. Potter's "knife easy in his hand to remove any friendly duty, any form" he might wish to maintain, with regard to the folks back in Yellow Sky, does not cut him loose from his law and order duties when he brings back his shadowy bride; the reader does not get the feeling that the bride will be scorned, spurned, or rejected—on the mere basis of her physical appearance or dress. Potter's intense disquiet and his guilty conscience *may be* the result of the knowledge—which he would desperately want to safeguard in his mind forever—that he obtained the woman from a place or from a set of circumstances so shocking and unforgivable to the townsfolk, if the truth got out, as to damn him forever in Yellow Sky and perhaps later in other communities where the news preceded him in his migrations.

Secondly, Crane's reference to the bride not being very young suggests (given the context) that she was somewhat older than Potter—else why would Crane have mentioned her advancing age? This in turn might mean that she was desperate or at least eager enough to quit San Antonio (things getting too "hot" there for her perhaps?), that she would marry and go off with a near stranger, someone she knew only slightly at best. If this string of *ifs* and *maybes* appears to stretch too thin, it should be kept in mind that Crane's Cora allowed herself to be transplanted too, by her man, and that while the bride was different from Cora in a number of ways, her being a cook was certainly no bar to social acceptability, nor was anything else about her that we are informed about such a bar. San Antonio seems a replacement of Jacksonville, Florida, in the domestic setting Crane created in his fictive self-examination; Potter's being so very bothered by his social duty suggests, finally, Crane's psychological projection and self-absolution.

The next two social issues are of a technical nature insofar as they bear on domestic relations within a cultural and historical setting. That is, they concern newlyweds and the embarrassment newlyweds were put to (given the time and place of the story) by the wedding audience and/or outsiders wanting to get in on the fun. The idea of a newly-married couple getting ready for bed and the delights of the wedding night, while no longer a big deal to a twenty-first-century audience, was cause for ribald mirth to a late nineteenth-century audience, which had various ways of dealing with the couple—ranging from kidding to mocking to harassing. There are at least two reasons for this. First, there was the rigid Puritan morality of the period, and the reactive need of some people (generally, the younger folk) to rebel in whatever way, against the sexual restrictions and censorship imposed by society; second, there was

the pattern, going back to ancient times, of folk practices and usages, involving some form of celebration, relating to the triad of sexual union, fertility, and new birth. In this connection, the combination of the wild revel (*komos*) and the domestic union of the sexes (*gamos*) may be traced back at least twenty-five hundred years, from ancient Greek comic-drama performance, to the endings of the comedies of Shakespeare (with their festive wedding ceremonies), and on into all the more recent practices and adaptations.

Certainly a wedding party in the early twenty-first century might still send the "Just Married" couple off on a honeymoon, with showers of rice or a pair of old shoes tied to their car's rear bumper, and possibly a following of several cars with horns tooting to signal the event and its supposed aftermath. But in this story's frontier-town society in the 1890s, public scrutiny could make sensitive people painfully self-conscious where their affectionate behavior was concerned. And since observers might snicker, smirk, smile broadly, roll eyes, drop a suggestive remark, or even make a public show in the presence of a newly-married couple revealing their insecurity, Crane's bride and groom coming to Yellow Sky were involved in a pair of intensely embarrassing comic sequences that involved strangers infringing on their privacy: what might be called The Honeymooners and The Shivaree.

A number of commentators on "The Bride Comes to Yellow Sky" have apparently missed the point of Crane's references to certain folk traditions—particularly in the case of the spectacle provided by the honeymooners—and this has further obscured the significance of the story for some readers. In his Honeymooners sequence Crane makes use of a conventional situation which around the turn of the twentieth century needed no elaborate explanation. Such a matter, for example, as the bride's "blushes caused by the careless scrutiny of some passengers" when she entered the Pullman car would have been easily understood. Well over half a century later, however, it seems to have puzzled a number of readers and commentators, despite a clear hint from the author himself. Crane refers to such matters as: the Negro porter, on the train, surveying the newlyweds "from afar with an amused and superior grin," bullying them, subtly using "all the manners of the most unconquerable kind of snobbery," oppressing them; and some of the travelers covering "them with stares of derisive enjoyment." After that Crane caps the description of the scene as follows. "Historically there was supposed to be something infinitely humorous in their situation."

There certainly was, and it had nothing to do with Potter announcing the expected time of arrival in Yellow Sky or the splendor of the Pullman car the couple occupied, as one commentator has claimed. It is no secret that a number of stories appearing in that general period reveal an intense antipathy on the part of the newly married, brides especially, to being taken for honeymooners. A few examples follow. William Dean Howells's autobiographical novel *Their Wedding Journey* (1872), whose action is set in 1870, makes very much of the newly-married Isabel March's determination not to have her status detected. Van Wyck Brooks in his Introduction to the Fawcett Premier Classics paperback edition (1960) of *Their Wedding Journey* writes: "Basil and Isabel March were a typical bridal pair, not least in their wish not to be taken for one." A short story by *Puck* editor Henry Cuyler Bunner, "The Nice People" (1890), depicts a charming, likeable couple at an elegant summer resort on the Eastern seaboard, who act in so suspicious a manner that the proprietor thinks they are not married, and confronts them in a humiliating manner, wishing to turn them out of his establishment. As the outraged couple are about to

leave in disgrace, it is suddenly revealed that they really are married, but were acting nervous and confused, giving inconsistent answers to direct questions about their background, in a strenuous effort to hide the fact that they are actually on their honeymoon. And in Henry James's *The Turn of the Screw* (1898), the governess relates as follows her difficult interview with Miles, the mysteriously abnormal child who has been put in her charge: "We continued silent while the maid was with us—as silent, it whimsically occurred to me, as some young couple who, on their wedding-journey, at the inn, feel shy in the presence of the waiter."

As for the Shivaree—a corruption of *charivari*—a cogent definition is provided by a British handbook, *The Wordsworth Dictionary of Phrase & Fable* (1994): "in the U.S.A. [it] means the mocking serenade accorded to newly married people." *Charivari*, according to this handbook, is a French expression "for an uproar caused by banging pans and kettles and accompanied by hissing, shouting, etc., to express disapproval." This fracas, resembling a cats' concert, began as "a common practice at weddings in medieval France, [and] was later used only as a derisive or satirical demonstration at unpopular weddings." (The American version of this custom applies here, needless to say.) Worried, guilt-ridden as he was by his (supposedly) unforgivable crime of not informing his friends in Yellow Sky about his sudden, surreptitious marriage to this questionable woman, Potter was also troubled somewhat by the anticipation of a clamorous shivaree waiting for him when he came back with his bride, and the town found out about it shortly after they got off the train.

Soon he would literally have to face the music: the shivaree music. As Crane puts it, "now the train was hurrying him toward a scene of amazement, glee, and reproach." The town "had a kind of brass band, which played painfully, to the delight of the populace." Thinking about it, Potter "laughed without heart." "If the citizens could dream of his prospective arrival with his bride, they would parade the band at the station and escort them, amid cheers and laughing congratulations, to his adobe home." Potter resolved to "use all the devices of speed and plainscraft" to travel from the train depot to where he lived. Once inside "that safe citadel," the marshal might give out some kind "of vocal bulletin," but after that "not go among the citizens until they had time to wear off a little of their enthusiasm." Then, getting off the train, Potter and his bride "slunk rapidly away"; however, as they fled he noticed their luggage being unloaded and the station agent coming toward him on the run, gesticulating. Laughing and groaning at the initial "effect of his marital bliss" on the town, Potter gripped his wife and the pair escaped.

However, two more social issues, of a very different nature, yet connected with the Honeymooners and the Shivaree sequences in such a way as to reveal something generally overlooked by readers, must be mentioned. Crane added to his lively Honeymooners and Shivaree elements a social issue concerned with law, justice, and human survival, as well as a social issue having to do with behavior, self-indulgence, and human safety. Thus, in the former instance, there is a dramatization of the continuing difficulty of attempting to maintain law and order in a frontier town: in Potter's periodic encounters with the rampaging, drunken Scratchy Wilson, who seems to be an actual deadly menace. And in the latter instance, there is the matter of the physical perils of two deadly temptations, drink and careless gunplay. Scratchy Wilson represents an unconvincing model of a potentially good man—when he is sober, according to the bartender of the local saloon, he is the "nicest fellow in town,"—but when he is drunk (by implication) there is no telling what he might do,

what harm he might wreak. These four concerns will come to represent important elements of an obscure but meaningful pattern (to be described below), suggesting one of the most interesting aspects of Crane's story. As that pattern indicates, his prehensile mind (or creative imagination) worked on several levels simultaneously and covertly, revealing the broader reaches of his human spirit.

Another social issue involves geography as well as social factors: the distinction between the East and Easterners, and the West and Westerners. Commentators have made so much of this contrast in the story (one writer even regarded San Antonio as an Eastern city, vis-a-vis Yellow Sky in the West) that attention has been shifted away from events and their significance in a specific locale. While it was only natural for an adventure- and danger-seeker like Crane to leave his Eastern home-base area of New Jersey and New York and go in search of other action zones—the great American West, Mexico, Florida, Cuba, Greece, before taking up temporary residence in England, visiting Ireland, and finally, spending his final days in a German sanitarium—he retained a decided East-West split perspective. (In Crane's 1898 story "The Blue Hotel" there is a minor character named Mr. Blanc, who is usually referred to by the narrator as the Easterner.) As a result of this dichotomous view, Crane was led to make certain curious observations in drawing distinctions between the two entities. The story in fact opens with such a statement, which has greatly impressed some of the commentators.

> The great Pullman was whirling onward with such dignity of motion that a glance from the window seemed simply to prove that the plains of Texas were pouring eastward. Vast flats of green grass, dull-hued spaces of mesquite and cactus, little groups of frame houses, woods of light and tender trees, all were sweeping into the east, sweeping over the horizon, a precipice.

The idea behind this optical illusion (as one commentator called it), in the annals of Crane criticism, is that the East is swallowing up the (wild) West, draining it of its substance, and pretty soon there will not be any West, or Western culture (i.e., civilization), as it has been known, left.

This idea of the predatory East taking in the once pristine and possibly even noble, West is reinforced, in those above-mentioned annals of criticism, by Crane's description of Scratchy Wilson's clothing. His "maroon-colored flannel shirt . . . had been purchased for the purposes of decoration, and made principally by some Jewish women on the East Side of New York. . . ." Scratchy's "boots had red tops with gilded imprints, of the kind beloved in winter by little sledding boys on the hillsides of New England." These references have been interpreted as a slur on those particular Jewish women and "little sledding boys": two groups that seem to have been targeted by an accusatory Crane for invading and corrupting the West. But then, as if to challenge the idea that he is casting aspersions on the influence of the insidious East, while applauding the exemplary West and its ways, Crane makes a curious remark. At the end of the story, when Scratchy, told off in effect by Jack Potter, is so dumbfounded at the news of Potter's marriage that he simply leaves the scene, there is this authorial explanation. "He was not a student of chivalry; it was merely that in the presence of this foreign condition he was a simple child of the earlier plains. He picked up his starboard revolver, and, placing both weapons in their holsters, he went away."

This East-West dichotomy, such as it is and notwithstanding some arguable interpretations by commentators who perhaps focus too narrowly when reading Crane's text, is part of a number of dichotomies or dual perspectives throughout the story, as will be made clear in due course. The view shared by some of the above readers that the old West was succumbing to the East because a few Eastern-made clothing items turned up in Yellow Sky (which is located in the Southwest, rather than the West proper) must be set against the realization that many items of clothing and other types of manufacture in common use—such as the railroad itself—came from the industrial and commercial East, which was by no means independent of, or alien to, the rest of the "land of the free and the home of the brave."

◆ THEMES ◆

Twenty-first century readers of "The Bride Comes to Yellow Sky," like its readers at the turn of the twentieth century, may well have widely differing views on essential themes, depending on how literally or broadly they interpret the actual text. Some may feel that the woman of mystery and her unexpected influence in curbing male passions represents a theme, as would the impact of the industrial and commercial East upon the wild and woolly West, to say nothing of the wondrous transforming power of marriage or the anticipation of a crisis or showdown that must somehow be resolved. Since most of these have already been discussed within different contexts, and in the remaining case—the wondrous transforming power of marriage—the subject requires a more suitable context than the present one, a different set of themes will be taken up. The three themes in this new group, though each is distinct from the other two, will be considered together, in terms of their dynamics and the way they interact among themselves. They are as follows: the individual in relation to society: insider as outsider, outsider as insider; role changes in relation to game playing; and a struggle for power.

Jack Potter when we first encounter him in the story is sorely troubled because he, the marshal of Yellow Sky, Texas, has placed himself outside the borders of what he considers his circle of friends and associates in the town, by withholding personal information from them. Potter's position as law officer of the town does not by itself guarantee him indefinite security of status in terms of a job or social standing. His realization that he may have forfeited his power in one area or both areas helps explain his feelings of disquiet and is also interwoven with his sense of self-reproach, or guilt. In this sense he is clearly the insider turned outsider. Potter's bride from San Antonio occupies an ambiguous position. As the wife of the marshal she could be expected to be on the inside, socially, but since she is an unknown quantity to the townsfolk, if negative information about her were to be made public, her status as an outsider would be reinforced, in effect doubled in significance.

On the train carrying the newlyweds to Yellow Sky, they have a Negro porter who in effect bullies them and subtly uses "the most unconquerable kind of snobbery," and a Negro waiter who attends them in the dining car, viewing them as would "a fatherly pilot" and deferentially patronizing them. Those two men are both examples of outsiders, socially, acting momentarily like insiders—toward insiders so insecure that they are not holding on to their earlier status. Finally, Scratchy Wilson, the resident outlaw who is a familiar fixture in Yellow Sky, is ipso facto both an insider and an outsider, but when the newlywed Potter disarms him with the weapon of his marriage and his disarmament, Scratchy ceases in effect to be an outsider, or even an insider for that matter—at least in terms of Yellow Sky society—simply by leaving the scene. By his withdrawal response to Potter's revelation Scratchy is *hors de combat*; and since he has placed himself out of the ongoing combat with Potter, such as it is,

his role in the little war game, like Potter's role in it, has ended.

Beneath this interplay of status positions in Crane's story (who is in, who is out?), as discussed immediately above, lies something more important than tedious scorekeeping. The main plot of the narrative is about power and power shifts: role changes in relation to power-game playing, and the struggle to be on top of things. The contest for power between the marshal and the town badman is won by the marshal because of, and despite, the marshal's unwillingness to fight (the equivalent of an apparent surrender), which exposes the cowardice and blustering pretense in the challenger: the hollow man, Scratchy. No objector to irony or reversal of intention, in his fictions, Crane enables the reader to consider this story's characters and their various interrelationships from different perspectives: social/occupational status, degree of authority or control or power over others, sustained willingness to play along or go along with an arbitrary code or game scenario, etc.

As already indicated above, Scratchy at the end of the story is described by Crane as being, in effect, on the level of a child. It is interesting that the psychiatrist Dr. Eric Borne, in his classic introduction to transactional psychology, *Games People Play: The Psychology of Human Relationships* (1964), offers a point of view that illuminates Crane's curious remark about Scratchy. Borne, in speaking of essential behavior and feeling patterns in people, begins with what he calls *ego states*. These are "psychological realities," rather than roles. The individual ego state is, practically speaking, "a system of feelings accompanied by a related set of behavior patterns." Every person, in Barnes' view, appears to possess a small number of these ego states, three choices to be exact. Thus at any particular time each human being within a social setting will display "a Parental, Adult or Child ego state, and . . . individuals can shift with varying degrees of readiness from one ego state to another." Not only does Crane refer to Scratchy as a child, but Potter, the adult figure in this transactional psychological situation, opens up to Scratchy something that clearly is for grownups only: marriage, putting away childish things such as guns, and assuming the responsibilities of a family man. As Crane puts it, "it was merely that in the presence of this foreign condition he was a simple child of the earlier plains."

◆ CHARACTERS ◆

So much has already been said about the three principal players in this Western extravaganza with dark overtones that this general overview will suffice here. "The Bride Comes to Yellow Sky" is—among a variety of fascinating matters—about new beginnings. The marshal is entering upon a radically different lifestyle, physically and psychologically (marriage), in a home base where his and his bride's social acceptance may be in question, and that is a real concern. Though he seems to have eliminated the town badman (or disturber of the peace) as a periodic threat, or nuisance, the strenuous duties of a law enforcer in rugged territory remain. Taking all the changes in his life into account, however, he may be considered a new man. As for his taciturn bride, she has taken a much greater leap into the unknown. A whirlwind courtship by a still unfamiliar swain, and a relocation in a frontier town of uncertain aspect, considerably smaller than San Antonio, intimidate her and place her in a position of vulnerability. Though this is a new life for her too, the timid woman retreats from it by withdrawing into the only realm where she may feel secure: her private thoughts. And in the case of Scratchy Wilson, beginning all over again once his relationship with Potter

is over, his end—so far as this story goes— is uncertain and open to wide-ranging speculation after he leaves Potter and begins tracking away over "the heavy sand."

◆ TECHNIQUES ◆

In this lively western yarn told in a third person, limited omniscient-observer style, and enhanced by certain autobiographical hints, Crane also uses a dual perspective to convey special meanings that might well be inaccessible or seriously obscured, if only a single line of thought were being projected for the reader. There are at least two instances of this dual perspective, each different from the other in format and purpose, but equal in that they are both necessary to the integrity of the story.

The first involves a special subtext by means of which Crane appears to make a running commentary on Potter's marriage and his honeymoon-return to Yellow Sky. Read closely the entire story takes on the appearance of an extended string of theatrical entertainment numbers, climaxed by the anticlimactic encounter with Scratchy, what might be called The Showdown That Was Not. This spoof of a gun battle between the marshal and the town badman (drunken or sober) highlights one of the staples of Western legend, fiction, and films. Perhaps more than other shoot-outs (over conflicting land claims or legal violations), it has for a very long time been a source of amusement for young boys wishing to simulate a quick-draw contest between the law and the outlaw, and a pastime for amateur performers and tourists (as well as some locals) at Western resort areas and amusement parks. In the summer of 1998 for example, a number of Wyoming towns offered such fare to anyone present in the late afternoon, at a particular site. In Cody, Wyoming, the advertisement for such an event, held in front of the Irma Hotel—once a sporty dance hall—read as follows: "Free Gun Fighters Shoot-Out, 6 p.m., Every Evening Except Sunday." The event featured a "drunken" badman exchanging bullets with a sheriff, with a gaudily dressed floozy running out of the Irma Hotel to stop the fray.

This terminal entertainment sequence in "The Bride Comes to Yellow Sky" is easy enough to identify as a burlesque element. While the story's opening sequence—The Honeymooners—has been misinterpreted by a number of commentators (who have taken it too literally and too seriously), others have discerned its comic intent. But what lies within the story material between these two sequences, to highlight them as part of an underlying pattern, seems to have made little impression on the story's interpreters. That middle portion actually contains vaudeville and stage-farce material that in its own way furthers the action of the story proper, while also offering amusement to the perceptive reader. But Crane, in shifting the action (while the newlyweds' California express was approaching Yellow Sky) to the town's Weary Gentleman Saloon, sets the stage first. "Across the sandy street were some vivid green grass-plots, so wonderful in appearance, amid the sands that burned near them in a blazing sun, that they caused a doubt in the mind. They exactly resembled the grass mats used to represent lawns on the stage."

Here then, in the saloon, Crane presents a new bit of entertainment which, had it only been completed in his story, would have been suitable for a vaudeville skit on its own merits. It was in effect a one-man show by an impromptu stand-up comic—a drummer (i.e., traveling salesman)—fast-talking and verbose, addressing a silent audience of three Texans and two Mexican sheep-herders. Leaning gracefully on the saloon bar, he told many stories "with the confidence of a bard who has come upon a new field."

The drummer's little entertainment number is cut short by a herald: a young man who rushes in and announces that Scratchy Wilson is on the loose again; in fact he is on a drunken rampage. This frenzied announcement of what will later be the grand finale turns out to be the prelude to another little skit involving some knockabout stage business plus a bit of comic wisecracking. Thus, the two Mexicans immediately exit, through the back door of the saloon. (It has been argued that Crane was a racist, but the complexities of Texas history, its connections with Mexico, and the resulting Anglo-Hispanic relations insofar as they might have affected Crane, make that issue hard to resolve.) The drummer, frightened and confused now by such apparently customary goings-on, seems almost to be the butt of some in-group joke concocted to discomfit him as an outlander. A paraphrase of the dialogue resulting from his nervous, destabilized condition and the response it evokes, is as follows. *There won't be a gunfight, will there?* he asks. *Don't know about that*, he is told by one of the three Texans, *but there'll be some mighty good shootin'*. When the bartender forces this poor rattled newcomer to get down on the floor, behind the bar, he seems even more like the fall guy in this little comic routine about a Western-style welcome to a lorn city-slicker stranger.

Another skit follows: a solo performance by the drunk and disorderly Scratchy Wilson (which is reminiscent of the drunken hall-porter interlude in *Macbeth*). He is wildly out of control, spoiling for a fight. Scratchy is also burdened by Crane with a heavy load of cliches from pulp and pop Westerns and possibly the temperance tracts as well. (His "face flamed in a rage begot of whisky ..." and "the cords of his neck straightened and sank, straightened and sank, as passion moved him.") He torments a dog by shooting around it, tries vainly to get through the closed door of the Weary

Gentleman Saloon, and fusillades "the windows of his most intimate friend." This last statement is one of Crane's loose ends in the story, unless he intended Scratchy (whom the barkeep described as "about the last one of the old gang that used to hang out along the river here") to still have one or two close cronies tucked away somewhere. Then Scratchy remembers his ancient antagonist, the marshal, and he decides to go to his home and "by bombardment" bring him out into the open for a fight.

Spectacle is all, here. Crane's language in this seriocomic approach to the hazards of frontier-town existence evokes the images and the feel of popular theater, including the vaudeville stage. The reader can almost see and hear the trained performers on the stage sets. Scratchy "was playing with this town; it was a toy for him." On his way to Potter's dwelling, Scratchy was "chanting Apache scalp-music." Once at the house, he howlingly challenges it but it "regarded him as might a great stone god," giving no sign. And, during the terminal sequence, at the confrontation of Potter and bride by Scratchy, Crane inserts what is perhaps the strangest of all his show business references. It has to do with the bride's reaction to seeing Scratchy's gun pointing at her husband's chest. "As for the bride, her face had gone as yellow as old cloth. She was a slave to hideous rites, gazing at the apparitional snake." This calls up an image of a stage magician producing a snake from out of nowhere, as a female volunteer from the audience is frightened almost to death at the sight of the stunt, yet cannot tear her eyes away from the spectacle.

The second instance of the dual-perspective technique that Crane uses is something more than simply a distinction between the glory of the married state and the implied lack of it in the unmarried state—a distinction that is made quite clear in this story. Specifically, Crane stresses the grandeur of the Pullman parlor car carrying bride and groom further West, as the outward and visible sign, the objective correlative, of their elevated existence. To their minds, the "surroundings reflected the glory of their marriage that morning in San Antonio; this was the environment of their new estate . . ." What this stage set represented greatly impressed them. The fittings were dazzling; the velvet was figured in sea-green; the brass, silver, and glass all shone; "darkly brilliant as" an oil pool's surface gleamed the wood. At one end of the car a sturdy bronze "held a support for a separated chamber" (men's and women's rest rooms?); and olive and silver frescos decorated the ceiling.

Throughout most of this story of a marriage that is framed in theatrical entertainment routines, Potter will retain this dual perspective. That is, on the one hand, the profoundly impressive, temporary dwelling of their Pullman parlor car (no matter their embarrassment or their being condescended to by everybody) and its allowing them momentary respite from certain troubles waiting for them after they reach their destination. On the other hand, the pervasive effect of those troubles permeates the couple's thoughts during the train ride and after, and become actualized when Potter feels that he may be at the point of death. That is, after Potter admits to the crazed and trigger-happy Scratchy that he is not carrying a gun, he realizes that Scratchy might do almost anything, no matter how drastic. Potter stiffens and steadies himself. At this crucial point in the story, the two facets of Potter's dual perspective come into play at the same time: " . . . somewhere at the back of his mind a vision of the Pullman floated," retaining the velvet and all the shining and gleaming surfaces of the original visual experience— "all the glory of the marriage, the environment of the new estate."

Because "The Bride Comes to Yellow Sky" appears so intensely personal, for all the reasons given or suggested above, it is difficult to cite a fictional work that might easily be tagged as a literary precedent. Michael W. Schaefer comments on this point, in his chapter on the story, in *The Reader's Guide to the Short Stories of Stephen Crane* (1996). Given the rich body of biographical material to be dealt with, Schaefer writes, "few critics have" made the effort to dig up

> literary sources for this story. The most obvious ones might perhaps more properly be termed sub-literary—the host of dime-novel Westerns that were so popular in Crane's day, the conventions of which regarding showdowns between bloodthirsty badmen and noble, straight-shooting marshals he deftly subverts here.

◆ RELATED TITLES ◆

Out of the five other important Western tales in the Crane canon with which "The Bride Comes to Yellow Sky" may be grouped—"Five White Mice," "One Dash-Horses," "A Man and Some Others," "The Blue Hotel," and "Moonlight on the Snow"—"The Bride Comes to Yellow Sky" may be closely linked only with the last named. "Moonlight on the Snow," which was published in 1900, two years after the publication of "The Bride Comes to Yellow Sky," includes in its cast of characters the marshal and the drunken badman of the latter story.

Jack Potter is described as "a famous town marshal of Yellow Sky, but now the sheriff of the county." Scratchy Wilson, described as "once a no less famous desperado," is his assistant. Not long before Tom Larpent, the operator of the largest gambling house in the notoriously evil town of Warpost, is to be hanged for shooting a man, Potter and Wilson arrive in town. Potter explains that Larpent is wanted in Yellow Sky, on a charge of grand larceny, and they have come to take him there. With only the slightest difficulty, and only token resistance, they take Larpent away from the rope and the town of dreadful reputation, Warpost.

For all its entertainment value as a grand program of vaudeville and sideshow sequences, "The Bride Comes to Yellow Sky" is graced with a seriousness and a haunting quality of elusive meaning. In this sense it is quite unlike "Moonlight on the Snow," which may appear to some readers as a story of convenience: another Western concoction written for the eager print media by the very needy and very ill Stephen Crane in his last months. The image of Tom Larpent may linger—with a rope around his neck, he bows, looking "handsome and distinguished and—a devil, a devil as cold as moonlight upon the ice"—but not much else does.

The issue of the passing of the wild, perhaps even wicked, West as it gives way to *a kinder, gentler* land, the civilizing East, which commentators on "The Bride Comes to Yellow Sky" have made so much of (as indicated earlier in this paper), is picked up in this story. Once again the reader is reminded that Crane is a deadpan satirist and mimic, prone to using cliches, stereotypes, and familiarities of plot episodes to spin out his yarns. In "Moonlight on the Snow," a venerable old man and his family also come into town, but in a coach, before Larpent is to be hanged. Crane explains the significance of the appearance of the white-haired gentleman (the new parson, as it turns out), "a beautiful young lady, and two little girls clasping hands" as "the rough West stood in naked immorality before the eyes of the gentle East." When these newcomers discover what will be done to Larpent, they are stunned and incapacitated.

The 1952 movie "Face to Face," directed by John Brahm, and with Bretaigne Windust, James Mason, Michael Pate, Robert Preston, and Marjorie Steele, is a two-part film comprising Joseph Conrad's *The Secret Sharer* and Crane's "The Bride Comes to Yellow Sky." Leonard Maltin in his *1999 Movie & Video Guide* gave it two and a half stars, and wrote (on "The Bride Comes to Yellow Sky" portion): "bland with Preston bringing bride Steele out West."

◆ IDEAS FOR GROUP DISCUSSIONS ◆

Stephen Crane's short story "The Bride Comes to Yellow Sky" has for many years continued to appeal to the imaginations of literary critics and other readers, because of its puzzling allusions and references, what seem to be its emotional excesses, and its colorful and diversified subject matter. Thus there are many interesting topics to discuss, a number of which are given below.

1. On first reading "The Bride Comes to Yellow Sky," did you sense something strange or puzzling about the plot and Crane's handling of it? Explain.

2. Why, in your opinion and based on your reading, has Crane's "Bride" story remained important to literary scholars as well as teachers and students in American literature classes? What are some of the story elements that might fix the tale in the reader's mind, or at least leave a lingering impression?

3. What factors, in your view, might have motivated Crane to make the marshal's bride such an ordinary, drab, low-profile figure, who despite the prominence given her by the story's title and by the requirements of the plot, is depicted as a kind of nonentity, rather than as a person to be reckoned with?

4. Crane's "Bride" story contains a number of nuances of meaning, hints of references to outside material, and other evidence of hidden agenda elements. What do you make of the guilt that Potter feels, which affects his bride also? Aside from the references to guilt, what other odd references have you been struck by in this story? Explain.

5. What was your reaction to the great showdown that never took place, at the end of the story? Did you regard it as a cop-out on Crane's part, as a credible event or nonevent, as a deliberate satire or burlesque on the wild West, or something else? Comment, with a well thought-out reason for your response.

6. How important in your view is the distinction Crane makes between the East and the West? What factors does he cite to point out the cultural differences between these geographic regions?

7. What does Crane, at the very end of the story, mean when he says that Scratchy Wilson "was not a student of chivalry" but that "in the presence of this foreign condition he was a simple child of the earlier plains"?

8. If you were to recommend "The Bride Comes to Yellow Sky" as a good read to a young reader or a mature older reader, on what solid basis would you recommend it? If you were not to recommend this story, why not? Explain.

9. After reading this story and considering these topics for discussion, what questions or issues do you feel should still be taken up, in order to help clarify important but neglected aspects of the story? Try to justify your suggestions.

10. After reflecting on a wide variety of aspects of "The Bride Comes to Yellow Sky," what in your opinion is its main organizing idea or principle? Explain.

Samuel I. Bellman
Professor of English, emeritus
California State Polytechnic University-
Pomona

THE BRIDE PRICE

Novel

1976

Author: Buchi Emecheta

◆━━━━━━━━━━━━━━━━◆━━━━━━━━━━━━━━━━

The very title of Buchi Emecheta's *The Bride Price* speaks to the double consciousness of the Ibo in postcolonial Nigeria. The novel opens in the urban center of Lagos in the home of an Ibo family, the Odias. Aku-nna, the central character, and her brother, Nna-nndo, stare silently at their father, Ezekiel, "properly khakied in his work clothes" but home in the middle of the day. Ezekiel Odia represents the place where tradition and modernity meet. His Christian name indicates a conversion of sorts. Yet, in the beginning of the tale, he has insisted that his wife, Ma Blackie "placate their Oboshi river goddess into giving her some babies." Though Ma Blackie is already the mother of two, only one of her children is a boy, and it is ultimately boys who carry on the family name. The sole benefit of raising a daughter is the bride price she will bring.

The bride price is just one of the traditions that remain intact, even in the metropolitan center of Lagos. The Odia family is one of many who have migrated from rural villages, abandoning the physical labor of farming to work a "white man's" job. Like Ezekiel, many of the male workers also fought in World War II, hoping to benefit economically upon their return. Many who actually made it through the war, including Ezekiel, maintain wounds that will not heal.

The distinctions between rural areas and urban centers are further illumined when Ezekiel's untimely death compels Ma Blackie and the children to return to their homeland in Ibuza. In Ibuza, traditions govern. After a sufficient period of mourning, Ma Blackie becomes the fourth wife of Okonkwo, Ezekiel's eldest brother. Okonkwo aspires to be a village politician, a chief, and taking on his brother's wife augments his wealth. Moreover, it entitles him to Aku-nna's bride price. Women in traditional Ibo society do not decide whom they will marry and Aku-nna, "trapped in the intricate web of Ibuza tradition . . . must either obey or bring shame and destruction on her people."

Aku-nna's family's refusal to accept Chike as her betrothed adds an interesting caste element to the tale. As part of an *oshu* or slave family, Chike is not deemed a fit mate for Aku-nna. Ironically, Chike's family can offer three times the normal bride price. When European missionary work replaced that of slave trading, many slave families, like Chike's were educated and appointed to high positions in education and government. However, in the traditional Ibuza community, families like the Ofulues still endure the stigma of *oshu*.

While *The Bride Price* explores the nature of change, it also reflects the manner in which people hold on to tradition. Perhaps most striking, however, is how both tradition and modernity leave women few choices and little autonomy. Aku-nna's tragic end acts as testimony for women who dare to disregard tradition, but it also offers a gleam of hope, for her daughter represents a new generation, potentially liberated from oppressive cultural mores and traditions.

◆ THEMES ◆

Emecheta's *The Bride Price* explores the conflicts between tradition and modernity, each seeking to dominate both land and woman. The land has served as a site of war and resistance as well as political, economic, and social upheaval. Emecheta contrasts the urban center of Lagos to rural Ibuza. In Lagos, many of the Ibo have succumbed to modern "European" ways or at least a fusion of the modern and traditional: "Lagos was such an unfortunate conglomeration of both [European and African] that you ended up not knowing to which you belong." Emecheta's text also displays a certain sense of nostalgia for the old ways, illuminating how Ibuza has not shifted from tradition. She notes, "There was something else different about the people here; they seemed more relaxed, more naturally beautiful than their relatives in Lagos. The women all had such long necks and carried their heads high, like ostriches, as if they had a special pride in themselves . . . " Ibuza "was on the western side of the River Niger" and Emecheta points out:

> However much the politicians might divide and redivide the map on paper . . . the inhabitants of the town remained Ibos. History—the oral records, handed down by word of mouth from one generation to

the next—said they migrated from Isu. . . . The traditions, taboos, superstitions and sayings of Ibuza were very similar to those still found at Isu.

Still, the traditions and mores—controlled by and most often beneficial to men—create a tragic dilemma for women and girls.

Perhaps one of the most pronounced themes in Emecheta's text is the condition of girls and women and the way in which their desire for autonomy forces them to relinquish tradition. The education of girls is a principal concern of the text. In Ibuza, the Odia family accepts that Nna-nndo continues his education, but they scoff at the idea of Aku-nna, a girl, gaining so much schooling, especially since neither Okonkwo's sons nor his daughter attends school. Residents of Ibuza remember the days when only slaves were sent to the European missionary's schools for spite. Moreover, none of Okonkwo's sons fancy school. Aku-nna's education, however, gives her a degree of power over her new brothers and an overwhelming message of the text is that education will ultimately pave the way for women's freedom. Okonkwo assuages his sons' contempt by pointing out that an educated Aku-nna will demand a higher bride price.

While Ibuza tradition allows Aku-nna to celebrate her development into womanhood with her age mates and provides a collective women's community for her and Ma Blackie, most of the cultural mores and taboos serve to keep women in submission. Women are expected to be chaste brides—and have the bloody sheet to prove it—yet they can be raped and ruined by any lustful man who deems it his right. Men can also take ownership of women they desire by cutting a lock of their hair or kidnaping an unsuspecting bride after she has started her menstrual cycle. Though Aku-nna's education does not prevent her from being a kidnapped bride, her wit overpowers Okoboshi enough for him not to have sex with her on their "wedding night." Having already shamed her family by feigning impurity, she does not have much more to lose by taking her fate into her own hands.

The Bride Price takes on the Shakespearian trope of "star-crossed" lovers through the unconventional romance between Aku-nna and Chike. Chike's family, the Ofulues, not only represent historical caste divisions in Nigeria but also "the lasting effects of such old-fashioned ideas about slavery." Though Chike is educated and his family can provide the necessary bride price, outdated ideas about caste eclipse Okonkwo's desire for a hefty bride price. But in line with most tales of forbidden love, Chike and Aku-nna defy tradition and escape Ibuza to be together.

Yet tradition and taboo continue to haunt the couple. Okonkwo uses traditional magic to taunt Aku-nna's spirit. Notwithstanding Okonkwo's deliberate taunting, Aku-nna's awareness of taboos surrounding the bride price could have attributed to her death. Whether by magic, madness, or anemia, Aku-nna's fate "substantiated the traditional superstition they had unknowingly set out to eradicate." At the same time, her girl child represents the potential for a new generation of females who will not be slaves to tradition.

◆ CHARACTERS ◆

The name Aku-nna literally means "father's wealth." It is Aku-nna who personifies the central theme of the novel, the tradition of the bride price. Though she is in many ways a "daddy's girl," her real wealth is the bride price she will demand and that her father will collect. Even upon her father's death, her uncle-turned-father Okonkwo sets his sight on her bride price. Aku-nna as wealth signifies girls as possessions, first of their fathers, then of their husbands. Chike makes his intentions known when he calls Aku-nna "Akum," meaning "my wealth." But as the heroine of the novel, Aku-nna also heralds new possibilities for girls and women. Her humility and deference to authority demonstrates her respect for tradition and elders. Still she recognizes early on that she has a mind and feelings of her own and she starts to resent the inability to make her own decisions. Aku-nna also hates her mother's passive acceptance of a woman's fate and wishes her mother were a source of support for her.

Ma Blackie, a giant woman with glossy black skin, enters the tale with a "family problem"—she is slow in getting pregnant again. Ma Blackie became a bride at a young age, demanding both a hefty bride price and an Anglican wedding to boot. The least she can do is grant Ezekiel another son, "Aku-nna [knows] she [is] too insignificant to be regarded as a blessing to this unfortunate marriage. Not only [is] she a girl but she [is] much too thin for the approval of her parents, who would rather have a strong and plump little girl for a daughter." Perhaps Ma Blackie's reluctance to bond with a child as fragile as Aku-nna—a potential *ogbanje*, "living dead"—is that Aku-nna, according to tradition, can die at any time. Ezekiel Odia feels sorry for his thin, frail daughter who resembles him more than his wife. "Aku-nna [knows] that there [is] a kind of bond between her and her father which [does] not exist between her and her mother."

Ezekiel Odia, as evidenced by his name, is a "typical product" of cultural syncretism. He belongs to the Christian church, but also relies on folk medicine and respects the taboos and superstitions of his native tradition. Ironically, the cause of his death is an injury acquired from his participation in a war that he fought on behalf of his colonizers. It seems appropriate that "he was buried in the same way that he had lived: in a conflict of two cultures."

It is up to Nna-nndo to decide which group of mourners will stand by his father's dead body. Like his father, Nna-nndo is impressed with the celestial images of angels and heaven. Though Nna-nndo is only eleven when his father dies, he is promoted to manhood and expected to take on a leadership role in his family. Nna-nndo is a flat character in the text whose purpose is to serve as a foil for Aku-nna. It is Nna-nndo who is the most desirable offspring, whose school fees are secure, who will carry on the family name, and ultimately who will assume leadership in the Odia family. The characterizations of Nna-nndo and Aku-nna symbolize the disparity in the ways in which boys and girls are treated in Ibo culture. Aku-nna's cousin, Ogugua, likewise serves as somewhat of an oppositional character to Aku-nna. Through Ogugua's character, Emecheta contrasts the upbringing of a rural Ibo girl to that of an urban one.

Ogugua and Aku-nna are age mates, born in the same week, but the geographical situation of their births steers their lives in dissimilar directions. Ogugua is more connected with Ibuza customs and she has already become a "woman," having begun her menstrual cycle. Ogugua knows what is expected of her as an Ibuza girl. Not formally educated, her world does not present many options for her. Aku-nna's exposure to traditional Ibo culture is limited to what she has gleaned from her family's household. She has not been exposed to women who farm the land, carry heavy loads atop their heads, and bathe naked in the river. Moreover, she has tasted knowledge. She appreciates the significance of education for girls and concedes that female autonomy and freedom may require defiance of tradition and even death. Still she tries to circumvent her duties and remain respectful to her people until she if left with no other option but rebellion.

Though Aku-nna does exhibit a quiet strength, her rebellious spirit is obvious. Yet Chike Ofulue is attracted by her vulnerability. He watches his lonely pupil, the only girl in her class, and yearns to reach out to her and fulfill some unspoken need she has. Chike falls in love with her, though he knows that as a "son of slaves," his pursuit of her will spark controversy. But Chike is a rebel in his own right. In a culture that expects their educated men to become doctors and lawyers, Chike commits himself to sociology and the improvement of his people. He also does not allow the *oshu* stigma to crush his confidence. A ladies man, Chike has had his share of affairs with local girls in the village and even the younger wives of chiefs. But he only has the best of intentions for Aku-nna—he wants to make her his wife. Although Chike's father, the elder Ofulue, warns his son against pursuing Aku-nna, his son's love for the girl eventually garners Ofulue's support. Ofulue even funds Chike and Aku-nna's elopement and—though in vain—he offers twice the required bride price to Okonkwo.

Okonkwo does not resemble the protagonist in Chinua Achebe's *Things Fall Apart* in name only, though the nomenclature does suggest "stubborn male pride." His thirst for power evidences itself in his desire for a higher title and more wealth. The addition of his brother's wife strengthens his standing in the community and since his own daughter, Ogugua, and Aku-nna will be courted at the same time, he has the potential to amass a great deal of wealth from their bride prices. Okonkwo's plan is foiled when Okoboshi kidnaps Aku-nna and his family pays only the minimum bride price for her. But the kidnapping does not infuriate Okonkwo half as much as Aku-nna's ultimate escape into the arms of a "slave." Even more emasculating for the proud Okonkwo, the Ofulues have English law on their side and there is nothing Okonkwo or Ibuza can do to repair the rupture of tradition triggered by Aku-nna and Chike. Publicly humiliated and his title averted, Okonkwo enacts vengeance on Ma Blackie and Aku-nna. A more superstitious reader may attribute Aku-nna's death to Okonkwo's supernatural assault on her spirit.

◆ TECHNIQUES ◆

Emecheta's principal technique in *The Bride Price* arises from African oral historiography and folk storytelling traditions. Her written account of history, tradition, and culture also reflects a shift from an oral "literature" to a written one—from tradition to modernity. While the mode of transmission has changed, the essence of the storytelling genre remains intact. As if to signify the tale's inherent orality, toward the end of *The Bride Price*, Emecheta tells how Aku-nna's story lived on after her death "to reinforce the old taboos of the land." It is storytelling and the storytellers who are the carriers of culture and traditions that, as Emecheta notes, continue in spite of modernization "until the present day." Yet the text also serves as a critique of traditions that outlive the rationale behind them, especially those mores that keep women subjugated.

While steeped in African tradition, Emecheta's text is a feminist narrative. *The Bride Price* and her other novels are concerned with the plight of African women caught in the midst of the conflict between tradition and modernity, slaves to men and/or motherhood, and seeking liberation through education. The end of *The Bride Price* may seem to assert that there is no compromise between freedom and tradition and that the price women pay for autonomy is isolation or death. But the birth of Aku-nna and Chike's little girl, Joy, implies that change may occur, but at a gradual pace, perhaps only one daughter at a time.

◆ LITERARY PRECEDENTS ◆

The Bride Price is an impressive addition to West African writers who compose in English. The mid-1900s witnessed a surge of West African writing dominated by males. Perhaps the most famous work produced during that time is Chinua Achebe's *Things Fall Apart*, a critically acclaimed first novel that reclaimed the voice of the African subject from colonialist literature. Like Emecheta, Chinua Achebe's works focus on the Ibo (Igbo) of Nigeria. Though he authenticates the stories of his homeland by writing from within, he also presents a masculinist perspective of Ibo culture.

The paucity of African women writers in the early to mid-twentieth century may be attributed to illiteracy and other restrictions on women's education that proliferated in Africa during that time. One of the forerunners of African women's writing and an additional predecessor to Buchi Emecheta is another Nigerian writer, Flora Nwapa, whose writing career spanned twenty years. Like Achebe, Nwapa's texts explore discord and change in Nigerian society. Yet Nwapa allows readers to view Nigeria through the eyes of women. It is African women writers who most often repudiate the paradisiacal stereotypes and nostalgia for the "old ways" that are thematic in African male novels. In the tradition of Flora Nwapa, Ama Ata Aidoo, Mariama Ba, and other West African women writers, Buchi Emecheta writes about the predicament of African women. In addition to Chinua Achebe's *Things Fall Apart* (1959) and Flora Nwapa's *Efuru* (1966), *The Bride Price* may share a bookshelf with: Ama Ata Aidoo's *Our Sister Killjoy* (1977), Mariama Ba's *So Long A Letter* (1981), and Bessie Head's *A Question of Power* (1973).

Buchi Emecheta has produced over ten titles to date, including an autobiography and autobiographical fiction that details her migration from rural Nigeria to London and the challenges the western world presents for a West African woman, struggling to survive in the urban ghetto. Though all of her works have to do with the multifaceted oppression of women, *The Bride Price* is most closely related to *The Slave Girl* (1977) and *The Joys of Motherhood* (1979). All three novels are set in Nigeria and based around a female protagonist caught somewhere between tradition and modernity. The heroine of *The Slave Girl,* Ogbanje, the nominal form of which means "living dead," witnesses the sacrifice of a slave girl at a chief wife's burial. A similar burial scene is repeated in *The Joys of Motherhood* in which Nnu Ego's barrenness is attributed to the malice of her *chi,* who, when she lived, had been the victim of a sacrificial burial. Again in Aku-nna, we witness the metaphor of the *ogbanje* for early in the text, Ma Blackie refers to her thin child as such. Midway through the narrative, Nbeke, Ma Blackie's co-wife, attributes Aku-nna's delayed onset of menses, her mark of womanhood, to the fact that she is an *ogbanje.* Tying these heroines together are an oppressive, patriarchal culture and the desire these women possess for change and autonomy. Tragically, the three aforementioned protagonists— whether they defy or succumb to tradition— all meet cataclysmic ends.

♦ IDEAS FOR GROUP DISCUSSIONS ♦

Changing social values are a universal concern, but for the postcolonial subject, those changes are rife with contention, trauma, and the challenges of restructuring fractured national and ethnic identities. The unstable marriage between tradition and modernity is a primary concern of postcolonial discourse as indicated by Emecheta's text. At the crossroads of this conflict stands the fate of women, forced to choose between self and tradition. *The Bride Price* takes on the challenge of grappling with these dilemmas and seems to insinuate that though tradition need not be supplanted by modernity, it does need to evolve to accommodate contemporary needs.

1. *The Bride Price* bears an obvious resemblance to Shakespeare's *Romeo and Juliet.* What conclusions may be drawn from Emecheta's use of such a familiar literary trope? What can be said about her borrowing a trope from Western literature and applying it to an African context? Might she be speaking to the universality of discrimination?

2. The color red occurs in the novel twice as a portent of death, once in the beginning and then again at the end. In the beginning of the text, when Ezekiel Odia leaves his home, never to return again, his children fix their eyes on the red color of the road, "The dust from the lorry obscured him completely, and when at last it cleared it seemed to have eaten him up, just as that prophet Elijah in the Bible was eaten up in his chariot of fire." Toward the end of the text, when the ambulance arrives for Aku-nna, the paramedics cover her with "horrid red blankets." Does the use of this symbol somehow connect Aku-nna and her father and if so, how? Why might Emecheta have compared Ezekiel with Elijah? What is significant about the novel both beginning and ending with death?

3. How is the nature of communalism or the "group mind" explored in the novel? How does a collective identity strengthen the community and maintain tradition? What challenges does it pose for in-

dividuality, particularly in the case of women?

4. "It is so even today in Nigeria: when you have lost your father, you have lost your parents. Your mother is only a woman, and women are supposed to be boneless. A fatherless family is a family without a head, a family without shelter, a family without parents, in fact a non-existing family. Such traditions do not change very much." In accordance with this statement, how are the roles of motherhood and fatherhood defined? What values are placed on these roles? Since motherhood does not exalt women very much, why does childlessness demean them to such a great degree?

5. Emecheta describes colonial Africa as a "mixture of the traditional and the European" with more emphasis "placed on the European aspect." What does her description suggest about the conflict between tradition and modernity, specifically the presumed superiority of European culture? How might this cultural clash impact African identity? How does Christianity factor into the overall imposition of European culture on African people, according to the novel?

6. Emecheta presents readers with a detailed illustration of Ezekiel Odia's funeral. How does her depiction reflect the importance of funeral rites in Ibo culture? What might such elaborate funeral rites communicate about the Ibo's perception of death?

7. In Ibuza, a collective women's community is highlighted as Aku-nna begins her rites of passage with her age mates and Ma Blackie settles in with her co-wives and other women in the village. Yet even with a women's support system in place, women do not join forces to change their condition. On the contrary, they concede, "This is the fate of us women. There is nothing we can do about it. We just have to learn to accept it." Does Emecheta critique women's fatalistic acceptance of their status and if so, in what ways?

8. *The Bride Price* has been characterized as a feminist text. What qualities inherent in the novel suggest such a distinction?

9. Some critics have suggested that a woman-centered African text like Emecheta's *The Bride Price* further impedes any constructive dialogue between women and men by portraying African men in a negative light. How might one respond to such a critique?

10. One of the most crucial themes of *The Bride Price* is the value of education for girls and women. In what ways does education liberate the oppressed?

Jennifer Williams
University of Texas at Austin

CRADLE AND ALL

Novel

2000

Author: James Patterson

◆

◆ SOCIAL CONCERNS ◆

The ultimate nightmare for mankind is a world in which Satan's legions, the forces of evil, are unleashed to wreak havoc on mankind. The great and ultimate battle between good and evil, the Christ and the anti-Christ, the survival of the human race, and the nightmares envisioned by Patterson if evil triumphs are the concerns of this novel.

Cradle and All is a retelling of a long out-of-print novel, *Virgin,* written by Patterson and published in 1980. Many of the characters and scenes are retold and expanded. A novel for the new millennium, the book emphasizes the continuing battle between good and evil.

The good is represented by the reappearance on earth of Christ, opposing the appearance of the anti-Christ. To focus on the seriousness of this battle, Patterson introduces Father Nicholas Rosetti, a priest who truly believes in God as man's savior and the Catholic Church as the protector of good. Rosetti is immediately attacked by a voice and a presence representing the evil force, an attack both mental and physical. Rosetti is able to maintain his equilibrium because of his strong faith, seeming in the end to triumph over the evil seeking to take over the world.

Anne Fitzgerald is hired by the Archdiocese of Boston to investigate the outbreak of polio in Boston and Los Angeles and the appearance in Boston of a young woman, eight months pregnant, who claims to be a virgin. The horrors of the polio epidemic raging in Los Angeles and Boston convince Anne that an evil force has been unleashed in the world. Children are suffering and dying. Doctors are trying to ease the suffering but have no drugs or vaccines that work. Health officials have no idea how the disease is spreading or where it is coming from. The horror in the hospital in Los Angeles is enough to convince Anne that she must try to solve this mystery.

The three female protagonists, two pregnant teenagers (Kathleen and Colleen) and Anne Fitzgerald, come from different backgrounds but have the Roman Catholic Church and their virginity in common. All consider themselves "good girls," a phrase often repeated by the teenagers. Both teenage girls need protection. Anne is a protector who in the end needs protection herself. Both young girls are ostracized within their communities. Anne, a former nun, has rejected her vows and the Dominican Order. She also experiences rejection by the community because of this. Although the Beavier family tries not to judge Kathleen, they do not believe in her either. The attempt on Kathleen's life by the housekeeper who was her childhood confidante and protector is evidence of evil at work. Children born out of wedlock are tolerated but not truly accepted by many people.

Colleen experiences ostracism by her community. She has a haven within her family because her father is dead and her mother's mind has failed, leaving her bedridden and unaware of events. Colleen, only fourteen years old, is enrolled in the Holy Trinity School for Girls, a convent school, but is being home schooled during the fall semester, since the other students and their parents are not being understanding about the situation. Whenever possible, Colleen remains at home to avoid the people of the community, whose cruelty to her is both physical and mental. Colleen tries to maintain her self-confidence by telling herself that she is a "good girl." She is profoundly relieved when her pregnancy is to be investigated by a priest from Rome, thinking that at last someone believes her. Sister Katherine Dominica is more supportive of Colleen after the visit from Father Rosetti, as she naturally respects a visitor, a priest, sent by Rome.

◆ THEMES ◆

The encompassing theme is the triumph of good over evil. The relationship of man to God and Satan is explored through secular and nonsecular characters being tempted, rewarded, and punished for actions taken. The protagonists do not have the opportunity to make the choices that change their lives. Other people who do not have their best interests at heart make their choices. The teenage girls are denied the chance to grow up and mature before adult responsibilities are pressed upon them, showing an unpleasant side of the coming-of-age process. The place of God and Satan in the beliefs of society and the part these beliefs play in decisions made for the good of all human kind is also a theme.

Nicholas Rosetti represents the good in all men and the battle between good and evil that is often fought on a personal level by all men and women. Because Rosetti truly believes in God, Pope Pius chooses to entrust him with the secret prediction made by the Blessed Lady of Fatima in her appearance in Portugal in the early 1900s. The pope hopes that Rosetti's belief in God will help him to identify the virgin who is about to give birth to the divine child and do whatever is necessary to rid the world of the satanic child about to be born to the other virgin. Rosetti has the ultimate responsibility of saving the world. The forces of evil are sure they will win, so sure they are beginning to inflict plagues and famine upon the citizens of earth.

The invisible enemy, working in the mind of Rosetti, represents the evil seeking to take over the world. Outward manifestations of the evil are the plagues and famines. The mysterious death of the pope signals the growing confidence of this force. Attempts on the lives of the teenage virgins add to a sense of futility. All the characters are sinking into depression and despair. The deaths of family members and others close to the young women add to the sense of growing danger. Hope is dimming. The battle between good and evil takes place on many levels, physical and mental, in all the characters. The protagonists must battle themselves as well as the difficulties they encounter.

Man's belief in God must be strong enough to overcome the forces of Satan. Each character finds his belief in God and the strength to play his or her part in the battle against evil. Anne must fire her gun for the first time, killing to save Kathleen. Rosetti must maintain his faith in the face of strong temptations of the flesh, keeping his vow of celibacy. Justin must assist Rosetti with the birth of Colleen's baby and then demand proof before accepting Rosetti's decision about the child. Later Justin is called upon to defend Anne.

◆ CHARACTERS ◆

The teenage female protagonists are young women from different walks of life, different countries, different goals, different ambitions. Each becomes pregnant while still a virgin. A third female character, whose importance grows as the story progresses, is Anne Fitzgerald, once a nun and now a private investigator. Because of her previous intimate connection with the church, she is asked to investigate the appearance of the two young virgins about to give birth. In light of the secret prophecy given the pope by the Lady of Fatima, these girls seem worth investigating. The prophecy says that a girl, a virgin, will bear a divine child; now there are two girls who appear to be virgins, soon to give birth.

Anne Fitzgerald, in whose voice most of the story is told, is a young woman in her early thirties, once a nun and now a private investigator. Anne thinks she has lost her religious faith. She still believes in God but questions the tenets set forth by the Catholic Church. Hired to interview Kathleen Beavier, the young woman in Newport, Massachusetts, who is near term with a pregnancy that appears to be virginal, Anne wonders why she is chosen for this job. When asked by Cardinal Rooney if she believes in "God the Father, Jesus, the Blessed Mother," she replies, "Yes. In my way." Anne's being licensed to carry a gun seems as important to the Cardinal as her belief in God, and she is hired to go to Newport to interview Kathleen. First, though, the Cardinal sends her to Los Angeles where she confronts the rising polio epidemic that is sweeping the United States. Returning to the East Coast, she asks herself why she is the one to be with Kathleen. Her own virginal condition and her reintroduction to the priest with whom she is in love add to her confusion.

Father Nicholas Rosetti is a priest sent by the pope to ascertain the validity of the claim to virginity of a fourteen-year-old, eight-month pregnant, Irish girl. The pope confides the prophecy made by the Lady of Fatima, that two virgins would give birth, one to a divine child and one to Satan. Rosetti must discover which virgin, the American or the Irish girl, is the mother of the divine child. As he leaves the Vatican, he is attacked mentally by an evil presence, threatening to end his life. The mental attacker reveals that it knows the secret of the holy child and predicts Nicholas's early death. He is ill for five days, and wonders then if he is truly well and sane. His will and belief in God keep him focused on his task. He battles this evil while attempting to discover the truth about the virgin births.

Kathleen Beavier is a sixteen-year-old American girl, who is pregnant and a virgin. She is one of the two girls being investigated to determine whether her pregnancy is the one prophesied by the Lady of Fatima. Her parents are wealthy enough to own a beach home in Newport, called Sun Cottage. She tries to have an abortion and when that fails, tries to commit suicide. She seems to sense many things but is unable to remember the circumstances under which she became pregnant. Her virginity is confirmed by several doctors, including one who is Jewish. He would not believe in a virgin birth or in Jesus, so his testimony is unimpeachable. She is living in a dream world, unable to distinguish reality from imagination and unable to provide details of a night in January when she went out with a young man from her school. When he dies in a car accident, Kathleen is left to wonder why he had to die.

Colleen Deirdre Galaher, the second pregnant virgin, is a fourteen-year-old Irish girl. Father Rosetti is tempted to break his vows of chastity when he sees her, one of the temptations sent to him by the presence he feels in his mind. Colleen tries to be the "good girl" she knows her mother would want her to be, enduring the taunts of the villagers and staying home to take care of her bedridden mother. Sister Katherine Dominica serves as Colleen's advisor and helper although she does not truly believe Colleen's story.

Justin O'Carroll, a priest, is sent by Cardinal Rooney to stay in the Beavier house. He was a caseworker for the Catholic Charities in South Boston, when Anne had first become acquainted with him. They were attracted to each other but respected their vows as a priest and a nun. He has remained in the priesthood although he is deeply in love with Anne. He is also a hero, trying to save Anne, Colleen's child, Father Rosetti, and himself. The pope sends him to Newport to protect both Anne and Kathleen, and then on to Ireland. He witnesses events in Ireland that give him direction, explaining to him what he must do with the rest of his life.

Pope Pius and Cardinal John Rooney serve as mentors to Anne and Justin. Their wise counsel and support allows Anne to sustain her faith and Justin to become her support.

◆ TECHNIQUES ◆

Patterson hints at the outcome of the story through his characters' names. Anne, the true protagonist, whose name means "grace" in Hebrew, gains strength throughout the story. She begins by doubting herself, her beliefs, her purpose, but finds her real place near the end of the story. The name Kathleen means "pure" or "virginal" in Celtic or Gaelic. Colleen is Gaelic for

"girl," not usually used as an Irish given name. Deidre, Colleen's middle name, means "sorrow," "sorrowful," or "wanderer." Justin is derived from "justice."

In an interview with Andre Bernard and Jeff Zaleski for *Publishers Weekly*, Patterson says that he has become aware that most people have short attention spans. "I just kept writing shorter, then cutting some chapters down, and making two chapters out of one," he says. "In my gut, it felt like this is the way it should be, for my books anyway." Many of the chapters in *Cradle and All* are only two or three pages. This adds to the feeling of movement, almost creating a window in time as the reader looks in on the characters.

Phrases usually associated with teenagers, such as "what's up with you?," "what a scene," "nearly tragic kicker," "it's pretty awesome," "a head case," and "bombed out of his mind," add to the youthful feeling of the story.

◆ LITERARY PRECEDENTS ◆

In 1980 Patterson published *Virgin* with a similar story line, many of the same scenes, and some of the same characters. *Cradle and All* is "an entirely reimagined version," reports Daisy Maryles in *Publishers Weekly*. The same article reports that Patterson has written seventeen novels that have boosted him to "one of the top six best-selling novelists in the U.S."

Patterson cites Stephen King as an author he likes to read. Charles L. Grant in *Twilight Zone* quotes King: "Almost all horror stories mirror specific areas of free-forming anxieties." Patterson says his stories are meant to reflect our deepest fears. King compares the violence in fairy stories, such as *Hansel and Gretel*, in which the witch states she is going to eat the children, implying cannibalism, with events in his stories. He concludes that his books have a milder form of violence and horror than many fairy tales. *The Three Billy-goats Gruff* is the inspiration for King's book entitled *It*. Lines from nursery rhymes provide titles for a number of Patterson's books.

Some of the psychological ploys used in *Cradle and All* are similar to those used by Dean Koontz in his thrillers. Rape and murder threaten Hilary Thomas, female protagonist in *Whispers,* by the villain in spirit form. The supernatural plays a large role in the events in this book, as it does in *Cradle and All*. Both use various forms of sadism practiced on women to build the climate of terror that drives the stories. In an interview with Sean Mitchell for the *Los Angeles Time Magazine,* Koontz says, "I think we're here for a purpose. . . . That's why I could never write cynical books or the classic hard-boiled book where it's all despair and we all die and it's meaningless." The ending for *Cradle and All* shows good and evil still at odds in the world, leaving humanity with the choice between the two.

◆ RELATED TITLES ◆

Patterson's first novel, *The Thomas Berryman Number* (1976), grew out of his reading William Peter Blatty's *The Exorcist* and Frederick Forsyth's *The Day of the Jackal*. He knew immediately that he wanted to write suspenseful thrillers, reported Bernard and Zaleski in their *Publishers Weekly* article. He did not, however, feel he could make a living writing, so he took a job as a junior copywriter at J. Walter Thompson, where he has risen to chairman of the North American division. About thirty publishers rejected *The Thomas Berryman Number* before it was bought by Ned Bradford for Little, Brown. The book was awarded the Edgar Award from the Mystery Writers of America for Best First Novel in 1977. Patterson

has gone on to write over seventeen novels, most in the suspense-thriller genre.

The "Alex Cross" series, including *Along Came a Spider* (1993), *Kiss the Girls* (1995), *Jack and Jill* (1996), *Cat and Mouse* (1997), and *Pop! Goes the Weasel* (1999), are Patterson's best known works. The protagonist, a black private detective who lives in Washington, D.C., is a hero in Patterson's eyes because he is trying "to bring up his kids in a good way, who tries to continue to live in his neighborhood and who has enormous problems with evil in the world." Bernard and Zaleski tell us that "it's most unusual for a white man to choose a black man as his lead character." Patterson believes many of his fans are women because his fiction is not "macho in tone," which is because one of his recurring nightmares is about "domineering men." Characters in this series include Cross's two children and his grandmother who was modeled on a cook in his grandparents' restaurant. In an interview with Time Warner Electronic Publishing, Patterson says of Cross:

> He's extremely human and very sensitive. He is raising these two kids by himself; he has this terrific relationship with his grandmother. He chooses to live in a tough part of town, even though he doesn't have to. He's raised himself up and has gotten a very good education. He's also larger than life in being this swashbuckling heroic king of guy, and he's genuinely a good person, too.

Other novels include *The Season of the Machete* (1977), *Virgin* (1980), *The Midnight Club* (1989), *See How They Run* (1997), *When the Wind Blows* (1998), and *Black Friday* (2000).

◆ ADAPTATIONS ◆

Cradle and All is published as an audio book by Time Warner AudioBooks, read by Ally Sheedy and Len Cariou.

Much of the story of *Cradle and All* depends on the mythology of the Roman Catholic Church. Church fathers are charged with explaining doctrine and dogma to the church members. Traditionally, the pope is considered by Roman Catholics to be the voice of the Trinity, the authority from God on Earth.

1. During the Middle Ages the Roman Catholic Church was the only Christian church in existence. Discuss the role religion played in the lives of Christians in the Middle Ages.

2. There are several places in the world that are considered shrines because the people believe the Virgin appeared there. Do research on some of these to find out what message, if any, is supposed to have been delivered there.

3. How did the physical appearance of each of the teenagers contribute to the confusion about which one was going to give birth to a holy child?

4. Why did Patterson use an Irish girl and an American girl as his virgins?

5. Describe characteristics of this book that you think would appeal to women readers? To men?

6. In an interview with Andre Bernard and Jeff Zaleski for *Publishers Weekly,* Patterson credits his awareness of how the audience responds to his books with some of the techniques he uses, particularly the technique of short chapters. He says he feel this technique helps make his books move faster, appealing to short attention spans. Discuss your feelings about the success of this technique.

7. Compare the major beliefs of three of the world's religions. What do they have in common? Where are their major differences?

8. Suggest ways the story could be strengthened or weakened using points of view not in the story, such as a Protestant minister, a Buddhist monk, or a Hindu priest.

9. Do you think the mythology of the Roman Catholic Church has outlived its usefulness?

10. Why was Justin's connection to Ireland important?

Ann Barton Sciba
Wharton High School Library

EASY PREY

Novel

2000

Author: John Sandford

◆

◆ SOCIAL CONCERNS ◆

Sex ripples throughout this novel of murder, usually in an unhealthy guise. In the first major scene, on the set of a fashion shoot, nipples are artfully manipulated while there is excitement over photographing a large male member. This overt sexual posing reeks of decadence, and even the lead model's mother, who sold out her morals for her daughter's fame long ago, cannot ignore how much the director is playing up the sex angle. The mother is concerned about the appearance of pornography because porno can kill a model's career—such is the moral concern of an entertainment media mother. Of course it is porno; the text makes that clear.

The next round of sex in the novel continues among the shallow, joy-chasing, drug-addict characters of the fashion shoot, focusing on female-on-female sex. Sandford uses sex consistently to titillate in this book. Among other things, Sandford inserts a teasing sex game with throwaway characters, and likes to keep the suggestive allusions and jokes coming. Unfortunately, since the sex never takes place between characters in any meaningful, healthy relationships, and since the sexual references include so many negative connotations, including a creepy, sex-obsessed father and siblings who have practiced incest, sex comes across as a social illness.

The protagonist of the novel, Lucas Davenport, seems fully enveloped in the immature side of sex. Although he has enough maturity to give good marriage advice, his own romantic life shows him to be as shallow as the joy-chasing drug addicts he condemns. During this novel, Davenport repeatedly has meaningless sex with an exotic woman despite the fact that the love of his life is simultaneously sending him signals she is ready to try out a new relationship. Simultaneously, Davenport is flirting with an old college girlfriend even though she is now married, and having coitus with her would obviously be a moral and emotional nightmare. He can only obsess on how great she used to be in bed. He is the hero of the novel, yet he does little to redeem sex's lowly status. On one hand, Davenport's sexual relationships are shown as fun flings, but on the other hand, in the larger context of his life, pursuing those relationships is not the most intelligent, fulfilling choice he could make.

Although the author may not have intended it, his novel develops the message that sex is dangerous. Sending visual images over the airwaves can hook people into fantasies and lead them to violent acts. Pursuing pleasure alone robs people of meaningful relationships.

While John Sandford's sexual message can be slightly ambiguous, his message on drugs is as clear as can be. The book opens with the drugged, confused perspective of the out-of-control, soon-to-be killer. The main focus of the beginning of the novel, the character Alie'e, immediately comes across as less than a worthwhile person because of her casual drug use. The people at the party also use drugs and then are painted as cowardly for lying about it. The main criminals in this book are all connected to drugs; Sandford clearly shows how drugs give rise to a criminal culture. The novel's message on drugs appears as simple as the hero Davenport's; Davenport has no tolerance for drugs. Despite his attraction to Jael, the beautiful former model, Davenport voices his disapproval of her drug use right away then alternately moralizes and offers advice about drugs. The entire chain of violence in the novel can be traced back to drug trade. While other things such as speeding and sex are painted as permissible, joyous pursuits, the message rings loudly that drugs are nothing but negative.

Sandford fills *Easy Prey* with all the major social concerns of modern-day America. Besides the sex and drugs, there is violence. By tradition, in any detective novel, the detective needs to catch the murderer for the sake of society. However, here that need to restore order is diminished by the low worth of the victims. The first victim is a drug dealer killed accidentally by her backer, so society appears to have little at stake. The second victim, Alie'e Maison, is an innocent bystander, but, despite her fame, she has been established as a vapid drug-addict who contributes little to society, so again society has little reason to avenge her death by capturing her killer. As with promiscuous sex, Sandford portrays violence as a modern illness of America, but again, unlike the situation with drugs, violence is shown as an issue without clear sides. For instance, the brother of Alie'e, Tom Olson, lives like a saint helping others, yet he brims with a passion that make other characters think he is dangerous. Lucas Davenport has been a violent person in the previous books in the "Prey" series, and while that behavior begins to change in this novel, his tendency toward violence is repeatedly referred to in *Easy Prey*. The first murderer, Spooner, on the other hand, kills by accident. His violence is passionless, yet he is obviously a danger as the number of people he kills to cover his original crime rises. The obsessed fan of Alie'e is the traditional psychotic, as he kills a string of people for strong emotional reasons.

Still, the message about violence is complicated. In one significant case, violence actually seems a more appropriate response than the "civilized" nonviolent resolution. After a peaceful settlement to a hostage situation wherein the captor, the obsessed fan Martin Scott, becomes a media darling, the former hostages reverse their previous acceptance of the situation and retaliate by beating their erstwhile captor. In this case, the violence is presented as a positive reaction in its emotional honesty.

In addition, as signaled from the beginning with the model shoot to the ending with Martin Scott's public capture, the entertainment and news media are another social concern in this novel. It is clear that people who "live with cameras" have no grasp of right or wrong or what is important in life. They will do anything to capture society's attention. John Sandford, a pseudonym of the award-winning journalist John Camp, does a strong job of portraying both the alarming behavior of the media and the unhealthy appetite of the American public with scenes such as the one where Jael talks about how she "made a lot of money with her scars" or the scene where the journalists high-five each other upon learning that they have a picture of the dress the murdered model was wearing. The preacher Tom Olson sums up the novel's warning about the media: "It's a death culture, and it's here, right now. It comes out of TV, it comes out of magazines, it comes out of the Internet, it comes out of video games." Like the media it criticizes, *Easy Prey* manages to capitalize on sex, drugs, and violence, even while explicitly condemning them.

◆ THEMES ◆

Most of the themes of *Easy Prey* are submerged in the large social concerns. For example, concerns regarding violence and the influence of the media find expression in the contrast between civilization and nature. When comparing the big city and its suburbs to small cities out in the country, Tom Olson says, "We see it in Fargo, but you can still fight it there. Here . . . this place is gone. Too late for this place. Too late. You'll see." Smaller, rural towns, closer to nature, are more protected from the dangers present in the big cities.

Sandford reinforces the contrast between nature and culture with his protagonist's entry into the story. Davenport begins the book out at his country cabin on a lake. He goes for a friendly morning of companionable fishing with a friend. We see how he allows a neighbor to store a tractor at his place, and then, as a favor, Davenport hauls a boat back to a farmer's house. The lake community appears to resemble an old-fashioned small town of friends. As soon as Davenport heads back into the big city, he meets the woman he is going to consider committing adultery with, and he is swept into the big, drug-related murder case. All the peace and quiet of the country have vanished.

Of course, even in the big city certain positive attributes exist. The city is not without friendship and loyalty. The tremendous concern all the detectives show for their wounded comrade, Marcy Sherrill, is very touching, reinforcing the theme of loyalty. After having so many unsympathetic characters portrayed and killed, it is refreshing for the reader to be concerned over the death of a character, or a potential death in this case, because through cheering for Sherrill to survive, the value of human life is reinforced.

Among the characters concerned for Sherrill, Davenport in particular shines. Though the two had a romance in the past, Davenport appears to do a better job of showing emotion for a woman he is not currently involved with than for any of his current romantic interests. That said, having a friend hovering on the brink of death is a relatively easy situation within which to show concern, so although the theme of emotional loyalty is present even in the city, not too much can be made of it.

◆ CHARACTERS ◆

As his is the viewpoint shared by the reader, Lucas Davenport feels realistic. The reader sees what he sees, hears what he hears, follows his efforts, and so he seems like a round character, one which has been well developed. On closer examination, Davenport is flat in certain areas: in this novel he does little thinking or self-examination, and it stands out. He is supposed to be a very smart man, a computer game entrepreneur and crack detective, and yet he often behaves more like a reactionary animal than a logical detective. On crimes, the reasoning given for his lack of reflection is that he lets his subconscious do the work and follows his hunches. As he does not usually make large leaps, this explanation is palatable. However, *Easy Prey* also focuses to a great extent on Davenport's romantic relationships, and here his lack of cognition is shocking. Davenport often puts aside his work to dwell on the women in his life, yet spends little time thinking. In this area, he appears immature and unintelligent, always focusing only on women's appearances, never on their personalities. When he gives his longest speech of the novel, offering advice to his ex-girlfriend Catrin on her marriage, he shows that he is capable of deep thought regarding relationships, which makes it all the more puzzling that he practices so little on his own. The novel highlights the fact that he has little control over his libido. He does not prioritize pursuing a healthy, long-term relationship over jumping into bed with whatever attractive woman offers, whether she be a drug-using, recent incest practicer who is only interested in casual sex, or whether she be a married woman. Since Davenport's thoughts are consistently shared with the reader, the lack of thought in this area is striking and creates an inconsistency in the supposed intelligence of the character.

Mirroring the main social concerns of the novel, after sex, Davenport's character is most involved with violence. In this area, there is some interesting character development, not so much within this novel as between books. In prior books, Davenport often displayed a violent streak, lashing out physically when he was frustrated or angry. In *Easy Prey*, Davenport finally seems in control. When his good friend Sherrill is shot, rather than seek vengeance, Davenport coolly explains to another police officer that it is a danger of the job. He pours his energy into caring for Sherrill rather than becoming enraged on her behalf, and it is this maturity that makes his ex-fiancee Weather interested in beginning a new relationship with him. We are reminded of his former violent nature by his flashbacks to college, when his college girlfriend Catrin was so concerned at the violence he dis-

played playing hockey that she feared he would hurt her. But in the present, we receive more evidence of his newfound maturity when he deals with a very annoying driver: whereas the old Davenport would have punched the inconsiderate driver who is causing trouble at a crime scene, the new Davenport acts with restraint. The wild Davenport still loves to speed in his Porsche and have sex with numerous women yet is finally becoming civilized in respect to violence, leaving open the possibility that he will improve in other areas as well.

The supporting characters in the novel appear flat in almost all regards. They help move the action and supply information but lack depth. Marcy Sherrill demonstrates some complexity, but her scenes are few in *Easy Prey*. Del, a narcotics officer, serves as Davenport's partner in the book, but for narrative purposes Del is simply a straight man: Davenport swaps information with and bounces ideas off of him.

◆ TECHNIQUES ◆

Point of view is very important in *Easy Prey*, as it is in all the books in the series. It is Lucas Davenport's series, and, except for the occasional experiment, the story is told from Davenport's third-person, limited point of view. The narrator is privy to Davenport's thoughts and impressions as they occur. There is never the sense that Davenport learns information the reader does not or that he is keeping thoughts secret. Where the text is not dialogue, which forms the bulk of the novel, it is Davenport's perception of the setting and events, and what he is doing and thinking, such as "Catrin. He didn't know what he thought about her, but she was on his mind. . . . " Most of the sentences in the book are short or medium length as in this example, keeping the pace fast and centered in the present, on what is being quickly said or described. The strong, highly inflected narrative voice adds to the intimate feeling of the point of view.

Having a strong sense of Davenport's personality is important because the "Prey" series is as much about Davenport's character as the crimes. As Sandford fuses together elements of the classic and hard-boiled detective genres, one of the key elements he brings from the hard-boiled genre is the focus on the detective's character and on the culture more than on the crime itself.

In the larger plot, *Easy Prey* roughly follows the formula of the classical detective story by introducing the detective, presenting the crime, having the investigation, offering the solution, explaining the solution, and apprehending the criminal. *Easy Prey* does complicate the classical formula greatly by having the crime occur first, having the investigation focus on the wrong victim, presenting and explaining an incorrect solution, having a second murderer, and only apprehending one of the two murderers.

In many ways, *Easy Prey* is more of a hard-boiled detective novel than a classical one because of its focus on the cynical detective and the society. However, *Easy Prey* does not contain many minor characteristics of the traditional hard-boiled detective story such as the betrayer-lover and the intimidation of the detective, and it also differs in some of the major aspects. Whereas the hard-boiled detective pursues a quixotic sense of justice, Davenport's motivation is defeating the criminal. As the narrator says, Davenport "[f]elt the dark finger of hypocrisy stroking his soul. All for justice, he thought. Or something. *Winning, maybe.*" Davenport pursues the threads of information, seeking to capture the criminals, because it is his job and because he likes to succeed, not out of a passion to see justice done. John Sandford shows an awareness of both the classical and hard-boiled traditions, forming a hybrid that contains aspects of the two, accompanied by new variations.

◆ LITERARY PRECEDENTS ◆

The classical detective novels that established the basic formula Sandford plays off of include all the classics of the genre including the Arthur Conan Doyle, Agatha Christie, and Rex Stout mysteries. The hard-boiled precedents most significantly include Raymond Chandler's and Dashiell Hammett's mysteries, which appear to influence Sandford's "Prey" series in regard to its cynical, tough detective and the corrupt nature of society.

◆ RELATED TITLES ◆

The considerable number of books in the "Prey" series attests to its popularity. Most of the "Prey" books spend time on Davenport's romantic relationships, but *Easy Prey* focuses more on this area than many, showing Davenport at a crossroads between multiple perspective partners. Also, *Easy Prey* is a milieu book more than usual, as it focuses on the media and its effect on society. As discussed under "Characters," Davenport appears to be evolving between books, here gaining control of his violent nature.

◆ IDEAS FOR GROUP DISCUSSIONS ◆

The primary purpose of genre fiction is widely held to be to entertain the audience. Entertainment appears a priority in the "Prey" series: these books are full of murder and detection, sex and violence. However, even though these novels are doubtlessly meant as an entertaining sideline to the author, the Pulitzer Prize-winning journalist John Camp, they do contain pertinent commentary on our society in addition to the action. This commentary is particularly sharp in *Easy Prey* where Camp explores a topic he is an expert on, the media, within his detective story.

1. In what ways does the media appear decadent in *Easy Prey*? Are there ways that the media could be coerced to behave more morally that would cause more good than harm?

2. Do big cities foster moral corruption and then spread that corruption into small towns via the airwaves? Is small-town life more moral than big-city life?

3. Is Lucas Davenport a sympathetic character? Does he seem a strong hero? Does he possess good morals?

4. How would *Easy Prey* be affected if it followed the classical detective formula more closely?

5. What do you think of the female characters in *Easy Prey*? Are there any generalities that can be made about how women are portrayed in it?

6. What are the advantages and disadvantages of working within well-developed literary traditions such as the classical detective novel or the hard-boiled detective novel?

Brian Forsyth

EMPIRE OF THE SUN

Novel

1984

Author: J. G. Ballard

◆

◆ SOCIAL CONCERNS ◆

*E*mpire of the Sun focuses on a young protagonist's strategies for survival in a Japanese prison camp in occupied China during World War II. In contrast to the privileged world he inhabited before the war, the reality of the world in which Jim finds himself involves merely staying alive by getting enough to eat, managing to maintain a relationship with his captors and the inmates of the camp, and remaining sane. Based on events from Ballard's childhood, this world is colored by childish imagination. The world Jim creates for himself in his imagination is more important to him than physical reality. In the *Paris Review* Ballard explained that he used his obsessions, setting up an "obsessional state of mind" within his characters. There is the fascination with a romanticized war contrasted with the truth of a real war with battlefields and dead bodies. Ballard examines "the relationships between the private fantasies of his characters and the public events and images of their environments" in order to build a world both real and surreal.

The protagonist, known as "Jamie" in his family and "Jim" in the camp, is eleven years old when the Japanese attack Pearl Harbor and the next day march into Shanghai, the city of his birth. Jamie's father owns a cotton mill on the Yangtze River, employing Chinese workers. This allows him and his parents to live a pleasant life of parties, private school for Jamie, friends in the European community, a large home with a swimming pool and servants in the years before the invasion. For Jamie it is normal to be driven by the chauffeur to and from school, church, his friends' houses, and anywhere else he wishes to go. He rides his bicycle out into Shanghai, without his parents' knowledge, in search of adventure to feed his imagination. The newsreels, shown everywhere, seem as imaginary as his dreams, playing over and over in his mind. His imaginary world is forming.

It is December 7, 1941. It will be December 8, 1941 in China when the Japanese attack Pearl Harbor. Jamie and his parents are invited to a party in the country outside Shanghai, one of a round of Christmas parties for the season. Jamie slips away from the home of Dr. Lockwood and his family, across a field containing a tumulus—a burial ground where he looks at the skeletons in their lidless coffins—to the aerodrome of Hungjao. He has visited the aerodrome other times, fascinated by a crashed and rusting Japanese fighter plane where he imagines he is the pilot. He has been trying for months to find a way to convince his father to move the derelict plane home to the house in Amherst Avenue. In his excitement at the visit to the plane, he sails his balsa wood model plane into the air, where the wind catches it and carries it across the field. As Jamie chases it, he becomes aware of a group of Japanese soldiers in the trenches by the blockhouse. He realizes he is in danger, but he wants to get his plane. His father calls to him to come, and he obeys, realizing he has put his father in danger also, showing an adult understanding of the situation while, childlike, still wanting to get his balsa wood plane. The plane and the dead pilot are part of the imagery of his private world.

Fearing that an attack is imminent, Jamie's parents decide they will spend the next several days in the Palace Hotel rather than their home. They think they will be less isolated and more protected in the hotel. The next morning, Jamie watches the British, American, Italian and Japanese gun boats on the Yangtze River, noticing that the Japanese gun boat is now anchored in front of the British Consulate. He notices the corpses put into the river every day by Chinese families too poor to afford burial of their dead. The corpses float toward the sea on the outgoing tide and return when the tide comes back in. Jim stands at the window, giving arm signals, and, with the ego of a child, thinks he has caused the war to start when the Japanese boat begins to fire on the H.M.S. *Petrel*, a British vessel. Jamie's parents decide the hotel is not safe with its proximity to the river, so they go to the car to be driven home by Yang. They are caught in the wave of Japanese soldiers invading the city. Jamie's father leaves the car to try to help the sailors from the *Petrel* by helping to pull them out of the river onto the mud bank. Jamie and his mother are forced from the car by a tank and are separated. Jamie finds his father on the mud flats, stays with

him and a wounded man for hours and is then separated from him at the hospital. The Japanese think he is a very young sailor because he is wearing his school uniform.

In the weeks that follow, Jamie is not successful in finding his parents or any of his friends. He lives by his wits, finding food in the abandoned houses of the European families. All the swimming pools are drained, a symbol indicating dereliction in this and other stories. The world gradually closes in on Jamie. He is forced to consider surrender to the Japanese but knows he must choose carefully in order not to be killed while trying to give himself up. Food becomes harder and harder to find. His bicycle is stolen, making it impossible for him to continue moving around Shanghai in search of food and shelter. Living on the street is certain death. He goes to the river, to the funeral pier, where he can sit and let his imagination dwell on the sunken Chinese ships he has admired. He imagines eating the Japanese ship, the *Idzumo*, a sign he is close to starvation. His imagination is so active that he uses a rotting sampan to reach a derelict vessel, boarding it as if he owns it, using it as part of his own private game. Frank, an American seaman who has managed to avoid capture by the Japanese, comes out to the ship in a small boat to get Jamie. Frank and his partner, Basie, are living on an unfinished boat in the shipyard. They feed Jamie with the intention of selling him to slavers and give him the name "Jim," "a new name for a new life," Basie says. Jim is able to keep Basie's interest by telling him about notable people he has met and using what Basie calls "interesting words."

From Basie Jim comes to understand that there may be people who want the war to continue, are profiting from it. They spend three days traveling around Shanghai bartering for rice while Basie and Frank try to sell Jim. The afternoon of the third day, they drive to Amherst Avenue, and Jim knows they are planning to leave him to starve or be killed. Jim suggests that they go to his house, where they meet Japanese officers coming outside and, to Jim's relief, are captured. Jim now understands that the only place he will be safe is in a civilian prison camp, fed and guarded by the Japanese. Everyone else is an enemy.

Survival is not easy. At the detention camp in the open-air cinema, something like a drive-in movie theatre, Jim entertains himself by watching the images created on the movie screen as the sun moves across the sky. The prisoners are fed only once a day, and Jim is sure he is not getting his fair share but has no idea what to do about it. Basie reappears, without Frank, and begins to tutor Jim in survival techniques. How to ingratiate himself to the people who control the food is Jim's first lesson. Jim puts this tutorial to good use all the time he is interned in the camps. His realization that there is not enough food to keep everyone alive makes this his most important lesson. He will need skills to obtain more than his share and insure his survival. Guilt disappears with this realization. The animal instinct to survive any way possible takes over.

The instinct to survive becomes paramount in Jim's life. He escapes from the open-air detention center to be transported to a camp by using his understanding of the guard and the guard's lack of patience. Jim needs to be in the truck because Basie is in it. Fortunately for Jim, Dr. Ransome is also in the truck. The trip to the camp is a nightmare of misunderstandings and near death experiences. The Japanese driver does not know how to get to the camp, becoming lost almost immediately. There is no food or water for the prisoners, most of them elderly. At the train station where the driver stops to get directions, Jim obtains water for himself and some of the prisoners, able to do this because he is a bothersome child. He

uses his knowledge of Japanese custom, drinking all the water in the first bottle himself rather than sharing, as the Europeans expect. His show of bravery coupled with the deep bow of respect earns more water that he can then share with the other prisoners.

◆ THEMES ◆

War and the consequences of war, death, reverence for life, the relationships between people who will make sacrifices to keep others alive are themes woven into the structure of the main theme—the psychological war waged by Jim. The internees of the prison camp have various agendas, shown in relation to a world Jim creates, the one in which he can survive. The people in Ballard's story move in landscapes that "are symbolic of his characters' psychological state" says *DISCovering Authors*.

For the foreigners who remain in Shanghai, life becomes a matter of survival rather than a good time. Those who flee the country before the invasion are better off only if they go far enough away with those in the Orient caught up in the struggle. The Japanese are not concerned with the survival of people they put into the camps. They are concerned only that they appear to be concerned. If an internee can survive on the small amount of food available, manage to fight off disease, and live through any attacks on the camp, he or she may survive the war. The death march from the camp to the edge of Shanghai is more than many of the prisoners can survive.

Another consequence of the war is the attitude of the Chinese toward the foreign community. This is illustrated by the amahs at the home of Jim's friends Clifford and Derek. The traditional Chinese amah is a combination housekeeper–child caregiver, often employed by the European families to care for their children. Clifford and Derek and their parents are no longer in residence, and the amahs are stealing furniture from the house. When Jim asks where his friends are, one of the amahs slaps him in the face, hitting him harder than he has ever been hit before. This, coupled with their refusal to talk to him, gives a clear picture of their true feelings for the Europeans. The Japanese are regarded as deliverers more than conquerors by much of the Chinese population during the first few days of the war. This sentiment will change.

In an effort to find his parents, Jim goes to the apartment building where his friend Patrick Maxted lives with his parents. The apartment has been ransacked by the Japanese, but Patrick's model airplanes still hang from the ceiling, representing order among chaos. The next morning Jim talks to the White Russian caretaker from the Shell Company in the building across the street. After showing Jim a picture of two British battleships being sunk by the Japanese, Mr. Guerevitch tries to send Jim after a group of British women and children the Japanese are taking to a camp. Jim refuses to follow because they are prisoners, but begins to understand that the Japanese may be able to win the war. He also suddenly realizes his parents may already be in a camp. He begins to consider the need to find a way to give himself up. An encounter with a Japanese soldier who bends the spokes on the front tire of his bicycle helps him decide that trying to surrender holds as many dangers as living on the street. He wonders how whole armies are able to surrender when he is having such a difficult time.

Part One ends with Jim and his fellow internees finally in a camp. They are to help captured Chinese soldiers build a runway for Japanese bombers to use. Jim knows chances of survival are slim, that they will be worked to death along with the Chinese. Part Two opens three years later, near the end of the war. Ballard puts the beginning

and ending in separate boxes, much as a child might do. For Jim, the war itself is not a first hand experience—the beginning and the end provide air raids and other actions that feed his imagination, the middle is routine. Part Three encompasses his last flight, the return to the camp, the rescue by Dr. Ransome, and his return to his parents in Amherst Avenue. Finally, he is to leave China for England. Writing in *The Nation*, Edward Fox says "the novel ends when Jim is sent by boat to a public school in England, presumably to continue honing his survival skills—the strangest and iciest twist of all." The war with the Japanese may be over, but the psychological war raging inside Jim is far from over.

◆ CHARACTERS ◆

Fox says "characters hardly matter in Ballard's decaying universe . . . [they] are no more than throbbing organic matter among futuristic objects, and the objects are slightly more interesting." Jim is the only character whose mind and thoughts are open. His ideas about the war and its consequences, whether it is actually beginning and then whether there can be an end, are generated by his imagination and colored by his childish understanding of events.

Jamie or Jim sees the war and its consequences through the eyes of a child aged eleven to fourteen. As Jamie, he is the pampered young son of a British couple, owners of a cotton factory in Shanghai, living with servants, chauffeur, a governess, private school, a swimming pool and attending a round of parties with other non-Asian families living in the area. Jamie is not prepared to live off the land, but he is prepared to protect himself enough to stay alive. When he is separated from his parents during the first wave of the Japanese attack on the city, he is able to get back to his home in the foreign section of the city—too late to be reunited with his parents. He manages to survive partly because of his experiences riding his bicycle around Shanghai before the war. He knows the city and which sections are dangerous. The danger is worse when war comes, but he manages to find food and a place to stay so long as he has his bicycle. When the bicycle is stolen threatening his physical survival, his imagination takes over, leading him to the river with its floating corpses and sunken boats. As he is subjected to the hardships of camp life, he sinks deeper into the world he has constructed for himself.

During the first several weeks after he is separated from his parents, he lives in a series of houses and apartments. The house in Amherst Avenue is the first. He is a little boy in this house, sleeping on his mother's bed, comforted by the smell of her clothes and cosmetics. He plays games in the garden, trying to identify the planes that fly over, eats food stored in the pantry, sitting in the dining room in his place at the table, and watches the water level in the swimming pool drop. The way of life he has known is slipping away as surely as the water in the pool. Even the house seems to change, "withdrawing from him in a series of small and unfriendly acts." Childlike, he uses the house as a racetrack on his bicycle, leaving chaos in his wake. At the end of his wild ride, he leaves the house in search of his parents.

At first Jim does not consider surrender. Surrender would not be honorable. He begins to realize surrender means survival, and honor becomes less important. The will to survive becomes the most important part of Jim's life. Physical survival is important, but for Jim, mental survival is more important. His fantasies help him with the mental survival, along with lessons in Latin and algebra and old *Reader's Digest* magazines.

As Jim travels around Shanghai looking for his parents, he has a series of encounters

with people he has known or seen in the past. Their attitudes have changed toward him—the Chinese, abusive; the Germans, worried. After managing to repair the damage done by the soldier to his bicycle, Jim's next journey through Shanghai reveals more changes in the city. The Chinese now seem to fear the Japanese soldiers. There are bodies of dead Chinese citizens littering the streets. Jim returns to the European quarter looking for food and help, finds neither, and retreats into books and magazines. He is building his fantasy world and changing, moving toward the place where he can survive. A group of Japanese soldiers feed him for a while, only to be replaced by a group who chase him away. He is barred from the houses he knows, the sanctuaries of his childhood, and ready to accept his new name from Basie. He is no longer Jamie. He is Jim.

Basie and Frank are Americans who manage to elude capture for a while. Basie is the thinker; Frank, the doer. Frank tells Jim that Basie, a former cabin steward, has a collection of gold teeth he has removed from the Chinese corpses floating down the river. Basie uses the teeth as trade goods. Jim is afraid Frank will try to remove one of his molars. Unable to sell Jim to slavers, Frank and Basie return with him to the house in Amherst Avenue where they are captured by the Japanese soldiers who are living in Jim's house. Frank is beaten to death; Jim is taken to the open-air cinema; Basie survives to be incarcerated in the open-air cinema, where Jim takes care of him, keeping him alive to be transported to the camp at Lunghua.

The other characters from the camp move in the background, occasionally coming into the light enough to see their features. Dr. Ransome feeds and educates Jim, giving him part of his food and lessons and homework. The Vincent family, with whom Jim shares a room, is blocked out by the makeshift curtains hung to separate the room. Mrs. Vincent speaks to Jim occasionally. Various old women come and go. Jim helps Mr. Maxted collect the rations for their group each day. Many of these people care about Jim and are trying to help him. He closes them out of his imaginary world, turning them into non-people.

◆ TECHNIQUES ◆

By using the point of view of the eleven- to fourteen-year-old child, Ballard is able to present the war as a never-ending story. Saturated with newsreels of the war in Europe, Jim tries to think of a way to help stop the Germans in Russia while the Japanese are poised to invade Shanghai. He watches the Japanese soldiers watching his father and other businessmen burning the papers from their businesses and is concerned about the soldiers' patience. He senses they are waiting for a prearranged signal but neither he nor his parents seem to understand that they will no longer be safe in Shanghai when the Japanese conquer the city.

Jim's fantasies are embodied in his interest in planes, pilots, and airfields. The incident at the Christmas party with the downed fighter plane is a window into Jim's imagination. The combination of his uncaring and thoughtless behavior with his fear at having put his father at risk from the Japanese soldiers camped on the deserted air field, sets the stage for Jim's reactions to the events of the next three years. He responds thoughtlessly as any preteen and early teenager would to most situations. He displays insight into the minds of his captors far beyond his years in matters of survival. He is able to stay alive and help to keep others alive because of this insight.

Symbols of death surround Jim, beginning with his dreams of newsreels without a sound track to the flies he tries to keep out

of Mr. Maxted's mouth as he is dying after the march from the camp to the Olympic Stadium at the end of the war. Empty swimming pools, burned out airplanes, weeds growing on lawns, houses and apartments left empty, the bodies of Chinese put off the funeral pier into the Yangtze River, sunken ships weave in and out of Jim's fantasies of flying. During the invasion of Shanghai, a traffic jam puts the war on hold when no one, invader or invaded, can move. Jim and his mother are forced from their car as it is run over by a tank. Sailors fleeing from the *Petrel* and the U.S.S. *Wake,* are stranded on the mud flats of the Yangtze River with the tide coming in and funeral flowers surrounding them. Jim's father is on the mud flat with a wounded British naval petty officer when Jim joins him. Jamie and his father survive the day on the mud flats, but many do not. The Japanese soldiers line the road above the flats, their bayonets forming "a palisade of swords that answered the sun."

Writing in *Contemporary Literature,* Roger Luckhurst observed that the story is "obsessed with the marking of boundaries and the logical inversions and displacements that attend them." Jim stays in the Maxted's apartment until the water and electricity have been shut off, and he cannot use the elevator to get his bicycle to street level. Jim looks for the end of his freedom, knowing he will be safer as a prisoner than a free man. The fence around the Lunghua Camp is not to keep him in but to keep the Chinese out. Basie sends him outside the fence, and Jim is almost lost there. He cannot find the end of the war, deciding that as one war ends, another is beginning. He hides in the Olympic Stadium among the dead and has to find his own way back to the camp. His inability to show how happy he is to find his parents, alive and at home, puts him on the wrong side of the fence once again.

Almost as a beacon leading Jim toward safety, recurring events involving a bright light move through the story. Newsreels are shown constantly during the year before the war. The patterns of light on the screen in the open-air cinema entertain Jim during the first weeks of internment. Near the end of the war, air raids light up the skies. While in the Olympic stadium, Jim sees the flash from the atomic bomb as it explodes over Japan. As Jim is trying to return to the camp, he finds a dead Japanese pilot and tries to revive him. When he puts his finger in the pilot's mouth and is bitten, he has a vision that he can bring all the casualties of the war back to life.

Counterpoint to Jim's vision and putting the world back into its tilt is Lieutenant Price. He is almost as great a danger to Jim's survival as any danger he has lived through until this time. In competition for the food and cigarettes being dropped by the allied bombers, Jim finds he must outsmart Price to survive.

◆ LITERARY PRECEDENTS ◆

Identifying precedents for Ballard's text is difficult because it does not seem to conform to other works within the genre of fictionalized autobiography. *Empire of the Sun* is his first work that is not science fiction. Many critics say his science fiction is explained by *Empire of the Sun*. Luckhurst noted "the difficulty of siting Ballard's work, of finding adequate contexts in which to read it, results from this uncertain nonsite between science fiction and the mainstream." Until *Empire of the Sun*, Ballard did not receive critical acclaim for his writing, since science fiction often is not taken seriously. This work, being autobiographical, allowed critics to include him in "mainstream" literature, "mainstream criticism celebrated his transformative reworkings of science fiction tropes as long as they remain within the genre," Luckhurst further commented.

Ballard's receipt of the Guardian Fiction Prize (1984) and the James Tait Black Memorial Prize (1985) and his nomination for the Booker Prize (1984) attest to the quality of the work.

Ballard's science fiction does not quite fit its genre, either. He does not have a hero who overcomes evil, but rather has heroes who accept catastrophe, finding death preferable to life. Science fiction critics praise him for writing an autobiographical novel rather than for his science fiction.

Ernest Hillen has written a memoir of a young boy in Java in World War II. Hillen is eight when his father and others working on a tea plantation in Java are taken away by the Japanese. He, his older brother, Jerry, and his mother are interned in a camp for the rest of the war. The book, *The Way of a Boy: A Memoir of Java*, recounts their experiences in the Bloemankamp prison camp, "where daily life was defined by random brutality, fear and unending hunger" reports *Publishers Weekly*. A reader might be led to wonder what brutality Ballard has chosen not to report.

◆ RELATED TITLES ◆

Ballard has written a series of novels dealing with catastrophes, beginning with *The Wind from Nowhere* (1962), and followed by *The Drowned World* (1962), *The Burning World* (1964), and *The Crystal World* (1966). In *Dream Makers: The Uncommon People Who Write Science Fiction*, Charles Platt quoted Ballard: "The hero is the only one who pursues a meaningful course of action—instead of escaping or trying to adapt to the material environment, he stays and comes to terms with the changes taking place within it and, by implication, within himself." The protagonists in these novels become loners who are at home in the ruined world around them.

Later work includes *Crash* (1973), *Concrete Island* (1974), *High-Rise* (1977). These novels deal with violence in modern society by presenting a disaster. *Crash* and *Concrete Island* deal with car crashes. *High-Rise* is set in a forty-story apartment building gone back to savagery after a power failure.

The Kindness of Women, also autobiographical, is the sequel to *Empire of the Sun*. In it, Ballard retells the story of the internment in China and continues with his life in England in boarding school through his marriage, the birth of his children and the loss of his wife. *Publishers Weekly* reports that "*The Kindness of Women* is full of scenes and moments that linger hauntingly in the mind, a piercingly honest, vibrant record of a very contemporary life." However, some critics have observed that certain details in *The Kindness of Women* do not agree with those in *Empire of the Sun*.

Also an author of many collections of short stories, Ballard has used this genre to explore his ideas of the inner self and the worlds created by his characters. *The Atrocity Exhibition* (1970), *The Venus Hunters* (1980), *Myths of the Near Future* (1982) and *War Fever* (1990) are some of these.

◆ ADAPTATIONS ◆

Empire of the Sun was adapted for film in 1987. It was directed and produced by Steven Spielberg from a script by Tom Stoppard and Menno Meyjes (uncredited). Peter Travers, movie reviewer for *People Weekly*, wrote that Christian Bale gives a remarkable performance as Jim. But, he continued, the chill has been removed from the movie. Spielberg even manages to romanticize the suicide of the kamikaze pilot. The ending "loses its resonance when Spielberg hasn't connected his spectacle to a larger moral theme."

An audiocassette recording consisting of eight cassettes of one and one-half hours each was made in 1996. Read by David Case, the recording is unabridged. It was called "an incredible literary achievement . . . brilliant," by the *Los Angeles Times*.

◆ IDEAS FOR GROUP DISCUSSIONS ◆

In a review for *Newsweek*, Donna Foote and David Lehman wrote that *Empire of the Sun* "explores the zone of 'inner space' that Ballard sees as 'the true domain of science fiction.'" The novel is autobiographical but edits out his parents during the time spent in the camp. Set during World War II, the book does not deal with the war, but with Jim's fantasies that grow around the machines for making war.

1. Japan invaded China before Pearl Harbor. Report on the war between Japan and China during the period before the Japanese attacked Pearl Harbor.

2. Dr. Ransome tried to educate Jim during the time they were in the camp. Why did he use subjects such as Latin in Jim's course of study?

3. Why would a shift from science fiction to autobiographical novel have gotten Ballard's work attention from the critics?

4. Why would Jim have believed that Dr. Ransome disapproved of him?

5. Jim and Dr. Ransome have a discussion about his lessons and having Mrs. Vincent help him with his Latin vocabulary. During the discussion (Chapter 25), Jim tells Dr. Ransome he has used his trig to calculate ways for the Japanese gunners to shoot down the American planes. Why did Jim feel loyalty to the Japanese?

6. As a European in China, Jim had enemies all around him. Jim's father could

have left Shanghai before the war began. What kept him there with his family?

7. Explain the reaction of the British prisoners to the execution of the Chinese coolie who had pulled the rickshaw from Shanghai to the camp.

8. What are some of the lessons Jim learns during the years he is in camp?

9. Describe instances that light is important to the story.

10. In what ways will the boarding school Jim is going to be like the camp?

Ann Barton Sciba
Wharton High School Library

EMPRESS OF THE SPLENDID SEASON

Novel

1999

Author: Oscar Hijuelos

◆

◆ SOCIAL CONCERNS ◆

The "empress" of the title is Lydia Espana, a Cuban emigrant living in New York City, post–World War II. It is mostly through Lydia's eyes that the city is revealed, and it is through Lydia's story that the difficulties of living as an immigrant in America from the late 1940s into the 1980s are depicted. Hijuelos tracks Lydia as she attempts to find her way in the city and figure out "how life really works for people without money and connections." She marries and has two children, Rico and Alicia, who embody the world of first generation Americans, estranged from their cultural past, puzzled by the actions of their parents and looking to an uncertain future. The city of New York is full of opportunities and grand possibilities for Lydia, who sees herself as an empress, the name given to her by her husband as he courts her before they are married. Forced to become a cleaning woman, Lydia's exposure to many new environments as she travels around the city shows us more clearly the relationships of immigrants to the new unfamiliar territory. Lydia's different jobs expose her to various facets of American life; she is exposed to many types of condescension, mistrust, and mistreatment that many immigrants face

when they come onto the shores of this land of opportunity.

One major source of hope and frustration is a particular household that Lydia cleans regularly; the high-class Manhattan apartment belongs to the Ospreys. Mr. Osprey befriends Lydia because she reminds him of his childhood nannies from South America, and the Ospreys, for Lydia, are the ideal American family. They are successful, happy, and very wealthy. Mr. Osprey is generous, kind, and friendly, while Mrs. Osprey, beautiful yet aloof, warms to Lydia and eventually befriends her as well. It is in this relationship between the two households, the Espanas and the Ospreys, that the differences in class, education, and opportunities are most striking. Lydia's fertile imagination brings her closer to their wealth and prominence, but it is only in her imagination. When Mrs. Osprey gives Lydia her cast-off clothing, Lydia wears it with pride, because it is the closest she will be to their wealth. This is most apparent with the fur coat that she inherits from the Ospreys. By surrounding Lydia with such impractical finery and showing Lydia's happiness in it, Hijuelos accentuates the distance between the society to which she belongs and the society to which she believes she should belong. This is echoed in the responses of her children to her admonishments about being well dressed and behaving properly. She forces them to abide by her own seemingly antiquated code of behavior, which accentuates her refusal to recognize her "place" in the world and the desire of her children to normalize themselves by taking on the practices of their adopted country. It is in her imagined superiority that she maintains the memory of her childhood in Cuba and the hope that the discomfort she and the rest of her family suffer is only temporary and can, at any moment, change, for she is in the land of opportunity.

Hijuelos shows that the only comforts that many immigrants have are their memories and their imaginations. He paints a picture of a bright immigrant community, that even though they are beset by daily hardships—little work, even smaller pay, condescension from non-immigrants—they manage to have hope and happiness in their relationships with each other. Through their music and dancing and late night parties, Hijuelos's characters attempt to maintain a connection to their past while seeking out their place in a new culture. In addition, various concerns that parents have in general are intensified for Lydia and her husband, Raul, as the attempt to negotiate the proper boundaries for their children in this unfamiliar place. When her daughter, Alicia, becomes friends with a local socialist café owner, Lydia is appalled at his values and beliefs and forbids the association, yet in the end, she befriends him herself, for he is someone to talk to, and his situation is much like her own. He is also a "stranger" in a strange land. Here, Hijuelos is working with the stereotypes of various characters and identifies these prejudgments to demonstrate that everyone has their own prejudices, which eventually need to be broken down.

Class stratification is a major issue for this novel. Lydia, as a cleaning woman, has for the most part, free access to the apartments of the very rich, as well as apartments of the middle class. She is alien to both, and as she moves through the different environments, it is easy to see her isolation and her desire to move to another level of society. She encourages her children to do so, as well. Rico, through the benevolence of Mr. Osprey, is allowed to go to a private school where he associates with the children of the very rich. He too, in this environment of extreme wealth to which he does not belong, manages to find his niche. He does this through his studies and the effect is that he is able to move up to another social level, to the level that his mother always belonged to in her mind, although she did not in terms of the physical world. Alicia likewise, makes her way, through marriage, into a middle-class life. Both children struggle with what it means to be Cuban and American, and in their struggles manage to make a way for themselves in the world through individuality, determination, and opportunity. These qualities, which are necessities for the American dream, are emphasized through the success of the children. Lydia, although she has determination, is unable to raise herself to the next social level, because of her sacrifices for her family, and because of her stronger connection to her past in Cuba. Opportunity and chance play a large role in the story, for it is only with the opportunities afforded him that Rico is able to succeed so fully. He is given the chance to go to a private school and thus gets the chance to remove himself from the stultifying world in which he finds himself in the public school. Hijuelos makes a point that it is only with opportunity can one exercise determination in order to succeed, that chance plays a large role in anyone's ability to succeed.

◆ THEMES ◆

Lydia Espana represents the common immigrant who comes to America with dreams fertilized by a healthy dose of Hollywood fare. As a young girl in Cuba she meets Errol Flynn and she imagines that in America, the land of the movies themselves, she can meet many more famous people, and among them, she would have her place. It is these unreasonable dreams along with her meager inheritance that are the first to go when she arrives in New York. Being displaced and looking for a place to belong are of extreme importance in this story. Lydia is forced from her home and finds herself in New York, where she becomes a seamstress in a factory in deplorable conditions. She falls from being the spoiled daughter of a prominent man to a common worker sewing fake pearls on sweaters. She finds herself in conditions that are utterly foreign to her; she mentions to her friend Concha that at that point she knew "how Marie Antoinette felt before going to the guillotine." As a result, she must find a way to survive. She does this by meeting people who are like her and find themselves in similar situations. The people of the community with their similar hopes and similar despairs unite together, and it is when they are together that they do not feel as out of place as all other times. Family becomes increasingly important as another safe place for dislocated people. This safe place is threatened from time to time, which affects Alicia and Rico the most. The difficulty of finding one's place as first generation Americans is mirrored in the awkwardness of youth and adolescence that they stumble through with Lydia's lectures, daydreams and forced ways of dress continually occurring around them.

Each member of the family and each of the other immigrants whose lives we peer into find individual ways to deal with their dislocation. Lydia resorts to her dreams of wealth, and believed superiority. As she demonstrates for her children in the fine antique store, she plays games with people of the higher class to demonstrate her rightful place among them. Raul finds his solace in drinking, but also in religious fanaticism. His religious fervor is contrasted with Lydia's conditional faith. He becomes ever more religious, until his dying day when he dies on his knees in supplication. Lydia, on the other hand, who is much more concerned with her and her family's own well-being, has a measure of faith when she needs it, seeing the church and God as neither needing her help nor devotion, for as she tells Raul when he attempts to give an offering during a service, "God is already rich!" Raul is more religious, and finds more comfort in his children. He treats them kindly and tenderly and seems to recognize the importance of genuine human interaction more fully than Lydia. He continues supporting his ex-wife and meets with his estranged first son; both actions cause much dismay for Lydia, and his relationships with his other two children are also warmer and closer than their relationship with their mother. Raul, as he becomes more religious, begins looking out for his fellow person more and more, no matter their social standing, whereas Lydia continues to distinguish the "good" from the "bad." Lydia refuses to interact with those she sees as "unsavory" for whatever reason and encourages her children to be similarly particular. It is in this action that she displaces herself even more, and perpetuates a cycle of stereotyping and mistrust that she herself suffers from. She has her own group of people that she believes are below the standards of her and her family, just as many for whom she works see her as below their own standards.

Rico and Alicia also have their own ways of coping with their displacement as Cuban-Americans. Bristling against Lydia's admonitions about proper friends, Rico draws into himself and finds solace in literary pursuits. He becomes friends with unsavory characters and as a result gets into trouble from which only Mr. Osprey is able to extricate him. His intentions were not misguided, but his quietness led him to be in an uncomfortable position. Alicia looks for her place in the spirit of the time by rebelling. She befriends a socialist café owner and investigates philosophies much different from those endorsed by her parents. She looks for a way to make her own way in the world, far apart from the well meaning but misguided Lydia.

Another way that many of the characters attempt to ease their displacement is dependence on the "American dream" as a source of hope and comfort. Lydia is surrounded by the stories of other immigrants, friends, relatives, and others who tell her their lives so that we may see how it really can be for immigrants in America. Many rely on the American dream. If only they work harder, spend even less, save more money, they can move away from the city to a place of their own far away. The dream is not all that it is thought to be, as one of Lydia's friends finds out. She makes enough money as a cleaning lady to buy a house in upstate New York for her and her husband to live in, and soon after dies. Many, many more find out that the American dream is all but impossible. The money is most often just not there even for day to day existence, much less for building a nest egg to use to propel one up the social ladder or to retire quietly. In the meantime, each person lives day by day, until one day, they hope, something lucky will happen, and like another of Lydia's friends, they will win the lottery or they, like Lydia herself, will have a rich benefactor, but winning lottery tickets and rich benefactors are few and far between and what these immigrants are left with is a mind full of hope and memories, and nothing in the bank.

◆ CHARACTERS ◆

Lydia is a complex character who provides a very good means for developing the different themes surrounding an exploration of immigrant life. She has a fertile imagination and a strong memory, but she is also determined and not unintelligent. She has very definite values about how she sees herself and how she feels is the proper way to act, which she enforces for herself and her family. She has a very high view of herself, which prevents her from slipping into despair over the turn of events in her life. She does experience isolated moments of despair, when reality manages to break through the defensive barrier of her imagination, and she feels that she will not win the lottery or be whisked away by a rich handsome gentleman, that she will never be rich, so she must make her way the best that she can, but for the most part, she remains in a world in which she is an empress. This reinforces the importance of the American dream in most of the characters' lives. Lydia dreams of an affair with Mr. Osprey, which would bring her into his social realm. She imagines that the movie stars she meets see her worthiness to be in their circle. She has been fortunate to work for Mr. Osprey, who as the great American benefactor has been kind to her, and has brought her the closest to fulfilling the American dream. Lydia's complexity allows Hijuelos to demonstrate various difficulties of Hispanic immigrants in America and to speak to the difficulty of establishing an identity of their own. Lydia's mixing of Spanish and English, neither of which she speaks extremely well, her freely imagined sexual encounters, her strictness with her own children, her unshakable awe of the Ospreys, all point to the difference between the identity she wants and the identity that she actually possesses in the eyes of those around her. She finds difficulty in her role as a mother, which emphasizes the importance of family in the contrast of Lydia's relationship to her children as opposed to Raul's gentler dealings with them. As she grows older she also slips from the role of the beautiful, desired woman, the role for which she feels best suited, and which she enjoys the most. As she no longer can exercise her feminine powers in this manner, she is forced to find another way in which to interact with those around her.

Rico is the character who Hijuelos devotes the most attention to after Lydia. He is the one great effect of Lydia's life. His manner of living is a result of her strict upbringing, and it is mostly her lectures and distance that causes the confusion that he experiences when confronted with considering his position as a Cuban-American, but despite this, as a successful psychiatrist he is the embodiment of all that Lydia worked and hoped for. Through his experience with Mr. Osprey's daughter, Marie, years after his intense infatuation with her, he realizes that he is glad that he did not have that particular wish fulfilled, and it is at this moment that a dream that has remained with him has come up short of its desired effect. This is a common theme for Rico; he has everything he could want, and yet he still finds himself distanced and feeling empty, which proves that reaching the American dream and being in a higher social stratum is not the measure of success, despite what Lydia believed. The importance of family and remaining true to his roots as a Cuban are emphasized as he realizes that he values the time spent with his one Cuban patient, but at the same time he realizes that perhaps he is too far separated from other Latinos. Rico values most the time he spends in the old neighborhood, among the people who have shaped him in the past. His connection to the history of his culture is the most important part of his life, and his discouragement is aroused when he feels that he is no longer able to enjoy and exult in it as he should; it

is this time when he feels like an outsider in every world in which he moves. Both he and Lydia move in two different spheres, and they each must negotiate a position for themselves in those worlds. Hijuelos uses Lydia's various employers to manifest the worlds in which she finds herself. She is confronted with people of all kinds who deal with their search for a place to belong in all different ways. The successful quiet businessman uses sex, one professor uses the occult, and another has built a life around death. In each case, Lydia is confronted with people of very different ideals, and in each case, she finds a place from which to interact with these varying views; most often it is a common ground that she assumed did not exist.

Each of the characters living within her community, who play a smaller role in Lydia's life, in his or her own way contributes to the theme of the importance of the American dream. The value of the dream is called into question as most do not succeed in real life the way they do in their dreams, but Hijuelos shows that just the way they live their life contributes something to their adopted culture. Mario, a friend of Lydia and Raul and Rico's godfather, dreams of being a famous bandleader. While he waits for his big break, he spreads joy among the community with his upbeat attitude. He never gets it, but he supplies the music that is the life force of the community. Mr. Fuentes the butcher, is a poet, eventually self-published and despite the thoughts of everyone in the neighborhood, not very good, but his contribution to the attitude of the neighborhood in general and for Lydia specifically is great. Both men are characters who may not be successful in the commonly accepted connotation of that word, or even in terms of Lydia's definition of success, but are successful within their own community, so in a small way, they did succeed in the American dream. Lydia does recognize this in her acceptance of them into her social circle. For Lydia, importance is placed on success, but even more important to her is a code of conduct that is befitting a person of high social standing. If one cannot be rich, then at least one can have the richness of decorum and gentility, which is what these men, and the other characters that Lydia deems worthy, possess. They exhibit this in their overwhelmingly positive attitudes, which enrich their lives and the lives of those around them.

◆ TECHNIQUES ◆

Hijuelos paints a biography of a career, beginning with the necessity for Lydia to become a cleaning lady, and ends with the termination of her employment. In the middle, the events of her life and the lives of those around her are recounted in relation to her work. It is through the use of this framework that Hijuelos is able to portray a wide spectrum of people for Lydia to meet. Hijuelos focuses on Lydia, yet uses a third person narrator to relate things that Lydia would not divulge herself as a narrator, and allows Hijuelos to explore the thoughts and feelings of other characters as well, to gauge Lydia's effect on others, to a great extent. The subject matter of the novel comes from the long history of social realism, with the impact of the more recent opening of the literary world to stories of immigrants, as long-ignored populations assert their rightful place in the literary marketplace. Hijuelos uses Spanish phrases in and out of dialogue to add to the realism of the story and to remind the reader of the context of the story and the importance of this community's story.

Additionally, the narration of the story is fragmented temporally. Anecdotes and other stories from the characters' lives are told out of order and are kept track of by section headings which often clue the reader in to the time frame of the vignettes. This fragmentation allows Hijuelos to deal with themes, rather than being bound to the strict chronology of relating a person's life. In this manner, the novel takes on the ways in which memory works, or the way that one person would tell the story of another outside the confines of a literary biography. A slight chronology is kept but is continually interrupted by significant foreshadowings and recognition of experiences from the past. Likewise, at the end of the novel, the focus shifts from the cleaning lady to the cleaning lady's son, as Hijuelos calls attention to the succeeding generation. This also comes from a tradition of familial stories, in which the guiding member of the family makes way for the younger generation to step in and become the focus, similar in this respect to *The Godfather* by Mario Puzo (although very dissimilar in many other ways).

◆ LITERARY PRECEDENTS ◆

This novel finds itself within a growing collection of Latino fiction. As the canons of literature expand and begin to be broken down by those who have been previously excluded from it, new opportunities for writers of cultures different from the Anglo-American culture are developed. One novel that works to tell the story of a particular ethnic culture in New York City is Toni Morrison's *Jazz*. In Morrison's novel, although to a greater extent but similar to *Empress of the Splendid Season*, music is of extreme importance, and its relation to the interaction between men and women is emphasized. Although focusing on an African American community, many similar themes arise as recently arrived people look for a reconciliation of their past and present and as different social classes come into contact with one another on the streets of the city. *Empress of the Splendid Season* also fits in with other novels with a Latino focus. Another book to investigate could be *Like Water for Chocolate*, by Laura Esquivel.

Empress of the Splendid Season is Hijuelos's fifth published work. Two of his other works also focus on Cuban immigrants in postwar New York, *The Mambo Kings Play Songs of Love* and *Our House in the Last World*. The *Mambo Kings Play Songs of Love* won a Pulitzer Prize and has been made into a motion picture. It also deals with issues surrounding Cuban immigrants in America, by focusing on the true story of a man and his brother who for a brief time led the band the Mambo Kings and achieved fame by appearing on the television show, *I Love Lucy*. Here, the lead characters are musicians, and this story demonstrates even more prominently than *Empress of the Splendid Season* the role that music plays in the Cuban American community. He also has written introductions to a collection of Latino poetry and a collection of Latino short fiction, so throughout his literary career thus far, Hijuelos places extreme importance on the validity of Latino fiction and the necessity for those from backgrounds such as his to tell the stories of their culture, sharing the richness and depth of it with those who are unfamiliar.

◆ ADAPTATIONS ◆

An abridged version of *Empress of the Splendid Season,* read by Rita Moreno, is available on audio tape through Harper Audio.

◆ IDEAS FOR GROUP DISCUSSIONS ◆

Oscar Hijuelos in many of his works includes Spanish phrases throughout the English narration. He manages to maintain a Hispanic flavor in his fiction, which remains true to his roots as the son of Cuban parents as well as to the subjects of his stories. As the debate for bilingual education and the rights of immigrants in America remains a very important issue, so are stories told by and for immigrants. Also, issues surrounding the working poor and the class stratification within American society are important in this novel.

1. Hijuelos uses various techniques to demonstrate the thoughts, feelings and other nuances of his characters. Often these techniques create a separation of these passages from the rest of the narrative. What is the significance of the use of italics for long passages within the novel? Is this similar to his use of passages within parentheses? What about his use of Spanish? What is Hijuelos trying to do by using these techniques, and is it effective?

2. Oscar Hijuelos is known for his novels based in postwar America, and specifically New York City. Does he provide an accurate background to his stories concerning the issues that were important to citizens at this time? How does he incorporate background information into his stories? What is the significance of the story being placed in New York City?

3. It seems that most of the people who are able to leave the community in New York and the social level on which they live for another place or level have done so because of opportunity. One of Lydia's friends saves enough money to buy a house, one wins the lottery, Rico becomes a psychologist, etc. Why would Hijuelos show that opportunity plays a large part in success? Once a character is presented with an opportunity, does it always lead to success? Happiness?

4. Hijuelos paints a portrait of the Cuban-American community in New York City. How do the men and women within

this culture relate to one another? Are there people who work against the grain in this respect? How does the relationship between Raul and Lydia compare to that of Mr. and Mrs. Osprey? What about the relationship between each set of parents and their children?

5. At Raul's funeral, Lydia shows her father to her children and tells them: "Always remember that your grandfather was Cuban." Rico is surprised at this comment. How do Rico and Alicia compare in terms of, as Rico puts it, their "Cubaness"? What point do you think Hijuelos is trying to make?

6. How do you think Hijuelos would feel about bilingual education?

7. Raul recites a poem he has written for Lydia before he proposes, and it is from this poem that the title of the novel originates. What is the significance of the poem, the environment in which it is recited, and the use of a line from it as the title of the book?

Jessica Horn
Pennsylvania State University

FALSE MEMORY

Novel

1999

Author: Dean Koontz

◆

Called "America's most popular suspense novelist" by *Rolling Stone* magazine, Dean Koontz demonizes authority figures who irresponsibly abuse their power and, under the guise of giving aid, injure and destroy. He normally focuses on government and corporate conspiracies, particularly ones involving biological experimentation that advances unchecked, but in *False Memory* he concentrates on a psychiatrist who practices brainwashing for diabolical personal motives and holier-than-thou academics whose ludicrous theories damage young people and lead to destructive patterns of behavior. His villains always have in common their willingness to play God, to experiment on the innocent, and to unleash nightmares with no care for the consequences. Koontz does not trust professions whose members see themselves as superior to the rest of humanity because he believes that arrogance and personal smugness lead to a contempt for humanity that invariably works itself out in dangerous patterns. Ironically, the villain in *False Memory* speculates on the "brave new millennium," Koontz's reminder to readers of the programming Aldous Huxley warned might come in *Brave New World*, and he proudly asserts that power trumps truth any day.

Koontz's most terrifying villain is a respected psychiatrist, Dr. Mark Ahriman, who enjoys controlling his patients and testing those controls. He is a megalomaniac and a sadist who has killed his father and then literally drilled through the heart of his father's live-in girlfriend. He keeps his father's eyes in a jar in a secret room at home, as well as tapes of some of his more sinister deeds. Yet, to all appearances he is a handsome, charming expert, kindly and concerned, and willing to sacrifice his private time for the needs of his patients. When he lived in Santa Fe, New Mexico, he used his position of trust and authority to implant a false memory in a child whose mother had come to him for treatment, a memory that led the child to accuse adults in a child care center of physically abusing him. Then, as the local psychiatric expert called in to use hypnotism and psychiatric forms of regression to test the memories of the other children in the center, he supposedly helped them regain detailed memories of such abuse. In fact, the accused adults were innocent, and the vivid memories of the children were false memories implanted to boost Ahriman's reputation, just as he had engineered the suicide of a child to seem like irrefutable proof of wrongdoing. Again and again Dr. Ahriman experiments on patients to test his own theories and wreak mayhem for the sheer pleasure of doing so. He betrays his female clients, using his brain control methods to make them sexually pliable and then to erase their memories of the perverse and degraded behavior he demands of them; when he is tired of these excesses, he might program a patient to kill his or her entire family and then commit suicide, just for the pleasure of causing pain and destruction. He sets in motion a complicated scheme involving brainwashing of several members of one family in order to get revenge on a university professor who has publicly mocked his books and professionalism in dozens of petty ways. Furthermore, he has helped found a corporation that employs these brainwashing strategies to produce assassins on demand—for a very high price.

The university professor who awakens Ahriman's ire, Derek Lampton, is himself an object of Koontz's social criticism. Koontz does not trust university professors, especially ones in the sciences and social sciences (like sociology). He finds them as a group arrogant, self-convinced snobs, capable of cold-hearted viciousness. Derek Lampton is typical. His power-hungry wife, Claudette, adores him for the heights of academic fame he has achieved, and he wickedly delights in rapier-thrust witticisms directed against his academic competition. Even more damning from Koontz's point of view is the effect of this attitude on Lampton's son, who at three years old was a promising child but who has been spoiled and pampered and taught that there are no rules. The son, at age fifteen, has become a selfish, destructive sadist who, near the end of the novel, shoots an intruder dead with his crossbow. The man had been disarmed and knocked down so there was no need for such extreme measures, but the boy sees an opportunity to kill and get away with it and

does so. His parents rally around him, praising him for his quick thinking and telling the police that the lad has saved them all—behavior that confirms him in his deviant ways and paves the way for another amoral sociopath like Dr. Ahriman. A final revelation places Claudette at the center of Koontz's attack, for, in addition to satisfying her cravings for fame and power in her ambitions for her son and husband and nurturing their egotism and their anti-social behavior, she smothered to death her first daughter (Ahriman's child) because of the possibility of Down's Syndrome and tried to smother her son Skeet, whose problem with drugs and a lack of self-esteem are her fault. Furthermore, her biting attacks on Ahriman's bad genes and her encouragement of Lampton to attack Ahriman's scholarship are what set in motion his murderous schemes for revenge. Thus, Koontz's social concerns are rooted in the individuals whom society places on pedestals and in his fear of the devastating effects of such misplaced trust.

◆ THEMES ◆

Koontz explores the social dynamics that produce sociopaths. More than anything else he blames families: self-obsessed parents who finance their offspring's every whim but who are completely indifferent to their child's psychological needs or cold, selfish parents for whom the child is a reflection of their own dreams and wishes, clay to be molded into whatever the parents want most—a miniature image of themselves, a genius who will bring them accolades, a social climber who will help them rise to the top. However, Skeet and Dusty share the same mother, and both had arrogant, selfish fathers or step-fathers, yet they both seem to have been born with good hearts and have resisted and rebelled against their parental models, so the individual, asserts Koontz, has some degree of free will in the matter. Skeet is the weaker of the two and has succumbed to drug abuse and self-destructive acts, but Koontz does not make clear how much this is a result of both his step-father's belief in medication as a panacea for wayward children and Dr. Ahriman's tampering with Skeet's psyche through brainwashing techniques.

Directly connected with this theme is the question of responsibility to one's community. Martie Rhodes's father is a model of community service. A fireman nicknamed Smilin' Bob, he risked his life time and again to rescue men, women, and children threatened by fire. Martie's recurring image is of him in his firefighter's uniform wading into the midst of a blaze, black smoke billowing up around him to pull out a child others had missed. Remembered too is his modesty, his refusal to accept special awards and medals for just doing his job. Though at the time the book begins he is dead from cancer, he lives on in the memories of his daughter, inspiring her with his strength and courage. During his lifetime, he had instilled in her the attitude of self-sacrifice that enables her to stand up against adversity and fears of personal madness and to struggle through to the truth. Clearly, Koontz believes that deeds count more than words and that parental behavior provides models that children imitate—for good or for ill. Smilin' Bob's public image, confirmed in his private persona, sets a standard for Martie to follow. In her moments of despair, Martie gains security from an almost supernatural sense of Smilin' Bob's spiritual presence, guarding her from evil. Even in the worst of times, she hangs on to the memory of her father's heroism and the strength of her love for Dusty to help her overcome the destructive fantasies Ahriman implanted in her subconscious.

Offsetting the villainous Dr. Ahriman is the genuinely kindly and concerned Dr. Closterman, a physician who truly cares about his patients and who distrusts Ahriman's smug arrogance. Though he has no concrete evidence against Ahriman, he is brave enough to warn the Rhodeses that something is awry and to support their story to the police once Ahriman is killed. Yet his hesitation to take on Ahriman suggests another recurring Koontz theme: the inability of good people to stand up publicly and credibly against well placed villains with academic credentials and high community standing.

Koontz's message is a democratic one: the ordinary working men and women in his stories are decent folk, who, despite sometimes rough exteriors, stand by their friends in times of trouble. Although they suffer the brunt of the evil and darkness that plagues Koontz's world, they somehow endure and ultimately thrive. The wealthy, in contrast, are always suspect in his stories, tainted somehow by the deeds it took for them to climb to the top. It is their own misdeeds that bring out the rage of the psychopaths, a fact they forever refuse to admit. At the end of *False Memory*, the wealthy psychopath who kills Ahriman has good lawyers who assure her no jail time and more sympathy than reprimand, and she remains at large to possibly kill again, immune to the punishments the law would exact on poorer citizens.

A southern Californian, Koontz finds eccentricities of lifestyle undisturbing as long as private obsessions do not produce negative public ramifications. However, when eccentricity turns kinky and takes violent forms, Koontz draws the line.

Ultimately, *False Memory* explores the power of fear to paralyze the mind and damn the body but also the power of love and friendship to provide a strong bulwark, a defense against "outrageous fortune."

Koontz's great skill lies in his ability to create credible, likable characters who are caught up in incredible situations that test the limits of their love and reason.

In *False Memory* the hero and heroine are Dustin (Dusty) and Martine (Martie) Rhodes, a happily married couple, affectionate and loving, whose world comes apart, whose friends and acquaintances are killed or injured, whose comfortable home is burnt to the ground, and whose sanity they themselves question. Dusty is a house painter and Martie a video-game designer. Both are hard-working, witty, compassionate, and personable. They watch out for their friends and go out of their way to help them in times of need. Martie spends time helping her friend Susan, once a successful real-estate agent, deal with a debilitating case of agoraphobia, a paralyzing fear of open spaces, of traveling between houses and buildings. Marie drives Susan to psychiatric appointments, purchases food for her, and runs a number of errands for her daily. Dusty, in turn, actually takes a high dive from a roof to a mattress below to save his suicidal half-brother Skeet from certain death.

Yet, Martie seems to have developed autophobia—a fear of herself and the horrors she might unintentionally inflict on those she loves, most particularly, Dusty. This innovatively imagined disease is very much an absurdist extension of modern paranoia: oneself as a danger to be feared. Both Dusty and Martie have had terrible dreams that haunt their waking hours, Dusty of a blue heron that enters his body and possesses his soul, Martie of a sinister presence expressed in a whirl of autumn leaves that invades her body and smothers her will to live. Normally wary of psychiatrists, both have been programmed to turn to the renowned therapist who has been treating their friend Susan to discover the reasons for Martie's sudden mental chaos. However, when Dusty realizes that Martie's description of a book she has been reading (*The Manchurian Candidate*) sounds programmed, he begins a process of inquiry that leads him to the shocking truth: brainwashing, as in Richard Condon's novel. This knowledge sends them seeking information in Santa Fe, where their fears are confirmed and where Martie must use her wits and her shooting skills to save them from Ahriman's murderous henchmen. In a crisis both Dusty and Martie prove competent and tough; they do what has to be done to protect each other and defeat Ahriman.

Before they fully understood their plight, their friend Susan Jagger left them a critical phone message that saved them from disaster. She had helped Ahriman get a deal on a house he purchased, only to succumb unknowingly to his twisted desires. Ash blonde with a trim and delicate figure, she is stunningly beautiful, both strong and vulnerable. Since meeting Ahriman her marriage and her life have fallen apart; her phobia has begun and worsened, and she has started to imagine that someone enters her locked door, sexually abuses her, and then leaves, the only sign of his presence the semen he leaves in her panties. However, she has been programmed to believe the perpetrator is her estranged husband Eric, and when she tries to capture him on a camcorder tape hidden behind a Ming vase, she discovers the real villain is Ahriman. By then, however, it is too late, for in replaying one of their sessions, he grows suspicious of her responses, returns unexpectedly, sees the tape, and orders her to slash her own wrists after writing a despairing suicide note. The power of his psychological control (through a sophisticated mixture of drugs and brainwashing methods) is such that, though she sheds a tear as she bleeds to death, she is powerless to disobey. The crime scene looks like a suicide, and the police have no reason to think otherwise, but Dusty has heard Susan's taped phone message and knows her death is a murder.

Dr. Mark Ahriman is, of course, the key villain, a sociopath from his youth who chose his profession because of the control it would give him over others and the respectable facade it would provide for his blood cravings. As a youth, he found the opposite sex both compelling and disturbing. As an adult, he seeks to gratify his sexual desires without the necessity of establishing a human relationship, for all too often his experience has been one of rejection, of women seeing through to the heart of him and turning away. Dusty and Skeet's mother, Claudette, had twisted an emotional knife in his youthful ego by seducing him and then repeatedly reminding him that the child their liaison produced suffered from Down's Syndrome, a defect from his side of the family, not hers. Ahriman's hidden persona is that of an adolescent, a voyeuristic teenager with a craving for quick gratification and dominance. He collects rare cars and relishes violent computer games in which he pits Nazi soldiers against the Mafia, alien spacemen, and the like, in an odd amalgam of historical and futuristic fantasies of conquest. The doctor studies the formaldehyde-preserved eyes he surgically removed from the movie director father he had murdered, hoping to see the secret of his father's success with women and his easily evoked tears. Unable to shed tears himself, Ahriman's pleasure comes from the tears of his victims and from the secrecy of his true role in so many public events: a mother who shoots her husband and son and then herself; a five-year-old child who loads a gun, undresses, and shoots herself through her vagina; a beautiful, modest woman who believes Ahriman is her father as he repeatedly rapes her. His arrogant overconfidence, however, ultimately proves his undoing.

Dusty's young half-brother Skeet Caulfield (his father had legally changed his own name to Holden Caulfield) is also an Ahriman target and, as the novel begins, Skeet tries to throw himself from a roof as Ahriman had programmed him to do. Skeet is high on drugs and claims he has seen the Angel of Death inviting him to experience the wonders of the next world, but his brother's fast action saves him. Later, Dusty again comes to Skeet's rescue in the psychiatric ward where Ahriman plans to reprogram him for death. Skeet is a damaged human being, befuddled by the drugs that his parents used to control his behavior as a child and by the drugs that he now takes to escape the hard edges of reality. His growing friendship with Fig Newton, a house painter who works with Dusty and who takes Skeet under his protection while Dusty gathers evidence against Ahriman, saves Skeet's life a third time and leads to a new career for him once he has recovered from the bullet of the "Keanuphobe" millionairess who thinks he is a robot working for the Ahriman "matrix."

♦ TECHNIQUES ♦

Koontz mixes the techniques of the amateur detective story, the psychological thriller, the tale of horror and suspense, the political thriller, and the social protest novel. Koontz's attack on academic frauds and his portraits of wealthy Californian types verge on satire, and his characters' analysis of and reflections on haiku are a twisted form of literary criticism. His villain stalks his victims and gloats over their bizarre and twisted deaths; he cuts off body parts, communes with coyotes, and reverts to a childish personality when in the midst of depraved acts. The narrator unveils a variety of phobias, of drug responses, and of obsessions that warp character and deed. His victims and heroes are afflicted by grotesque nightmares, waking compulsions, fear and loathing, psychotic fugues, and suicidal impulses. The brainwashing strategies he explores are straight out of the spy story and, in this tale, are used, in part, for political ends: to force the president to bow to political interest groups. The hero and heroine look within themselves for clues that will help them understand the horror that has rocked their lives; Dusty also follows the clues in *The Manchurian Candidate* to deduce Ahriman's method, and he and Martie travel to Santa Fe to interview witnesses and trace motives and means. Their logical reasoning and their intuition guide them to the truth about who, what, and why. This story is a romance as well, for its hero and heroine cling to their love as the steadfast rock that enables them to endure and overcome when all the world seems mad. Then there is the inevitable animal story, for Koontz is a devoted dog lover, and Valet is a kindly Golden Retriever, gentle and obedient, loving and playful, a balm to injured psyches. He is too gentle to injure the villain, but his presence reassures; Valet is, as Koontz affirms through Dusty, "almost as good for the soul as prayer." Most of all, however, *False Memory* is a psychological suspense story that explores the ability of the human mind to torment and destroy not just the vulnerable and the weak, but the seemingly strong and self-confident.

Koontz is a skilled stylist, a master of strategies for building horror and suspense. He carefully layers his plot through an intricate contrapuntal design that heightens tension. Like Frederick Forsythe's technique, Koontz's trademark structural pattern is to alternate between sets of characters, first Skeet and Dusty, then Martie and Suzanne, then Dr. Ahriman and Susan, and so on, building his story a bit at a time. As Ahriman engages in more and more horrific practices, as Susan's life is threatened and then ended, and as Dusty and Martie begin to discover the nightmare within themselves,

Koontz moves back and forth from suspenseful moment to suspenseful moment (Martie having a panic attack, Dusty struggling to protect her, Susan being physically abused, Ahriman suspecting her responses) so that the reader is led to read faster and faster as the suspense, tension, and potential for disaster build and accelerate. As Martie collapses into a drugged sleep, her phone rings repeatedly: it is Susan, desperate to pass on her discovery of Ahriman's betrayals, reaching out to her friend one final time before Ahriman asserts control and punishes her terminally for her knowledge. This suspenseful alternating between sets of characters and sets of action hurtles the plot forward as the danger builds to frightening heights and the atmosphere becomes more menacing. One seeming climax is followed by another until evil is routed in unexpected ways.

Another Koontz trademark is his movement between physical surface action and psychological action to capture the way in which people are trapped by their imaginings, by the dark side of obsessive behavior. For example, while Susan and Martie talk on the phone, their conversation is punctuated by the nightmare obsessions that have begun to afflict Martie. Susan reveals the facts that have led her to conclude that someone is breaking into her locked room, having rough sex with her, and then leaving in such away that the room seems totally safe and secure; despite Susan's desperation and the disturbing possibilities of her situation, Martie's responses are distant, for her mind is fixed on the sounds of household objects inviting her to acts of violence: the *klick-klick* of snipping scissors echoes again and again as Martie imagines them calling out to her from the desk drawer, inviting her with their gleaming blades, pivoting against each other, to slash and pierce.

Related to this technique is one that is a tour de force in this novel: a catalog of the violent potential of household goods and products extended sporadically over more than one hundred and fifty pages as readers see through Martie's crazed vision. Ahriman had programmed Martie to become obsessed with plunging some weapon into Dusty's blue eyes and in some way killing him, and Koontz captures Martie's psychotic fears of engaging in such violent acts with the weapons at hand. Thus, everything she sees as she goes from room to room, she sees in terms of its potential as a tool of destruction—in the kitchen, in the bathroom, in the bedroom, in the living room, in the garage. The knives, scissors, rolling pins, hammers, pry bars, hedge trimmers, spading forks, fireplace poker, knitting needles, and other such tools come alive in her imagination. She sees in a car key and a corkscrew the potential for gouging and slashing eyes, in a wine bottle and a vase solid, blunt, effective skull crackers, and even in potato peelers and corncob holders, cheese graters and spoons objects for ripping, tearing, scraping, and thrusting.

Koontz's descriptions are often tongue-in-cheek or reflect a certain offbeat sense of humor. Construction worker Ned Motherwell produces books of haiku with titles like *Ladders and Brushes,* while another member of Dusty's construction team, Fig Newton, makes a fortune with Skeet on "Strange Phenomena Tours," which follow the trail of Big Foot, explore the sites of the most famous alien abductions, track Elvis's postmortem wanderings, and so on. Ahriman often sees the world with a peculiar twist, for example, labeling his would-be trackers "the two idiot nephews of Miss Jane Marple" and thinking that they would have been blind to him even if he had been atop "a Rose Parade float, wearing a Carmen Miranda banana hat." Just before he is shot to death, Ahriman obsesses over how Skeet, shot four times in the abdomen, could have staggered six to eight miles in over eighteen hours to point a blood-stained finger of accusation at him.

◆ LITERARY PRECEDENTS ◆

False Memory breaks the boundaries of genre classification. It is in the detective fiction tradition of the amateur who ferrets out crime where the professionals see none, with Koontz's interesting addition that makes his detective also an unwitting victim, with the clues to events locked away in his own subconscious. More particularly, the novel is in the subgenre of the mass murder/serial killer story. Mass murderers are more often the subject of thriller/horror stories than tales of detection because their focus is on the mad impulses that lead to insane acts of mass violence; while the villain of Koontz's novel is led by mad impulses to insane acts of violence and kills untold numbers of people, he kills them one at a time instead of en masse. Thus, he is more properly labeled a serial killer; and serial killers are very much a staple of the detective genre, from the early stories of Jack the Ripper (including Marie Belloc Lowndes' classic thriller, *The Lodger,* 1913) to the more recent Hannibal Lector stories like *The Silence of the Lambs* to Caleb Carr's *The Alienist* and Michael Connelly's *A Darkness More Than Night.* Authors such as John Harvey and Patricia D. Cornwell concentrate on the murderers' psychopathologies and the medical and forensic knowledge that lead to their undoing. Koontz is more interested in the psychological trauma experienced by the victims and the sadism and lunacy of the victimizer. Koontz calls attention to the limits of the serial killer mystery subgenre through a detective story Susan and Martie discuss, one in which it is the nun, not the butler, who is the murderer— and a serial murderer at that, with ax, hammer, wire garrote, acetylene torch, and nail gun. The murder of Susan Jagger is a locked-room mystery, on the pattern of Edgar Allan Poe's "The Murders in the Rue Morgue," Wilkie Collins's "A Terribly Strange Bed," Arthur Conan Doyle's Sherlock Holmes mystery "The Adventures of the Speckled Band," and Jacques Futrelle's "The Problem of Cell 13."

At the same time, Koontz intentionally builds on the pattern of Richard Condon's espionage thriller *The Manchurian Candidate,* in which brainwashing methods are used to create and control a political assassin. In a parody of the Condon story, one of Koontz's brainwashed characters is programmed to bite off the nose of the American president in order to convince the president to follow the mandates of shadowy figures manipulating political events from behind the scenes. In both Koontz and Condon's novels, a cruel and politically ambitious mother is responsible for her son's brainwashing, and in both a psychological trigger sets in motion behavior over which the individual has no control. To this source book, Koontz adds the Keanu Reeves movie *The Matrix* to bring in the paranoid possibility of programming that totally overrides reality and replaces it with a fantasy world, a computer construct with no foundation in reality. Finally, Koontz taps into the dark paranoia, the fear of conspiracies and plots exploited in Thomas Pynchon's *Crying of Lot 49* and in so many other postmodernist novels. The common parent of such works is, of course, Franz Kafka.

◆ RELATED TITLES ◆

Dean Koontz's canon consists of novels much like *False Memory,* story after story of the world turned upside down, of deceptive appearances, of conspiracies and plots that make ordinary citizens fear they have entered a realm of madness from which there is no escape. Such paranoid fantasies have become the stuff of modern fiction.

John Sanford's *The Devil's Code* (2000) is typical of the tradition in which Koontz works. It features a vast electronic conspiracy that involves both a large technological corporation and a cadre of U.S. government bureaucrats who use technology and their vast resources to cover up murders and to blackmail prominent citizens, but who are ultimately defeated by a renegade band of hackers and telephone wizards.

At the same time, Koontz also writes in the Stephen King tradition of frightening psychological horrors, though with Koontz these horrors ultimately have a solid grounding in real acts. John Saul's *Nightshade* (2000), a macabre and terrifying tale of a household torn apart by malevolent forces from within, including child abuse, torture, and deadly dreams, is in the tradition of this other aspect of Koontz's novels.

A psychological mystery focused on a serial killer, Jonathan Kellerman's *Monster* (1999), like Koontz's novel, depicts a serial killer who thinks he can outwit authorities. However, in Kellerman's novel consulting psychologist Alex Delaware is the detective hero, not the villain, and he uses his training to unlock the secrets in the minds of the victims rather than to create secrets and to lock up memory. In this case the hacked-up body of a woman psychologist has been found abandoned in a car trunk, one of a series of murders like those committed by Ardis "Monster" Peake, who is imprisoned in the Starkweather State Hospital for the Criminally Insane. "Monster" had brutally murdered his mother and the family she worked for and had ripped out their eyes, but has been too heavily drugged and too carefully guarded to have committed the two recent murders. Jeffrey Deaver's Lincoln Rhyme novels, *Bone Collector* (1997), *The Coffin Dancer* (1998), and *The Empty Chair* (2000) all deal with the forensic evidence that guides a paraplegic detective to a serial killer. However, unlike Koontz,

Rhyme focuses on the careful scientific analysis of crime scene physical evidence rather than on the victim's terror and the killer's craft.

◆ IDEAS FOR GROUP DISCUSSIONS ◆

Dean Koontz combines deep pessimism with unexpected optimism. His villains are horrifyingly evil despite their respectable facades, while his good characters are vulnerable and at times terrified but have an expected strength that helps them survive hard times and ultimately prevail. His vision of present and near future realities is a postmodernist one: terrifying, bleak, alienated. At the same time, friendship, love, and the companionship of dogs transform the world into a place of personal warmth and hope.

1. What qualities do characters like Zina and Chase Glyson and Martie and Dusty Rhodes share that are lacking in Koontz's villains?

2. Name the villains (besides Ahriman) and explain what qualities Koontz criticizes in them.

3. How does Koontz's introduction of the Bellon-Tockland Institute in Santa Fe broaden his warning about the pathologies of secretive corporations engaged in private scientific research?

4. What final events suggest truth is vindicated?

5. What final events warn that the battle for truth and goodness is never fully won?

6. Find two examples of Koontz's humor. What exactly is humorous about them? Is the humor a positive or a negative experience? Is it black humor? Satiric humor? Or good-natured?

7. Watch the movie, *The Manchurian Candidate*. How many parallels can you find between the movie and Koontz's novel?

8. Are there any indications that Ahriman wants to be caught or is he simply so arrogant that he believes precautions are truly unnecessary? List the mistakes he makes that a careful police investigation could uncover and use against him. What mistakes enable Dusty and Martie to outwit him?

9. What is the significance of the title?

Gina Macdonald
Nicholls State University, Thibodaux, LA

FIERCE INVALIDS HOME FROM HOT CLIMATES

Novel

2000

Author: Tom Robbins

◆

◆ SOCIAL CONCERNS ◆

At the beginning of his picaresque novel, *Fierce Invalids Home from Hot Climates,* Tom Robbins quotes a Hindu verse, "Sometimes naked / Sometimes mad / Now the scholar / Now the fool / Thus they appear on earth: / The free men." Thus, Robbins reveals the crux of his story—the world and its people are full of contradictions; the ones who understand this are the free men, or in the words of the protagonist, "enlightened *and* endarkened."

The protagonist embodies some of the contradictions Robbins wishes to illuminate. Switters is an unorthodox CIA agent who takes the designer-drug, XTC, for enlightenment, a vegetarian who eats red-eye gravy, a hacker who hates computers, a tough guy who is squeamish about bodily functions, a lover of innocence and purity who lusts after his teenage stepsister and has sex with a nun. Even Switters cannot decide whether he is a hero or a rogue, or in his words, a "cowboy" or an "angel." Although extreme, such strong contrasts mirror those evident in the popular culture of America at the turn of the century, a time of simultaneous "politically correct" and "anything-goes" mentalities.

As he is not known for his realism, Robbins can begin with these contrasts, mix them with several outlandish coincidences, and end up with an entertaining story. *Fierce Invalids Home from Hot Climates* tells of a CIA operative who is in love, or at least in lust, with his teen-aged stepsister. On a CIA mission, he embarks on a trip to Peru, bringing along, at his grandmother's request, her aging parrot, Sailor Boy. The parrot knows only one phrase: "People of zee wurl, relax." Because the parrot's statement so aptly describes their religion (one based on humor), the native Kandakandero Indians become enamored with the bird, leading Switters to confer with their shaman, "End of Time." As a result of their conference, Switters ends up in a wheelchair, or what he calls his "starship." From there—by way of numerous coincidences—Switters almost has an affair with his stepsister while helping her to research the prophecies of Our Lady of Fatima, gets fired from the CIA (a result of his honest explanation about his wheelchair), races paper boats with art students, and finally winds up in a convent in the middle of the Syrian desert, having everything-but-sex (according to the late 1990s meaning) with a nun called Sister Domino Thiry (pun intended). Here, he meets the abbess, or Masked Beauty, who was the model for Matisse's Blue Nude (the very painting that hangs in his grandmother, Maestra's living room). Masked Beauty, adding coincidence to coincidence, knows the third prophecy of Fatima. Customarily, fiction writers refrain from relying so heavily on coincidence and fantastical chains of events, but Robbins embraces coincidence, using it, together with the contrasts, as a literary device in the story.

Along with the stark contrasts he shows among truths of the late 1990s world, Robbins documents a number of signs-of-the-times. For example, suspicious of authority, Switters is alarmed by what he terms to be world control by corporations and "governments—and the armed agencies that [serve] them." He views advertising to be symptomatic of many American cultural ills. "Human societies have always defined themselves through narration, but nowadays corporations are telling man's stories for him." In talking about members of sixteen-year-old stepsister Suzy's generation, he says they are "rather blissfully unaware" of "being lied to by corporate America—through the movies, TV shows, and magazines . . . a hundred times a day." Opining about action-adventures, or what he calls "boom-boom movies," Switters tells a disinterested seat mate on the plane: "Subconsciously, people feel trapped by our culture's confining buildings and its relentless avalanche of consumer goods. So when they watch all this shit being demolished in a totally irreverent and devil-may-care fashion, they experience the kind of release the Greeks used to get from their tragedies. The ecstasy of psychic liberation." Thus Switters expresses a late 1990s angst about the conquest of the world, or at least the culture, by commercialism.

Another conflict indicative of the times is the factor of excessive "political correctness," the confusion around the proper or most respectful term for, as example, African-Americans. Switters has a discussion with

an African-American fellow-rogue spy, who tells him that he cannot detect "a hell of a lot of *difference* between the terms 'colored people' and 'people of color.'" Switters agrees. "The distinctions are subtle all right . . . [t]oo subtle for the rational mind. Only the political mind can grasp them." Switters cannot conceive of the extreme liberal view, calling its adherents "new-age fluff heads." Nor can he conceive of the extremely conservative "dour-faced, stiff-minded, suck-butt, kick-butt, buzz-cut, macho dickheads" view, either. Switters's reaction to both extremes mirrors that same end-of-twentieth-century tension between extreme liberalism and conservatism.

Also indicative of the times, is the characters' use of the Internet for communication. From Switters's sending pornographic e-mails to his stepsister out of state, to his researching Our Lady of Fatima, to cross-the-world communications with Bobby Case, the Internet plays an important role in the plot. Even cybersex is discussed, disdained by Switters, who says, "I'm not gonna sit around for hours every day having nonorgasmic sex with a computer or TV set." Yet Switters is not afraid of technology. He tells Suzy, "virtual reality is nothing new . . . books . . . have always generated virtual reality." Ultimately, the Internet plays a positive role; because, using a battery-powered laptop computer and wireless connection, Switters is able to e-mail the Vatican on behalf of the nuns and negotiate a visit to the Vatican.

Switters's contacting the Catholic Church by e-mail is one very modern means of communication. Even more modern is the message he sends on behalf of the nuns. They ask the Vatican—in return for keeping secret the third prophecy of Our Lady of Fatima—for an "unabashed appeal for papal sanction of birth control." Switters agrees, saying, "too damn many people [are] using the roads, using energy . . . using everything except good taste and birth control. I mean, did you get a look at the parents of the American septuplets . . . That one couple's one tasteless test-tube tumble could dork down the entire gene pool." With this subplot, Robbins not only makes a statement about the necessity of the church's control of its members' lives, but also he makes a statement about those people who choose to play God in their own lives.

So, the nuns have the secret third prophesy of Fatima. Here the story follows the truth closely. The Catholic Church did in fact keep the third prophecy of Our Lady of Fatima a guarded secret for almost a century, until ten days after the release of Robbins's book. On a trip to Portugal in spring 2000, the Pope revealed the third prophecy. According to *Time* magazine, Robbins suggested that the Vatican's release of the statement was more than a coincidence, that the prophecy from his book—that the salvation of mankind will come from somewhere other than the church—was more accurate than the Catholic Church is comfortable admitting.

Robbins is not afraid to satirize or challenge the authenticity of the Catholic Church. Such irreverence is a rule, rather than an exception, in his work. In fact, it should be noted that in depicting turn-of-the-century American culture, humorist Robbins takes serious issues such as incest, casual drug use, and organized religion in general about as seriously as he takes himself. Those easily offended by such humor and/or deliberate irreverence may want to avoid this book, or at the very least, take the advice of the parrot, Sailor Boy: "People of zee wurl, relax."

◆ THEMES ◆

Fierce Invalids Home from Hot Climates has as its core the universal theme of good versus evil; however in this book, neither good nor evil wins; it is a draw. The central point of the text is that in order for good to exist, evil must exist in tandem. The idea of the co-existence of good and evil in all things answers some of the difficult questions raised in this book: How is it that a holy institution like the Roman Catholic Church can be corrupt? How should one view the modern fascination with the Virgin Mary, when she appears only a few times, in passing, in the Bible? Why would a CIA agent take drugs and lust after his stepsister? Switters sees no conflict in these questions; he sees the good and evil in things simultaneously. Rather than fearing or fighting evil, he embraces the inherent good *and* bad in all that he does. He finds that "no matter how valid, how vital, one's belief system might be, one undermines that system and ultimately negates it when one gets rigid and dogmatic in one's adherence to it." So the danger is dogmatism, not evil.

This contrast, at least according to Switters, illuminates a related theme, the pursuit of enlightenment. Laughter is a mark of enlightenment—to see the contradictions and find joy in them causes one to be enlightened, or as Switters says, "enlightened and endarkened." Switters discusses the feeling of enlightenment, saying, "you strip the layers away, one by one, until the images grow fainter and fainter and the noise grows quieter and quieter, and *bing!* you arrive at the core, which is naked emptiness, a kind of exhilarating vacuum . . . each layer is a separate dimension, a new world." Later, Sister Domino Thiry asks Switters whether anything is making him "glad to be alive." He tells her yes, because "I'm in a foreign country, illegally, in a mysterious convent, inappropriately, and in conversation with the blue nude's niece, improbably. What's not to enjoy?" This statement captures the very spirit of enlightenment for Switters.

A third theme Robbins toys with is a question about the nature of innocence, or purity. At the outset, Switters is seen to be lusting for his stepsister. He and Bobby Case find older women less appealing, but Case sees a difference in their reasons. He says, "I chase after jailbait. I'm a midlife adolescent, I can't make commitments, I'm scared of intimacy . . . but with you, Swit, it's something different. I get the feeling you're attracted to . . . innocence." Switters's pursuit of innocence does not change as a result of the action in the story, but his definition of it does.

Switters's considerations about beauty help to alter his definition of innocence. Early in the story, Maestra explains "the six qualities that distinguish the human from the subhuman." Those are "humor, imagination, eroticism . . . spirituality, rebelliousness, and Aesthetics, an appreciation of beauty for its own sake." She goes on to observe, however, that many so-called humans are subhuman in their lack of one or more of the qualities. Switters, who shares her high standards, considers the innocent and the pure to be beautiful. However, until he meets Masked Beauty, he misses some of the subtler implications of beauty. He explains to her that beginning in the late 1980s, "socio-political dullards had chopped up beauty and fed it to the dogs . . . on grounds ranging from its lack of pragmatic social application to the notion that it was somehow unfair to that and those who were by beauty's standards, ugly." The abbess argues that beauty is purposeless and indeed it does oppress the plain and give the beautiful "a false sense of superiority." Switters disagrees with her, but when she removes her veil, and he sees her septuagenarian's face is beautiful, yet marked with an ugly wart, he considers her point of view. Once a beautiful young woman, she had prayed for the mar on her beauty because her beauty was "a distraction for others and an onus" for herself. By the time

Masked Beauty, much later in the story, allows that perhaps she should have accepted her beauty as a gift from God, Switters has developed a more sophisticated and encompassing view about beauty. What he had once thought of as beautiful might be "just too goddamn vivid."

◆ CHARACTERS ◆

Switters considers himself to be a "free man," as in the Hindu quotation that opens the first part of the book. When Maestra accuses him of not liking animals, he denies it, saying, "It's cages I dislike. Cages and leashes and hobbles and halters. It's the taming I dislike . . . domesticity shrinks the soul of the beast." To Switters, dogmatism is the same as cages, leashes, hobbles, and halters. He refuses to be bogged down in absolutes. Robbins uses Switters, a self-styled "absurdist," to illustrate both the conflict between good and evil and the quest for enlightenment central to the book. When approached from a dogmatic perspective, Switters easily could be viewed as a drug-using pederast who disrespects the sanctity of a nun's vocation. But Switters has rules about drug use, and in a confused manner, about women as well.

First, he sees there are drugs that expand one's ego and drugs that cause revelations. He limits his use to the revelatory kinds, because he favors "awe over swagger." So, his rules about drug use are fairly clear; his pursuit of girls, rather than women, is not so clear.

Without any doubt, Switters breaks a taboo of Western culture by lusting after girls, rather than women. Indeed he is obsessed with the idea of femininity: one of his points of pride is that he knows "the word for vagina in seventy-one separate languages." However, he ponders the reasons why in particular he prefers the young ones, at one point hypothesizing that it is because "they [give] off the organic equivalent, the biological equivalent . . . of new-car smell." Yet, when presented with an opportunity to consummate his urges for stepsister Suzy, he cannot. He desires youth not as much as he desires innocence and purity.

His pursuits, then, of both Suzy and of Sister Domino Thiry, represent a quest for innocence. Bobby Case, who shares his predilection for girls, warns him against his longing for Suzy, reminding him of the cultural taboo. "Our girls are culturally unprepared for . . . emotional *intricacies* . . . I know you wouldn't want to muddy her sweet waters." Switters reluctantly agrees. Yet when faced with someone his own age, like the Peruvian Gloria, he thinks she is "a tad old for his specialized taste."

Switters flashes back to time he spent in Bangkok (a city notorious for child prostitution) "in the company of an actual adolescent." It is unclear what happens between the two, but it is clear that Switters understands his own cultural taboos about the young girl, even if they are not shared by her culture. "He bought her a new silk dress, jeans, and a compact disk player. Then he put her on a bus back to her native village with six thousand dollars . . . her brief career as a whore over." He goes on to explain that she will experience no shame, since sexual shame in the way that Westerners experience it does not exist in Thailand. "Not much given to self-analysis," Switters does not stop to consider the contradictions in his own beliefs and behaviors. Switters says, "I think sex *is* filthy and nasty—and I can't get enough of it." Bobby Case responds, "Paradox! . . . or we could say that innocence and nastiness enjoy a symbiotic relationship." "It is a matter of cultural context," they conclude.

No matter how the reader may feel about this taboo, Robbins, via Switters, does his best to justify it. He reasons that "Ancient Greeks had a concept they called 'eating the taboo,'" in which men would "deliberately break any and all of their culture's prevailing taboos in order to loosen their hold, destroy their power . . . a casting out of demons." Bobby Case is not convinced. "I sure hope Hell has wheelchair access," he tells Switters.

However, Switters's conversations with Masked Beauty and Sister Domino Thiry expand his views of what is beautiful and pure. When Switters finds himself to be attracted to Sister Domino, who is his own age, he surprises himself. At first, though, Sister Domino does not appear to reciprocate and suggests that he might want to be with Fannie, the randy nun. "She's not so bad," he says, "for a woman her age." But when, almost by accident, he becomes involved with Sister Domino Thiry, he notices only her beauty.

Without a doubt, Switters inherits his irreverence from his very modern grandmother who, before he is two, insists that he call her, "Maestra," lest she be known by "one of those declasse G words, like granny or grams or gramma." Maestra, as "tough as a plastic steak," very obviously influences the way Switters speaks, which Robbins calls "overly flowery, formal speech but always done tongue-in-cheek." Maestra is instrumental in one of the critical coincidences of the story. She tells Switters, "I did intercept an e-mail message in which you promised little Suzy you were gonna take her 'all the way to grandma's house.'" By blackmailing him, Maestra coerces Switters to take her parrot, Sailor Boy, to Peru with him, thus beginning the chain of coincidences that lead Switters to his starship and on to Syria and the Vatican.

Maestra, whose name, she tells Switters, in Italian means "teacher," or "master," acts as a guide for Switters, the external superego to Switters's lustful id. Her not-so-gentle reminders cause him to learn to balance good and evil, to distinguish for himself between freedom and license. Maestra serves, perhaps, as a spirited representative of the mainstream American opinion. "This business with little Suzy is not funny," she warns him. "It's sick. What's more, it's criminally prosecutable." Unfortunately, it turns out that Maestra's hacking has gotten her in trouble. Such technology expertise might be considered unusual for a senior citizen, but as she tells Switters, it is "easy as pie. Child's play." As a result of the stress related to her conviction in a hacking case, Maestra has a stroke, and although she is not paralyzed, her speech becomes slurred. Thus, she won't see Switters until she recovers, because he would "try to take advantage of my vocal impediment to win his first argument with me in thirty years." Switters learns from her attorneys, before he departs for Syria and meets the *real* blue nude, that she is bankrupt. He agrees that she should sell Matisse's blue nude (which she owns and has willed to him), in order to finance her recovery. His agreement to sell one thing he considers beautiful helps him to reconsider his entire concept of beauty.

Switters's one "bosom buddy" and meditation teacher is "no Thai monk or Himalayan sage ... [but] a CIA pilot from Hondo, Texas, by the name of Bobby Case, known to some as Bad Bobby and to others as Nut Case." Since Switters keeps in touch with him by e-mail during all of his journeys and detours, Bobby Case as a character acts to further the plot. His advice to Switters, and Switters's responses, ties together Seattle, Syria, and Peru. In the end, information he learns about Switters's trip to Peru and the resulting shaman's spell is enough to propel Case down to Peru to rescue Switters from the sentence of a permanent ride in the "starship." Case understands how to help Switters because the two have in common "a cynical suspicion of politico-eco-nomic systems and a disdain for what passed for 'patriotism' in the numbed noodles of the manipulated masses ... and that they actually believed in freedom." Like Switters, Bobby Case embraces all the contradictions of the true free men.

Thanks to R. Potney Smithe, Switters survives the shaman's curse. A cultural ethnographer who is studying the Kandakandero Indians, Smithe claims to be an objective observer and documenter of behavior who longs for a second audience with the shaman, End of Time. Switters disapproves of Smithe's science, claiming that it exploits the natives and that his objectivity is "as big a hoax in science as it is in journalism." But he is impressed with Smithe's vocabulary and his entreaty. When the Indians hear the parrot Sailor Boy repeat his stock phrase, "People of zee wurl, relax," Smithe translates it, and having heard of the bird, End of Time summons Switters. At first, Switters is reluctant to go, wanting just to release the bird and get out of "South too-goddamned-vivid America." Thus, Smithe entreats Switters, "I've boiled my pudding in this bleeding hole for five bleeding months, petitioning, pleading, flattering, bribing, doing everything short of dropping on all fours ... to win another interview with End of Time, and you come along ... oblivious ... and fall into it." So Switters makes his fateful journey, agreeing to take notes for Smithe. But when Smithe comes back the next day to retrieve him, eagerly awaiting details about End of Time, he meets his end. Since End of Time placed a curse on Smithe as well, Switters asks him to test it, to see if the curse is "for real." When Smithe tests it, he finds that indeed it is. Thus, as the Kandakandero says, "this mister is very, very dead." Smithe represents the kind of dogmatic rule-follower that Switters (and evidently Robbins) dislikes. He meets his just end in service of the principal theme of the book.

End of Time, or (depending on the translator) Today is Tomorrow, plays a relatively small part, but his role is critical in the formulation of the plot. This leader with a head in the shape of a pyramid analyzes the superiority of white men and thinks he has found their mysterious power in laughter. Since his fellow Indians "don't know from funny," he decides that his people must "fashion shields out of laughter" to "withstand the assault of the white man." But although he may be deficient in regard to humor, End of Time knows secrets about the universe to reveal to Switters. These revelations are so startling that Switters cannot put all of them into words. And the cost of these revelations, according to Switters, is "henceforth I must never allow my feet to touch the ground . . . and if I ever do . . . I will instantly fall over dead." End of Time's curse leads Switters to contemplate the meaning of enlightenment. Much later, he remembers a guru who likens the state of enlightenment to "orbiting the earth from a height of two inches," which for practical reasons is what he must do on his stilts or in his wheelchair. Furthermore, when Switters considers the third prophecy of Fatima—that the salvation of mankind will come from somewhere other than the church—together with the secrets revealed by End of Time, he is able to hypothesize that mankind's salvation will come from the Amazonian Indians. Thus, End of Time serves to lead Switters to enlightenment.

Suzy is the daughter of Switters's stepfather, not a biological sister, but closely enough related and young enough to be off limits, or taboo. Switters views her as "a freshly budded embodiment of the feminine archetype . . . a glimmer of primal Eve." Suzy's fascination with the Virgin Mary and the prophecy of Fatima leads Switters to assist her in the research she needs for a term paper. Coincidentally, this research proves extremely helpful to Switters

later at the convent. He ponders the nature of "Marian fantasies of healthy girls," observing that like the love of horses, those fantasies, "tend to wane . . . once they become sexually active." He attributes Suzy's fascination with Mary to her "status as Super Virgin," despairing that this "casts a monstrously mixed message—motherhood is divine, sex a sin." Switters tries to urge Suzy toward writing a daring thesis, but she just wants to "write [the story] down for everybody." Switters lies and says he is not disappointed. Suzy's lack of sophistication makes her an unchallenging conversationalist. Switters wonders, before she walks in and discovers that he has lied to her and that he can really walk, what right he has "to teach her *anything*?" Suzy as a character exists in order for Switters to learn the difference between being innocent and *too innocent*. At the end, Switters must decide between Sister Domino Thiry or Suzy. "He loved them both. He wanted them both. It was only natural. He was Switters." Although the narrator does not reveal the answer, Switters's greater sophistication and his deeper understanding of what is pure and beautiful make it unlikely that he chooses Suzy.

Switters's first words to Sister Domino Thiry are "I love you." A French nun who grew up in the United States, Sister Domino provides the very combination of innocence and experience that Switters seems to crave, "a woman who would stick to your ribs." After she rescues him from heat stroke in the Syrian Desert, he observes that "she was older than her voice and mannerisms had led him to believe. Older, but no less sparkling of eye." When he compliments her "I am most taken with . . . your eyes," he finds her response "refreshing" since she does not protest at all. "Tonight they are ruined. But as a rule, they *are* my nicest feature." In their discussions about the origins of the convent, she asks him about his knowledge of nuns, and his response to her is a clue to the reader about the advancement of theme involving the pursuit of innocence. "Nun . . . is an old Coptic Christian word meaning *pure*." Switters is charmed by her near-grasp of the English language. "Don't try to butter me off," she tells him. Another time she explains that her English vocabulary is coming back "like the swallows to San Juan Cappuccino." Further, Sister Domino's name explains one of the book's mysteries: When the name John Foster Dulles is mentioned—which occurs frequently in the text—Switters and Bobby Case spit on the ground. Coincidentally, the nun got the nickname while she lived in the United States during the Cold War. Dulles used the term "Domino Theory," according to Switters, "to hoodwink the American public into supporting our criminal war against Vietnam." Switters says "don't remind me" when she asks if he understands the origin. Sister Domino sets in motion Switters's domino effect of a deeper understanding and appreciation of innocence and beauty.

It astounds Switters to learn that Masked Beauty, the abbess of the Syrian convent, was the model for Matisse's blue nude, the very painting that hangs in Maestra's living room. His fascination with the blue nude foreshadows Switters's auspicious arrival at the convent. He describes the painting this way: "Matisses's nude was nude but not really naked . . . she was far from brazen. . . . In her way, she was more innocent than Suzy, wiser than Maestra; a woman such as Switters had never known nor would ever know—or so he thought." The blue nude becomes symbolic to Switters of the perfect woman, innocent, yet wise, naked, but not ashamed. When he meets Masked Beauty, he debates the nature of beauty with her, and he assists her in her research project about birth control, Fatima, and the world's religions. Masked Beauty argues

"much of the poverty, violence, addiction, ignorance, mental illness, pollution, and climate changes plaguing human kind in general" has "roots in careless or coerced reproduction." As a result of his debates with Masked Beauty (and her niece, Domino Thiry), he no longer finds it so easy to consider wisdom and purity to be exclusionary. Thus, Switters gains a deeper understanding of the nature of beauty and of innocence.

◆ TECHNIQUES ◆

At the beginning of *Fierce Invalids Home from Hot Climates*, the narrator takes a break from narration to comment on technique, saying, "[n]ow, it appears that this prose account has unintentionally begun in partial mimicry of the mind." Here Robbins reveals a technique he has used in every novel, a stream-of-conscious narrative. Almost every one of his novels is told in the third person, using what one reviewer has called a "single omniscient meta-narrator . . . a device [that] allows him to take the reader on a spiritual journey." This narrator-as-guru helps Robbins to develop a theme common to all his novels: the quest for enlightenment.

If, according to the narrator in *Fierce Invalids Home from Hot Climates*, the mark of enlightenment is laughter, then another technique Robbins uses might also develop this idea. Figurative language and wordplay in general decorate Robbins's prose. Strong (if unorthodox) images abound from similes and metaphors. The reader pictures the gelatinous "cool as clam aspic" air of Seattle, or sees Maestra's eyes "like the apertures through which Tabasco droplets enter the world." He speaks of turtles that weigh "as much as a wheelbarrow load of cabbages" and describes "heavy-lidded caimans [that] did Robert Mitchum imitations, seeming at once slow and sinister and stoned." Robbins can take a common word apart and make a joke of it, as in, "a view that was all pan and no orama." Switters orders food from a Thai restaurant, remarking that the names of the dishes sound like "a harelip pleading for a package of thumbtacks." Another time, a group of clouds is compared to "a herd of white-trash shoppers just crawled out of shacks and sheds and trailer homes for the end-of-winter sale at Wal-Mart." Although some of the word play is extreme, even scatological ("If innocence was toilet tissue, Godzilla could have wiped his butt with Switters's smile"), the effect is usually humorous, keeping the reader on the brink of enlightenment throughout the story.

Also at the beginning of this novel, the narrator hints at plot, saying this, "is probably not the way in which an effective narrative ought properly to unfold—not even in these days when the world is showing signs of awakening from its linear trance." *Fierce Invalids Home from Hot Climates* is one of Robbins's most carefully plotted novels, but even a somewhat linear progression of events does not cause Robbins to shy away from tangents. On a discourse about bats, he discusses the winged creatures, explaining that women are afraid of bats because the creatures can become entangled in their hair. From the topic of bats, he further deviates to the notion that St. Paul decreed that women's heads must be covered in church "because of the angels," which, like bats, have wings. He explains, "In Paul's era, words for *angel* and *demon* were interchangeable." From here he continues his discourse of the "line between cowboy and angel," which, he says, is "no wider than an alfalfa sprout." So Robbins connects these tangents thematically with the rest of the story. His willingness to deviate from the Western, linear notion of the progression of a story is proof of Robbins's

own study of and appreciation for Eastern literary techniques, which tend to be more circuitous.

◆ LITERARY PRECEDENTS ◆

The title of *Fierce Invalids Home from Hot Climates* comes from Arthur Rimbaud's farewell-to-literature poem, "A Season in Hell" (1872). In addition, other relationships to Rimbaud's work and his life exist in Robbins's novel. One critic cited lines from "The Drunken Boat": "If there is one water in Europe I want, / it is the black cold pool / where into the scented twilight / a child squatting full of sadness / launches a boat frail as a butterfly in May." This verse is evocative of Switters's paper boat races with the "art girls." Further, the notion of the main character whose feet cannot touch the ground may relate to Rimbaud's life story. Rimbaud's leg cancer and Switters's curse from the shaman, End of Time, both cause them to be carried around, "two inches off the ground." Judging from the book's title, the possible relationship to "the Drunken Boat" and the resemblance between Switters's and Rimbaud's plights, one may, at the very least, assume that Robbins was reading Rimbaud at the time he wrote his novel.

Robbins's style of writing, with its plays on words and non-linear storytelling may seem unique to the modern reader. However, stream-of-consciousness narration in this vividly descriptive style—particularly with the picturesque subject matter—is seen in Henry Miller's work. Books such as *The Tropic of Cancer* show similarly non-linear and intensely descriptive storylines. In addition, Robbins's work has been compared—in terms of plot and Eastern influence—with that of J. D. Salinger; both writers create stories that are difficult to summarize, in which the whole is somehow greater than the sum of its parts. In interviews, Robbins has said that among his influences are Thomas Pynchon (specifically, his *Mason & Dixon*), Franz Kafka, Gabriel Garcia Marquez, and Vladimir Nabokov.

◆ RELATED TITLES ◆

Tom Robbins's first novel, *Another Roadside Attraction,* was published in 1971. Although the hardcover release was not a great success, the book became a cult classic. In fact, one of Elvis Presley's close associates claimed Elvis had been reading it at the time of his death. This novel is the story of two young hippies and their encounters with the more mainstream American culture around them, a contrast revisited in *Fierce Invalids Home from Hot Climates*. Similar elements include experimentation with drugs and the irreverent subplot involving the Roman Catholic Church, only the irreverence in *Another Roadside Attraction* involves a botched Second Coming and a corpse at a roadside zoo.

Robbins's second novel, *Even Cowgirls Get the Blues,* published in 1976, is best known for its 1994 film adaptation by director Gus Van Sant. Actress Uma Thurman stars as Sissy Hankshaw, who is born in a small town with an extra-large thumb. Sissy hitchhikes from Virginia to Manhattan then to "the Dakota Badlands," where she meets Bonanza Jellybean, the lesbian cowgirls of the Rubber Rose Ranch, and Dr. Robbins, her reality instructor. The film received poor reviews, but like *Another Roadside Attraction*, the paperback garnered a strong cult following. In *Even Cowgirls Get the Blues,* Robbins shows his strong tendency for tangential rants, this time about yams, yin & yang, and whooping cranes. Although his attempts to combine the many tangents of the story are similar to his efforts in *Fierce Invalids Home from a Hot Climate*, in *Even Cowgirls Get the Blues*, this effort is less successful. Although the book is humorous and appreciated by real Robbins fans, it is not one of his best.

Still-Life with Woodpecker (1980) is one of the most widely-read of Robbins novels. This complex love story takes place inside a package of Camel cigarettes. Here also, Robbins begins his fixation on "neoteny," or staying young. The tangents, or "interludes," as they are called in the novel, continue in this book somewhat more successfully, explaining the difference between criminals and outlaws and the problem with redheads. Robbins makes a reference to the woodpecker bomber in *Fierce Invalids Home from Hot Climates* when he describes the sounds of End of Time's laughter: "Sounds a lot like Woody Woodpecker. Friend of mine used to cackle like that."

Robbins's fourth novel, *Jitterbug Perfume* (1984) is an epic that begins in ancient times and ends at "nine o'clock tonight, Paris time." The hero, "neotenous" ancient king-turned-janitor and his love, Kudra, travel through time, never aging because they refuse to let age catch up with them. The story continues Robbins's fascination with youth, expanding it to include living forever. Fewer tangents and an exciting storyline (the janitor and his love are in search of an ancient bottle with a priceless fluid that may be leaking out) make this a very readable epic.

In *Skinny Legs and All* (1990), the reader must suspend disbelief long enough to accept the notion of a group of objects (a stick, a shell, a spoon, a sock, and a can of Van De Camp's baked beans) having discovered the secret to movement. They travel to New York, where they find a restaurant run by an Arab and a Jew across from the United Nations. The story is another in the tradition of *Another Roadside Attraction*, offering commentary on the popular culture and the issues of the day by contrasting them with fantastical counterculture elements.

Robbins's *Half Asleep in Frog Pajamas,* released in 1994, chronicles the 1987 crash of the stock market. Told in second person point of view, it is the most traditional of Robbins's novels, if traditional means the protagonist chasing her boyfriend's lost monkey, having a 300-pound Tarot card-reading friend, and finding enlightenment with a terrorist. Robbins's writing style here remains appealingly chatty and metaphoric, but it is more refined than his previous works, leading to the most sophisticated of his novels, *Fierce Invalids Home from Hot Climates.*

◆ IDEAS FOR GROUP DISCUSSIONS ◆

Because of its concern with good and evil, *Fierce Invalids Home from Hot Climates* lends itself well to discussions about morality. Since Switters can be viewed as part-hero and part-rogue, debate about the nature of the change he undergoes in the story may ensue.

1. The principal theme of *Fierce Invalids Home from Hot Climates* is good versus evil, or in this case that good is the same thing as evil. Since the singular notions of good and evil govern the popular idea of morality, can Switters (who believes in this duality) have a moral sense? Identify specific ways this sense is shown in his behavior.

2. Critics have complained that Switters's views show "contempt for the citizens and institutions of modern democracies." What evidence supports or contradicts this statement?

3. Switters thinks that "[t]he stiff-witted and academic seem not to comprehend that it is entirely possible to be ironic and sincere at the same instant; that a knowing tongue in cheek does not necessarily preclude an affectionate glow in the heart." Is he correct? Are there times when it is not appropriate to be "tongue-in-cheek" or ironic? If so, what set of rules should one use to decide?

4. If enlightenment comes from recognizing the contradictions in life and finding joy in them, which characters in the novel are enlightened or become enlightened, and which do not? What process enlightens them?

Heidi R. Moore
Northern Virginia Community College

FLAUBERT'S PARROT

Novel

1984

Author: Julian Barnes

◆

◆ SOCIAL CONCERNS ◆

Though certainly concerned with social issues of the time, the concerns of *Flaubert's Parrot* affect relatively few people. Rather than worry about issues of race, ethnicity, gender or class division, Barnes, with a flamboyance which betrays a faith in Oscar Wilde's aphorism about art being useless, considers various ethical issues pertaining to the related (but not synonymous) tasks of reading and literary criticism. What, Barnes asks in various ways, should be the relationship between a reader and his or her favorite author, or a critic and his or her favorite victim?

Flaubert's Parrot chronicles an amateur scholar's attempt to solve mysteries about his favorite author, nineteenth-century French novelist Gustave Flaubert. Geoffrey Braithwaite, a doctor by trade, tries to answer an innocuous question: Which of two stuffed parrots actually sat on Flaubert's desk while he composed a story in which a parrot played a crucial role? In the course of answering this question (or not answering it), he encounters other professional scholars who variously pay Flaubert too much and too little respect. Barnes suggests that either task causes problems for the casual reader.

One social concern *Flaubert's Parrot* explores is the capacity of literary criticism to destroy the beauty of a work in its attempt to expand the public's understanding of it. Chapter VI opens with the rather ominous sentence, "Let me tell you why I hate critics." The narrator's ire toward academicians is focused narrowly on a single woman, Dr. Enid Starkie. Braithwaite is flabbergasted by her claim that Flaubert was inconsistent in describing the eyes of *Madame Bovary's* protagonist. Starkie claims that they are variously described as brown, black and blue. Braithwaite counters her assertion with the observation that this variation is Flaubert's point; Emma Bovary's eyes had the mesmerizing quality of shifting color as the men who gazed at her changed their vantage points. Dr. Starkie has, in Braithwaite's opinion, committed the sin of becoming too close to her subject. Casual readers, he asserts, are able to forget an author's small errors and inconsistencies and maintain their admiration for the overall quality of the author's work. Professional scholarship, Barnes suggests, perverts the relationship between reader and writer, creating a mercenary exchange instead of one based on a mutual love of literature.

Perhaps the social concern that garners the greatest share of attention is the inability of scholarship to ever fully document a life or solve a literary mystery. The problem, Barnes suggests, is not that individual researchers like Dr. Starkie will make mistakes, but that research into an author's life will, invariably, lead the scholar astray. This, clearly, is not a social concern of the same urgency as the failure of ethnic groups to reconcile differences and live in peace, but, to the lover of literature, it is significant. How, Barnes' narrator wonders, can so many men and women make a living from the study of an author's life and still fail to answer important questions? Barnes demonstrates this failure in part by giving multiple accounts of Flaubert's life—each valid but contradictory. Chapter II, for example, contains three chronologies of Flaubert's life, each from his birth in 1821 to his death in 1880. The first could be called the official version, presenting the man's accomplishments without calling attention to his embarrassments. The second is the inverse of the first, citing the same years but recounting only deaths, failures, and transgressions. The third consists wholly of Flaubert's own words: diary entries, letters, etc. Though attempting, by moving from different vantage points, to come closer to the author, this experiment only highlights the failure of any chronology, biography, or critical work to capture the complete artist. Each version seems to claim objective truth, but in juxtaposition with the other two, each seems inadequate.

What Barnes seems to advocate is the kind of research done by his narrator. Braithwaite never ceases to wear his heart on his sleeve. His love for Flaubert's work is ever-present; his desire to see the author in the best light, though often overwhelmed by the enormity of his subject's callousness, is never denied. Furthermore, Braithwaite uses his journey into Flaubert's life as an opportunity for telling the story of his own life. It seems as though Barnes suggests that a scholar's life will invariably emerge in

any assessment of an artist. The narrator of *Flaubert's Parrot*, at least, does not attempt to deny this fact.

◆ THEMES ◆

The most pervasive theme of *Flaubert's Parrot* is the nature of love, whether for a book, an author, or a spouse. The narrator, Braithwaite, simultaneously loves all three. Barnes, through Braithwaite, explores how unreciprocated love affects the lover and his view of the beloved. There are profound psychological consequences, in the world of Barnes' novel, for adoring anyone or anything that cannot return such affection.

Obviously, any one who would dedicate the time to amateur literary scholarship that Braithwaite does must be deeply enamored of his subject. The retired doctor makes many trips across the English Channel to root around in Flaubert's hometown, to revisit his haunts, hoping for some new insight. Love of an author and his books becomes, for Braithwaite, akin to obsession. It seems as though once committed to the task of finding out more about this intriguing French novelist, Braithwaite is unable to stop. He remarks, "if you love a writer, if you depend upon the drip-feed of his intelligence, if you want to pursue him and find him—despite edicts to the contrary—then it's impossible to know too much. You seek the vice as well." Love for an author works in a way similar to the cliched notion of romantic love; it accepts completely, good and ill. Braithwaite, it seems, is in love with Flaubert the author. Whatever he may have been in person, whatever ill-treatment he may have doled out to his friends and lovers, Braithwaite can see only the beauty of his writing. He defends the long-dead novelist at every turn. In Chapter X, for example, he lists all of Flaubert's most commonly cited faults, then tirelessly defends him on every count. His defenses are sometimes impassioned, sometimes ludicrous: "3 *That he didn't believe in progress.* I cite the twentieth century in his defence."

This unfailing dedication to defend a loved one is carried over, by Braithwaite, to his account of his wife's life and death. Barnes demonstrates the relationship between literary and romantic love by drawing parallels between his narrator's love of his favorite dead author and of his dead wife. Ellen, who Braithwaite claims to have loved absolutely, did not reciprocate his love any more than Flaubert does. She led a separate, private life of affairs which were only crudely concealed. Her infidelity widened the space between them, making Braithwaite unsure that he knew the woman he loved. Her inner life "lay in the . . . inner chamber of her heart, inaccessible to me." Authors' lives, Barnes asserts, are unknowable; so too, however, are the lives of those closest to us.

One of Flaubert's anecdotes, repeated numerous times by Braithwaite, involves a pair of boys planning to visit a brothel. They discuss and prepare for the excursion but never actually visit the house of ill-repute. This, Braithwaite says, is a perfect example of desire in its purest form: the never-attained, long-anticipated something remains always just beyond reach. That yearned-for something about a lover or an author, which will never be possessed fully, and never known completely is, Barnes' work suggests, what fuels love.

Barnes also considers the nature of memory. This theme is important because it demonstrates possible, psychological reasons for the failure of literary inquiry, one of his primary social concerns. He suggests that the impossibility of writing complete histories or biographies becomes apparent when one recognizes the impossibility of fully categorizing one's own memories. The past is always irretrievable, whether the past one seeks is in an archive or one's own mind. The reason, Barnes suggests, for the failure of memory is its subjectivity: every memory is one's own, individual version of the story. Thus, his narrator concludes, "history is merely another literary genre: the past is autobiographical fiction pretending to be a parliamentary report." Remembering is itself a creative act, as is reconstructing another person's past. The past cannot be related journalistically but only as an imaginative act.

To demonstrate this, Barnes' narrator enters into a kind of debate. Throughout Chapter X Braithwaite defends Flaubert from a list of charges. In each case he cites documentary evidence to show that Flaubert was not, as his critics claim, a reprehensible man. Such a documentary defense, however, does not hold up to Braithwaite's own imaginative capacity. Chapter XI, aptly titled "Louise Colet's Version" is an imagined narrative in Colet's, one of Flaubert's longtime mistresses, voice. Braithwaite, who imagines her ambiguous verdict on her often indifferent lover, is clearly not satisfied with the empirical data he has collected to defend his favorite author. Such information only challenges the version of Flaubert's life which Braithwaite, as a dedicated fan, has already settled upon. Whether Flaubert was a saint or a demon depends more on who answers the question than does any definitive fact of his life.

◆ CHARACTERS ◆

Dr. Geoffrey Braithwaite is the protagonist and narrator of *Flaubert's Parrot*. He is an elderly Englishman, a retired doctor, and a widower. Each of these aspects of his person is relatively important for Barnes' book. He moves between roles as teller of tales, relater of encyclopedic information, and bereaved husband. He is at various moments erudite, funny, and sad.

His character's most important development is related to Barnes' concern with the
uses and usage of literary inquiry. At the
opening, Braithwaite is in awe of Flaubert.
He views the long-dead author with a kind
of reverence. His stance toward scholarly
research is also, in the novel's opening pages,
fairly orthodox. Faced with a dilemma in
the shape of conflicting claims of the two
parrots' authenticity, Braithwaite delves into
archives, writes to experts, and rereads primary sources in an effort to answer defini-
tively a question about a parrot's authenticity. By the novel's end, however, he comes
to accept the impossibility of ever knowing
fully which, if either, of the two birds actually sat on Flaubert's desk. He comes to this
conclusion in part through his confessions
about his wife's affairs. He realizes that he
continues to love her in spite of her death
and in spite of what she kept from him.
Why then, he asks, can he not leave Flaubert
what he keeps hidden? In the end he can
satisfy himself with what "was an answer
and not an answer . . . an ending and not an
ending." His faith in and love for the author
allow him to give up a pursuit which consumed a great deal of his energy.

Braithwaite has a foil named Ed Winterton,
an elderly, failing scholar who Braithwaite
meets by chance. Both the professional and
the amateur biographer reach for the same
rare book one day, and though their interests lie with different authors (Winterton is
working on a biography of the English man
of letters, Sir Edmund William Gosse), they
feel an immediate kinship. Winterton's commitment to dredging for information on his
author's life is at once more mercenary and
more noble than Braithwaite's. Though he
searches out biographical minutiae for professional gain—whereas Braithwaite does
it for sheer joy—Winterton demonstrates
an ethical standard far above Braithwaite's.

About a year after their first meeting,
Winterton sends Braithwaite a letter in which
he claims to have uncovered letters by
Flaubert concerning Juliet Herbert, one-time
lover and possible fiancee of the French
novelist. Braithwaite is overcome with delight and agrees to meet Winterton. The
professional scholar tells the amateur one
some of the details of the letters (which he
came across by chance), then mentions that
he had burned them, in accordance with
the wishes Flaubert expressed in the letters.
Braithwaite is shocked and concludes "the
man was a maniac, that much was plain."
Quickly, though, that much becomes less
plain. Winterton counters Braithwaite's indignation by asking, "if your business is
writers, you have to behave towards them
with integrity, don't you?" Thus, Winterton
represents the moral scholar, the rare dig-
ger into a writer's papers who will read all
but share nothing the author asked not to
have shared. He is, then, the opposite both
of Braithwaite, who is so fueled (at this
point in the novel) by his obsession for
answers that he would secure them at all
hazards, and of Dr. Starkie, who fails to
consider the author's intentions, thoughts,
or feelings. For the most part, Barnes presents Winterton's decision in a positive light.
Perhaps, the passage suggests, all the discoveries made in letters, manuscripts, and
novels kept against an author's expressed
intent imperil the author's right to control
the destiny of his or her own text. Through
Winterton, Barnes raises a question, which
is never fully answered, about whether the
reader or the writer owns a piece of literature.

It is not surprising that in a novel about
an individual's effort to make sense of an
author's life the author becomes an important character. Though he does not take
part in the action, Flaubert's personality is
considered and developed through the
course of the novel. The book opens by
presenting the author, literally, on a pedes-
tal; in the opening scene Braithwaite stands
contemplating his statue. By the book's conclusion, the reader knows much more about

Flaubert than just his successes. Not only his failures but also his most embarrassing moments are recounted. Furthermore, Barnes takes imaginative flights of fancy when he speculates on what Flaubert, his friends, and his lovers might have meant to and thought of one another. The Flaubert Barnes creates as a character is certainly not entirely accurate. Neither, however, is the Flaubert created by official biographers.

The author's friends and lovers also insinuate themselves into the narrative and become fully-fledged characters. Flaubert's close friend, photographer Maxime du Camp, becomes something of a shadow to Flaubert. It seems that with every unpleasant story Braithwaite uncovers, du Camp appears again, somehow colluding in Flaubert's excesses. The most notable example revolves around the pair's trip to Egypt and the Orient, a trip which may have cost Flaubert the love of Louise Colet, a poet and his long-time mistress.

What caused the fracture between Colet and Flaubert, though, is, like all trivia of literary lives, unknowable. Colet does, however, become something of a living, breathing character through Braithwaite's imaginative attempts to document her life with Flaubert. As noted above, Chapter XI is entirely in her voice, rather in Braithwaite's imagined version of her voice. She emphasizes the fact that the final version of an author's life is invariably affected by the stature of those around that author. Colet's literary career has been derided, Barnes suggests, because she drew the personal scorn of so lofty a figure as Flaubert.

◆ TECHNIQUES ◆

Barnes' most useful technique for making *Flaubert's Parrot* a success is his blending of scholarly and entertaining elements. The novel is alternately funny, sad, and encyclopedic. Long discussions of Flaubert's

body of work and literary connections are relieved by Braithwaite's sad confessions regarding his wife and his hilarious tendency to poke fun at academics, his countrymen and himself.

Barnes' brand of humor is rather unorthodox. The humor in *Flaubert's Parrot* is closer to Thomas Pynchon's than to humorist Dave Barry's. Barnes demands of his reader a substantial understanding and knowledge of literary history. More specifically, Barnes' ideal reader is one with a love of French literature who understands the nuances in his discussion of Flaubert's life and foils.

Barnes clearly knows the annals of French literature. His ability to weave his clearly extensive research of Flaubert's life and work into the narrative is one of his most important talents. *Flaubert's Parrot* reads like fiction but educates as exceptional literary history. Flaubert's travels with du Camp, his relationship to the realists who followed in his wake, and the triumphs and tribulations of his personal life are all recorded in fine detail. Significantly, though, these biographical scraps of information are not catalogued, not related in a dry, academic manner. Instead they are sprinkled through the text, constantly teasing the reader with trivia, inviting deeper research.

◆ LITERARY PRECEDENTS ◆

Flaubert's Parrot fits into a long tradition of metafiction, that is, fiction which radically departs from the norms of narrative and which is often concerned with the nature of fiction. It also shares two of its primary concerns, the impossibility of memory and the nature of literary criticism, with many prominent pieces of literature. Many novels work, like Barnes', to educate the reader about how and why literature works even while it attempts to entertain.

James Baldwin's short story "Sonny's Blues" (1965) tells the tale of an African-American math teacher and his brother, a jazz pianist and a recovering junky. The story is not told in the usual straightforward narrative manner; instead, it jumps from the past to the future to the present, moving in an improvisational style akin to the aesthetics of jazz. It thus reflects, in its form, the content. In this way, Baldwin's story, like Barnes' novel, reveals a great deal about the nature of fiction. Baldwin's message is similar to Barnes in that both authors assert that texts are inherently unable to fully capture an individual.

More prominent examples of metafiction come from James Joyce, who constantly experimented with the form of his work. His masterpiece, *Ulysses* (1922) relates the events of a single story in a constantly shifting style. Each chapter adopts a different literary mode. Joyce, then, introduces alternate methods for presenting narrative material in close juxtaposition, allowing the reader to assess their relative strengths and weaknesses. In his final chapter, Joyce presents a prolonged narrative in stream of consciousness. This form, one free of punctuation, attempts to mimic the flow of an individual's thoughts. It attempts, as Barnes' narrator does, to recover experience and memory.

In Barnes' blending of encyclopedic detail and a compelling story, he is clearly indebted to what many consider the great American novel, Herman Melville's *Moby Dick* (1851). Like *Flaubert's Parrot, Moby Dick* is a historical catalogue and a novel in one. Instead of recounting details of literary history, however, Melville's book gives the reader every piece of information he or she might ever want about nineteenth-century whaling vessels.

Barnes' thematic concerns also have noble predecessors. His fascination with memory recalls Marcel Proust's masterpiece *In Search of Lost Time* (1927). This enormous book (actually a collection of six volumes) details the memories inspired by an innocuous experience. It meditates on what memory loses and the importance of the small details it retains. Proust dwells on minute events such as turning down a bed or biting into a cookie to demonstrate that these moments, lost to memoirs or journals, are essential aspects of life's pleasure.

Braithwaite's antipathy for literary critics echoes sentiments expressed in many earlier works. One succinct example can be found in Marianne Moore's poem "Poetry" (1921). This poem opens with the rather unusual line "I, too, dislike it: there are things that are important beyond all this fiddle." Poetry does not reveal the high truths that critics ascribe to it, Moore suggests. Like Barnes, she is principally enamored of literature because of the joy it brings to the reader.

Similarly, Vladimir Nabakov criticizes the reverence paid to literary critics in his novel *Pale Fire* (1962). The novel, purportedly the work of a critic closely acquainted with a major poet, implies, in its surprise ending, that criticism is in fact fiction. The narrator, who misleads the reader about his knowledge of the poet's life, is no less creative in his writing than other critics who claim authenticity.

◆ RELATED TITLES ◆

Though none of Barnes' other novels continue the journeys of Dr. Geoffrey Braithwaite, many feature the same themes as *Flaubert's Parrot*. Barnes is a prolific author with over ten books to his credit. Any reader who enjoys *Flaubert's Parrot* has a wealth of other material to choose from.

Barnes's most recent work, *England, England* (1999), is one of a handful concerned primarily with his native country. It tells the story of the egotistical mogul Sir Jack Pitman and his effort to rebuild England as a theme park, or, in his words, a "heritage center." The project is planned for the Isle of Wight, just off England's southern coast. The story allows Barnes to parody the efforts of media moguls to make culture accessible and easy to digest.

In 1995 Barnes published another book about England, *Letters from London*. This collection of essays, all originally written for the *New Yorker*, considers many aspects of English life with Barnes' characteristic wit and insight. He discusses the delicacy of relations between the French and English, the people of two nations with a long history of animosity.

Regardless of any ill-feeling his countrymen might have toward the French, Barnes, as demonstrated by *Flaubert's Parrot*, is an unabashed Francophile. Some of his other novels, including *Cross Channel* (1996) and *Talking it Over* (1991) are set in France. In addition to their settings, both books share thematic concerns with *Flaubert's Parrot*. *Cross Channel* dwells on the nature of memory and the impossibility of recovering the past. Where *Flaubert's Parrot* considers the effect of losing the past on literary endeavor, *Cross Channel* considers its effects on individual lives. *Talking it Over* is a twisting, turning tale of adultery. Thus, Barnes addresses again the subject of infidelity begun with the tale of Ellen Braithwaite in *Flaubert's Parrot*.

◆ IDEAS FOR GROUP DISCUSSIONS ◆

Flaubert's Parrot is an exceptionally erudite blend of fiction and literary history. The story of Dr. Braithwaite and a commentary on the life and work of Gustave Flaubert co-exist in a way which makes the work both highly entertaining and enormously informative. It also raises questions (many

more than it answers) about the ethical implications of critiquing either a work of literature or its author's life. Perhaps the biographer does, invariably, do violence to an author's life; perhaps the critic does destroy the vitality of the author's work. Barnes' outlook, however, is not entirely pessimistic; he does not advocate a moratorium on literary scholarship. Instead, he calls the reader's attention to the inadequacy of history and memory, to point out that all writing is, in a way, creative, and that each reader and every writer will interpret books and events differently. The subjective nature of reading is not, to Barnes' mind, a problem, so long as it is recognized.

While concerned with such high-minded topics as the ethics of literary study, *Flaubert's Parrot* also tells a touching story about a marriage gone wrong. This tale of failed love enhances the reader's understanding of how one forms and maintains a relationship with books. The story of Ellen Braithwaite's affairs and death acts, in a way, like an extended metaphor for the narrator's engagement with the life and works of Gustave Flaubert.

1. What do you think of Barnes' premise about the moral problems raised by literary research? Do academics owe some level of respect to their dead subjects? Does literary criticism kill the beauty of art?

2. Do the personal and historic stories told in *Flaubert's Parrot* fit well together? In other words, does this book seem like a coherent whole, or is it two books in one?

3. The book presents two versions of Flaubert's relationship with Louise Colet, one official, one imagined. Which, to your mind, comes closer to the truth? Why? Is there any way to tell which is more accurate?

4. Does *Flaubert's Parrot* inspire you to read more of Gustave Flaubert's work?

5. What are Barnes' ideas concerning memory and the depiction of the past?

6. What kind of character do you consider Braithwaite to be? Is he a sympathetic character? Is he likable? Is he reliable?

David Slater
University of Minnesota

FOR THE RELIEF OF UNBEARABLE URGES

Short Stories

1999

Author: Nathan Englander

◆

◆ SOCIAL CONCERNS ◆

The stories in Nathan Englander's collection *For the Relief of Unbearable Urges* all address issues of Jewish identity. In general, the stories tell tales of individual people and families who do not fit into society because of their religious background. Englander's Jewish characters are, for the most part, orthodox in their beliefs, so they stand out from the crowd even more than secular or less strict Jews might. Because Englander's stories span a large period of time, the social concerns addressed are not particular to a single era; instead, they address the persecution of Jewish people that has occurred since ancient times. Thus, Englander's stories strive to capture the totality of Jewish experience.

The first two stories consider the social concern which has, historically, most directly affected Jewish people: persecution. Set in World War II Poland and Stalinist Russia respectively, "The Tumblers" and "The Twenty-seventh Man" tell the stories of Jewish groups subject to the worst kind of persecution, mass slaughter. The Jewish men and women in these stories are condemned to death for no reason other than their Jewish faith. In both cases, though,

Englander does more than relate the horror of genocide.

In "The Tumblers" Englander shows off his skill at black comedy and asserts that absurd situations call for absurd responses. The story tells of how the Nazi regime came to Chelm, a tiny, isolated village. Its Jewish residents removed themselves so thoroughly from the outside world that even as they are relegated to the ghetto and herded onto trains, they do not fully understand what is happening. A small band of Chelm residents manage to slip past the Nazi herders and onto a train filled with circus performers. Finally comprehending their fate, the group decides to "pass as acrobats and tumble across the earth until they found a place where they were welcome." This wandering desire for a homeland persists today as Jewish and other native peoples continue to fight over the land which makes up Israel. Though World War II denotes a high water mark of Jewish persecution, Englander's concern for the homelessness of the people is not peculiar to the era in which he lives or in which his stories are set.

"The Tumblers" ends with the first performance. Obviously, an underfed band of Jews with no experience at gymnastics could not pass as professional tumblers. But an act of providence sees them through; an audience member (presumably Hitler himself) laughs at what he believes is the act's intentional humor. Then, one of the tumblers moves to center stage and stretches out his hands toward the audience, finally occupying a space where "there were no snipers, as there are for hands that reach out of the ghettos . . . no angels, waiting, as they always do, for hands that reach out from chimneys into ash-clouded skies." Though ending with an infectious optimism and a sense of hope in the power of divine providence, the story remains a disturbing account of the violence perpetrated by the Nazi regime. Only through cosmic good fortune is a small band able to escape the camps and furnaces into which the Jewish people were systematically herded by the Nazis.

In "The Twenty-seventh Man," Englander underscores the arbitrariness of ethnic persecution, thus teasing out some of its motives rather than simply relating its horrors. The fate of Pinchas, the character that gives the story its title, demonstrates the anonymous, almost random nature of Stalin's campaign against Jewish people. The story's opening shows that, though he knew his motive for rounding up dissidents, Stalin was not particular about who fell into the hands of his police:

> It was not an issue of hatred, only one of allegiance. For Stalin knew there could be loyalty to only one nation. What he did not know so well were the authors' names on his list. When presented to him the next morning he signed the warrant anyway, though there were now twenty-seven, and yesterday there had been twenty-six.

This passage points to the motive that people have cited since ancient times in justifying their campaigns against Jewish people: suspicion. Stalin demands that all his countrymen declare allegiance to him alone. The Jews' dedication to God diminishes their commitment to their secular state,

so Stalin, as Hitler had, becomes suspicious of their allegiance.

One effect of this suspicion against anyone who shows dedication to a god other than a political leader is the arbitrariness of punishment inflicted. All the names on Stalin's warrant are of authors who either write anti-Communist tracts or continue, after the Communist Party's ban, to write in Yiddish. Pinchas, though he does write Yiddish, never publishes his work. A recluse, Pinchas lives in a backroom of an inn, writing for the joy of the practice and never venturing into the outside world. Such reclusiveness, coupled with his Jewish identity, provokes enough suspicion for one of Stalin's underlings to place his name surreptitiously on a list condemning him to death. Englander's work uncovers the absurdity of such arbitrary sentencing of people simply because of their ethnic difference. Pinchas could not harm the Soviet state. He is a gentle, harmless man. Nevertheless, the force of paranoia is strong enough in Englander's imagined version of communist Russia to doom a gentle, reclusive man.

Obviously, such systematic aggression against Jewish people does not exist in today's world. No governments have committed themselves to the systematic extermination of all Jews. Nevertheless, violent hostility toward Jews does exist in Israel and its environs where a low-level war between Jews and Palestinians has persisted for decades. Englander turns his attention to this social concern in his final story, "In This Way We Are Wise."

The story relates the personal consequences of a terrorist bombing in central Jerusalem. The protagonist, Natan, hears the blast while sitting in a café, waiting for his girlfriend. The two experience a kind of near-death experience as both suspect that the other was caught in the blast. While relating the horror of living under the shadow of terrorist activity, the story, perhaps unwittingly, uncovers at least half of the entrenched ideology that keeps the two sides of the conflict from resolving their differences. While thinking back on the previous day's bombing, the narrator muses, "Today is a day to find religion. To decide that one god is more right than another, to uncover in this sad reality a covenant— some promise of coming good." Unfortunately, the assertion that "one god is more right than another" lies at the heart of the conflict between Israel's official, Jewish residents and its marginal, Palestinian inhabitants. Both sides claim the land as their historic and religious center and both claim that the presence of the other is an abomination in the face of their god. Resolution of the conflict depends not on the conclusion of Englander's narrator that one god is more right but on the recognition that peaceful co-existence requires flexibility on the side of all parties.

Unfortunately, more mundane motives than peace force Jewish people to show flexibility. Englander, in his comic tale "Reb Kringle," betrays his concern about the modern world's potential to insinuate itself into the lives of the most pious Jews. Itzi, a rabbi whose parish has grown too small to support itself, has taken to using his long white beard to make money at the local shopping mall. Though he objects viciously, he dons the red suit every season and portrays Santa Claus for the Christian children.

This foray into the secular world is necessary for Itzi to sustain himself and his parish. Nevertheless, he shows hesitancy about his occupation:

> He was not one of the provincial Jews who had never crossed the Royal Hills bridge into Manhattan, the naives who'd never dealt with the secular world; it was not the first time that he'd put on the suit, and he very well knew the holiday kept him afloat. But even after all those years, the

words "Merry Christmas" remained obscene to him.

Englander concedes that Jews must function in the secular world to survive. The need for a Jewish environment cannot be taken to the extreme of isolation, for such isolation breeds economic disaster. However, there are limits beyond which Englander's rabbi cannot go. So long as he does not himself blaspheme by bidding children a merry Christmas, his flexibility remains contained. One can achieve a compromise between religious and secular identities, but the story's conclusion demonstrates that this compromise remains tenuous.

Englander explores the corollary of this social concern in "The Gilgul of Park Avenue." Instead of focusing on a rabbi dabbling in secular life, this story narrates the conversion of a middle-aged Christian man to Judaism. The conversion comes suddenly: "Charles Morton Luger understood he was the bearer of a Jewish soul. *Ping!* Like that it came. Like a knife against a glass." The sudden and inexplicable nature of Charles' conversion suggests that Englander is less concerned with the theological dynamics of conversion than with the social impact of a secular man adopting Jewish faith. Shocked and disturbed by the change, Charles' wife wonders "why do people who find religion always have to be so goddamn extreme?" The problem, it seems, is that most people, even when outwardly accepting of religious difference, remain unwilling to accept the behaviors that they see as deviant in their loved ones. Charles' wife has no problem with Jewish faith so long as she remains untouched by its more obscure traditions. But with her husband's conversion, she must experience these traditions firsthand. Though she takes the changes her husband makes as an affront, an intentional effort to make her life more inconvenient, Charles wants only simple acceptance: "He struggled to stand without judgement, to be only for Sue, to be wholly seen, wanting her to love him changed." "The Gilgul of Park Avenue," is, then, a modern day fable about the difficulty of acceptance. Charles' wife, like most non-Jews, never knew what Jewishness truly meant until she was forced to make room for it in her life. Truly accepting ethnic or religious difference does not entail an absence of discrimination but actual, personal sacrifice.

◆ THEMES ◆

In his first story, "The Twenty-seventh Man," Englander takes on his most self-reflexive theme. The character of Pinchas demonstrates more than the randomness of religious persecution; he embodies the driving passion of writing as well as its power and importance independent of publication. Pinchas is different from his fellow inmates in two ways. First, his voluminous writings are unpublished. The other Jewish authors rounded up by Stalin's cronies published scathing attacks against the Communist regime. They represent half of writing's purpose: to change minds through mass readership.

Pinchas, on the other hand, represents the often unrecognized second half. Unlike the other prisoners who argue bitterly about their respective techniques in an effort to assert their superiority, Pinchas has no interest in either fame or esteem. Though the other authors write for political purposes as well as glory, Pinchas writes only because he loves to: "he had written because it was all that interested him, aside from his walks, and the pictures at which he had peeked. Not since childhood had he skipped a day of writing." The posturing of his fellow prisoners seems shallow in comparison to Pinchas' deep passion for literary production. The value of language, it seems, is not in the reading but in the composition.

Pinchas is one of many characters who give Englander an opportunity to turn his attention to the persistence and strength of Jews. This theme appears most clearly in "The Twenty-seventh Man" where "an eminent selection of Europe's surviving Yiddish literary community was being held within the confines of an oversized closet." Though clearly destined for the firing squad, these members of the literati remain defiant of their Soviet captors. They continue to debate the best strategy for uncovering Stalin's hypocrisy. The foundation for their strength, of course, lies in their religious faith. The characters in the story remain confident that they lie on the right side and that their persecutors will suffer after their deaths. When arrested, one of the writers says to his guards, "I did not say you were without orders. I said that you have to bear responsibility." Only by relying on God's power to punish can Jews remain sane in the face of the religious persecution suffered throughout their history. At every turn this faith proves invaluable for Englander's characters as they are denied the usual comforts awarded members of secular society.

◆ CHARACTERS ◆

Pinchas, the protagonist of "The Twenty-seventh Man," is the vehicle for two of Englander's most important themes, the compulsion to write and the calming force of tradition. Pinchas is condemned to death for his eccentricity. Though he never publishes a word, he spends all his days isolated in a room, writing. The authorities suspect that he intends to dismantle the Communist regime with these writings. In fact, his motive is purely self-serving: he loves to write. In fact, he has a compulsion to write that, in his last days, becomes his only solace. For Pinchas, writing is a tradition, like the rites of prayer. Rather than reverting to prayers, however, Pinchas begins composing a final story at the outset of his internment. In part, he does this out of habit, but on a deeper level it works as his sole psychological ballast. While the guards tortured him to coerce a confession of disloyalty, "Pinchas had focused on his story, his screams sounding as if they were coming from afar. With every stripe he received, he added a phrase, the impact reaching his mind like the dull rap of a windowpane settling in its sash." His own writing becomes a mantra, giving Pinchas peace in the face of his unreasonable execution.

The protagonist of "The Wig" may be Englander's most dynamic female character. Through Ruchama, a maker of wigs, Englander expounds on a universal theme: the desire for acceptance. Ruchama lives in a strict, somewhat isolated Orthodox community. Nevertheless, she has strong urges to make forays into the outside world; she spends afternoons, for instance, surreptitiously reading the forbidden fashion magazines at a magazine stand. She wishes, not at all unreasonably, to be more than a Jewish mother. These twin identities are, she feels, stifling and reductive. Sometimes, "to take off her makeup slowly, to look in the mirror and be sad, that's all she wants." The demands placed on her because of her identity often deny her these simple wishes. Englander thus makes an important point about the essential nature of categories such as Jew and mother: they reduce the possibilities of personal expression available to an individual. Ruchama finally breaks free of the constraints placed on her, but this only happens through a hilarious and Herculean effort on her part.

In "The Reunion" Englander considers the tricky, sometimes shifting boundary between sanity and insanity through Marty, an institutionalized man who believes he is, in fact, quite sane. Unorthodox behavior in Synagogue and at home prompt his wife to send him to an asylum. Every transgression, though, is accompanied by a rational explanation on Marty's part. The outrage he enacts in the temple is, to his mind, justified by the word of the Torah. He believes it was not he but the Rabbi who erred. The reasonableness with which Marty excuses his past actions raises interesting questions about both insanity and religious practice. Who really has the power to say that Marty suffers from a mental illness? More interesting, however, is the question Marty raises about religious practice: If a worshiper breaks religious practice but adheres to the word of God, who is to say he has transgressed? Is Marty in fact more right than the Rabbi who supports his wife's desire to keep him institutionalized?

◆ TECHNIQUES ◆

Though concerned with a rather dark topic, Englander's stories consistently retain a light, often funny tone. He employs several techniques to maintain this tone. For example, he carefully orders his stories to avoid drawing the reader down a slope to despair. The pointless tragedy of "The Twenty-seventh Man," for instance, is balanced by the divine redemption of the Jews in "The Tumblers." This balance is important because it give the reader a sense of the strength in Jewish identity. Even while ruminating on the oppression suffered by his people, Englander does not give in to self-pity but strikes back in a clear, comic voice.

The clarity of the voice with which Englander endows his characters underscores the force of personality that *For the Relief of Unbearable Urges* exudes. None of the characters is flat or stereotypical. Though they often repeat Yiddish phrases common to the shtick of a farce like *Seinfeld,* the Jews of Englander's stories are not parodies or stick figures. They are, for the most part, complex characters that all have individual quirks. Thus, Englander is able to tear down stereotypes by resisting the urge to make his characters fit the reader's expectations of Jewish behavior. Itzi's reluctant acceptance of a job as Santa Claus is almost unbelievable to the reader who suspects that all Orthodox Jews are rabid in their conviction. The story reveals, however, that people of all religious faiths and ethnic origins must pay homage to the world outside their community in order to survive. Englander's careful rendering of character reminds the reader that Orthodox Jews are not naive, isolationist, or, most reductively, weird.

Another technique Englander employs to give voice to Jews is the detailed description of obscure Jewish traditions. Non-Jewish readers will find *For the Relief of Unbearable Urges* fascinating simply because of the insight it gives into religious practices unknown to them. In all the collection's stories the non-Jewish reader occupies the position of Charles' wife in "The Gilgul of Park Avenue." The traditions described and names used by Englander might at first seem strange to those not familiar with Jewish tradition. Englander's sympathetic rendering of character, however, easily tempers the foreignness of the practices. By the end of the collection, the quirks of Jewish Orthodox worship appear less like curiosities than ancient and majestic traditions.

◆ LITERARY PRECEDENTS ◆

Englander's attention to the problems of contemporary Jewish-American identity places him in the company of several contemporary authors with similar concerns. Published, like Englander's collection, in 1999, Ehud Havazelet's book of short stories, *Like Never Before*, focuses on the conflict between the twin Jewish needs of assimilation and traditional practice. The stories all center on one family and the generational differences it experiences. The patriarch, Max, is angered and hurt by his son David's desire to fit in with the people of his new home. Max worked hard to bring the Old World with him, and he cannot comprehend his son's desire to live fully in the New World. Such tension is explored in many of Englander's stories. Most notably, "Reb Kringle" and "The Gilgul of Park Avenue" consider the difficulty of balancing secular life and religious needs.

For the Relief of Unbearable Urges also has precedents in older, more prestigious quarters of the American literary tradition. Nobel Prize winning novelist Saul Bellow has written several works with similar concerns of Jewish-American identity. *The Victim* (1947), for example, deals with the often problematic relationships between Jews and Gentiles. Englander also takes on this theme in "The Gilgul of Park Avenue" and the title story. In both tales an individual member of one community makes a foray into the other with consequences that are both funny and indicative of incompatibility of Jewish and Christian lifestyles.

Englander's interest in the treatment of Russian Jews has a precedent in Bernard Malamud's best known work, *The Fixer* (1967). This novel tells the story of a Jewish jack-of-all-trades who lives in Russia shortly before WWI. His community's rabid anti-Semitism comes to the fore when he is falsely accused of murder. Malamud's character, like Pinchas of "The Twenty-seventh Man," is the victim of an arbitrary system of oppression and violence.

Thomas Keaneally's *Schindler's List* (1982) is a well-known precedent for Englander's depiction of Jews subject to the violent hatred of the Nazi regime. Though Keaneally's book focuses on the heroic efforts of a German businessman to save hundreds of Jewish workers, it gives a vivid picture of what life in the Jewish ghettoes was like. Also, the characters in Keaneally's novel who are saved are the benefactors of the same sort of divine providence which keeps "The Tumblers" from the camps and ovens.

Students should also read works which do not take sympathetic views of Jewish people in an effort to gain a fuller understanding of the struggles they endure. Casual readers often cite William Shakespeare's *The Merchant of Venice* (1600) as a play which ennobles its Jewish character through the famous "hath not a Jew eyes" speech. The drama actually expresses rather anti-Semitic sentiments. Shylock, the Jew, is not a sympathetic character but a money-grubbing usurer who demands a pound of flesh for an unpaid debt. The drama concludes with the forfeiture of half his wealth and his conversion to Christianity. In addition to this antiquated, fictional source, Adolf Hitler's *Mein Kampf* (1926) gives a useful but disturbing view of a madman's motivations for killing millions of Jews. In the two volumes of this book, Hitler outlines his "final solution," the plan for exterminating all of Europe's Jews. Though painful to hear, the voice of the oppressor often provides a more profound understanding of the plight of the oppressed.

◆ IDEAS FOR GROUP DISCUSSIONS ◆

Englander's stories all focus on Orthodox Jewish characters who struggle to either isolate themselves from or fit into secular society. The stories in *For the Relief of Unbearable Urges* cover the entire gamut of Jewish experience from the horror of Nazi camps to the terror of bombs which still explode in downtown Jerusalem. In between these extremes, Englander situates the small struggles to survive in a world that views Jews with suspicion.

Because Jews have endured the struggles described by Englander for thousands of years, the social concerns he addresses are somewhat timeless. Though his first two stories relate events set in two particular eras of genocide, one can imaginatively recreate the violence against Jews in almost any era. Stories such as "Reb Kringle," however, reveal that Jewish people do not only suffer during times of ethnic cleansing. Though funny, many of Englander's stories endeavor to make a rather serious point: that Jews remain a minority, subject to the same sort of prejudice and discrimination as African-Americans. If the prejudice is different in degree, it is not in kind.

1. Do you think Englander's depiction of Orthodox Jewish life is somewhat exclusionary? In other words, do you think that one should strive to represent the broadest possible cross-section of an ethnic group when lending that group a voice through fiction?

2. What effect does the juxtaposition of comic and tragic elements in a story such as "The Tumblers" have? Does the comedy make the tragedy more disturbing, or does it relieve the tension created by the story?

3. How does divine providence operate in Englander's stories? Is fate, luck, or the work of a higher power always beneficent?

4. If you are not Jewish, what aspects of Jewish religious tradition did you learn about by reading *For The Relief of Unbearable Urges*? If you are Jewish, how do your traditions differ from those of Englander's characters?

5. Which of Englander's stories might one make into a film? Why? How might such a film be cast?

6. What do you make of Englander's construction of female characters? Does he create strong, dynamic women, or are they all either naggers or schemers?

7. Do you think Marty, the protagonist of "The Reunion," is crazy? Clearly, he has only good intentions and jus-

tifies all of his actions with reasonable argument and the support of the
Torah's words.

David Slater
University of Minnesota

A GATHERING OF OLD MEN

Novel

1983

Author: Ernest J. Gaines

◆

Fiction by Ernest J. Gaines interprets the layers in the society of rural life in Louisiana. The setting for this novel, the quarters on the Marshall plantation, the town of Bayonne, and the area where the Cajun population lives, is based on Pointe Coupee Parish in Louisiana, where Gaines was born and lived until he was about fifteen. What can be learned from the older generations, what can be handed on to the next generation, and how the history of the people influences all lives are of concern to Gaines in *A Gathering of Old Men*. In *Christian Science Monitor*, Sam Cornish writes that the "characters—both black and white—understand that, before the close of the novel, the new South must confront the old, and all will be irrevocably changed." Social change and how it comes about, peacefully or violently, and what this change does to the people who bring it about is at the center of this novel, explaining how the groups within the parish relate to each other and how they see each other. The people within each group find that the way they see each other and themselves is not what they expect.

The society of rural Louisiana in the 1970s was divided into three layers: descendants of the white plantation owners, the Cajun farmers, also white, who lease the land belonging to the plantations, and the African-American descendants of the slaves who are now laborers for the Cajuns. The central character, Beau, is dead when the story opens. He was a Cajun farmer, a man who bullied his workers until one of them turned on him. His claim to superiority was the color of his skin. His death unites the older African-American men in the community, symbolizing defeat of the white men they have been afraid to stand up to all their lives, and allowing them to become real men. They are finally able to defend the people they love from a society that has oppressed them.

The Cajun farmers are the decendents of Frenchmen who came to Louisiana when they were expelled from Acacia, Nova Scotia, by the British in the 1755. They settled in the Bayou Teche region, then under Spanish rule. Americans were also moving into what would become Louisiana, demanding that the Mississippi River be kept open so they could ship the produce from their plantations to the markets of the world. Spain was forced to retrocede Louisiana to France in 1800, opening the way for the Louisiana Purchase of 1803, thus doubling the size of the United States.

The Cajuns in Louisiana today often live in small communities, speaking a French patois that incorporates words from other languages spoken in the area. In 1970 the Cajuns were the middle layer in Louisiana society as they had been for many years, looking down on the African-American population, and looked down on by the white population not of French extraction. Many leased plantation land for farming, paying a set price in money for the use of the land, implying an equality with the land owners not shared by the black share-croppers. The sharecroppers paid for the use of the land in actual farm produce, implying an inability to function as business people equal to the land owners.

In the novel, the Boutan family are Cajun farmers leasing the Marshall plantation land for farming. They are known for violent reaction to events where they feel their family honor is at stake. Thus, the sheriff and his deputy expect the Boutan family men to appear as a group, armed and ready to lynch the black man they decide is guilty of killing Beau. The sheriff shows he realizes the times are changing when he has the body taken to town and sends a deputy to the Boutan home to keep the family there. The usual violent reaction from the Boutans cannot be permitted, heralding an increased awareness of social changes.

Candy Marshall, the heiress to the Marshall plantation property, is the first to plead guilty to the murder. She is protecting "her people," not realizing that by doing so she is perpetuating the myth that these workers need to be protected. In its own way, that is as insulting as Beau's ridiculing his workers. The nicknames the black men have given each other, nicknames these old men are known by in the community, are child-ish, giving the impression that these men need to be protected. "Dirty Red," "Rooster," "Clatoo," "Rufe," and "Coot," have other names, names that would lend dignity to their owners. Unintentionally, Candy is living with the prejudices inherited from ancestral slave-owners. While she thinks she has overcome these attitudes, the fact that she sees the men as needing to be protected shows she has not. Mathu is the only father figure Candy has known. She is protective but does not see there could be a different explanation, that Mathu perhaps has not told her the whole story. She thinks she is protecting Mathu when in reality she is protecting herself. She is fighting the change that is coming but encouraging it by sending out a message to get help. Everyone knows that an explanation of self-defense is not viable.

Never before in the history of this community have the members been united and willing to stand up for themselves. The individuals express over and over that they want to do at least one honorable thing before they die. The community has watched the loss of their graveyards and homes in the quarters as the tractor claims more and more land to farm. Men such as Yank have lost a way of life, with the changing needs of the community. No more horses or mules to break, no more land to plow as the sharecroppers are forced out, their land swallowed up by the Cajuns who lease the plantation lands.

The sheriff Mapes, white and male, begins his interrogation by dismissing Candy's claim that she committed the murder. The only way he knows to deal with this group of people is to choose the one he thinks is the weakest and use force to break him down. To his surprise, his use of force unites the group. Suddenly, for the first time in the history of this community, all the men are standing tall, looking him in the eye, and are not intimidated. Realizing he has misjudged this group, he chooses Mathu, the one person there that he truly respects, thinking that Mathu will dismiss the others. Mapes understands the power of the group, and his deputy fears it. Mapes begins to understand that he will have to work with the group rather than ordering these people to do what he wants.

Signs of change in the people and the community continue. Members of the group tell of abuses and insults to themselves or family members, giving these as reasons for murdering Beau. Each has an incident in his past, something that happened to him or someone he cares about, which he now wishes to avenge. By bringing these events to the attention of the group, they are teaching the children that they have a history. The children will need to move forward from this time and place, remembering the things in the past so that change will not erase the proof they have been there. By remembering, the young people in the community will be empowered to keep their history, maintain their dignity, and claim their place in the community.

◆ THEMES ◆

All of Gaines's fiction has, as an overarching theme, the place of the characters in their society. This theme encompasses the lives of the people within the strata of the society, within the area in which they live, and within the family circle, whether that family circle involves blood relations or adopted relations. The theme of father-son relationships is expanded to include father-daughter relationships. Change with all the upheaval it brings is a theme that grows as the story progresses. A way of life is passing as a generation passes; a generation involving all the levels of the society included in the narrative.

If these men were young, this would be a classic coming-of-age story. But the sharecroppers have waited until they are old to find the manhood hiding within them. Chimley and Mat wonder why they have waited until they are old to become brave.

When they decide they will go to Marshall as Candy has asked, they show the first sign that they will stand as men from now on. There will be no more hiding in fear for these men. The second sign of change within Chimley is signified by the order he gives to his wife to clean the fish and have them cooked and ready when he gets back home. Mat tells his wife that "anytime we say we go'n stand up for something, they say we crazy." He has a fight with his wife about whether he will go to Marshall, leaving after telling her he has one last chance to do something with his life.

This newfound manhood shows itself over and over. Griffin chooses Uncle Billy, the oldest, smallest man, to be the first person Mapes questions. When Mapes hits Uncle Billy, who would have backed down quickly the day before, Mapes finds that force does not work. Uncle Billy may hold his hat to his chest and be afraid to look Mapes in the eye, but he does not change his story. Gable is the second man to be questioned. Again Mapes uses force to no avail. As Griffin brings him the third man, the Reverend Jameson, Mapes begins to realize his strategy is not working. The Reverend is even less satisfactory as a witness than the other two. Suddenly, everyone is forming a line in front of the sheriff, with Candy at its head. Faced with this show of unity, Mapes calls off the questioning.

Changes in the social structure are surfacing in places other than the Marshall plantation. Gilbert "Salt" Boutan, attending college at Louisiana State University, is a football star on his way to becoming an All American and possibly a professional football player. Calvin "Pepper" Harrison, already nominated for All American, is the other half of the football team's "Salt and Pepper" duo. They are the first black and white players in the same backfield in football history. The fact this this history-making lineup is tolerated in the deep South lends added meaning to the situation. Both could make All-American, if they continue to work together. The killing takes place the day before the biggest game of the season, making it difficult for Gil to maintain his loyalty to a black player. Gil understands that change has come, that the old ways of dealing with honor will not work anymore. He is working for change because he knows everyone will have a better life. Gil's father Fix knows change is coming; his concession to the changes taking place is his refusal to go to Marshall unless all his sons agree to go with him. Gil and Jean refuse. Fix saves face by banishing these two sons, telling them never to return to their home. Fix is not able to take the responsibility for his choice; he must lay the blame elsewhere. In this situation, the father-son theme is reversed. The father requires the strength of the sons and is willing to tear his family apart unless he gets his way. By playing in the game the following day, Gil shows he can stand up for himself and what he believes in.

Lee Papa, writing in the *African American Review,* says religion and a change in the attitudes of the people in the quarters at Marshall toward their religious beliefs is a part of the social change taking place in the story. The "black people of the Marshall quarters complete a conversion begun with the alienation of Reverend Jameson from the community. This process continues through the denial of the white god and reaches its culmination with the raising of Charlie to martyrdom. As a consequence, a new, communal religion is forged." Charlie's return from the swamps to face what he has done, telling the group he heard a voice call him back, heralds a mystic experience to be shared by the whole group. When Charlie dies, the men, women and children gathered at Mathu's house lean over and touch him, hoping to get a taste of what he found in the swamps. They have the courage to make even their religion into

a new image, one that suits their new pride and self-confidence.

Death is another theme in Gaines's novel. Beau's demise causes the deaths of other characters. The deaths of the old men in all the plantation's social groups would signal the end of an era. The deaths of people in the families of all the characters has an effect on how they see the world. For Candy, the death of her parents allows her to see that skin color is not the important part of a man. For Mat, the racially motivated death of Oliver has soured his life. For Dirty Red, the deaths of the other members of his family helped motivate him to stand up and be counted.

◆ CHARACTERS ◆

The story is narrated by a different character in each chapter, from a first-person point of view. This allows the reader to see all sides of the community's life through the eyes of its members. The effect of this narrative technique is that the reader feels as if he or she can rotate the community and view it from all its sides. Reynolds Price of the *New York Times Book Review* says the various narrations "are nicely distinguished from one another in rhythm and idiom, in the nature of what they see and report, especially in their specific laments for past passivity in the face of suffering."

Beau Boutan, the murder victim, becomes the center of the story, as each character claims responsibility for his demise. A member of a violent, prejudiced Cajun family, Beau farms the land belonging to the Marshall plantation. The plantation owners are no longer in charge of the day-to-day farming operation; the African-American population does the physical work, work that is changing as it becomes more mechanized. The man with the mule and plow has given way to the tractor. The black men, sharecroppers for generations after the Civil War, are now laborers. The Cajuns lease the land that once was worked by slaves, and Beau treats the blacks as if they were still slaves.

Candy Marshall is the latest member of the Marshall family to take responsibility for the plantation property. She is the heir to the land, raised by an uncle and Mathu, an African-American man who has been on the plantation all his life. Her parents have been dead since she was a child, killed in an accident. Candy is the first to reach the scene of the killing and, since she believes Mathu guilty, claims to have shot Beau herself. She is trying to protect "her people," as she always has. She does not realize that she feels a sense of ownership in matters pertaining to Mathu and the rest of the community. Candy must face, in the end, the injustices committed by her immediate family against the people of the quarters. As she acknowledges the truth about how her father and grandfather actually treated the people, she becomes a woman able to allow Mathu to be a man.

Mathu is an African-American, elderly but still vigorous, the one man in the quarters that has always held up his head. He is the one man Mapes respects; he and Mapes hunt and fish together. He is also the only one Mapes feels is capable of the act of murder. Fix, who respects and hates Mathu, also thinks Mathu is the only possible suspect; there was a history of trouble between Mathu and Fix because of a fight that Mathu won. Mathu has dark skin, a source of pride to him since he says this proves he has no white blood. He does not respect many of the old men who gather at his home. He truly loves Candy, is her surrogate father, and is unable to express his feelings to her, because he loves her too much.

The Boutan family and their hatred of the black population is central to the story. William "Fix" Boutan is the patriarch of the family, feared in the community and in his home. He sees no reason not to ridicule his sons and sees every reason they should obey him. He has no respect for opinions different from his own. Claude, an older son, mimics his father's attitudes. Gil, Gilbert "Salt" Boutan, a younger son, attends college at Louisiana State University in Baton Rouge. He is also a possible candidate for the All American football team. Gil has worked for understanding between the races for most of his life. He is on good terms with both the black and the white communities. His success on the football field serves as a catalyst to unite the two communities. Gil tries to help his father understand that the Boutan name will be dishonored if the family lynches a man, using his chances of becoming an All American as a reason for the family to let the sheriff resolve the problem. Jean, a younger son, owns a butcher shop in Bayonne. He knows the success of his business depends in large part on the black community. Fix addresses Jean as "Mr. Butcher of hog-gut fame" and is surprised when Jean sides with Gil. Fix refuses to act unless all his sons will act with him. Fix realizes he will not be allowed to lynch a black man and have the sheriff look the other way. He uses the family division as an excuse to back down.

Calvin "Pepper" Harrison, also known as Cal, is a black football player at LSU. Gil and Calvin, as "Salt" and "Pepper," symbolize the ability of the races to work together for the common good. They are also symbolic of two people who know each other well enough to rise above skin color and see inside each other. They are friends, dependent on each other on the football field, caring about each other off the field. Cal has been nominated for All American and hopes Gil will join him in that honor.

The old men who gather at Mathu's home at Marshall have much in common. Some are given a special voice; others share in the event. There are eighteen who come to back Mathu and all are armed with 12-guage shotguns, recently fired. All have empty number five shells, the size shell used to kill Beau. Among them, Robert Louis Stevenson Banks, called "Chimley" for his dark skin, knows Mathu is the only one who ever stood up to the white people. Mat (Matthew Lincoln Brown) says, "I have to go. . . . This could be my last chance." Cyril Robillard, aka Clatoo, comes prepared. He realizes there will have to be a showdown of some sort with someone, and motivated by his newfound pride and bravery, makes sure his group will be able to defend themselves. He brings live shells and hides them where everyone else can get them and load their guns. Uncle Billy (Billy Washington), the first to be questioned and beaten by the sheriff, maintains he killed Beau. Sidney Brooks, aka Coot, comes in his moth-eaten World War I uniform, the uniform he has been forbidden to wear since returning from his tour of duty. He fought with a unit trained in France. These old men and the rest who are gathered at Mathu's house weave in and out of the story, each finally having the strength and pride to stand up to the white community, even in the face of the threat of death.

The Reverend Jameson tries to send the old men home, fearing what will happen when Fix and his group appear. In the name of religion, Jameson preaches fear and self-contempt. He loses his leadership role in the group because he tries to do what the white sheriff wants and is not able to stand up for himself. He is the nineteenth man, the only one unarmed.

Luke Will, a Cajun friend of Beau's, is a living symbol of all that the old black men are standing against. He does not sense that times are changing, that his hatred of the black community will no longer be tolerated. When Fix refuses to go to Marshall, Luke Will feels he is obliged to go. He cannot allow the death of a white man to go unpunished, regardless of what the white man may have done. He cannot trust the law to dole out punishment as he feels it should be done.

The African-American women and children at Mathu's house provide a sense of family, strengthening the resolve of the gathering. The children learn what it is to have pride in one's self and one's community, giving them a start toward a new way of looking at themselves and their lives.

♦ TECHNIQUES ♦

In an interview in the *National Forum*, Gaines said that he writes "for the black youth of the South to let them know that their lives are worth writing about, and maybe in that way I can help them find themselves . . . [and] for the white youth of the South to let them know that unless they know their neighbor of three hundred years, they know only half of their own history." By narrating *A Gathering of Old Men* through the voices of many different characters, Gaines allows the many sides of the story to become apparent.

At first the movement of the story is slow, as it should be after a tragedy. Few people know what has happened or why it has happened. As more people become aware of events, the story picks up speed, as the added characters build momentum to the final conflict between the members of the different layers of society. The group of black men who gather at Mathu's house are a counterpoint to the group of men who gather at Fix's house. The group at Mathu's house gathers strength from the changes in each other; the group at Fix's lose their strength, as key members do not agree that vengeance will solve the problem.

The community is unraveled and laid bare, first by the black men as they tell of the insults they and their loved ones have suffered in their lives. They tell of rapes, murder, lynching, unfair fights, all sorts of belittling treatment at the hands of the white community. The Cajuns feel that their place in the racially stratified society should have been different. It is only by accident that they are not in the position of the plantation owners, land owners instead of renters. The plantation owners, feeling their uselessness, have retreated into alcoholism. They are an aristocracy gone sour.

The language of the narrators is used to set each apart and give insight into his or her personality. Janey shows her terror by repeating prayers and worrying that Miss Bea will be bitten by a snake while she looks for pecans in the weeds under the trees in the back pasture. The weeds are a sign of the decadence of the property. Had the pasture been mowed, the pecans would have been easier and safer to gather. Miss Merle gives a picture of the relationship between Candy and Mathu, strengthening the impression that Mathu is the killer, when she thinks about how many times she has observed Candy and Mathu talking at his home or the plantation house. The chapters narrated by black characters are typical of the language structure of African-Americans in the South. The chapters move from layer to layer of the community, showing the divisions and differences in thought patterns. Narration also shows the divisions within the layers—the prejudices felt within each group in the community. As the characters confront changes in themselves, some find they must move between the groups since they no longer fit where they had been before. Some find that growth and change are not pleasant.

◆ LITERARY PRECEDENTS ◆

The autobiographies of Maya Angelou begin with the memoir *I Know Why the Caged Bird Sings*, describing life in a small Arkansas town in the 1930s. The town is rural and deeply segregated. Angelou's grandmother, with whom she lives, runs a store where the black community can purchase groceries and other supplies. The rest of the books in the series—*Gather Together in My Name* (1974), *Singin' and Swingin' and Gettin' Merry Like Christmas* (1976), *The Heart of a Woman* (1981), and *All God's Children Need Traveling Shoes* (1986)—chronicle her life from her teen years through her four-year stay in Ghana. Like Gaines, Angelou is deeply bound to the heritage of place. While Gaines's writing reveals his connection to his childhood in Louisiana, Angelou's memoirs draw more generally on her identity as an American. Wanda Coleman tells us in the *Los Angeles Times* that Angelou's work is "an important document drawing much needed attention to the hidden history of a people both African and American."

As Gaines gives his characters a place in history and community, Angelou grants herself a place also. Each of these authors gives insight into the political and social attitudes and realities of the eras they write about. Angelou's connections to many of the people involved with the civil rights movement—Malcolm X, Martin Luther King, Jr.—have led to her personal involvement in the feminist and civil right movements. Gaines and Angelou use the themes of hardship in the lives of people of the lower classes to inspire a desire for social change for a better life.

◆ RELATED TITLES ◆

The novel *The Autobiography of Miss Jane Pittman* is the work which has thus far brought Gaines the most critical recognition. Told in the first person by Jane, the story spans over one hundred years of history from slavery, Reconstruction, two world wars, and segregation to the civil rights movement. *DISCovering Authors* calls the character of Jane Pittman "an embodiment of the black experience in America." Made into a film for television in 1974 starring Cicely Tyson in the title role, it won nine Emmy Awards.

A common thread in all Gaines's stories is the town of Bayonne, a fictitious setting based on Pointe Coupee Parish, near New Roads, Louisiana, where he was born and lived until moving to California at age fifteen. His first novel, *Catherine Carmier*, is the story of a daughter of a Creole family, proud of their light skin color. Catherine becomes involved with a man whose skin is dark, leading to clashes of loyalty. The man, Jackson, has returned to the community after being educated elsewhere. Catherine is torn between Jackson and her family, Jackson between the community and his knowledge of the outside world.

Of Love and Dust pits a black parolee and a white overseer in a contest for the love of the overseer's wife. The story ends in tragedy for the parolee when the overseer kills him after discovering the romance. In *Dictionary of Literary Biography* Keith E. Byerman says the novel "more clearly condemns the economic, social, and racial system of the South for the problems faced by its characters."

The theme of father-son relationships is paramount in Gaines's fourth novel, *In My Father's House*. A son—abandoned for twenty years—seeks to kill his father. The father in turn must face the consequences of that act of abandonment with all the ramifications to the woman and children he left. The father, now a pastor and civil rights leader, must search for this lost family, discover what has happened to them, and try to find a way to remedy his mistakes.

A Lesson Before Dying is the story of Jefferson, a young black man falsely accused and convicted of murder. Set in the late 1940s, the novel focuses on a black schoolteacher's visits to Jefferson in jail, and the teacher's attempts to gain his confidence and raise his self-esteem. By the end of the story, Jefferson has taught his teacher how to be a man and accept responsibility for his life and the betterment of the community.

Each of these novels portrays the layers of the cultures that make up the community as a whole. In an interview for *San Francisco*, Gaines says, "So many of our novels deal only with the great city ghettos; that's all we write about, as if there's nothing else. We've only been living in these ghettos for 75 years or so, but the other 300 hundred years—I think this is worth writing about."

◆ ADAPTATIONS ◆

Aired on CBS television, May 10, 1987, the movie adaptation of *A Gathering of Old Men* starred Louis Gossett, Jr, as Mathu, Richard Widmark as Mapes, and Holly Hunter as Candy.

There have been two sound recordings on cassette tape made of the novel. The first, made in 1987, is currently out of print. The second is a set of six cassettes reviewed in *Booklist* by Ted Hipple (1997). He wrote, "the multiple voices provide a stirring listening experience." The narrators, including Peter Francis James, Michelle-Denise Woods, and Dally Darling give the recording an authentic feeling.

◆ IDEAS FOR GROUP DISCUSSIONS ◆

A Gathering of Old Men addresses issues unresolved in many communities today. Though set in 1970, the story could take place at any time. Members of a community can take a stand against injustice at any time. Members of a community must find their history, learn to apply it, and find ways to respect each other, no matter where the community is or who is living in it. In order for the people in the world to live and work together, without racial prejudice and hatred, all people need to develop an understanding of those who may be different.

1. Snookum and several other children were present at Mathu's house during the day. What did these children learn from the men who gathered to support Mathu?

2. Why did the Cajuns not own the land they were farming? Why did the plantation owners choose the Cajuns to lease the land?

3. How does Candy's perception of her relationship with the black community change? How do you think she will now relate to that group of people? What will change with her relationship with Mathu?

4. What could Candy have done to avert the tragedy? What do you think she could do to avert future problems and unite the community?

5. What event in Mathu's past allowed him to maintain his self-respect?

6. Why is the graveyard important? Why would losing the graveyard be important? Why are many of the graves unmarked? Is this a sign of disrespect?

7. What clues do Mathu and Candy give that hint at the ending of the story?

8. Was Fix fair to Gil? If the story continued, do you think Fix would have changed his order to Gil?

9. Research the changes in the duties of African-Americans in the armed forces since World War I. Why have these changes taken place?

10. Reverend Jameson's brand of religion is rejected by the people of the quarter. What sort of religious beliefs will the community have after this incident? Will they stop attending church? Will they need a new preacher? Why does this show a new community spirit?

Ann Barton Sciba
Wharton High School Library

GERTRUDE AND CLAUDIUS

Novel

2000

Author: John Updike

◆

Long recognized as one of the most acute observers of the American scene during the last half of the twentieth century, John Updike's special strength has been novels set in the immediate present, in which the manners, styles, and sexual mores of American culture are dissected under the microscope of his fiction. The four novels concerning the life and times of ex-athlete Harry Angstrom (*Rabbit, Run*, 1960; *Rabbit Redux*, 1971; *Rabbit Is Rich,* 1981; *Rabbit at Rest,* 1990) constitute a chronicle of a man whose best years ended when he was eighteen years old; but they also tell with uncanny prescience the narrative of an America increasingly consumed by media superficialities, racial tensions, sexual revolutions, and a credo of material success that legitimates greed and self-interest as a way of life. Similarly, his novels *Couples* (1968), *A Month of Sundays* (1975), and *Marry Me* (1976) along with the powerful collection of short stories, *Too Far to Go* (1979), explore from a variety of perspectives evolving preoccupations with sex, marriage, religion, and failed relationships. Finally, his stories about growing up in the American depression and thereafter, collected in *Pigeon Feathers* (1962) and *The Olinger Stories* (1964) add to the sense that Updike has served his coun-

try well as one of its most astute and observant cultural commentators.

During the final decade of the twentieth century, however, Updike modified his habitual contemporary perspective, emphasized in *Rabbit, Run* by the use of the present rather than the past tense for the narrative voice. *Memories of the Ford Administration* (1992) looks at events from twenty years before the time of the novel's publication and *In the Beauty of the Lilies* (1996) traces the lives of four generations of an American family. *Toward the End of Time* (1997) is set in the year 2020, but includes narratives about Egyptian grave-robbers and an important section narrating a Viking invasion and slaughter of an English monastery sometime in the medieval era. This seeming digression anticipates the subject matter of Updike's nineteenth novel, *Gertrude and Claudius* (2000).

With his first novel published during the new millennium, Updike has moved further back into history than ever before. Even his under-appreciated play, *Buchanan Dying* (1974), which imaginatively chronicles the final months in the life of a minor president whose bad historical luck it was to precede Abraham Lincoln, seems recent by comparison with *Gertrude and Claudius*, Updike's "prequel" to William Shakespeare's

Hamlet. Set at a transitional if undefined moment in Danish history, this novel daringly tells the story of the adultery and murder that constitute the situation for England's best-known play, a staple of American high-school and college curricula. As filmmaker George Lucas told the opening chapter of his *Star Wars* saga in the fourth film, America's foremost cultural observer deploys modern perspectives to tell, 400 years after Shakespeare's play was first produced, his story of passion, lust, intrigue, and regicide/fratricide in a Denmark that is, as is Updike's America, evolving through transformations in manners, technology, religion, and politics. As Shakespeare's Elsinore Castle resembled a feudal British duchy more than a medieval Danish monarchy, so Updike's Elsinore, while fastidiously medieval in dress and climate, reminds us of modern America in its evolution from one mode of existence into an uncertain future.

In his play Shakespeare nearly eliminates historical time and social conditions to concentrate on one man's relationship(s) with his destiny, so much so that a mid-twentieth century production and subsequent film of *Hamlet* were set in contemporary dress, including v-neck sweaters and worsted slacks, with little negative impact on the timeless power of the story itself (the production starred Richard Burton). Many other productions have set the action in the eighteenth and nineteenth centuries. We may infer that time in Shakespeare's play is "internal"; that is, we as readers or playgoers are concerned with the fact that Hamlet is 30 years old (a detail withheld until Act 5), that his father killed the Norse king on the day of Hamlet's birth, that two months have passed since the king's sudden death, that the queen re-married only a month after her husband's death, that the ghost has been seen on the castle wall for two consecutive nights before the play begins, and so forth. Readers and playgoers alike do not particularly care whether the events take place in the thirteenth, sixteenth, or even nineteenth century. In *Hamlet* time is internal, a pressure that is felt within the play but not with specific reference to external conditions.

By contrast, *Gertrude and Claudius* is very much about time and the inevitability of change. Like the end of the century in which Updike penned his story of the Danish throne and the end of the century in which Shakespeare wrote *Hamlet,* Updike's Denmark is a monarchy in transition. Several crucial social changes are underway, which affect the characters' ability to relate to one another and to the world they occupy. For example, the king's advisor, Polonius, complains that Gertrude gets dangerous ideas from her reading "Gaulish" (French) novels to pass the time while her husband is doing kingly business. By implication, she assimilates Renaissance influences from southern Europe, which proves to be a crucial differentiation between her provincial husband and his cosmopolitan brother. Shakespeare's Gertrude was probably illiterate (the play does not mention her reading or writing skills); moreover, most literary scholars date the invention of the novel as a literary form to the sixteenth century or even later. Polonius, unlike the character (who boasts that he once played Julius Caesar) in Shakespeare's play, laments the emerging theatrical profession, and especially its impact on Prince Hamlet. The novel's character's positions, that acting companies blaspheme by mimicking God's creative genius, and that acting companies further contribute to a general decline in religious and ethical values, were widely voiced by conservative and moralistic persons in Shakespeare's time. Stephen Gosson, for example, lamented the insidious moral influence of acting companies in a pamphlet influential enough to cause Sir Philip Sidney to respond with his great essay, "An Apology for Poetry" (1595). Minister Thomas White cleverly if illogically proved that plays are a principal cause of plagues in a sermon delivered in 1577. Updike inserts fragments from Shakespeare's play, in which Hamlet and Polonius exchange views of the theater and its role in society (Hamlet offers the classical view that players "hold the mirror up to nature"), but he wants to make us constantly aware of a civilization in cultural change, whether in its methods of entertainment, its economy, its religion, or its theories of marriage.

In Updike's novel, the transition between King Hamlet and his brother corresponds directly with an important shifting cultural paradigm, the transference of wealth and power from the traditional baronial estates to the new burgher or merchant class. Hamlet senior laments the collapse of the traditional lines of fealty and authority, as do the conservative factions in many of Shakespeare's English history plays, most notably the deposed king in *Richard II*. Claudius seems to align himself with the less traditional modes of government, perhaps because his journeys into Mediterranean Europe and Constantinople have taught him that authority takes many forms. At any rate, the conflict between the brothers, for a queen's love and a kingdom's throne, is further aligned by Updike with emerging patterns of power and wealth that would lead to the end of the feudal system in Europe and with the beginning of guild and mercantile capitalism that would in turn drive the forces of colonialism, leading to the settlement of the New World and several less fortunate consequences.

It is a convenient model, if nonetheless an oversimplification, to suggest that Updike associates Claudius with forces of progressive thinking and emerging definitions of wealth and power, whereas he aligns the elder Hamlet with traditional forms of loyalty and obligation. Claudius adroitly manipulates the *"thing,"* Updike's playful invention for the assembly of barons and merchants who elect the king, to select him upon his brother's sudden death by creating alliances with the emerging class. Even the election process Updike assesses as a precursor to modern democracy. If Hamlet complains at least twice in Shakespeare's play that Claudius "Popped in between th'election and my hopes," Updike provides an answer to the question that comes up in almost every college discussion of *Hamlet*, why the hero, at age 30, did not become king upon his father's death. Shakespeare was not interested in the mechanics of succession in *Hamlet*, even if he was politically obsessed with such themes in his English history plays, but Updike observes that this process of selecting leaders, like the displacement of chain mail by plated armor because of technical improvements in archery, is due to the inevitability of change and perhaps a precursor of modern democracy.

In Updike's narrative, then, Claudius seems to be a man of the future, and Hamlet the elder a man of the past. The senior brother clings to traditions and forms that are slipping away as Denmark grudgingly absorbs influences from Mediterranean and Atlantic nations. But Updike compounds his own irony in that Claudius shows preliminary signs of devolving into a carbon copy of his elder brother once he assumes the royal diadem. He changes his name from Feng (the brother's name in one of Shakespeare's sources) to Claudius to symbolize the new era Denmark is entering. But he becomes increasingly preoccupied with his royal obligations and his shaky claim to the throne. Even though the novel ends with an illusory hope ("The era of Claudius had dawned. . . All would be well, " itself echoing the final line of Claudius's soliloquy after his guilt has been disclosed in Act 3 of the play), Updike depends on his readers' familiarity with Shakespeare's play for one final irony—to remember that within months all the major, and several minor, characters in this novel will become indirect victims of Claudius's regicide. Like so many of Shakespeare's English Kings, notably Henry IV and Richard III, Claudius learns that power is easier to get than it is to hold and wield. As the cultural paradigms shifted under the elder Hamlet and Gertrude's father before him, they continue to shift during the brief era of Claudius.

◆ THEMES ◆

Although Updike has from time to time been charged with being a misogynist blessed with a graceful style by critics of various persuasions, the first characteristic one observes about this novel is the sequence in which the characters' names appear in the title. By contrast, Shakespeare's three plays, named after joint protagonists, consistently exhibit a patriarchal priority characteristic of his age (*Romeo and Juliet, Troilus and Cressida, Antony and Cleopatra*). Updike's title, however, gives the privileged position to the woman who drives the male characters in *Hamlet*: the mother upon whom Hamlet obsesses; the wife Claudius genuinely adores, to the degree that he endangers his throne to keep her beloved son nearby; and the widow whom the Ghost (an ectoplasmic inconsistency that overwhelms young Hamlet) tells young Hamlet to spare while wreaking vengeance on her lover. Although she is the center of three men's universe in the play, Shakespeare's Gertrude is hard to comprehend fully. Is she complicit in her husband's murder? An adulteress who rushed to the altar with her lover after her husband's sudden death? A traditional, weak, woman incapable of living without a strong male presence? Any of these may be true of Shakespeare's character; but none is provable by data or statements within the play. In Updike's novel both the priority and the sympathy are clearly with Gertrude, a lively young woman whose body,

love, and loyalty are negotiated by her dynastic father, a man who cares much more about Denmark's future than his daughter's happiness.

Gertrude's victimization, defensible only under patriarchal attitudes characteristic of late medieval and early modern Europe, begins with a father who subdues his captive Wendish princess by forcing himself on her. He actually boasts to Gertrude that Ona, her mother, attempted suicide after Rorik (Gertrude's father) in effect raped her. The captive bride/mother died when Gertrude was three years old, so the theme of maternal nurture, so absent in her own childhood surrounded by carousers and whores in the Danish court, accounts for the mature Gertrude's taking Ophelia under her wing. In Shakespeare's account, the queen's sudden lament at Ophelia's gravesite, "I hoped thou shouldst have been my Hamlet's wife. / I thought thy bride-bed to have decked," seems abrupt. Updike fills in the motivation as well as the past in Shakespeare's story by emphasizing Gertrude's own lack of maternal nurturing, her alienation in the macho cultures of her father's court and the one her husband imposes on his son, and her sympathy with Ophelia, whose mother she sees as a sickly victim of old Polonius's patriarchal lusts. According to Gertrude, Polonius continued to impregnate his wife despite her several miscarriages, and she believes this was the cause of Ophelia's mother's unhappiness and early death.

Updike's narrative, however, is not merely a jeremiad about patriarchal authority in late medieval Europe. Gertrude is simultaneously a resenting victim and a contributor to the suppression of women in this novel. Although she sees her own arranged marriage and motherless childhood mirrored in the young woman's vulnerability, her interest in Ophelia is not solely a matter of feminine sympathy. She sees Hamlet's marriage to Ophelia as a means for her son to settle down and become more prince-like. Trying for a second time to persuade Hamlet senior that diplomatic interests are less important than their son's mental health and personal happiness, she professes that marriage might cure the prince of his "sterile egotism" because "marriage ties us to the established order." Thus Gertrude (and Updike) have it both ways: marriage is a trap for women, an institution that robs them of their autonomy and ultimately their spirit, and yet it is very good for the social order—and for their sons.

Moreover, the adultery itself, certainly Updike's critical interest in the Hamlet story and a theme that is both timely and time-less, is in considerable measure an expression of Gertrude's private, if largely unconscious, resentment of the patriarchal system that commodifies her. When her father approaches her with his expectation that she (at age 16) honor his bargaining her hand in exchange for Denmark's dynastic and territorial interests, she expresses resentment of the arrangement and contempt for Rorik's claim that the proposed groom's vicious slaughter of an enemy proves his worthiness as a husband and leader. She refers to herself as "plunder" in the exchange between her suitor and her father, and is resentful of the barbaric custom of a counselor's verification of the broken hymen by inspecting the wedding sheets and presenting the evidence to the court. Yet the rebellious young woman, like many heroines in early Shakespearean comedies, notably Hippolyta in *A Midsummer Night's Dream* or Kate in *The Taming of the Shrew*, comes to accept the role of the wife as the help-mate. She eventually resigns herself to her role as part of the currency in the Danish body politic. She accepts that the power and decisions are appropriately her husband's, now that Rorik has died the month her son was born. Her sole failing is that she cannot conceive another heir, and there is royal concern that Hamlet is both sickly and a little strange.

The language Updike uses to describe the initial stage of Gertrude's settling into the role of wife and queen, moreover, suggests a profound resentment lurking beneath the social adjustment: "A good woman lay in the bed others had made for her and walked in the shoes others had cobbled. . . . In much of her being she could not help revering the man who possessed her, who housed and protected her and—this the key to all right relations—*made use* of her" (Updike's emphasis). When her brother-in-law returns to Denmark a cosmopolitan soldier of fortune who has learned diplomacy in Italy and Provencal poets in France (he mentions Bertrans de Born, a troubadour poet who influenced T. S. Eliot and Ezra Pound), her simmering resentment, at age 48, boils over. Courted by a passionate, attentive lover who values her opinion and physical body over her capacity to produce offspring and unite dynasties, the mature Gertrude re-discovers her lost youth and passion. She ultimately comes to believe that the sophisticated Claudius restores the value her father and husband took from her by bartering her. Moreover, she discovers her own libidinal sexuality, long repressed by the demands of a proper Danish court and a husband who values his and his wife's decorum over passion and spontaneity. Updike claims, whereas Shakespeare did not, that Gertrude's adultery expresses an element of overt political as well as gendered rebellion: "Protest had been lurking in her, and recklessness, and treachery." Shakespeare's Hamlet naively denies the possibility of his mother's sexuality while upbraiding her for not remaining true to his father's memory. "You cannot call it love," he tells his mother, in reference to her feelings for Claudius, "For at your age, / The heyday of the blood is tame, it's humble, / And waits upon the judgment." These remarks assign Gertrude's feelings for Claudius to some innate depravity of the soul. By contrast, Updike, with his modernist sensibility, describes the union of Gertrude and Claudius as a nearly-metaphysical synthesis that recalls the great poet of the generation after Shakespeare, John Donne: "their souls' emissaries, those lower parts so rich in angelic sensation." Thus in Updike's narrative, Claudius liberates, rather than entraps, Gertrude. He is her path to transcending a narrowly dynastic patriarchal system. But his influence predictably creates conflict within Gertrude on a spiritual as well as political level; and that conflict enables Updike to take a fresh look at one of the overriding themes throughout his fiction, the relationship among religion, morality, and passion.

One of the chief social changes in Updike's narrative is the recent introduction of Christianity into Danish culture. Shakespeare's *Hamlet,* drawing on sources in pagan Scandinavian lore, contains Christian motifs such as the Ghost being freed from Purgatory to walk the night; the Church's refusal to sanction full burial ceremonies for Ophelia because of suspicion that she committed suicide (and its unwillingness to deny burial in sanctified ground to the daughter of a high-ranking government official no matter how uncertain her death); and Hamlet's reservations about killing Claudius while at prayer because his soul might find heaven rather than hell. For Updike, the transition from a pagan to a Christian culture constitutes a central theme. Long one of America's more controversial self-proclaimed Christian writers, Updike takes in *Gertrude and Claudius* his most historic look at the origins of several contradictions in modern Christian practices, a look that contrasts with the invasion and slaughter in the monastery in *Toward the End of Time.*

Inevitably, the themes relating to religion impinge on those dealing with ethics and politics. As has been true since late medieval Christianity, often the line between politics and religion is hard to draw in *Gertrude and Claudius.* The new religion was introduced to Denmark three generations before Gertrude was born, but its assimilation and combination with the polytheisms of nature and the celebration of the senses create tension for individuals asked to subject the urges of nature to the guidelines of religion. Nothing in the political or personal constitution is unaffected by this new and pervasive element.

Among those elements is Christianity's potential as an ally of the status quo power elite. Gertrude's father, although himself lax in practicing the new religion, sees it as a political asset appealing to peasants and slaves, presumably because, as Marx put it centuries later, religion teaches obedience and endurance as preparations for the reward of a blissful afterlife. At any rate, Rorik feels that although the elite class is under no obligation to submit to the pieties and mortification of the flesh the new Christian culture teaches, it is a valuable instrument for suppressing a potentially restive working class, a position with which his hand-picked successor, Gertrude's new husband, enthusiastically agrees.

It is a convenient shorthand to one central theme of *Gertrude and Claudius* to suggest that Hamlet the elder represents the new believer, who adapts Rorik's cynical appreciation for the practical, class-control effects of Christianity to a profound internal belief as well. His younger brother, who with his wider experience in Rome and Constantinople (and thus exposure to Roman and Byzantine forms of Christianity), represents the kind of doubt that would characterize much of Renaissance humanism. In addition to his embracing Rorik's respect for the Church as a political ally, Hamlet the elder despairs of the enlightened education his son is receiving at a German university. He worries about Hamlet absorbing pernicious influences from eastern and Mediterranean Europe, but his greatest anxiety is that Hamlet is learning to question the conventional wisdom on which his father governs: "My son is . . . learning how to *doubt*—learning mockery and blasphemy when I'm trying to instill piety and order into a scheming, rebellious conglomeration of Danes." Moreover, Updike insinuates that the elder Hamlet has internalized the strict order the new religion has taught him. His brother, who vividly describes contradictions in the pieties and cruelties of Christianity as practiced in Constantinople, believes that he, his brother, and his nephew are victims of "Danish small-mindedness—Viking blood-hunger crammed into the outward forms of Christianity." But the elder Hamlet's piety conflicts with his private identity. Gertrude, after she becomes intimate with his brother, comes to believe that the post-coital *tristesse* that habitually affects her husband traces to his religion and its teachings concerning the mortification of the flesh: "a nature-hating piety, learned in Jutland, had unmanned him."

By contrast, Claudius's interest in religion seems anthropological, rather than internal or exploitative. With his greater worldliness, his wider scope, he feels comfortable with new theories combining the love of the world with the appetites of the flesh, especially variations on the courtly love traditions of late medieval Europe. A key symbol supporting this motif is his second gift to Gertrude, a Byzantine chalice that fuses traditional religious, pantheistic, pagan, and hedonistic motifs—she is delighted to learn that the chalice is a "*chimaira*." At one level, what Claudius gives her is a representation of himself: a hybrid, part Danish warrior, part European diplomat and soldier of fortune, part courtly lover in the medieval tradition that produced such figures as Bertrans de Born, Chaucer's hero Troilus, the Italian poet Petrarch, the British poet-courtier Sir Philip Sidney, and satirically,

Shakespeare's Duke Orsino in *Twelfth Night* and Orlando in *As You Like It*. As his politics evolve toward the conservative and authoritarian, however, Claudius leans toward orthodox religion once he becomes king. Moreover, the "pontificating" that Gertrude silently resented in her late husband becomes evident in the speech of her new one: the rhetoric of power, punctuated, in the tradition of modern politicians, with sound-bytes from religion. Moreover, Claudius's piety is not merely a matter of public relations. Although he is a sinner doubly damned by murdering his king and his brother with one vial, Claudius lectures Gertrude about her "unease of soul," or guilt over Hamlet the elder's death, in language fit for the most pious ecclesiastic: "This unease, this guilt for our first father and mother's original sin, is what calls us to God, out of our unholy pride. It is the sign He has placed within us of His cosmic rule. . . ." Quite a leap backward for a man who brought back to Denmark new ideas about everything from the rationale for the Crusades to the viability of traditional codes of conduct.

Claudius's transformation, whether intended as suggesting his spiritual regression or confirming his political manipulation, is another way in which Updike suggests the possible collusion of religion and political life. Having committed mortal sins, Claudius convinces himself that he can repurchase his soul: "The Church made its intercessions as available as daily bread, and scarcely more expensive." In yet one more way, we are reminded of certain materialistic aspects of early Christianity in the acknowledgment, early in Claudius's brief rule, that the Crusades, in which he participated, were a "long-range failure" and the death knell for the heroic tradition. Taking a post-colonialist stance on the Crusades, Updike implies that these great adventures were really little more than religiously-endorsed piracy.

As in all things, however, the issue of religion ultimately revolves around Gertrude, who struggles with the austere codes of the new religion and its support for the suppression of women. Even as a child, she felt intuitively that the chapel was an inhospitable place, one that condemned her as a creature of nature and as a woman. To her the space itself felt "doomed," with its otherworldliness and its call toward mortification of the body: "Being in the chapel frightened her, as if her young body were a sin. . . ." The effect on the child was the disconnection of her soul from her body: the "chill, the Latin, the fusty smells made her feel *accused*; her natural warmth felt chastened." Updike centers here on the practice, not the substance, of medieval Christianity, which produced a patriarchal Mariology—that is, a blanket dismissal of women as the source of sin (daughters of Eve), evidence of which can be traced to their very menstrual cycles; and a profound veneration for the intercession and holiness of the virgin Mother of Christ.

After spending her youth and middle years learning to accept the Church-sanctioned role of mother, wife, and queen—in short, subordinating herself to her lord and master, in his divinely-sanctioned role—Gertrude's rebellion is as much against the established order sanctioned by the Church as it is against political repression. She tells her would-be lover that she repudiates a "duty laid upon the wife by the stiff-mouthed priests, to whom we are sinful poor animals." In discovering her love for Claudius and her new-found sexuality, Gertrude once more speaks of a religion of nature, arguably a synthesis of the pagan religions of nature and a rejection of the *contempto mundi* traditions of late medieval Christianity. Updike risks letting Gertrude stand on a soapbox for him in this marvelous statement of a natural religion: "To waste life in fretful care for the next . . . that, too is a sin. Birth lays upon us the natural

commandment to love each day and what it brings."

Updike is, however, more interested in the conflict between such a position and the orthodox teachings of the medieval Church than in the validity of any of these positions. Gertrude's religion of nature serves her quite well while she seeks a sanction for moving toward adultery with a man who has fascinated her since she was "bargained" to his elder brother. But after that brother dies unexpectedly, the superstitious element of religion re-asserts itself for her. She feels that her infidelity somehow caused her husband's death, as if some cosmic cause-effect machine were set into motion by her betrayal. As the novel ends, and the play *Hamlet* begins, Gertrude feels the presence of her husband's ghost within the castle and raises a question central to the first act of *Hamlet* (one raised not by Gertrude but by Hamlet and Horatio in Shakespeare's account): What Shakespearean theological position does the ghost represent? Does the existence of the ghost suggest some purgatorial penance, as the Ghost subsequently suggests? The question beneath the issue of Hamlet's ghost has to do ultimately with the nature of God, the afterlife, and the fate of a virtuous person dying without last rites. Moreover, in act 4 of the play, Gertrude cannot see the ghost when he comes to chide Hamlet's delay in getting revenge; but in Updike's story her guilt in betraying her spouse causes her to feel the presence of a "perturbed spirit." And although her new husband finds comfort in the outward forms of a corrupt clergy, Gertrude cannot reconcile a religion of nature with one that condemns women, yet seems to be right about the inevitability of guilt and punishment.

On the whole, therefore, Updike does something more than provide history and context for the behavior of the characters in this drama, which we all know will unfold in near-universal disaster by the end of Shakespeare's play. He also develops two themes that are implicit, but hardly fleshed out, in *Hamlet*: the roles of women and the role of religion in the lives of the ruling class of a transitional culture, moving from an age of paganism to one of Christianity and reacting to enormous changes in culture and even technology. He brings a modern perspective to these issues, and tries to learn by writing the history behind the play the origins of certain tensions that remain central to our twenty-first century.

◆ CHARACTERS ◆

As has been argued throughout the sections on social concerns and themes, Updike, by shifting the narrative perspective, encourages us to take a new look at the supporting characters in Shakespeare's grand drama of revenge.

We are seldom aware how many of our impressions of *Hamlet* derive from the point of view, a phenomenon in itself somewhat unusual for a play. But upon reading Updike's "prequel," we become conscious that, more than any Shakespearean play with the possible exception of *Richard III, Hamlet* privileges the protagonist's subjective view of other characters and events. Almost like a Henry James novel, the play revolves around the revelation of one man's consciousness. An obvious example is Hamlet's misogynistic condemnation in his first soliloquy, "Frailty, thy name is woman." He has generalized from his disillusionment with his mother, who in his judgment compounded her failure to honor his dead father by marrying his brother without sufficient mourning. Thus Hamlet's generalization pervades the play, and his cruel mistreatments of Ophelia in acts 2 and 3 reflect this transfer of his resentment from his mother, whom he loves and may be unable to confront directly, to his lady friend who is not protected by the cloak of maternal invulnerability. The critical point is that, because this play reflects Hamlet's privileged point of view and no other, we have no data to determine the truth or extent of Hamlet's hasty generalization from his mother's marriage to his blanket condemnation of women. Similarly, other characters are exactly what Hamlet makes of them: Claudius is a bad king, a brutish lover, a drunk, therefore an embarrassment to Denmark, and a wretched criminal, "vice of kings" because that is how Hamlet sees him; we seldom see Claudius as a more complex character, except for his prayer after the play within the play exposes his guilt. The list could be extrapolated further: Horatio is the trustworthy friend, whereas Rosencrantz and Guildenstern exploit the claims of friendship for their own benefit; Ophelia as a woman is Eve's daughter, and therefore, by Gertrude's example, bound to be unfaithful; Polonius is a foolish, garrulous, bureaucrat; Laertes is a shallow, boastful seeker of respect and reputation; Osric is a courtier and sycophant; and so forth.

The genius of Shakespeare's play depends on Hamlet's coming to terms with his own subjectivity and learning to cope with his destiny. Updike, by contrast, takes a more "volitional" view of the characters. As a novelist, he distributes the point of view between his principal characters, and, as the last two sections of this analysis argue, suggests that Gertrude's and Claudius's lusts were not acts of depraved wills, but rather expressions of a vital and in some ways ennobling passion that grows from the clash between provincial Danish culture and the emerging, cosmopolitan, southern Europe. Claudius is developed by Updike as a very complex character, a man driven by his obsessive passion, near veneration, for Gertrude. He even tells her at one point that his extended exile from Denmark, when he acquired his cosmopolitan polish, was undertaken out of his love for her and his duty to his brother. Speaking like a true courtly lover, Claudius explains that his exile was his way of preventing his envy for his brother's wife and crown to lead him to forbidden acts like those in his dreams, in which "you [Gertrude] were wanton, and I wore a crown." Although ambition, largely unacknowledged as in his dream, and love lead Claudius to the same evil acts that drive the Shakespearean character, the motivation takes up a complex and a lengthy section, narrated from Claudius's first-person point of view, that brings sympathy and understanding for a man consumed by a love that is, initially at least, an ennobling passion. Unlike the circumstances in Shakespeare's play, moreover, Claudius did not murder his brother because of envy or even self-preservation, but for a reason directed at protecting Gertrude's life and reputation. Moreover, the murder is not even his own idea.

Similarly, as the above sections argue, Gertrude is a very complex character in this narrative,: a mother with a surly son, a daughter with an indifferent and autocratic father, a wife with a demanding but statesman-like husband, and a mistress with an attentive and adoring courtier. Her vacillation, between rebellion against and acquiescence to, the social and religious demands these roles impose on her, constitutes the core of Updike's novel. But it is the transformation of Hamlet that will startle most readers.

Like Tom Stoppard's play *Rosencrantz and Guildenstern Are Dead* (1967), *Gertrude and Claudius* moves Hamlet from the narrative's center to its perimeter. Whether we admire or despise the protagonist (and a good case may be made for either position) *Hamlet* is about Hamlet's inner world projected onto the outside. In Updike's version, the red-bearded hero is a thirty-year-old ne'er-do-well who enjoys acting, teasing Polonius, and making his mother anx-

ious. Hardly "Th'expectancy and rose of the fair state" of Ophelia's lament upon observing Hamlet's apparent madness, this Hamlet is represented as a cranky, precocious child who, spoiled as the only son of a royal couple, grew up as "a foppish rude brat" according to his uncle. Although Claudius sees much similarity between himself and his nephew, and even courts Hamlet's sympathy as a fellow victim of the long shadow cast by the late king, the Hamlet who speaks in riddles and asides in the first act of Shakespeare's play, creates a sense of alienation and wit with his gnomic utterances. Updike's Hamlet is a proud, arrogant, distant man who rudely rebuffs Claudius's attempts to establish his nephew as his heir and protege. Whereas in Shakespeare's play Claudius's refusal to permit Hamlet to return to the German university is motivated by his love for Gertrude, in the novel she actually wants Hamlet to go back to school, because his aloof arrogance is a constant reminder of her failure as a mother and her infidelity as a wife. She captures Updike's characterization of Shakespeare's tragic hero cryptically but well: he is "too charmed by himself" to be charmed by Claudius, Gertrude, Ophelia, or anyone else for that matter. "He is the only man in his universe," she laments.

Other characters from the Shakespearean text are modified, much as Shakespeare transformed the old counselor of the sources into the garrulous, memorable comic character Polonius. Updike reinvents that character, making him much more politically astute and ruthless. We often wonder, upon reading Shakespeare's play, how such a silly man could have survived the political upheaval and kept an important place in the new king's court. Although Updike's character is also long-winded and self-important, he is a Machiavellian at heart—a counselor who secretly despises the senior Hamlet and looks for subtle ways to undermine the king. His covert strategies include discretely encouraging, then facilitating, the queen's adultery. As Shakespeare's Polonius does, this character also hides behind a curtain to spy on the royal family—but with markedly different results. His fate, moreover, is another victim of Claudius's transformation as king: by the end of the novel, Claudius has decided on the same course of action his brother did for Polonius—early retirement, and Updike insinuates that permanent silence will be the key element in these golden years: after all, Polonius knows much too much and is willing to use what he knows to gain power.

Aside from Hamlet, the most striking character distinction between Shakespeare's and Updike's version of the story involves King Hamlet. Again, the technical issue of perspective should be considered. In the play we see the senior Hamlet as his son does,: an object of veneration and awe. Hamlet compares his father with ''Hyperion,'' ''Jove,'' ''Mars,'' and ''Hercules,'' suggesting an exaggerated veneration for a father whose sudden death precluded the psychological process of leave-taking. Playgoers have no reason to doubt Hamlet's account. Moreover, the Ghost's version of his assassination, while urging his son to commit regicide and murder, is a sympathetic narrative about a virtuous man condemned to Purgatory because his murderer took his life with ''No reck'ning made, but sent to my account / With all my imperfections on my head.'' We have no reason to question the senior Hamlet's virtue in the play, and we therefore may assign Gertrude's infidelity to innate moral depravity as well as bad taste.

_ Quite different is the king in Updike's narrative, an able leader but a boorish, crude husband and a generally inattentive lover except for a brief span during Gertrude's affair. His brother and his wife nickname him ''the Hammer,'' suggesting blunt, single-minded, one-dimensional leadership as well as a bawdier pun. He is indifferent to Gertrude's feelings as a person and generally insensitive to his son's (except as a potential heir) but attentive to Denmark's political interests. Gertrude interprets her husband's public character by saying ''pomp is his element,'' whereas her lover believes that kingship has driven his brother mad. This last description must be placed in context, for Claudius may want to justify his former crime (adultery) and his pending one (murder) against his brother. These judgments, therefore, made by other characters must be taken in their narrative context, and Claudius has every reason to demonize the brother he has wronged.

Judged objectively by his behavior, however, the elder Hamlet is not an appealing character. He is throughout the text represented as a lout, and a touch of sadistic cruelty surfaces when he confronts Claudius with his knowledge of the adultery. Adapting a popular Shakespearean trick (see, for example, *Henry V,* act 2, scene 2) Updike has Hamlet the elder entrap Claudius into suggesting a severe punishment for a lesser, hypothetical crime, then disclosing that he knows about Claudius's and Gertrude's adultery, which is, because the cuckold is a king, treason by extension. The splendid scene discloses Hamlet senior as maniacally controlling with a sadistic tendency even in exercising his power over a brother and a wife who have betrayed him. With this scene, Updike explains the murder with which the play begins.

◆ TECHNIQUES ◆

Symbolism has always been a strength in Updike's writing. His capacity to invest literal images with contextual signification may be unrivaled among the writers of his generation. Many objects and scenes are invested with symbolic association in *Gertrude and Claudius,* but this discussion will limit itself to a brief commentary on the cluster of symbols associated with birds as signifiers for freedom and entrapment. One of the novel's most charming sections concerns a visit Gertrude makes to Claudius's rookery, in which his retainers train falcons. Gertrude is fascinated and a little troubled by the systematic breaking of these fierce predators' spirits and by the cruelty she witnesses when one is loosed to hunt and kill a crane. Her mixed feelings are well placed; what she is witnessing is a symbolic extension of the process she herself underwent when she was "tamed" by Horwendil to become an obedient wife. She feels this intuitively, thinking even as she watches fascinated as the bird kills and returns to its captor: *"What a cruel and boylike business."* Petruchio in Shakespeare's early comedy *The Taming of the Shrew* explicitly if crudely invokes falconry as the model for his plan to starve, sleep-deprive, bully, and confuse his new bride into total submission. Whether Fengon/Claudius knows he is exhibiting the process of wife-breaking to Gertrude is not completely clear. If he is aware, he may be modeling the mind-control of Horwendil as part of a strategy to disillusion Gertrude with her marriage, thus to set the stage for adultery. If he is not aware, the implication is even more disturbing: as worldly-wise as he may be, he never doubts the notion of bullying and "taming" a natural creature.

This seems the more probable reading. Updike clusters this association with two gifts Gertrude receives from her two suitors. Before they marry, Horwendil gives her two caged linnets, obviously creatures confined to serve human desires for music. Updike reinforces this association of the caged linnets with male power by noting that when the linnets fell silent, Horwendil gave "the cage a shake and in alarm, the poor things would run through their song again"—in short, singing not out of joy or natural causes, but out of fear to entertain a man who in this scene is represented as a bully. Similarly, before he leaves for an extended trip to southern Europe, Claudius gives the falcon Bathsheeba (the name itself recalling a Biblical adulteress whom a lusty king coveted enough to have her husband killed) to Gertrude. Unlike most of his gifts, this one brings Gertrude distress. She is annoyed by Bathsheeba's sudden, often destructive, "baiting" or attacking objects in the castle. More importantly, she empathizes with the falcon's cries "lamenting her loss of freedom, as I imagined it." Updike suggests by this comparison of the tamed falcon and the "broken" woman the no-exit situation traditional patriarchy created. Bathsheeba cannot be placed in the royal mews, because as a half-wild creature the royal falconer fears that she would be "slaughtered" there. She cannot stay in Gertrude's apartments because she is too wild to be among the precious objects, and her incomplete adaptation to domestic situations unconsciously reminds Gertrude of her "broken" role as mother, wife, and queen. Finally, with help from Claudius's servants, she returns Bathsheeba to the wild, seemingly her natural condition. But Updike reminds us, through Claudius's judgment, that Bathsheeba cannot survive there either because she is incompletely wild. In this cluster of symbols Updike adroitly suggests the predicament of a wife in a patriarchal culture.

A final technical device that charms fans of the bard is Updike's inclusion of soundbytes from the play, often in different contexts or even voices from those in Shakespeare. A full list would deprive readers of the fun of discovering unexpected bard-phrases in the novel, but one illustration will suggest the cleverness of such a scheme. Herda, Gertrude's lady-in-waiting, confides to Gertrude when she inquires about her new role as queen, that "There's a shape in things, fiddle and fuss however we will around the edges." Her homely acceptance of destiny parodies Hamlet's greatest single discovery, that a man cannot be the author of, but rather must be an actor in, the drama of his life, as evidenced by his remark that "There's a divinity that shapes our ends, / Rough-hew them how we will."

Throughout this discussion it has been necessary to associate Updike's novel with Shakespeare's play as well as Stoppard's *Rosencrantz and Guildenstern Are Dead*, a play that depends on the audience's knowledge of *Hamlet* for much of its effect. While Shakespeare's tragedy is one of the most important works in the western literary tradition, it is not in itself an original narrative. Upon examination of the known and surmised sources Shakespeare drew upon to craft his great play, we may infer that Updike has staked out a position similar to that which Shakespeare took in the creation and refinement of an existing narrative. In fact Updike calls attention to the continuity of authorship he implies by appropriating and modernizing the *Hamlet* narrative. His Foreword acknowledges his debts to two of the sources many scholars believe Shakespeare drew upon. That acknowledged debt accounts for the three-part structure of Updike's narrative as well as a certain pedantry that pervades the text.

The earliest probable source, direct or indirect, is the *Historica Danica* of Saxo Grammaticus. In Part I of Updike's story, concerning the youth and marriage of the queen and her growing attraction to the brother-in-law recently returned to Denmark, Updike uses the names of characters in Saxo's version. Thus Gertrude is "Gerutha," Claudius is "Feng," and the husband-to-be is "Horwendil," who names his son "Amelth."

Appropriating the names in the original version, however, Updike holds generally to the narrative data of Shakespeare's play, ignoring the profound changes Shakespeare, or one of his lost sources, made. For example, the king in Saxo was a "rower," or a pirate chieftain, and his murder by Feng was no secret. Amelth feigned madness to keep from getting himself killed and to buy time to plot his revenge. Updike adapts the names while ignoring the substantive changes Shakespeare and his probable predecessor, Thomas Kyd, made in a crude and violent tale of murder and revenge.

Having established these archaic names for the central characters, Updike changes them twice, to indicate both the maturation of the *Hamlet* plot in the early Renaissance and his own characters' evolutions and transformations. In Part II, the section dealing with the courtship, decision to reform, and eventual seduction, as well as "Geruthe's" transformation because of her love for "Fengon," Updike uses names from Francois Belleforest's *Histoires Tragiques*, a play printed in French in 1576 and translated into English after Shakespeare's play was performed. Part III of *Gertrude and Claudius* treats the events of the first act of *Hamlet* and in that section the characters are assigned the names with which we are familiar. Updike cleverly explains Fengon's changing his name to Claudius and Corambis's simultaneous adoption of Polonius as politically motivated. The characters' decisions reflect the Latin and Renaissance humanism that was taking hold in southern Europe and thereby reinforce the culture-clash issues discussed in the "Social Concerns" section of this essay. He does not offer comparable explanations for the updating of other characters' names.

Throughout all three sections, Updike moreover casts a perspective on the literal physical space of the play. Elsinore is a work in progress; rooms are added and their purposes change constantly between the time of Rorik's ancestors and Claudius's coronation. As playgoers or readers, we tend to think of Elsinore as "static space," an unchanging place, very much like the story with which it is associated. Updike reminds us that places, persons, events, and even stories are dynamic rather than static.

A final element of Updike's narrative technique is his effective use of landscape and symbolism. As we have seen, the ice-world of Denmark is represented as harsh, cruel, indifferent, a test to the body and the spirit. Despite the inevitable association of the cold world with rationalism, decorum, and iron codes of duty, Updike's description of the Danish spring, which is traditionally associated with the blossoming love of the adulterers, is lush and evocative. Much like his descriptions of seasonal change in *Toward the End of Time,* his description of the coming of spring in a northern climate powerfully evokes the association of natural and human rebirth that animates traditional English texts back as far as *The Canterbury Tales* and many middle English lyrics.

By contrast, the world of Mediterranean Europe, primarily evoked in Fengon/Claudius's stories for Gerutha/Gertrude but also mentioned in connection with Laertes's Paris education, associates with new ideas, a more lax moral code, the dawning of the modern age. In fact, Fengon's servant Sandor misses the opulent Mediterranean world, from which he was exiled when his master chose to follow his heart back to Denmark, so much so that he betrays Fengon to his brother in return for safe passage back to Italy. With this small event, Updike not only reinforces his paradigm associating locale with culture, but he also reminds us that in an hierarchical society, the governing class may be so callused to the feelings of the lesser classes that they forget that such persons may have rights and may also have the will to act upon them.

◆ RELATED TITLES ◆

Several of Updike's novels, and his play *Buchanan Dying,* speak to his growing interest in the literary and cultural history that contributes to our modern experience. He has never, however, reached so far back into literary history, and only a few writers have had the audacity to re-write the narratives of the masters. His retrospective narratives have generally been confined to the American experience of the past two centuries, except for the fragments of historical narrative about Egyptian grave-robbers and the Norse invasion of an English monastery in *Toward the End of Time* (1997). Two additional literary and cinematic phenomena provide a context for Updike's approaching Shakespeare to re-cast and reinterpret one of our culture's widely-accepted core narratives.

First, the final decade of the twentieth century witnessed a resurgence of Shakespearean drama adaptations into commercial films. Kenneth Branagh (to whose 1996 "four-hour film" version of *Hamlet* Updike attributes a "revivified image of the play" in his "Afterword") also produced critically and commercially successful films of *Henry V, Much Ado about Nothing,* and *Othello* during the decade. Other important films of the 1990s include the Mel Gibson and Glenn Close *Hamlet,* Trevor Nunn's *Twelfth Night,* Ian McKellan's *Richard III,* and Michael Hoffman's *A Midsummer Night's Dream.* Sir Anthony Hopkins' adaptation of the revenge play *Titus Andronicus,* while a commercial as well as critical failure, gives convincing evidence that the 1990s were the Shakespearean decade on film. In no other time period would anyone have put up capital to produce a play that has never been popular, and has occasionally been the object of claims that it was not the work of the bard. The Shakespeare revival was also reflected in stage performances in national, regional, and local theaters. *Shake-*

speare in Love, a film about the bard's life and love, contained several references to lines and events from Shakespeare's plays, as well as the ubiquitous theme of androgyny in his golden comedies, as the heroine, with whom the young Shakespeare falls in love, disguises herself as a young man in order to break into the exclusively male profession of acting.

In addition to film interest in Shakespeare and especially his plays, several of Updike's predecessors and contemporaries had begun to re-visit established narratives, both literary and cultural, from a contemporary perspective. The ground-breaking text is of course James Joyce's *Ulysses* (1922), in which a day in the life of a modern Dublin Jew resembles, or in some ways parodies, events in *The Odyssey*. Updike also emulated Joyce's appropriation of classical narrative in his third novel, *The Centaur* (1963), which superimposes the story of the centaur Chiron on the life of a Pennsylvania high school teacher.

Several of Updike's contemporaries also built upon this model of re-telling a classic story from a contemporary perspective. Playwright Tom Stoppard tells the *Hamlet* story from the perspective of the fated and very limited school chums in *Rosencrantz and Guildenstern Are Dead* (1967). American novelist John Gardner re-told the epic *Beowulf* from the monster's point of view in *Grendel* (1971). Adapting less distinctly literary sources to explore past events from contemporary perspectives, William Styron in *The Confessions of Nat Turner* (1967) and Toni Morrison in *Beloved* (1987) explore the origins and effects of slavery in America, whereas Thomas Pynchon re-examines the establishment of the surveyor's line that would eventually distinguish between slave and free states in *Mason and Dixon* (1997), along the way creating portraits of the founding patriarchs that challenge our general historical view of these individuals. Finally,

Joseph Heller and Norman Mailer take us even further into our cultural past, Mailer's *Ancient Evenings* (1983) telling the story of all four lives of his protagonist, who in one incarnation is the Egyptian pharaoh Menenhetet, and Heller's *God Knows* (1984) narrating from a complex temporal perspective the ancient Hebrew warrior-king David's quarrel with God. Like these fellow writers, Updike revitalizes old narratives, literary, sacred, or cultural, with the modern or even postmodern imagination to explore their continued relevance to the modern human condition.

◆ IDEAS FOR GROUP DISCUSSIONS ◆

Much spirited conversation might center on the audacity of Updike's narrative. How do readers feel about the contemporary author's appropriation of one of literature's most cherished texts, and his re-casting the roles of villain and heroine? Is this heresy of a sort? Do modern authors breach some kind of literary decorum by amending stories by great authors of the past? Or is Updike doing what Shakespeare did, adding his culture's vision and variety to a story that has become nearly archetypal? Do such models as James Joyce's *Ulysses*, John Gardner's *Grendel*, or Jean Rhys's *The Wide Sargasso Sea*, which re-tell traditional narratives from a new perspective, apply to Updike's telling this classic story? Here are other questions upon which groups might focus.

1. Are Gertrude's transformations, from spirited girl to Horwendil's wife, to Fengon's mistress, to his wife and the grieving widow, fully motivated?

2. Does Updike overstate the arrogance and aloofness of Hamlet? Is this representation consistent with that character's role in the play? Should it be?

3. One of Shakespeare's great strengths is his creation of minor characters. Do Updike's come to life for you? Are these characters merely names from the play, or do they take on motives and habits of their own? If not, is that due to the novel's focus on three powerful characters' perspectives?

4. Are Updike's original characters, who do not appear in Shakespeare's or his predecessors' accounts, such as King Rorik, Sandor and Herda, fully realized? Has Updike succeeded in bringing these characters to life?

5. Is Updike's account of the Church's support of the suppression of women too harsh? Is it historically accurate (several recent books study early modern history and the place of women, and such studies might cast perspec-

tive on *Gertrude and Claudius*)? Can the harshness of this account be reconciled with Updike's public profession of his role as a believing Christian?

6. Did you like the murder scene itself, as told from Claudius's point of view? Or is this better a story indirectly told (by the victim) as in Shakespeare?

7. Do Claudius's efforts to establish common bond with Hamlet, as victims of "the Hammer's" assumed superiority and male modeling, establish sympathy for this character after he has committed a murder?

8. Does Updike's switching of names from the Icelandic narrative through Shakespeare's version, amuse or annoy you? Why?

David Dougherty
Loyola College in Maryland

HOT SIX

Novel

2000

Author: Janet Evanovich

◆ ———————————◆——————————— ◆

◆ SOCIAL CONCERNS ◆

*H*ot *Six* is Janet Evanovich's sixth novel about Stephanie Plum, a former lingerie buyer, forced through redundancy to take on a job as a bail enforcement agent, which is a polite way of saying a bounty hunter. The setting for all six of Evanovich's Stephanie Plum novels is a part of Trenton, New Jersey, known as the Burg. In *Hot Six*, the Burg is described thus:

> The Burg is a residential chunk of Trenton with one side bordering on Chambersburg Street and the other side stretching to Italy. Tastykakes and olive loaf are staples in the Burg. "Sign language" refers to a stiff middle finger jabbed skyward. Houses are modest. Cars are large. Windows are clean.

The Burg is a very close community, based on extended families. As Evanovich writes in *High Five*: "no one ever really leaves the Burg. You could relocate in Antarctica, but if you were born and raised in the Burg, you're a Burger for life." Due to Evanovich's focus on the closeness of the community, and its influence on Stephanie's character, it is impossible to analyze the specific social concerns in one work without first analyzing the Burg and its inhabitants.

The Burg is a second and third generation Italian-American immigrant community that, while proud of its Italian heritage, fiercely asserts its naturalization as American. This attitude is best represented in the work by Stephanie's father's assertion of the superiority of American goods over foreign imports, a superiority that takes on almost a moral aspect: American equals good, foreign equals bad. Stephanie says: "My father was a second-generation American, and he loved bashing foreigners, relatives excluded." This moralizing tone extends to the level of daily routine: Burg meals are always ready at six in the evening, prepared and served by women, and the kind of food that is eaten is dictated by the man of the house. In this patriarchal society, there is a pressure on couples to get married early and a pressure on daughters to provide their mothers with grandchildren, a pressure that sometimes drives Stephanie insane. Finally, there are many people who suggest to Stephanie that she should get a more feminine job. In *Hot Six*, the unattractive prospect suggested by Stephanie's mother is a packing job at the Personal Products Plant.

The closeness of the community inevitably means that the Burg gossip mill, or grapevine, soon broadcasts any and all goings on. This is mostly presented in the series as being an irritation and a hindrance to Stephanie's sex life. But there is a sense of claustrophobia in the novels, however humorous Evanovich makes it. The upshot is that everyone knows everyone else's business. It is in this closed space that *Hot Six* takes place.

The work deals specifically with organized crime and the ways in which the criminal underworld very much represents a hidden government and economy beneath the surface world of the Burg. Stephanie is drawn into this as she finds out that her friend and mentor Ranger, Trenton's finest bounty hunter, has himself skipped bail on a minor charge, one step ahead of being called in for questioning about the murder of Homer Ramos, a son of Alexander Ramos, an international arms dealer. As Stephanie's investigations continue, she discovers that this seemingly isolated incident has come close to starting a crime war over control of Trenton. Evanovich paints a picture of a hidden criminal government and criminal economy, thinly veiled beneath the law-abiding community. While the existence of a criminal underground is no surprise to any reader, Evanovich does not simply focus on the most noticeable elements of this underground, like the street gangs, which get so much publicity. They are strictly minor players, and it is the major players, the families who control various areas of crime on a city-wide or a state-wide level, that are examined. Evanovich describes an unwritten policy document dividing crime by type amongst the rival families and organizations in this government of crime. This division of criminal territories that allows these organizations to run crime as an effective business must be strictly respected. Only in this way can the families avoid wasting time and resources by embarking on wars of mutual annihilation. This balance is threatened by Homer Ramos who, in an attempt to recoup

his gambling losses, has been poaching outside his family's territory of gun smuggling by running drugs. Consequently, he risks starting a war with the Mafia, whose criminal territory includes the drug trade.

Evanovich has Stephanie stumble around in this increasingly tense situation as she attempts to determine Ranger's innocence, which she eventually manages to do. What Stephanie also stumbles upon is the fact that both the police and the Federal Bureau of Investigation (FBI) are in contact with the various crime families in order to prevent just such a war that seems to be in the offing. At the same time, Joe Morelli, Stephanie's on again/off again lover, is serving as an intermediary with Vito Grizolli, the local Mob boss, in order to get assurances that Homer's poaching will not start a major underground crime war. Morelli eventually explains to Stephanie the role that he is playing—and which he has been hiding from her.

> "[Drug smuggling] was an extracurricular activity for Homer Ramos," Morelli said. "Drugs, extortion and numbers go to organized crime. Guns go to the Ramos family. Alexander Ramos has always respected that."
>
> Except, in Trenton, it was more like *disorganized* crime. Trenton fell in the middle of New York and Philadelphia. No one cared a whole lot about Trenton. Mostly Trenton has a bunch of middle-management guys who spent their days running numbers through social clubs. The numbers money helped give stability to the drug trade. And the drugs were distributed by black street gangs.

Here, Evanovich demonstrates the importance of etiquette in respecting the division of the crime pie. Also, she shows the interlocking layers of the underground economy and the problems posed by border areas in the geographical territory break down: many major criminal players have marginal interests in Trenton, so any crime war could swiftly escalate to encompass New Jersey and even the surrounding states. In this explosive situation, the figure of Ranger is a vital one.

Ranger is presented throughout the series as a man of mystery, a man who knows the underworld of the underworld, in Evanovich's words. Ranger can shift instantly from the speech of Stark Street, the poorest street and the area with the worst crime rate in Trenton, to the speech of Wall Street, speaking of his investment portfolio. In addition to being the best bounty hunter in the area, Ranger has a small army of employees, most ex-military, to aid him in his various "almost-legal" enterprises. Ranger is almost an extra-legal force, capable of dealing with almost any situation. The police know of him, but turn a blind eye. Ranger's actions are always governed by a strict sense of ethics, and thus he is valuable as a peacemaker who, unlike the police, is not obliged to go through legal channels.

He is perhaps the only figure who can be said to have a foot planted firmly in both the criminal underworld and the world of legitimate business and politics. Fittingly, Ranger has been serving as a go-between in this crisis, attempting to reestablish the division of territories. In his words: "[I was an] arbitrator. I was acting as liaison between the factions. Everyone, the feds included, would like to avoid a crime war." Like any other corporation, every criminal organization wants to avoid a war over trade. This would adversely affect their profits and put their assets—in this case personnel—in jeopardy. But even Ranger, the man who slips effortlessly from the criminal world to that of legitimate business, is here caught in the middle of a criminal power struggle. Homer Ramos, in his drug-addled weakness, has allied himself with Arturo Stolle. Stolle sees a possibility to add to his organization's allotted territory by means of a hostile take-over of

Mafia controlling interest in the drugs market. Together, Stolle and Ramos set up Homer's faked death in such a way as to implicate Ranger, so as to muddy the waters and buy themselves more time to set up their drug operation.

Thus, Evanovich presents the reader with a legal world, the Burg, which is based on extended families, and implicitly parallels this with the criminal underworld, which is controlled by a group of extended families. In both instances, there is a sense of claustrophobia, of boundaries being firmly drawn, and in the underworld, Evanovich describes a pressure building that threatens to explode, upsetting the underworld's fragile division of crime. Amidst this tension walks Stephanie Plum, bounty hunter extraordinaire.

◆ THEMES ◆

In her characterization of Stephanie, Evanovich parodies a stereotype that dates back to the 1930s. Through absurd humor, Evanovich asserts that the traditional depiction of the private investigator and bounty hunter as hard-boiled heroes is both naive and sexist. From film noir to the novels of Dashiell Hammett, Raymond Chandler, and Mickey Spillane, the audience is presented with a brave hero who faces corrupt police officers and vicious criminals alone, and ensures that justice prevails against all odds. The critic Sally Munt, writing in *Murder by the Book? Feminism and the Crime Novel* (1994), describes this hero perfectly:

> The low-lit, monochromatic, American *film noir* of the 1940s springs to mind, with its city of mystery and shadows, violence and vengeance. Through the mist steps the messianic "man in the mac," dispenser of commonsense justice, alone in his mission. The image is archetypal—the warrior knight, the tough cowboy, the intrepid explorer—he is the representative of Man, and yet more than a man, he is the

focus of morality, the mythic hero. He is the controlled centre surrounded by chaos, and an effective reading must involve identification with this mediator of action, truth, and finally pleasure and relief through closure.

Against this mythic hero, Evanovich's Stephanie Plum is distinctly unheroic, a woman with very human failings and concerns. Her job is not the glamorous job of the heroic cowboy explorer, full of derring-do. Very often, it consists of finding someone who has forgotten her court appearance and taking her to the police station to reschedule, somewhat like a legal taxi service. Evanovich has Stephanie comment on the difficulties of surveillance: trying to stay awake against the boredom of watching nothing happen, and the problem of needing to go to the toilet while on a stakeout. While the hard-boiled hero gets shot or beaten up, Stephanie has to deal with a pimple on her chin. Like Chandler's Marlowe, sometimes during a case, Stephanie feels the need to drink, but unlike Marlowe, she drinks her whisky in her cocoa with her grandmother and becomes violently ill the next day. It is hard for the reader to identify with the mythic detective heroes on a personal level, as the reader cannot imagine being able to do what they do in the course of the investigation. Conversely, readers may find it easy to identify with Stephanie Plum, and Evanovich has a great eye for noticing the little problems in life that cause so much stress and anguish. This point is best exemplified during that most heroic of *film noir* moments, the stand off with the villain.

> We both had guns drawn, standing about ten feet apart.
>
> "Drop the gun," I said.
>
> [Homer Ramos] gave me a humorless smile. "Make me."
>
> Great. "Drop the gun, or I'm going to shoot you."
>
> "Okay, shoot me. Go ahead."

> I looked down at the Glock. It was a semiautomatic, and I owned a revolver. I had no idea how to shoot a semiautomatic. I knew I was supposed to slide something back. I pushed a button and the clip fell out on the carpet.
>
> Homer Ramos burst out laughing. . . . I threw the Glock at him.

This is not to suggest that Stephanie is without skills; indeed, she escapes captivity and torture at the hands of the hitmen Habib and Mitchell, as well as repeatedly gives her various pursuers the slip. Furthermore, Stephanie does not feel a macho need to face things alone and, in Joe Morelli and especially Ranger, she has help who make hard-boiled heroes look average. This does not mean that Stephanie's partnership with either is a partnership that approaches equality: both Ranger and Morelli milk Stephanie for what she knows, while offering little or nothing in return. Evanovich takes delight in depicting Stephanie's struggles for information and for professional respect against these two, in which Stephanie sometimes comes out on top. In describing the struggles for professional respect, Evanovich shows Stephanie battling against the sexism implicit in Burg society, as both Morelli and Ranger try to protect her and to keep her away from trouble by not telling her about it: it is a measure of Stephanie's determination that she gets any information at all. Also, while Stephanie does bring this case to its conclusion, it would be difficult to say that she does this by imposing order, as the traditional detective hero does. Rather, she works by intuition: "intuition is the big gun in my arsenal. I can't shoot, I can't run all that fast, and the only karate I know comes from Bruce Lee movies. But I have good intuition. Truth is, most of the time I don't know what the hell I'm doing, but if I follow my instincts things usually work out." Stephanie is a courageous, feisty, and successful detective, but she is no superhuman hero.

To return to a more personal aspect of Munt's messianic "man in the mac," one of the key features of these hard-boiled men is their chosen status as loners. They avoid personal relationships, which they see as compromising their effectiveness. In contrast, Evanovich foregrounds Stephanie's sexuality as an important part of her character. Through Stephanie, Evanovich examines the change in sexual mores between different generations of the tightly knit Burg community.

This theme is explored through Stephanie's relationship with Morelli. While they lived together in *Four To Score,* Stephanie still feels the inbuilt need to protest the innocence of her relationship with Joe to her mother, Joe's mother, and Joe's fearsome Grandma Bella. Armed with the magical ability to put the evil eye on people, Bella represents a matriarch for the whole Burg. The older generation, while they are not completely blind to what is going on, still expect sex and/or cohabitation to lead to marriage and children. Stephanie's mother especially is presented as eternally hopeful that her daughter will take a safer job, learn how to cook, get married and, after having borne children, become the local patriarchal culture's ideal of maternal femininity. Stephanie, on the other hand, wants sex on her terms and wants to make her own decisions about whether to commit to marriage or not. The closest thing she has to a child is her hamster, Rex. Her mother's repeated anguished cries "Why me?" could be a comic plaint for the older generation as a whole about the incomprehensible actions of the younger generation. In this respect, Evanovich's exploration of the Burg resembles a comedy of manners.

◆ CHARACTERS ◆

The protagonist and first person narrator of all six books, Stephanie Plum is perfectly described in the words of her mentor, Ranger: "Nothing is ever simple with you. Men blow themselves up. Cars get flattened by garbage trucks. I've been in full-scale invasions that have been less harrowing than meeting you for coffee." Stephanie, while not deadly herself, is a lethal disaster area to all those around her. Usually caught in ridiculous situations, seldom in control of either her investigations or even her love life, she nonetheless gets to the bottom of each case, always by the most circuitous of routes. The series of novels chart the slow growth in Stephanie's proficiency as a bounty hunter, along with the rapid fluctuations in her love life: *Hot Six* begins with Stephanie's humorously defensive confession that she is a nymphomaniac.

The main ongoing love interest for Stephanie is police officer Joe Morelli. Stephanie describes him as a good cop, while adding that the jury is still out on whether he is a good human being. Morelli represents a kind of hard-edged competence and control, seldom telling Stephanie all he knows about her case, as their personal relationship is always cast aside when Morelli assumes his law enforcement persona. When this happens, his face goes blank, and he refuses to divulge any details of his investigations to Stephanie. Despite being unconventional in his methods, he always manages to keep a lid on possibly explosive situations. More than this, the series charts his struggle against admitting to himself that he truly cares for Stephanie, which culminates, in *Hot Six,* in his protestation of love. Finally, a self-confessed sexist in some respects, Morelli tries to keep Stephanie out of danger, as he feels that women should be protected by men.

If Joe Morelli is hard-edged competence, then Ricardo Carlos Manoso, better known as Ranger, is a cross between a hard-boiled detective, a deadly mercenary with ethics, and Batman. In contrast to Stephanie the walking disaster, Evanovich presents Ranger as almost superhumanly competent, breezing in and out of locked buildings, tracking down and capturing Trenton's most violent criminals with ease. While he is dark and dangerous, he nonetheless becomes increasingly attractive in Stephanie's eyes. As with Morelli, Ranger represents a touch of the sexism and the valorization of traditional gender roles implicit in the patriarchal hardboiled detective.

A woman who definitely does not fit the traditional detective novel's conventions of the damsel in distress is Lula, a former prostitute turned bond enforcement office filing assistant and part-time sidekick to Stephanie. Her character first appeared in *One for the Money*, where she was brutally raped and tortured in the course of Stephanie's investigations and left on Stephanie's fire escape as a warning to abandon the case. Lula is a cause of concern for Stephanie, who feels responsible for Lula's safety after almost getting her killed. However, Lula is also a resourceful character in her own right, adept at picking locks and puncturing the bad guys' car tires. Always talking a good fight, Lula's bounty hunting exploits are often described in grand language to comic effect: in *Hot Six*, Lula bravely muscles out an old woman in order to steal her dog excrement. Evanovich is not content with this ludicrous event, but has the excrement turn into an impromptu firebomb, which accidentally burns Mitchell and Habib's replacement car to the ground. Finally, Lula also represents an exaggerated version of the mythology of gun culture, which characterizes the inhabitants of Trenton between the ages of nineteen and ninety-nine. A veritable one-woman arsenal, Lula carries a Tech-9, which Evanovich refers to, tongue in cheek, as the urban assault weapon of choice. Lula boasts that "I could invade Bulgaria with the [stuff] I've got in my handbag."

Stephanie's Grandma Mazur is another comic character with a signature firearm. Toting her .45 long barrel, given to her by her retired friend Elsie, she is probably the most unlikely Dirty Harry ever, with a bad habit of getting the words in Harry's "the most powerful handgun in the world" speech the wrong way around. Hidden amidst the laughter is a serious point: a great deal of the humor in Grandma Mazur's actions and appearance stems from their incongruity for an elderly lady. However, Grandma Mazur is emblematic of those elderly retired widows in good health, who find themselves without the husband who was the dominant partner in the marriage. Indeed, Stephanie wonders in the novel whom Grandma Mazur might have been if she had not married her husband. These women find that they want to enjoy single life and feel that they can do whatever they please, as they no longer live for their husbands. Though Grandma Mazur drives her daughter to despair when she wears the same clothes as Stephanie, learns how to drive after having bought a red Corvette, goes to strip clubs, and speaks about her sexual desires, Evanovich underlines the fact that what Stephanie's mother really worries about are opinions of the Burg community. Stephanie's mother is ultimately concerned not with Grandma Mazur's outrageous exploits, but rather how they reflect on the community's opinion of the family. This raises the question of ageism in the community, questioning the assumptions made about proper behavior for the elderly.

The Ramos family, international drug runners, are comic characters with deadly dangerous sides. Alexander Ramos is a pitiful character in that he has to evade the bodyguards/nursemaids that his son has placed around him to get even a cigarette. However, he is still a man who has built an international arms business, and he has not done that by being nice. The elder son,

Hannibal, controls the family business. He represents the parallel between the world of legitimate business and the world of underground criminal activity. An old, calculating man, Hannibal nonetheless looks fatigued by the long hours and high stress of his post. The youngest son, Homer, whose faked death is the event that drives the plot of the novel, is Evanovich's symbol of the danger posed by unscrupulous figures looking to make quick money to feed their various addictions, as he almost brings about a state-wide crime war.

In the hitmen Mitchell and Habib, Evanovich offers a study in menacing ineptitude. In *Hot Six*, they provide a humorous element, showing that most bad guys are not mythic villainous masterminds, but rather thugs with very human failings. Both hurl racist and xenophobic stereotypes at each other, particularly through the characterization of Habib and his descriptions of Pakistan. This could even be said to represent racist humor on Evanovich's part.

To turn to the Plum family, Stephanie's parents are the typical Burg family. In Stephanie's mother, readers see the ideal housewife, as well as a woman who continually worries about what constitutes acceptable behavior in the Burg. Stephanie's father is a presence in the background of the narrative. Through him, Evanovich explores the phenomenon of "foreigner-bashing" as an assertion of naturalization in second-generation immigrant families.

Of the remaining characters, the most important is Stephanie's arch-enemy, Joyce Barnhardt, a regular in the series of novels. She is emblematic of the people who make children's lives a misery at school, and her pantomime villain status is assured by the fact that Stephanie walked in on her now ex-husband having sex with Joyce on the dining room table. Joyce's use of her own body to get ahead is underlined by her appearance, which is described as

"Dominatrix Barbie." Evanovich hints that Joyce has slept her way into her job as a bounty hunter, and authorial condemnation can be seen in the hints that Joyce has had sexual knowledge of large dogs. As with all comic villains, the reader expects to see Joyce thwarted, and Evanovich always offers delightful vignettes of Joyce's humiliation, often at Stephanie's hands.

◆ TECHNIQUES ◆

Evanovich's technique in *Hot Six* is characterized by slapstick and parody. Written in the first person singular, so as to increase the immediacy of events for the reader, Evanovich describes fantastically disastrous events that spiral out of Stephanie's control, as opposed to the usual first person detective protagonists, who control events through their proficiency and stoicism. Evanovich raises the reader's expectations by lavishly describing recognizable stock vignettes of detective fiction, such as the aforementioned standoff between protagonist and villain, only to frustrate those expectations with disaster. This frustration of reader expectations serves to heighten the almost manic humor. An even more ludicrous example is Habib and Mitchell's attempted kidnaping of Stephanie's dog, Bob, who, like her hamster, is like the child that Stephanie has never had. Evanovich describes Stephanie's horror as she watches the villain's car race away only to have the car stop dead. The doors burst open, Habib and Mitchell stagger out, followed by a happy and unharmed Bob. But it is not the protagonist's quick thinking that has thwarted the bad guys: it is the cumulative laxative and emetic effects of the two boxes of prunes that Bob had eaten, which puts their car out of commission.

Evanovich, however, does not rely solely on slapstick and parody. She provides a detailed narrative framework on which to mount the hilarious vignettes described above, a combination that has earned Evanovich a long list of crime fiction accolades and awards. She deftly manipulates her swift-paced plot to pull her readers into the story. By making her protagonist a bounty hunter, Evanovich can spin multiple subplots around the various people that Stephanie has to track down in the novel, which Evanovich neatly dovetails together with the main plot. The complexity is further increased by the fact that the author has Ranger and Morelli investigating the same case as Stephanie. By keeping these parallel investigations as hidden plot lines which Stephanie is seldom party to, Evanovich skillfully draws a complex whodunit.

◆ LITERARY PRECEDENTS ◆

In writing crime fiction in the first person, Evanovich places herself in a long tradition of American writers, of whom the most famous is probably Raymond Chandler. In Chandler's novels, his protagonist, the private eye Philip Marlowe, is a hard drinker, a loner, cynical about women and love, and very competent at his job. He always moves one step ahead of the police to bring the guilty to justice, and this is especially evident in *The Lady in the Lake* (1944). Part of the delight in reading Evanovich comes from her self-conscious sending up of this hard-boiled school of writing. When Marlowe is having difficulties, he turns to Old Forester whisky for comfort: when Stephanie finds herself in dire straits, she turns to Boston Creme doughnuts. Marlowe is a loner, a ghostly figure in the background, whose life is never complicated by personal relationships: Stephanie is constantly at the mercy of her hormones, relentlessly teased by both Morelli and Ranger, and frequently hindered when her family loyalties are called upon.

While a knowledge of the hard-boiled tradition of Hammett and Chandler allows the reader to see some of the ludicrous humor in Evanovich's work, there are more profitable comparisons to be made. In having a single, assertive, sexually active female protagonist, Evanovich could be compared with writers like Val McDermid and especially Sara Paretsky. In *Tunnel Vision* (1994), Paretsky's V.I. Warshawski is, like Stephanie, carrying out an investigation that is also being pursued by the police. The professional tensions caused by this are heightened by the fact that Warshawski is involved with Conrad Rawlings of the Chicago Police Department, and Warshawski's determination to complete her investigations increase the tensions on her relationship. Furthermore, as an investigator specializing in financial crime, Warshawski's investigation also explores the linkages between politics, business, and the supposed underworld of crime. However, there is an important contrast between the competent and controlled Warshawski and Evanovich's disaster-zone Stephanie, and the difference between Paretsky's dark, menacing works and Evanovich's humor.

Stephanie's shortfall in ability, compensated for by determination and intuition, and the complicated intersections between her professional and her personal life brings to mind Emma Victor, the protagonist in Mary Wings' books *She Came Too Late* (1987) and *She Came In A Flash* (1988). As in the Stephanie Plum novels, Wings' protagonist is a parody of the hard-boiled detective, played for humorous effect.

◆ RELATED TITLES ◆

Over the course of the six Stephanie Plum novels, it could be said that what has drawn readers is a certain lack of development: the reader knows to expect parody, slapstick humor, and a tangle of multiple plot lines when they pick up any Stephanie Plum novel. This is not to say that the novels are poorly constructed or repetitive: rather, this shows Evanovich's constant use of humor to explore serious issues and her gift for convoluted plots. Indeed, reading the books as a series deepens the reader's appreciation, as the ongoing romance of Stephanie and Joe Morelli, the sexual tension between Stephanie and Ranger, and the development of supporting characters like Lula all represent long-term plot developments. However, perhaps the most marked change is that of Grandma Mazur. Having initially appeared as a fairly traditional widow in *One for the Money*, she is now Dirty Harry in a red Corvette, looking for a job as a bounty hunter, and hungry for sex. Finally, Evanovich's situation of her novels within the Burg has allowed her to create, over the course of the six novels, a cast of supporting characters increasingly fleshed out with individual histories. While *Hot Six* works perfectly well as a stand alone novel, it represents new developments in the plot lines that run through the series.

◆ ADAPTATIONS ◆

In an abridged form, *Hot Six* has been adapted to an audio book format, read by Debi Mazar and produced by Audio Renaissance (2000).

◆ IDEAS FOR GROUP DISCUSSIONS ◆

In *Hot Six*, Evanovich succeeds in using humor to analyze serious issues about identity in traditional patriarchal communities, the agreements between criminal organizations as unwritten laws for an underground government, and the inter-generational

problem of changing sexual mores. By writing detective fiction, Evanovich adds manic humor by frustrating reader's expectations through a succession of spectacular slapstick episodes without sacrificing complexity of plot line. Through the series, the author has built up a hilarious supporting cast of characters and on-going subplots, all of which add to the reader's enjoyment and amusement. While it is tempting for readers simply to read the work as comic light entertainment, in doing so they might miss out on Evanovich's multifaceted appropriation and adaptation of the traditionally patriarchal, conservative, and sexist hard-boiled detective fiction genre.

1. Is the depiction of inept Pakistani hitman Habib racist? Why or why not?

2. How does the setting add to characterization? How would the work be changed if it were set in a large, anonymous city?

3. To what extent could Stephanie Plum be considered to be a feminist character?

4. Does the humor of *Hot Six* add to or detract from Evanovich's analysis of social concerns?

5. Consider the attitude of the police to Stephanie's interference in their investigations. Is Evanovich's depiction of the police investigation positive? Why or why not?

6. Discuss Evanovich's presentation of Grandma Mazur. As people live longer, more healthy lives, do you think that ageist views on appropriate behavior for elderly people will be a problem?

7. Do you agree with Evanovich's presentation of the mythologizing of gun culture in New Jersey? Do you think that opinions on gun ownership and use change from state to state?

8. Some critics have accused detective fiction of being simply formulaic and unchanging. Where do you see the originality in Evanovich's work?

Scott Bunyan
University of Sussex

HOW THE DEAD LIVE

Novel

2000

Author: Will Self

◆

◆ SOCIAL CONCERNS ◆

It is difficult to speak of a few, specific social concerns in Self's *How the Dead Live* because the novel is *full* of social commentary. Large sections of the book are devoted to minute historical and political critique. As Lily Bloom lays on her deathbed—and later as she sits and reflects after her death—she spends a great deal of time going over major political and cultural events of the last fifty years. Self criticizes the popularity of psychoanalysis in the fifties, nostalgically commemorates the political activism of the sixties, satirizes the weight-loss crazes of the seventies and eighties, and jokes about the political scandals of the nineties (i.e., the Clintons). And, through it all, he is, of course, quite merciless in his critiques of the middle class and its banal, homogenous desires. However, if readers were to attempt to articulate a handful of major issues that seem to organize the book's social commentary, they should consider the following four key issues: death's position in contemporary life, society's increasingly instrumental approach to human life, ethnic identity and racism, and drug addiction.

While the novel is certainly concerned with death's effects on the individual, it is just as interested in the ways death fits into social networks: the way doctors line up to make a profit of it, the way the best of friends and family do their best to pretend it is not there. When Lily is dying, she begins to understand that the entire medical system treats the human body in a rather instrumental way:

> I also liked the doctors' being at my beck and call—or so I thought. I realise now that all I ever represented to them was diseased throughput; another sick shell of a human requiring a missing component to be bolted on. Modern Times—no wonder these assembly-line workers find themselves unable to cease making diagnoses when their day's work is done.

The medical establishment begins to seem like a system that slowly feeds on death. Self is implicitly criticizing the way that medicine operates as though the body were a mere object to be input and then output either dead or alive. Hospital food, for instance is as bland as possible, in Lily's words, put together "for the express purpose of sliding through us near-cadavers as fast as possible. . . . The other thing about this slick cuisine is, natch, that it doesn't repeat on you. Or rather, neither its odour nor its substance is likely to rise up in the faces of those poor overworked nurses." When Lily's daughter Charlotte and her husband, Richard Elverse, go to the magnificent Dr. Churchill in search of fertility solutions, this attitude of the human body as merely an instrument is taken to an extreme. Churchill admires Charlotte because she has "long since ceased to view her body as anything other than a vessel for procreation." When Richard visits Churchill himself, "the doctor [talks] to him, man to sperm." Indeed, when Charlotte and Richard finally get around to "having sex," Self suggests that "they were really having sex, owning sex the same way that the Elverses possessed two hundred Waste of Paper outlets, three homes," and so on. Though not all of these scenarios precisely parallel one another, their common thread is an absence of regard for the aspects of the human being that the novel as a whole seems intent on valuing. Self seems wary of systems, markets, and bureaucracies that threaten human creativity. Ironically, when Lily actually dies, she ends up facing a "Deatheaucracy" almost as stifling as the networks of control that occupy the living.

One of the novel's other pervasive concerns surrounds ethnic identity and racism. Lily Bloom and her first husband are both Jewish, but their relationships to their own identities are complex. Lily is constantly referring to both herself and her social circle (including, especially, her first husband, Kaplan) as Jewish anti-Semites. "I married Dave Kaplan, I understood later, because of his own—soon to be manifested—Jewish anti-Semitism. 'Y'know Kaplan isn't my real name,' he used to say to people, 'I changed it in order to appear Jewish—my real name's Carter.'"

Lily is highly self-conscious in her own "Jewish anti-Semitism." Her narrative voice is absolutely aware of itself when she sets herself in opposition to her sister Esther and her "UESNYJF" (Upper East Side New York Jewish Face). And Lily realizes the she is "unable to hide [her] racial self-disgust from [her] mongrel kids." However, while

Lily does indeed make a point of distinguishing herself from her own roots, at certain moments she is keen to identify with them. This "positive" side of her ambivalence takes center stage when she distinguishes between American Jews, like herself, and English Jews:

> The indigenous Jews were too dull and conformist a group to crack real jokes. They were the ones left behind in Liverpool while the rest of us headed on to the New World. As soon as they made some money they retreated, Rubens-like, to the 'burbs, to live out their days in colourless indifference. Jewish Anglicans. The English had to turn to American Jewry for entertainment, and so began the proper Jewing of London.

One recurrent trend in all of Lily's remarks on her Jewishness is her attempt to create an identity that makes her feel "different" or "special." At a certain point, she comes to believe that even Jewish anti-Semitism is not as "special" as it used to be: "To be a Jew-hating Jew used to mean something, you could take pride in it; it put you up there with some of the finest minds of the last two centuries—but nowadays any little cut-about prick with an attitude can get away with it."

The entire issue of both Jewish identity and Jewish anti-Semitism actually has more to do with the "mystical" themes of the novel than one might think at first glance. All of Self's nods to Eastern philosophy and religion—such as the *Tibetan Book of the Dead*, the possibility of reincarnation, and the possibility of transcending the boundaries of the self to "get off the circle" of reincarnation—are actually participating in the same investigation into the concept of identity. Once dead, Lily learns: "our sense of self was nothing but mannerisms and negative emotions." Self borrows from Eastern mysticism to create a parallel for the paradox of Lily's ambivalent relationship to her own Jewishness. Identity is, in a sense, all one has, but one's relation to it can be entirely negative; indeed, one's own identity can seem "alien."

The obverse of her first husband's self-conscious Jewish anti-Semitism is her second husband, Yaws's "gentle" bigotry: "never hating anyone because they were black, or a Jew, or a woman, but simply disliking them for themselves alone—*and incidentally* their blackness, their Jewishness, their femaleness." The rather more conventional hatred of the other that readers find here is also prevalent in Self's novel. This overt racism has actually left visibly traumatic wounds that haunt Lily until her death itself, and even beyond that. In a flashback to her childhood on Long Island, Lily remembers kissing and cuddling with her family's black maid, who "defined the world itself" for the young girl. But just as Lily is being absorbed in "Bettyness," her mother bursts in to yell at her, slapping Lily "the way British actors playing Gestapo officers were later to slap their interrogation victims." From this moment on, Lily cringes at the very idea of being touched by black hands: "we both knew we could never touch each other ever again; that for me black flesh was an anathema. An evil substance." Self suggests at points that even Lily's children may be filled with this "inherited racial prejudice."

Later, in 1957 to be exact, this scenario tragically repeats itself, as Lily admonishes her own son for covering himself in mud while playing with his friends and shouting that he's playing the "nigger game." Though Lily, unlike her mother, is attempting to act *against* racism, her response is eerily similar: "I grasp his blond hair, I smack his head once, twice, three times. The way British actors playing Gestapo officers smack their interrogation victims." Lily's son immediately runs away into the street and is struck by a car. David Kaplan is devastated by the loss, and he and Lily are soon divorced.

This traumatic event, coupled with Lily's own childhood experience, severely complicates her relations with the black people she encounters in the novel.

If the novel attempts to point towards a tenuous resolution to Lily's anxieties about race, this possibility is most evident after her death when she meets her "spirit guide," an Aboriginal Australian man named Phar Lap. As Lily comes to terms with the afterlife, Phar Lap attempts to guide her beyond many of her prejudices—racial and otherwise. At the same time, another possible resolution to the novel's racial problems seems to arrive when Lily's daughter Charlotte and her husband adopt an Afro-Caribbean child. This child itself ends up being oddly twinned with Lily herself when, in the novel's denouement, she is reborn as her younger daughter's baby.

Finally, when reading *How the Dead Live*, the issue of drug addiction difficult is to avoid. Throughout the novel, Lily's daughter Natasha struggles with heroin addiction. Of course, Self's own heroin use has garnered a great deal of notice in the press, and thus it is not a surprise to find that he addresses heroin dependency with a combination of sympathy and humor that avoids the sort of dehumanization one often finds in descriptions of "junkies." Some of Natasha's behavior is indeed rather scandalous: as Lily is about to get her diamorphine from the nurse, Natasha swoops "in its wake like a seagull. Jesus—how grotesque. You're dying and your junky daughter comes over to rip off your pain relief—'Natty!'" Yet one must note the humorous tone of such passages. Lily is always jokingly, if cynically, realistic about Natasha's addiction. When Natty is off heroin she is a "nightmare"; when "she's on it she's a peach." Self is more interested in using addiction as a metaphor to approach broader thematic concerns than he is in demonizing drug addiction in the manner of the popular press.

The major thematic cruxes of *How the Dead Live* are the slippery life/death opposition, the body, and addiction.

Perhaps the most obvious of the novel's themes involves the life/death barrier and its permeability. This threshold is crossed a number of times in the novel, sometimes realistically, sometimes fantastically. Over the course of the novel, Lily Bloom moves from life to death and back again, and in doing so she discovers that there was always already death in life and vice versa. She comes to believe that "the boundaries between life and death [are] provisional, confused and indeterminate." For Lily, the living imagine themselves concerned with the present, with life, when, in reality, "Their minds are full of dead ideas, images and distorted facts. Their visual field is cluttered up with decaying buildings, rusting cars, potholed roads . . ."

As we have seen already, death's presence in life is very much a factor when Self is describing the medical system. But the novel's discussion of death and bodily decay extend beyond social critique (as it is conventionally defined, anyway) and move towards introspective interrogation of the body's status as the cause of both life and death. As Lily lies in bed, waiting to die, she becomes highly conscious of her own body, its weight, its decay, even its pleasures. At times, her body becomes terrifying and "other." When Lily becomes convinced that the cancer has taken over her liver, she speaks of this as a sort of revolution in metaphors taken from the exterior world: "like a filthy sponge, it oozes poisons. The body's oil refinery is itself polluted. The crazed enzymes have taken over the asylum." The key point here is that this is not "just" a metaphor. The vehicle (the refinery) does not dissolve into the tenor (the liver) the moment we decode the trope. The movement from liver to refinery is important because it signals a shift in the way Lily understands her own body. As she nears death, her body becomes a prison: "I've been buried alive in the flesh-eating box of my own body." Self describes her comatose state in stunning detail, revealing again the dominant theme of the body's strangeness. Her body is made increasingly alien as it takes on the attributes of a "mere" animal. She can no longer control the sounds her body makes, lamenting "I don't sound human. I sound like a[n] . . . animal. A gurgling cow. My brain's been vaccinated—with cancer." She begins to refer to this phase of her life as "the live burial, the uncoupling of mind from body."

Ironically, the fact that Lily Bloom leaves her earthly body behind halfway through the novel actually provides Self with more opportunities to articulate his main character's anxious relation to her body. A key example of this involves one of Self's more entertaining conceits about the afterlife: "the Fats." These three "disgustingly obese" dopplegangers follow Lily everywhere in the world of the dead; as it turns out, the women are made from all the fat Lily has shed in dieting and gained back on eating binges over the years. Self's targets here are "those Weight Watchers meetings" in the seventies and eighties, but also, more generally, the systematic, ascetic approach to life these dieting fads involved.

As we saw in the last section, many of Self's moments of social commentary are devoted to critiquing medicine's instrumentalization and dehumanization of the human body, but readers cannot overlook the fact that other instrumental attitudes towards the human body are particularly troubling for women. In this novel, Lily's appetite for sex, for instance, is tempered by her knowledge that men are using her as a mere object. When Lily Bloom describes her affair with a younger man (she is in early middle age at the time of this affair) she says "Every time we did it I was amazed that he wasn't discommoded by my sour smells and puckering cellulite. But I guess there was plenty of vagina, heaps of bosom." Some readers may detect a typically misogynist representation of a middle aged woman attempting to hold on to her sexuality "for a little too long." Self is certainly open to criticism on this front, but readers should also point out that he is both attacking the instrumental use of women and providing another deft analysis of the general "otherness" of the human body as such.

The body's ability to betray its owner is, in a sense, also the basic idea behind *addiction's* thematic importance in this novel. Indeed, the unmanageable desire that comes with an addiction is itself yet *another* instance of the body's otherness. Readers may have already noted the novel's interest in the issue of heroin addiction, but this narrower sense of addiction is certainly not Self's only concern. Lily Bloom is *addicted* to sex; the novel's middle class characters are *addicted* to commodities. The clearest instance of this sort of non-drug addiction is manifested in Charlotte and Richard's mad desire to procreate. Each night Richard has to "shoot up his wife with more human chorionic gonadotropin." Self makes the parallel completely clear when he writes that the Elverses (Charlotte and Richard) "*parodied*" Russ and Natty (the heroin addicts) "with their sniffing and shooting up drugs." Finally, Lily's inability to "transcend" the cycle of birth and death (in Phar Lap's words, "to get off the go-round") must itself, inevitably, be linked to the model of heroin dependency. It is a rather daring move on Self's part to connect the mystical/religious idea that desire connects one to the world (the cycle of life and death) with addiction, but the move works very well.

◆ CHARACTERS ◆

As the novel's central character and main narrator, Lily Bloom dominates *How the Dead Live*. Lily's name connects her to Leopold Bloom, the hero of James Joyce's *Ulysses*, and readers of the classic high modernist novel will no doubt detect some similarities between the two Blooms (their fascination with bodies, their earthy pragmatism, and so on). Lily's relationships with the novel's other characters propel the narrative.

Lily's two daughters, Natasha and Charlotte, are set up as opposites from the very beginning. Natasha is tall and thin; she has striking black hair and perfect cheekbones. Lily describes Charlotte, on the other hand, as "a big, blonde, lumpy thing, like me." These physical oppositions are not merely superficial; they are clearly meant to signify deeper personality traits. Charlotte is stable, secure, and reliable, while Natasha is hysterical, unpredictable, and addicted to heroin. Such contrasts between sisters are common in literature—the blonde-brunette opposition was a staple of much Victorian fiction, for instance—and in this case the opposition is one of the key structures that propels the narrative.

Lily's ex-husbands, Dave Kaplan and David Yaws, are both located in the distant past. Kaplan is the more tragic figure, having had a nervous breakdown when Lily's first child dies. Incidently, this breakdown affords Self yet another opportunity to attack the medical system. Yaws, on the other hand, is appallingly dull. Self's characterization here is very skillful; he manages to portray everything readers need to know about Yaws in one damning passage: "Yaws was an ecclesiastical historian. He wrote his thesis on Trollope and the nineteenth-century clergy as depicted in his novels. I'm not saying it was a second-rate subject, but it was amazing how many second-rate minds were engaged by it."

Once dead, Lily encounters another, equally important set of characters. The two strangest characters—Lithy and Rude Boy—are, in fact, both Lily's children. As Phar Lap informs Lily when she reaches the world of the dead, stillbirths, miscarriages and abortions "snag round yer head some." Rude Boy is the son hit by the car in 1957. "Lithy" is a more confusing character. "A minuscule cadaver of a child," Lithy was conceived and died "mislodged in the folds of [Lily's] perineum." Lithy, short for "lithopedion," is Lily's "little dead fossil baby"—literally, her "stone-child." Rude Boy, Lithy and "the Fats" (the women comprised of Lily's lost weight) are all very enigmatic. Certainly they add to the sheer strangeness of Self's world of the dead, but, as Lily's second family, they also help to define Self's main character as well.

Finally, Phar Lap Dixon, Lily's spirit guide, seems to tie together a number of loose threads for the novel. First, he is the "sage" of the afterlife, providing Lily with all she needs to know to "get off the go-round." Second, as indicated above, he seems to help resolve the racial tensions of the novel—Lily's traumatic childhood wound is balanced by the authority invested in this Aboriginal Australian. Third, he is the only character who exists simultaneously in the world of the living (Natasha encounters him in Australia) and the world of the dead.

◆ TECHNIQUES ◆

Self structures most of his works around a central conceit—in this case the possibility of a life after death that is contiguous with the world of the living. He has long been praised for his ability to write extended, complex works based on rather simple, if fantastic, scenarios (in *Great Apes*, for instance, monkeys control London). When reading *How the Dead Live*, one should note the ways in which these conceits allow Self

to offer political, social, and psychological commentary from unusual perspectives.

Self's prose itself is very worthy of analysis. Like Joyce, Self makes use of puns and neologisms. When a pub explodes early on in the novel, items are cast everywhere in a chaotic mushroom cloud, including "the artworks formerly known as prints" (a nod to one of pop-icon Prince's various incarnations). However, Self is also capable—again, like Joyce—of seamlessly oscillating between such playful moments of hilarity and moments of high seriousness and pathos. Such an ability is absolutely crucial for an author working with the sort of satirical prose Self writes.

Self focalizes the entire narrative through Lily Bloom; as Phar Lap suggests, it is all in her head. Self thus makes extensive use of both Lily's stream-of-consciousness and her interior monologue. By repeating a number of passages from Lily's interior monologue word for word (i.e. the passage about the British actors playing Gestapo officers), Self is able to indicate the persistence of memory and trauma. As all of these techniques are standard devices in British modernism, one could argue that Self's prose owes much to both Joyce and Woolf.

◆ LITERARY PRECEDENTS ◆

There are quite a number of relevant literary precedents for *How the Dead Live*; these literary precursors can be divided into two groups: the first group are various literary treatments of the afterlife or the voyage to the underworld, the second group are formal precursors, that is, novels with stylistic similarities but not necessarily thematic similarities.

The key texts grouped under the first heading are Homer's epic, the *Odyssey*, Virgil's *Aeneid*, Dante's *Inferno*, and *The Tibetan Book of the Dead*, the last of which Self actually quotes in his epigraph. Self is constantly referencing these "intertexts." Though he indeed echoes a number of these text's characters, his versions are most often playful parodies. Phar Lap Dixon plays the role of the underworld guide, but he is exactly the opposite of Virgil in Dante's *Inferno*. Likewise, Self's parodic version of Charon—the ancient Greek's ferryman of the dead across the river Styx—is a London cab driver who gives Lily a lift to London's "Dead" suburb "Dulston."

As far as formal precursors go, many compare Self's work to that of Nabokov, Pynchon, Gaddis, and Ballard. Self himself sometimes compares his work, particularly its use of conceits, to that of Kafka. It seems safe to assert that Self is working in a postmodernist tradition that develops out of Joycean High Modernism. As mentioned above, Joyce's *Ulysses* is an extremely important precursor—not only does Lily Bloom recall Joyce's Leopold Bloom, but the styles of the two novels are also comparable. Self's similarity to Pynchon (often compared to Joyce himself) will probably strike the reader most at moments such as the lengthy digression about the invention of the ballpoint pen. This interest in the simple materials of everyday life, their origins in engineering, and their determining relation to larger social issues will seem familiar to readers of Pynchon's work, particularly *Gravity's Rainbow*, *V*, and *The Crying of Lot 49*.

A much earlier writer with whom Self shares a great deal is Jonathan Swift. Swift's *Gulliver's Travels* is also organized around a simple conceit: Gulliver travels to lands where he encounters beings radically different from himself in size or even in species. Swift's conceit, like Self's, offers him an opportunity to defamiliarize certain aspects of his world, allowing for devastating critiques of politics, society, and psychology that are astute, hilarious, and sometimes misanthropic.

◆ RELATED TITLES ◆

Self has published collections of short stories (*The Quantity Theory of Insanity* [1991], *Grey Area* [1994], *Junk Mail* [1995], *Tough, Tough Toys for Tough, Tough Boys* [1998]), novellas (*Cock and Bull* [1992], *The Sweet Smell of Psychosis* [1996]), and novels (*My Idea of Fun* [1993], *Great Apes* [1997]). Those interested in *How the Dead Live* will find his short fiction interesting because it often serves as a testing ground for ideas and characters that show up in his novels. "Between the Conceits" (published in *Grey Area*) for instance, brings up the idea of the "eight people that matter," an idea that reappears in *How the Dead Live* when Lily discusses the "eight couples that mattered" during her first marriage.

Those interested in Self's other works would be well served by reading the novella *Cock and Bull*, which is probably as representative as any of Self's works. It is composed of two thematically related novellas that are queer modern versions of Kafka's *Metamorphosis*. In *Cock*, an abject housewife grows a penis, while in *Bull* a cabaret critic wakes up to discover a vagina in his leg. Again, as with *How the Dead Live*, Self uses fantastic scenarios to create possibilities for cultural critique (in the case of *Cock and Bull*, inquiry into one's understanding of gender).

◆ IDEAS FOR GROUP DISCUSSIONS ◆

How the Dead Live presents many problems for the reader. Lily Bloom's stream-of-consciousness is often difficult to follow; indeed, Self purposefully confuses the reader at important moments. With this problem in mind, one cannot simply look past the confusing form of the novel to discuss the thematic elements immediately. The novel's formal features must be carefully examined if one is to gain an appreciation of the novel.

Once these initial barriers to understanding are broken down, one can then attempt to interpret and link the novel's various thematic concerns.

1. Why does Self choose to represent Lily's thoughts in a "stream-of-consciousness"? What is gained by this technique? Does it merely cause confusion or does it help the reader to a deeper understanding of Lily's character? Is it an effective way for Self to get his social commentary across?

2. Why does Self shift so often between the present and the past? How are these transitions marked? How are they meaningful? Can you notice any points where past and present seem to comment on one another?

3. One of Self's major concerns is undoubtedly the body: the dying body, the decaying body, the erotic body, the discarded body. What are Lily Bloom's attitudes towards her own body? towards the bodies of others? Is she comfortable with her body? Is the reader meant to be?

4. Why did Self, a young male writer, choose an elderly woman as the focal point of this novel? Self, like many modern novelists, is interested in observing and critiquing society. What does he gain by using Lily Bloom as the point-of-view for this sort of critique? Are certain social problems more easily perceptible from a senior's perspective?

5. Self's own relation to drugs has been tabloid-fodder since his career began. Is it possible to detect his sympathetic, knowledgeable understanding of drug addiction in this novel? How do drugs function in the novel? Is their inclusion merely arbitrary, or are they integrally related to the novel's dominant themes?

6. One of the novel's most stunning conceits is Phar Lap Dixon's restaurant, "Nowhere"—a perfect simulation of the Australian outback in the middle of London. When Natasha goes on her own "walkabout" in Australia, she not only encounters Phar Lap, but she also finds a "portal" of sorts in the middle of the Australian outback that leads back to "Nowhere." The mystical "purity" of the Aboriginal desert seems understandable, but why would this pristine site lead directly to its own simulation in the heart of London? Is Self suggesting that the desert is not as pure as it seems? Or is he suggesting that there is a sort of purity that resides even in the heart of the artificial?

7. At one point in the novel, Self satirizes the public's unending desire for Nike products: "It's struck me that I've been living with millions of worshippers of the wind goddess. Everywhere you look, NIKE is emblazoned on sweat pants and tops, jackets and hats, shoes and even socks. Often there's only the ubiquitous tick that's the shmutter vendor's logo." How does Self's conceit allow him to critique consumerism? Does the world of the dead have a special perspective on commodification?

Marlon Kuzmick
Cornell University

HUGGER MUGGER

Novel

2000

Author: Robert B. Parker

◆

◆ SOCIAL CONCERNS ◆

S penser, the brash private eye with one name, one girlfriend, and more scars and minor injuries than most sports heroes, returns in *Hugger Mugger* to try, in his unusual but effective way, to right some wrongs in his corner of the world, which in this case stretches south to include the fictional town of Lamarr, Georgia. Hugger Mugger is a two-year-old thoroughbred stallion that the Clive family hopes will be the next Triple Crown winner, but the prize horse is in danger from some unknown sniper who has shot three other horses belonging to the Clives and has tried to shoot Hugger Mugger. Thus Spenser is hired to catch the bad guy.

Perceptive and acerbic as always, Parker uses this situation to observe and point out—via the cutting words of his well-known detective—the foibles, vanities, and perversities of the worst of current southern aristocracy. The Clive family, headed by patriarch Walter Clive, represents all that is bad about the New South and quite a few things that have always been bad about rigidly stratified societies—for example, the way some members of the upper class take unfair advantage of their old money, silver-spoon prestige, and enormous power to further their own private interests while abusing other people in the process; and the fact that racism and prejudice are often perpetuated by means of the accepted social order. Unfortunately, like the caste system in India, American society, especially in the South, retains its unyielding class structure with its built-in rancor and pain, despite centuries of progress toward the egalitarian ideals of its founding fathers, and this ugly truth often shows through the humorous, jaundiced commentary of Spenser as he goes about discovering who is doing what to whom.

Dalton Becker, the honest and talented deputy sheriff in charge of the official investigation is "a big, solid, slow black man [with] short graying hair," and he readily admits that he is treading lightly in deference to the Clives' elite position in the county's social and political circles. As Becker points out to Spenser, the sheriff is an elected official, and getting elected requires the support of the Clives and others like them. Therefore, there are some lines of enquiry closed to the deputy sheriff. He cannot energetically press the family for information if he wants to keep his job, and the fact that he is an African American does not help him gain the respect and cooperation of the Clives. As Parker demonstrates here, the surface of the New South is more attractive, but prejudice and racism are still sinewy monsters in the shadows.

Unlike many of the other Spenser novels, *Hugger Mugger* does not feature Hawk, Spenser's black sidekick, who is away on an extended vacation. The sleuth's most important helper in this case is Tedy Sapp, an openly homosexual bouncer at the local gay bar, the Bath House. Sapp looks like a professional wrestler but has dyed his hair "the aggressively artificial blond color that musicians and ballplayers were affecting that year," in an effort, as he says, "to gay [himself] up." Spenser jokes with Sapp about gay stereotypes and helps Sapp kick out a gaggle of rednecks who want to hurt some of the bar's clientele. Spenser also jokes with Becker about black stereotypes and helps the deputy sheriff in his investigation. Implicitly, Parker is representing an ideal society in which people treat each other as equals and help each other achieve important goals, while at the same time dealing with prejudice and other human flaws by acknowledging them and even having fun with them.

The Clive family, which has a background steeped in incest, adultery, and drunkenness, stands in opposition to such an ideal society and openly tries to discourage it by attempting to maintain the status quo at almost any cost. Penny, one of Walter's three daughters (the sources of the name for his Three Fillies Stables), is a charming but astute businesswoman who is virtually in charge of the family business. Following her father's death, she forces the break-up of her sisters' marriages in order to preserve the "purity" of the family. She shuts out Spenser to prevent him from discovering any inconvenient truths or damaging secrets, and she constantly shows the steely reserve behind the magnolia sheen. More than any other character, Penny represents that particular Southern ability to smile politely and offer icy, delicious drinks while destroying enemies with a ruthlessness that borders on vicious cruelty.

◆ THEMES ◆

As Lord Acton correctly pointed out, absolute power corrupts absolutely, and although the Clives do not have absolute power, they are nonetheless almost totally corrupt. Penny's sisters, SueSue and Stonie, spend their time trying to seduce strangers for fun, and their husbands Pud and Cord, respectively, are equally immoral, Pud being an alcoholic who indulges his sexual appetites with prostitutes and Cord being a pederast. These perversions obviously contrast with the unshakable, long-lasting love shared by Spenser and Susan Silverman, two very different people who fit together like yang and yin. Quoting Shakespeare's Sonnet 116, Spenser points out to Penny, "Love is not love which alters when it alteration finds." He is also fond of telling people that his name is spelled like that of the English poet Edmund Spenser. These references to poetry and romance are integral to his character and point up one of the main themes in any Spenser novel: love is stronger than evil. No matter what the intrepid private eye must face in his blood-spattered career, he can always depend on the fact that Susan loves him and he loves her. This is the Rosetta stone behind all the wisecracks, courage, and caring in Spenser's world: it is the one true thing to which he can always return, the proof that everything can really be all right, and the source of much of his legendary personal strength.

Another familiar theme in *Hugger Mugger* is that being humane increases, and sometimes even salvages, the humanity in others. After Spenser shows that he values

SueSue, Stonie, Pud, and Cord as people, even with all their horrendous faults, they begin to heal and respect themselves and each other. In his first solo encounter with SueSue, she epitomizes the Clive philosophy when she says, "Money makes the world go round, darlin'. And sex makes the trip worthwhile." This is after Spenser has spurned her advances and mentioned his love for Susan. "Love?" SueSue laughs. "Only some big dangerous gun-totin' Yankee would come around talking 'bout love. My God—love!" Yet it is Spenser's inherent love for his fellow human beings that ends up saving the lives of SueSue and Stonie, and helping Pud and Cord reclaim some dignity in their lives. In a very real sense, love is Spenser's God.

As mentioned, the continued prevalence of racism and prejudice is also an important theme here, especially as it exists alongside the official pronouncements that American society is the best on Earth and that Americans have made great strides in stamping out such anachronisms. Parker has often shown, as he does in this novel, that human nature can be quite stubborn when it comes to getting rid of the sins of the fathers and that a person is better served by being realistic about such insidious flaws than by glossing over them. People will always be people, and some of them will be small-minded, retrograde villains. This type of person is represented in *Hugger Mugger* by Jon Delroy, the Clives' Nazi-like security chief who tellingly wears an "SS" pin on his lapel, the "SS" standing, in this case, for Security South, the company he manages. Delroy is as rigid as an oak and, it turns out, just as dumb. As such, he is the perfect foil for the easy-going, quick-thinking Spenser, who is treading on his territory, but Delroy's brand of evil is tiny compared to the evil that surrounds him, both in the novel and in reality.

◆ CHARACTERS ◆

Spenser has proven to be one of the most durable characters in crime literature, taking his place alongside Sam Spade, Mike Hammer, and even Sherlock Holmes as a classic sleuth with his own methods, his unique and unfailing morality, and his razor-sharp wit. When he suggests to Penny and her father that he will handle Delroy's objections to his intrusions with his "northern charm," Penny points out that this might be an oxymoron, and he acquiesces, "You're right. . . . Maybe I'll just threaten him." Spenser later sums up the character of a Southern lawyer by saying that he smiles "a wide smile, a good old Georgia boy, friendly as lemon cake" and by noting that the lawyer selects a cigar "slightly smaller than a Little League bat."

Staunchly humanistic, altruistic, and romantic, Spenser does not think twice about blithely accepting those who are gay, putting his life on the line for what he believes in, or freely admitting to Susan that he finds other women, including Penny, attractive. After he discovers that Penny may be having an affair with Delroy, he lets Susan know that his initial reaction was disappointment. "Life is full of heartbreak," Susan says, to which Spenser jokingly replies that he is lucky to have "a fallback position." Then he admits that Susan is really his main position: "Everything else in life is fallback." His love for her is an absolute, not subject to change, as is his firm belief in the potential for goodness in the human spirit, even as he dodges bullets and fends off roundhouse right hooks.

Spenser is physically up to most tasks, being an ex-boxer who tries to stay in shape and knows a good deal about hand-to-hand combat and the use of various weapons. Perhaps his biggest flaw, however, is the hubris that such toughness can engender, and even though his high opinion of his physical prowess is often a source of humor, Spenser nonetheless gets himself into some very tight spots by overestimating himself and being overconfident in his physical abilities. At the same time, he is well aware of his shortcomings as a sleuth and of his unconventional methods, which involve trying to learn as much as he can about a case while stumbling in what he hopes is the right direction. At one point in *Hugger Mugger* when he does not have a clue as to what is going on, he refers to himself sarcastically as "Spenser, Ace Detective."

Susan, a Harvard-trained psychologist, has her own brand of toughness, often shown by her willingness to stand by Spenser when he does show his faults and when she realistically fears for his life. So small that she can sit in a bathroom sink to put on makeup, she is the rock of sanity and strength that Spenser needs to get him through his battles. She also serves as a sounding board for his theories, always standing ready to tell him frankly that he is talking nonsense when they both know that he is. In *Hugger Mugger*, Susan's role is primarily in the background, as it usually is in Spenser novels, but she does come on stage during a trip they take to San Francisco and during a period of time when Spenser is back in Boston after Penny has fired him. (Dolly Hartman, Walter Clive's mistress, later rehires him.) As always, Susan and Spenser have some of the sexiest, funniest, most urbane repartee since that of Nick and Nora Charles in Dashiell Hammett's *The Thin Man* (1934), yet in the midst of the rapid-fire banter, there is often a moment that shows how much they mean to each other, as when Susan laughs at one of Spenser's jokes during a long-distance call and he tells the reader, "Susan's laugh . . . was immediate and intimate and as much of home as I was ever likely to have. It made my throat hurt."

Penny Clive rarely laughs, because that would break her veneer of decorum, but she has a ready smile that is charming, warm, and winning, a smile that effectively masks her Machiavellian nature and completely fools Spenser for quite a while. He finds Penny "adorable," and their conversations are sublimely witty and frothy, until someone kills her father. Then Spenser gradually begins to see the machine behind the veil and begins to wonder exactly who Penny is and how she got to be so strange and devious. All three Clive sisters are beautiful, but Penny is especially gorgeous: blond and perfectly, subtly, healthily tan. Her teeth are as white as those of the models in toothpaste ads, and her sharp, bold intelligence serves to make her even more alluring. However, Penny's mind holds surprises and secrets that turn out to be as shocking and disconcerting as any Spenser has had to face, and her power over others is the force that ultimately proves the most destructive in the novel. Yet she is no match for the undaunted Spenser. At one point, she looks at her family with "a very cold gaze. Scary almost," he notes, "unless of course, you were a tough guy like me."

The name of the Clive family is appropriate in at least two ways: the most famous Clive in history is Robert Clive, an eighteenth-century English baron who established the British Indian empire, and the Clives are regal and colonial in their bearing and style. Secondly, the name sounds like the word *cleave*, and the family is split apart emotionally and, by novel's end, physically. There develops a deep hatred born of selfishness and greed, which are the motives for the murder of Walter Clive and for the subsequent imprisonment of his daughters Stonie and SueSue in the family home, until they are liberated by Spenser and Pud, a former football player, while Cord waits for them in a safe place (he is not prepared for such physical battles). There is hope for these daughters and their formerly profligate husbands, but even if Penny is never sent to an actual prison, she will be forced to live within the prison walls of her own warped and rigid mind while she gradually deteriorates like the mansion around her.

The sisters' mother, Sherry Lark, following her divorce from Walter, has moved to San Francisco to become a latter-day hippie, and it is obvious from her carefree, egocentric demeanor that she has little emotional attachment to her daughters. They tolerate her, and she makes a show of keeping in touch with them; however, SueSue and Stonie openly dislike her, and Penny is probably only more civil because she is more mannered. Readers can readily see why Walter would have preferred his mistress, Dolly, to the ditzy Sherry, whose name neatly sums her up: someone who wants to laugh, drink, and have a lark with life, avoiding responsibility at all costs while wearing her freedom like a political campaign button.

Dolly Hartman, whose name and appearance resemble Dolly Parton, is a relatively minor character, but she lights up the page whenever she appears, being not only lovely but forthright, smart, and supremely confident. As Spenser describes her, "She was iridescent with cool sexuality that made me want to run around the desk and ask to die in her arms." Dolly is also determined that her son, Jason, now a young man, get what is due him from the Clive estate, so she hires Spenser to help her, which allows him to resume the investigation of Walter's murder and reacquaint himself with those other characters in Lamarr, Georgia, whom he has learned to love and hate, namely Deputy Sheriff Becker and Tedy Sapp on the one hand, and Jon Delroy and his henchmen on the other.

Becker might be viewed as an older, Southern version of Hawk: his laid-back manner belies his quick mind and his hard-won toughness, and he has a ready sense of humor that matches Spenser's in its irony and offhandedness. When Spenser asks if Becker has any suspects in the horse shootings, he answers, "Well, so far I'm pretty sure it ain't me." Becker tells Spenser that Hugger Mugger's groom, a small black man named Billy Rice, is sleeping in the horse's stable with a ten-gauge shotgun, "case a hippopotamus sneaks in there." However, because of legitimate political concerns, Becker is only able to play a minor, though important, role in the investigation. He must sit back and be supportive while Spenser does most of the heavy lifting.

As mentioned earlier, the detective gets much of his direct help from Tedy Sapp, one of the most interesting of all the characters—especially interesting and unusual as Spenser's main ally. Though Spenser has never been prejudiced or homophobic, he has also never been known to enjoy hanging around gay bars, and he has occasionally had funny things to say about those who do enjoy such a lifestyle, not being a man to let a good joke pass him by, although it might be offensive to the politically correct. Even here, summing up Sapp's effectiveness as a bouncer, Spenser quips, "Most people don't anticipate a tough fairy." A former soldier and former policeman who lifts weights and has studied karate, Sapp never has a problem convincing people to leave the bar when he wants them to. Being a man who values courage and honesty, he does not hesitate to help Spenser in his quest, going so far as to provide a safe haven for Stonie, SueSue, Cord, and Pud, and providing armed back-up for Spenser when the bullets start to fly.

Like most of the other people Spenser instinctively feels comfortable with, Sapp also has a good sense of humor. When Sapp learns that Spenser used to be a policeman, too, but was fired for disobedience, he says, "I'll bet you're pretty good at disobedience," and Spenser replies, "One of my best things." When Spenser sees that Sapp has been using an M1 rifle during the shootout scene, Spenser calls the gun "an oldie but goodie," and Sapp says, "Like me." Through the humor and camaraderie between these two quite different, though in some ways very similar, men, Parker is showing the possibilities for an open, tolerant society, while through Spenser's obvious disdain for the despicable aspects of the other characters, Parker effectively demonstrates the need to be disobedient to any social system that would valorize and nurture such corrosive, self-centered, and narrow-minded attitudes.

One product of such a social system is Jon Delroy, who has built his reputation for toughness on his claims of being a former marine and a former FBI agent, neither of which is true, and on his militaristic, storm trooper stance, which Spenser immediately sees through and has the temerity to make fun of. None of Parker's characters is a caricature, however, and Delroy, who has often made a living by scamming women, is eventually undone by his heartfelt love for Penny. The scammer gets horrendously scammed, but in the process he shows that he really does have some toughness and does possess enough genuine emotion to be true to his one and only love. His other traits overbalance these good ones, though. Of the black grooms at Three Fillies Stables, he says, "They wouldn't tell a white man the truth if it would make them rich," and his opinion of Sapp is even lower and more profane. Delroy's favorite problem-solving methods center on cruelty, fraud, extortion, and even murder. Sapp sums him up succinctly by referring to him as "a mean, dangerous jerk."

◆ TECHNIQUES ◆

Parker, who has a Ph.D. in literature from Boston University, is especially well versed in the detective genre—he focused his dissertation on Dashiell Hammett, Raymond Chandler, and Ross Macdonald—and he is also well aware that this genre has much older roots than those found in the works of Arthur Conan Doyle. The fictional sleuth is merely one of the most popular versions of the hero on a quest, as delineated in Vladimir Propp's seminal *Morphology of the Russian Folk Tale* (1928), a hero who is often tempted but who steadfastly remains true to his beliefs and his determination to complete the quest. Spenser is clearly a Lancelot figure, and knowing in detail the history of such characters allows Parker to take Spenser out of the mold enough to be interesting but not enough to destroy his deep ties to the genre. In other words, Parker both uses and plays against the stereotypical hero-centered detective novel.

Spenser always solves the case and brings the villains to justice, while protecting and worshiping his favorite damsel, Susan, but he does so in a roundabout, sometimes hilarious way, complete with several self-deprecating quips. In *Hugger Mugger* as in his other Spenser novels, Parker shows his deft ability to walk the tightropes between sentimentality and brutality, between farce and melodrama, and between pulp fiction and overly serious literature. Spenser's important but idiosyncratic relationship to the detectives who have gone before him is a constant source of both solidity, in the sense that the reader has certain touchstones that remain firm, and play, in the sense that Spenser often makes fun of his own profession. When another character asks how he knew some secret, he always has the deadpan reply ready: "I'm a detective."

In fact, comic relief may be the most important literary technique that Parker employs. After all, there are always the elements of tragedy in a Spenser novel: people are killed; people dishonor themselves; people betray each other in horrible ways. But during and after all the violence and pain, Spenser maintains his semi-detached, world-weary, and indestructible wit. He may not agree with or understand the events swirling around him, but he is wise enough to know himself and to know how valuable laughter can be, especially in the face of disaster.

Parker's talent for characterization is also important to the success of the Spenser novels. Like the best portrait painters, Parker can capture the essence of his characters with a few poignant strokes. Walter Clive, for example, is "tall and athletic and ridiculously handsome [with] a lot of white teeth and a dark tan. His silver hair was thick and smooth." He has a smile that says, *Of course I'm superior to you, and both of us know it, but I'm a good guy and am not going to hold it against you.*" His daughter Penny "had big eyes, the color of morning glories. Her eyes were nearly as big as Susan's, with thick lashes. Her smile was not superior. It was friendly . . . and maybe a little more." People are also quickly characterized by what they say and how they say it. Shortly after meeting Spenser and Susan, Sherry Lark claims that Lamarr, Georgia, is "stifling to the spirit. . . . All that rampant machismo, all that rancorous capitalism. . . . You know the two are really mirror images of each other." But then she goes on to tell Spenser, "You're a man, you probably don't understand it." As Susan plays along with Sherry's tirade, readers can easily see that Sherry Lark has meticulously made herself into the butt of a joke that she will never get. Parker's gift for dialogue adds immeasurably to the power of his characterization.

Imagery is another literary technique that Parker uses with dexterity, but not with heavy-handedness. He sets the scenes with just an occasional touch of poetry, as when Spenser describes the Three Fillies horses working out in the early morning: "The horses' hooves made a soft chuff on the surface of the track. Otherwise it was very still. . . . There was nothing else in sight but this ring in the trees where the horses circled timelessly, counterclockwise, with an evanescence of morning mist barely lingering about the infield." On another occasion, he describes the climate: "It was hot in Lamarr. The sky was cloudless and the sun hammered down through the thick air." Occasionally one notices the influence of Ernest Hemingway on Parker's spare but effective prose.

A technique that he rarely uses but expertly puts into play in *Hugger Mugger* is the careful changing of tenses to create a certain effect. In a novel about horse country, including a horse race is obligatory, and Parker makes it more exciting by having Spenser narrate the race in the present tense, whereas his normal (logical) choice is to narrate in the past tense. Thus, the action speeds up with the horses.

◆ LITERARY PRECEDENTS ◆

There were many detectives plodding their way through thousands of mysteries in popular fiction before the dime novel became a twenty-five-cent paperback, but only a few of them stand out in such a heavily littered genre. Sherlock Holmes is, of course, the most well-known nineteenth-century detective, but Edgar Allan Poe's Monsieur Dupin was the first classic sleuth in American fiction. Spenser can be compared, or more properly, contrasted, with both. Though he shares with Holmes the knowledge of how important it is to rely on a trustworthy helper, he certainly does not have the meticulous, almost insane attention to detail that served Holmes so well. In fact, Spenser readily admits that he is often just stumbling around in the dark with good intentions and little inspiration. And while he has the dogged determination of Dupin, he does not ruminate or concentrate too well. As he says in *Hugger Mugger*, when he thinks "long thoughts," Susan sometimes remarks on his snoring.

Spenser's closest literary precedents are the heroes created by Hammett, Chandler, and Ross Macdonald, along with John D. MacDonald's Travis Magee and Mickey Spillane's Mike Hammer. Spenser has the toughness and jaundiced eye of Hammett's Continental Op and Sam Spade along with the sophistication of Nick Charles, and Parker pays direct homage to Hammett in *Hugger Mugger* when Spenser alludes to *The Thin Man*. As he and Susan are zipping along in her Mercedes convertible, he says, "I feel like Nick and Nora Charles," and Susan replies, "Of course, darling. Would you like to stop at the next Roy Rogers and have a martini?" Susan's remark is funny but also points up the comparative ugliness of the current American landscape as compared to the wide-open beauty of the countryside during the days of Hammett's novels. The ugliness in the minds of the villains remains about the same, though, and Spenser is just as relentless in his pursuit as any of the detectives that preceded him in the genre.

Like Spenser, Chandler's Philip Marlowe was named after a well-known English writer, in this case Christopher Marlowe, but the two Marlowes were similar only in their quick temper and clever turns of phrase. Chandler's Marlowe differs from Spenser mostly in his somber, almost morose, attitude and his dark reflections on evil and life in general. Marlowe is anti-romantic, even cynical, and Chandler's prose is grittily realistic. The tone is heavy, especially compared to the bright wittiness and breezy optimism of Spenser.

Unlike Chandler and Hammett, Ross Macdonald chose to veer away from the hard-boiled style and create a more detached, more sophisticated detective in Lew Archer, who is well read and an aficionado of Japanese art. Spenser shares with Archer his intelligent, no-nonsense view of human nature, but both Archer and his creator took themselves far more seriously than do Spenser and Parker.

Travis Magee, on the other hand, shares many characteristics with Spenser: he is romantic, tough, resourceful, and often light-hearted. He also has a regular helper, in the form of Meyer, the bearlike accountant. However, Magee is more philosophical and methodical than Spenser, and is an unrepentant playboy. Settling down with one woman seems to be anathema to the free-wheeling Magee, even though he does believe in love and does occasionally fall in love.

Mike Hammer is also a ladies' man but is a loner in the style of the cinema cowboy. Arguably the most popular modern detective, in terms of sheer volume of sales and media adaptations, Spillane's creation shares Spenser's tough-guy stance and traditional American values, but he is more force than finesse. Whereas Spenser is subtle and playful, Hammer is much closer to his name in his approach to cases and to villains, and although Spillane is an excellent storyteller, he could never match Parker in terms of literary or comic abilities.

◆ RELATED TITLES ◆

While the Spenser novels, after the first one, *The Godwulf Manuscript* (1973), could be viewed as a series of sequels, each one also stands on its own merits, and each one is a novel in the full sense of the word, not just a detective novel. Parker's genius is shown in his ability to maintain a strong central character through a series of entertaining novels and at the same time to create other believable characters and wide variations in storylines so that his novels can be read singly and enjoyed just as much as when a reader is familiar with all of them.

Hugger Mugger is related to all the other Spenser novels, of course, in the sense that it continues the story of Spenser and Susan while introducing the stories of other characters, but it is especially related to two recent Spenser novels, *Hush Money* (1999) and *Small Vices* (1997), in that it shows Parker's continuing concern with class-driven politics and with virulent prejudice as a still-prevalent and destructive force in American society. Spenser is still feeling the effects of his serious injuries in *Small Vices*, too, because he finds it hard to climb a flight of stairs.

However, in a way *Hugger Mugger* balances out the heaviness of the two earlier books with its many instances of comedy and with its overall tone of optimism, in spite of the evil inherent in Penny Clive and Jon Delroy. These illicit lovers and conspirators are lightweights compared to the villains in *Hush Money* and *Small Vices*, the latter of which features a cold, professional killer named Rugar, who comes very close to ending Spenser's life. *Hush Money* shows Parker at his acidic best as he pushes the political commentary envelope almost to bursting, and the climax of the novel, which shows the mean-spirited leader of a right-wing paramilitary group literally in bed with an African-American leader who has a high position in the academic community, comes close to satirical farce in its overtly bitter sarcasm. *Hugger Mugger* returns Parker and Spenser to the familiar territory of the detached-but-concerned detective who mildly, but pointedly, comments on the injustice and ludicrous behavior he sees around him. Violence is rare in the book, and when it does occur, it is not graphic. Thus, Parker seems to have mellowed a little after getting some vitriol out of his system in *Hush Money* and *Small Vices*. (An intervening Spenser novel, 1998's *Sudden Mischief* centers on Susan and some deep trouble that her ex-husband has fallen into, and Parker seems more concerned in this case with domestic love, illicit passion, and social justice than with politics and prejudice.)

◆ IDEAS FOR GROUP DISCUSSIONS ◆

The so-called hard-boiled school of detective-fiction writers, whose most well-known representatives were Hammett, Chandler, and Spillane, presented realistic, often depressing pictures of American society as being deeply, irreparably corrupted by greed, cruelty, and dishonesty. This was a society from which the ruggedly independent private eye must rebel yet must also, ironically, protect by maintaining a basic code of law and order. This romantic, heroic viewpoint is echoed in the stance of many comic-book heroes, such as Superman and Batman, who battle both villains and corruption, as well as in the tales of King Arthur and his knights. In his Spenser novels, Parker shows his debt to and understanding of the writers who formed and popularized the genre of detective fiction, along with his broad knowledge of the similar literature that preceded it.

1. How does Parker make his hero different from all those who have gone before him? What are some of the similarities that Spenser shares with his predecessors?

2. In what ways is Spenser a superhero? Are there any comic-book heroes that are very close to him in terms of strength and attitude? Do they have helpers like Hawk, or in the case of *Hugger Mugger*, Tedy Sapp?

3. How is Spenser's quest in *Hugger Mugger* related to the adventures of the Knights of the Round Table? How do his practices of chivalry and morality compare to theirs?

4. Spenser's love for Susan Silverman is always an integral part of any Spenser

novel and is an important source for his internal resilience and positive attitude. Why do you think that the couple has remained unmarried? Does this fact undermine Spenser's firm belief in the need for morality (a strong sense of right and wrong)? If so, how does it?

5. "Noblesse oblige" is a French phrase that means nobility comes with obligations, that those in positions of prestige and power must behave themselves so that they remain good examples for the rest of society. Enumerate the ways in which the Clives fail in their duties to their employees and their community. Do Penny and Walter Clive get what they deserve? Why or why not?

6. Some readers may be offended by Parker's valorizing of the openly gay character Tedy Sapp, even though Sapp makes it clear that he is not "recruiting" people. In other words, he does not care whether others become gay or not; he is simply being true to his own personality. Parker depicts the homosexual community in a favorable light here, but at what point does fiction become polemic and lose some of its power as literature? Does Parker approach or pass that point in *Hugger Mugger*? Is his portrayal of Sapp and his friends realistic?

7. What are some of the contributions Parker has made to the detective-fiction genre? Has he refined, expanded, or changed it significantly? Do you think Parker's fiction will have much of an impact on society itself? Why or why not?

Jack Turner
Wesley College

THE HUMAN STAIN

Novel

2000

Author: Philip Roth

◆

In a *New York Times* review of *The Human Stain* Michiko Kakutani argues that it takes "all of Mr. Roth's favorite themes of identity and rebellion and generational strife and refracts them not through the narrow prism of the self but through a wide-angle lens that exposes the fissures and discontinuities of 20th-century life," which is a way of saying that the novel reflects virtually a catalogue of major social concerns of the United States in the twentieth century with the exception of the environment and energy conservation. Whether race, the private conduct of politicians, political and social consciousness in the academy, violence (in sports, marriage, politics, higher education, or society at large), post-traumatic stress syndrome, the nature of work, and the possibilities of economic advancement for members of the "lower" classes, literacy and illiteracy, this work has much to say.

The novel's themes revolve around or spring from sensitive social issues. For instance, the thematic concern of how individuals create and define their identity is given flesh here as Coleman Silk denies his black heritage, his mother, his brother, and his sister all to "pass" as an American Jew.

And, of course, Roth is deliberate in his ironies. What comprises one's identity? Reconstituting or inventing one's identity has a long history in the United States; one may redesign one's identity to hide or alter a genetic heritage, a political affiliation, or an economic or social condition. All it takes is the will to do it, an individual's decision and resolve to create actions and gestures that over a lifetime can create a new life—and deny the old. But Coleman Silk is not the only character in this novel to create a new identity and deny the old. Faunia Farley, Coleman's lover in the last two years of their lives, has recreated herself as an illiterate in response to the horrors of her previous life. Identities may be invented; they may also be destroyed. Coleman Silk deliberately denied his mother, his birth family, and his racial heritage to take on the identity of another group, one that traditionally was a race cast out from many European communities, its members condemned to renounce, hide, and deny their Jewish heritage or be put to death. Coleman Silk's action constitutes a powerful statement about the nature of racism and its consequences for individual and community.

But even as Coleman Silk was successful in creating his new identity and then his career as a Jewish intellectual, scholar, and administrator, he was unwittingly laying the groundwork for the terrible and consequential irony of his downfall. Just as Sophocles' Oedipus, diligently inquiring after the manner of the former king's death, unwittingly brings about his own catastrophe, so too does Coleman Silk bring about his own downfall. On a fateful day, calling the role for his class and noting two names who even after six weeks of the term have yet to show up, he asks if anyone knows them or whether they are "spooks." His meaning, character Nathan Zuckerman assures us, was that of the first definition in the dictionary, ghosts or "ectoplasmic presences," but in an atmosphere charged with the ideals of academic "political correctness" the term is taken for an ethnic slur. The two students are, it turns out, African American. And the second definition of "spooks" in the dictionary is a derogatory term used to refer to African Americans.

Thus the ironies of fate fall upon Coleman Silk in much the same way that they do for Sophocles' Oedipus, who had created his new identity in Thebes by saving the city from the curse and riddle of the Sphinx, a riddle the answer to which is of course man. Oedipus, in attempting to escape his own fate foretold by prophecy, plunged headlong to meet it. Coleman Silk, having taken on and lived a new identity as arguably the most powerful man at Athena College, is not able to tell the world who he is, that he is himself black, that he has been "passing" all these years, and that to do so he sacrificed relationships with his own mother and brother and sister. He is caught, as Oedipus was, in the web of his own willful weaving. What more powerful theme can there be in literature (and in life) than learning who one is? Is there a denial more consequential than denying one's parents, one's birth family, one's racial and genetic and cultural heritage?

One of the great social issues of the twentieth century has been the struggle not only to identify one's heritage and take possession of it but also to take pride in it and find strength in it. The perversion of this struggle, Roth argues, is the silly and hateful side of "political correctness," which so angers Coleman Silk that his temper and his intellectual pride combine to cause him to surrender the field in a fit of anger and disbelief. That he could be so misunderstood he blames on the fad for being so "anti-racist" and so "anti-sexist" as to expect less of those one seeks to recognize and assist. One result according to Roth is academic and social policies of faculty and administrators that coddle "disadvantaged students" by making class attendance and scholarship unnecessary, thus seriously harming them and the institutions which harbor such policies.

Another social issue that recurs frequently (some might say obsessively) in Roth's fiction is the relationship of sex to identity. *The Human Stain* follows true to form. It is all, finally, about sex. Here Coleman Silk is rejuvenated by his sexual relationship, assisted by Viagra, with Faunia. She, however, has a history of being involved, since her stepfather raped and abused her, with abusive men, none more so than Lester Farley, now her ex-husband. Farley, a Vietnam veteran who has been seriously traumatized by being a warrior, stalks Faunia and terrorizes her. That Les Farley murdered Coleman Silk and Faunia Farley by running them off the road is certain in Zuckerman's mind. But how to prove it? Zuckerman confronts the police officers who investigated the "accident" scene. He asks about the disposition of the bodies and whether there is any evidence that a sexual act's being performed caused Silk to lose control of his automobile, a story circulating about the community. He is rebuffed with an official denial that extends as well to the possibility of Coleman's and Faunia's being murdered. At the same time Delphine Roux, the young French scholar and Coleman's anima, is desperately seeking a male lover. She composes the draft of a personal ad for *The New York Review of Books,* an ad, however, that instead of deleting she mistakenly sends to the faculty in her department. And, ironically of course, the ideal man she describes is Coleman Silk whom she then accuses of breaking into her office, entering her computer, and composing and sending the message. Coleman Silk, the black man passing as white, is symbolically lynched by both the "outraged but innocent and wronged" ex-husband and by the "hysterical female" whose false accusations against him contribute to his downfall and destruction.

Thus, the relationship of sexual activity, sexual identity, and sexual reputation to the creation and destruction of human beings is presented in a wondrously complex and densely textured novel. Roth's words flow like hot lava over the New England landscape, a site of sexual hysteria, ever since the Salem "witches" and later Nathaniel Hawthorne; the "human stain" of the book's title, it always had enormous and generally fatal consequences for its human denizens.

Roth appears to be making complex claims about the relationships of literacy and illiteracy, of head to body, of sex to brain, of feeling and desire to knowing and repression. In fact, the issue of literacy vs. illiteracy forms an interesting counterpoint to the other themes and issues addressed in this complex piece of fiction. Coleman's beloved daughter Lisa attempts to teach children of immigrants how to read English, but she is unsuccessful and frustrated. Everything is a question of reading, of knowing, of being able to interpret signs and signifiers whether on the printed page or on the page of the frozen white landscape where, at the end of the book, Zuckerman

interviews Lester, seeing him finally "as the only human marker in all of nature, like the X of an illiterate's signature." Since he killed Coleman Silk and Faunia Farley, he "X-ed" them out. Does this complex of allusions and images at the end of the novel symbolize the ultimate ineffectualness of knowledge, of reading, the failure of literacy to remove "the human stain"? Blood, then, in its meaning as genetic heritage, as family, as the fluid of life, seems frozen upon this field of snow and ice. Blood and denial, knowledge and ignorance, family and heritage, community and isolation, life and death are thematically linked then in the human capacity to express, read, and successfully decode the human condition in all its complexity.

Related to the issues of literacy is the issue of language. Indeed, part of Coleman Silk's tragedy may be laid to the careless and thoughtless use of language at every level of our society. When Zuckerman reveals the reason for Silk's sudden retirement from Athena College to Ernestine, Silk's sister, she regards the entire "spooks" business with amazement.

> "I don't believe," she says, "I've ever heard of anything more foolish being perpetrated by an institution of higher learning . . .; To persecute a college professor, whoever he is, whatever color he might be, to insult him, to dishonor him, to rob him of his authority and his dignity and his prestige for something as stupid and trivial as that. I am my father's daughter, Mr. Zuckerman, the daughter of a father who was a stickler for words, and with every passing day, the words that I hear spoken strike me as less and less of a description of what things really are."

Roth is impatient with persecution and stupidity, with the careless use of language especially in the worlds of academe and politics.

Even though the consequences of Coleman's aggressive self-shaping behavior on his life and his career have been for thirty-six years a successful professional and personal life, his pride led finally to rash behavior that became his undoing. As dean of the faculty at Athena College, he was a powerful administrator who brought the faculty up to his standards of performance and productivity, to better teaching and more original scholarship all for the good of the students and the society as a whole. Yet, these laudable ambitions and actions destroyed personal and professional relationships while enhancing his prideful arrogance. Resigning from the college in anger over the sheer stupidity and awful irony of being falsely accused of having uttered a racial slur, he discovers that the faculty does not support him, sees his high standards of academic performance crumble, and witnesses the death of his wife, Iris, from a stroke, which Coleman attributes to the relentless onslaught of his enemies under the ensign of "political correctness." His anger and bitterness are all consuming.

But then he meets Faunia Farley, a woman half his age with whom he has incredible sex because of Viagra, a popular product created by the medical and chemistry industry to help people prolong or enable sexual activity beyond the range of ages heretofore thought "normal" and "human." Faunia's two children had died in a home fire; her husband beat her into a coma; she has nothing. As a child she had been abused by her stepfather and ran away from a wealthy home at the age of fourteen. And this relationship becomes a new nexus of community outrage.

◆ THEMES ◆

While Roth's treatments of the human condition often argue that life makes no sense (see, for example *American Pastoral* in which Seymour "Swede" Levov, his paragon of decency and convention, learns just

that lesson), *The Human Stain* argues a profound question, one that poets have been examining for thousands of years. How do you know who you are, the Sophoclean question? And what are the consequences of either not knowing or of denying one's identity? At the heart of this thematic question is the related one of knowing and recognizing one's parents. When a parent denies a child or a child denies his parent, the consequences for the individual and society are profound. When Coleman denies his mother because she is black, Roth has created one of the most painful and moving scenes in all his work. Here is the most fateful, intensely painful emotional transaction possible between parent and child. In denying his mother, Coleman ironically denies his own ethnic and cultural heritage and cuts himself off from his family to "pass" as a Jew, which for Coleman is to pass for "white," so that he may avoid the consequences of being black in a racist post-World War II America.

Another equally ancient theme in this novel is the effects of war on individuals and the community. This theme, related to the social concerns analyzed above, is embodied in the character of Lester Farley, a veteran of the Vietnam War who suffers intensely from post-traumatic stress disorder, the disorder from which Odysseus suffered, according to some scholars, and for which he is exiled for ten years before being allowed to return to Ithaca. Supposedly cured by his exile just as Farley has been "cured" by the efforts of counselors, he still wreaks terrible "vengeance" upon his community when he returns to restore himself to leadership of family and community. Apparently, neither veteran has been entirely cured of "the war sickness."

Other classical allusions are woven into the novel. Athena was the goddess of wisdom for the Greeks; she was Odysseus' patron and protectress, but she leaves

Odysseus for a period of ten years because he and his men desecrated her shrine during the sack of Troy. Supposedly, Athena is the "patron" of Athena College, but as wisdom she has absented herself from Athena College where Coleman Silk has served as a professor of classics and then as dean of the faculty. Crossroads are a classical locus for fateful actions and decisions; for example, it was at a crossroads far from his home that Oedipus met a cranky old man and killed him, only to learn much later the man was his father. The rural crossroads post office that Faunia Farley cleans twice a week is where Coleman first sees Faunia. The ancient myth expresses much about the complexities of the human condition and of knowing the truth, especially about oneself, and continues to do so in Roth's story. As Sophocles put it, only expiation of blood for blood and banishment can purify a community of the stain that results from patricide and incest. Roth has woven an intricate tapestry on this old and complex theme and invites his readers to consider the ancient Greek story in its new dress.

A number of other themes are likewise related to the social issues of the novel. For instance, the novel illustrates how good values may be perverted by their extreme and unintelligent application; the value of the classic "middle way" as the best means to achieve the good life is suggested by its absence; and the consequences of crossing boundaries and borders are reflected in plot, especially as they result from the choices the characters make. Even the physical setting functions in *The Human Stain* as it does in most good novels to reinforce the mysteries of borders.

Then there is the theme posed in the novel's title. What is the nature of human nature? What is the "human stain"? What is finally ineradicable? Is it sex? Is it pride? Is it anger? Is it racism? Or is racism merely a consequence of pride and sex and territorial desire? And there is the theme of the Jew and the black, both figured as outcasts and as wanderers in the white-anglo-Christian-American landscape.

◆ CHARACTERS ◆

The Human Stain is the eighth of his novels that Roth tells through his narrative alter ego, Nathan Zuckerman, who serves as the filtering consciousness and narrator of this especially complex moral fiction. Zuckerman has aged appropriately since his first appearance as a twenty-three-year-old apprentice writer in *The Ghost Writer* in 1979; he now lives (without prostate or sex drive) alone in a two-room cabin near a small western Massachusetts college town, the home of Athena College. As a professional writer, he has long observed his fellow human beings and listened to them. He is fascinated at what moral suffering can do to a person, operating more insidiously than even a physical illness to render someone weak and vulnerable—and nearly unrecognizable.

Roth's use of the narrative voice and moral consciousness of Nathan Zuckerman to tell this particular moral fiction is perhaps the single most important technique deployed by Roth. Zuckerman is the authorial eye, the sponge, the always on and always focused video camera, the truest reporter who does not stay aloof from his subject but who soaks up every conversation, every encounter, remembers every detail of gesture, conversation, confession, and action with a wonderful devotion to detail, and is proxy therefore in his responses for the reader as well as the author. Zuckerman's narrative voice is as rich and fully nuanced yet accessible as any in American literature. To present and interpret the main character of Coleman Silk, as well as all of the attendant players in his tragedy, Roth presents

Zuckerman as Silk's neighbor, a man like ourselves, but who as a writer, is a trained and empathetic observer of life as well as a competent, believable, and reliable narrator of what he observes. Thus, Roth creates Zuckerman as the reliable witness who appears on the stage in classic Greek fashion to tell not only what happened but to guide us in the fashion of the chorus to an appropriate understanding of why it happened and its significance to the protagonist and to the audience. Zuckerman thus perceives and reveals Coleman Silk's *hamartia,* that collection of errors, frailties, mistaken judgments, and missteps through which his fortunes are catastrophically reversed and from which he suffers grievously and dies. Zuckerman's narrative role is so powerful and so successful because of its classical Greek contours. Roth's reliance on the power of the ancient tradition moves his readers to pity and terror because the ironic actions of Silk's abundant human virtues are so fiercely destructive.

Coleman Brutus Silk, "Silky" Silk, is the protagonist. Because of the time and place into which he has been born and because of the choices he has made to shape himself within that time and place, Coleman must finally face the judgment of the mob that seeks to make him a scapegoat for their—and his—sins. He grew up in East Orange, New Jersey, the child of Gladys, a hospital staff nurse, and Clarence Silk, a man of vast learning, who, although a trained optician, had to earn his living as a steward for the railroad. Coleman Silk, the second of two sons, learned to box, became the protege of "Doc" Chizner, who taught the Jewish kids how to box, and learned to slip the punches and slough the racial insults that were part of the time and the place. Although black, Coleman is fair of skin and green eyed, and he learns the power of *self*-discovery after his father's death and upon entering the Navy during World War II—"passing" as a Jew, as a "white" man. "The passionate

struggle for singularity. . . . Self-knowledge but *concealed* [self-knowledge]. What is as powerful as that?" And that became Coleman Silk's guiding principle, his passionate means of "slipping the punch" of the racism of the time, of creating and recreating himself as a white sailor, as a Jew whose father was, in Coleman's invention of him, a saloon keeper of considerable learning and physical power. After being discharged from the Navy, he lived in Greenwich Village, graduated from NYU (New York University), became a professional boxer for a while, and fell in love with a beautiful blonde from Fergus Fall, Minnesota. When he took her home to meet his family, Coleman did not tell her that they (and he) were black nor did he tell his family that his new girlfriend was white. His mother and brother and sister greeted her warmly and treated her as his girlfriend, no questions asked. She bore up during the visit despite the surprise, but she was unable to absorb the shock of discovering that he and his family were black, and on the way back to New York City, she literally ran out of his life.

Roth creates Coleman Silk as an intelligent and strong man determined always to create his own fate and not to allow the ignorant, hostile world of others to do it for him. The wonderful tension of the novel develops from this resolve, from this determination, and it is this core quality that makes Coleman Silk a classic tragic hero. *Hubris,* the pride of self, was Oedipus' tragic flaw, and Coleman likewise has the same pride, a pride that propels him to create himself and to do it very, very well, and yet not know fully who he is. Coleman Silk is a man proud of his strengths, proud of his achievements. Thus, his *hubris,* finally, one might say, is what kills him, but his life is a magnificent one, and, despite the "low" Viagra humor of Coleman's affair with Faunia and the Rothian allusions to President Clinton's sexual activities in the White House during the summer of 1998—the time frame for the present action of the novel—Silk emerges as a powerful and genuine tragic hero, one with whom readers can identify and sympathize and whose *hamartia,* errors, mistaken judgments, and missteps raise pity and terror within our own hearts so that catharsis results.

Silk becomes a classics professor. Roth tells us that Silk's academic career as a professor and teacher and then as an administrator at Athena College was excellent, but he shows us very little of the detail of it. Perhaps it is Roth's judgment of the successful career of a professor that causes him to gloss over it all and to let us actually see only his ruthless and relentless purge of his senior colleagues once he becomes dean of the college. As Dean Silk, he becomes a feared administrator with a mandate and the power to raise Athena College's standards of scholarly performance and teaching prowess by pruning away the "dead wood" and making hires of bright young scholars full of energy and promise. Dean Silk is not portrayed as an administrator who by example, persuasion, and rewards can exact both scholarship and exemplary teaching from all but the deadest of the deadwood. Rather Silk operates through fear and intimidation, bullying his (former) colleagues to shape up or ship out so that he can bring in "new blood." Roth does make it clear, however, that it is the president of the college, not Dean Silk, who receives—and takes—the credit for raising the standards of academic excellence—and who uses his enhanced reputation to move on to a better job, leaving Silk to return to the classroom where he asks an unfortunate but innocent question analogous to Oedipus' asking about the circumstances of the death of the previous King of Thebes. Just as Oedipus' envied and enviable position as savior of Thebes, ruler of the city, and happy family man changes suddenly and catastrophically, so Silk sees his entire life and career of thirty-six years and his marriage to Iris brought to an end all because Silk is judged to have uttered a terrible racial slur, and it is the judgment of the academic community that he must suffer for his "racism." The irony is that the "spooks" are not "ghosts" of the ectoplasmic sort Silk had in mind but are rather the "ghosts" of his own denied ethnic heritage. His denial as a young man of self and family leads to the catastrophe in good Sophoclean fashion, the result of his *hamartia.*

The three principal female personages in the novel are each connected with Coleman Silk in some profound way: Gladys Silk is his mother; Delphine Roux, his nemesis; and Faunia Farley, his lover. Gladys Silk, his mother, is a registered nurse who becomes "the first colored head nurse on the surgical floor of a Newark hospital." She believes that Coleman was wrapped like a gift in every ameliorating dream she ever had, but Coleman decides that he can and will "pass" as the white son of a Jewish saloon keeper to avoid any problems for his career. Coleman disowns her in an act of denial, dispassionate yet fiercely savage and cruel.

Delphine Roux is a young French scholar who leaves France in a desperate attempt to recreate herself and escape the overbearing presence of her mother and the depressing shadow of her family, the Walincourts, an ancient French aristocracy, by establishing her own identity with an academic career in America. Coleman Silk hired her to chair the French department at Athena College as part of his reformation of the faculty. Like Coleman Silk, she has made herself something different from what she was at birth, creating an identity in defiance of her family, especially of her mother. That she should be one of the agents of Silk's destruction is yet another irony to tease the careful reader. At one point she, close to hysteria and lamenting the condition of her life, reflects that while she has an understanding of American academic English, she lacks cultural fluency in "real" American English, the American English of courtship and social intercourse. Thus, like Silk, she bears the "human stain," the stamp of her birth, the mark of Cain, and blunders about lonely and disoriented in a culture not her own. And she, like Silk, like the other characters in the novel, like the rest of the human race in general, is unable finally to be her brother's keeper; in denying her family, as Silk has denied his, she destroys a critical part of what is necessary to be a fully functioning human being. Both she and Silk are bound together by having created themselves against the grain of the familial heritage, by denying their birthright, their heritage. Thus, when Delphine in her hysteria composes an e-mail personal ad for the *New York Review of Books'* notorious personal column for lonely intellectuals, she describes the ideal man she is looking for as a

> mature man with backbone. Unattached. Independent. Witty. Lively. Defiant. Forthright. Well educated. Satirical spirit. Charm. Knowledge and love of great books. Well spoken and straight-speaking. Trimly built. Five eight or nine. Mediterranean complexion. Green eyes preferred. Age unimportant. . . . Graying hair acceptable . . .

And then she finally sees in her created portrait the picture of a man she already knows, Coleman Silk, Dean Silk. Moving quickly but in her highly emotional state erratically to delete the message, which she has habitually and unwittingly addressed as she does most of her e-mail messages to her faculty colleagues, she hits the send button, not the delete button. She knows for a certainty that she is ruined and exposed. Yet she is saved in a way from total ruin and exposure by the coming together of Lester Farley with Silk and Faunia in the final catastrophe on the same night as Roux's hysterical performance. Thus, because he is now conveniently dead, she is able to blame him for breaking into her office, of compos-

ing and sending the e-mail, of making a shambles of her files.

Coleman Silk's disowned and denied mother might have said at this point, "What goes round comes round." She would have been right.

After the catastrophe of the "spooks" incident and Coleman's subsequent resignation from Athena College, his wife, Iris, suffers a massive stroke and dies, murdered, Silk charges, by his attackers. About a year later he begins an affair with Faunia Farley, a woman half his age whose marriage to Lester Farley has ended in divorce and whose two children have died in a farm fire. Faunia is presented as illiterate but she is not. She supports herself by working as a custodian for the college and the post office. With the aid of Viagra, Silk begins a passionate affair with her that further outrages the sensibilities of the Athenian community. Coleman characterizes her to Zuckerman as "an ignitable woman" who has "turned sex into a vice again," as a woman made wise by her life of disasters and catastrophes that combined every day to grind her down beginning with a stepfather who molested her and continuing with marriage to a Vietnam vet who suffers from serious post-traumatic stress disorder. She is a woman who in bed is a "powerful, coherent, unified being." Thus, Roth characterizes Faunia as a creature created by her life circumstances and her defensive reactions to them, a deeply sympathetic character who combines with Coleman Silk in a final relationship, fatal to them both, murdered, Zuckerman believes, by her ex-husband.

◆ TECHNIQUES ◆

Perhaps the most important element of Roth's technique in this, his twenty-third novel, is his choice of Nathan Zuckerman as his technical narrative point of view. Telling the story from the point of view of his "creative alter ego" gives Roth a certain useful distance from the characters and the action while at the same time creating a condition that commands belief in the fiction. Zuckerman as narrator and as a created character bears witness to the life, rise, and fall of Coleman Silk. Roth creates him as a reliable and credible witness not only to the "facts" of the narrative but to the qualities of Silk's mind and person, to what Aristotle called *hamartia*, that combination of choices, decisions, and actions that lead to a tragic figure's destruction. Zuckerman is the messenger, come to tell us the whole story, the truth.

Readers of Roth's seven other "Zuckerman" novels (*The Ghost Writer, Zuckerman Unbound, The Anatomy Lesson, The Prague Orgy, The Counterlife, American Pastoral,* and *I Married a Communist*) will note the development and change of this character/narrator. They might also observe that just as Roth himself has somehow become sixty-seven years old when *The Human Stain* was published (Roth was born in 1933), so too has Zuckerman arrived at his mid-sixties. And he appears to have changed in other ways as well, most noticeably in his responses to different social issues and in the conditions of his personal life—one might call his changes the "normal" and "expected changes" that result in one's having lived for six decades. He has also become "wiser" thus becoming in Roth's characterization an even more credible witness than before.

Zuckerman is by turns contemplative, ruminative, and reflective as he meditates on all the old sins, and he is also capable of outrage over the treatment afforded Silk. He empathizes with his pain and is baffled by the pettiness and stupidity and cowardice of the academic community, and playful at times such as when he and Silk dance to some old 1940s tunes. Zuckerman is also courageous, especially when he approaches Lester Farley ice fishing alone in the middle of an isolated lake in an attempt to learn what Farley is and whether he will confess to having murdered Coleman Silk and Faunia. Zuckerman reveals an interesting connection with Farley in this act; as a writer Zuckerman discovers that there "is no such thing as a back road that doesn't lead headlong into your obsession." It is at this point that Roth reveals a principal reason for his creating and using Zuckerman in this story. "Writing personally is exposing and concealing at the same time, but with you [Coleman] it could only be concealment and so it would never work. Your book was your life—and your art?" Being white was Coleman's art, his creative fiction. Zuckerman as narrator gives Roth the creative freedom to tell such a story and to testify to its truth, its "reality," its power. The narrator/witness/writer must have the courage to tell the truth.

◆ LITERARY PRECEDENTS ◆

As an academic novel, a novel set in the context of a university or college campus and involving academic personnel, *The Human Stain* has many precedents including Kingsley Amis' *Lucky Jim,* David Lodge's *Changing Places: A Tale of Two Campuses,* Jane Smiley's *Moo,* Saul Bellow's *The Dean's December,* and Bernard Malamud's *A New Life.* If one categorizes *The Human Stain* as mainly a "Jewish" novel, then, of course the work of Saul Bellow and Bernard Malamud must be considered as must also Roth's own work since these three are arguably the "big three" of twentieth-century Jewish novelists.

Roth characterizes *The Human Stain* as the third and final novel (when taken together with *American Pastoral* and *I Married A Communist*) in a trilogy, though some critics cannot see much in them that would make a "trilogy." The three novels do, however, explore a pervasive and continuing concern (some might say "obsession") with the issue of being Jewish in America. However, Roth's themes are broader than that, his focus being on what it means to be human, anywhere, to be fallible and obtuse and small; to suffer from, as Aristotle put it, *hamartia,* a collection of flaws and actions and decisions that lead to the sometimes small but often large catastrophes that seem a part of human nature and that prevent humanity from reaching its fullest potential. Taken individually or as a trilogy, these three novels are powerful additions to Roth's body of work and should be considered along with the work of Saul Bellow and Bernard Malamud as some of the most significant fictions of the twentieth century.

◆ RELATED TITLES ◆

The Human Stain may be compared, for example, with Saul Bellow's *Ravelstein,* both of which, despite their obvious differences in style, make use of many comparable devices including that of the narrator. Chick, the narrator of *Ravelstein,* has produced a novel about Ravelstein; Zuckerman, the narrator of *The Human Stain,* has produced a book entitled "The Human Stain." Critics suggest that in both cases, the identification of narrator with author is very close, indeed. Among other recent "academic novels," one might consider *Blue Angel* (2000) by Francine Prose, a much younger writer than either Bellow or Roth, and Brian Morton's *Starting Out in the Evening* (2000).

◆ IDEAS FOR GROUP DISCUSSIONS ◆

The following four areas of inquiry may be especially fruitful of excellent discussions: classic (Sophoclean/Aristotelian) ideas of human tragedy and responsibility; the American Jewish experience as represented in fiction; "passing" as a survival strategy among African Americans; and the nature of the American academic community at the end of the twentieth century. In each of these general areas, the questions of individual responsibility and the consequences of one's actions seem dominant. While society and the zeitgeist exert pressure on individuals, minorities such as Jews, African Americans, and women have struggled to achieve acceptance and success in the United States, but often at great costs and often with serious but unintended consequences for the individual and his or her family and community.

1. Is Coleman Silk a tragic figure? Explain why or why not. Is he a victim of prejudice, be it racial, gender, or age-based? What is the relationship between the actions he takes and the various forms of societal and individual prejudice that he experiences? Is Coleman ultimately responsible for his fate?

2. Is Roth's satire on "political correctness," a fact of academic life of much of the last quarter of the twentieth century, appropriate and well-targeted or is it based more on caricature and personal animus than on a serious condition in American cultural life that needs to be corrected?

3. Much is made in the novel about literacy and illiteracy of various kinds. Identify and analyze the causes, consequences, and cures of illiteracy as presented by Roth. Is literacy related more to truth and happiness or to power and responsibility? What is the relationship of literacy and illiteracy to the fates of Coleman Silk and Faunia Farley?

4. Relate the question of Delphine Roux's sexual frustration to her function in the academy. Is she simply a caricature, a straw-man (woman) for Roth to attack,

or does her characterization raise issues of serious concern to the academy and the larger community?

5. Research the phenomenon of "passing" (African Americans pretending to be "non-African Americans" of some sort or another). What other literary works, especially by black authors, have examined this issue? Has the development of "black" pride and other ethnicity-based pride movements hurt or helped the development of racial harmony in our multi-ethnic society? Has "passing" hurt or helped? What are the most fundamental social issues today that are related to race or ethnicity? Does Roth's treatment of the issue shed important light on the problem?

6. Roth raises the issue of chemically aided sexual performance for men, specifically Viagra. How important is such an issue in our culture? What about the disparity of ages between Coleman and Faunia? Is Coleman guilty of abuse in his sexual relationship with Faunia as the feminists at Athena College charge or is the relationship entirely one between consenting adults and therefore of nobody's business?

7. A number of authors have chosen to create fully developed narrators who are participant-observers of the fictional action at the center of the story. Assemble a number of novels told by a participant-observer (that is, not the main character) and analyze the function of this narrative stance. (Think about, in addition to the novels mentioned earlier in this article, F. Scott Fitzgerald's *The Great Gatsby*.) Why do you think writers find such a point of view useful and effective?

8. Allusions to classical literature abound in *The Human Stain*. Read *Oedipus Rex* by Sophocles and the section of Aristotle's *Poetics* that analyzes it. Compare and contrast Roth's use of *hamartia, hubris,* and *fate* with their use by Sophocles. Do you see any other classical allusions in Roth's novel? What are they and what is their significance?

9. Read Roth's other novels narrated by Nathan Zuckerman. Analyze the nature, growth, and change in Zuckerman's characterization as Roth has developed him in the eight novels. Are there inexplicable inconsistencies in that characterization or has Roth created a character in Zuckerman who grows and changes and develops in an acceptably realistic and believable manner over the nearly thirty years of his fictional existence?

Theodore C. Humphrey
California State Polytechnic University,
Pomona

IN THE TIME OF THE BUTTERFLIES

Novel

1994

Author: Julia Alvarez

◆ SOCIAL CONCERNS ◆

A fictionalized biography of the lives of four young women growing up in the Dominican Republic under the dictator Raphael Leonidas Trujillo, *In the Time of the Butterflies* brings alive the terror and anxiety of living in that time and place. The overarching concern is human rights, played against the consequences of a dictator's ability to gain total control over a nation, holding the lives of the people hostage to his whims. Underlying concerns are the rights of women in any society, freedom to make choices, and the right to live in a free society. "May I never experience all that it is possible to get used to"—Violeta's prayer while in the prison cell with the sisters—is a poignant reminder that people can lose their freedom if they allow themselves to become unconcerned.

Alvarez, having fled to New York as a child with her family to escape Trujillo, has noted that she finds her identity divided, a trait common among people who find they have to adjust to a new country and new culture. In *DISCovering Authors*, she said: "I am a Dominican, hyphen, American. As a fiction writer, I find that the most exciting things happen in the realm of that hyphen—the place where two worlds collide or blend together." Validation of these feelings is a universal concern in Alvarez's writing.

Born in 1891 to impoverished parents, Raphael Leonidas Trujillo, also known as El Jefe, entered the Dominican Republic's National Guard in 1919. Established by the Americans during their occupation of the country from 1916 to 1924, the Guard eventually became the Dominican Army. In 1927, Trujillo was appointed a general. In 1924, the Americans withdrew their occupation of the country after Horacio Vasquez was elected president. In 1930, Trujillo and the army removed Vasquez, who wanted an illegal second term as president, and engineered Trujillo's election to the presidency, beginning his dictatorship. His campaign methods set the stage for his rule; the opposition surrendered in the face of bands of thugs and army personnel armed with machine guns.

A month after Trujillo's election, the country was devastated by a hurricane, and Trujillo used the event to consolidate his power. With the suspension of the national constitution, Trujillo could control all necessities such as food, medicine, and building materials. He increased his personal wealth by confiscating property and wealth from his opponents and solidified his stranglehold on the country. Thousands were murdered or imprisoned and tortured. The United States was willing to overlook his human rights transgressions since the worldwide depression and the fascist movement encouraged President Roosevelt to work for the friendship of the Latin American nations. Because strategic interests such as the Panama Canal needed to be protected, the United States was willing to overlook human rights violations to ensure a stable Caribbean. On the positive side, Trujillo was successful in repaying the foreign debt, balancing the budget, reorganizing the currency and the banking system, and improving medical services. However, "Murder, kidnapping, and imprisonment were established methods of dealing with dissent," according to an article in *DISCovering World History.*

Charles D. McIntosh, writing for *American Heritage,* observed that "We Americans don't understand very well what it is to live under a dictatorship, so we tend not to become too disturbed when our government helps some general stay in power." Generalissimo Dr. Rafael Leonidas Trujillo Molina, Benefactor of the Fatherland and Father of the New Fatherland, as he styled himself, reigned as dictator over the Dominican Republic for almost thirty years, with the help of the American Central Intelligence Agency. Communism appeared to be gaining a foothold in Central and South American countries, enough to make the Americans concerned that the United States would become one of only a few democratic countries on the continents of North and South America. The American government again was willing to overlook Trujillo's human rights transgressions because he was an anti-Communist. During that time, Trujillo became careful not to antagonize his American supporters.

McIntosh, who grew up in the Dominican Republic from 1928 to 1939 while his father managed the National City Bank of New York, gave a picture of life in that country in 1957, after he returned to the island to work for the Porto Rico Sugar Company. The week McIntosh arrived for his new job, Trujillo raised the minimum wage for the sugar workers from $.75 to $1.50 per day, much to the consternation of the company. Trujillo, using his extensive spy network, had assessed exactly what the company could afford. So extensive was the spy network that the foreign employees, living in the company compound, knew that their servants were spying for Trujillo. McIntosh said, "It took a while for newcomers to grasp that spies were everywhere and that one's tongue must be constantly guarded."

The severity of the political situation was brought home to McIntosh when his bicycle was stolen and, after reporting the theft to the military police, recovered. He witnessed the brutal beating of an elderly peasant man, in whose possession the bicycle was found. McIntosh went on to describe Trujillo's attitude toward stealing, begging, and prostitution. Anyone caught engaging in any of these forbidden pursuits simply disappeared into La Fortaleza, a waterfront prison in Ciudad Trujillo—the new name for the city of Santo Domingo—never to be seen again. Shark-eaten bodies washed up regularly on the beach under the chute coming out of the back wall of the prison. No one dared complain.

Summing up life in a regime such as this, McIntosh wrote, " . . . life in a totally controlled society buys its vaunted orderliness at an intolerable cost. That cost is the demise of the human spirit. Even for those who reside, as my wife and I did, as guests in a totalitarian regime, the pressure can become insupportable." If a foreigner, much better protected than a native, has these feelings, one wonders how much worse is the lot of the native?

In the Time of the Butterflies

The daughters of the Mirabal family begin to hate Trujillo even before their family suffers a loss to the regime. "There are the Perozos, not a man left in that family. And the Martinez Reyna and his wife murdered in their bed, and thousands of Haitians massacred at the border, making the river, they say, still run red—*Ay. Dios Santos!*" are the thoughts of Patria, as she begins to understand Minerva's rebellion. The hatred is concealed, as it must be, to preserve their lives. The four young women will make different choices in their crusade against Trujillo, and they will eventually be instrumental in his downfall. They refuse to allow the demise of their human spirits.

Alvarez said in the postscript to the book: "November 25th, the day of their murder, is observed in many Latin American countries as the International Day Against Violence Toward Women. Obviously, these sisters, who fought one tyrant, have served as models for women fighting against injustices of all kinds."

◆ THEMES ◆

The disastrous effect of a dictatorship on the lives of the citizens of the Dominican Republic is the main theme of *In the Time of the Butterflies*. In addition, the relationships between the members of the Mirabal family shape the story. The bonds among the sisters and the social influences of the time set the goals for these brave young women. They are willing to sacrifice themselves for the good of their nation. "Political and personal themes are thus interwoven with powerful effect," wrote Elizabeth Martinez in *The Progressive*. Martinez also observed that a powerful theme is the "journey from traditional Catholicism to revolution—a journey made by many priests also . . . as in Latin American liberation theology."

Beginning during the time of their convent education, the sisters witness Trujillo's obsession with beautiful young women. Trujillo woos and wins a young woman in the convent school, eventually taking her away from the school to live in a large house outside the capital. When his wife discovers her, she is discarded, sent to Miami to live alone. Papa uses the story to lecture all four girls about the dangers of the world, explaining that "hens shouldn't wander away from the safety of the barnyard." But Papa is unable to protect Minerva at the Discovery Day Dance when Trujillo begins making advances to Minerva. Papa knows the family will pay dearly if Trujillo does not get what he wants. He delegates his responsibility by saying the young ones know what is best as they leave the party. Minerva is strong enough to stand up for her principles, the principles taught to her by her family and religion.

The Roman Catholic Church takes the position that God will eventually deliver the people from the bondage of Trujillo. Gradually, the priests begin to understand that unless they take an active part in the deliverance, it may not happen. After the retreat at the motherhouse where the women and priests are almost killed, the priests decide "they could not wait forever for the pope and the archbishop to come around. . . . The word was, we were all brothers and sisters in Christ." The priests plan to organize the people, telling them they cannot continue to carry out the orders of Trujillo. Murder is a mortal sin. Castro's revolution shines as a beacon of hope for the Dominican underground. No one knows as yet of Castro's ties to Communist Russia.

Women were beginning to look for ways to gain full rights within the society at this time. The fact that these sisters were willing to take an equal role with their husbands in planning and carrying out the plans of the underground revolution became an inspiration to all the women of their country. Their story provided inspiration to all the women of the world. The sisters were treated in a "somewhat condescending fashion" said Ilan Stavans, writing in *DISCovering Authors,* "which of course doesn't exclude the oppressive power from annihilating them in the end." That the women were stronger than their oppressors suspected is encouragement for all women.

◆ CHARACTERS ◆

Told in a journalistic style, the voice changes from chapter to chapter, presenting the point of view of each of the four sisters. In the background, Trujillo's sinister omnipresence is like a black cloud hovering over the nation. The secret police, the SIM, is there to enforce El Jefe's whims and desires. He is, in many ways, the main character of the story, involving totally the thoughts and feelings of the rest of the characters.

Patria Mercedes Mirabal, eldest of the sisters, is the religious one. "I was afraid that you wouldn't live long, that you were already the way we were here to become," says her mother because Patria has such concern for everyone else and is generous to everyone. Patria is sent to a convent school, where for a time she considers becoming a nun. She falls in love with Pedrito Gonzales, whose family has a farm in the next town, and marries three days before her seventeenth birthday with the entire village in attendance to wish her well. Her first child is a son, the second, a daughter, and then she loses a baby boy, a devastating blow. The first eighteen years of her marriage are devoted to her home and family. She becomes pregnant with another son in 1959, and discovers her oldest son, Nelson, is involved with her sisters and their husbands in the revolutionary movement. She sends him from the capital to Santo Tomas de Aquino, a seminary without the obligation of the priesthood to try to keep him out

of the movement. Patria is protecting him also from the SIM, the secret police, who are forcing young men to join their ranks. The church remains neutral; she sees it as a sanctuary. She tells Nelson "God in his wisdom would take care of things," when he begins to talk of joining the rebels in the hills if Cuba invades. This is what the church is preaching.

Involvement in the revolution being planned by her sisters and their husbands begins slowly. Patria allows the group to meet in a grove of trees on the farm, her first small involvement. While she is attending a retreat with other women and several priests in the mountains, the motherhouse is shelled and they witness the killing of several *campesinos* and the capture of four others by members of the National Guard. The killings are brutal. Patria fears the ones captured are to be tortured. She makes the decision to take part in the revolution to save not only her children, but also the children of the nation.

Dede, the second sister and the only one to survive and keep the memory of her martyred sisters alive, thinks she is the one without courage. She marries a conservative man who makes her promise not to become involved with her sisters; he remains free while the sisters' husbands are in prison. Her marriage to Jaimito is the one thing she will not risk, so she lives when the other three die. However, she finds that living under those circumstances is the more difficult thing to do. Jaimito tells her "This is *your* martyrdom, Dede, to live without them" when she wishes to die on the trip to return their bodies home for burial. She eventually becomes a modern woman—divorced, a top life insurance salesperson, the keeper of the museum dedicated to her family members lost in the revolution, and the surrogate mother for all her nieces and nephews.

Minerva, the third sister, is the leader, the revolutionary. When she discovers that her father, whom she adores, has a secret second family, her life changes. She realizes she, her sisters, and her mother are stronger than her father, a realization that gives her courage. She even takes responsibility for her father's other family after he is imprisoned and dies, trying to be sure that her half-sisters attend school. Minerva wants to go to the university to study law. However, her life is irrevocably altered when she and her family attend a dance given by Trujillo on October 12, celebrating Discovery Day. Trujillo shows interest in having her for his mistress, and she slaps him, incurring his displeasure and causing her father's arrest. Trujillo also blocks her entrance into the university. At age twenty-nine, she marries Manolo, and together they begin to plot a revolution to free their country. Her experiences and observations of El Jefe, beginning while she is in the convent school, convince her that his regime is enslaving the people of the Dominican Republic. Her experience when he wants to make her his mistress drives her farther down the revolutionary path. In prison Minerva is the leader, organizing lessons, chores, and times to look out the one small window. She uses her courage and spirit to sustain her sisters and the other women in the cell and spends her life trying to live up to her convictions.

Maria Teresa, Mate for short, is the youngest, the one who follows her heart into the revolution. She keeps a diary whenever possible, recording events, thoughts, and feelings. She meets "Palomino," whose real name is Leandro Guzman Rodriguez, and marries him on February 14, 1958, in the San Juan Evangelista Church in Salcedo. "Mariposa and Palomino, for now! Maria Teresa and Leandro, forever!" is her desire and dream. She and Minerva are arrested and spend months in prison. A diary is smuggled in to her so she can write. She is tortured to get a confession and provide the names of others in the movement. With Patria and Minerva, she refuses to give up

the visits to the men, even when they must travel to the far end of the island to see them.

The sisters draw strength from each other, love and support from family members, and spend their lives working for the betterment of their families and the people of the Dominican Republic. Each contributes a different strength while supporting the others.

Trujillo's enmity hangs over the family after the Discovery Day Dance. Until that time, Papa, Enrique Mirabal, is a "Trujillista." Minerva tells her sisters, after Papa's death, that "his advice was always, don't annoy the bees, don't annoy the bees. It's men like him and Jaimito and other scared *fulanitos* who have kept the devil in power all these years." Minerva discovers her father's second family, a woman with four daughters, half-sisters to the girls. Mama, Dona Mercedes Reyes Viuda Mirabal, is instrumental in giving the girls a good education. She insists they go to the convent boarding school and encourages Minerva to further her education at university. She is a strength when Minerva and Mate are in prison, finding ways to get information about them and sending everything she thinks they will need when they have the opportunity to smuggle supplies into the prison. Mama is practical enough to accept her husband and all his faults. She is caring enough to forgive him and do everything she can to help her children.

◆ TECHNIQUES ◆

The story is broken into four parts in each section with each part told from the point of view of one of the four sisters. Maria Teresa tells her part of the story through her diary entries. Patria Mercedes' point of view accentuates her strong religious beliefs. Minerva is the leader, her principles upheld with each decision she makes. She lives her beliefs, whether at home or in prison. She does not allow her inner fears to change her decisions or her actions, standing up for what she sees as right. Each of the sisters is strengthened by the use of her personal point of view. Stavans wrote, "we have a quatrain of novellas, only one of which doesn't end in tragedy." Dede's novella may not end in death, but tragedy is there nonetheless.

Alvarez add richness and depth to her characters by using many Spanish words and phrases in the text. Stavans commented that "when you ask somebody what's up and no easy reply can be found, people are likely to say, '*Entre Lucas y Juan Mejia.*'" "'Between the devil and the deep blue sea' isn't the right equivalent in English," Alvarez added, "because you aren't describing the sensation of being caught between a pair of bad alternatives. . . . " What are you caught between? How did you get there? And how does it feel to be there?

He went on to say that Alvarez "stands apart stylistically, a psychological novelist who uses language skillfully to depict complex inner lives for her fictional creations."

The journal entries include drawings and diagrams; correspondence is included. Stavans observed that "Alvarez allows each Mirabal to acquire her own voice. Pasted together, their voices provide a sense that Truth, capital 'T,' is a collective invention." Alvarez inserted herself into the narrative at the beginning and the end, *la gringo norte americana*, not speaking very good Spanish but truly wanting to answer the question that led her to write the novel: "What gave them that special courage?"

◆ LITERARY PRECEDENTS ◆

Mother Tongue, by Chicana poet Demetria Martinez, is the story of a young Chicana who falls in love with a refugee from El Salvador. The young man is exiled to the United States after being tortured as a coun-ter-insurgent in his own country. Reviewer Elizabeth Martinez said that "good novels with political themes are a rare treat. Here we have not one but two: along with *Butterflies* comes *Mother Tongue.*" She went on to compare the books interwoven personal and political themes, maturation of young female characters, links between spiritual and political matters, journal structures, and the different voices used. She claimed, "Both are treasures."

Stavans likened Alvarez's style to that of Israeli writer A. B. Yehoshua. He wrote that "by intertwining disparate literary forms (journals, first-person accounts, correspondence, drawings, etc.) Alvarez allows each Mirabal to acquire her own voice." Writing in *DISCovering Authors,* critic Carla N. Spivack said: "One of Yehoshua's fundamental beliefs is that Israelis must break free from their past in order to live successfully and freely in the present and future. . . ." Minerva and the revolutionaries also believe their country must break free of Trujillo's rule if the people are to live successfully and in freedom.

◆ RELATED TITLES ◆

How the Garcia Girls Lost Their Accents, published in 1991, is Alvarez's first novel. Largely autobiographical, the work features a collection of stories about Dominican sisters who grow up in *el norte,* America, having escaped from Trujillo's tyranny. Sybil Steinberg, reviewing the book in *Publishers Weekly,* noted that Alvarez "has an ear for the dialogue of non-natives, and the strong flavors of Dominican syntax and cultural values." Told from multiple points of view, the stories record the rebellion of young, first-generation American women against their parents. Alvarez uses each of their accounts of the events in their lives to show

how they adapt themselves to the new country and society. These adaptations do not always please the parents. Alvarez won the Pen Oakland/Josephine Miles Award for excellence in literature for this debut novel.

The Other Side: El Otro Lado, a book of poems by Alvarez, was published in 1995. It traces "a lyrical journey through the landscape of immigrant life . . . [and] ends with the title poem 'The Other Side/El Otro Lado,' a multi-part narrative recounting her return to her homeland as a woman transformed—translated—by the years she has lived in America from native to guest," as described by a reviewer in *Publishers Weekly. Homecoming: New and Collected Poems* (1996) adds to her collection of the same name published in 1984.

A 1997 novel, *Yo!*, was called "a delightfully humorous exploration of cross-cultural and feminist issues," by Cynthia Tompkins in *World Literature Today.* Tompkins wrote that the focus of the Garcia sisters, introduced in *How the Garcia Girls Lost Their Accents*, shifts to a middle-age viewpoint, assessing the choices made while growing up. Plume/Penguin has published a translation of *Yo!* to Spanish by Dolores Prida.

Alvarez continues with insights and recollections of her Dominican Republic childhood and transplantation to New York in *Something to Declare* (1998). Laura Jamison, writing for *People Weekly,* observed that Alvarez has learned that she is "a cultural hybrid who could never truly go home." In *USA Today Magazine*, Steven G. Kellman recorded that

> Alvarez confesses fondness for gossip, and *Something to Declare* imparts innocent intelligence about its twice-divorced author, now married to a doctor from Nebraska. Her conflicted impulse toward revelation, she explains, derives from a Latin culture that cherishes storytelling, but also demands reticence in well-bred daughters. The chatter of family maids most helped her find her narrative voice.

The essays are meant to answer questions from readers about her life and writing, according to a critic in *Publishers Weekly.*

♦ IDEAS FOR GROUP DISCUSSIONS ♦

Trujillo ruled the Dominican Republic with an iron fist for over thirty years. He maintained his dictatorship by any means necessary in the beginning and by any cruel whim in the end. He was supported by his secret police and by the Central Intelligence Agency of the United States. He was also aided by the attitude of many of the people, expressed by Papa Mirabal as "don't annoy the bees."

1. Find out what other countries in Central and South America have been ruled by dictators. Which of these have been allies of the United States? Why?

2. Alvarez spoke of finding the place where her worlds collide or come together to be the most interesting when she is writing fiction. We all live in more than one world, some private and some public. Discuss ways we overlap and divide these worlds.

3. Identify and discuss problems in our nation that are "between the devil and the deep blue sea."

4. What happened in the Dominican Republic after the assassination of Trujillo?

5. What kind of government does the Dominican Republic have today?

6. Compare the lives of the people in the Dominican Republic today with their lives under Trujillo.

7. In an article for *Library Journal*, Alvarez gave her formula for choosing books to add to her personal library. She said she chooses authors whose work she has found add to her understanding of

life, books recommended by other readers whose opinion she trusts, new books in a subject area of interest at the time, or books to use for research. How could you use these ideas to choose particular books you might wish to add to your personal library?

8. Alvarez said in an article for *The Writer* that the first thing she does each morning when she goes to her writing studio is to read poetry and then prose. She wrote, "I read my favorite writers to remind me of the quality of writing I am aiming for." Discuss one writer who has influenced any writing you have done.

9. In the same article, Alvarez went on to tell us "that it's by what people have written and continue to write, our stories and creations, that we understand who we are. . . . It [writing] clarifies and intensifies; it reduces our sense of isolation and connects us to each other." Discuss an author who has helped you to discover who you are. What was it about this author that allowed this to happen?

10. Compare the work of Julia Alvarez to the work of Chicano writer Sandra Cisneros.

Ann Barton Sciba
Wharton High School Library

In the Time of the Butterflies

JACK MAGGS

Novel

1997

Author: Peter Carey

◆

◆ SOCIAL CONCERNS ◆

T he social concerns addressed in *Jack Maggs* may be divided into two categories: those of the past and those of the present. This is not to suggest that the two groups are mutually exclusive, for one of the text's major concerns is the way in which the past has shaped the present. While the nineteenth-century issues are evident to the sensitive reader, the twentieth-century concerns are more subtly embedded within the narrative.

Carey picks up on the need for radical social reform so often encountered in the works of Charles Dickens. Carey's city of London is just as bleak, dark, and pestilent as that of his literary forebear, and the despair of the metropolis is heightened by occasional comparisons to the prosperity that Maggs has left behind him in Australia. The state is depicted as having neglected the impoverished children it has failed to provide for, with figures like Percy Buckle and Mercy Larkins being saved from lives of toil or degradation through individual acts of kindness. Percy receives a legacy, whilst Mercy's redemption from a life of prostitution is dependent upon the whims of her master, leaving her far more vulnerable to sliding back into the gutter and without any hope of assistance from the society at large.

Maggs, as an outsider returning from exile, serves as a device to comment upon this world of squalor, the source of so much misplaced nostalgia for nineteenth-century Australian settlers and their descendants. Whilst England is initially a highly attractive place for the outcast Maggs, Mercy Larkins gradually brings Jack to an awareness of the futility of his quest to be accepted by his alarmed protege, Henry Phipps. She also makes him realize the ludicrousness of leaving behind a life of abundance in the colonies, not to mention his own children, to risk death from a state which demands that he remain in exile. In giving voice to these opinions, Mercy, who implicitly takes on the authorial voice here, seems to be striking a blow for modern Australian identity. She declares with passion of Jack's sons who are, by extension of the parent-child allegory, Australia itself, "And while these little boys wait for you to come home, you prance round England trying to find someone who does not love you." She, alone of all the characters, seems to recognize Britain as a society in decline and understands that Maggs, and by implication Australia, will not be able to progress until they are able to leave the past behind them. Carey's novel, then, is concerned with dispelling the sentiment attached to the mother country and with forging an independent, autonomous identity.

◆ THEMES ◆

The novel is a deliberately loose adaptation of Dickens's *Great Expectations* (serialized 1860–1861), and in order to appreciate fully the subtleties of Carey's revision at least some knowledge of the plot of *Great Expectations* is desirable, although of course, there is no substitute for the text itself.

In brief, and focusing only upon the elements of the story which resurface in Carey's reinterpretation, *Great Expectations* is the story of Philip Pirrip, or Pip, an orphan who is raised by his ferocious older sister and her weaker husband, the blacksmith Joe Gargery. One Christmas, when he is a child, Pip aids an escaped convict, Abel Magwitch, by stealing food for him. Magwitch is subsequently re-captured and banished to Australia for the term of his natural life. Thus, having made the briefest of appearances, Magwitch vanishes from the narrative for several years. In the meantime Pip is taken to meet Miss Havisham, a wealthy old woman who was deserted by her lover the night before her wedding was due to take place. Miss Havisham has remained dressed in her bridal attire ever since and has cloistered herself in her house with her ward, Estella, whom she has reared to use her beauty and wiles to hurt and punish men as a form of revenge for her own abandonment. Pip falls in love with Estella and wishes to become a gentleman so that he may be in a social position to marry her. When an anonymous benefactor intervenes by bestowing money and status upon him, with the promise of more to follow, Pip assumes that Miss Havisham is responsible. He shuns his lowly roots and

those who have been kind to him and departs for London to become a gentleman. He is later horrified to discover that Magwitch the convict is the source of his wealth, having made a fortune in Australia and never forgetting Pip's early kindness to him. Magwitch risks his life to return to England (returned transported convicts were hanged) so that he may be with the gentleman he has created. As a returned convict, or "transport," however, Magwitch has been ejected from the dystopian England which has failed to provide for him. Thus, his freedom of movement is restricted by a need for concealment which leads to Jaggers' constant reiteration to Pip that "You can't have verbal communication with a man in New South Wales, you know." For Dickens, then, in spite of its negligence as a parent, the mother country is still perceived as a home to which the convict will want to return.

Although initially repelled at the "low" origins of his money, Pip later feels a degree of compassion for Magwitch and assists him in an attempt to escape from Britain, where he is in grave danger of being captured once more. The escape bid fails and Magwitch dies in prison, a broken man, but at last having gained Pip's affection. As a criminal, Magwitch's assets may not pass to Pip and the latter is left penniless, but with a heightened awareness of the fact that status alone cannot make a gentleman. He therefore leaves Britain and goes to work in Egypt, returning years later to encounter Estella once more.

As an Australian writer trying to come to terms with his own position in relation to the English literary canon, Carey concerns himself with textual silences and brings Magwitch from the story's periphery. *Jack Maggs* is a novel particularly concerned with the themes of expulsion and return, excision and revision. Carey has challenged the Victorian impulse towards closure which frequently killed off problematic individuals or jettisoned them into the colonies, never to be seen again. He instead attempts to make sense of his own post-colonial identity and roots in a society of convicts by revising the narrative of the returned "transport" and reinventing Magwitch. In *Great Expectations* Magwitch is largely portrayed as an inert spectator once he has returned to Britain. He declares to Pip, "And this . . . and this is the gentleman what I made! The real genuine One! It does me good fur to look at you, Pip. All I stip'late is, to stand by and look at you, dear boy!"

The very nature of his existence as a returned transport necessitates stealth and a deference to Pip, who has the freedom to wander through the city. Carey, on the other hand, finds this static Magwitch to be a frustrating figure, and when reinventing him removes him from the margins and awards him a far greater prominence.

On one level, it is possible to construe Carey's conception of the static Magwitch as an analogy to his perception of the relationship between British and Australian culture. Just as Magwitch cannot be incorporated into mainstream British society, so too is the (white) Australian writer excluded from the canon of classic British texts. However, because of their colonial roots such authors are unable to assert a uniquely Australian identity (a problematic concept anyway, in the light of the third-class status accorded to Australian Aboriginals) free from the cultural baggage of the past. In reworking *Great Expectations*, Carey displays an unwillingness to abandon this past altogether and instead attempts to re-order it. However, in working from an established text, rather than creating anew, Carey places his relationship with the parent country on a somewhat Oedipal footing. He attempts to challenge a legacy of British hegemony through revising or "killing" the master narrative, which itself has been complicit in

mirroring life and repeatedly condemning to death the Australian transport.

While the Magwitch of *Great Expectations* is the subject of both Pip's and Dickens's accounts, Carey's reincarnation of the convict Jack Maggs is a far more reticent subject who constantly insists on his need to tell his own tale. At the beginning of Chapter 42 of *Great Expectations*, Magwitch declares to Pip and Herbert Pocket,

> "Dear boy and Pip's comrade. I am not a going fur to tell you my life, like a song or a story-book. But to give it you short and handy, I'll put it at once into a mouthful of English. In jail and out of jail, in jail and out of jail, in jail and out of jail. There, you've got it. That's my life pretty much, down to such times as I got shipped off, arter Pip stood my friend."

While Magwitch does then proceed to offer a more expansive account of his life, this information constitutes only one small element of Pip's narrative. Maggs, on the other hand, is all too aware of his potential as subject matter for Tobias Oates and is depicted as constantly resisting the exuberant young author's urges to mesmerize him in order to extract his story. Towards the close of the novel when the literate Maggs has perused Tobias's notebooks and has uncovered Oates's projected end for the story of his life, he attacks the author's sense of omnipotence and sinisterly insinuates that Toby's ending could also be revised:

> "You are planning to kill me, I know that. Is that what you mean by painful? To burn me alive?"

> "Not you, Jack, a character who bears your name. I will change the name sooner or later."

> "You are just a character to me too, Toby"

Maggs reiterates his point on several occasions by explicitly accusing Oates of theft and revealing that he has already written his story for himself. However, it is the notion of the author as a mere character which is crucial to Carey's revisionist agenda. The author no longer enjoys an unchallenged position of control as historically marginalized figures such as Magwitch/Maggs are brought to the fore and given voices.

Equally as important as Maggs's sense of his own voice is Carey's view of the England to which his convict returns. In creating a returned transport who can read, write, and quote Shakespeare, Carey attempts to undermine a complacent British sense of cultural superiority. The irresponsibility of the mother country—which was noted by Dickens in his grimy microcosm, Little Britain—is emphasized through the allegorical figure Ma Britten, Maggs's gruesome adopted mother, a seller of back street abortion pills who leads her ward to a life of crime.

A strong sense of the stagnation of British culture is exemplified through the now peripheral Pip, who is reinvented as the selfish and irresponsible Henry Phipps, as well as through Oates's sister-in-law Lizzie's abortion of the author's unborn child. The aborted fetus and the subsequent death of its mother represent the colonizer-artist's creative irresponsibility. Oates's impregnation of his wife's sister may be viewed as an analogue for his interference in the "other" territory of the Australian settler or, to extend the analogy even further, for the imperial nation's interference overseas. Indeed, the destructive nature of Oates's intervention is evidenced when he vengefully burns the blood-soaked linen in which Lizzie has died:

> It was Jack Maggs, the murderer, who now grew in the flames. Jack Maggs on fire. Jack Maggs flowering, threatening, poisoning. Tobias saw him hop like a devil. Saw him limp, as if his fiery limbs still carried the weight of convict iron. He saw his head transmogrify until it was bald, tattooed with deep wrinkles that broke apart and floated glowing out into the room.

A few pages earlier, Maggs had forced Tobias to burn his notebooks, and in this passage the two acts of immolation become equated. A new Maggs emerges phoenix-like from the flames in a dramatic travesty of the revisionist process, and Oates is finally able to envisage the violent death of his subaltern convict in the wake of the sordid accident of Lizzie's death.

Peter Carey, however, is not faced with the same problem of closure as his nineteenth-century predecessors and unlike Dickens or Oates, he has no ordering impulse to destroy Maggs. Note that Oates's novel is entitled *The Death of Maggs*, while Carey's is the less destructive *Jack Maggs*. Carey is far more concerned with the future which must emerge once the past has been redefined. Hence, the Magwitch of the 1990s is persuaded by the appropriately named Mercy (a trait decidedly lacking from the institutions depicted in *Great Expectations*) to return to his children and his state of affluence in the new colony and to abandon his nostalgia for the "old country." Implicit in this revisionist ending is a message to modern-day Australia to free itself from a similar nostalgic allegiance to British culture and to move forward to forge a new sense of national identity which will enable the Australians, as a people, to come to terms with their colonial legacy.

◆ CHARACTERS ◆

Carey's novel merges elements of *Great Expectations* with events from Charles Dickens's life, blurring fact with fiction, or as he states in his epigraph, "The author willingly admits to having once or twice stretched history to suit his own fictional ends." The novel's eponymous hero is moved from the margins of the nineteenth-century text—where he was little more than the troublesome source of Philip Pirrip's wealth—to the center of this late twentieth-century re-working. In contrast to the insipidity of the British characters surrounding him, Maggs is a vibrant and strong protagonist who represents—albeit unwittingly—the opportunities on offer in Britain's penal colonies. In contrast to the rather nondescript clothes of the other characters, Maggs dresses in a bright red waistcoat. Physically he is an imposing figure, in direct contrast to the stunted growth that adds to the feelings of inadequacy which dog Tobias Oates. A self-made man, Maggs is industrious and obviously resourceful, having converted the infertile land given to him with his ticket-of-leave into a brick-works. Although lacking in social refinement, he possesses compassion, both for his dead first-love, Sophina, and also for the fatherless Mercy Larkins.

Indeed, Carey seems to have transferred Dickens's well-documented empathy and kindness to Maggs, for the author's textual representative is almost completely devoid of these traits. This act of transference is reflected in the surname Maggs, which has been drawn from Thomas Mag, who was to have been the hero of *Mag's Diversions*, one of many titles Dickens considered for his semi-autobiographical novel, *David Copperfield*. In renaming Charles Dickens Tobias (to bias) Oates, Carey exemplifies his awareness of authorial subjectivity and the way in which all narratives reflect the positioning of their writers. Through removing Dickens from his authorial position of omniscient power and planting him within the narrative as a protagonist, Carey mounts an assault on the canon through demonstrating that *no* narrative can be fixed, not even a history. Moreover, Oates's name is also loaded with connotations of unfulfilled potential, since it is the same name as of one of Pip's dead brothers in *Great Expectations*. In a novel so concerned with fabrication, its resemblance to that of the perjurer Titus Oates can hardly be a matter of coincidence.

The author depicted by Carey is an exaggerated Dickens figure who is morbidly fascinated by the Victorian underworld to the point of obsession. Unscrupulous, ambitious, and living well beyond his means, Oates exploits Maggs's affliction with tic doloureux, a painful facial convulsion, to hypnotise him, thus enabling him to extort Maggs's life story and appropriate it for himself—the implication being that the novelist is lacking in imagination and can only steal stories. Carey's reinvention of Dickens—often regarded as the greatest English novelist—as a libidinous hypocrite is clearly bound-up with a desire to reconfigure his artistic relationship with the English literary tradition. Carey's hostile portrayal perhaps results from the creative constraints that the literary canon has imposed upon him and from which he is seeking to liberate himself through overturning the "master narrative" and the authority of its writer simultaneously.

Oates's wife, Mary, is a fairly minor figure, but the narrator clearly has a great deal of sympathy for the way in which her husband's financial and personal carelessness has left her in an extremely vulnerable position, while his vibrant and strong personality seems to have eclipsed her own altogether. Unlike Dickens's wife, Catherine, who is usually portrayed by biographers as a rather passive and dull figure, the reader is offered some insight into Mary's psyche, and she is also given a degree of autonomy that could not have been enjoyed by a middle-class woman in the nineteenth century. Thus, when Mary guesses that her sister is expecting Tobias's child, she does not turn a blind eye to her husband's misdemeanors as one would expect a model Victorian wife to do, but instead takes the unlikely step of procuring some of Ma Britten's abortion pills. Just as Carey frees Maggs/Magwitch from the margins of the text, so he also liberates Catherine Dickens/Mary Oates from both social and spatial restrictions by allowing her to walk across London. The journey itself mirrors one of Dickens/Oates's "slumming expeditions" into the East End to see the lives of London's underclass, but it is also of importance because the character is permitted to enter territories that would have been off-limits to her nineteenth-century counterpart. Mary truly comes into her own in the wake of Lizzie's death, and it is clear that she is far from being the "slow and famously dim-witted creature who was commonly thought not to understand half of what her famous husband said." Rather, it is Mary who, while racked with guilt at having, as she believes, killed her sister, takes control of the situation and manages to make the death appear as a tragedy, thus saving both herself and her husband's reputation.

Lizzie Warriner herself is a far cry from the young and innocent Mary Hogarth upon whom she is based. Apparently more attractive and intelligent than her sister, Lizzie's transgression with her brother-in-law is at odds with the moral propriety that is usually (albeit erroneously) ascribed to the Victorians. Her death scene is, whilst entirely plausible, completely at odds with the demise of Dickensian heroines like Little Nell. Instead of welcoming death as a just atonement for her crimes or embracing it as a passing to a better place, Lizzie oscillates between remorse and aggression, at one point rejecting her sister's ministrations with the response, "No, damn you!"

As the vendor of the concoctions which kill Lizzie and as Jack Maggs's foster mother, Ma Britten is an important catalyst. Her rise to prosperity at the expense of the misfortune of others mirrors Britain's own economic and industrial advancement during the nineteenth century, while her selfish neglect of Jack parallels the mother country's lack of concern with either the poor or with colonial exiles. With the exception of the opening pages, when Jack returns to visit her and the scene in which Mary obtains the tablets, Ma Britten is, along with her scheming son Tom, the criminal Silas Smith, and Maggs's first love, Sophina, presented to the reader through Jack's eyes. It is therefore difficult to obtain an unbiased perspective of this figure, and in a novel so concerned with the subjectivity of the narrator, this is an important point of which to be aware.

Just as un-endearing as Ma Britten is Percy Buckle. Initially presented as a philanthropic figure, Buckle is responsible for saving Mercy Larkins from the life of prostitution that her mother has been forced to consign her to. A former grocer and seller of fried fish, Percy has inherited a fortune and an extremely chaotic household. His physical appearance is slightly ridiculous and he walks like a duck. He initially seems to be an innocuous enough figure: bookish, kind, and totally uncomfortable with the social niceties that should have accompanied his sudden rise to prosperity. Yet instead of conforming to the Dickensian stereotype of the slightly quirky gentleman with the heart of gold, Percy succumbs to jealousy of Jack Maggs when it becomes obvious that Mercy is attracted to the convict. Buckle is rapidly transformed into a malevolent schemer, willing to manipulate other characters, like Henry Phipps, in order to rid himself of Maggs.

The English characters on the whole are presented as deeply flawed and selfish. Having received Maggs's money, Henry Phipps flees his benefactor because of his criminal past and lack of gentility. Significantly, none of the English relationships are fruitful, thus pointing to a fundamental sterility and lack of creative impulse in the mother country. Phipps and the footman Constable are both homosexual and therefore cannot reproduce. Oates's child with Mary is sickly, while the child conceived by Lizzie is unwanted and must be destroyed at all costs. Finally, Mercy and Buckle's relationship does not yield any offspring. Of all the English characters it is Mercy alone who possesses charisma and vitality; she is also the only figure who is willing to tell the truth. She jeopardizes her future by incurring Buckle's wrath through aiding Maggs. She is also concerned enough about Maggs's well being to tell him some home truths and to point out that his future should not lie in England. It is therefore inevitable that she returns to Australia with Maggs to care for his children and, in a new and more stimulating environment, to bear infants of her own. Since there is no mercy in Carey's rendition of Victorian England, Mercy must be transplanted overseas where she is able to reinvent herself as "a disciplinarian." She is also able to build a strong, prosperous, and loving family that is identified not only as a "clan," but also, significantly, as a "Race," putting her practicality to good use in a land willing to offer opportunities to those with skill and energy.

◆ TECHNIQUES ◆

Jack Maggs is a text obsessed with writing and rewriting. When Maggs agrees to allow Oates to mesmerize him every day for a fortnight he stipulates, "I won't have nothing written down," thus manifesting a deep suspicion of the written text. There are multiple narratives in play in the novel, and each narrative has multiple layers. Maggs is afraid not only of exposure to the authorities, but also of having his story stolen. Whilst Oates keeps two sets of books in a bid to outwit the convict, Maggs writes his own version of events in invisible ink so that the story of his life may only be read by Henry Phipps.

Passages from Oates's work in progress, *The Death of Maggs,* are interspersed with Carey's narrative and Maggs's own version of events. It is therefore, at times, somewhat confusing for the reader who is required to tease out "fact" from "fiction" and to determine which of the narratives are "true." Carey himself plays with facts as a way of drawing attention to the relativity of all writing. Although he is scrupulously accurate in recording key dates that correspond to important moments in Dickens's life (for example Lizzie Warriner's death coincides with that of Dickens's sister-in-law, Mary Hogarth), his attitude to naming is much more cavalier. The forenames of characters belonging to Oates's family are all drawn from figures surrounding Charles Dickens, yet Carey deliberately jumbles them up, naming Oates's son after Dickens's father, Oates's wife after his sister-in law, Mary, and his lover, Lizzie, after Dickens's mother. This technique is a means of making the reader suspicious of facts and history and it also serves as a constant reminder of the revisionist process. Indeed, the novel's final paragraph acknowledges that rewriting can never be definitive, by depicting Mercy Larkins as having expunged the Oates's dedication from no fewer than seven volumes of his novel, *The Death of Maggs.* Thus while the novel, along with Maggs's letters to Phipps, becomes a piece of archive material in Sydney's Mitchell Library, it is, like all documents that purport to be authoritative, both incomplete and flawed, having been revised itself.

◆ LITERARY PRECEDENTS ◆

Jack Maggs belongs to a long line of adaptations of *Great Expectations*, including David Allen's play *Modest Expectations* (1990), in which Dickens and his mistress Ellen Ternan visit Australia, and Michael Noonan's *Magwitch* (1982), which expands the convict's story without significantly revising it. As Australia has come increasingly interested in its colonial past, rather than seeking to forget its origins as a penal settlement, concern with figures like Magwitch/Maggs has increased. Robert Hughes has produced a compelling history of British settlement in Australia, *The Fatal Shore* (1988), which vividly depicts the privations endured by those condemned to transportation. Equally, Marcus Clark's *For the Term of His Natural Life* (1874) and George Dunderdale's *The Book of the Bush* (1870) provide graphic, and at times startling, accounts of life in the outback.

Carey is certainly not alone in his need to engage with Dickens's novels. Most recently John Irving has drawn upon Dickens texts, notably *David Copperfield* in *Cider House Rules* (1986), and *A Tale of Two Cities* in *A Prayer for Owen Meany* (1990). Looking forward to post-Carey adaptations, Susanne Alleyn's *A Far Better Rest* (2000) fleshes out the character of Sydney Carton and rewrites *A Tale of Two Cities* from his perspective.

◆ RELATED TITLES ◆

Much of Carey's work reflects upon what it means to be Australian, whether in the present day as in *Bliss* (1981), *Illywhacker* (1985), and *The Tax Inspector* (1991), or in the past. Both *Illywhacker* (the word is Australian slang for a charlatan) and *The Tax Inspector* are concerned with deception and forgery (interestingly, both texts feature used car salesmen), themes that are important to Carey and his quest for an "authentic" Australian cultural identity that does not simply imitate Britishness. Several of Carey's works, including his collection of short stories *The Fat Man in History* (1974) and *The Unusual Life of Tristan Smith* (1994), are set in imaginary societies that are identifiable as Australia. This technique is employed as a means of critiquing both contemporary Australia and, what is for Carey, the nation's troubled relationship with Europe. Set in the imaginary land of Efica, a decolonized country that was formerly governed by European powers, *The Unusual*

Life of Tristan Smith allegorizes Australian anxieties regarding its past. The deformed central protagonist's quest to find acceptance for his unconventional appearance is representative not only of the country's fear that as a society it is somehow "tainted" because of its origins, it is also analogous to the independent Australia's own need to find a niche for itself on the world stage.

The text most obviously related to *Jack Maggs* is *Oscar and Lucinda* (1988), a novel that portrays a lapsed clergyman, Oscar Hopkins and his efforts to transport a glass church through the Australian bush. The highly impracticable church in which parishioners would have been roasted alive in the Australian heat is the result of a lifelong obsession with glass by Lucinda Leplastrier, who, like Oscar, is a compulsive gambler, but who is also a woman of business. The fragile church comes to represent the settlers' failure to understand the new landscape, the frailty of established religion in nineteenth-century Britain, and also, through its resemblance to Joseph Paxton's Crystal Palace, British cultural imperialism. Symbolically, the edifice shatters spectacularly on arrival at its destination, before finally sinking into the river while Oscar, who becomes trapped inside it, is drowned.

◆ IDEAS FOR GROUP DISCUSSIONS ◆

1. Given his previous highly original works of fiction, consider why Peter Carey has chosen to re-write *Great Expectations*. Why does he adapt the novel so loosely?

2. *Jack Maggs* is a text concerned with silences and giving voices to those "others" who have traditionally been denied a voice in "great" literary texts. On one level it might be possible to view the text as a work of post-colonial Australia. Thinking about the idea of

suppressed voices, why might this view be subject to challenge?

3. How is the outsider from the colonies used to comment on British society in the nineteenth century?

4. Do you consider Phipps's rejection of his benefactor to be tragic? Why or why not?

5. What roles do the women of *Jack Maggs* play? Consider how they might be regarded in allegorical terms.

6. Maggs is haunted for most of the novel by the "phantom" of his repressed memories that Oates taps into when he mesmerizes him. Do you agree with Maggs that Oates has planted the phantom there himself? Why does Maggs mistake Henry Phipps for the phantom?

7. Percy Buckle moves swiftly from being a weak character to become a schemer who seeks to manipulate others in order to rid himself of Maggs. How does Carey use Buckle to propel the plot's action? Did you find the sudden altera-tion/development of his character to be convincing?

8. As well as being a re-working of a text, *Jack Maggs* contains texts within texts. Why might that be, and why is Carey so concerned with undermining the authority of the written word?

9. Why does Maggs want to return to Britain? How does the novel's narrator feel about this ambition? Compare the descriptions of London to the recollections of Australia revealed in Maggs's trance. Does either place represent an "ideal" society? Contrast the London figures to Maggs. Why does Maggs return to Australia? Why do you think Carey decided to send his character back?

10. The novel begins with a lengthy passage from de Chastenet and de Puysegur's *Du Magnetisme Animal* which seems to frame the narrative and perhaps to place the reader in a type of trance. Why might that be?

Grace Moore
University of Exeter

THE KNIFE THROWER

Short Story

1998

Author: Steven Millhauser

◆

◆ SOCIAL CONCERNS ◆

"The Knife Thrower" begins with a community puzzled and bewildered with the knowledge that the infamous Hensch, the knife thrower, is coming to town. Thus begins a tale that explores the deep recesses of desire, the formation of identity and the fascination with controlled (and sometimes not so controlled) danger. Hensch is an outsider, a transgressor; he has crossed the boundary of his professional code. He has become a fascinating figure because he is on the outside of society, and he has turned his ostracization into a crowd drawing act: "in his early carnival days he had wounded an assistant badly; after a six-month retirement, he returned with his new act." His act draws crowds because it titillates the community's sense of guilty pleasures—tapping into their desire for the ability to watch what one is not supposed to watch and enjoy that which should only inspire disapproval. His popularity calls attention to where the community draws the line between entertainment and the infringement of decency, because Hensch is a transgressor; he does what he is not supposed to do: he wounds people.

The community goes into the performance willingly, with full knowledge of its dangerous potential. Again and again in the story the boredom of safety is contrasted with the excitement of danger as the community grapples with its own attraction to supposedly "unnatural" or "disapproved of" actions. For example, during the performance, the marking of the assistant has the mask of failure, at which the audience is disappointed: "The knife struck beside her neck. He had missed—had he missed?—and we felt a sharp tug of disappointment, which changed to shame, deep shame, for we hadn't come out for blood, only for—well, something else." It is the exploration of this "something else" that provides the basis for the story and the value of the performance for the community. As the audience chastises itself for its disappointment at the idea of the failure to harm and explores its inner feelings about the need to see the assistant be marked, it is revealed to the audience, and the reader, that the marking was successful.

The audience is grateful for "the touch of the master, who had crossed the line, who had carried us safely, it appeared, into the realm of forbidden things." The community is pleased that it was able to go through the experience of the marking with no harm to its view of itself, or to its ethical sensibilities. The community believes this until the final act of the performance, after the "ultimate sacrifice," has been made by a member of the community's own. Laura is stabbed, and after this occurs, the community is haunted by the images of the reality of the performance. The community attempts to rationalize the feelings away by guaranteeing to themselves Laura's safety: "Of course the final act had probably been a setup, the girl had probably leaped smiling to her feet as soon as the curtain closed," but the images remain, which cause them to "remember the traveling knife thrower with agitation and dismay." They are able to satisfy themselves throughout the performance, but instead of being able to leave their emotions in the theater, the indelible images caused by their own acquiescence to visceral attraction, and the possible effects it had on one young life in particular, remain.

◆ THEMES ◆

The knife thrower can be seen as a cult figure for this community, a momentary visitor who incites strange and deeply felt emotions. Like many cult figures, part of his appeal is the offer of an identity of sorts from association with him. He gives out identifying marks that can be used by the receiver as a testament to their belonging somewhere, that they are brave and willing to risk injury for something worth doing. His followers are "many, young women especially, who longed to be wounded by the master and to bear his scar proudly." This is reiterated during the performance itself as many offer themselves to be marked: "then there were other hands, young bodies straining forward, eager." The people who are marked are new members going through initiation, which is demonstrated by the assistant who is transformed from purity, marked by gleaming white and silver gown, to the initiated, in a dark full-bodied gown; likewise, each of the members who are subsequently marked are dressed in dark colors.

Those who are initiated have demonstrated their bravery and their willingness to risk their own safety for the benefit of the master, for they do benefit him, as they become a part of his act. These people are looking for a place to belong, and they find it in the path of the Hensch's throw. The community, while encouraging the performance by their attendance, silently discourages this that is a slight step too far: "We wanted to cry out: sit down! you don't have to do this! but we remained silent, respectful." The community allows this to happen because they feel that it is their duty to be respectful and supportive of the young girls' decision. The people of the audience will return to this feeling after Laura is stabbed; part of their rationalization is that none of the three marked people were forced or coerced—they made their own decision and thus should be allowed freedom to do as they choose. The community's dilemma then arises as they consider what led them to the need for marking in the first place, and if anything could have been done differently.

At the same time, the community is fascinated with the ability of this man to transgress the boundaries set up for him. Codes and laws govern almost every section of our lives, whether it is our own personal moral code or the rules of the country in which we abide. The citizens who break these laws are considered transgressors and often a type of punishment will result, and those who are punished serve as a reinforcement of our own role as law-abiding citizens. Defying codes of conduct and assumed paths of life become stories and myths that we look to for renunciation of bad behavior, but also entertainment, titillation, and perhaps encouragement for our own minor transgressions. A result of this is a fascination that develops with those who transgress laws and codes and gain some kind of success because of it. Hensch is a person like this; he has broken the rules of his profession and as a result has a successful act. His bold indifference to codes of conduct and unspoken rules baffles and intrigues the audience in the theater. He begins the act when he pleases, defying the necessity of obliging the audience in their late arrival, and refuses to throw at a certain point, defying the assumptions made by the audience about the course of his act. He does not acknowledge the audience until his final throw has been completed and he has committed his ultimate transgression. He does not need the community, except for their attention, and this is an interesting facet of his performance for those who do need the community and draw their identity from it.

◆ CHARACTERS ◆

The story is told in the first person plural, and the effect is such that an entire community is speaking collectively and is a character unto itself. The narration seems to come from one perspective while maintaining the notion of a collection of voices. This allows judgment to be placed on the entire group and devotes attention to a group of people rather than singling out just one person who is responsible for fascination with Hensch—the fascination is the effect of a society, not of one single person's individual experiences. The group experiences the show together, and together the community must deal with the effects of the show: "as we left the theater we agreed that it had been a skillful performance, though we couldn't help feeling that the knife thrower had gone too far." The audience experiences a complexity of feeling, from understanding, to confusion, to sympathy, to a measure of betrayal. A link between the knife thrower and the community, they attempt to draw him in, "like the rest of us, he had to earn his living, which admittedly wasn't easy in times like these," but in the end, Hensch is still an outsider, and the community must deal with the feelings they are left with.

The knife thrower himself follows the stereotype of the dark magician, alluring, independent, and somewhat threatening. Dressed in all black, he strides out on stage and holds himself confidently. Ignoring the audience until the very end and the only recognition in the form of a bow, his silence demonstrates his perceived superiority in demeanor and in his art. He is labeled a freak, by the narration, which is his reason for his act. He accepts his separation from "common" society, but he will do so only on his own terms. He has tempted the audience and draws them into his dark world in which all that they have come to expect about themselves and their children is brought into question. His assistant is his mouthpiece, a beautiful, leggy blonde with smooth skin and a gentle voice; she is the comforting side to the strict and uncompromising master. Soothing the new initiates and thus the audience, she masks Hensch's threat. The volunteers are each shy, somewhat withdrawn, and young. This creates a feeling that the audience is somehow responsible for them. In each case, some part of the audience attributes to them each a measure of joy or ecstasy at their experience of being marked. This is another way that the community attempts to justify its preoccupation with Hensch and his art. If the three people had received a measure of joy from their experience, then the community can rest at ease at their own encouragement of it.

◆ TECHNIQUES ◆

Millhauser uses color as a manifestation of the sides that the community is battling between and to demonstrate the rite of passage that the initiates must go through. The story is built around the white of purity, the black of the master and the initiated, and the red of the blood that is the process and effect of transgression. Likewise darkness and light are used as examples of the differences between what the community knowingly becomes involved with, what they do not know or expect, and what they wish to ignore in the service of their own excitement.

Millhauser also focuses on one night and one performance by Hensch to tighten the focus of the story. This, in addition to his choice of narrative voice, emphasizes the community and the emotions and difficulties it experiences as a result of Hensch's performance.

◆ LITERARY PRECEDENTS ◆

This story's closest literary relative is the work of Vladimir Nabokov, who wrote many short stories in addition to his numerous novels. The magical realism of this story finds a likeness with Nabokov's fiction, which often uses everyday events and lives to explore otherworldly dimensions and themes. A good example of a short story that explores similar themes is "The Aurelian," which takes as its subject a butterfly collector who is eerily watched by the specimens mounted in his shop. Another group of fiction that is somewhat similar to Millhauser's is Roald Dahl's fiction for young adults, as collected in *The Umbrella Man*. Dahl's stories, like Nabokov's often take unexpected turns at the end, or end unexpectedly, often leaving the reader to complete the train of thought at the end of the story. This can be used to explore different assumptions that the reader has made throughout. These authors play with literary traditions, manipulating stock characters and prejudices to manifest their themes.

◆ RELATED TITLES ◆

Millhauser's collection of three novellas, *Little Kingdoms*, also explores in similarly magically realistic ways the different desires that can consume and enchant. In each story a different art is considered, but in extremely different ways. The art begins to dictate reality to some extent, which is similar to "The Knife Thrower," and the community surrounding the art must deal with the effects of being consumed by a particular idea. The motif of the dagger, as well as the emphasis on a community's response to particular stimuli is present in the second novella, "The Princess, the Dwarf and the Dungeon."

◆ IDEAS FOR GROUP DISCUSSIONS ◆

Millhauser explores the odd fascination that some societies seem to have about things with which they are not supposed to be fascinated. Guilty pleasures seem to be the best kind for many people. From these "unnatural" pleasures comes a sense of identity, for those participating and for those just watching. Whether priority is placed on independence or community vigilance also seems to be a primary concern for this story.

1. Is the community's fascination with Hensch similar to the popularity of "reality television"? In what ways is it alike or different?

2. Should the audience have stopped the three volunteers from being marked? Why or why not? Would it have been different if the volunteers had been older? Why or why not?

3. Why would they each want to be marked? What is Hensch's appeal?

4. Do you think that the final act, "the ultimate sacrifice," was staged? Why

or why not? If it was real and not a setup, how would that affect the community's opinion of the performance? How does that affect your view of the performance?

5. Should Hensch be held responsible for those that he harms? For example, should his act be stopped? Does it matter that the members of the act are volunteers?

Jessica Horn
Pennsylvania State University

LESS THAN ZERO

Novel

1985

Author: Bret Easton Ellis

◆

◆ SOCIAL CONCERNS ◆

E llis' principal social concern is particular to the time and place in which he sets *Less Than Zero*. Implicitly, however, Ellis' work critiques American society at large and concludes that the prosperity of the eighties was squandered by self-interest. The specific acts of depravity he chronicles—drug abuse, sexual promiscuity, violence, etc.—are part of a much larger problem: personal isolation. A culture that privileges the rabid individualist must accept the consequences of their ethic; Ellis' book outlines these consequences in gritty, shocking detail.

On the surface, *Less Than Zero* seems concerned with the excesses of young, rich Californians living in the eighties. Clearly, Ellis, unlike authors such as Hunter S. Thompson, sees the drug culture as decadent and depraved. This fact is often missed by critics who detect a sympathetic attention in Ellis' careful rendering of drug-abusing characters; there are no clearly good characters against which to compare the clearly bad characters. Those individuals who do provoke sympathy, however, are, at times, apathetic to the point of negligence or self-loathing to the point of narcissism. The reader's response is, then, ambivalent at best. *Less Than Zero*, therefore, is more complicated than an after-school special, but it is also more powerful.

Ellis' book outlines the damage caused to individuals by the abuse of hard drugs. Ellis demonstrates this capacity for self-destruction when he describes the decomposing body of a rich young man who has apparently overdosed. Even for those not killed by drug abuse, there are profound psychological effects, including apathy and aimlessness.

Ellis seems troubled by drugs' ability to transform earnest young men and women into apathetic malcontents. His characters, so long as they are inured by cocaine and alcohol, are utterly unaffected by the horrific behaviors of those around them. Clay's mother, for instance, shows indifference to his drug habit. Alana, one of Clay's friends, most concisely articulates their emotional insensitivity when, after an abortion, she says "I think we've all lost some sort of feeling." Each character shows this loss in a different way.

Clay never betrays deep concern for his friend Julian's need to work as a prostitute to pay off a drug debt. Instead, having seen his boyhood cohort injected with heroin and led to a bedroom, Clay remarks monotonously, "I turn away and leave the house." Clay turns away from all disagreeable appearances, rarely commenting and never making any but the most feeble attempt to ameliorate unpleasant situations. Even the loss of his girlfriend, Blair, leaves him disturbingly untroubled: "She tells me that she doesn't think that Blair likes me much anymore. I shrug and look out an open window." Clearly, Clay's drug use causes this disconnection from his personal experiences. Such apathy, even at the loss of a loved one, makes reading about Ellis' characters an eerie experience.

Another side of apathy is aimlessness. Of all the members in Clay's set, only he and his friend Daniel leave the Los Angeles area in an effort to begin the rest of their lives. Though Clay has, at the novel's opening, just finished his first term of college, he seems unsure of what he will do with his life. Even so, Clay seems highly motivated by comparison to his friends. Some of them who are enrolled in college are unsure even when the new semester starts. Several wonder aloud if classes have already begun. Clearly, education and self-advancement is, at best, a ploy to kill time in the lives of Ellis' young characters.

Ellis describes a generation of children without the slightest notion of how they might contribute to society. In part, of course, this aimlessness derives from their economic backgrounds: without the need to work, few of Ellis' characters have any desire to find jobs. Unfortunately, this lack of direction and absence of productive pursuits lead them to fill their days and nights with destructive activities. Each day Clay moves through a series of social interactions and parties. There is, in short, never anything for him to do. Ellis thus criticizes any group, whether a social set or an entire nation, without clear goals. In Ellis' view, dissipation necessarily follows when one loses sight of a definite purpose.

The absence of parental guidance might cause the lack of direction in Ellis' teenaged characters' lives. The parents Ellis describes are as narcissistic and apathetic as their children. They never take any interest in their kids lives, except to give them some money. The children reciprocate by taking no notice of their parents, to the point that one character, Kim, remarks that she is unsure of her mother's whereabouts because *Variety* and *Vogue* had printed conflicting reports. Ellis' characters actually learn how to live a degenerate life from their parents. *Less Than Zero* suggests, then, that the children of the privileged inherit their forbears' iniquities as much as their money.

Ellis is also concerned about the effects of personal isolation. American society, it seems, has made a horrible mistake in its lauding of individualism. Rugged individualism was important for pioneers such as Daniel Boone, but members of a civil society must live together. Ellis' wealthy Californians have, through their prosperity, withdrawn from civil society to create their own world, one with the unpleasant appearances of the poor moved to the margins. Co-existing with the idle rich is the unfortunate majority of working and homeless poor. Members of the underclass appear briefly on Clay's radar from time to time. They are always remarked upon in brief, however. Clay recognizes a homeless woman, for example, but does not even condescend to give her change. His friend Daniel remarks on the drug abuse of his Mexican maid but does not demonstrate an interest in her. The poor appear only when they stand in the path of Clay and his friends. Even then, they are merely dismissed with a turning of the head.

In addition to removing themselves from American society, Ellis' idle rich have withdrawn from each other. Left to make their own laws, each of Ellis' characters become laws unto themselves. This rabid self-involvement allows them to laugh at a snuff film and even perpetrate their own acts of violence. In the novel's closing pages, Clay's friends bring him to their home where they have tied up a twelve-year-old girl they use as their sex slave. Clay, whose own emotional capacity has atrophied to almost nothing, can only say, "It's . . . I don't think it's right." His friend's reply might be the most concise summary of the callousness lying at the heart of American culture: "What's right? If you want something, you have the right to take it. If you want to do something, you have the right to do it." Though coming from the mouth of a young man who coldly abuses a twelve-year-old, these words invoke the principal tenants of American freedom. Capitalist ideology advocates succeeding at all hazards; freedom means the right to define one's own moral code. When taken to their extremes, these ideologies can, Ellis asserts, become green lights for individuals to commit violent, anti-social acts. In fact, these freedoms can, it seems, provoke individuals to actively degrade themselves and others so that they might sense the force of their freedom.

◆ THEMES ◆

Ruminations on the nature of memory pervade *Less Than Zero*. The impossible desire to recapture lost moments clearly interests Ellis as a theme. The book, which is made up of short vignettes usually about a page long, is sprinkled with italicized sections that retell events in Clay's past. Many focus on a trip to Palm Springs he took the summer before college. Others are centered on his grandmother's last days and death. In all these vignettes, there is a sense that Clay looks upon his past with a mixture of sadness and desire. He recognizes the pain the events inspired, yet he longs to experience them again. His descriptions of long

past events are both more lucid and more emotionally charged than his narration in the present tense. Ellis thus suggests that the passage of time endows experience with a kind of certainty. Only upon reflection can Clay be certain of what he felt at a particular moment. Surely, such an ordering of experience through memory is a universal experience. *Less Than Zero* adeptly demonstrates how the surplus of stimuli received at the moment of an event confuses one to the point of stasis. Only afterward can events be ordered and understood.

The banality of popular culture also interests Ellis as a theme. His characters constantly tune into MTV or discuss the latest record from their favorite rock band. Unfortunately, their musical interests do not seem to provide them with any emotional solace. Even the bands they are most excited about hearing do not move them in any profound way. Instead, the parade of musical acts which make up their culture only serve to mark time. The same applies to the movies they watch. At one point Clay and his friend Trent meet a friend in the lobby after a movie. None of the three can remember the name of the movie they had just seen. The only effort any of the characters makes to assimilate high culture occurs early in the novel when Trent takes "the Cliff Notes to *As I Lay Dying* out of his glove compartment and hands them to Blair." This passage underscores the inadequacy of Clay's friends' attention spans and their disinterest in the finer points of culture.

Familial interactions also occupy Ellis' thematic attention. Specifically, Ellis is interested in the causes of family dysfunction. For his characters, dysfunction arises, simply, from a lack of interest in others. When Clay's father takes him out to lunch, for instance, he spends most of his time speaking with business associates he meets at the restaurant. In the course of the same lunch, Clay's father asks what he wants for

Christmas numerous times. This indifference by and for family members seems to spill over into the larger world. Ellis takes pains to highlight the similarities between Clay's loveless family and his emotionally vacuous social set.

◆ CHARACTERS ◆

Clay, *Less Than Zero*'s disaffected narrator, guides the reader through Ellis' world of ennui and self-destruction. Significantly, Clay is as involved in the degradation of his set as his friends. He, too, snorts cocaine, drinks, and engages in casual, indifferent sex with women and men. There is some degree of objectivity to his perspective, however. Clay has spent the past several months at college in New England. The novel's opening sees him disembarking from his plane home, and the conclusion depicts his departure. The novel then relates his becoming reacquainted with his hometown. Things seem moderately foreign to him. Nevertheless, he is not an outsider. Furthermore, he is, at best, only marginally more likeable than Ellis' other characters. Clearly, he at least understands that his generation has somehow gone astray. Nevertheless, his drug habit has left him unable to do anything to withdraw from the depths of debasement he and his crowd have fallen into.

Clay is also the vehicle through which Ellis meditates on memory and desire. The narrator repeatedly turns his attention from the present to the past. There seems to be an effort, albeit a futile one, to recover the past. Ellis makes it impossible for Clay to succeed in this endeavor to demonstrate the impossibility of reliving past experiences.

Clay's hunger of memory takes as its principal objects two of his childhood friends, Blair and Julian. Blair is actually Clay's girlfriend, but it takes some time for this to become clear. Blair picks Clay up from the airport, and though they have not seen each other in months, the lovers do not show any sign of their affection. This coldness persists throughout the novel. Both think nothing of sleeping with other people, and neither is affected by the news of the other's infidelity. Thus, Blair demonstrates the extent of Clay's apathy. Their relationship is the archetype of love in a generation of emotional bankruptcy.

Julian seems to occupy more of Clay's attention than Blair. Though Julian is only rarely present during the novel's action, he seems to occupy the thoughts of every character. Clay and his friends constantly ask one another if they have seen or know the whereabouts of Julian. When he finally discovers what is happening with Julian, Clay is characteristically underwhelmed. Apparently, Julian has taken to prostituting himself to pay off his drug debts. Ellis uses him, then, as a study in the depths of degradation one reaches when abusing drugs.

Perhaps more interestingly, though, Clay's discovery of Julian's occupation gives Ellis an opportunity to ruminate on one of *Less Than Zero*'s most pervasive themes: the power of memory. Sitting in a hotel room, watching a middle-aged man strip and caress Julian, Clay is struck with "an image of Julian in fifth grade, kicking a soccer ball across a green field." Memory is triggered at a traumatic moment to provide Clay a measure of comfort. He can recall the simplicity of the past and disappear into it as a relief from the ugliness of the present. For the reader, however, Clay's memory of Julian only marks the depth of his descent. Bearing witness to an image of his innocence only makes his debasement more deeply disturbing.

Another thematic element of *Less Than Zero* becomes apparent through the interaction of Julian and Clay. In spite of the apathy and emotional bankruptcy which touches every one of the novel's characters,

Julian and Clay demonstrate an attachment to one another. At one point Julian asks Clay to borrow a large sum of money. When asked what the money is for, Julian lies, saying it will pay for an abortion. Though he knows Julian lied, Clay produces the money. Clay understands, almost instinctively, that his friend needs help and provides it willingly. Julian returns the favor by, in the end, revealing the severity of his need. Rather than paying Clay back, Julian introduces his friend to the world he now occupies. Though he cannot tell anyone else about his foray into prostitution, Julian shares his most humiliating secret with Clay, trusting his closest friend to understand his desperation.

◆ TECHNIQUES ◆

Less Than Zero is a realist novel in the naturalist vein. Naturalism, as practiced by authors such as Gustave Flaubert and Stephen Crane, is concerned not with nature but with brutal honesty. Naturalist authors endeavor to neither romanticize their subjects nor exaggerate their shortcomings. The monotonous candor of Ellis' narrator, Clay, gives the novel a strong sense of authenticity and of honesty. Much of the novel's emotional impact lies in its deadpan delivery; events are simply chronicled and not expounded upon. The reader is thus left to supply his or her own judgement.

Ellis employs an episodic structure in *Less Than Zero*. Rather than long narrative chapters, he breaks his novel down into vignettes, short passages, often less than a page, which tell a minute portion of the story. For the most part, each passage relates only one event or detail. Ellis thus breaks with narrative convention. His novel does not begin with event "A" and then, through a sequence of orderly occurrences, reach event "Z." Instead, the narrative meanders aimlessly. This technique is useful and interesting because it allows the form to follow the content. In other words, Ellis' book about young men and women wandering listlessly through life wanders listlessly itself. The reader enters the lives of Ellis' characters through a medium which mirrors the fragmented, disorganized lives they lead.

◆ LITERARY PRECEDENTS ◆

Ellis' portrait of a generation gone awry is an excellent example of what some critics have called the oldest American form, the Jeremiad. This genre, popular with the Calvinist preachers of colonial New England, is, essentially, a complaint against the morality of the time and a warning that such laxity might inspire the wrath of God. American Jeremiads, unlike their European forbears, also emphasize the fact that the sinners chastised are actually a chosen people, destined to find their way to the right path. Ellis' novel fits this pattern. The privileged characters he describes are indicted for debauchery in the face of providential blessings. The rich, California elite of the 1980s are endowed with an economic prosperity beyond comprehension, yet they shun their good fortune by their flights of excess. Ellis' novel is at once a criticism of this excess and a reminder that plenty abounds.

Another work that engages in this simultaneous criticism of and praise for contemporary American morality is Hunter S. Thompson's *Fear and Loathing in Las Vegas* (1971). This nonfictional (but wildly imaginative) account of Thompson's trip to Las Vegas to cover two stories looks back on the failed experiment of sixties counterculture. The wave of freedom which the sixties ushered in broke, Thompson argues, with the election of "the forces of old and evil" in the guise of Richard Nixon. American democracy was, in Thompson's mind, nearly achieved by the counterculture's efforts.

But in the early years of the seventies, Thompson sees a return to the conservative oligarchy and a general apathy about serious political issues. Thompson's book, like Ellis', depicts an American people who shun their privileges and wallow in excess and apathy.

For the character of his narrator, Ellis is clearly indebted to J. D. Salinger's *The Catcher in the Rye* (1951). This novel's legendary narrator Holden Caulfield addresses his surroundings with a sneer that looks remarkably similar to Clay's. Both are disaffected with their cohorts to the point of physical illness; both are socially inept young men who would rather be alone than deal with others. Clay and Holden both exude a fury that purports to echo the sentiment of their respective generations. This anger makes both classically unreliable narrators; their description of events is colored by the strength of their emotions. The similarities between Ellis' protagonist and Salinger's narrator do not suggest a lack of vision or originality on Ellis' part. Instead, the recasting of Holden, one of American literature's best known mouthpieces, firmly entrenches *Less Than Zero* in the tradition of American letters.

◆ RELATED TITLES ◆

Though he does not follow Clay, Blair, and their friends in subsequent works, Ellis does focus on similar concerns with a similar style in his later publications. In *The Rules of Attraction* (1987), *American Psycho* (1991), and *The Informers* (1994) Ellis dwells on the disintegration of American society. The American people of the late twentieth century are, in Ellis' view, selfish, isolated, and morally depraved. Each of the works in which he has made this assertion has drawn some degree of criticism for actually perpetrating the societal ills the author critiques.

The Rules of Attraction is, in a way, a continuation of *Less Than Zero*. It does not involve the same characters, but it focuses on college life in New England, the life Clay returns to at the end of Ellis' first book. Again set at the height of the Reagan eighties, the novel describes the moral laxity and stunted emotions of a set of self-consciously bohemian youngsters. They are sexually promiscuous drug abusers without goals or purposes in their lives. Again, Ellis presents them as a privileged people, endowed with the money and intelligence to do good, who turn their attentions inward rather than out toward the needy world.

In his third novel, *American Psycho,* Ellis trumps his previous forays into the description of depravity by recounting the descent into madness of Patrick Bateman, a twenty-six-year-old investment banker. This young, handsome yuppie comes across mass murder almost by chance, but once involved he becomes an efficient killer. Ellis allows his mad protagonist to narrate the novel, giving it the same chillingly unreliable narrative voice as *Less Than Zero*.

Both as a book and as a movie (directed by Mary Harron in 2000), *American Psycho* drew criticism for its violence and its apparent misogyny. One critic for the *National Review* betrayed his racist/classist views by saying of the plot, "Manhattan may be crawling with serial killers, but I find it highly unlikely that any of them are doubling as investment bankers." It is this very "it can't happen to us" spirit that is, Ellis asserts, at the heart of the horror of eighties society. The economic and intellectual elite, usually considered immune from the depravities of society, take center stage in Ellis' depictions of anti-social behavior. Thus, Ellis consistently adheres to the conventions of the American Jeremiad. The people of the eighties, who experienced immense prosperity, were, in Ellis' mind, a chosen people who went terribly off course. A generation that could have done great work for all became horribly, violently, and totally self-interested.

◆ ADAPTATIONS ◆

Less Than Zero was made into a film in 1987. The movie was directed by Marek Kaniesvska and followed a screenplay written by Harley Peyton. Peyton's script makes radical departures from Ellis' novel. The story told by the movie is, in essence, entirely different than that told by Ellis. The film is still a useful companion to the book because it displays the California landscape in rich detail. Ellis' sense of detail is strong, and his descriptions are excellent. Nevertheless, the movie's visuals add a more immediate understanding of the space in which the book's events occur.

The most substantial difference between the novel and the film adaptation is the shift in the narrative stance. Clay (played by Andrew McCarthy) is clean in the movie; his character is a far cry from Ellis' strung-out, confused narrator. This constitutes a reformulation of the narrator's position in relation to the reader. Peyton's screenplay transforms Clay from an unreliable narrator to an objective voice of reason with which the viewer can feel an easy kinship. It is difficult to sympathize with Ellis' Clay; he is as deeply involved in drugs as the unlikable characters he describes. Thus, Peyton's changes make the movie much easier to watch. Characters are easier to categorize with simple definitions like good and bad, sober and wrecked. Though clearly a function of his medium, this simplification robs the text of much of its narrative complexity.

The story's sequence of events also changes a great deal in the translation from book to movie. Unlike Ellis' character, Peyton's Clay returns from college with a strong desire to resume his relationship with Blair (played by Jami Gertz). Unfortunately, Blair has taken up with Julian (Robert Downey, Jr). Thus, Julian, who functions as a shady, undeveloped character who is the subject of an unexplained fascination of Clay's, becomes a principal character with a great deal more time on screen than he occupies on Ellis' pages. A convoluted but clearly presented sequence of events sees Blair and Clay back together and Julian, worn out by fear of his dealer's reprisals and the shock of trying to get clean, dies quietly. This clarity and neatness of this narrative line is an unfortunate departure from Ellis' vision. It is void of the ambiguity which makes Ellis' a haunting and complex story.

◆ IDEAS FOR GROUP DISCUSSIONS ◆

Less Than Zero is a grim representation of eighties youth disaffection that aspires to a brutal honesty. It can be read either as an indictment of a particular social set's excesses or as a criticism of the ethics which transform American individualism into American narcissism. Ellis suggests that personal isolation breeds anti-social, self-destructive, and outright violent behavior in groups without accountability. Such freedom of responsibility is, unfortunately, easily available to those with the financial wherewithal to free themselves of the burdens associated with adult life. Ellis' characters are spoiled children, whether they are eighteen or forty-eight.

Ellis' presentation of these criticisms alternately compels and shocks the reader. Though distant and enigmatic, *Less Than Zero*'s narrator is sympathetic, if ambiguously so. The novel's action, more than a logically ordered sequence of events, orders itself along the lines of a crescendo of degradation. The details Clay relates become more disturbing, the things characters do become more deviant. Ultimately, the book ends without resolution. One cannot be sure whether Clay has cut himself free from his cohorts' degrading influence or has recognized the inevitability of his connection to them.

1. Ellis' characters all occupy a tiny fraction of the general population; they belong to an economic elite. Is it difficult to sympathize with characters, however painful their experiences, who are the beneficiaries of such material excess? In other words, is it hard to feel sorry for the rich kids that fill the novel?

2. Why might the film version of *Less Than Zero* take such radical departures from the novel?

3. Did you find the book lacking in structure or does the narrative hold up? Were you disturbed by the book's failure to resolve itself?

4. How might Ellis' book have misled those who see it as condoning drug use?

5. Why might Ellis have set the book in Los Angeles during the 1980s?

David Slater
University of Minnesota

LITTLE KINGDOMS

Novellas

1993

Author: Steven Millhauser

◆

◆ SOCIAL CONCERNS ◆

T he three novellas that make up *Little Kingdoms* greatly vary in their subject matter—a cartoonist/animator, a fairy tale, and an art catalogue—but the concerns that they touch upon are strikingly similar. Each of the little kingdoms is a realm of art, and through the three different disciplines that are explored, Millhauser raises questions concerning the nature of art and its relationship to the artist that creates it and the society that consumes it. The branch of philosophy known as aesthetics has explored these questions as long as art has existed, and Millhauser adds his own interpretation through emphasizing the stories of the artists themselves.

The kingdom of the first novella, "The Little Kingdom of J. Franklin Payne" features the art of cartooning, both comic strips and animation. The story of this gifted artist begins with a fantastical emergence from his third-floor study onto the roof of his house, thus setting the tone of magical realism for the rest of the story, and in fact, the rest of the collection. Always surrounded by comics and cartoons—whether an editorial cartoon that he must draw for his job at the *World Citizen* or the animation that grows to his obsession—Franklin thrives in a world

of fantasy and imagination. He is an artist who is successful within the milieu of his created worlds, but not in the real world that continually infringes on the time and energy that he would rather devote to his creations. As he gets deeper into the process of creating a cartoon, he becomes exhausted and physically ill, as the energy from his real life is pumped into the cartoons he creates. The boundary between art and life moves for Franklin, and as the lines blur, Millhauser's fiction becomes equally ambiguous. This occurs especially towards the end, for as Franklin reaches a fever pitch with his longest and most intricate cartoon, the world outside seems to melt away as he is drawn further and further in to his own cartoon-worlds.

The descriptions of Franklin's cartoons echo the feelings demonstrated by his isolation in his study and in the memories of his father. As Franklin continues to obsess over his art, he neglects those around him. This takes its toll, and his wife, Cora, leaves him for an artist who is based more in reality and thrives not on his art, but the use of art for practical purposes, namely, making a profit. The only person who truly remains connected to Franklin throughout, and who becomes even more of a stabilizing figure as the story wears on, is his daughter, Stella.

Franklin realizes that he must be faithful to his art, for that is his legacy, just as the legacy of his father remains with the emergence of images from the pure white of photographic paper. The purpose of art is lost with Rex, who sees it only as a means to an end, cutting corners when he can, whereas for Franklin, part of the beauty of the art is the process itself.

There is a similar consideration in the second novella, "The Princess, the Dwarf and the Dungeon." In this story, the art is that of storytelling, and the artist is the community itself. In this case, the final product varies tremendously from telling to telling, but it is the process that is most revealing about the community's basic ideology. Through the way that the community chooses its stories and the manner in which it tells the story, one can begin to understand the nature of the community itself. The community uses its story to remember its history, enforce its present, and imagine its future. Cultural stories are devices that link people to their surroundings, to their history, and to each other. They are also a way of maintaining the status quo and settling minds that fear the invasion of outside forces that could wreak havoc on their way of life. An example of this is the repeated assertion of the ability of the town to defend itself. This is significant to the community because it is used to set minds at ease, yet the threat of the margrave remains within the story to encourage vigilance.

"The Princess, the Dwarf, and the Dungeon" takes the form of oral tradition; it is fragmented and composed of short, focused vignettes or themes. It is in this manner that Millhauser is able to demonstrate an instance of community story-telling, which is not consistent or smooth. Stories come into being through mixing, forgetting, creating, and repeating, each reflecting a cacophony of voices, rather than one authoritative voice. Through the stories, members of the community create links to each other, through separating themselves from those across the river in the castle and through the shared history that is related in the tales.

The third novella, "Catalogue of the Exhibition: The Art of Edmund Moorash (1810–1846)" tells a story of painting, with an emphasis on the career of one particular artist through descriptions of his artwork gathered together for an exhibition. The story is narrated by one authoritative voice, but the stories themselves relate much more than the background of the paintings. Information begins to be related that has very little to do with the art itself. What results is a portrait of an artist, the disturbing paintings that he creates, and the detrimental effect he has on all of those with whom he is involved. Here, the story again relates the extreme emotional impact that art can have on its creator as well as its viewers. Each of those who have viewed his art regularly, or have met with him regularly (including himself) die within the same year; four of the five people involved with his art die within moments of each other in response to one painting in particular. This effect is the direct opposite effect of the first novella, in which the art is beneficial in at least one way for the artist. In that story, the art brings about reconciliation, rather than chaos. In between the two extremes of art is the second novella, in which the artists benefit at the expense of the characters themselves. In each case, the society that surrounds the art, whether it is a society of one or of an entire town, is susceptible to the whims and effects, good or bad, of the art that it creates.

◆ THEMES ◆

One of the themes of "The Little Kingdom of J. Franklin Payne" becomes most clear at the end of the story during the first screening of his most precious cartoon. All of the people that have meant anything to him gather together, and it is his art, the world that he creates out of his imagination that brings them together. This is the power of art for Millhauser; it has the ability to reconcile and remember, even if it is only for an audience of one or perhaps two. Franklin realizes that no one in the public will ever see his final cartoon, but this is not the purpose of the cartoon. The purpose of his cartoon is to create a legacy of himself, just as his father did with his photographs. He is creating a link with his daughter through the creation of images from the blank white screen, similar to the link that his father created with him through the creation of images from the blank white photographic paper. The process that allows for animation—"the persistence of vision"—is the very thing that allows a continued link from one generation to the next. It is this persistence of vision that Franklin is seeking for himself and his daughter. Similarly, the community of "The Princess, the Dwarf and the Dungeon" links together its individual stories to create a legacy for itself.

Thus, the persistence of vision phenomenon articulates a major theme running throughout the three stories. Franklin's cartoons are composed of a series of still images, and the second and third novellas use a similar technique. The second novella uses smaller stories linked together to create a larger, more complete story. The third novella uses a series of paintings to create a biography. Each of these stories points to the creation of larger stories from smaller ones. What our mind does next is link them together to create a larger, more complete story. This is, for the most part, the way in which readers view their society and their identity. Memories are made up of individual stories, fragments of emotions, and physical sensations that are linked together to form one's view of him or herself and the surrounding world. Likewise, societies are made up of individual people linked together to create a bigger, more complete whole. Millhauser then demonstrates how part of the artist's role is to be able to step back and recognize this, which is precisely what he does in his fiction.

◆ CHARACTERS ◆

Franklin is the portrait of the misunderstood artist. He is the artist who sacrifices his own health because of the importance of his art and his purpose. He is a stock character in this regard, but he gains depth through the fertility of his imagination and his recognized duty to his wife and child, which causes him a measure of remorse. He is a sympathetic character, patient and understanding with the villainized boss, and even understanding of Cora, who is the antithesis of his imaginative creation. Cora, on the other hand, represents the stifling nature of close-minded people who refuse to recognize the validity of "lower" forms of art—such as cartoons, television, and advertisements—as worthy areas of concentration and study. Her eventual move to be with Rex is expected as throughout the story she seems to be solely discouraging of Franklin's pursuits. She is not painted in an entirely unsympathetic way, as Franklin continues to love her, but the necessity of losing her for the sake of his art is the important response to her departure. Stella, on the other hand, is another stifled genius who benefits from Cora's absence. She comes out of her shell and begins to explore her own artistic pursuits, creating a comic of her own and wanting to take piano lessons. In an effort to reconcile the opposing forces in her life, she merges the two arts of her parents, drawing and playing the piano, as a gesture of her ties to both. She begins to replace Cora for Franklin, becoming almost the wife that he should have had all along— she encourages his art and allows him the distance that he needs, while remaining supportive and present when he needs her attention. Her matronly actions irk Franklin, but it is most likely disapproval of the situation (caused by himself and by Cora) that has led her to be in such a position.

This idea of extreme closeness between family members is also a facet of "Catalogue of the Exhibition." The narrator of the story repeatedly denies that the close relationship between Edmund and Elizabeth, as evidenced by their refusal to part and their almost psychic connection, is anything unnatural, but the emotional picture that is drawn cannot help but suggest a more than sibling relation. This is not an uncommon suggestion; there have been examples in the past of suggested pairings (for example, the alleged relationship between sisters Virginia Woolf and Vanessa Bell), and the effect here, especially in the case of Edmund and Elizabeth, is to separate these characters from the society in which they live, essentially mirroring the physical move that each of the artists makes, Franklin to his tower and Edmund to his cottage. Although not an artist herself, Elizabeth is similar to Franklin in her utter devotion to the art that she values. She is fascinated with that which disturbs her and is able to create a response within her. She faithfully serves Edmund and provides one of the only sources of information about Edmund and his work. Her faithfulness becomes a detriment to her well-being in the end and eventually causes her death. Although not fatal, the princess of the second novella experiences a similar effect of faithfulness to a less-than-worthy partner. She is led by her devotion to wrong another, which in turn sets the entire group on a path towards despair and destruction, similar to the effect of Elizabeth's refusal of William's proposal of marriage.

The princess of the second novella is a variation on the stock character of a prin-

cess in a fairy tale. She is the purest of the pure, and the most devoted of all, which are standard characteristics of fairy tale princesses, but she reaches a depth of emotional torment that is unusual. The prince, likewise, is granted certain characteristics that are unusual for a fairy tale. The result is an emphasis on the emotional state of each of the characters and an exploration of their psyches, which is usually entirely lacking in the fairy tales from childhood. It seems that Millhauser has taken the characteristics of fairy tale characters and has let them loose to see how people with such characteristics would react and interact if they were presented with "real life" situations rather than having the sole purpose of being a means to a "happily ever after" ending.

Edmund, of the third novella, is again a portrait of a tortured artist, a slave to the perfection of his art. His paintings spring from his tortured soul, and it is in this way that Millhauser again explores the relationship of the artist to his art. This process is complicated by the nature of the narrative in this story, as it is being told by a narrator who is set a considerable way off from Edmund's milieu. It is in this way that Millhauser uses the paintings, in a way as characters themselves, things to which Edmund relates that readers can then investigate for information about his life. The way one looks at Edmund is through shadow images through the story created by the exhibition which is created through the writings of others surrounding Edmund; this is the very nature of his paintings, which show slight images through coats of paint, leaving things questionable and at times utterly unrecognizable.

♦ TECHNIQUES ♦

Millhauser finds himself among very good company in terms of experimental forms of narrative. The style of "The Princess, the Dwarf and the Dungeon" is similar to Italo Calvino's *Invisible Cities*. *Invisible Cities* presents the stories Marco Polo tells Kubla Khan after he returns from his journeys. The novel is divided into independent sections that are related to each other by their categorization. Likewise, "Catalogue of the Exhibition" is extremely similar in tone, theme, and format to Vladimir Nabokov's novel *Pale Fire*, in which a fictional poem is analyzed by a fictional critic who claims to be a displaced member of royalty. Questions arise as to the narrator's authority and the creation of a narrative from examples of an isolated piece of art created by the main character of the narrative. Thus, the story of the artist is told by the interpretation of the art he makes. Both Calvino and Nabokov are descriptive in the same vein as Millhauser; all three use intricate descriptions of their own creations to enrich their story and examine their chosen themes.

◆ LITERARY PRECEDENTS ◆

Millhauser would best be classified under the amorphous heading of "magic realism." One major author who is synonymous with this type of fiction is Jorge Luis Borges, whose short stories such as "The Babylon Lottery" and "The Library of Babel" mix the fantastical with the banal and everyday in ways that arouse one's imagination and create new discussions surrounding the societies involved and the assumptions that they are based upon. Similarly, Calvino and Nabokov could be considered in this category. Both writers use the methods of this tradition to explore the process of writing and reading, and the creation of meaning from these two processes. Calvino's *If on a Winter's Night a Traveler* is a very good example of this. An example from another author is Umberto Eco's novel *Foucault's Pendulum*, in which all of history is at the mercy of rewriting and reconnecting in the search for meaning. Millhauser uses many of the motifs present in Nabokov's fiction, such as the preoccupation with windows, the appearance of dark imagery, and especially the obsession of the main character with worlds that he creates. Two notable examples of Nabokov's work would be *The Defense* and *The Gift*.

◆ RELATED TITLES ◆

Millhauser touches on many of the same themes in his other fiction that he is concerned with in these three novellas. His novel *Edwin Mullhouse* relates the story of a boy genius who dies mysteriously at a very young age and in some ways is very similar to "Catalogue of the Exhibition" in its concentration on one particular artist. A close friend of Edwin's narrates this novel, which is similar to the reliance on Elizabeth's journal for information. Likewise, Millhauser's novel *Martin Dressler*, for which he won a Pulitzer Prize, takes the form of a biography about an entrepreneur. Millhauser's short stories vary in the use of fantastical elements; "The Visit" from his collection *The Knife Thrower and Other Stories* is a particular example of mixing the extraordinary with the ordinary.

◆ IDEAS FOR GROUP DISCUSSIONS ◆

One of the most interesting facets of collections, whether it is a collection of poetry, short stories, novellas, or anything else, is not only being able to deal with each story in isolation, but also finding intersections among the pieces of the collection. Millhauser uses many of the same themes, motifs, and types of description throughout his fiction. He returns to the fantastic again and again, but always places it in a very particular context, and it is through his very particular lens that images of societies begin to emerge.

1. What are some motifs that run throughout all three novellas?

2. The relation of art to society is very important in all three of these stories. What are some ways that art intersects with our society and in our daily lives? What are the similarities between those ways and these stories?

3. What is the significance of Franklin's choice of comic strips and cartoons? Why would this form of art be used instead of film or sculpting?

4. Does Cora's absence benefit the family? Is her leaving a good or bad thing?

5. In "The Princess, the Dwarf and the Dungeon," Millhauser calls upon the form of the fairy tale, using motifs and iconography from tales of Rapunzel, Sleeping Beauty, Rumpelstiltskin, and the like. These stories are told again and again in various forms from those of the Brothers Grimm to James Finn Garner's *Politically Correct Fairy Tales*. How these stories are used, then, is telling of the person or community that uses it. What motifs can you pick out of this story and how are they significant? What is Millhauser trying to do? How does it relate to the other two novellas?

6. The narrator in the second novella explains that the community has developed various ends to their story of the princess. What are some other ways that you think the story could end?

7. How would you classify the relationship between Edmund and Elizabeth? Should Elizabeth have married William? What effect do you think it would have had? Would the story have ended the same way? What if Sophia had married Edmund?

8. What is going on in America at the time that Edmund is painting? Does his work reflect or respond to any movements or manners of thought that are occurring at this time?

9. The line "In October 1846 Charlotte Vail died, after a lingering illness" ends the third novella and the collection itself. What is the significance of this line? Why end with Charlotte Vail, who seems to be a very minor character in the story?

10. Critics often compare Millhauser to Edgar Allen Poe. Can you find any similarities? In which novella is the connection most striking?

Jessica Horn
Pennsylvania State University

THE MAMBO KINGS PLAY SONGS OF LOVE

Novel

1989

Author: Oscar Hijuelos

◆ SOCIAL CONCERNS ◆

In 1990, *The Mambo Kings Play Songs of Love* won the Pulitzer Prize for fiction. It was the first time that award was given to a Latino author, and it signaled that Latino fiction was no longer considered marginal, but was in fact a vital part of American literature. One of Hijuelos's major achievements in the novel is its range of themes that reflect both general American and specifically Cuban American experiences. *The Mambo Kings Play Songs of Love* comments significantly upon the American Dream, gender roles and relationships, the immigrant experience, and nostalgia for Cuba.

In the novel, Cesar and Nestor Castillo, two brothers from Oriente Province, Cuba, come to New York City in 1949. They hope to escape their pasts and find new career opportunities in the thriving New York Latin music scene epitomized by such real-life musicians as Xavier Cugat, Machito (also known as "The Mambo King"), and Tito Puente. The brothers are soon working in a meat packing plant by day and playing Cuban mambos, boleros, and rumbas by night. They achieve their greatest success and recognition when the Cuban musician and actor Desi Arnaz asks them to perform on his television show, *I Love Lucy*. This leads to record sales and more appearances in clubs.

At first glance, it would appear that the Castillo brothers live out the traditional American Dream, in which immigrants come to the United States, take menial jobs, and over time and through hard work, acquire better jobs and financial security. In this paradigm, the United States is the "land of opportunity" where immigrants can ascend the socio-economic ladder through their own efforts. Hijuelos, however, challenges that concept. First, the opportunities available to the brothers come at a steep price. Cesar starts a Cuban orchestra, the Mambo Kings, but he soon finds that the night club world is stacked against musicians. He refuses to sign an exclusive contract with any club owner because such contracts are biased in favor of club owners. As a result, the band is forced to continually hustle for gigs, and at times Cesar and his musicians are cheated by racketeers who "forget" to pay them. In addition, the Mambo Kings cut several records, but because Latin music is regarded as a specialty item rather than something with mass market appeal, their recordings sell at most a few thousand copies.

Hijuelos further questions the American Dream of economic advancement when

Cesar opens the Club Havana, a small nightspot that serves up traditional Cuban music and food. All goes well until Fernando Perez , Cesar's financial partner, takes over the club and turns it into a drug operation. The local residents shun Cesar when their children become addicted to Perez's wares, and Cesar eventually has to abandon the club to Perez. Hijuelos suggests that the cherished American value of financial success through hard work can be undermined by a darker American ethos, that economic success is to be attained at any price.

Although the story of the Club Havana illustrates the dark side of American success myths, Hijuelos also finds entertainment in them. He parodies American success manuals, which have been popular in America since the early nineteenth century. Success manuals promise that their readers can move up in society through studying and applying general principles that often are ridiculous in their banality. During many of the novel's scenes, Nestor reads a hilarious self-improvement book called *Forward America!* Nestor's dog-eared paperback exhorts its readers to have self-confidence and be "men of the future," so that they can win "respect and love of others ... the *American Way!*" Despite Nestor's best efforts to absorb this philosophy, he drifts into gradually increasing despair that culminates in his death at age 31 in a car accident. Nestor cannot be this new man of the future because he is too distracted by what he left behind in Cuba. There he was in love with Maria Rivera, a glamorous dancer who married another man. Nestor's obsession with Maria, which continues once he moves to the United States, drives a wedge between him and his wife, Delores. This is no surprise, considering that Nestor writes Maria imploring letters and spends months composing a melancholy song about her, "Bellisima Maria de mi Alma" ("Beautiful Maria of My Soul"). Ironically, the song that gives Nestor so much exquisite

pain as he composes it is the one that draws Desi Arnaz's attention and becomes the Mambo Kings' biggest hit.

Critics have remarked that Nestor's haunted longings for Maria echo many exiled Cubans' desire for Cuba. After the 1959 Revolution in Cuba when Fidel Castro came to power, the emigre Cubans in the United States became exiles. That is, they were no longer able to return to Cuba because that country had become Communist. For many in the exile community, Cuba became a powerful symbol of a way of life that was irreparably lost, as well as the subject of bitter political arguments that polarized Cuban enclaves in the United States for the rest of the twentieth century.

Nostalgia for a forever-vanished golden past characterizes the literature of exile, a category to which many Cuban American novels can be said to belong, especially those written before 1990. Although *The Mambo Kings Play Songs of Love* is too strongly rooted in classic American themes to be a true novel of exile, Hijuelos borrows from the genre. He depicts first Nestor and then, after Nestor's death, Cesar, as men "plagued by memory." Just as Nestor becomes increasingly more melancholy and unable to focus on what is around him because he longs for the unattainable Maria, Cesar's prolonged grief for his dead brother plunges him into depression. Cesar seeks to alleviate his sorrow through alcohol and frenetic sex. Tellingly, he abandons music, his means of creative expression, during his darkest days.

The Castillo brothers' unsuccessful struggle to escape their personal histories contradicts a classic myth of America, that the past can be left behind. Hijuelos does this not only through the plot he creates, but also though the novel's narrative structure. *The Mambo Kings Play Songs of Love* skips forward and back in time and place, from 1920's Cuba to New York in 1980. The plot unfolds in an order that is anything but chronological. Just as Cesar's memory is "scrambled like eggs," the novel's events are jumbled together. This produces an eternal now in which all events are present at once, much like exiles holding the nostalgic past together with the actual present in their minds. At the same time, however, Cesar knows that these places and people now live only in his own thoughts, not in the real world. As Cesar says to Lydia Santos, his final girlfriend, "See, the worst part of it is that things don't exist any more." He speaks here about Cuba, but he could also have been referring to the tight-knit New York Cuban community that also dissipated over time, or any of his memories of past places and people. Of course, exiles are not alone in their inability to revisit the past. In essence, time makes exiles of everyone because the past is a place to which no one can return. Nevertheless, Hijuelos suggests that memory can be particularly debilitating to exiles. While the past may not physically exist any longer, it still can trap exiles in their old national identities, no matter how much they wish to become "men of the future." "Look, brother, there goes the future," Cesar jokes to Nestor as they pass by a cemetery. For Cesar and Nestor, time most readily points backwards. They cannot reinvent themselves as men without histories that weigh them down.

◆ THEMES ◆

One of the strengths of *The Mambo Kings Play Songs of Love* is that it shows the price exacted by adherence to rigid gender roles. In its world of New York Cubans, many men are machos: physically strong, capable of silently enduring great pain, but also prone to mistreating women. Cesar is such a man, and he gives Nestor traditional ma-

cho advice, "A little abuse never hurt a romance. Women like to know who's the boss." Nestor, who is more sensitive than his brother, nonetheless applies this counsel to his relationship with Maria, to disastrous effect. He shoves her, insults her, and looks lustfully at other women in her presence. In response, Maria becomes quiet and unhappy, eventually leaving Nestor to return to her previous lover. Likewise, Cesar cannot settle happily with one woman. In Cuba, he marries and has a baby daughter, but he destroys his marriage through his inability to stay away from other women. In the United States, he beds a vast parade of women, and Hijuelos explicitly describes Cesar's passionate, sometimes violent sexual encounters with them. The net result for both Cesar and Nestor is alienation. Although courtship and sex promise release from emotional pain, acting like machos backfires, leaving the two brothers distant from women and their offers of love.

In contrast to men, who are to go out and experience what the world has to give, the role of women in the novel is to be wives and mothers, their lives centered around home. As Nestor tells Delores, "a woman with two children should never spend more time than's necessary away from home." It is important to note that Hijuelos sharply criticizes this attitude rather than applauds it, and he does this chiefly through the character of Delores. A bookish Cuban who yearns to attend college classes, she wonders why she does not feel emotionally fulfilled by life as a housewife. She asks herself, "why did she act willingly like a slave, attending to all the men, and yet feel no satisfaction or closeness to the women, like her sister, Ana Maria, and Pablo's wife, Miriam, who went happily about the business of cooking and happily rushed into the living room with trays of food?" However, we do not know what the other women truly feel because the novel never enters their minds. Whether they are as genuinely contented as Delores thinks they are remains a mystery.

Hijuelos also questions another common gender role practice. In traditional Cuban society, women always take orders from men. However, the novel's female characters are often emotionally stronger and more sensible than the men. The marriage of Delores and Nestor nicely illustrates this point. As Nestor withdraws further and further from Delores, sinking into his private despair, Delores goes to night classes at a high school and keeps the family fed and the house clean, even though her own heart deeply aches. She acquires a longing of her own, to attend classes at nearby City College, which was then well known for its open enrollment policies, but Nestor will not allow her to do so because he thinks it would challenge his authority as the head of their family. He tells her, "You go, and that will be the end of normalcy for us!"

The issue of who is in charge in a heterosexual relationship also plays out in Cesar's six-month-long romance with Celia. Celia is an unconventional woman who is used to making her own decisions, and at first it looks as though she will be able to stop Cesar's grief-driven slide into alcoholism and unhappiness. However, the relationship hits an insurmountable crisis one night when Cesar has drunk too much. Celia ties him up with a clothesline to force him to stay home. Literally roped down by domestic life, Cesar is furious. He cannot forgive her for having "tried to reduce me in my stature" and breaks up with Celia, telling her that no woman "can be allowed to do that to a man." Although Celia went too far, ultimately it is to Cesar's detriment that he leaves her and refuses to take her wise advice: "What you have to do is learn to be content with what you have in this world, *hombre.*"

Celia is the rare woman in the novel who is not economically dependent on a man.

She does not appear to have children, and thus she has to support only herself through her small retail enterprises. This frees her to act as she pleases. Many of the novel's other female characters are not so fortunate. They not only have children, but, unlike Celia, they are unable to overcome the three significant financial strikes against them. First, they are living before the women's movement dramatically opened up the career opportunities available to women. Second, they are Latinos, which constricts job choices still further, due to prejudices of the time. Finally, they lack education, a deficiency that in large part results from male fears that educated women will be too independent, as in the case of Delores and Nestor.

The financial dependence of women upon men is powerfully dramatized in the plight of Cesar's last girlfriend, Lydia Santos. Almost thirty years younger than Cesar, she has two children but no financial support from her husband, who lives outside the United States. She works full-time in a factory making eyeglasses, but has no insurance and no money for anything more than the barest essentials of life. Even though she is physically repulsed by Cesar's aging and ill-cared-for body, she has a sexual relationship with him, primarily because he brings her presents and food for her children. Similarly, when Delores remarries after Nestor's death, she selects a man whom she does not love, but who will take care of her and her children financially. The inability to earn a good wage coerces women into sexual relationships and marriages of convenience they would not otherwise choose, a situation that is by no means Hijuelos's invention.

Hijuelos's revealing portrait of the economic reality behind many heterosexual relationships helps to counter one possible criticism of his novel. It is possible, although misguided, to think of the novel as anti-woman because Cesar's sexual exploits so often degrade women. Cesar at his most self-indulgent reduces his lovers to mere objects who are there to bring him sexual release from his emotional pain, and the characterizations of these women do not rise above that level. Some female characters are merely a collection of body parts and graphically described sexual behaviors. The one-dimensionality of these descriptions can be annoying, especially in the early sections of the novel. At some point, however, the reader realizes that the women are seen through Cesar's eyes, not Hijuelos's, and that Cesar pays a price for his callous treatment of them. Because Cesar repeatedly refuses to become a monogamous family man, even though he has a daughter, he must continue playing the Romeo to the end of his life or be alone. He undergoes repeated humiliations as a result. Some are small, such as when Lydia keeps him waiting on a date, something he never would have tolerated in his younger days. Some are large, such as the terrible shame he experiences when he pressures Lydia to grant sexual favors she does not wish to give because his body repulses her. Through the story of Cesar, Hijuelos portrays the profound alienation and loneliness that can result from a lifetime of being a traditional macho.

◆ CHARACTERS ◆

Cesar and Nestor Castillo are the two central characters of *The Mambo Kings Play Songs of Love*. At first they appear to be opposites. Cesar is confident and worldly, and Nestor is sensitive and withdrawn. However, both are driven to destructive treatment of women by their own psychological flaws. Furthermore, Hijuelos gradually reveals that both are haunted by recollections of a troubling past that they can never reclaim and make right. A Castillo man, Hijuelos writes, was prone to moments when "melancholia abruptly came over him and he would suffer from his own plague of memories." For both Cesar and Nestor, these bouts of unhappiness are tied to childhood. Pedro Castillo, their father, was a violent and melancholy man who physically abused his family. As a result, Cesar turned his pain outward and became a macho while Nestor retreated inward. To further escape their difficult family life, they both became musicians at an early age, thus embodying the archetype of the artist who turns his suffering into beauty. Nestor's preoccupation with his composition "Bellisima Maria de mi Alma" is the ultimate expression of this in the novel. Not only does it reflect his obsession with his lost love Maria Rivera, but Maria was also the name of Nestor and Cesar's mother. Cesar's endless quest for hedonistic pleasure, or as the narrator puts it, "rum, rumba, and rump," can also be read as the desire to recapture a mother's enveloping love.

Against these overly high expectations of what can be recovered through love stand the major women in the novel: Delores Fuentes, Lydia Santos, Vanna Vane, and Maria Rivera. Of the four, the reader most comes to know the thoughts of Delores and Lydia, who are the most fully realized female characters. Less detailed is the character of Vanna Vane, "Miss Mambo for the month of June 1954," a curvaceous blonde American who is essentially the stock type of the party girl, a woman who lives for going out in the evening. She is Cesar's steady girlfriend for several years, despite his affairs with other women. He enjoys her for the public status she confers on him, as well as for the private pleasure she brings him. Although Hijuelos downplays the discrimination that Latinos experienced in twentieth-century New York, he still notes the racial calculus that occurred—the paler the skin and lighter the hair color, the higher the person's social status—and Vanna Vane appeals to Cesar as a high-status girlfriend.

In return, she indulges in her own fantasies about Latin lovers, based on the stereotype that Latinos are more sexually passionate than men of other ethnicities.

Something of a mystery is the fourth major female character, Maria Rivera. The object of Nestor's obsession, she is present throughout the novel less as a real woman than as an abstraction. She quickly loses her last name and instead is usually referred to as Beautiful Maria. This new appellation suits her function in the book as a symbol of what has been lost and can never be recovered.

Moving out from the center of the novel, there is a wide range of secondary characters. These include additional Castillo family members, Cesar's discarded girlfriends, Mambo King musicians, and two celebrities from real life (Desi Arnaz and Lucille Ball). Of the minor characters, the most fully portrayed is Eugenio, Nestor's son, who narrates the novel's opening and closing. Hijuelos briefly but vividly describes the other minor characters, so that they appear as though in a snapshot. The reader gets a momentary glimpse, enough to establish who the characters are but not enough to tell us everything about them. This approach reinforces Hijuelos's overall strategy of slowly depicting Cesar and Nestor through a swirl of fragmented memories that must be reassembled by the reader into a story that has meaning and significance.

◆ TECHNIQUES ◆

Hijuelos informs readers from the very first page that they will have to work to understand his novel. The novel's epigraph, a relevant quotation from another work that provides readers with important clues about what they are about to read, appears to be taken from the album liner notes of an old record called *The Mambo Kings Play Songs of Love*. Many readers will wonder whether there actually was a band called the Mambo Kings and thus whether the novel they are about to read is completely fictional. Hijuelos further confuses reality and fiction as the novel proper opens. Eugenio Castillo eagerly summons his Uncle Cesar to watch an episode of the popular television series *I Love Lucy*. Cesar and Nestor, we learn, were musicians in an orchestra called "The Mambo Kings," and they performed one of their songs on the program. The motif of the repeating television episode that can be seen forever in reruns sets up a major theme of the novel: recurring memories packed with nostalgia for a not-quite-real past. Readers continue to discover that the novel will not develop in a simple fashion after Hijuelos elaborately describes how the Castillos met Desi Arnaz and Lucille Ball, the stars of *I Love Lucy*. The meeting may not have happened that way at all, Hijuelos tells us, and he then provides a much shorter, more prosaic explanation. This is a major moment in the novel, for it acknowledges the fundamentally unreliable nature of memory.

The problem of knowing which memories in the novel are to be trusted is not one that can truly be solved. The novel's point of view changes repeatedly, sandwiched between Eugenio's first-person narration at the beginning and end. Much of the narrative appears to represent Cesar's perspective, and we also get brief glimpses of Nestor's and Delores's thoughts. Hijuelos's decision not to tell the story in chronological order also suggests the state of Cesar's disordered memories more intensely than a straightforward telling of the tale would. Essentially, *The Mambo Kings Play Songs of Love* is a psychological novel. The emotional realities of its characters are more important than knowing the "truth" about what happens to them.

One of the pleasures of the novel is its many allusions to music. Like an old-fashioned record, it has a "Side A" and a "Side

B," the names of two sections in the book. At one point the narrative stops altogether, taken over by "nothing but drums," a page and a half description of drumming, much like a conga drum solo in the middle of a mambo song. In addition, just before Cesar and Nestor die, Hijuelos switches to a fluid stream-of-consciousness technique that captures the brothers' thoughts without trying to make sense of them, giving each man one last moment alone in the spotlight before his performance ends. Music is also vitally important to the lives of the Castillos because it preserves their Cuban culture in a country where immigrants are pressured to assimilate. That the novel's form is influenced by a musical sensibility further helps to drive home the significance of music.

◆ LITERARY PRECEDENTS ◆

The Mambo Kings Play Songs of Love has deep roots in early twentieth-century American novels of immigrant experience, such as Upton Sinclair's *The Jungle* (1906) and Abraham Cahan's *The Rise of David Levinsky* (1917). These older works chart immigrants' attempts to rise on the economic ladder and explore the price that must be paid for financial success. The world Hijuelos depicts is not as harsh as that of Sinclair and Cahan, however, as can be clearly seen in a scene from *The Mambo Kings Play Songs of Love* that strongly evokes *The Jungle*. Once they arrive in the United States, Nestor and Cesar work in a meat packing plant, just as many characters in *The Jungle* do. Sinclair's meat packing plant is a place of horror, where a moment's inattention results in maiming or death, and where readers were shocked to discover what found its way into the sausage vats. In contrast, *The Mambo Kings* depicts Nestor absent-mindedly composing his ballad of lost love while working near the sausage grinder. He is blissfully unconcerned for his safety, which he can

take for granted. The difference between the two scenes stems from a variation in focus. Sinclair wanted to improve working conditions for immigrants and so dramatized the direst threats to their physical beings. Hijuelos, on the other hand, writes about a world where the threats to immigrants are more psychological, in that they may not be able to mentally adapt to their new country.

Classic autobiographies about the experiences of immigrants in the United States can also provide useful comparisons with *The Mambo Kings Play Songs of Love*. For example, Mary Antin's *The Promised Land* (1912) explores Americanization and assimilation more directly than does Hijuelos's novel and could assist students in getting at those key issues.

◆ RELATED TITLES ◆

The Mambo Kings Play Songs of Love is Oscar Hijuelos's second novel, and it continues the exploration of Cuban American experience that he began in his first book, *Our House in the Last World* (1983). Interestingly, Hijuelos was not afflicted by the sophomore curse, the common phenomenon of an author's second book being not as strong as the first. *The Mambo Kings Play Songs of Love* not only won the Pulitzer Prize, but it remains one of the most technically flamboyant of his novels, with its allusions to music and its fractured narrative. His third novel, *The Fourteen Sisters of Emilio Montez O'Brien* (1993), focuses more on women's experiences, but was regarded by critics as not entirely successful. It has not been until his fifth novel, *Empress of the Splendid Season* (1999), that Hijuelos has been able to fully realize his female characters. In that novel, Hijuelos takes a commonplace figure from modern American life, the Latino cleaning lady, gives her an individual history, and explores in detail the connection between low-wage jobs and poverty. The resulting creation, Lydia Espana, is more detailed and three dimensional than his previous female characters. In *Empress of the Splendid Season* Hijuelos also dramatizes the conflicts between Cuban emigres and their Americanized children to a far greater extent than he did in *The Mambo Kings Play Songs of Love*.

◆ ADAPTATIONS ◆

A film version of the novel, titled *The Mambo Kings,* saw its theatrical release in 1992. Written by Cynthia Cidre and directed by Arne Glimcher, it varies significantly from Hijuelos's novel. First, it lacks Eugenio's narration as a framing device and does not move forward and backward through Cesar's memories. Instead, it dramatizes the novel's major storylines in chronological order, with important changes in characterization and incident. Cesar is no longer a womanizer, and his decline into alcoholism after Nestor's death is downplayed. In addition, Nestor becomes a less sympathetic character. In a plot development not in the novel, Nestor secretly schemes with Fernando Perez to leave the Mambo Kings and start his own solo singing career. When he later attempts to abandon the plan, Perez says that he will make sure the Mambo Kings never find work as musicians again. This development causes Nestor to feel tremendous guilt, which impels him to fatally crash Cesar's beloved DeSoto automobile. In the novel, on the other hand, it is Nestor's steadily worsening depression that precipitates the accident. The movie ends with a chastened Cesar opening the Club Havana in New York and singing "Beautiful Maria of My Soul" while he sadly remembers his brother. Furthermore, the movie strongly hints that Cesar and Delores may become romantically involved in the future. These changes make the movie more sensational than the novel and also less interesting. Without the book's fragmented, drenched-in-nostalgia narrative structure, the relationship between memory and exile remains unexplored.

The film's version of the song "Beautiful Maria of My Soul" marks another departure from Hijuelos's novel. In the book, the song's lyrics portray a tormented lover bemoaning the ill treatment he has received from the woman he adores. In the movie, however, the words have been changed so that the lover is no longer agonized, just nostalgic. Instead of a traditional Cuban lament, the song becomes a lushly romantic remembrance of past passion. The new version was recorded by both the actor Antonio Banderas, who played Nestor in the film, and by the band Los Lobos. Here, it is easy to see that commercial considerations were at work. The movie's song is much more emotionally upbeat and thus more likely to be a mainstream success.

An abridged version of *The Mambo Kings Play Songs of Love* was also released on cassette by Dove Audio in 1991. The actor E. G. Marshall read the novel.

◆ IDEAS FOR GROUP DISCUSSIONS ◆

Discussions of *The Mambo Kings Play Songs of Love* can focus on both topical issues in American life and on artistic form. One possible area to be examined is the novel's depiction of the Cuban emigre experience in comparison to that of other groups who have immigrated to the United States. Hijuelos's portrayals of female characters and the tensions between men and women in the novel also could spark worthwhile discussion. In addition, Oscar Hijuelos has said in interviews that he thinks of himself more as a New York author than as a Latino writer, and attempts to define those categories could lead to interesting conversations about identity and genre. The novel's technical aspects and how they express the book's themes would make a good final area of study.

1. How is the *The Mambo Kings Play Songs of Love* similar to and different from the works of other Cuban American novelists publishing at the same time as Hijuelos, such as Roberto Fernandez, Cristina Garcia, and Elias Miguel Munos?

2. How would you describe the difference between an exile and an immigrant? How does the exile experience differ from the immigrant experience? Which characters in the novel would you consider exiles and which would you consider immigrants?

3. Does the Castillo "melancholy" truly run in the family, as the narrator says it does, or is it a reaction to the circumstances of Cesar's and Nestor's lives?

4. Are there factors other than Nestor's obsession with Beautiful Maria that contribute to his sadness?

5. Can any of the novel's women be considered strong? Are they sympathetically portrayed?

6. Why are neither Cesar nor Nestor able to find happiness in family life, in contrast to the characters of Pablo, their cousin, and Julian Garcia, a musician in Cuba?

7. Can artists or musicians have a settled domestic life, or does the production of great art or music require them to live emotionally apart from other people?

8. What images of masculinity can you find in the novel? Do any of them seem to be more desirable than others?

9. Why do you think Hijuelos took some characters from real life, such as Desi Arnaz and Lucille Ball, instead of using only fictional characters?

Kelly Fuller
Claremont Graduate University

O IS FOR OUTLAW

Novel

1999

Author: Sue Grafton

◆

" A n Unsuitable Genre for a Feminist?" is the title of Cora Kaplan's article in *Women's Review* discussing women writing detective fiction (1986). The question is a valid one, for the drive of detective fiction, the genre to which *O Is for Outlaw* belongs, is toward a goal that upholds the law and maintains or restores social order, and sees that justice is done. Subsequently, the detective novel tends toward a conservative ending in support of the *status quo*. Since this *status quo* favors the masculine, how, indeed, might women make use of the genre without perpetuating the patriarchal ideologies that underlie it?

Into the generic framework Sue Grafton inserts her central protagonist, Kinsey Millhone, a thirty-six-year-old female private investigator. But, can a woman's presence in what is conventionally thought of as a man's role, both in life and in literature, make any difference? Although Millhone's character stems more from the hard-boiled detective genre rather than overtly feminist concerns, her very presence raises some issues of social import. It may be argued that women are accustomed, like the lone hero of detective fiction, to being on the margins of society. For centuries their voices have not been heard, their skills have not been developed or valued, and their identities have been viewed as "other" to the mainstream male identities around which western social existence is structured. While contemporary conditions for women have greatly improved, it is plain that equality has, as yet, not been achieved.

As a single (twice-divorced) working woman in what is traditionally conceived of as a man's role, the character of Kinsey Millhone raises awareness of the choices available to women in society of the mid-1980s, the time at which this novel is set. The character is a marked example of a woman adopting a masculine-identified role and succeeding at it, although Grafton is quick to inform the reader that the character is "lacking" in what are conventionally conceived of as "feminine" traits by the fact that she possesses one multipurpose dress which can be scrunched into the bottom of a bag without too much damage, she lives for the most part in jeans, and, in an earlier novel in the series, she states that she has never understood the concept of accessories. In social terms, therefore, Millhone in some respects also exists on the margins of conservative expectations of "womanly" behavior—and it is important to remember that these are simply conservative expectations—and her position thereby questions society's conception of womanliness itself, exposing it to be something of a masquerade. Although not depicted as overly organized, Millhone shares some traits of the image of the successful businesswoman of the 1980s, the latter characterized by her rather masculine shoulder-padded business suit. The novel thus reflects on debates which are relevant today: how a woman can negotiate the world of work which is predominantly male-oriented. However, the degree to which Millhone might be held up as a feminist role model is questionable as she conforms mostly to the stereotypical male detective role and, if a woman can only succeed if she masquerades as a man, this does not forward the value of women as a social group.

The novel's movement between past and present provides opportunities for reflection on the ambivalent degree of change in the status of women in society. The present of *O is for Outlaw* is 1986 but the novel is also concerned with uncovering events which occurred some fifteen years before this, in 1971. In one instance, the first-person narrator, Millhone, recalls living through the Women's Liberation Movement in her twenties, a time when she used to "barhop" in order to pick up men:

> What Women's Liberation "liberated" was our attitude to sex. Where we once used sex for barter, now we gave it away. I marvel at the prostitutes we must have put out of business, doling out sexual "favors" in the name of personal freedom. What were we thinking?

Millhone's characteristically sardonic tone is, shortly after this reflection, applied to her overhearing, in the present of the novel, a woman in the ladies' room of a bar vomiting to the accompaniment of encouragement by her friend:

> I could hear two women in the adjoining stall, one barfing up her dinner while the other offered encouraging comments.

"That's fine. Don't force it. You're doing great. It'll come." If I'd even heard of it in my day, I'd have assumed Bulimia was the capital of some newly formed Baltic state.

The women emerge from the cubicle, "both of them thin as snakes":

> The barfer pulled out a prepasted toothbrush and began to scrub. In five years the stomach acid would eat through her tooth enamel, if she didn't drop dead first.

Millhone's despondency at the status of women in society is made clear here, although her comments on bulimia are somewhat discomforting. The freedom that the women of the eighties might ostensibly have gained from the feminist movement of the preceding decade continues to be curtailed by societal expectations for which they put their health at risk. The novel thus questions the progression of women's positions and offers little that is positive for women who accept conventional representations of themselves, that is to be actively sexual in the seventies or to be thin in the eighties. Presently, Millhone is something of an outsider as far as women are concerned also, yet this, it is implied, is one of the reasons she is successful at her job.

While the position of women is founded upon societal inequalities, suggested by the incident in the restroom, the novel's depiction of unseemly or corrupt behavior is that it is a matter of individual conscience. Many of the characters in the novel are discovered to be having extramarital affairs, and at the heart of Millhone's ex-husband's shooting is a further tale of adultery and the fathering of a child outside of marriage during the Vietnam War. This, in turn, gives rise to the discovery of attempted concealment of corruption in a person running for public office. These extramarital entanglements and the sins of a public figure split apart the correlation between what is seen on the surface and what is occurring below the social mechanisms, the stuff of which detective fiction is made. Although the adulteries are treated as relatively minor infringements of society's codes, the public figure is ousted at the novel's finale and this canker of society's fate lies in an unlawful modern-day equivalent of the guillotine, restoring order to society once more.

◆ THEMES ◆

This quotation from early in the novel sets the scene for one of its central concerns:

> Our recollection of the past is not simply distorted by our faulty perception of events remembered but skewed by those forgotten. The memory is like orbiting twin stars, one visible, one dark, the trajectory of what's evident forever affected by the gravity of what's concealed.

O Is for Outlaw handles the concept of distorted memories primarily through the personal story of Millhone. The mystery in which she is engaged pertains to her personal history and requires a reappraisal of the behavior of her first ex-husband, whom she discovers she judged wrongly. What she reveals in her investigation of his shooting reverses what she had thought about him: now she finds he was "guilty of infidelity, innocent of manslaughter." Such a reappraisal touches upon the novel's concern with the dislocation between appearances and reality. Millhone had judged her ex-husband, Mickey Magruder, upon circumstantial evidence when he was accused of manslaughter. The fact that he had been a cop who "chafed at the limitations set by policy and, on a broader level, at legal restrictions he felt interfered with his effectiveness", and that he had asked Millhone to provide him with an alibi for some crucial hours for which he could not account, made her leave him. Millhone has lived with the version of the past that she created, and her misjudgement, for fifteen years.

Echoing this plot-centric revision of the past, the effects of the Vietnam War on its participants reverberates throughout the novel, mostly in the form of physical damage. The character in whose death Magruder was implicated was a veteran, with a metal plate in his head as a result of the war. This contributes, ultimately, to his death in the year following its end. Living with a physical reminder of the war is also central to another character's life—Eric Hightower, who lost both legs. He presently runs a successful business manufacturing equipment for people with disabilities. Interestingly, it is Hightower's disability, which can be seen, that is integrated into society successfully while that which cannot be seen, the victim Benny Quintero's, is excised, a reversal that rehearses the surface/reality dichotomy running through detective fiction as a genre. This dichotomy is made much more explicit between Hightower and Mark Bethel, the Vietnam veteran whose sins during the War and subsequent to it are exposed during the course of the novel. As an open and visible totem of the past, Hightower is embraced by society, but Bethel and his secrets are not. Bethel does not suffer from a physical handicap as a result of the War and his corruption is represented as an individual matter, not resulting from any social factors. His character is the epitome of the split between surface and reality, for he presents himself as the upright figure running for public office, concerned, in fact, with obtaining a fair deal for Vietnam veterans, while his actions attempt to conceal his own dishonorable behavior. In its representation of the veterans, the novel does not question the involvement of the United States in Vietnam—the subject of contemporary debate—but upholds the conservative version of events of the past.

The version of the past that Millhone had created for herself on a personal level, however, is overturned by her discoveries. As she gradually realizes the error of her judgement, she becomes concerned that she set right that misjudgement by finding the person who shot Magruder, reinforcing the sense of justice and personal integrity which courses through the central protagonist: "if I'd been an unwitting accomplice to his [Magruder's] downfall, I needed to own up to it and get square with him." This sense of attaining justice on a personal level is intertwined with the overarching concerns of the detective novel genre, and finds its literalization in the final scene where the perpetrator is brought to an end in a rather Biblical "eye for an eye" fashion. In this sense, forms of justice and its very nature come under scrutiny. For, one way the novel does question conservative values is in the violent and unlawful manner with which the criminal, Bethel, is dispatched by another criminal, Marlin Duffy, with whom Millhone has displayed some empathy, sharing a few beers with him on one occasion:

> Often I identified with guys like him. As crude as he was with his racist comments, his tortured grammar, and his attitude toward crime, I understood his yearning. How liberating it was when you defied authority, flaunted convention, ignoring ordinary standards of moral decency. I knew my own ambivalence.

At the end of the novel, Duffy avenges the death of his brother by killing Bethel, saving Millhone from danger. Although Duffy is imprisoned, his previous description of spells in jail is recalled: "with its volleyball, indoor tawlits [sic], and color television sets." Compared to Duffy's existence outside of jail, currently living in a shed in a garden center with no basic facilities, these conditions are fine. Additionally, he has described jail as "kind of like a time-out till I get my head on straight." The implication is that Bethel was the worse of these two criminals and that imprisonment might have been too good for him. Impor-

tantly, Duffy, in contrast to Bethel, has never attempted to conceal what he is. This is evident in an early conversation with Millhone:

> "Okay, so maybe sometimes I do something bad, but it's nothing *terrible.*"
>
> "You never killed anyone."
>
> "That's right. I never robbed nobody. Never used a gun . . . except the once. I never done drugs, I never messed with women didn't want to mess with me, and I never laid a hand on any kids. Plus I never done a single day of federal time. It's all city and county, mostly ninety-day horseshit. Criminal recklessness."

Duffy, therefore, lives by his own rules, which he considers never seriously harm anyone and it is this "outlaw" quality with which Millhone can empathize, as her response to Duffy here demonstrates: "It's fun breakin' rules. Makes you feel free," he tells her. She replies by saying "I can relate to that." Millhone relates her tendency to break small rules to Duffy in the following:

> I was split down the middle, my good angel sitting on one shoulder, Lucifer perched on the other. Duffy's struggle was the same, and while he leaned in one direction, I usually leaned in the other, searching for justice in the heart of anarchy. This was the bottom line as far as I was concerned: If the bad guys don't play by the rules, why should the good guys have to?

While justice is found in the heart of anarchy in Duffy's murder of his brother's killer, the question is raised as to who is the "outlaw" of the title. For there are many characters who exist outside of the law in varying degrees. Magruder and Millhone inhabit a space of occasional transgressions of the law, whereas Duffy does this in a more serious manner and Bethel, the most outwardly upright of these characters is shown to be the most inwardly corrupt. Justice, likewise, is seen to exist in degrees.

◆ CHARACTERS ◆

Characterization in hard-boiled detective fiction is typically not overly developed, as the emphasis is on investigation into events rather than character analysis. The genre requires a detective (in this case Millhone), and a criminal (Bethel), and other characters are encountered mostly as conduits for information. *O Is for Outlaw* possesses a rare character, however, in the form of Magruder. The discovery of his behavior and values is at least as important, if not more, than the discovery of the criminal.

The character of the detective is part of the genre's constitution, and its foundations go back to the nineteenth century and Edgar Allan Poe's tale, "The Murders in the Rue Morgue" (1852) in which Dupin makes his appearance. Along with Arthur Conan Doyle's Sherlock Holmes, first appearing in 1888, Dupin demonstrates the utility of rationalism in the face of the inexplicable. The first female detective created by a woman writer is also of this period. Anna Katherine Green's *That Affair Next Door* (1897) introduced the amateur aristocrat detective Miss Amelia Butterworth, the template for the infamous Miss Marple, created by Agatha Christie in 1930. Both of these detectives are extensions of the stereotype of the nosey woman since, being amateur, they have no legitimate business in the mystery, although they are far from gossips, keeping their findings to themselves until the appropriate evidence has been gathered. Both women are asexual spinsters, thereby posing no threat to the male police detectives working on the case and also posing no threat to the concept that a woman cannot be both intelligent and sexy at the same time.

What is known as the "hard-boiled" detective is characterized by an intensely masculine personality, often physically violent in the line of duty and with an attitude to women that is filled with mistrust (and this is frequently founded due to the negative portrayal of women in the hard-boiled genre) and contempt. This character is sexually active, without the aloofness of his antecedent nineteenth-century detective, and he possesses a rough charm. Dashiell Hammett's Sam Spade is a founding archetype of this character, appearing in *The Maltese Falcon* (1930). The hard-boiled detective, a professional private investigator, is a hero figure at odds with mainstream society.

An Unsuitable Job for a Woman, by P. D. James (1972), in which Cordelia Gray is introduced, makes clear by its title the conflicts that occur when a female is placed in the role of professional detective. This is complicated further when women characters, such as Millhone, are placed in the role of the hard-boiled detective, for they cannot take on the "macho" attitude to violence and to women without looking ridiculous and neither ought they to. The fact that female characters do not sit comfortably in the role without altering it exposes its masculinist presumptions. Millhone, incarnated in *A Is for Alibi* in 1983, is not alone in straddling this field, however. Sara Paretsky began her series of V.I. Warshawski novels in 1982 with *Indemnity Only* and Warshawski is perhaps the character who comes closest to Millhone in contemporary women's hard-boiled detective fiction.

Differences that the female character brings to the role are largely related to attitudes to violence and sex. The female hard-boiled detective does not engage as much in violence as her male counterpart, withdrawing from conflict situations if she can, rather than embracing them as does her male counterpart, which results in gritty realistic fight descriptions. Millhone's only close encounter with violence in this novel is when she is faced with Bethel's gun at the novel's climactic action scene. Here she runs away rather than challenge him. Additionally, she does not always carry her gun, another characteristic of the female detective. For women the gun does not hold the same phallic power as for the male detective and it might be just as easily taken out of her hands and turned on her, something which does not appear to be a consideration for the male detective (Grafton, in a discussion on the Barnes & Noble Web site, has provided an elementary reason for Millhone not carrying her gun often in that the author gets tired of the "gun nuts" informing her that she has the details wrong). With regard to sex, here we have a female character who is both sexual *and* intelligent, but her attitude to sex is not exploitative as is the male hard-boiled detective's attitude. In *O is for Outlaw,* Millhone's sexual activity is portrayed as occurring in the past although she devours junk food with the same relish as she devours sex:

> I steered with one hand while I munched with the other, all the time moaning with pleasure. It's pitiful to have a life in which junk food is awarded the same high status as sex. Then again, I tend to get a lot more of the one than I do of the other.

This is far from the spinsterly nature of Miss Marple for, although Millhone's sexuality is currently latent, it definitely exists. In previous novels in the series, the character does engage in sexual acts and in this novel, she believes Eric Hightower to be flirting with her in one instance. This concept of sexuality is important as it helps to break down the dichotomy between spinster, as detective, or *femme fatale,* as villain, which were really the only options available to female characters in hard-boiled male-centered stories in which female desire was coded as dangerous.

Millhone's position as first-person narrator encourages the reader to empathize with her and view characters and events from her perspective and this must be borne in mind when considering the other characters. The villain of *O Is for Outlaw,* Mark Bethel, shares with many of his predecessors in the hard-boiled genre the fact that he is a wealthy, powerful man. Along with the *femme fatale,* this is one of the most common stereotypes of the villain in this genre. A lawyer who advised Magruder at the time of his manslaughter accusation, Bethel's duplicity comes to the fore as he is discovered to have been involved in this crime and in others. He is presently running for public office and is the epitome of the surface and reality divide thematic of the novel. In contrast to the detective's noble lower middle class status, money and power are seen to hide corruption.

Carlin Duffy is another character caught up in criminal behavior. His criminality is depicted as lesser than Bethel's in part because of his openness about it and in part because of his social position. Duffy is poor, homeless apart from a shed, and his crimes are seen as minor infringements by himself, and to an extent by Millhone, and, by extension, the reader as we are enticed into her outlook by virtue of her being the narrator. However, Duffy breaks his own rule of non-serious crime when he kills Bethel. Although the law is not allowed the opportunity to put Bethel to trial, Duffy's executing his own form of justice raises serious questions about the nature of justice and about penalties given murderers. Because we have empathized with Duffy through Millhone earlier in the novel, our opinion of his behavior is skewed when he kills his own brother's murderer. Although by no means justifying his behavior, the novel does not dictate the reader's response. Duffy's character is removed from the stereotypical "low-life" criminal by virtue of the degree of empathy he is shown in the novel.

The ghost of Millhone's past, Mickey Magruder, is fittingly comatose for the duration of the novel, never appearing as a tangible character in the present. As such, he represents a kind of a spiritual journey for Millhone, enabling her to grow as a character. Fans of the alphabet novels and of Millhone have never been treated to the story of her first ex-husband until now and, along with the detective herself, have excavated this spectre and laid him (literally, courtesy of his death at the novel's close) to rest. It is the function of this character rather than his nature that makes Magruder stand out in this novel and the tradition of the genre. For, the character is basically another hard-boiled detective, complete with the attitude to women and to violence attendant upon that role. However, as Millhone's ex-husband, his presence personalizes the story beyond the expectations of the genre. Henry, Millhone's elderly neighbor and landlord, functions as a friend and allows a more emotive side of Millhone to be explored as he encourages her to face her emotions in relation to Magruder.

The remaining cast of characters consists primarily of cogs in the machinery moving toward the discovery of the villain. Two barmaids (a suitable job for a woman?) are represented in the forms of Dixie and Thea. Dixie in the 1970s is the picture of the effervescent barmaid, with a "bawdy self-assurance", in her mid-twenties, "rail thin", long auburn hair, plucked eyebrows, false eyelashes and she "was usually braless under her T-shirt, and she wore miniskirts so short she could hardly sit down." Dixie is a stereotype here, down to the fact that she is cheating on her husband, and is the type of character encountered in masculinist hard-boiled narratives. However, we also encounter her in 1986 and discover that she is still married to her husband and still having an affair with the same man. This redeems Dixie somewhat in that she is at least duplicitously faithful. As a forty year old,

Dixie is still "glamorous", in her skintight jeans and spike-booted heels. The fact that she wears no make-up makes her "features more delicate." Seeing Dixie's transformation across two decades softens, like the lack of make-up, the stereotypical features of her character to give her a little more depth. The other barmaid, Thea, also proves to be unfaithful although useful to Millhone's investigation. There are no successful women professionals represented in the novel, apart from Millhone herself, and in this respect the novel fails to break away from the stereotypical portrayal of women.

Requisites of the genre, police officers are represented by Detectives Claas and Aldo, with whom Millhone finds herself in an antagonistic relationship at first but with whom she then colludes in the entrapment of Bethel. Her relationship with the detectives is therefore as is expected of the genre. Other characters that Millhone encounters are either friends of her ex-husband's, Eric Hightower and Shack, for example, or the sons of the veterans, Tim Littenburg and Scott Shackleford, the latter pair of whom are involved in a credit card scam, or are incidental informers, as are Magruder's neighbor and Dixie's manservant, for example. Not much development is given these characters and they are noteworthy mostly only in relation to the plot.

◆ TECHNIQUES ◆

As befits its genre, *O Is for Outlaw* is plot-driven toward a definitive ending and its tone of voice characterized by a wry sense of humor or sarcasm. The narrative also presents characters, events and action in great detail, sharing this aspect with the nineteenth-century realist novel, alongside which the genre grew. The style suits the focalization through the detective, who is a character from whom no minute detail escapes and the reader is closely aligned with the detective in this observatory and analytical role through the almost mathematically precise descriptions. Although characters are not given much depth generally, they are usually subject to close physical scrutiny of the narrator's eye which effects a sense of judging by appearances and again aligns the reader closely with the detective's perspective, as in this description on first meeting Mr. Rich:

> His face was a big ruddy square, his sunburn extending into the V of his open-collared denim work shirt. He wore his dark hair combed straight back, and I could see the indentation at his temples where he'd removed the baseball cap now sitting on the table next to him. He had a wide nose, drooping upper lids, and bags under his eyes. I could see the scattering of whiskers he'd missed during his morning shave. His shoulders were beefy and his forearms looked thick where he had his sleeves rolled up.

No character, however minor—and Mr. Rich never appears in the narrative again—escapes this ever-watchful eye of the detective, which makes the detective all-seeing if not quite all-knowing. However, the same detail is proffered to describe the most insignificant events so that Millhone's rising from bed, getting dressed and getting breakfast can take up a page or more of narrative. This technique of following Millhone's moves very closely further aligns the reader with her perspective and adds to a sense of real time, for no moment in the day, or night, is unaccounted for. Correlative to this is the amount of dialogue in the novel. Whenever Millhone gathers information from an informant the conversation is generally presented as direct speech, giving the impression of immediacy and that the reader is encountering the information simultaneously with Millhone. All of these techniques are componential to the hard-boiled detective genre.

◆ LITERARY PRECEDENTS ◆

The history of the genre is, to a large extent, the history of the detective's character, detailed earlier in this essay. Early detective novels combined elements of the Gothic, that which could not be explained, with crime stories, both popularized in the eighteenth century. By the end of the nineteenth century, schema were in place for the writing of detective fiction, as an article by S. S. Van Dine published in 1929 entitled "Twenty Rules for Writing Detective Stories" attests. In 1930 Dorothy Sayers founded The Detection Club, which set up rules for "fair play" in detective fiction. Many of the characteristics of the early fiction are recognizable in *O Is for Outlaw,* such as the emphasis on observation and the powers of rationalism, identification of a criminal, and a solution based on information within the fiction.

The genre has always been popular with women writers, perhaps initially because it offered them a freedom from writing novels of manners or romance. Women writers have contributed greatly to the genre's development, and Grafton continues in the tradition of pushing its boundaries. In particular, women contributed enormously to the "Golden Age" of detective fiction, the 1920s and 1930s when the genre reached the heights of popularity. Writers from this period include Agatha Christie, Dorothy L. Sayers, and Margery Allingham. More recent precursors of Grafton's work include the fiction of P. D. James and Ruth Rendell, both of whom began writing in the 1960s. Grafton's contemporaries who attempt to negotiate feminism with detection include Amanda Cross, who utilizes a female academic as amateur detective, and Sara Paretsky, Katherine V. Forrest and Mary Wings, whose works feature female private investigators.

Interestingly, Grafton sets her novels in the 1980s, when the detective has little more in terms of resources than her 1930s predecessors. The 1980s is the period immediately prior to the advent of the Internet and e-mail, which would make much of the footwork of the detective obsolete. This raises the question of whether the hard-boiled detective can survive into the twenty-first century without revisions of the role.

◆ RELATED TITLES ◆

Grafton, like many detective fiction writers, builds her novels around a series character, to whom she refers as her alter-ego. Grafton intends to take Kinsey Millhone all the way through the alphabet, producing a novel a year, although the timescale of the novels means that Millhone does not age synchronically with her author. *O Is for Outlaw* is a departure from its predecessors in that so much of the focus is on a matter very close to Millhone personally. Speaking in a forum on the Barnes & Noble Web site, the author, when asked why she has left it until now to reveal details concerning Magruder, lays the cause at the feet of her character: "the cranky Ms. Millhone rules the roost around here." In this same discussion, Grafton states that she is not consciously altering or developing the character of Millhone as the series progresses. Indeed, as integral as the fact that there is a murder in every novel, Millhone's presence is the element of constancy in Grafton's fresh plots, maintaining her wit, her intellect and her little black dress throughout them all.

◆ ADAPTATIONS ◆

O is for Outlaw is available as an audio book in both abridged and unabridged versions (on both tape and CD) read by Judy Kaye (Random House Audiobooks). Kaye, who has also read all of the preceding alphabet books on tape, has received much praise from fans as the voice of Millhone and Grafton states that she is *"crazy* about her" (http://www.barnesandnoble.com).

◆ IDEAS FOR GROUP DISCUSSIONS ◆

The enduring popularity of the detective novel in its variant forms is a testament to the cathartic comfort it brings in a perceived unstable and shifting world in which values and morals seem to be declining. The sense of maintaining society's standards is just as relevant today as it was in the nineteenth century and the detective remains the hero who returns the chaos to order. While *O Is for Outlaw* does not portray justice and criminality as clearcut, it does offer closure at its end, in contrast to the trend in recent fiction toward the open ending which replicates society's uncertainties. As far as feminism is concerned, Grafton's alphabet novels are problematic, for although their feisty, witty, sexy *and* intelligent hero might prove an admirable role model in some respects, her deployment as exorcist of corrupt individuals conceals the corrupt mechanics of patriarchal society as a whole.

1. What are the strengths and weaknesses of the hard-boiled detective genre from a feminist perspective?

2. To what extent is Kinsey Millhone a good role model for women?

3. Does the novel's representation of justice seem fair or might it be seen to promote anarchy? Can anarchic behavior ever be justified?

4. How relevant is the character of the hard-boiled detective to contemporary society?

5. Examine the ways in which the novel's theme of concealment is represented

and consider how the surface/reality dichotomy permeates contemporary life.

6. Discuss whether examining the darker side of life, the murders and crimes in this novel, for instance, can enlighten our awareness of our individual values and those of society. Does this novel challenge, or make you rethink, your own values?

7. To what extent are the minor characters stereotypes?

8. Millhone learns that she needs to reappraise the version of events she has created and lived with for fifteen years. Consider the notion of history as a collection of stories. Might the versions of these stories with which you are familiar have been colored by who told, or is telling, them? Are the official versions necessarily correct? How can we determine what happened in the past and why is it important?

Julie Scanlon
University of Sheffield, England

ON MYSTIC LAKE

Novel

1999

Author: Kristin Hannah

◆

◆ SOCIAL CONCERNS ◆

G iven the current divorce rate and the ever-changing roles of women in contemporary society, the story of one woman's marital crisis and the resulting journey of self-discovery will resonate in the lives of many readers. As her only child leaves home and her husband abandons her for a younger woman, Annie Colwater must come to terms with her loss and reinvent her life. Through Annie's experiences and those of the two wounded characters with whom she joins forces, the novel tackles a number of other issues as well, among them suicide, alcoholism, domestic violence, drug addiction, and blended families.

Annie's shifting perception of her own role is the novel's main focus. Raised by her father after the death of her mother, Annie escaped her hometown of Mystic, Washington, when she went off to Stanford. Rather than pursuing her own dreams of becoming a writer or opening a bookstore, Annie married right after college, becoming pregnant soon after, and fell into a life that revolved around her husband and child. Afraid even to travel alone, Annie has always felt safest "in the center of the ordinary, with her family gathered close around her."

When her husband, Blake, shocks her by asking for a divorce, Annie leaves California, fleeing back to Mystic. There she reexamines her relationship with her father, Hank, and becomes the caretaker for the daughter of old friends. Gradually she realizes that her father raised her to doubt herself, define herself through men, and have no other goals beyond marriage and children. Not only does Annie recover her own dreams, but she also discovers that her mother once had similar dreams for her own life. Annie assesses her life and her faults without casting blame, recognizing that she herself has played a role in allowing others to limit her dreams and failing to grow. She realizes that "in her quest for perfection, she'd let Blake become a bad husband and father."

Annie arrives at her realizations in the course of caring for Izzy, the daughter of Nick and Kathy, Annie's childhood friends. Traumatized by Kathy's suicide, Nick and Izzy are falling apart: at six, Izzy is convinced that she is disappearing and she has stopped speaking; Nick takes refuge in alcohol. Annie falls backs into a care-taking role, assisting Nick in becoming sober, helping Izzy to deal with her loss and begin speaking again, and making the three of them into "a patchwork family." In feeling helpful to and appreciated by Nick and Izzy and in gaining understanding of her father, Annie comes to value herself and her dreams again.

Along the way, the novel touches on other serious social issues, including alcoholism, suicide, murder, and poverty. Nick's temptation to drink remains a daily struggle for him, even after he begins recovery; Kathy's suicide creates a complex web of pain and self-blame for Nick and Izzy. Nick's memories of childhood poverty and homelessness as well as of his mother's murder add to his difficulties as a police officer when he answers domestic violence calls.

Despite these harsh realities, *On Mystic Lake* is at heart a romance, affirming love, marriage, and families. As a result, Annie is not free to simply reinvent her life; she is, after all, still married, and within a few weeks Blake tires of his less domestic lover and wants Annie back. Discovering that she is pregnant with Blake's child, Annie returns to him to try to rebuild their marriage. Finally, though, Blake is unable to do his part and Annie returns to Mystic with the new baby, intending to open a bookstore and continue her relationship with Nick and Izzy. Annie's journey of self-discovery leads to her becoming more independent while still valuing her role as a caretaker.

◆ THEMES ◆

Returning to a literal or spiritual home to recover a lost self is a common literary theme. Hannah emphasizes the idea of losing and finding oneself through her repeated references to silence, disappearance, and invisibility. The child Izzy serves as the most obvious representative of this theme; silent since her mother's suicide and convinced that her fingers are becoming invisible, Izzy symbolically reenacts the disappearance of her mother into death.

Annie's instinctive understanding of Nick and Izzy's grief is partially tied to her own experiences of loss—of her mother, her marriage, and her sense of self. Annie knows about "mothers who disappeared one day and never came back" and sympathizes with the daughter "who no longer spoke and the father who had no idea what to say." Annie helps Izzy to see that she cannot follow her mother; as a result of Annie's love and insight, Izzy becomes visible to herself again. A compass given Annie by her father so she would "always know where she belonged" comes to symbolize Annie's process of finding her own center again: "If only there were some internal mechanism that pointed unerringly to the true north of ourselves," she thinks.

Repeated references to absence and invisibility resonate with the losses suffered by these characters as well as with Annie's process of recovery and self-discovery. Annie says that over the years, she became a "poster child for a missing soul"; she tells her husband that in his shadow, she let herself "become nothing." When she goes back to Blake she feels herself "fading" and imagines herself "searching in mirrors once again for evidence of her own existence." The gradually disappearing ghost of Kathy only Izzy can see represents her gradual acceptance of her mother's death; the child's insistence on moving a Candyland piece for Annie during every game after she leaves suggests Izzy's faith in and love for Annie despite her absence. Nick, too, becomes associated with the image of disappearance when, as a result of his flagging self-confidence before sobriety, he sees himself as "nothing."

The foggy, rainy, verdant landscape Hannah describes lends itself to related recurring images of sunlight and shadows. After leaving California, Annie thinks of her life in Los Angeles as comparatively cold and sterile, a life in which sunlight was taken "from [her] soul" and she was left "stranded in a cold, gray landscape." The wilder, greener scenery of Mystic becomes symbolic of the restorative powers of returning home.

The major characters of *On Mystic Lake* are types: Annie, the plucky heroine and eternal optimist whose major faults are her passionate love and her willingness to sacrifice her own needs for others; Blake, the overworked, inattentive, often cold and condescending husband who is overly concerned with appearances; Nick, the idealist with a painful past and a capacity to love "more deeply, completely than others" that has allowed life "to pummel him so brutally"; and Izzy, the traumatized child.

As a result of these characterizations, the lines are clearly drawn between villains and heroes. While Blake eventually sees the error of his ways, there is little to redeem him; ultimately he simply cannot recreate himself into a loving husband and father. He does give the reader some satisfaction though when he at least realizes what he has lost in Annie. Annie, in contrast, has few qualities presented as real faults, and despite her questioning of her role, she is often stereotypically feminine. She always believes "the best of everyone," always cares for others, and is described by her father as someone who does not "understand despair or weakness, not really. You can't get your mind wrapped around hopelessness." Annie is very much a typical romantic heroine, with the standard "heart-shaped face" and a strength and resolve that enable her to unwaveringly stand up to Blake within weeks after he has left her.

Nick is Annie's male counterpart, on his own journey of self-discovery as he tries to recover the idealism "hacked away" by the harsh realities of his job as a police officer and by Kathy's death. With Annie's help, he transforms back into the loving, involved father he used to be and is able to return to his job. Also idealistic and idealized, his daughter Izzy's frequently-mentioned tear-filled eyes and scraggly appearance seem primarily designed to tug at the heartstrings.

A number of other characters assist in Annie's journey, primarily Hank, her father. Though he once failed to encourage his daughter to pursue her dreams, Annie understands that he was a grieving widower and a product of his times. Unlike Blake, Hank is able to see his mistakes and compensate for the past. In sharp contrast to Blake and Hank, from early on Annie's daughter Natalie roots for her to become her own person and possesses an independence and self-confidence that Annie envies. Somehow escaping Annie's pitfalls, Natalie is strong, sensible, and inspiring to her mother.

Numerous other more minor characters serve to add color and lend contrasts to Annie that subtly reinforce her integrity, strength, and good taste. Terri, Annie's "wild" friend with an "over-the-top actress lifestyle" and a "steady stream of divorces and marriages" gives Annie support and perspective while reminding the reader of Annie's more traditional values. Similarly, Mystic hairdresser Lurlene is a quirky, good-hearted woman who lives in a triple-wide mobile home and wears clashing colors, making her something of a caricature who adds humor as well as contrast to Annie's quieter personality.

Hannah's background as a romance writer is evident in her lush descriptions of nature as well as in the metaphor, hyperbole, and personification that often cross over into sentimentality. From the first line, in which rain falls "like tiny silver teardrops from the tired sky," the climate and the landscape frequently foreshadow or reflect the emotions of the characters. Rain and tears appear in abundance and are often linked. More than once the reader is reminded that the rain is "an angel's tears"; Annie tells Izzy that rain is her mother's tears, "and the sunshine is her smile."

The descriptions of Mystic are equally idealized and sentimental, the sky starting "deep in the palm of God's hand," dusk portrayed as day rounding "the bend into a lavender evening." Descriptions of characters are also cliched and hyperbolic: one character has "breasts the size of the Alps" and another character's smile falls "faster than a cake when the oven door was slammed." Such language does underline the friendly colloquialisms of Mystic natives and the conception of nature as a beautiful refuge, thus linking such details to Hannah's thematic concerns.

A number of plot contrivances contribute to the novel's emotion if not its credibility, including when Izzy is—illegally—kicked out of school because she refuses to speak; when a supposedly trained therapist tells Izzy that she "had to talk or else she wouldn't get over her mommy"; when Nick says that the "technical term" for his late wife's illness is the outdated "manic depression"; and when Annie's baby is kept in an incubator and allowed no physical contact because she weighs "only" five pounds. Hannah's writing is most likely to appeal to readers who enjoying suspending disbelief for the sake of being manipulated.

◆ LITERARY PRECEDENTS ◆

American literature's prototypical novel of a woman's mid-life attempt to recreate herself is Kate Chopin's *The Awakening*. Edna is the foremother of Annie and characters like her, discovering a deep discontentment with her marriage and her life and beginning to gain new awareness as she seeks to find herself. In her artistic pursuits and her love affairs, Edna casts about for a new center but ultimately cannot find a way to fit into her society.

While *On Mystic Lake* borrows from a Chopin-influenced literary tradition, Hannah's story is also strongly shaped by the romantic tradition—one that elevates and seeks solace in the natural world—as well as the romance genre, in which happy endings are paramount. Hannah's novel of awakening is one in which the heroine trades one love affair for another, and, unlike Edna, finds fulfillment in family life, develops clearly defined goals, and is presumed to live happily ever after at the close of the novel.

◆ RELATED TITLES ◆

Hannah's eight previous paperback romances include *Waiting for the Moon* and *Home Again*. She made her hardcover debut with *On Mystic Lake*, an attempt at a more mainstream novel in the vein of Luann Rice, Anne Rivers Siddons, and Barbara Delinsky. Hannah's follow-up novel, *Angel Falls* (2000), returns to northwest Washington State and to themes of identity and family connection, though as in *On Mystic Lake*, the influence of the romance genre remains evident.

◆ IDEAS FOR GROUP DISCUSSIONS ◆

Hannah appears on the surface to promote a feminist ethic, advocating that women define themselves rather than letting others do it for them. At the same time, Annie finds her inner self in caring for Nick's family and bearing another child, and these are the activities she seems to find most fulfilling. Whether or not Annie truly challenges traditional roles and undergoes significant change is a subject likely to engender controversy among students. Furthermore, Annie's changes may strike some readers as less convincing because of cliched writing and implausible plot twists, while others are willing to overlook those because of the familiar experiences the story taps into and the familiar emotions it evokes. The novel can serve as a springboard for a discussion on what makes some literary manipulations more effective than others, and what, finally, constitutes good literature.

1. Is Annie a feminist heroine? In what ways does the novel question traditional roles and in what ways does it affirm them?

2. How convincing is Annie's change at the end of the novel? Does it matter that, though she plans to open a bookstore, she has never read a book in the course of the novel except to Izzy? Is her change toward Blake believable and consistent with her character? How independent is she finally?

3. Once afraid to travel, Annie later goes to Mexico alone for an afternoon and sums up the benefits of travel afterward, focusing on the self-esteem gained upon going "to a wildly different place" and learning "that you could negotiate for a silly trinket in a foreign language." Discuss the authenticity of this revelation.

4. The novel frequently relies on sentimentality to stir the reader's emotions. Izzy, for instance, is described in ways that emphasize her state of neglect and grief and that underline her childish innocence. In addition, Hannah compares the rain to tears and shows tears springing to her characters' eyes numerous times. How effective are they at creating emotional responses? Do these details make you care more or less about what happens to the characters?

Nancy McCabe
Presbyterian College

OUT OF AFRICA

Novel

1936

Author: Isak Dinesen

---◆---

I sak Dinesen's novel, *Out of Africa* written five years after she returned to her native Denmark, describes Africa as she remembers it: an Eden, a lost paradise and a place of innocent beauty that regrettably changed with the passage of time.

Dinesen begins her work with a simple description of her African home: "I had a farm in Africa at the foot of the Ngong Hills. The Equator runs across these highlands, a hundred miles to the North, and the farm lay at an altitude of over six thousand feet." To Dinesen life in Africa was preferable to life in Denmark, where a person's social status was given undue importance. She wrote, "Here at long last one was in the position to not give a damn for conventions, here was a new kind of freedom that one usually finds only in one's dreams." However, due to the immigration of Europeans, "their boots and constant hurry that rudely broke into the natural rhythm of the country," the Colony began changing. Several times Dinesen expressed her contentment with life on the farm: "Up here in this high air you breathed easily, drawing a vital assurance and lightness of heart." Another time she wrote, "In the highlands you woke up each morning and thought: Here I am . . . where I ought to be." The tone of the book is set with these two phrases. For, in Africa, Dinesen discovered her niche in life, and shortly after settling in Kenya, Dinesen became a part of the early settlers' aristocracy.

Almost from the beginning of her life in Africa, Dinesen felt affectionate toward the Native tribes. She felt especially that the Kikuyu, a tribe who worked on the farm, were her friends. However, Dinesen was not certain that they felt the same emotion toward her, but her introduction to the Natives' lives enlarged her world. After living on the farm a while her acquaintance with the Natives, who worked on the farm, developed into a deep and lasting relationship. Dinesen believed the Natives understood life and nature in a deeper way than the white settlers ever could. The Natives represented Africa in flesh and blood, and were united with nature. The colonists' constant hurry was out of place in a country where the natural pace of the Natives was more suitable to Africa.

The Kikuyu people and the farm became Dinesen's life. As the owner of much land and a friend to the natives, Dinesen willingly performed many duties for the Kikuyu squatters living on the farm. For example, when the squatters on the farm had disagreements, she sat in and observed them, then acted as an arbitrator when they could not settle their disagreements alone. Often she served them as hunter, caregiver and doctor. The Natives had no guns, so Dinesen would kill birds and wild animals for them to eat. If her cures for their illnesses did not work, Dinesen traveled with them to Nairobi's hospital for medical aid. She carried out all her responsibilities to the natives with understanding and sympathy and felt pleased in her role.

Dinesen's description of life on the farm reveals her sensitivity toward the natives who lived nearby in their shambas, or villages, and worked on the farm. In exchange for the Kikuyus working a certain number of days a week, they were allotted a few acres of land to plant and harvest as their own. Dinesen realized that her squatters probably felt differently about the land that they had occupied for so many years and probably considered her a "superior squatter" on their land. Even though managing the squatters, experiencing crops ruined by drought or disease, and harvesting with worn machinery was difficult, Dinesen enjoyed her life and persevered.

Probably the worst experience on the farm was the year a raging fire destroyed their warehouse. That night the farm lost a year's coffee crop that was bagged and ready to transport into Nairobi. Still Dinesen did not quit; instead she remembered how pleasant it felt to lay contentedly in her bed listening to a convoy of loaded wagons moving out at night toward the market in Nairobi.

Dinesen felt that her early years in Africa represented a time in Africa's past when people accepted the hardships of living in a primitive land, and she felt that here people were more genuine. She wrote, "one might be hard up for cash, but life was still rich in many ways."

In some ways Dinesen preferred life in Africa to the artificiality of life in Europe, and she felt saddened by the changes she observed happening in Africa. Dinesen remembered the days when Africa had no cars, and they rode into Nairobi in a cart drawn with a team of six mules. She wrote, "The colony was changing and has already changed since I lived there. When I write down as accurately as possible my experiences on the farm . . . it may have a sort of historical interest."

During her years in Africa, Dinesen experienced many local customs. Her first introduction to the village and home of her personal Somali servant, Farah Aden, surprised her. The outside of the buildings looked poorly put together, "but once inside, the home surprised her, because she found it neat, fresh, and scented with Arab incenses." The floors were covered with fine carpets and woven hangings decorated the room. And Dinesen discovered the Somali women were dignified, and made her feel quiet comfortable in their homes. She found them dignified and gay company. She said, "I was much at home in the Somali village through my Somali servant Farah Aden, who was with me all the time I was in Africa. I went to many of their feasts and sometimes arbitrated in the Somali tribe's disagreements."

The Masai, Dinesen's neighbors and a nomadic, cattle owning nation, sometimes came to her home and asked her to shoot lions that were taking their cattle. During her stay in Africa Dinesen became an excellent hunter and always killed the marauding animals for them. If her good friends Denys or Berekley were visiting they would go hunting together to kill the lions for the Masai's safety. Once lions hunted too near the village school and, fearing for the children's safety, Dinesen and Denys hunted and killed the animals.

Often Dinesen opened her home to visitors. She records in her novel that "Sometimes visitors from Europe drifted into the farm like wrecked timbers." The welcome guests remained until they were rested and renewed, then left.

One of her visitors, Old Knudsen, a Dane, came to her farm sick and blind. She allowed him to stay in an empty bungalow. Knudsen shared stories of his life with her. He often helped with chores and remained on the farm until his death.

After Dinesen divorced her Danish husband, Baron Bror von Blixen-Finecke, her good friend and lover Denys Finch-Hatton and his friend Berkeley Cole often came unannounced from a long safari to rest. They brought her gifts of fine skins and furs to be made into coats and shoes when she traveled to Europe. Also, they purchased gramophone records, books, and wines as gifts for all of them to enjoy. And Kamante, her cook, took great pride in his culinary skills and prepared fine feasts for the hunter and other guests to enjoy. Kamante would prepare feasts for them to enjoy after being on long safaris. When resting from a safari, Denys stayed with Dinesen, and he also watched the house when she was away on a trip to Europe.

In 1931 the farm had to be sold, because of the constant battle with the farm's debts, and the lack of needed money to keep it functioning. The developer who bought it divided the farm into small plots for housing, and her home became the new settlement's clubhouse. After selling the farm government officials required that the natives should be resettled in some other place. Dinesen felt that moving the natives away from the area they had lived in for many years destroyed their Eden. The natives silently protested, because they did not want to live on land apart from their friends. The Kikuyu believed that in losing the land they lost their identity.

In behalf of the Kikuyus, Dinesen wrote in protest to the officials in Nairobi. "It is more than their land you take away from

the people whose native land you take, it is their past as well." She understood that they reacted more strongly about leaving their land than other people did, and sympathized with the squatters. In order to convince the authorities to resettle the natives on land of their own, she visited Nairobi many times. Eventually the government authorities complied with a large parcel of land for the Kikuyu to live on together.

The sale of her farm combined with the untimely death of Denys Finch-Hatton were stunning blows to Dinesen. She wrote to her loyal friend, Thomas, at the peak of her unhappiness, that she returned to Denmark as a dead woman.

◆ THEMES ◆

The major themes in Dinesen's novel seem relatively clear. She deals with Africa and its culture as a lost paradise because of the influx of immigrating Europeans, who are thoughtless and insensitive to the native tribes' cultures and needs. And for Dinesen this Eden released her from the strict social rules and constraints of European society. Here at last she had found herself and her place. Dinesen stated, "Here I am—where I ought to be." Another strong theme is the place of God and the devil in society. Although Dinesen was not connected to any religion, it is safe to state that she believed in a creative power, which she called God, and that he and the devil somehow worked as a team in the world. For instance, Dinesen wrote that Kamante's fine culinary art made her feel it might be divine and predestined.

" I felt like a man who had regained his faith in God because a Phrenologist showed him the seat in the human brain of theological eloquence . . . if that theology could be proved," then in the end God's existence is true. Then when Kamante lost his fear of snakes and became brave, because of his belief in God, Dinesen wrote, "He did show off a little bit, as if to boast of the power of his God." In these two references to God, Dinesen illustrated both her doubt and belief in a Creator of this Eden, Africa. She expresses her concerns about the life of the African natives and what will happen to them and to their culture because of the brash materialism she sees destroying the Natives' Eden. Of major importance to Dinesen were the eternal existential problems of who is God and what is his intention for his creation, and the Natives of Africa.

♦ CHARACTERS ♦

True to the role of storyteller, Dinesen remains objective and unemotional when relating her relationship with the characters in this novel. However, because she had so many relationships with so many characters, one must choose the more outstanding ones to discuss: Denys Finch-Hatton, Berkeley Cole, the Kikuyu Kamante, and Farah Aden, and the Kikuyu natives.

Dinesen's lover and closest friend, Denys Finch-Hatton, and his friend Berkeley Cole hold major parts in the novel. Denys, an English safari hunter, came to live with her after Dinesen divorced her Danish husband. Denys and Dinesen had much in common. Both were good hunters and enjoyed music and books, and Denys kept his books and gramophone at the farm when he was out on safari. He felt happy with her and free to come and go at will. Dinesen portrays Denys as a solitary person and a humble and truthful man who enjoyed listening to her tales. Between Denys' visits Dinesen would plan stories to tell on his return from a hunt.

Denys and Dinesen often flew above the Ngong Hills to view the animals in his airplane. Shortly before Dinesen moved from Africa, he came to stay a short time, then took his things and moved into town. Still, she remembered his trips to the farm and that Denys once told her that she might be happier in Denmark, because of the changes occurring in Africa. Shortly before Dinesen left Africa, she was devastated when told about Denys' death in an airplane crash. She remembered a place they had chosen as a burial spot on a high ridge in the Hills of the Game Reserve. After his death, she and Farah Aden made arrangements for Denys' body to be buried in that spot.

As a caregiver, Dinesen tended to the natives' illness and injuries. One small Kikuyu boy, Kamante, stands out. She noticed that he had terrible running sores on his legs, and when her cures did not work, Dinesen took him to the Scotch Mission's doctors. Kamante returned home three months later and took great pride in displaying his healed legs. As a result of Dinesen's help, a lasting friendship developed between them. When she discovered Kamante's natural skills in preparing food, she sent him to Nairobi, so he could fine-tune his skills. He returned and became her chef, and often prepared fine meals for her guests. Kamante was described as an astute observer of his surroundings, and he often watched the animals that came on the land. Once he tamed a young deer, Lulu, whom Dinesen gave the freedom to roam about her home. When Lulu had a doe, Kamante watched and cared for them, until she left the farm.

Another major figure is the Somali servant, Farah Aden, who is educated and speaks fluent English, French, and Swahili. As Dinesen's personal servant, Farah was her constant companion and advisor about African culture. For instance, an African tribe asked her to arbitrate a tribal disagreement; Farah Aden accompanied her and acted as her interpreter. He often invited Dinesen to his home and to his village's festivals, which she found delightful. And after the farm was sold, Farah helped her close the house. She confided to him that empty, it was a fit place to live and should have been like this all the time.

Farah faithfully accompanied her to the government officials when she pleaded with them to give the Kikuyu land. And, as his final act of friendship toward Dinesen, he accompanied her to the Nairobi train station and remained with her until they reached the Samburu station, where they visited before she departed for Europe.

◆ TECHNIQUES ◆

Dinesen began telling and writing stories as a young child and had a reputation for being a fine storyteller. The novel *Out of Africa* fits the techniques of an earlier time when simple and effective stories about personal relationships and shifts in social values arose and created conflicts within society. The title of this novel designates one leaving a place and the search for a new home. Thus Dinesen, who had found a place of contentment in Africa, was forced by the failure of her farm and unpaid debts to return to Denmark. Five years later, Dinesen wrote her memories of life on a coffee farm in East Africa. In Africa she felt at home with the land and with the Natives. Her stories relate tales of her personal interaction with the native tribes, and her distress when the farm because of debt was sold and she was forced to return to Denmark.

Dinesen wrote about native African people, who worked on the farm and relates her experiences with Farah Aden, a Somali servant, who introduced Dinesen to his society, and with Kamante, a young boy whom she befriended and who eventually became a chef in her home. She told the difficulty of raising coffee at an altitude of 6,000 feet. Even though Dinesen liked the Kikuyu natives, she did not write sentimentally about them or experiences that

occurred during her seventeen years in Africa. In fact Dinesen distanced herself from events and objectively dealt with her memories. Still, Dinesen's stories illustrated her friendship and sensitivity toward the natives and to others visiting or working on the farm. One good example of her sensitivity was to the blind Dane, Old Knudsen, who came to the farm in ill health. "He was," she stated, "a singular figure to have on a highland farm: so much a creature of the Sea that it was as if we had had an old clipped albatross with us." Eventually, Knudsen is discovered on a path dead, and she and Kamante cared for his body.

In the novel, Dinesen uses the formal language written and spoken in the Romantic period of literature. She creates pictures of persons and events through her use of language. For example she once wrote an impression of a Kikuyu native: "When you walk amidst the Kikuyu's shambas, the first thing that will catch your eye is the hind part of a little old woman raking in her soil, like a picture of an ostrich which buries her head in the sand." Instead of simply giving the facts about an event or person, the reader visualizes the Kikyku women and children reaching high into the trees and picking coffee beans from the trees. In the story about Kamante, Dinesen writes so clearly that one sees the running sores on Kamante's skinny legs. Later the reader watches him dramatically and proudly unwrapping his healed legs so Dinesen can see them.

And Dinesen clearly shows her disagreement with the authorities on the use of land. She writes, "In my day, the Buffalo, the Eland and the Rhino lived in the Ngong Hills—and I was always sorry that the whole Ngong Mountain was not enclosed in the Game Reserve." Instead as the colony grew, Dinesen watched the young Nairobi shoppeople, recklessly run their motorcycles into the hills on Sunday and shoot at any herd they saw. The changes were bound to occur, and she believed that the animals would drift away into the thorn thickets, and the peaceful animal kingdom would disappear. Dinesen still wished that the African authorities had expanded and maintained the reserve as a special paradise.

◆ LITERARY PRECEDENTS ◆

Dinesen's primary technique in *Out of Africa* is a first-person reminiscence focusing on personal relationships and the conflicting values in Africa between a new generation's commercialism and the ways of the original colonist. Her title signifies the memorable stories of the loss of the Eden that once existed in that country. Thus Dinesen's numerous tales illustrate to the reader the conflicts and positive relationships that she experienced on the farm, where she believed her life began and ended.

Dinesen strongly resisted the changes that occurred with the influx of the young Europeans who with their noise and boots disturb the African Eden. She resented these new colonists' indifference to the natives' right to live on the land and their callous attitude toward nature and strove with the officials to permit her Kikuyu natives to remain on a parcel of land together. In the end Dinesen won her battle. Like other authors of that era—such as E. M. Forster—she is concerned with materialism ruining humanity. Dinesen wishes for man to soften materialism and balance life with nature's rhythms.

◆ RELATED TITLES ◆

A major criticism of Dinesen's work is that it seems a little difficult to read, perhaps due to her use of a more formal language. This is the reader's loss, because few modern writers possess Dinesen's ability to tell a good tale. Another reason is that her stories demand the reader's attention and the ability to interpret the subtle meaning of her work. However, *Out of Africa* is well worth the reader's effort. Other short novels of Dinesen's are *Shadows in the Grass* and *Letters from Africa*. Criticism of these novels is generally focused on the manner in which she portrays the African natives.

One of her harshest critics is the Kenyan novelist and critic Ngugi wa Thiongo. He views her as a racist author who tries to explain the colonized world to the European colonizer. Dinesen's constant reference to her servant Kamante as "'a civilized dog' who has lived too long with people,'" is a supreme insult in Thiongo's view. This critic finds her work insulting and is angered by her inability to give Western society a more complete picture of Kenya and her people.

However, other critics disagree with Thiongo's point of view; instead they find Dinesen's view a noble but somewhat artificial description of Africa and its people. No matter how realistic *Out of Africa* might appear, it remains a portrait drawn from memory after she returned to live in Denmark.

◆ ADAPTATIONS ◆

In 1985 Columbia Pictures developed a screenplay of *Out of Africa* with Robert Redford cast in the role of Denys Finch-Hatton and Meryl Streep in the lead as Isak Dinesen. The movie won numerous awards and played to a huge audience of moviegoers. However, this movie adaptation of *Out of Africa* is not based on this novel alone. The movie includes stories from two other of Dinesen's novels, *Shadows in the Grass* and *Letters from Africa*.

Dinesen's novel deals with a lost paradise, caused by the influx of immigrant Europeans who had no sensitivity to the African natives' rights and thoughtlessly invaded their land. She believes that harmony in life is exhibited in wild animals that, in contrast to domestic animals, live in complete harmony with God's plans. Thus, the European's immigration in the colony disturbed this harmony. However, the African natives live in harmony with nature and thus this places them in a higher position than the overcivilized settlers. Thus, the natives live with nature's rhythms, but the Europeans break that rhythm, because they are blind to it.

1. Explain why or why not, the Kikuyu and other African tribes might be used to represent tragic figures in this novel.

2. Discuss Dinesen's thematic description of Africa as a lost paradise. How does her description relate to the lives of the early colonists, to her life, and to the lives of Africa's native tribes?

3. One of Dinesen's harshest critics is the Kenyan critic and novelist, Ngugi wa Thiongo. His essay accuses Dinesen of being a racist author who tries to explain the colonized world to the European colonizer. He cites Dinesen's constant reference to Kamante as a "'civilized dog' who has lived too long with people." Thiongo finds her work particularly insulting because she is educated and has a particular place in society, which gives her views credibility with many readers. Discuss whether you agree or disagree with his thoughts.

4. Although Dinesen expresses a religious belief in a God, her thoughts and beliefs about God and the devil being one and acting as a team is unusual. Explain how she tries to prove this union to be true.

5. The character Denys Finch-Hatton is an interesting one. Discuss his personality and place in Dinesen's life and how his death affected the colony and her.

6. The young Kikuyu boy, Kamante, stands with Dinesen's Somali servant, Farah Aden, as a major character in Dinesen's novel. Explain their relationships to Dinesen and her response to them.

7. Explain why Dinesen finds the colonists's ideas on society more acceptable than the society of her native Denmark. Give specific examples for Dinesen's preference.

8. Relate the question of Dinesen's loss of the farm and the natives' loss of their land, to the question of who eventually inherits Kenya.

9. Discuss specific instances when Dinesen acted as an arbitrator between the African tribes when they experienced conflicts, and when she functioned as a caregiver to Kamante and to other natives living on the farm.

10. Dinesen is widely considered a spellbinding teller of tales. Chose one or two tales from *Out of Africa* and discuss what makes these tales so riveting.

Martha Smith Lane

THE PERFECT STORM

Nonfiction

1997

Author: Sebastian Junger

◆

◆ SOCIAL CONCERNS ◆

*T*he *Perfect Storm*, like Arthur Miller's classic play, *Death of a Salesman*, focuses the attention of the general public on the least noticed members of society, in this case the fishermen of Gloucester. The recurring phrase in Miller's work is "attention must be paid" to the life and death of Willy Loman, the salesman of the title who is a "low man" in his profession and in his life, an unimportant cog in a large mechanism that serves the interests of others. Whether consciously or not, Junger follows Miller's model of forcing us to pay attention to the common man, in this case the men who put fish on our tables, the usually anonymous workers in an extremely hazardous and low-paying industry whose agonies when things go wrong are rarely explored in the mass media. *The Perfect Storm* employs a wide variety of techniques to make sure that "attention is paid" to fishermen and their families; by its insistence on viewing its characters as complete human beings with full and complex lives, it forces readers to regard the loss of men at sea as more than just a filler news article on the inside pages of the newspaper.

The Perfect Storm begins with a two page chapter titled "Georges Bank, 1896," a short recapitulation of the despair a fisherman went through on a doomed boat in the nineteenth century. For most readers, recollections of the Rudyard Kipling *Captains Courageous* literary tradition remain vivid enough to sustain an awareness of how dangerous fishing was in the days of sail and oar, and Junger does describe some historical losses of vessels and men off Georges Bank and the Grand Banks. However, his point in doing so is the opposite of what readers might expect, not to celebrate twentieth century progress in safety but rather to show how fragile and tenuous modern safeguards actually are. A loss of electronics quickly sends a boat back to the nineteenth century, leaving its sailors unsure of their true location and completely ignorant of the changing conditions around them. While fishing boats are equipped with automatic distress signals known as EPIRBs, the device on the *Andrea Gail*, the boat whose loss is explored in *The Perfect Storm*, fails to function as it should. Sideband radio, weather faxes, even cellular phones serve to inform the fishing fleet of danger and to link individual boats into a network, but these communication devices which are so sturdy on land are far more vulnerable at sea. When an extraordinary storm puts men and machines under stress, the battle to survive the sea reverts to timeworn nautical strategies rather than to high-tech solutions.

The Perfect Storm also establishes how cavalier government and industry oversight of the fishing fleet can be. The *Andrea Gail* is a well set-up boat, but she has been modified to carry more fuel and supplies without benefit of testing or analysis of how these changes will affect her seaworthiness. An extended and carefully written disquisition on why and when boats founder makes readers appreciate how dangerous casual modifications to fishing boats can be, and even worse, how stability can be affected by where gear is stowed, how fish are stored in the holds, and how a captain and crew react to fairly trivial breakdowns in equipment. The seeming strength and safety of steel-hulled boats is somewhat of an illusion; in fact, while they will endure far more pounding than will wood boats, whose seams eventually open, steel boats turn over and founder more readily than wooden ones. Unlike, say, trucks or airplanes, which are fairly standardized and therefore fairly predictable in their handling, fishing boats can be modified by "eyeball engineering" and then loaded in perilous fashion, making them potential disasters in challenging conditions.

Given the level of unpredictability in vessels and equipment, it is not surprising that fishing is still among the most dangerous of occupations, just as it was in the days of dories rowed out to Georges Bank. Then, the Gloucester fishing industry lost several hundred men a year to drowning, or four per cent of the town's population. A large storm could result in half a dozen ships and hundreds of men lost overnight, with bodies littering the beaches of Newfoundland. In fact, an estimated ten thousand Gloucestermen have perished since 1650; Junger points out that going out to sea to fish has been far more perilous to Gloucestermen than journeying abroad to fight in foreign wars. Given such technology as global positioning by satellite pinpointing a space smaller than an average suburban house, readers can be forgiven for thinking of offshore dangers as distant and dated as frontier gunfights, but in fact, fishing remains the most dangerous occupation in the United States: more fishermen are killed per capita than police, taxi drivers, or convenience store clerks. While fishing gear, electronics, and helicopter rescue have revolutionized some aspects of the trade, it remains inherently perilous, especially when out of reach of the shore (helicopters can carry only about four hours worth of fuel) or during bad weather, which can wipe out communications with electronic "noise." The day-to-day life of a fisherman offers multiple chances to be swept overboard by a "rogue" or freak wave, to be bitten by a dead shark hauled on deck (the reflex survives death), or to be pulled underwater by a fishing line paying out rapidly (baiters put squid on large hooks which are clipped to the "longline" drifting behind the boat; a second's inattention is paid for by being hooked through the hand and dragged down, a death sentence unless a shipmate notices and reacts within seconds). One horrendous scene describes a fisherman gone overboard being pulled on deck with a gaff, just like a fish, the damage done by the gaff secondary to saving his life in a rough sea.

Why would men (and today, some women) put themselves at such risk in such a thankless trade? While a share of the profits of several weeks of fishing can amount to several thousand dollars, normal life is suspended while at sea, and many in the profession spend a good deal of their earnings in compulsive celebrations when they arrive back home. Junger is at pains to deconstruct the romance of fishing: "Most deckhands have precious little affection for the business . . . for them, fishing is a brutal, dead-end job that they try to get clear of as fast as possible." The young men of Gloucester fish to make money fast, to get themselves out of financial trouble. In *The Perfect Storm,* for example, Bobby Shatford has a bad feeling about his current berth on the *Andrea Gail* and wants desperately to stay with his new love, Christina Cotter, but forces himself to make the trip to keep up his alimony payments. The working class people who end up on fishing boats have sometimes made a bad bargain between immediate necessity and long-term benefit, but once in the life, they find it hard to return to the far less lucrative forms of manual labor that are a safer alternative. Junger makes us feel the reluctance of a crew to return to sea, as well as the brutal economic forces that require them to do so again and again. The fishing life often leads to alcohol abuse, divorce, and reckless behavior on shore; these consequences of having normal life routines suspended for weeks at a time make the practitioner of the trade even less able to seek other forms of work. At least miners and factory workers are protected by unions and government agencies; workers offshore tend to be individualistic free spirits, contracting their persons and their labor for short periods and trusting their captains and boat owners to treat them decently. They operate offshore, beyond the psychological and sometimes even legal attention paid to onshore workers, and Junger's goal is to make their lives visible and affecting.

◆ THEMES ◆

Like a good novel, *The Perfect Storm* returns to a series of general ideas evoked by the particular situations endured by its characters. The main theme might be summed up in the old cliche, "men against the sea," but Junger imbues this venerable idea with numerous contemporary relevancies. Primary is the aforementioned stress on the unchanging danger of fishing at sea and the unrecognized continuity between the days of sail and modern steel and diesel technology. Quotes from Samuel Johnson, Melville's *Moby Dick,* and the Bible make this point by linking the ancient and the new: the human risks and terrors endured by fishermen have changed little if at all. Nature is still unconquerable by the pitiful efforts of men; though the connection is established only indirectly, the confidence and even arrogance that declared the *Titanic* unsinkable is still at work in captains like the owner of the *Sartori,* who insists his small sailboat can survive hurricane force winds and waves. In the case of Bob Brown, the owner of the *Andrea Gail,* such confidence in human power is entangled with the profit motive, which dictates scores of small decisions (Should stability be risked against extra fuel-carrying capacity?) which cumulatively can put a boat in an irrecoverable situation. Part of Junger's argument against the conventional idea that "fate" governs deaths at sea is that in fact fate is shaped by countless small choices, most of which seem trivial at the time they are made.

Like Brown, captain Billy Tyne is sure of his boat and his ability to find a way out of peril; however, he risks his own life as well as those of his men if he goes a step too far. All the crewmen are putting themselves at risk to escape poverty or dysfunctional lives on shore; Junger asserts that none would choose fishing if other options were available. A mitigating factor, however, is the camaraderie enjoyed by the fishermen at work and onshore, for, once in the life, they seem unable to escape each other's company even in barroom celebrations. Fishing provides a powerful identity and gives pride to men who have little education or privilege.

This identity, however, can be the despair of the wives and families. Divorce is common among men who spend weeks and months at sea, and the women who love them are both attracted to their toughness and uncomplaining competence and terrified at the prospect of becoming widows, unsure even if their loved ones are truly dead. For the most part, fishermen simply disappear; there are often no bodies to bury and funerals to signal their end. Junger is very good at capturing the far-flung effects of the storm. Just as tiny ripples in the Caribbean can eventually become hundred-foot waves off New England, so the human consequences, personal and social, can have effects far distant from their source. The general theme of the interconnectedness of nature is thus applied to human nature as well: "Like a war or a great fire, the effects of a great storm go rippling outward through webs of people for years, even generations. It breaches lives like coastlines and nothing is ever again the same."

Another theme is the casual heroism of rescue workers. Parajumpers, pilots, rescue swimmers, and aircrews, all train for years to go to the aid of complete strangers under appalling weather conditions. By following the actions of a couple of rescue operations during the storm, and by briefly sketching some of the life stories of the crews, the book allows the reader to form a picture of the kind of people who would choose such careers and the enormous sacrifices some make. This kind of heroism is rarely celebrated in popular culture, and Junger sees his task as making readers understand its nature.

◆ CHARACTERS ◆

Sebastian Junger is the author of *The Perfect Storm,* yet he is also in many ways the main character. He is part of the story, as he recognizes to his discomfort: not really a journalist in his own mind but rather "just a guy with a pen and paper and

an idea for a book." While Junger is a first person presence in the foreword and afterword, he is also very much present throughout, unapologetically taking the reader aside on digressions to explain the dynamics of waves, the physics of storms, and the physiology of drowning. He is overtly uncomfortable about his standing in Gloucester: he is an outsider, he has never fished, and he is intruding on the lives and grief of real people, whose misery he will write about for all the world to read. Even worse, neither Junger nor anyone else knows what happened in the last hours to the *Andrea Gail,* and thus the climax of the book, the fulfilment of its opening promise stimulated by the sinking of the fishing boat off Georges Bank in 1896, to answer the question, "How do men act on a sinking ship?", must be pure speculation. Fictional characters can be made to run a gamut of literary emotions, but what is the protocol when the men were real and family members still mourn them? Junger builds credibility with his ethical punctiliousness and restraint, repeating "undoubtedly" and "maybe" as the case requires when actions and feelings must be inferred, and further by establishing his own thoroughness and familiarity with fishing practices, equipment, and situations through researched information. His self-evident respect for the particular families and the people of Gloucester in general is admirable, a restraint unusual in an age when journalists encourage victims to vent their emotions while they are still in shock and when irresponsible speculation is the order of many news reports. Junger avoids both emotional voyeurism and speculation unfounded in scientific and technological fact. Junger the character, then, comes across not as a researcher nearly obsessed with finding the truth, but one with a firm moral sense about boundaries he must not cross.

Billy Tyne is somewhat mysterious since as the captain he is the ultimate decision-maker responsible for the fate of the *Andrea Gail*. But Junger has few land-based close relatives who can give insight into his thinking. Tyne is a Gloucester boy who grew up in non-fishing work settings, yet became a whole-hearted competitor when he went to sea. His less-than-stellar performance at finding fish on the *Andrea Gail*'s previous trip perhaps provokes his aggressive search on the final, fatal trip, with forays into fishing grounds at the limits of safety given the time of year. He is the key figure in the failure of the *Andrea Gail* to survive, for even trivial, harmless decisions might have built on each other pyramid-like to seal the fate of the boat. However, as Junger is at pains to point out, the last hours of captain and crew are sealed in mystery, and perhaps a freak wave drove the boat past the point of recovery. Words like "perhaps" and are used to describe Billy Tyne's thoughts and acts, emphasizing the speculative nature of Junger's reconstruction of events. Nevertheless, Tyne comes across favorably, as a true Gloucester fisherman, who will do all within his power to return his crew to land safely. The reader inevitably identifies with Tyne's predicament, and thus feels his loss more deeply than that of the other men on the boat, who have fairly passive roles once the storm begins to rage.

Bobby Shatford and, to a lesser degree, his mother, Ethel, who works behind the bar at the Crow's Nest where Bobby drinks and sometimes stays, come into sharper focus as fully rounded characters in the literary sense. Ethel was Junger's first personal informant about Bobby and the crew, a grieving mother who trusted a personable working man (Junger was then working as a tree cutter) with ideas for a book about the *Andrea Gail*. In the dynamic of the story, Bobby is portrayed as a reluctant fisherman in contrast to the driven Billy Tyne, a young man with a new girlfriend and the promise of a happy life ahead of him if he can pay off his debts with a successful outing.

Christina Cotter, Bobby Shatford's girlfriend, also served as an informant for Junger, especially about the aftereffects of the tragedy. Junger's point about death at sea is that it offers no "closure," in current jargon: the sailors just "disappeared off the face of the earth and, strictly speaking, it's just a matter of faith that these men will never return." Both Ethel Shatford and Christina Cotter cannot "willfully extract" their loved ones "from their lives and banish them to another world." A Bobby Shatford look-alike gives Ethel a bad turn, while Christina cannot get on with her life. Those "lost at sea" leave equal numbers lost on shore.

The crew of the *Andrea Gail* in general are often considered as a collective, sometimes in opposition to Billy Tyne, who must drag them out of the Crow's Nest bar and out to sea, and sometimes as frightened human beings putting all their trust in their captain to bring them back alive. Bobby Shatford is given a great deal of individuality, largely through information provided by Christina Cotter and Ethel Shatford, but at times he is simply part of the work force on the boat. Readers find out some personal information about Michael "Bugsy" Moran, Dale "Murph" Murphy, and David "Sully" Sullivan, but the fifth crew member, Alfred Pierre, is an outsider with a new "site" or berth on the *Andrea Gail* and is sketchily drawn. Unlike Billy Tyne, who "really, truly loved to fish," all the crew see fishing as demanding, dangerous work to be gotten through as quickly as possible, but all are trapped by circumstances into continuing the life and venturing out one more time. The tight bonding created by demanding, dangerous work for weeks on end, isolated from the rest of society, survives squabbles and shore-leave drunken excess, and accounts for the crew staying together over the years: they all know each other in ways shore workers can never fathom.

Bobby Brown is the land-based owner of the *Andrea Gail* and as a highly successful former fisherman turned entrepreneur, he is perfectly cut out to be seen as a villain by the people of Gloucester and the grieving friends and relatives of the lost men. Since he had the *Andrea Gail* rebuilt and refitted, he bears possible legal liability for the loss of her crew, but the fishing industry is so loosely regulated he escapes with financial payments to survivors. Junger quotes the generally negative feelings about Brown held by the people of Gloucester (the author is clearly on their side) but is careful to depict the pressures and difficulties inherent in ownership of boats in such a hazardous occupation. As both owner and general manager of the *Andrea Gail*, Brown has personal knowledge of her refitting and potential for foundering that even Billy Tyne might not have known about. He is thus another shadowy figure, perhaps himself a victim of his own success at managing boats, but also in the difficult moral position of sending men out under circumstances which might well kill them. War justifies such decisions on the part of officers; here, only the profit motive is involved.

Rescue jumpers provide the perfect contrast to Bob Brown and the self-interested side of the fishing trade. Rescue jumpers put their lives at risk to save complete strangers. Without hesitation, parajumpers/rescue swimmers launch themselves out of helicopters into the sea, sometimes at night, trusting their colleagues will recover them but well aware that storms at sea can overwhelm even modern technology. While readers can see that one of the attractions of rescue operations is belonging to an elite outfit doing very dangerous and exciting work, there is no question about the willingness of these public servants to put their lives on the line for others. Their stories leave the reader astonished at their physical bravery and their psychological toughness.

Finally, "The Perfect Storm" itself is anthropomorphized into a near-living creature. The sea has always been romanticized into human terms, and the sailors in the book are no different: "It's a beautiful lady . . . but she'll kill ya without a second thought." The storm, however, a product of a named hurricane and an unusual concatenation of weather fronts, is not given the benefit of a human personality, only raw and destructive emotions: "Thirty-foot seas are rolling in from the North Atlantic and attacking the town of Gloucester with a cold, heavy rage." The virulent unpredictability of the storm is repeatedly equated to a living, organic force, but not as personification; rather, it is nature itself showing both its irresistible power and its utter unconcern for human wishes. Even the shorefront itself is under assault, houses are lost, and widespread flooding takes place; away from land, the magnitude of the storm tests the limits of measurement techniques. Weather systems at sea are simply beyond human comprehension, let alone human ability to control their effects on flimsy fishing crafts and even ocean liners.

◆ TECHNIQUES ◆

Junger organizes his narrative around both spatial and chronological principles. The spatial development takes the reader out of Gloucester onto the open sea and then the narrative attention ranges widely across the North Atlantic, encompassing the swordfishing fleet, the sailing yacht *Sartori*, various freighters caught up in the storm, Sable Island and important coastal points, and even Caribbean weather systems which will eventually impact the North Atlantic. The chronology follows the last days of the *Andrea Gail*, but also goes back in time to the days of dory fishing off

Georges Bank and literary and historical references from the nineteenth century (for example, to *Moby Dick*). Junger also courageously interrupts both spatial and chronological development with learned technical disquisitions on how waves form, how people drown, how boats turn over, and so on. These mixed developmental patterns and disquisitions are held together by a clear, forceful prose that nevertheless conveys great human feeling for the doomed fishermen whose story it records.

Junger also occupies a position somewhere in between pure factual reporting (as mentioned, he does not consider himself a journalist) and a novelist writing a dramatized version of a historical event. The author steadfastly resists the temptation of fictionalizing the last hours of Billy Tyne, Bobby Shatford, and the others, instead relying on parallel situations, both historical and contemporary, to establish what "undoubtedly" happened. Aware of his obligation to living relatives and friends, Junger records only what someone highly informed about the sea and shipwrecks believes transpired. He acts as a form of advocate for the missing men, giving them voices and imagining their fate (sometimes by offering alternate possibilities) but never shying away from the fact that they are truly dead. In a sense, Junger is helping the relatives come to term with the deaths by making their last hours concrete and imaginable, the absence of bodies or debris notwithstanding.

◆ LITERARY PRECEDENTS ◆

The Perfect Storm is in the tradition of the disaster story. Sometimes written as fiction, sometimes as researched historical fact, these stories trace the development of a natural disaster and give a precise accounting of its human costs.

Walter Lord's *A Night to Remember* (1955) is one of the most influential of modern disaster stories. It provides a chronological, moment by moment recreation of the sinking of the *Titanic* based on interviews of surviving passengers, so that readers experience a gripping you-are-there account of the last moments of the seemingly unsinkable great ship. Lord captures the ironies in details—a falling funnel that, while almost hitting a lifeboat, knocks it thirty yards away from the wreck, and thereby saves it from being sucked into the foundering ship's downpull; a survivor calmly riding the sinking vertical boat down until he can step into the sea without even getting his head wet while waiting to be successfully rescued. Lord's cold logic, dry, bitter wit, and meticulous scholarship set a high standard for others to follow.

Following in Lord's tradition A. A. Hoehling's *They Sailed into Oblivion* (1959) dramatically recounts more than twenty great sea disasters that shocked the world while William Hoffer's *Saved! The Story of the Andrea Doria, the Greatest Sea Rescue in History* (1979) recreates the events of the collision between the *Stockholm* and the *Andrea Doria* that left the latter sinking and put the lives of hundreds of passengers at risk.

Shortly after Lord's influential novel, John D. MacDonald set another fictive standard in his *Murder in the Wind*. Therein, five sets of characters try to outrun a hurricane in western central Florida and finally seek refuge in an old house only to have the forces of nature overcome them. The storm itself, based on a hurricane that hit Florida in the late 1940s, becomes a violent, destructive character. Twenty years later in *Condominium* (1977) MacDonald again captures the destructive fury of a hurricane, as he tells what happens to Golden Sands, a "dream" condominium built on a weak foundation in a bad location, the result of secret real estate swindles, political payoffs, shoddy maintenance, and construction in violation of building codes.

◆ RELATED TITLES ◆

A number of recent titles concern disasters at sea. Among them are John Protasio's *To the Bottom of the Sea: True Accounts of Major Ship Disasters* (1990), Edgar Haines's *Disasters at Sea* (1992), Rhoda Nottridge's *Sea Disasters* (1993), Keith Eastlake's *Sea Disasters* (1999), editor Logan Marshall's *The Sinking of the* Titanic *& Great Sea Disasters* (1998), William Allen's *Accounts of Shipwreck and Other Disasters at Sea* (Notable American Author Series-Part I, 1998), editor Phyllis Raybin Emert's *Shipwrecks: The Sinking of the* Titanic *and Other Disasters at Sea* (Perspectives on History Series, 1998), and Michael D. Cole's *The* Titanic: *Disaster at Sea* (American Disasters, 2001).

However, the most striking recent parallel with Junger's book is Jim Carrier's *The Ship and the Storm: Hurricane Mitch and the Loss of the Fantome* (2000). *The Ship and the Storm* tells the story of a 282-foot steel-hulled, four-masted schooner, the *Fantome*, which, in October 1998, disappeared at sea with its thirty-one crew members (mainly twenty-year-old West Indians) during Hurricane Mitch, a savage storm with 180 mile-per-hour winds and fifty-foot seas. Hurricane Mitch devastated Honduras and left 18,207 people dead or missing. Carrier interviewed the crew members' families, National Hurricane Center authorities, the Windjammer cruise company passengers and staff, and Honduran survivors of the storm, among others, and conducted on-site research to bring to life of story of pride, courage, and the overwhelming forces of nature. His story alternates between the National Hurricane Center, shipboard, research planes in the eye of the storm, cruise

company headquarters, and island and coastal villagers who struggled to survive the storm surges. The *Fantome* disappeared completely. Possibly following Junger's lead in bringing to life a real disaster, Carrier questions the seaworthiness of the vessel, plays the dangerously exposed Caribbean coastline off against the wisdom of the captain putting to sea in the face of the storm, and predicts what experiences a ship like the *Fantome* might endure when it crosses the eye of the worst hurricane in two hundred years. The result is riveting forensic journalism and real-life drama.

◆ ADAPTATIONS ◆

The Perfect Storm was made into a film of the same name which premiered the summer of 2000. Bill Wittliff's screenplay focuses efficiently on the main ideas of the book, while state-of-the-art visual effects by Industrial Light and Magic translate a surprising amount of Junger's descriptions onto the screen. The film was directed and produced by Wolfgang Petersen and stars George Clooney, Mark Wahlberg, Diane Lane, and Mary Elizabeth Mastrantonio.

◆ IDEAS FOR GROUP DISCUSSIONS ◆

Even Sebastian Junger was surprised at the success of his book, a project which might seem unpromising if described in a publisher's proposal: a nonfiction work, part narrative, part history, part technical description, which dramatizes the effects of a major storm which hit New England a decade earlier. For all the mixture of genres and approaches, Junger grounds his discussion in a number of traditions, including the sea disaster story and a narrative which celebrates a way of life, but also relies on carefully written set pieces about wave actions, weather phenomena, and fishing boats. It is the artful combination of these elements that brought success to the project.

1. How does Junger locate his discussion in the tradition of the sea disaster story? What reminders to the reader show the long history of disasters at sea?

2. Much popular fiction is escapist fare which avoids reminding readers of unpleasant realities. Junger goes in exactly the opposite direction, focusing on working class labor and tragic events. How does he create reader interest in an industry lacking almost all the qualities that make a profession dramatic or romantic?

3. How does Junger create sympathy for the gritty, sometimes pub-crawling fishermen whose lives he traces?

4. The book builds slowly, like the storm itself, before it gathers rhetorical force and sweeps its many subjects together. Trace this development by listing the general topics each chapter covers. Where is the climax of the book? Is this climax identical with the climax of the storm?

5. One writing problem Junger faced was an unhappy ending known from the start of the book. How does he handle this problem? Does he provide any ameliorating elements which might lessen the effect of this unhappy ending?

6. Junger's prose is highly informed and sometimes a model of technical description. Choose the passage you think best describes a difficult technical question then decide what techniques the author uses to convey complex information in interesting and comprehensible ways. Give examples to make these techniques clear.

7. Another way *The Perfect Storm* goes against the grain of current practice is in its depiction of real heroism, as opposed to the superhero antics of Hollywood action stars. What does heroism consist of in this book? What personal and psychological qualities are involved?

Andrew Macdonald

THE PILOT'S WIFE

Novel

1998

Author: Anita Shreve

◆

◆ SOCIAL CONCERNS ◆

A plane crash resulting from an act of terrorism kills everyone on board; the wife of the pilot subsequently discovers that her husband was leading a double life. In portraying the ultimate marital betrayal along with the large-scale tragedy and disaster of a plane crash, Shreve touches public nerves on both a personal and global level. The title character Kathryn's stages in uncovering the truth about her husband and, in the process, of discovering what caused the plane crash humanize a seemingly sensational event and raise uneasy questions about limits of marital trust.

The novel opens at the moment that Kathryn's life changes; not only does life as she has known it explode as she is notified of her husband's death, but her perception of her marriage begins to disintegrate. The plane crash, at first rumored to be caused by pilot error or mechanical failure, soon is suspected to be the result of suicide or an act of terrorism on Jack's part—these latter theories a result of the revelation that an object pulled from her husband's flight bag caused the explosion.

Kathryn's belief in the solidity of her marriage continues to shift as facts emerge that throw into doubt her image of Jack and her trust in him. Though Jack told her that his mother died when he was nine, Kathryn learns that his mother is actually alive, an Alzheimer's patient in a nursing home. Kathryn finds brief notations with another woman's name in Jack's office. Jack, it turns out, did not spend his last night in the crew apartment—information forcing Kathryn to wonder about their agreement that Jack would always be the one to phone her because of his erratic schedule and need to sleep without being awakened. Kathryn also begins to wonder about a time that she tried to call him under unusual circumstances and was unable to reach him. When Kathryn tracks down, in London, the woman mentioned in the notations, Kathryn's vague suspicions turn to absolute knowledge: Muire holds a child with eyes that are different shades of blue, a characteristic that Jack shared.

Kathryn is shocked to learn that Jack and Muire married in the Catholic church several years before and had two children, despite the fact that Jack was already married. The Jack presented by Muire is someone Kathryn barely recognizes; a Catholic who never attended mass at home, Jack had been a devout churchgoer during his time in London and through Muire and her family had become involved with the Irish

Republican Army, using his position as a pilot to act as a smuggler. Muire also reveals that Jack's mother deserted him when he was nine, running away with another man, offering a motive for his insistence that his mother was dead and his decision to maintain two families rather than abandon his and Kathryn's daughter Mattie.

Kathryn's illusions about her marriage unravel entirely like the scarf she pulls apart thread by thread during the frenzy of shock and grief that follows her encounter with Muire. Knowing that her husband was "two different people" throws Kathryn's own identity into question as she wonders if she herself was "the pilot's wife"—or if Muire was. Kathryn grapples with her anger at Jack for "gutting" her memories, struggles with the best way to help their daughter through her grief, and blows up at the pilot union's grievance expert, Robert Hart, who has assisted her through the disaster's aftermath, accusing him of "using" her to extract information about Jack's activities. The gamut of emotions that Kathryn experiences before she comes to terms with her husband's death and betrayal call into question all of her beliefs about what constitutes a good relationship. At the same time, her incipient romance with Robert reaffirms possibilities.

◆ THEMES ◆

Despite its tense subject matter and tight plotting, The Pilot's Wife is above all the portrait of a marriage through the lens of grief and shifting realities. "How do you ever know that you know a person?" Kathryn wonders continually, thinking about how one first gets to know another by forming a picture, filling in "missing brush strokes, wait[ing] for form and color to materialize." As the novel meticulously sketches out the anatomy of grief, it also fills in the form and color of Kathryn's marriage.

Repeated references to and metaphors involving vision reinforce the necessity of self-examination and self-knowledge.

Kathryn moves through typical stages in her grief process, worrying about details such as Jack's last words, wondering if she will ever sleep again, imagining that she hears her husband on the stairs, marveling at "the way the body kept moving forward, past the shock and the grief, past the retching and the hollowness inside, and kept wanting sustenance, kept wanting to be fed." She notes with surprise that the shock begins to wear off, that gradually the thought of Jack's death "didn't rock her as violently as it had the day before." Still, Kathryn has to constantly negotiate the memories "like mines in a field, waiting to detonate." And on a plane to London, she finds herself obsessing over Jack's death, reliving it in her imagination.

Kathryn's experience of grief is sometimes intensified, sometimes ameliorated by her need to think about her teenage daughter, Mattie, who alternately feels guilty, sinks into depression, and blames her mother for her father's death, mostly because Kathryn is an available target for her anger. Kathryn wishes that her daughter could simply go into a coma "and then awaken to a consciousness dulled by time, so that she would not be hit again and again with the pain that was always absurdly and cuttingly fresh." Kathryn is a philosophical parent, understanding that children are always in the process of leaving, "incrementally at first, and then with head-spinning rapidity." Still, Kathryn's revelations about how little she knew Jack are paralleled in her grief over the gradual loss of her daughter. When Mattie confesses to her mother that she has had sex, Kathryn is disturbed mostly because she had not suspected and because her daughter's experimentation has resulted from curiosity rather than love. It saddens Kathryn that she has known so little about the people she loves the most: "I didn't know about my daughter's sexual life, and I didn't know about my husband's sexual life."

What is perhaps atypical about Kathryn's grief process is the complication of her husband's infidelity, the need to reinterpret her entire life with Jack and re-examine herself. Kathryn has previously seen her relationship with Jack as passing "out of being in love to just loving," an interpretation thrown into further doubt with each revelation. Each of Kathryn's memories becomes infused with new insight as she recalls her few fights with Jack, the way he once was angry and out of sorts on his mother's birthday, the ways that he seemed distant and once alluded to divorce, and the dynamics of an argument that escalated out of control as Kathryn veered back and forth between repentance and grievance. Kathryn must reconsider her entire conception of a normal marriage as one in which a couple lives "in a state of gentle decline, of being infinitesimally, but not agonizingly, less than they were the day before . . . which means, on the whole . . . a good marriage." As Kathryn's view of her marriage and her image of her husband shifts, she does find that she knew her husband well enough to come to some understanding of his motives. She realizes that he would have been drawn to Muire's intensity and passion as well as to the adventure and idealism of involvement in dangerous political conflict. Her new vision and self-knowledge also allow her to move toward forgiveness and great self-reliance and open the door for future relationships. Nevertheless, she remains shaken by the "impossibility of ever knowing another person . . . the fragility of the constructs people make."

◆ CHARACTERS ◆

Kathryn, the "pilot's wife," is the most dynamic character, moving from a kind of complacency through grief to a new vision of herself and her marriage. A music and history teacher fifteen years younger than her husband, she is a sensible, practical person who takes things in stride and easily puts trust in others—too easily, she eventually recognizes. Having once struggled with her and Jack's shift "from being lovers to being a couple," that transition she once accepted as normal shifts meaning as a result of her discoveries. While flattened somewhat by the numbness of the grief process, Kathryn does undergo significant change. A direct and honest person, she unflinchingly pursues the clues left by her husband, becoming more clear-sighted about her relationship with him and even beginning to consider the possibility of forgiveness: If a woman forgives a man who betrays her, she wonders, is it "an affirmation or was it merely foolishness?"

While the novel filters all events through Kathryn's point of view, distancing other characters somewhat, and while those characters often remain static, Shreve is masterful at using brief details that cause Kathryn's supporting cast to come to life, achieving at least the illusion of roundness—the illusion that we know these characters even when they are relatively flat. Even Jack, who is absent from the current action because the novel starts after his death, is a constant presence. Shreve creates a sense of a complex character through the constant reversals in what Kathryn thought she knew about him. Trying to describe Jack to the priest preparing for a memorial service, Kathryn reinforces the novel's theme about how difficult it is to truly know a person: as she says that he was an only child who grew up in Boston, served in Vietnam, and liked to fish, play tennis, and spend time with his daughter, Kathryn feels as if "the real Jack, the Jack she knew and loved" is somehow missing from the bare facts of his life. Jack's attraction to excitement and adventure drove his career choice as much as it did his

---

The Pilot's Wife

eventual double life; Kathryn is awed by how as a pilot he does "tricks with gravity, with physics, with fate." While Jack only appears in flashbacks, he becomes a dynamic character in the sense that the reader's understanding of him deepens as Kathryn's does. She comes to recognize how Jack's political activities and relationship with Muire would have offered instant meaning to a life grown stale and routine: "The falling in love itself, the romantic idealism, the belonging to a righteous organization, and even the religion would have been part of a whole."

Teenage daughter Mattie becomes both a reflection of Kathryn's grief and a distraction from it, and also through her confession about her sexual experience, is a catalyst for Kathryn's revelations about how little she knew her loved ones. Close to her father and devastated by his death, Mattie is typically mercurial, emotional in her reaction but distant from her mother, at once sophisticated and immature, usually "plugged into headphones as if they delivered oxygen through her ears." Mattie's independence eventually leads her to withdraw even further from Kathryn and move on with a life more influenced by her peers than her mother, moving toward healing. Mattie was, Kathryn realizes, the reason that Jack stayed rather than leaving as his mother left him when he was nine. Kathryn protects Mattie from the knowledge of Jack's double life, and though Kathryn has lost most of her illusions, she remains determined to believe the Mattie is the last person Jack thought of, hers the last name he spoke.

Julia, Kathryn's grandmother, serves as the novel's voice of wisdom, offering her support and insight about the grief process, telling Kathryn early on that "the only way to the other side is through it." From the time that Kathryn was very young, her family lived with Julia, who provided sta-

bility for Kathryn in a way that her alcoholic parents did not. Julia, while not a highly developed character, still comes across as an individual rather than a type, someone who remains a source of stability and strength for Kathryn, offering her the support and Mattie the care that allows Kathryn the freedom to take care of details, and eventually giving her the courage to confront her illusions.

In her first appearance, Jack's "other" wife, the Irish Muire, appears to be cold, calculating, and angry, a beautiful and sophisticated woman who took what she wanted even knowing that Jack was married. This first view of Muire proves a facade when she makes her second and final appearance, seeking out Kathryn and apologizing for her cruelty. The conversation deepens her character and reveals her passion and desperation. On the verge of arrest and on the run, Muire tells the truth about Jack's involvement with the IRA and her own loss of family members through Loyalist violence. While never a fully developed or fully sympathetic character, Muire is presented as a complex woman with complicated motives.

Curiously, Robert Hart, who appears on the page far more than most of the other characters, remains somewhat flat, shadowy and indistinct. A quiet, supportive presence throughout Kathryn's ordeal, he is doggedly concerned and caring, apparently very experienced at notifying families of plane crashes and the deaths of loved ones, yet also attracted to Kathryn. Robert's character parallels Jack's in some ways, choosing his career because he is "drawn to moments of intensity." Kathryn gets to know Robert, a divorced recovering alcoholic, at the same gradual pace that she uncovers truths about her husband. Some reviewers have criticized Kathryn's realization that Robert has "used" her, given that it is his job to look for signs of knowledge about her husband's activities and convince her to name others involved. However, Kathryn's sudden anger at him occurs during her shocked response to her husband's betrayal and though irrational, highlights Kathryn's too-easy trust in others. The fact that Robert makes no attempt to detain Muire is more puzzling and left unexplored. Robert Hart functions as a rather flat love interest for Kathryn, a more trustworthy stand-in for Jack who enables Kathryn to move toward a more stable future.

◆ TECHNIQUES ◆

Described by one reviewer as "part detective story and part interior monologue," *The Pilot's Wife* moves at a brisk pace through Kathryn's discoveries about her husband, dwelling only on her psychological processes, which Shreve details lyrically. Though the book contains many elements of a thriller, ultimately the solution to the mystery and the details of the plane crash are too vague to allow the novel comfortably into that category; the emphasis is on psychological exploration, Kathryn's interior monologue of grief and her reassessment of her marriage.

At one point, Kathryn says that if Jack's motive had been suicide, "there'd be one small thing that maybe wouldn't register at the time, but would after the fact." This quotation describes the novel's structure: past tense chapters telling the story of Kathryn's reactions to the loss of her husband alternate with present tense chapters that sketch out scenes from Jack and Kathryn's courtship and marriage, reminding readers of the eternal presence of that past for Kathryn. Shreve uses each new discovery that Kathryn makes about Jack as a trigger for a present-tense memory in which suddenly, some small detail registers for Kathryn and she sees it in a new light. These recast memories are at the heart of the novel, emphasizing the ways that new informa-tion can radically alter the meaning of an event.

The very close third person point of view that filters all events, characters, and observations through Kathryn lends itself to metaphors that resonate thematically. When Kathryn thinks of getting to know another person—in this case Robert—as like painting a portrait, she also might be describing Shreve's technique for accruing details that gradually deepen our knowledge of the characters while underlining the elusiveness of knowing them entirely. Other metaphors revolving around vision and visual detail function similarly; Kathryn thinks early on about how "night would settle in like slow blindness, sucking the color from the trees and the low sky and the rocks . . . until there was nothing left in the window but her own reflection." This description captures the coastal Massachusetts setting and Kathryn's grief while also reinforcing themes of vision and self-examination.

Shreve often relies on symbolism rather than direct commentary to suggest her themes, in one case using an architectural detail to imply the completion of Kathryn's shift in vision. In one of the early flashback chapters, Shreve describes the former convent that had become Kathryn and Jack's home. Idly, Kathryn often wonders where the chapel used to be. At the end, her shifted vision helps her to recognize that what she thought was a marble bench was in fact the old altar, a recognition that substitutes for a more developed exploration of Kathryn's changed viewpoint.

◆ LITERARY PRECEDENTS ◆

The Pilot's Wife is a contemporary bildungsroman, detailing a protagonist's movement toward greater self-knowledge. The novel falls into the tradition of the female bildungsroman, which differs from the male version that concentrates on a male hero becoming initiated into adulthood and finding his place in the community. Instead, like many female heroines, Kathryn experiences a disillusionment that teaches her about her separation from her society. Also like many other female protagonists of novels in this category, Kathryn is the nurturer, the one who stays home and has created a life there rather than embarking on adventures like classic male heroes such as Goethe's prototypical Wilhelm Meister, Fielding's Tom Jones, or Twain's Huck Finn.

The Pilot's Wife shares much in common with one of the cornerstones of the female bildungsroman, Charlotte Brontë's Jane Eyre. Brontë's novel traces its title character's development from dependence to independence; along the way she discovers that others are not what they seem, particularly Mr. Rochester, who is leading a double life, intending to go through with his marriage to Jane even though he is already married.

Loosely similar to Jane Eyre in its plot elements, The Pilot's Wife also resembles Brontë's work in its emphasis on self-examination and its imagery surrounding blindness and vision. Jane, who comes of age and gains self-reliance by the novel's end, only reunites with Mr. Rochester after he has been blinded in a fire that also killed his first wife. Jane and Mr. Rochester are able to come together on more equal terms than their previous master-of-the-house/ governess relationship partly because of the self-knowledge both achieve due to his loss of sight and both characters' new insight.

Of course, symbolism involving sight and wisdom are at least as old as ancient Greek characters such as the blind seer Tieresias and the proud Oedipus, whose blindness results from a lack of self-knowledge but whose loss of sight parallels his increased insight. Like The Pilot's Wife, Sophocles' Oedipus centers on a character who must pursue a mystery at all costs,

even when it destroys him. Though Shreve's work loosely draws from this tradition, Kathryn avoids such dire consequences, her renewed sight opening the door for a probable happy ending.

◆ RELATED TITLES ◆

Shreve tends to use similar New England coastal settings in her other work, and her 1999 novel Fortune's Rocks takes place earlier in the twentieth century in the same house Kathryn now occupies, a converted convent. That Fortune's Rocks deals with marital infidelity from a completely different angle—the point of view of the other woman—creates an interesting interplay between the two novels.

◆ ADAPTATIONS ◆

Blair Brown reads the audiobook version of Shreve's novel.

◆ IDEAS FOR GROUP DISCUSSIONS ◆

Shreve's spare style and the multiple layers of her novel—some more developed than others—provide for a variety of discussion possibilities. The changes that Kathryn undergoes are more psychological and gradual than one might expect from a suspense novel, making the book difficult to categorize and causing it to operate on more than one level. Shreve's very interior writing style allows her to mention layers of background material that hints at motivations, but she chooses not to explore the characters' pasts in much detail, instead leaving the reader to draw conclusions. In the same way, she often substitutes symbolic detail for more developed exploration. The lack of development in some areas may be considered flaws by some readers and strengths by others. At any rate, what Shreve examines and what she leaves vague raises many questions about character, genre, and technique.

1. Some reviewers have complained that Kathryn is too passive a character. In what ways is she passive? In what ways does she actively determine her own fate?

2. Shreve clearly draws on a tradition that emphasizes the importance of self-knowledge, but devotes more time to Kathryn's examination of what she knows about others than her examination of what she knows about herself. How much self-knowledge does Kathryn finally gain as a result of the novel's events?

3. While containing many elements of a mystery/thriller, *The Pilot's Wife* skims over many of the specifics of the disaster in favor of focusing on Kathryn's reactions. In what ways does the novel resemble a thriller, and what other genres does Shreve draw from? How would you categorize this novel?

4. Though Kathryn never fully examines her own past, we learn about many parallels: Mattie is named after Jack's mother; Kathryn's parents were alcoholics as is Robert; Kathryn and Jack both considered themselves "orphans"; and Kathryn's husband and father both prove to have been unfaithful. Why does Shreve mention these details but choose not to develop them? How do they add to or detract from her thematic concerns?

Nancy McCabe
Presbyterian College

PLAYBACK

Novel

1958

Author: Raymond Chandler

◆———————◆———————

◆ SOCIAL CONCERNS ◆

"Murder laced with lust, mayhem spiced with nymphomania: this is the formula for the chief surviving form of the murder mystery in America, though, indeed, that form has not surrendered its native birthright of feminism. It insists, however, on undressing its bitches, surveying them with a surly and concupiscent eye before punching, shooting, or consigning them to the gas chamber. Not only in the cruder and more successful books of Mickey Spillane, but in the more pretentious ones by Raymond Chandler, the detective story has reverted to the kind of populist semi-pornography that once made George Lippard's *The Monks of Monk Hall* a black-market best-seller." So wrote Leslie Fiedler in 1960, perpetrating a tendentious and prejudicial myth about the hard-boiled genre in general, and Raymond Chandler in particular.

As every Chandler fan knows, such charges could be cooked up only by someone with no first-hand knowledge of his novels or his hero. Philip Marlowe, a hard-boiled P.I., is an almost impossibly ethical romantic who not only does not punch, shoot, or consign women to the gas chamber, but whose infrequent episodes of love-making are invariably rendered in under-stated, lyrical terms. Fiedler's aggravated assault is simply a case of a highbrow critic projecting his dislike of the genre to one of its most celebrated and consummate practitioners. For although Chandler's novels are unquestionably of the hard-boiled school, they have shot and punched their way out of the crime-fiction ghetto and into literary excellence.

Even in 1933, when most whodunit hacks hacked out a million words a year to make a living, Chandler's first pulp story, "Blackmailers Don't Shoot," was a product of five months of tireless revisions. A quarter of a century later, his last novel, *Playback* (if one does not count the unfinished *Poodle Springs*), is another testimony to his literary ambitions, playing a tongue-in-cheek game with the entire hard-boiled school of writing. Chandler's unflagging attention to style, mood and character has always separated him from run-of-the-mill purveyors of crime thrills, earning him acclaim from such luminaries as T. S. Eliot, Anthony Burgess, W. H. Auden, Ernest Hemingway, J. B. Priestley, Somerset Maugham, and S. J. Perelman. A writer of power, vision, and endurance, Chandler was quite simply a contemporary American novelist who, as Auden put it, was "interested in writing not detective stories, but serious studies of a criminal milieu, the Great Wrong Place." And as such "his powerful and extremely depressing books should be read and judged, not as escapist literature, but as works of art."

What kind of Great Wrong Place does *Playback* evoke for the reader? Published in the '50s, when every TV commercial implicitly reassured Americans that they lived in the best of all times and in the best of all countries, *Playback* is closer in sensibility to Chandler's novels from the dark '30s and the war-ravaged '40s. Nobody is outraged by crime, graft, vice or corruption because they are so widespread and commonplace. When the novel takes a sleepy, peace-abiding little town of Esmeralda and eviscerates it right before the reader's eyes, it does it without fanfare or righteous indignation. After half a lifetime of sifting through society's human garbage, Chandler's hero has seen it all, and his tired, almost complacent view of crime is the author's vehicle for suggesting that the line between criminals and society at large is about as real as a lawyer's promise.

Chandler takes many potshots at guns and lawyers, two icons of the uneasy relationship between America and American law. Neither of them, in his opinion, can settle anything satisfactorily. Guns, drawls Marlowe, "are just a fast curtain to a bad second act," and the bad second act is played out in today's reality, filled daily by reports of firearm massacres. The justice system is another nightmare, designed to profit the lawyers at the expense of the rest of us. Not that the public is reluctant to use the lawyers' services: if one is to believe one of Joseph Wambaugh's unforgettable characters from *Glitter Dome*, these days the next word a child learns after "Mom" is "sue." In *Playback*, Betty Mayfield, the dame in distress whom Marlowe is hired to tail, makes no distinction between lawyers and blackmailers when told that she may need a

good attorney. "That's a contradiction in terms," she sneers. "If he was good, he wouldn't be a lawyer."

Another target of Chandler's criticism is the state of American cities, conveyed through his characteristically brooding and melancholy descriptions of urban landscape. There is little to cheer about: at the beginning of Chapter 7 Marlowe contrasts the fictional town of Esmeralda with the dismal reality of Anytown, USA: tawdry, shabby, littered, with a parade of false fronts, glaring billboards, smoky poolrooms, street toughs, and hamburger joints serving paper food on paper plates. Such pictures of urban blight, roadside wreckage, abject poverty and backyard slums, which accompany Marlowe's investigation of the town's underbelly, are a fitting prelude to the entire Chapter 20 in which the plot takes a back seat, while an inconsequential motel owner deplores the transformation of Esmeralda. This type of socioeconomic analysis, not common in the genre driven typically by a murder mystery, is not uncommon in a writer who has always deemed plots superfluous to the spirit of hard-boiled realism. Chandler's reflections, all the more effective in the mouth of an average working Joe, conjure up the decline in the social and urban landscape, the splintering of communities, the loss of neighbourhood group identity and cohesion, and the emergence of the me-first dog-eat-dog mentality.

Although *Playback* lacks the type of a sadistic cop which appeared regularly in earlier of Chandler's books, the fact that Marlowe is moved to thank the local law-enforcers for treating him like a human being hints at a permanent enmity between cops and private citizens. As the author realized, the very existence of private detectives (and, in general, private security agents who, in our day, well outnumber the regular police) is an implied censure of the latter's efficacy and competence. In *Play-*

back, where a tycoon like Henry Cumberland deems himself above the law because he owns the town in which the law is dispensed, and where an ex-gangster like Clark Brandon lives the life of a nouveau riche instead of languishing in jail for racketeering, we see the same two-tiered system of social justice as in *The Great Gatsby.* Just like Jay Gatsby, Brandon is a former racketeer and bootlegger who buys himself respectability by moving to a new place, acquiring lavish property, throwing crime-tainted money around and mingling with the local establishment (and, when needed, arranging a hit on those who would stand in his way).

A discussion of the novel's social themes would not be complete without a mention of the situation of women in 1950s' America. Two separate passages, striking in the manner of an iceberg, tell the whole unwritten story. When Marlowe is first given the assignment to shadow Betty Mayfield, looking at her photograph he remarks the absence of a wedding band. As it is, Betty had indeed been married; yet, the implication is glaring: a girl in her late twenties ought to have a husband or else there is something wrong with her—wrong enough to prompt a comment from an investigator. Much in the same manner, when the detective is invited to the house of Miss Vermilyea, the executive secretary of his employer, he says flatly: "You've been married, of course." This instinctive assumption once again underlies the precariousness of a woman's economic position, making it (and her) de facto much less independent than we would care to believe. If she owns property, after all, it is a safe guess that it must be from her marriage/husband, a fact confirmed by Vermilyea in the next sentence.

◆ THEMES ◆

One of the major themes in *Playback* is the author's self-conscious treatment of the hard-boiled genre. In the later stages of his career Chandler would frequently express his discontent with its limitations, insisting: "From now on I am going to write what I want to write as I want to write it. Some of it may flop. There are always going to be people who will say I have lost the pace I had once, that I take too long to say things now, and don't care enough about tight active plots. But I'm not writing for those people now." Indeed, he was not. *The Long Goodbye,* his second last and probably best novel, is a far cry from the shoot'em-first-ask-questions-later whodunit of the type perfected by a Hammett or a Spillane. In this poignant, at times almost reflective book, Chandler writes about crime in order to write about friendship, love, and middle-age compromises, transforming a story of double murder into a psychological drama, character study, mood piece and a novel of manners.

"I am not satisfied that . . . a novel cannot be written which, ostensibly a mystery and keeping the spice of mystery, will actually be a novel of character and atmosphere with an overtone of violence and fear." Statements like these reveal the author's ambitions to exceed the limits of the formula by leaving a lasting emotional effect on the reader. Such a controlled half-poetic emotion should combine with a lingering image of the mood and aura of the places and people described. In this context it is significant that his protagonist is almost never hired to unravel a murder mystery; instead, he gets entangled in it while dealing with people-oriented investigations. Increasingly preoccupied with writing contemporary fiction using the crime-story form, Chandler would go as far as to apologize for his early *Black Mask* stories which pandered to the pulp tradition by piling on murders and violent deaths.

Playback is surely Chandler's most self-conscious and over-the-top performance. While fully delivering on hard-boiled goods, it displays a flamboyantly self-reflexive attitude to the genre and its cliches. To begin, in a tribute as ironic as deferential, the novel swarms with allusions to Dashiell Hammett's classic, *Red Harvest*. The most prominent among these is the Kansas Op, Goble, "a middle sized fat man and the fat didn't look flabby," who not only is a ringer for the Continental Op, but ends up beaten to a pulp by a red-haired gangster, Richard (or Red) Harvest. Marlowe runs into a cabbie who protests that car tailing is something from crime books; Vermilyea greets him as "Mr. Hard Guy in person," while the hero himself quips about TV detectives who never take their hats off, or pulp-fiction sleuths who always drive dark inconspicuous cars. Moreover, *Playback* deviates from the standard elements of the genre in so many ways that it verges on becoming an anti-mystery. Larry Mitchell is presumed dead but no formal investigation is initiated, and no one is ever brought to trial. Justice is not meted out, at least in the legal sense: the detective does not enforce the law by arresting the likely culprit, Brandon, nor does he report him to the police. To top it all off, there is not even a clear-cut case of murder, although no less than three people (Betty's husband, Mitchell, and the night watchman Ceferino Chang) die a sudden death. There are plenty of guns around but nobody fires one; there are long passages of stark philosophical reflections or sociological vignettes; and there is a quaint ending, with the hero in love and looking forward to impending marriage.

Even Marlowe, ostensibly a gumshoe hireling for a fee plus expenses, is not like the Op or Sam Spade, those perennial hustlers and money pinchers. In *The Long Goodbye* he returns a $5,000 bill he got from Terry Lennox when he realizes that it was meant to buy his silence; in *Playback* he rejects a similar $5,000 "gift" from a gangster. This perennial test of integrity forms one of Chandler's recurring themes. By common standards the detective is, of course, a social failure. As Robert B. Parker's Marlowe tells his millionaire wife in *Poodle Springs*, "They [her friends] will laugh at me because I'm a failure. I don't have any money. In this great Republic that's how the judgement is made, darling." Yet, ironically, we measure the failure of others by judging their moral and ethical standards against Marlowe's.

The last major theme inextricably bound with Chandler and hard-boiled fiction in general is the deluge of violence, crime, and vice on both sides of the law. If anyone should doubt that crime fiction's repeated portrayals of crooked cops, corrupt judges, criminal (in the full sense of the word) lawyers, and untouchable racketeers is a true reflection of American society, the facts speak for themselves. A Police Commissioner by the name of Teddy Roosevelt had this to say to the public in 1895: "I have the most corrupt department in New York on my hands." In 1929 Frank Loesch, President of the Chicago Crime Commission, actually went to Al Capone and asked him to help Chicago hold an honest election. In the same year, a full decade before Chandler's *The Big Sleep*, the National Commission on Law Observance and Enforcement met for the first time, concluding: "The general failure of the police to deter and arrest criminals guilty of many murders, spectacular bank, payroll, and other hold-ups and sensational robberies with guns, frequently resulting in the death of the robbed victim, has caused a loss of public confidence in the police in our country."

In this climate which has only gotten worse since, it is small wonder that the cops and detectives in Chandler's novels nourish such a jaded attitude toward law enforcement. The real criminals are never brought to court because graft and corruption are everywhere. Crime, money, and power are all in the hands of the people who can afford to buy legal and political immunity from even the most tenacious investigators. Although Marlowe will usually get the man who pulls the trigger, he is painfully aware that the capture of the murderer is nothing to cheer about; the corrupt system remains intact. In a symbolic scene at the end of "Smart-Alec Kill", a *Black Mask* story from 1934, the detective and a police captain go for a drink after closing the case. "What'll we drink to?" asks the cop. "Let's just drink," answers the hero.

◆ CHARACTERS ◆

In his famous essay, "The Simple Art of Murder," Chandler insisted that in a crime narrative the hero "is everything." In his private notebooks, published since as "Twelve Notes on the Mystery Story," he was equally resolute: "The hero of a mystery story is the detective. Everything hangs on his personality. If he hasn't one, you have very little." In Philip Marlowe he created one of the most famous and most memorable characters of the twentieth century, a hero so vivid and real that even his offstage life has become the subject of interest, eventually leading the author to flesh it out for the public. From his 1951 letter to D. J. Ibberson, listed as "The Facts of Philip Marlowe's Life" in *Selected Letters of Raymond Chandler*, we learn, for example, that the P.I. is around forty, has no living relatives, did a couple of years of college, was an investigator for an insurance company and later for the D.A. of Los Angeles county, is over six feet tall, and tips the scales at 210 pounds. These and a welter

of other details add up to the picture of a handsome, husky, intelligent, sensitive, and morally nuanced hero. Clearly a romanticized composite of features that have precious little in common with real-life sleuths. His creator summed the difference in this way: "The real-life private eye is a sleazy little drudge from Burns Agency, a strong-arm guy with no more personality than a blackjack. He has about as much moral stature as a stop and go sign."

Chandler, for whom the hard-boiled novel has always been a vehicle for mood and character rather than plot, deliberately developed Marlowe as an urban knight. In the first scene on the first page of his first novel, when the hero enters General Sternwood's mansion to get his first assignment, he notices a stained-glass panel showing a knight in dark armor rescuing a lady tied to a tree. "I stood there and thought that if I lived in the house, I would sooner or later have to climb up there and help him," reflects Marlowe, articulating his creator's vision of romantic sordidness. Gradually emerging from the hard-boiled mold of the stories and early novels, the detective in *Playback* is a complex character with complex inner life, a man of feeling as well as action who no longer hesitates to become involved with people around him. "To me," admitted Chandler, "Marlowe is the American mind: a heavy portion of rugged realism, a dash of good hard vulgarity, a strong overtone of strident wit, an equally strong undertone of pure sentimentalism, an ocean of slang, and an utterly unexpected range of sensitivity." Although the hard-boiled hero is a distinct fixture on the American literary horizon, his roots can be traced to Huck Finn: undereducated, poor, solitary, pragmatic, independent, with plenty of common sense, good coping skills, distrust of phony intellectualism, flair for the vernacular, and a heart of gold—a representative of the American.

In all other respects, Marlowe from *Playback*—older, more tired, slower and more cynical as he may be—is still pure hard-boiled Chandler. Phoned at 6:30 in the morning, he is ready with an ironic repartee for a big-shot lawyer who tries to cow him with authority and bluster. He talks tough when the occasion requires, does not sleep nights, calls the shots by virtue of being in the centre of the action, smokes, drinks, and gets beat up, all in a day's work. Better educated and more eloquent than other hard-boiled gumshoes, he is still a model of raw masculinity, and the dames, no matter how blonde, sharp, or cool, warm up to him quickly. He knows the ways and byways of the city, its train stations, police stations, taxi ranks, restaurants, hotels, offices. The knowledge of the streets, fluent Spanish, the ability to size up people and situations, and an understanding of human psychology make him a smooth professional operator, who rarely needs to use muscle. Yet make no mistake: he is as tough as a refugee's life. Armed with a tire iron he faces a professional gunman sent by Brandon to teach him a lesson and, risking his own life, instead of killing, only cripples the assailant.

Yet for all the hard-boiled veneer Marlowe is always ready to save the damsel in distress, full of compassion for the weak and defenseless on whose behalf he will often endure physical hardship. For these reasons, the case often becomes a crusade which pits him against the evil that defines the society he has to live in. In *The Long Goodbye* Marlowe says: "I'm a romantic. I hear voices crying in the night and I go see what's the matter. You don't make a dime that way. You got sense, you shut your windows and turn up more sound on the TV set." Naturally we love Marlowe and feel the need for heroes like him precisely because he refuses to shut the window. For that matter, there may be existentialist echoes in his Sisyphus-like choice to roll the stone of virtue up the hill of corruption and decay. Even though, unlike many movie detectives, he does not consider himself above the law, in the spirit of American self-reliance (maybe even civil disobedience) he is not above using the law to his advantage when necessary. In a typical hard-boiled understatement he may claim to have only shreds of ethics left, yet in reality he is a superlatively ethical P.I. whose internal moral code simply outweighs the letter of the law (which he nonetheless always tries to follow in spirit).

If every hard-boiled novel must have its femme fatale, Betty Mayfield certainly fits the bill. Moreover, if Brigid O'Shaughnessy, the red-haired looker from *The Maltese Falcon*, can be said to typify the character, the redheaded Betty could be her twin sister. A runaway from a troubled past, she wants nothing better than to start a new life and yet is curiously unsurprised when her previous life always catches up with her. She is a drop-dead knockout, a consummate actress who readily uses her body, wits and charms to her advantage, and an inveterate liar. Yet she is completely unapologetic and cynical about it, sounding almost indifferent when she concedes to Marlowe: "All right, I'm a liar. I've always been a liar." Although she is drawn to the hero like to a magnet, and even goes through the motions of daydreaming about their future, everyone (including Betty) knows that it will not happen. A femme fatale uses men like pawns and, although Betty seems to be a victim of circumstance and not a premeditated murderess of her rich husband, for Marlowe this is simply a playback of many temptation scenes from previous novels. As a character type, Betty (and the femme fatale in general) is a fascinating incarnation of a modern woman: fiercely independent, sexually liberated, not much of a homemaker but able to get on with her life independent of men, and determined to fend for herself in a man's world—be it in shady business, sex, drink, smoke, or tough talk as an equal.

Besides these two central figures, *Playback* is not different from other Chandler novels in presenting a broad cross section of society, from melodramatically hyperbolic power figures to everyday people in everyday jobs. In the order of Marlowe's investigation, we meet with the expensive lawyer, Clyde Umney; his secretary, Helen Vermilyea; the runaway suspect, Eleanor King (who is now Betty Mayfield); a train station porter; a petty hustler and hotel lounge lizard, Larry Mitchell; cabbies; motel receptionists; a cleaning woman; another P.I., Goble; a taxi driver by the name of Joe Harms; a garage night man, Ceferino Chang; a hotel detective, Javonen; an old hotel guest, Henry Clarendon IV; several cops; Captain Alessandro of the local police; the hatchet man, Red Harvest; Mr. Cumberland, tycoon, city-owner, and Betty's father-in-law; and the racketeer and ex-gangster, Clark Brandon.

One character that must be singled out is Henry Clarendon IV, whose presence in the book might be one more self-reflexive bow towards Dashiell Hammett. Just as Hammett featured in his own novel as Dan Rolff, the thin man with T.B., in *Playback* Chandler makes his own cameo appearance in the guise of the aging hotel-lobby philosopher, Henry Clarendon. The notion for this little stunt may have germinated in the writer's mind since his 1950 collaboration with Alfred Hitchcock (who put in a cameo in all of his films) on the script for Patricia Highsmith's *Strangers on a Train*. Chandler writes himself into his last novel as an old, wealthy, intelligent and cynical hotel patron, his hair neatly parted, hands in white gloves (in later years the author was plagued by a skin condition), his eye as astute in observation as enamoured of the female form, and, self-reflexively engaged in conversation with his own creation, Philip Marlowe.

◆ TECHNIQUES ◆

Some critics have raised doubts whether Chandler has the same narrative abundance as other crime-fiction writers. In a letter from 1957, i.e., around the time he was finishing *Playback*, the author admitted: "I'm a good dialogue writer, but not a good constructionist." Whether this self-deprecation is true or not is open to debate. It may take readers a while to realize that the real target of Mitchell's blackmail is not Betty but Clark Brandon, which would suggest that Chandler may be a more intricate constructionist than he would allow. What is not open to debate is that he had a Technicolor eye for image and a Panasonic ear for language. Trained and educated in England, he acknowledged: "I had to learn American just like a foreign language. To learn it I had to study and analyze it. As a result, when I use slang, colloquialisms, snide talk or any kind of off-beat language I do it deliberately." Consistently hard-boiled in style, Chandler uses two distinct voices for the purpose of creating atmosphere. The first is typified by his vernacular, rollicking, snappy and wisecracking dialogue; the other by the more meditative, at times even melancholy, descriptive passages. The dominant mood in his novels is that which surrounds losers in life, drifters, grifters, minor hoodlums, drunks, washouts, lonely people coming together for a few moments during which even their togetherness is tinged with the certainty of solitude; people who saw too much of the wrong side of life, broken by life; cynical people who lost their ideals, so that even their dreams are only in black and white.

For all the harsh, hard-boiled veneer, there are many elements of melodrama detectable in Chandler's last novel. He writes about crime with the assurance that it will be solved; creates a pure, romantic, sensitive, compassionate hero who will inevitably triumph in the end; gives us a couple of durable girls, Betty and Helen, who shine with solid gold from under the chromium exterior; ends the book with a vision of love and impending marriage; and renders sex scenes with an almost sentimental delicacy. Still, Chandler's ironic attitude to himself, to his characters and the genre is never far below the surface, as when Marlowe undercuts a poignant scene by walking away and scolding himself: "A little more of that and I'd be falling in love with myself. I might even give myself a small unpretentious diamond ring."

Keeping the novel's mood in balance, scenes like this once again reveal Chandler to be a master of image and simile, fresh and apt to a degree perhaps unequalled in American letters. The quality and abundance of his wit has certainly few equals in the hard-boiled genre, and the startling effect with which he yokes disparate concepts or images together seems to belong to the metaphysical school of English poetry from the seventeenth century. The stylist who wrote in *The Big Sleep:* "The General spoke again, slowly, using his strength as carefully as an out-of-work showgirl uses her last good pair of stockings," is back in *Playback* with similes like: "One was a Hertz rented car, as anonymous as a nickel in a parking meter." Although first and foremost a master of the hard-boiled style, Chandler embeds within it longer descriptive passages, internal monologues, descriptions of settings bearing an almost Hemingway-quality attention to detail, and a gallery of colourful secondary characters. In this way he remains faithful to Cap Shaw's editorial manifesto for *Black Mask*: "We wanted simplicity for the sake of clarity, plausibility and belief. We wanted action but held that action was meaningless unless it involves recognizable human character in three-di-

mensional form." While acknowledging the formulaic character of much of hard-boiled prose, Shaw wanted his writers to emphasize "character and the problems inherent in human behavior over crime solution." Without shying away from the seamy and seedy details of modern urban life, *Playback* describes them in a way that makes the reader experience and respond to them emotionally, in terms of human triumphs and sorrows.

◆ LITERARY PRECEDENTS ◆

Much as Chandler admired Hemingway's titles, he vacillated a lot about his own. Some that he contemplated but did not use were: *The Corpse Came in Person, A Few May Remember, The Man with the Shredded Ear, Zone of Twilight, Parting before Danger, The Is to Was Man, All Guns Are Loaded, Return from Ruin, Lament but No Tears, Too Late to Sleep, The Cool-Off. Playback* refers, of course, to a replay of Betty's nightmare of being accused of murder with circumstantial evidence pointing in her direction: barely exonerated of her husband's death, in Esmeralda she faces the spectre of being held responsible for the death of Mitchell. Yet Chandler's title resonates in yet another way, inasmuch as the novel is in many ways a replay of an original movie script that Chandler wrote for Paramount in 1947. After the smashing success of his scripts for *Double Indemnity* (1944, co-credited with Billy Wilder) and *The Blue Dahlia* (1946; both films Academy Award nominees), Universal offered him a groundbreaking contract ($4000 a week, percentage of profits, minimum supervision) to write the script for a movie called *Playback*, which Chandler completed early in 1948.

Suffering from the post-World War II recession, Universal never got around to shooting the picture, yet as it stands, the script remains one of the writer's outstanding achievements. It was "one of the best films I wrote," confided Chandler who, after the first stab in 1953 at turning it into his final Marlowe novel, completed the job in 1958. The book preserves the main outline of the plot, i.e., the story of Betty Mayfield who runs from a playback of her tragic past, as well as a number of principal characters, but is in many ways quite different from the script. The setting is Vancouver, British Columbia, where Betty arrives on a train with Larry Mitchell who, after playing around with her and Margo West at Brandon's penthouse party, ends up dead on her balcony. The investigation is conducted by a sympathetic Canadian detective, Killaine who eventually (and not so convincingly) falls in love with the heroine after clearing her of blame for the death.

The one source which cannot be left without a brief mention is *Poodle Springs*, the first four chapters of which Chandler wrote before his death. In 1989 it was completed by Robert B. Parker, another well-known writer of crime mysteries, and appeared at book stands as the last Marlowe adventure, co-authored by both writers. Married to Linda Loring, Marlowe chafes at the millionaire lifestyle while trying to preserve his dignity by returning to sleuthing, this time on a case involving pornography, quadruple murder, and a lot of soul-searching about his identity. Perhaps buoyed by his literary coup, Parker returned to Marlowe in a subsequent novel of his own, a sequel to *The Big Sleep* entitled *Perchance to Dream*.

◆ IDEAS FOR GROUP DISCUSSIONS ◆

Playback is in many ways Chandler's farewell work, at once typical in taking a hard look at contemporary society, and untypical in turning into a self-conscious and at times almost nostalgic retrospective of his entire career in the hard-boiled genre. In forming your response to this unique novel you may wish to consider the following questions:

1. In what ways does Marlowe differ from the stereotype of the hard-boiled detective?

2. Are Mitchell and Chang victims of murder, or of accident and suicide, respectively? What are the implications of either interpretation for the novel?

3. What elements imitate or even reverse the conventional features of the genre?

4. Did you find Chandler's style vivid and colourful? To what can it be attributed?

5. How would you describe the mood of the novel and how is it evoked?

6. What is the significance of Henry Clarendon's philosophical musings for the rest of the novel?

7. Why does Marlowe not report Brandon to the police? Why does he refuse to shake hands?

8. Have the themes of *Playback* lost pertinence in the intervening decades? Why?

9. Is Chandler just a better mystery writer than most, or a qualitatively different novelist who just happens to write about crime in contemporary society?

Peter Swirski
Comparative Literature, University of Alberta

RABBIT IS RICH

Novel

1981

Author: John Updike

◆

*R*abbit Is Rich is the third novel explor-ing the inner life of Harry "Rabbit" Angstrom, a former high-school basketball star in a small Pennsylvania city who finds it difficult to adjust to life outside the lime-light of sports stardom. John Updike, also from a small Pennsylvania city much like Rabbit's Brewer, reveals in his introduc-tion to the Everyman's Library edition of the collected novels that Rabbit is his way of seeing the country and American cul-ture through different eyes. Those eyes be-long to an ordinary blue-collar man who is driven to live his life in a way that feels right to him. In the first novel, *Rabbit, Run* (1960) Rabbit is twenty-six and searching for redemption and grace in a late-1950s America in which most other young white men are seeking a ride on the wave of prosperity. *Rabbit Redux* (1971) features a thirty-six-year-old Rabbit, abandoned by his wife Janice, raising a pre-teen boy alone and coping with the massive cultural changes wrought by '60s activists. Janice returns and by the time Rabbit is forty-six and *Rabbit Is Rich* opens in 1979, he has in-advertently become prosperous despite eco-nomic chaos in America—gas lines are lengthening as double-digit inflation undercuts the national confidence and spirit.

A social and emotional history of the United States in the late '70s, *Rabbit Is Rich* opens with a sly reference to the verb "run" that has propelled Rabbit into the national consciousness: "Running out of gas, Rabbit Angstrom thinks. The . . . world is running out of gas. But they won't catch him, not yet, because there isn't a piece of junk on the road gets better mileage than his Toyotas, with lower service costs. Read *Consumer Reports*, April issue." Ironically, the Rabbit who has never been materialistic has now, along with his wife Janice, inherited the lucrative Toyota dealership, Springer Motors. The "rich" in the title forecasts an obsession with money, and Rabbit's interior mono-logues are indeed often consumed by thoughts of getting and spending. The novel is filled with newsworthy economic events such as rising OPEC prices, the decline of the dol-lar, and a sixty percent rise in the value of gold, but Rabbit is interested only in how such worldly events affect Toyota sales or his own investments. Rabbit's fascination with establishing a Keogh investment plan mirrors his fascination with finding "it," his word for transcendence, in the original novel. Rabbit's only reading material in the novel, *Consumer Reports*, underscores the consumerism of Americans during the period.

The novel also provides a snapshot of the culture of the late '70s. Skylab falls. *The Amityville Horror,* a popular book and subsequent film, is critiqued, as is Warren Beauty's film *Shampoo.* Farrah Fawcett and her television show, *Charlie's Angels,* disco on the radio, Pete Rose batting .400, and dealerships offering a free Chevette with the purchase of a gas-guzzling Cadillac Eldorado get equal time in the narrative with the terrorist murder of Lord Mountbatten. Updike sends Rabbit's son, Nelson, to a college whose very name represents the tumult of the early '70s student protest movement: Kent State. However, Nelson, the first person on either side of the family to attend college, lacks interest in his alma mater's activist history: "As far as Nelson is concerned, they could have shot all those jerks. During the '77 trouble about Tent City, he stays in his dorm."

Sexuality plays an important role in *Rabbit Is Rich,* as it does in most other Updike novels. Rabbit's thoughts have always been filled with sexual images. In the first novel he confuses the search for physical fulfillment with the search for grace, but he is bitterly disappointed by his wife's drowning of their baby and by his lover Ruth's threat to abort her pregnancy. In the second novel, he still thinks about sex, but is rarely able to perform. In this novel of his middle age, however, the sexually explicit scenes are more numerous than ever, and sex for Rabbit has become fun. When Rabbit invests in South African Krugerrands and brings them to bed to entice Janice, Updike playfully juxtaposes Rabbit's sexual and economic obsessions. "Gods bedded among stars," the couple later panics when post-coitally they count only twenty-nine Krugerrands scattered among the bedclothes. "He does not rest until, naked on his knees on the rug . . . he finds the precious thirtieth."

Updike also captures America's casual attitude toward pre-marital and extra-marital sex during this time before awareness of AIDS and other sexually transmitted diseases helped rein in sexual behavior. Nelson, Rabbit's son, who has impregnated a Kent State secretary, nonchalantly discusses marrying her while having intercourse with one of her friends. Melanie, the aforementioned friend, has numerous sexual liaisons going on simultaneously, including one with Charlie Stavros, Rabbit's chief salesman and former lover to Janice. And although sex with Janice is better than ever, Rabbit still longs for Cindy Murkett, the sensual twenty-something wife of his golfing buddy, Webb. This longing precipitates a three-couple swap on a Caribbean vacation, a swap that ironically pairs Rabbit with the prim and seemingly repressed Thelma, not Cindy.

Rabbit is nonetheless quite content with America and his life at age forty-six; "For the first time since childhood, Rabbit is happy, simply, to be alive." *Rabbit Is Rich* is a novel of commonplace domestic issues and events of middle age—financial stability, marriage, family, grandchildren. Between 1969 and 1979 Updike divorced, remarried, and moved to another town. Between 1969 and 1979, Rabbit reconciles with his wife, sees his son marry and produce a beloved granddaughter, and moves into his ideal home in another town. The Rabbit of this novel may make only $40,000 per year, but he considers himself "rich."

◆ THEMES ◆

Updike introduces a theme of the novel in the two epigraphs. The first is a definition of the ideal citizen from Sinclair Lewis's *Babbitt:* "At night he lights up a good cigar, and climbs into the little old 'bus, and maybe cusses the carburetor, and shoots out home. He mows the lawn, or sneaks in some practice putting, and then he's ready for dinner." The second is from Wallace Stevens' poem "A Rabbit as King of the Ghosts": "The difficulty to think at the end of day,/ When the shapeless shadow covers the sun/ And nothing is left except light on your fur." *Babbitt* is an ironic look at the solid middle-class businessman, the role Rabbit plays now as chief of Springer Motors. Sure enough, Rabbit often cruises around in any one of his Toyotas, and after he has checked his garden to make sure the vegetables are doing well, he most often heads to the Flying Eagle, the golf and racquet club where his social set drinks, swaps stories and hits the links.

Stevens' poem exposes a rabbit that imagines himself puffed up to heroic stature. Rabbit, too, is somewhat the hero in the midst of a town running down. He is now "King of the lot . . . the man up front. A center of sorts, where he had been a forward." With his sports headlines on the showroom walls, "yellowing, toasted brown by time," he still "has that look" of a famous basketball player, according to the young woman he decides may be his and Ruth's long-lost daughter. Rising gas prices have made Rabbit even more satisfied with his fleet of fuel-efficient Toyotas, which "sell themselves," and he likes having this money to "float in," the other guys at Rotary and Chamber looking up to him again as they did when they all played ball back in high school. Rabbit is comfortable in his status, both at the lot and at the country club, where his golf game and storytelling prowess keep him in the center of attention. However, Harry is not completely fulfilled, and his search for what is missing in his otherwise happy life fuels the action of the narrative.

Harry's quest is no longer for "it," that elusive spark of grace found only in the spiritual world. That was the object of a young man's search. Rabbit's middle-aged quest in this novel is much more down to earth: to be rid of his son Nelson, to bed the exotic Cindy Murkett, to have a home of his own, to find the daughter he has never known. It is as if achieving these goals will stave off the aging process. Although he is happy at the moment, there is a specter of death looming not too far out of reach. In fact, the statement about his newfound happiness follows a paragraph cataloguing his dead friends and family members. Since childhood, aging has troubled him. He remembers grade school in which he had "suffered another promotion, taken another step up the stairs that has darkness at the head." Harry's Herculean task is to secure these desires before it is too late, while he is still among the living.

A principle threat to his happiness is the arrival of his son, Nelson, who has dropped out of Kent State to move into the old-fashioned home Rabbit and Janice share with her mother, Bessie Springer. Rabbit's attempt to rid the household of Nelson's unwanted presence drives the narrative. Although Rabbit loves his son, he can barely control his animosity toward him. The father has been "blissfully" content both at the dealership and at home until the son demands a job and seems to take up more than his share of the house. Rabbit feels threatened by him, perhaps more so because Nelson is also repeating many of Rabbit's youthful indiscretions. At twenty-three, Nelson too gets his girlfriend pregnant, conducts two sexual relationships at once, and finally, runs out on his wife who has just had their baby. But what Rabbit really despises about his son is his lack of grace, his awkwardness, his lack of spiritual qualities. When the young Rabbit made the same mistakes, he was at least in search of redemption; when Nelson runs, it is simply to avoid responsibility.

The father-son conflict pervades the novel, with Nelson's complaining, whining, and shirking weighing more and more heavily on Rabbit. The antagonism is mutual. Near the end of the narrative Updike reveals Nelson's thoughts, "Why doesn't Dad just die? He knows he can manage Mom." But Rabbit cannot die yet, he has to be there to support and protect Pru, his son's wife, when Nelson abandons her just before their baby is born. In the last scene of the novel, Rabbit staves off the specter of death as he cradles his beloved granddaughter in his arms, Nelson safely far away back in Ohio. As welcome as this child is, however, she forecasts his fate: "Fortune's hostage, heart's desire, a granddaughter. His. Another nail in his coffin. His."

A second quest has similarly bittersweet results. From the first moment that Rabbit spots the bikini-clad Cindy Murkett, his golfing buddy's wife, he is consumed with longing. "It hollows out Harry's stomach, makes him faintly sick, to think what a lucky stiff Webb is . . . it isn't *fair* to have a young wife but no old lady Springer on the other side of the walls." Much later, observing Cindy at the Murkett's home during a party, "the vehemence of his lust dries his mouth." When Harry discovers Polaroid shots of Cindy and Webb in various sexual positions, the urgency of his desire is quenched only by thinking of his other "secrets": "His daughter. His gold. His son coming down from the Pocono's to claim his place at the lot." Thinking of Nelson temporarily blunts his lust, but on returning to the party, he discovers that the shared trip to the Caribbean has been planned in his absence. He is convinced that fate has conspired to award him Cindy on the trip. When the moment of swapping arrives, however, it is the prim-looking forty-six-year-old Thelma who takes Rabbit's hand and leads him to her room for a long night of uninhibited sex. Cindy is scheduled for the next night, but Bessie calls them home because Nelson has deserted his pregnant wife. Rabbit fumes, "You mean we can't

stay here tonight because of something Nelson has done?" Updike cannot allow Rabbit all his desires. So again the quest fails, but Rabbit is not crushed: "That trip was fun. I feel satisfied," he tells Janice as they fly back to Pennsylvania.

Rabbit's desire for his own home, his own space, is a theme of the novel as well. He and Janice have been sharing Bessie Springer's "old barn of a house" filled with musty antiques and antimacassars for years, and as Janice puts it, "It's a great sacrifice on Harry's part, a man of his income not having a house he can call his own." For Rabbit, the presence of both women is sometimes comforting, but often frustrating: "Day after day, mother and daughter sharing that same house, it's not natural. Like water blood must run or grow scum." Rabbit's need for his own space is also fueled by house envy of the Murkett's modern tasteless ranch coupled with a desire to entertain Cindy and Webb in style. He repeatedly dreams of a "sunken living room" for parties. By the end of the novel, Updike allows Rabbit to move into a home befitting his newfound status, a stone cottage in Penn Park "with all those nice divorce lawyers and dermatologists." Rabbit exults, "I've always kind of dreamed, ever since we used to play them in basketball, of living over there somewhere." But after moving in, even as "the king of the castle" prepares to watch the Super Bowl on his "brand new Sony," Rabbit feels he and Janice are "trying not to panic here in this house where they shouldn't be at all . . . lost in space . . . he's ruined himself."

The most pressing quest in the novel is Rabbit's overwhelming need to find the daughter he believes he fathered twenty years previously. Having buried his weeks-old daughter, Rebecca, and having watched daughter-figure Jill, from *Rabbit Redux,* die in a fire, he yearns for a girl child. He needs redemption for these failures even as he longs for a girl to give birth to his offspring. Convinced he has found her when young Annabelle Byer appears on the lot in the opening scene, Harry immediately feels "an unwitting swimming of her spirit upward toward his." His need to confront his former lover, Ruth, to verify his paternity is a thematic device that pervades the entire narrative. Several times he tracks Annabelle down to a rural Galilee farm, where scenes of Rabbit hiding in the hedges and frantically dodging Ruth's call extend the mystery. At the end of the novel, emboldened by advice from Thelma, Rabbit summons the courage to meet with Ruth, whose protestations about Rabbit's paternity are a bit too much. When she ambiguously tells him, "Suppose she *was* yours. At this stage it would just confuse her," Rabbit reluctantly lets go of the possibility—for now. In the closing scene, Rabbit again recounts the dead in his life, sadly adding "his daughter Annabelle Byer snuffed out with her whole world . . . like those entire planets obliterated in *Star Wars*."

Despite the looming specter of death that pervades the novel and the qualified failure of most of his quests, Rabbit refuses to contemplate his own demise: "He sees his life as just beginning, on clear ground at last, now that he has a margin of resources, and the stifled terror that always made him restless has dulled down. He wants less." In the end, cradling his longed for female offspring, Rabbit may not be running any longer, but he still refuses to give up.

◆ CHARACTERS ◆

Harry Angstrom at forty-six has retained his memories of grandeur on the basketball court, and despite the fact that his waist is now ten inches larger and the image in the mirror often appalls him, he stands tall and attractive in the eyes of the bevy of women who surround him in this novel. Harry's most significant characteristic in this novel is his contentment, a condition that has eluded him since his high-school glory days. Yet problems with his son, Nelson, provide the narrative's necessary conflict to fuel the story. Harry's parenting skills, never exceptionally strong, are much more sorely tested by the adult Nelson. Harry veers from feeling sorry for Nelson to being jealous of him—of his youth, his girlfriend, his freedom that Harry never had at that age. All of these characters, Harry's women and Nelson, are developed only in relation to how they supply or thwart his wants and needs.

Janice has improved with age. Not only does her Springer inheritance supply the family's material comforts, but her newfound sexual appetites also supply most of her husband's physical needs. Trim and tanned from her regular tennis matches at the country club, Janice has forsworn the cotton nightgowns she favored for the first decade of their marriage and now "comes to bed in just her skin, her little still-tidy snake-smooth body" challenging Rabbit's virility. He realizes that he is a lucky man, that his "dumb little moneybags" in her bikini is the envy of the other husbands at the Flying Eagle Club. Updike underscores Janice's dual assets, sensuality and money, in a memorable scene in which she and Rabbit make love among their golden coins. Despite Janice's charms, however, Rabbit still longs for what he cannot have, the younger, even more sensual Cindy Murkett.

Cindy's character is not highly developed. Twenty-nine and the mother of two young children, Cindy exists in the novel only as a tantalizing and elusive dream. Updike writes lovingly about every part of her anatomy, especially in describing the Polaroid self-portraits of Cindy and Webb's sexual positions. Rabbit's scrutiny of these photos when he accidentally stumbles upon them during a party is hilarious: "*Consumer Reports* had a lot to say a while ago about the SX-70 Land Camera but never did explain what the SX stood for. Now Harry knows." Cindy remains an unattained dream, yet Rabbit does not mourn his inability to bed her.

Thelma, the gray-haired, prim wife of his long-time rival from high-school, Ronnie Harrison, serves to remind readers that Harry still retains the "gift of life" which has affected so many women in the past. In the Caribbean when Thelma "with gentle determination pulls him along" as the women choose new partners, Harry is stunned to learn that she "adores" him. The night of totally uninhibited sex that follows is in some ways a payback for Ronnie's sexual activity with Ruth, Rabbit's former lover, twenty years earlier. Their intimacy also serves another purpose. Thelma lovingly encourages Rabbit to confront Ruth about his paternity of Annabelle, thus precipitating the climactic encounter at the Galilee farm.

Annabelle, like Cindy, is an unattained dream, the daughter he has longed for since Rebecca June's death. Rabbit's desire to have a girl-child is ferocious: "Her eyes his blue . . . a secret message carried by genes all that way through all these comings and goings all these years, the bloody tunnel of growing and living, of staying alive. He better stop thinking about it, it fills him too full of pointless excitement." Annabelle is not well developed, but she appears at every key point in the narrative, even driving by the church just as Nelson and Pru enter to get married. One of his "riches" is this secret knowledge that he has another child. Annabelle's mother, Ruth, plays an important role in the novel in that only she has the truth about the girl's paternity, but she appears fully in just one scene. A former prostitute who used to dress in satin and sling-back heels, Ruth is now a caricature of a fierce rural Pennsylvania farmwoman, her iron-gray hair pulled back in a Mennonite bun, her man's red lumberjack shirt and dungarees dirty, her eyes nearly buried under wrinkles and fat, but nonetheless blazing with hostility for the man who deserted her twenty years before. Ruth's revenge is to kill Rabbit's secret dream of having a daughter.

Rabbit does, however, gain a daughter-in-law. Prudence, the young working-class woman Nelson has impregnated, serves as a way of bringing the family together, if only temporarily. Rabbit is entranced with her from the start: "Harry could hardly take his eyes from this grown woman. . . . She breathed that air he'd forgotten, of high-school loveliness, come uninvited to bloom in the shadow of railroad overpasses . . . " He feels "an instinctive" bond with this girl, intuiting that she is pregnant long before it is obvious. Perhaps one reason he and Pru are so in sync is that she shares his opinion of Nelson's shortcomings. As she tells him after their marriage, "You're a little Napoleon. You're a twerp, Nelson. . . . You're horrid about your father when all he wants is to love you, to have a halfway normal son."

Nelson, his father's "enemy," is portrayed in exclusively negative ways. Nelson is so awful that readers may wonder why Updike is so merciless in his characterization, but the author has acknowledged in interviews that his empathy is reserved for the father. Nelson wants to be on the fast track, hoping to major in computer science at Kent Sate, but he is so willfully ignorant that he fails to put forth the effort to pass even the introductory math courses. Underscoring Nelson's academic weaknesses, Updike allows readers to see a misspelled note from the twenty-three-year-old in which he promises not to be any "troble" if he can come back home. Having dropped out of college and failed at his summer job, he arrives in Brewer in a "denim jacket, bought at a shop in Boulder specializing in the worn-out clothes of ranch hands and sheep herders," oblivious to the fact that the price was double that of a new one.

He wrecks Rabbit's beloved Corona, finances gas-guzzling American convertibles which fail to sell at the Toyota lot, and infuriates his father by answering the minister's question about love and commitment to his pregnant fiancee by whining, "I *said* I'd do it, didn't I?" Nelson's woes, as well as his father's antipathy, may result partially from the boy's lack of height and coordination: "that fury against limits had been part of Nelson since he had known he would never be taller than five nine though his father was six three." The last readers hear from Nelson is a postcard from back at Kent State where he has fled after the baby is born: "Need certified check for $1087 . . . plus living expenses. $2000–2500 shd. be enuff. Will call. Melanie says hi." Harry, happy with his granddaughter and daughter-in-law all to himself, seems relieved to write the check. The father rests easy only with his problem son out of the house.

◆ TECHNIQUES ◆

Updike continues the use of the literary techniques he has employed in the previous Rabbit novels: the present tense, intricately detailed descriptions of even the most mundane scenes, a narrative uninterrupted by chapter markings. His use of the present tense gives the reader a sense of immediacy, an even stronger sense that we are living Harry's life along with him. In the closing scene of the novel, when Harry, who "resettles himself in one of his silvery-pink wing chairs," receives his granddaughter, the use of the present tense highlights his bittersweet emotions: "Teresa comes softly down the one step into his den and deposits into his lap what he has been waiting for. . . . Fortune's hostage, heart's desire, a granddaughter. His. Another nail in his coffin. His."

Updike's intricate descriptions, filtered through Harry's decidedly ineloquent consciousness, retain their ability to stun the reader. In this passage, Harry contemplates his failure to grasp the meaning of life, which at forty-six, he believes should have "showed up by now":

> Yet at moments it seems it has, there are just no words for it, it is not something you dig for but sits on the top of the table like an unopened dewy beer can. . . . A ball at the top of its arc, a leaf on the skin of a pond. A water strider in a way is what the mind is like, those dimples at the end of their legs where they don't break the skin of the water quite. When Harry was little God used to spread in the dark above his bed like that . . . and now he has withdrawn, giving Harry the respect due from one well-off gentleman to another, but for a calling card left in the pit of the stomach, a bit of lead true as a plumb bob pulling Harry down toward all those leaden dead in the hollow earth below.

Updike's technique of allowing the narrative to run with only the occasional spatial break also pulls the reader more and more into the consciousness of his characters.

As befits a middle-aged Rabbit, the breaks are more frequent in this novel than in the previous narratives of the younger, more frenetic Rabbit.

A technique in this novel that has not appeared in the previous ones is the use of a frequent comic touch. Perhaps because Rabbit is financially sound, his sex life is fulfilling and his buddies are often around to build him up, he has the luxury of laughter for the first time in his life. Numerous scenes take place after golf at the Flying Eagle Club, as the crowd swaps jokes and crude stories. However, the laughter in the novel is often at Harry's expense. The night before Nelson's wedding, Janice confronts Rabbit with yet another example of Nelson's incompetence, defending her son who has wrecked her car: "It wasn't his fault exactly, this other man just kept coming, though I guess the Stop sign was on Nelson's street." The wedding scene is also written with a light comic touch, the minister emerging with a "*What? Me Worry?* grin" and Rabbit suppressing "a crazy impulse to shout out" when the spectators are asked to speak or forever hold their peace. Another highly comic scene takes place as Rabbit follows Annabelle home, darting from bush to bush to hide from Ruth, now hugely fat and menacing.

◆ LITERARY PRECEDENTS ◆

The most closely related literary precedents are the first two novels in the series, *Rabbit, Run* (1960) and *Rabbit Redux* (1971). In the first, a twenty-six-year-old Rabbit flees his pregnant wife and their toddler son to search for the elusive spark of the divine, or "it," as he so crudely puts it. He is convinced that God does not want him to settle for his "second-rate" life, and so he runs, in ever-tighter circles, ultimately ending the novel back at the starting blocks. Ten years later, Rabbit reappears in *Rabbit Redux,* a novel which portrays the character struggling to cope with life in the tumultuous '60s. On the jacket flap to the first edition of this novel, Updike gives Webster's definition of his title term, "redux": "Lit., led back; specif. *Med.,* indicating return to health after disease."

For *Rabbit Is Rich,* however, it appears that Updike has turned to two much earlier works of American literature for inspiration. Updike acknowledges his debt to Sinclair Lewis' early twentieth-century satire of middle-class America, *Babbitt* (1922), by including a quotation from the solid citizen George Babbitt as an epigraph. He also appears to have been inspired by Frank Norris' novel about the importance of money in middle-class life, *McTeague* (1899). Critics Donald Greiner, in *Updike's Novels,* and

James Schiff, in *John Updike Revisited,* point to scenes in *McTeague* in which the wife takes sensual pleasure in playing with her gold coins, possibly inspiring Updike to create Rabbit and Janice's sex scene with their Kruggerrands. In Norris' novel, the wife is also the one who possesses the money and the couple rekindles their passion for each other by buying a new house.

In interviews Updike has cited Proust as inspiration for his sentence length and the qualities of the perceptions he attempts to convey. Furthermore, a somewhat obscure English novelist, Henry Green, is the "master of the voice in fiction" and inspiration for *Rabbit Is Rich*'s "pick and roll and quickness," Updike claims in an interview published in connection with the novel's winning the National Book Award.

◆ RELATED TITLES ◆

Updike revisits Harry "Rabbit" Angstrom once more in *Rabbit at Rest,* published in 1990. This novel, winner of the Pulitzer Prize, the National Book Critics Circle Award and the Howells Medal, is a long elegy for the fifty-six-year-old character, who becomes convinced in the opening scene that "he has come to meet . . . his own death." The ending of *Rabbit Is Rich,* with its reference to Harry's coffin, foreshadows the subject matter of this final work in the series, and Updike wanted readers to know that *Rabbit at Rest* would be the final visit to the character's inner life. According to James Schiff, in *John Updike Revisited,* Updike published an essay "Why Rabbit Had to Go" two months before publication of the novel and encouraged publishers to use the image of a tombstone on the book's dust jacket. Harry's heart, hardened by selfishness in the first novel, has now become physically hardened by overindulgence in junk food. The novel spans nine months, includes Harry's first heart attack in the opening section, and ends with a scene that echoes the opening basketball scene of the first Rabbit novel. Finally in Florida, yet with the specter of Hurricane Hugo hovering, Rabbit joins a rough pick-up game of basketball with a young black man, during which "His torso is ripped by a terrific pain, elbow to elbow. He burst from within." Harry does survive long enough to enter the hospital, finally sharing conciliatory words with his son "to put the kid out of his misery: 'All I can tell you is, it isn't so bad.'"

◆ ADAPTATIONS ◆

The book has not yet inspired any adaptations to other genres. However, in March of 1983, Books on Tape, Inc. published an audio version of the novel.

◆ IDEAS FOR GROUP DISCUSSIONS ◆

Although this novel is perhaps the most optimistic of the four with Harry "Rabbit" Angstrom as protagonist, it nonetheless offers many controversial themes and characters that stimulate strong debate. Rabbit's treatment of women and his simultaneous disdain and affection for his son are topics that evoke strong reader reactions. The unflattering portrait of America in the 1970s is another theme that can provoke further study about this decade that for many young readers is merely historical. For those who have read the previous novels, inevitable comparisons of previous themes and characters will emerge naturally. Some specific topics for discussion or debate follow:

1. Although Rabbit is "rich," he estimates his income at $40,000 a year. Discuss whether the "rich" of the title is ironic. In what ways is he rich?

2. Rabbit's wealth has been thrust upon him by luck and by economic condi-

tions that are beyond his control. Discuss the circumstances and economic forces that created his good fortune. What might be the psychological implications of this type of wealth?

3. In *Rabbit, Run* circumstances always conspired to keep Rabbit from his quest for spirituality. Discuss how circumstances in this novel seem to conspire to favor him.

4. A central character of *Rabbit, Run* was the Episcopal minister, Eccles. Discuss the role played by Eccles' successor, whom Rabbit refers to as "Soupy." How does he serve to heighten the tensions between father and son?

5. The father-son conflict is the most dramatic clash in the novel. Discuss whether the information readers learn from Nelson's point of view makes him more sympathetic. Is Rabbit justified in his opinions about his son?

6. Many critics have faulted Updike for the attitudes toward women expressed by his characters. In this novel, key women characters are presented more favorably. Discuss how Updike treats Janice, Mrs. Springer (Bessie), and Pru in this novel.

7. The Mt. Judge house plays a significant role in the narrative. Trace its importance in the major conflicts of the novel.

8. Some readers have been put off by the graphic nature of the sex scenes in *Rabbit Is Rich*. Updike has granted countless interviews in which he argues that sexuality should be treated like any other part of life. Discuss the validity of this belief. What would be lost if these scenes were not included?

9. Although granddaughter Judy does not arrive until the final scene in the novel,

her presence is felt throughout. Discuss how her existence propels the action of the narrative.

Harriett S. Williams
University of South Carolina

RABBIT, RUN

Novel

1960

Author: John Updike

With the publication of *Rabbit, Run* in 1960, John Updike began a series of four novels exploring the inner life of Harry "Rabbit" Angstrom, a former basketball star who struggles to find meaning in his chaotic life. In this first novel, twenty-six-year-old Rabbit has left the basketball court where he excelled to find himself failing at work and in his marriage. The remaining novels in the series include *Rabbit Redux* (1971), *Rabbit Is Rich* (1981), and *Rabbit at Rest* (1990). Updike, born in 1932 in Shillington, Pennsylvania, is the same age as Rabbit, who inhabits the world of Mt. Judge and Brewer, Pennsylvania, fictional towns much like Shillington. According to the introduction to the Everyman's Library edition of the quartet of novels, Rabbit is Updike's way of seeing the country and American culture through different eyes. Those eyes belong to an ordinary blue-collar man who refuses to be trapped in a life that he sees as "second-rate."

Rabbit, Run is a portrait of America in 1959. Readers are immersed in the minutia of popular culture: the Mickey Mouse Club, the top ten songs, news of President Eisenhower, the search for the Dalai Lama. It is a time in which Rabbit can support his stay-at-home wife and child on his meager salary from demonstrating the MagiPeel vegetable peeler at the five-and-dime store, a time in which a Chinese dinner for four totals $9.60, monthly rent on an apartment, $110. The economic and political stability of the late 1950s provided many young white men just out of the army, as Rabbit is, with opportunities to build the American Dream.

Rabbit Angstrom, however, suffers from the angst that inhabits his name. He is a feeling, not thinking, man who is ruled by his own worse instincts. He leaves work one March evening, when "things start anew," and crashes a pick-up game of basketball. Discovering that the boys he plays with have not just forgotten him, "worse, they never heard of him," Rabbit nonetheless is elated that the touch still lives in his hands. "Liberated from long gloom," he runs home, but there he feels trapped, "glued in with a lot of busted toys and empty glasses and television going and meals late and no way of getting out." He panics, then runs. The narrative begins, then, with his walking out on his pregnant wife, Janice, his toddler son, Nelson, and his sales job at the dime store. In the balance of the novel, Updike attempts to convey both the shock and the necessity for Rabbit's running.

This ordinary man's quest for "it," for that indefinable something that he knows is missing in his seemingly adequate life, is at the heart of this novel. This psychological search is particularly significant because it takes place not in the 1960s, the turn-on, drop-out decade, but in the tranquility of the Eisenhower years. Harry defines his choices in life as a dead-end job and a burned dinner with Janice or the freedom to run but with no place to go. Updike poses this dilemma which has no good answers, only uncertainty and ambiguity. Even though Rabbit abandons his family and moves in with a prostitute, even though he blindly follows his own sexual urges with no regard to his partners' wishes, he is at times portrayed as a mystic. Mrs. Smith, an elderly woman who hires him as a gardener, explains his unique quality as the "strange gift" of life. As his lover Ruth explains, "You haven't given up. In your own stupid way you are still fighting."

Updike refuses to takes sides in his treatment of Rabbit: readers get the thrill of breaking free from stultifying domesticity, but then we are forced to experience the terrible consequences of the lives he ruins by running. Much of that ruin is the result of Rabbit's sexual urges, which are played out in what was for the time highly explicit detail.

Rabbit finds a brief glimpse of satisfaction in sexual release, but this joy, too, is fraught with danger. His wife Janice is pregnant when he leaves, and his refusal to compromise his sexual satisfaction with Ruth by allowing her to use birth control results in yet another trap, another domestic crisis. In the novel's last scene, Ruth offers him the ultimate trap: marriage to Janice or marriage to her. At the end of the novel, Rabbit runs uphill once more, feeling as though he is a "blank space in the middle of a dense net," still searching, having violated the social contract once again.

◆ THEMES ◆

Updike establishes a central theme of the novel in the epigraph, a quotation from French philosopher and mathematician Pascal: " . . . the motions of Grace, the hardness of the heart; external circumstances." Rabbit, the star athlete, has mastered the motions of grace, but he also yearns for the grace of God, and his search for satisfaction in life is, in large part, religious questing. It is the hardness of Rabbit's heart, usually accompanied by sexual frustration, and the messy external circumstances of his life that ultimately come between him and justification for his sins. Until the final scene of the novel, Rabbit seems secure in his faith that there is something that lies beyond, a something that can elevate him from this second-rate life to a better existence, so he keeps running. Unfortunately, his actions toward grace are guided by his own worse instincts.

The novel begins and ends with flight. Rabbit first runs just after he comes home from selling the MagiPeel peeler to discover Janice, pregnant with their second child and high on Old-Fashioneds, staring blankly at the Mickey Mouse Club. Ironically, head Mousekeeter Jimmy motivates Rabbit's flight when he quotes "a wise old Greek" who warns, "Know thyself . . . be what you are. Don't try to be Sally or Johnny or Fred next door; be yourself." The fastidious Rabbit looks around at the chaos of his apartment that "clings to his back like a tightening net," rejects this unbearable life, and heads out for the straight and clear road ahead.

Impulsively, he takes his car from Janice's parents' house, "hops" onto the highway and turns instinctively south. Hoping to find the mythic land of peace and order on a Florida beach, he instead finds himself hopelessly lost, traveling for hours only to reach West Virginia. Rabbit turns down a dirt lover's lane as "the naked tree-twigs make the same net. Indeed the net seems thicker now." His journey, and the map that represents it, form yet another trap: "The names melt away and he sees the map whole, a net, all those red lines and blue lines . . . a net he is somewhere caught in." He is eventually pulled home, returning not to Janice but to his old coach and mentor, Tothero. Expecting guidance for the "game of life," Rabbit instead receives from Tothero an introduction to Ruth, a former classmate now earning her living from "dates."

Returning home completes the first cycle in the novel and sets the pattern for each of Rabbit's successive flights, futile moves in which he runs in ever-tightening circles. He is always running, from one woman to another, between Brewer and Mt. Judge, between the "good way" and "the right way," searching for transcendence. Because Rabbit's verbal skills are so limited, he can refer to this object of his desire only as "it" or "this thing that wasn't there." He fails to find the elusive "it" except briefly during a game of golf, but he does not stop questing. Rabbit searches through sex, orthodox faith, and family for a sign that life is not meaningless, conceiving of that thing he wants to find as embodied in the perfectly hit golf ball whose trajectory is straight and true, a way "straight out of this mess."

Rabbit appears to long for God's grace, stopping to pray even on the morning after he first commits adultery. Across from his lover Ruth's apartment is a church, and the vision of its rose window comforts him: "this circle of red and purple and gold seems in the city night a hole punched in reality to show the abstract brilliance burning underneath. He feels gratitude to the builder of this ornament, and lowers the shade guiltily."

At two points in the narrative he seems within reach of spiritual grace. When Rabbit is summoned by Eccles, Janice's minis-

ter, to come to the hospital for the baby's delivery, he abandons Ruth and immediately runs to his wife's side. Awaiting the baby's birth, Rabbit tries to repent, to clear his way to the "brilliance." As the Catechism says, "The grace of the Holy Spirit has the power to justify us, that is, to cleanse us from our sins." Rabbit, however, cannot take the last step, asking for forgiveness:

> He is certain that as a consequence of his sin Janice or the baby will die. His sin a conglomerate of flight, cruelty, obscenity, and conceit. . . . Though his bowels twist with the will to dismiss this clot, to retract, to turn back and undo, he does not turn to the priest beside him, but instead reads the same sentence about delicious fried trout again and again.

Returning to his family after Rebecca June's birth, Rabbit finds the "straight path" but is then "too elevated with happiness to ask forgiveness." After attending church and giving incoherent thanks for his daughter among "senseless eddies of gladness," Rabbit's sexual urges again devastate the family. He pressures Janice for sex too soon after the baby's birth, and when she angrily rejects his advances, Rabbit, "thinking of the air and trees and the streets stretching bare under the street lamps," once more goes out the door. Janice lapses in his absence, and drinks until "the worst thing that has ever happened to any woman in the world has happened to her." She accidentally drowns Rebecca June in the bath.

At the child's graveside funeral Rabbit again almost achieves the grace he has sought. As the coffin is lowered, Rabbit recalls the words from the hymn, "*Casting every care on thee* . . . The sky greets him. A strange strength sinks down into him. It is as if he has been crawling in a cave and now at last beyond the dark recession of crowding rocks he has seen a patch of light." However, once again the external circumstances of his life interfere, and as he turns, "Janice's face, dumb with grief, blocks the light." Rabbit's acceptance of God's love seconds before is negated when he reacts by angrily exclaiming to the remaining mourners, "Don't look at *me,* I didn't kill her."

After bolting from the funeral, Rabbit searches in vain for the spiritual light: "Afraid, really afraid, he remembers what had once consoled him by seeming to make a hole where he looked through into underlying brightness, and lifts his eyes to the church window." However, because of "church poverty or just carelessness" it is unlit, merely a dark circle in a stone facade. True Grace denied, Rabbit in the final words of the novel has nothing left but motion itself, so he "runs. Ah: runs. Runs."

◆ CHARACTERS ◆

Updike centers not one, but four, novels around Harry "Rabbit" Angstrom, so it is to be expected that his development, or lack of it, commands most of the narrative. Rabbit's inner life and his quest for meaning and grace occupy most of the omniscient narrator's focus, but on three occasions, the narrator takes readers into the consciousness of other characters: Janice, his wife; Ruth, his lover; and Eccles, his wife's Episcopal minister.

Janice is portrayed as the principle stumbling block to Rabbit's happiness, an immature wife and careless mother who has "just yesterday stopped being pretty." In contrast to Rabbit's physical grace and personal fastidiousness, she is "especially clumsy when pregnant or drunk." Her failure at housekeeping has produced clutter that frightens her husband away: " . . . the Old Fashioned glass with its corrupt dregs, the choked ashtray balanced on the easy-chair arm, the rumpled rug, the floppy stacks of slippery newspapers, the kid's toys here and there broken and stuck and jammed . . . the continual crisscrossing mess clings to his back like a tightening net." Ironically,

Janice does not suffer significantly from Rabbit's first desertion. Eccles tells Rabbit that she and her young son have moved back into her parents' comfortable home, where she enjoys "her own version of your irresponsibility."

Readers get only these brief unflattering glimpses of Janice until near the end of the novel. Then, when Rabbit deserts her again after the birth of the baby, Updike for the first time provides an extensive look into Janice's mind. Drinking heavily to blot out the pain of losing her husband, Janice reviews how she became dependent on alcohol early in her marriage: " . . . she was still dumb little clumsy dark-complected Janice and her husband was a conceited lunk who wasn't good for anything in the world Daddy said and the feeling of being alone would melt a little with a little drink." Ironically, the more Janice drinks in this segment, the more insight readers have into her character. Janice veers from picturing her life happy and single as if in the movies to wishing that Rabbit would abandon his aspirations toward the unknown and come "settle" for their domestic routine. She bitterly resents his need for more than she can offer. Her mother calls to say that her daughter has brought "disgrace" on the family, accusing Janice of incompetence by saying, "The first time I thought it was all his fault but I'm not so sure anymore. . . . I'm not so sure." Realizing that she has lost even her parent's approval, Janice desperately tries to clean the apartment and bathe the baby to impress her mother. It is this drunken need to appear in control to her dictatorial mother that causes her to accidentally drown Rebecca June, unwittingly fulfilling Rabbit's waiting room prediction that his sins would cause either the baby or Janice to die.

Ruth, the lover with whom he lives for two months, is a woman also wounded permanently by her relationship with Rabbit. Ruth, too, is presented in a most unflattering light: her face "caked with orange" makeup; her poorly dyed hair "red and yellow and brown and black . . . like the hair of a dog." She is overweight, crude, and when Rabbit offers her money to "help pay the rent," he calculates his investment as "a dime a pound. And that's not counting the restaurant bill." However, Ruth ironically refers to Rabbit as a "Christian gentleman," and for the two months they live together, he indeed does treat her as a loving spouse, even referring to their first sexual encounter as "our wedding night." Ruth serves as a catalyst for Rabbit's exploration of his spiritual desires as well as his sexual desires. He confesses his belief in God to her, and he is walking with her at the foot of Mt. Judge when he formulates his most coherent vision of man's spirituality: " . . . bothered by God. It seems plain, standing here, that if there is this floor there is a ceiling, that the true space in which we live is upward space."

Ruth, though outwardly tough, succumbs to Rabbit's charms, admitting grudgingly to him that "the whole *world* loves you." Because of his urging, she stops using birth control ("Don't do it. I know what it is. I hate them.") and gets a legitimate job at an insurance company. By Memorial Day Ruth, too, is pregnant. Rabbit, however, does not know about this child, since the information is implied in an omniscient aside to the reader. Ruth does not tell Rabbit about her pregnancy until the last scene of the novel. This information, delivered just after Rabbit has buried his beloved Rebecca June, pleases him inordinately: " . . . he has regained that feeling, of being on top. 'Oh,' he says, 'good. That's so good.'"

But Updike again uses Ruth as a catalyst, this time to propel Rabbit into his final flight. When Ruth demands that he divorce Janice and marry her, threatening to abort the child if he refuses, Rabbit is sent into a tailspin of indecision: "On this small ful-crum he tries to balance the rest, weighing opposites against each other: Janice and Ruth . . . the right way and the good way . . . —and the other way, down Summer Street to where the city ends." He looks at her for the last time, "fat and flushed, her many-colored hair straggled and damp," and runs off the "other way."

Eccles, Janice's family's Episcopal minister, is the third character that Updike develops through an extended stream-of-consciousness narrative. A humanistic, secular preacher whose main concern is pleasing his biological father, Eccles is confused about his own role in society. The bumbling ecclesiast attempts to counsel Rabbit on the golf course, begging Rabbit for his company because of the difficulty of finding partners; "Everyone works except me," he confides. Eccles veers between quoting Belloc and blurting out inane statements such as "Now if *I* were to leave *my* wife, I'd get into the car and drive a thousand miles." Rabbit expects the minister, like the coach, to give him conventional advice, to tell him to go home, get a job, take care of his family. However, just as Tothero made it possible for Rabbit to continue his escape by introducing him to Ruth, Eccles assists Rabbit by arranging for a job with an elderly parishioner, Mrs. Smith, in whose extensive garden Rabbit finds great pleasure and meaning by "lopping, lifting, digging." Eccles interferes in Rabbit's life because he cannot fathom Rabbit's pursuit of "it," and he unwittingly contributes to the coming tragedy. As Ruth puts it, "You've got Eccles to play golf with every week and to keep your wife from doing anything to you. You've got your flowers, and you've got Mrs. Smith in love with you. You've got me."

In an extended passage just before Janice drowns the baby, Eccles, always the social worker, visits both Rabbit's and Janice's families, then introduces himself to the Angstrom family's minister. Fritz Kruppenbach, a Lutheran, has devoted himself to a God of fire and brimstone, to becoming an exemplar of faith. He shames Eccles by thundering: "I was listening to what was said about you . . . the story of a minister of God selling his message for a few scraps of gossip and a few games of golf. . . . I say you don't know what your role is or you'd be home locked in prayer. In running back and forth you run from the duty given to you by God." As Eccles leaves, "His depression is so deep that he tries to gouge it deeper by telling himself *He's right, he's right.*" Instead of heading home to pray, however, Eccles visits the drugstore in the center of town where he drowns his sorrows in an ice-cream soda.

Although Eccles is a concerned, decent man, he is of no help in guiding Rabbit toward grace; indeed, he seems oblivious of the existence of Rabbit's "it." He once asks sarcastically, "Have you ever seen it? Are you sure it exists?" Rabbit's reply helps readers to understand the humanistic character of Eccles: "Well if you're not sure it exists don't ask me. It's right up your alley. If you don't know nobody does."

Ronnie Harrison, a character who is present in only one scene in the novel, nonetheless serves an important role in this and the following novels. Harrison is a former teammate of Rabbit's during their basketball heyday, one of the "other four who were for that time unique in the world," but "never one of his favorites and he has not improved." A salesman in an Ivy League suit, he is now fat and half bald, goading Rabbit about his selfishness on the court: "You were too much a queen to dirty your hands. . . . Harry the bird, he was on wings. Feed him the ball and watch it go in." More important, Harrison goads Rabbit about Ruth's promiscuous past, making it clear that he and many others have purchased Ruth's time. This revelation completely changes Rabbit's attitude toward Ruth, the woman he has treated as a beloved wife for

two months. When they return home, he forces her to commit a sexual act they have not shared previously, and the balance of their relationship, both sexual and personal, shifts. On that same night the call comes from Eccles that Janice is in labor and Rabbit leaves Ruth easily. By introducing athletic competition and sexual jealousy to the narrative, Harrison serves as a bitter rival in this and the subsequent Rabbit novels.

◆ TECHNIQUES ◆

Updike employs the present tense in this novel, a powerful literary technique which was somewhat unusual for the time. The sense is that readers are living Rabbit's life along with him, that no one knows when and where this running will lead. This technique establishes an immediacy that pulls the reader along, as in the opening: "Boys are playing basketball around a telephone pole with a backboard bolted to it. Legs, shouts." And of course, in the conclusion: " . . . he runs. Ah: runs. Runs." Movement is a central theme of the novel, and there would be precious little movement in " . . . he ran."

Updike trained as an artist in the Ruskin School for Fine Arts in Oxford, England, and his visual acuity is evident in the incredibly detailed scenes he sketches, often writing beautifully about the most sordid vistas:

> He hides in the lavatory. The paint is worn off the toilet seat and the washbasin is stained by the hot-water faucet's rusty tears; the walls are oily and the towel-rack empty. There is something terrible in the height of the tiny ceiling: a square yard of a dainty metal pattern covered in cobwebs in which a few white husks of insects are suspended.

Updike devotes as much detail to sexual encounters in the novel, counter to the norms of 1950s literature. The initial sex act between Rabbit and Ruth covers six and one-half pages, including a vivid description of Ruth's post-coital cleansing rituals.

Another Updike technique, which echoes the chaos of Rabbit's life, is the use of a dense narrative, with few official interruptions of the action. Rabbit rarely pauses to think before he acts, so this format echoes the main character's sensibilities. Occasionally, Updike uses a spatial breather, but the book rockets on with only two true stopping places. The first division happens just after Rabbit gets his first glimpse of "it," watching his golf shot recede along a line "straight as a ruler-edge." He finally has escaped the traps, both on the golf course and in his consciousness, and has delivered the ball arcing toward its intended destination. For Rabbit, who earlier could not follow a road south without becoming hopelessly lost, this success is amazing. The narrative stops here, and when it begins anew on a separate page, he is happily laboring in Mrs. Smith's garden, an occupation that seems ideal for any rabbit. The second division is just after Janice drowns the baby, and it signals the final cycle of the novel.

◆ LITERARY PRECEDENTS ◆

Updike revealed his fascination with the notion of a downwardly mobile ex-basketball player in two previous short works. A short story, "Ace in the Hole," originally appeared in the *New Yorker* and was anthologized in 1955. Ex-basketball star Ace drives home to his ineffectual wife, Evey, after being fired from his job, feeling "crowded" by his mother and his wife. Running the last few blocks, he is mesmerized by the sight of a kid across the street "dribbling a basketball around a telephone pole that had a backboard and net nailed on it." This scene, with few alterations, forms the opening of the later novel.

In 1958, he published the poem, "Ex-Basketball Player," about Flick, a player "with hands like wild birds" who holds the county scoring record "still." Also lost after his early athletic success, Flick now "sells gas/Checks oil, and changes flats." He once in a while "dribbles an inner tube," but "most of us remember anyway." At the gas station, Flick "stands tall among the idiot pumps," but he spends his life vainly awaiting the missing crowd's applause.

◆ RELATED TITLES ◆

Updike periodically revisits Rabbit throughout the rest of his life, exploring both Rabbit's inner consciousness and the social and political climate of the United States at ten-year intervals. In *Rabbit Redux* (1971) Updike explores the summer of 1969, complete with racial and cultural tension, as the country first puts men on the moon. Janice is the run-away this time, leaving Rabbit for another man. Rabbit and his son Nelson bring Jill, a real teenage runaway, into their home, and both soon see Jill as a member of the family. Skeeter, one of Updike's rare African-American characters, enters the narrative as a drug supplier for Jill. Ten years later, America is embroiled in an oil crisis, and Rabbit and Janice, together again, have fortunately inherited a Toyota franchise. Set during a time of sexual indulgence, *Rabbit is Rich* (1981) explores the territory of the wife-swapping country-club set, a fairly familiar Updike theme. The final book in the tetrology features Rabbit, age 56, dealing with Reaganomics and his own mortality. This novel, *Rabbit at Rest* (1990), is divided into three segments: "FL," set in the Angstrom's condo on the Gulf coast (Rabbit finally makes it to that beach he headed for in the first novel); "PA", set back in Brewer in familiar territory; and "MI," which readers come to learn is set in the strange land of "myocardial infarctions."

According to Donald Greiner in *John Updike's Novels,* Updike originally subtitled the manuscript of *Rabbit, Run* "a movie," and he wrote the opening scene of Rabbit playing basketball with two young boys after work as background for the title and credits of the film. Greiner reports that Updike later realized that the film medium could not show the ambiguous nature of Rabbit's questing and therefore abandoned the screenplay idea.

However, in 1970 Warner Brothers produced and Jack Smight directed the film version of *Rabbit, Run,* which starred James Caan as Rabbit. Also featured were Jack Albertson and Anjanette Comer. The film, rated R, is still offered for sale, its topic listed as "A former high-school basketball player struggling with an unhappy marriage buckles under the pressures of responsibility." The film version, perhaps because of its inability to convey the moral ambiguities of the novel, was not well received by critics or the viewing public.

◆ IDEAS FOR GROUP DISCUSSIONS ◆

The central contradictions of this novel are ones that most readers face as well and therefore lend themselves to often strong debates. Some readers sympathize with Rabbit's reaction to his circumstances, others condemn him for his selfishness. Learning the difference between lust and love, learning that freedom carries responsibilities, and finding some meaningful work are all issues that young adults must face. In addition to these concerns, the novel provides fodder for analysis and debate about many other issues:

1. Updike has said that he has presented a portrait of American life in the late 1950s in this book. Using the text as an historical document, describe what the country was like, specifically as to gender relationships, the economy, work, and popular culture.

2. Some critics have argued that Updike's novels, especially this one, offer a perspective that is too exclusively male. What evidence is there to support and to contradict this belief?

3. Discuss how Rabbit's early athletic success has ironically condemned him to failure as an adult.

4. Focus on the scenes that precede Rabbit's various flights in the novel. What do they all have in common?

5. The reader may see Rabbit as an ambiguous character, but the women in the novel seem to have unconflicted opinions about him. Discuss how these various women view Rabbit: Mim, his mother, Janice's mother, Janice, and Ruth.

6. Like many young people, Rabbit turns to people in leadership positions for advice when he finds himself in trouble. Discuss the guidance Rabbit receives from his former coach (Tothero) and from his wife's minister (Eccles).

7. One frequent criticism of Rabbit's behavior in the novel is that whereas his abandonment of his wife may be somewhat understandable, his leaving his child is not. What evidence is there in the text that Rabbit really does care for his son?

8. Focus on the scene in which Rabbit works in Mrs. Smith's garden. Discuss why he seems so contented there.

9. Rabbit's relationship with Ruth has, from the first, been more like another marriage than an affair. Discuss what happens at the Club Castanet scene to make Rabbit re-think this relationship.

10. Readers disagree on assigning blame for Rebecca June's death. Analyze how Updike avoids taking sides on this issue by offering readers Janice's own interior monologue. How is this event precipitated by both parents?

Harriett S. Williams
University of South Carolina

THE READER

Novel

1997

Author: Bernhard Schlink

---◆---

◆ SOCIAL CONCERNS ◆

Originally published in German as *Der Voleser* in 1995, Bernhard Schlink's *The Reader* deals with one of the weightiest possible social concerns: the Nazi Holocaust that wiped out over six million people—the majority of whom were Jewish, although Slavs, gypsies, Communists, homosexuals, and Jehovah's Witnesses were also targeted. Set in the 1960s, the novel is concerned with the legacy of collective guilt inherited by the post-war generation, and it raises important questions about complicity and what could have been done differently. Schlink attempts to make his subject-matter manageable by reducing his focus to a single cross-generational relationship—that between the narrator, Michael Berg, and the much older Hanna Schmitz, with whom he has his first sexual encounter.

Michael initially meets Hanna when he is stricken by hepatitis outside her apartment block. She comes to his aid, and months later he visits her to thank her for her assistance. Michael is clearly attracted to her and, in spite of their differences in age, the pair begin a relationship in which Hanna is the dominant partner. Michael's involvement with Hanna is analogous to the post-war generation's engagement with the past.

When years later he learns that his lover was a guard at a concentration camp, he undergoes a period of angst, which forces him to dredge up not only his own emotional past, but also his nation's recent history. The questions he is forced to ask himself are akin to those faced by Germany in the post-war years when he, like many in his country, has to question how he could have loved a Nazi and the extent to which he was seduced and deceived. The novel is concerned with both personal and public justice, and the tensions between the two.

◆ THEMES ◆

The Reader addresses the legacy of guilt that the Holocaust has left behind, and Hanna's question to the judge at her trial, "What would you have done?" is the question that every reader must ask him or herself. The extent to which Hanna is guilty is a complex question and one that Michael attempts to unravel when he demands:

> But could Hanna's shame at being illiterate be sufficient reason for her behavior at the trial or in the camp? To accept exposure as a criminal for fear of being exposed as an illiterate? To commit crimes to avoid the same thing?

Readers may ask themselves these same questions. If Hanna's motive was fear of exposure—why opt for the horrible exposure as a criminal over the harmless exposure as an illiterate? Or did she believe she could escape exposure altogether? Was she simply stupid? And was she vain enough, and evil enough, to become a criminal simply to avoid exposure?

On the one hand it appears that Hanna had no alternatives in a society that stigmatizes illiteracy and values learning. On the other, the not altogether reliable evidence presented at the trial suggests that she took pleasure in carrying out her orders with efficiency and even cruelty. Since he is attempting to reconcile matters for himself, Michael Berg cannot be relied upon for a definitive answer. His recollection that Hanna was startled when he suggested "horse" as a suitable nickname for her leads him to conclude that she was alarmed because of comparisons made between herself and a particularly sadistic guard known as "mare". Yet later, Michael concludes that Hanna was neither stupid, nor evil, nor vain. Instead, he argues that Hanna is struggling for some kind of private truth and justice whose precise meaning must elude all others. Michael's explanation is evasive, and its credibility is open to debate, since he too is attempting to rationalize his own failure to speak out in support of his former lover.

There are also a number of important class tensions in play in *The Reader*, of which Hanna's illiteracy is only one symptom. As a member of the working class, the only time that Hanna is given a chance to speak is at her trial, and even then she is not able to tell her story as she sees it, but must instead answer a series of questions aimed at incriminating her. We are never given any evidence to suggest that she is, before the trial, haunted by recollections of her past and at least a partial explanation for

this must be that Hanna is a character who is forced to live in the present. She needs to earn a sufficient living to stay alive, all the while concealing her inability to read. Unlike the leisured middle classes, she does not have the luxury to spend time contemplating life as both Michael and his philosopher father are able to. Whilst Michael is more or less oblivious to class tensions, Hanna is deeply uncomfortable when he cooks for her in his parents' home. Thus while he is able to inhabit both worlds, Hanna registers the material difference in their backgrounds and feels culturally displaced.

◆ CHARACTERS ◆

The only characters of any real significance in *The Reader* are the narrator, Michael Berg, and Hanna. Although Michael has a mother, a father (who is a professor of philosophy), two sisters, and a brother, they are almost completely excluded from his version of events. Indeed, along with his former wife, Gertrud, and daughter, Julia, the members of Michael's family never attain the status of what E. M. Forster would describe as "rounded" characters. Michael's account is so caught up in his own feelings and with analyzing his relationship with Hanna that for much of the novel he appears completely oblivious to anyone else.

Michael is, by his own admission, far from being a reliable narrator. Early on in the novel he confesses that he has poor recall and that there are details of his time with Hanna which he is simply unable to remember. However, later, when he is musing upon the void left by Hanna's departure, he speculates,

> I had no difficulty with friendships, with relationships or the end of relationships— I had no difficulty with anything. Everything was easy; nothing weighed heavily. Perhaps that is why my bundle of memories is so small. Or do I keep it small? I

wonder if my memory of happiness is even true. If I think about it more, plenty of embarrassing and painful situations come to mind, and I know that even if I had said goodbye to the memory of Hanna, I had not overcome it.

In this unusually candid moment, Michael registers the subjective and selective nature of his memory. It is obvious that he considers himself to have been emotionally damaged through his involvement with Hanna and that to a degree much of his apparent forgetfulness is a willed act of self-preservation. Ernestine Schlant has argued in *The Language of Silence: West German Literature and the Holocaust* that ''the gaps in his [Michael's] memory do not disclose a subtext'' in terms that suggest that this is a flaw in the novel. However, this very absence of any form of sub-text is important because it lays his authority into question and demonstrates the ways in which memories and histories are subjective and can be revised.

Michael's narrative of his involvement with Hanna is clearly a cathartic exercise in which he endeavors to deal with the adolescent pain and feelings of rejection and abandonment that he experienced when Hanna disappeared from his life. However, on a deeper level, he is also attempting to make sense of how he could possibly have loved a woman with a past like Hanna's. The latter question is inextricably bound-up with a wider debate on German national identity and how an entire nation could either have fallen in love with, or been seduced by, the Nazi regime. Since Michael presents his account with the benefit of hindsight there are a number of clues embedded in the text which indicate both Hanna's capacity for cruelty and also her illiteracy. Hanna certainly possesses a number of traits popularly associated with members of the Nazi SS; for example, she is scrupulously, almost obsessively clean, as if she is trying to wash away either guilt or blood. A latent sadism

is also manifested when she and Michael visit Amorbach and have their one serious argument. Hanna's behavior in this instance is confused and irrational; she awakes to find that Michael has disappeared and because she is unable to read the note that he has left for her, she pretends that she has not seen it and removes it. Although Michael returns with a breakfast tray and a rose, Hanna irrationally vents her anger on him with physical violence:

> She was holding the narrow leather belt she wore around her dress; she took a step backwards and hit me across the face with it. My lip split and I tasted blood. It didn't hurt. I was horrorstruck. She swung again.

> But she didn't hit me. She let her arm fall, dropped the belt, and burst into tears. I had never seen her cry. Her face lost all its shape. Wide-open eyes, wide-open mouth, eyelids swollen after the first tears, red blotches on her cheeks and neck. Her mouth was making croaking, throaty sounds like the toneless cry when we made love. She stood there looking at me through her tears.

This scene is of particular importance because it neatly encapsulates the contradictions within Hanna, which become obscured in parts two and three of the novel, where the focus shifts to her trial and her past. Here, Michael is shocked by his lover's violence, but, since the couple make love in the immediate aftermath, he is also aroused by the act, which consolidates Hanna's dominance in the relationship as well as reveals an emotional vulnerability that she had previously succeeded in hiding. Her behavior, though impulsively cruel, is completely at odds with the ruthless and calculating Hanna constructed by the witnesses at her trial and this complicates the Manichaean discussions of good and evil which are normally applied to the Holocaust. She quite literally lashes out because, one assumes, she had thought that Michael had abandoned her, but as soon as she realizes that she has hurt someone she cares about, she collapses.

In the second and third sections of the novel readers gain even less of an insight into Hanna's psyche since Michael reports all of her answers during the trial and he can only speculate as to what she might really be thinking. It is here that Michael's shortcomings as a "reader" come to the fore. He is certainly able to read texts aloud, but he is unable to understand or interpret people. He is also rather lacking in empathy and at key moments in the novel, such as when he visits the site of a concentration camp, he can only speak about what he *thinks* he should be feeling, rather than what he actually feels. Michael's interest in the Holocaust, it must be remembered, does not stem from his relationship with Hanna but from a quest to try to fill an emptiness in his life.

Although Michael seems to hold Hanna responsible for his failings and suggests that her sudden departure caused some form of deep psychological scar, he admits that he had begun to outgrow her and had started to take an interest in other women in the weeks before she left. His reasoning raises questions about the apportioning of blame and the extent to which individuals are prepared to take responsibilities for their actions and the consequences. Michael's own life is an act of evasion. As his wife observes, he becomes a researcher in a bid to avoid the type of engagement with the real world that was foisted upon him when he learned of Hanna's former existence. He is able to read to Hanna, but he will not visit her in prison until the governor requests his presence, and in this respect, he is unable to allow the past to coexist with the present. Like Germany's collective consciousness of the Holocaust, Hanna cannot simply be dismissed through imprisonment or death. She, like the past, is a presence that will stay with Michael and shape his identity, just as Schlink implicitly argues the Holocaust must remain a reality for all.

◆ TECHNIQUES ◆

One of the most important issues raised by *The Reader* is the subjectivity of human justice and the dangers of reducing right and wrong to simplified binary categories. Hanna's acts are certainly never condoned. However, the narrative raises questions about her motivation and demonstrates how socio-economic pressures can foster evil regimes. Indeed, as Hanna asserts towards the end of her life, "I always had the feeling that no one understood me anyway, that no one knew who I was and what made me do this or that". Schlink also presents his readers with different levels of justice and uses the technique of an unreliable narrator, himself recounting unreliable evidence to reveal the fundamental subjectivity of all versions of history. Michael himself is a procrastinator, as he muses:

> But today I can recognize that events back then were part of a life-long pattern in which thinking and doing have either come together or failed to come together—I think, I reach a conclusion, I turn the conclusion into a decision, and then I discover that acting on the decision is something else entirely, and that doing so may proceed from the decision, but then again it may not. Often enough in my life I have done things I had not decided to do.

He makes this admission at the commencement of his version of events and it is certainly endorsed by his failure to speak or act at times of crisis, such as Hanna's trial. Indeed, if one juxtaposes Michael's non-actions with Hanna's actions there is little to choose between the two, and both lead to evil. Schlink's aim above all is not to make his readers judge, but rather to bring them to a point of self-awareness at which they are able to register that it was ordinary people like Michael and Hanna who facilitated the atrocities committed by the Nazis. The Holocaust was not simply the result of a giant, sweeping force of evil, but was caused through complicity and passivity—traits possessed by most people.

◆ LITERARY PRECEDENTS ◆

As Ernestine Schlant has observed, *The Reader* belongs to a category she has labeled "literature about fathers and mothers", penned by the children of the generation of Germans who lived through the Nazi regime in an attempt to make sense of what took place. Michael asks himself, "What should our second generation have done, what should it do with the knowledge of the horrors of the extermination of the Jews?" These novels attempt to grapple with how the new generation should channel its collective guilt and its knowledge of the human capacity for evil. Such works are also usually a way of examining the blame that is apportioned to the parental generation, either because of its complicity with the Nazis or because of its failure to act against the Third Reich. Michael Berg enacts such a process when he goes to speak to his father about Hanna and, like the authors of these works who condemn the previous generation, his failure to speak at crucial moments raises questions as to whether he could or would have behaved differently.

Guenter Grass is one of the most obvious influences on Schlink's novel, and *The Tin Drum* (1959), his magic realist story of the dwarf Oskar Matzerath, presents the reader with a grotesque and macabre allegory in which Oskar's physical degeneration mirrors Germany's moral degeneration. One day Oskar, an inhabitant of the town of Danzig, announces that he will not grow any more and begins to bang a tin drum, which becomes an inane accompaniment to Germany's descent into chaos—a process which is depicted through a dual first and third-person narrative technique.

The Reader also fits into the bildungsroman tradition, which deals with the development and coming of age of a character. It is therefore interesting that the first work Michael chooses to read to Hanna is Homer's epic poem *The Odyssey*, which details Odysseus's adventures whilst returning from war. Odysseus is, of course, in a way that eludes the dysfunctional Michael, able to discover himself and find peace at home with his wife, Penelope. Michael, on the other hand, is left to mull over the past and to ponder on the extent to which Hanna may be held responsible for his failure to sustain relationships.

Thomas Mann's *Doktor Faustus* (1947) and *The Genesis of Doktor Faustus* (1949) are also important predecessors in that they examine Nazism and the relation and responsibility of the artist to society at large.

◆ RELATED TITLES ◆

The philosopher Theodor Adorno famously observed in his essay "Cultural Criticism and Society" that "to write poetry after Auschwitz is barbaric", and Michael Wyschogrod later expanded this comment, explaining:

> I firmly believe that art is not appropriate to the holocaust. Art takes the sting out of suffering. . . . It is therefore forbidden to make fiction out of the holocaust. Any attempt transform the holocaust into art demeans the holocaust and must result in poor art.

While for the likes of Adorno and Wyschogrod, transforming the event into art is a trivializing attempt to contain it, for many survivors and indeed for subsequent generations, writing about the Holocaust has become a way of dealing with feelings of bewilderment, despair, nihilism, and guilt.

Literally thousands of responses have been published since the end of the Second World War, and any selection is bound to be a subjective one. Some of the best known novels dealing with the period include Thomas Keneally's *Schindler's Ark* (1982, later *Schindler's List*), which tells the true story of the industrialist, Oskar Schindler, who saved Jews from being sent to their deaths by employing them in his factory. William Styron's *Sophie's Choice* (1979) attempts to deal with the guilt of an individual Auschwitz survivor, the Polish Catholic Sophie who has resettled in the United States and who is involved with a Jewish paranoid schizophrenic, Nathan. The story is recounted by Stingo, a struggling young writer, and it gradually emerges that Sophie is haunted by flashbacks to her time in the camp and a devastating decision she was forced to make. Paul Celan, one of the most famous poets of the Holocaust, is a Romanian-born writer who worked in France but wrote almost entirely in German. His parents died in a Romanian concentration camp, and he himself was imprisoned for two years in a labor camp. Celan's first collection of poetry *Poppy and Memory* (*Mohn und Gedaechtnis*, 1952) included his 1948 poem "Death Fugue" ("Todesfuge"), which offers a depiction of the camp at Auschwitz.

In terms of literature by survivors, *The Diary of Anne Frank* (1952—posthumous) is perhaps the most widely-known. Elie Wiesel's *Night* (1958) provides a useful starting point and raises a number of weighty questions about the role of mankind in this systematic mass destruction, as well as the types of crises of faith it induced in many survivors. Like Wiesel, Primo Levi also spent time in Auschwitz and his *Survival in Auschwitz: The Nazi Assault on Humanity* (1959) provides a graphic, moving, and at times even humorous account of day-to-day camp life. An invaluable primary source for those interested in first-hand accounts by camp inmates is Dr. Sid Bokosky's archive *Voice*

Vision: Holocaust Survivor Oral Histories, an internet site which holds transcripts of interviews with over 150 survivors. The site is still under development, but may be found at http://holocaust.umd.umich.edu.

For those interested in learning more about the history of the Holocaust Martin Gilbert's *A History of the Jews in the Second World War* (1978) provides the reader with a thorough and authoritative historical overview. Daniel Jonah Goldhagen's *Hitler's Willing Executioners* (1996) raises similar questions to those of Schlink by asking to what extent the German people were willing participants in genocide and what their alternatives might have been.

◆ IDEAS FOR GROUP DISCUSSIONS ◆

Discussions on literature of and about the Holocaust by their very nature often become highly emotive. While the following questions deal with incidents and characters from the novel, the allegorical nature of the text makes it inevitable that the debate will branch out to address wider issues of human behavior and justice. It is important to recognize that Schlink himself does not offer his readers a right or wrong answer, nor is the conduct of any character lauded over that of another. Underlying any discussion on this powerful novel will be Hanna's own demand, "What would you have done?" and this question will allow students to develop their understanding of the text and to suspend immediate moral judgement.

1. Hanna is more concerned that her illiteracy may be discovered than her past as a concentration camp guard. How do the two pasts become intertwined?

2. Why can Hanna only settle to learn to read once she has been incarcerated?

3. How reliable is Michael Berg as a narrator? Why is his unreliability significant to the novel as a whole?

4. In the final chapter, Michael admits that there are several different versions of what he refers to as "our story". He claims that the version we read is the correct one, stating, "The guarantee that the written one is the right one lies in the fact that I wrote it and not the other versions. The written version wanted to be written, the many other versions did not". Does the fact that the story "wanted to be written" necessarily make it right? If it is the definitive account, then why are there other stories that Michael is unable to write?

5. After Hanna's death Michael visits the daughter who testified at Hanna's trial. She insinuates that Michael has been damaged through his involvement with the older woman. To what extent do you agree with the daughter's assessment? Can Hanna be held solely responsible for Michael's shortcomings?

6. Hanna's bookshelf contains a combination of works by concentration camp survivors, Nazis, and Holocaust scholars. What might she be trying to achieve by reading this range of materials?

7. Why does Michael not speak to the judge about Hanna's illiteracy? How could this failure to speak out be connected to the wider concerns of the novel?

8. The work's title identifies Michael as a reader. How effective a reader is he?

9. Michael tells us that he initially enrolled in a seminar dealing with the trials of alleged Nazis out of curiosity. He declares, "I wanted more; I wanted to share in the general passion." Consider the extent to which his interest in the trials is bound-up with an attempt to find himself. Is Michael a voyeur or is he seeking a cause?

10. Why do you think Michael regards it as "both natural and right that Hanna should be in custody"?

Grace Moore
University of Exeter

SOUTHERN CROSS

Novel

1998

Author: Patricia Cornwell

◆

◆ SOCIAL CONCERNS ◆

P atricia Cornwell's central law enforcement concern in *Southern Cross* is the
law's inadequate method of dealing with
juvenile offenders and the growing problem with juvenile delinquents from privileged homes. Her youthful villain Smoke, a
"special needs" child whose real name is
Alex Bailey, had been written up fifty-two
times and arrested six times for crimes ranging from extortion, harassment, sexual assault, and larceny to murder (killing a crip-
pled elderly woman). Charges of activities
that began with disruptive dress, bus mis-
conduct, cheating, plagiarism, truancy, gambling, and indecent literature have escalated to more and more serious wrongdoings
while his parents have turned a blind eye to
his nature. Cornwell blames the parents for
not recognizing the psychopathic and criminal nature of their son and for not taking
steps to control him or institutionalize him
instead of excusing, covering up, and defending his behavior. Yet their motivations
for protecting him are to some degree understandable: a beloved son, he is so very
clean-cut, handsome, and well-mannered
around them and their friends that he simply does not look or act the part of the
juvenile delinquent in front of adults; and
since their image of him does not match the

view of authorities, they assume that he is
being punished because of their money
and position and therefore act to insulate
him from such seemingly unwarranted
accusations.

Smoke is indeed good looking, neatly
attired, and unusually bright, but at his
center he is angry, mean-spirited, sly, sadistic, and irreparably warped. His father is a
banker so he is accustomed to wealth and
privilege, and his mother, who has always
spoiled and protected him, believes he can
do no wrong in spite of the evidence before
her. Her explanation is that he has been set
up by jealous classmates, resentful teachers, and corrupt police. His parents do not
provide Smoke a set of demanding rules
because, in their opinion, any teenager
would just naturally feel challenged to break
the adult imposed strictures. Smoke spent
time in C. A. Training School in Butner for
juvenile offenders, despite scathing letters
from his parents to the district attorney,
governor, and U. S. Senator, but his juvenile
records have been expunged, his finger-
print records and mug shot destroyed. When
Smoke turned sixteen, the age of accountability by North Carolina law, his family
moved to Virginia where he would still be
deemed a minor. These actions reveal that
despite their protestations about their son's

---

innocence, somewhere deep inside his parents understand that all is not well.

Cornwell clearly believes that evil is genetic, that some people are just born to be trouble, no matter how upscale their family environment. Despite his youth, Smoke's predatory, destructive relationship to the world is clearly adult in its malignancy. As the novel begins he is victimizing and robbing ATM users, but such acts quickly escalate to include the murder of a helpless old woman who resists and whom he takes pleasure in tormenting. He shoplifts ten garage remote controls from Sears and uses them to break into the garage-stored weapons locker of a local working man (a stereotypical redneck in the view of the Charlotte investigators); the collection of high powered weapons from this one robbery could arm a small militia. When police officers Brazil and West visit the local high school, Smoke asks them tantalizing and self-revelatory questions about whether a person is born bad or chooses evil and about how police can protect citizens from such bad seeds, and he goes on to argue that these people are probably smart and hard to catch. Their cocky replies about personal responsibility and police competence make Smoke anxious for open combat with them. He fantasizes about shooting off a continual stream of bullets with an AR-15 assault rifle from a downtown rooftop, taking out half of the city cops, "shooting down helicopters and slaughtering the National Guard" (55)—fantasies he later tries to enact on a lesser scale.

A charismatic gang leader, Smoke spurs fellow juveniles to violent acts, and he tortures and terrifies the young males at his school. His Richmond gang consists of Divinity, a dark-skinned teenage exhibitionist obsessed with sex, alcohol, and violence, and three "slaves" (called Dog, Sick and Beeper), younger boys Smoke takes pleasure in ordering around and sending on crime sprees. He tells them where to go and what to do and they follow instructions to prove their manhood and worth (and to avoid Smoke's ire). At the start of the novel Smoke has used intimidation and violence to recruit another youth nicknamed Weed, but the initial tattooing while high on vodka is enough to send Weed running. At the close of the novel Smoke, wearing tool pouches containing a stolen Beretta, four ten-round clips, two fifteen-round clips, and a Glock with three seventeen-round clips, plans to make himself "king" of the Azalea Parade by shooting as many participants and bystanders as he can. His nickname Smoke sums up his ability to mingle with any crowd, look the part of the bystander, and fade out of sight like drifting smoke, but where there is smoke there is fire, in this case firepower, and this juvenile psychopath plans to "smoke" (in the sense of "kill") as many victims as he can.

Thus, through Smoke, Cornwell addresses a number of tough modern concerns: the generation gap, gangs, inept parenting, motiveless violence, drugs and alcohol for minors, the nature of evil, nature versus nurture, the judicial question of the age of accountability, and the legal loopholes through which psychopathic juveniles can escape full retribution or tracking by law enforcement officials. At a time in which mass killings are perpetrated by high school students at good schools, Cromwell's subject matter leads the reader to wonder about the kind of youth that would explode in public violence that results in multiple deaths of strangers. Her answer is a seemingly bright, normal, well-brought up, well-adjusted youth from a moneyed family, a youth who has been forgiven every wrong, who has always had what he wanted, who is brighter than many of his teachers—a bully with a taste for violence—alienated, disfunctional, and criminal.

A recurring theme of *Southern Cross* is regional differences, the differences in mindsets and ways of acting between northerners and southerners and between the citizens of Charlotte, North Carolina, who look to the north for models of propriety and efficiency, and those of Richmond, Virginia, whose southern attitudes are still shaped by the Civil War. From a Richmond point of view, the citizens of Charlotte are "Yankees," "turncoats," and "carpetbaggers." Cornwell mocks Richmonders for their continued devotion to the Lost Cause, the Confederacy, the Southern Cross (the Rebel flag), and Jefferson Davis, the first and last Confederate president. The novel begins with a tongue-in-cheek description of the history of Richmond, from its founding in 1607 by "fortune-hunting English explorers," its "firewater" trade with the Indians, its importation of African slaves, its part in the secession from the Union in 1861, its moment of glory as the capital of the Confederacy, its survival of "other terrible wars that were not their problem because they were fought elsewhere," and its modern-day plight of a shrinking tax base, abandoned downtown businesses, knife-wielding schoolkids, a homicide rate that is the second highest in the nation, and a location on the traffic route of drug dealers moving north and south. Cornwell calls the social chaos and violence of the city "clear evidence that the Civil War continued to be lost by the South."

Furthermore, Richmond's new police chief, Judy Hammer, has come from Charlotte to bring "enlightenment" to the beleaguered Richmond police department, to "hammer" home her ideas. Cornwell says tongue-in-cheek, "She decided it was her calling to move on to other southern cities [from Charlotte] and occupy and raze and reconstruct." Her blueprint for reconstructive action is the New York Crime Control Model, COMSTATE, or computer-driven statistics, a northern "battle plan" for mapping crime patterns and identifying city hot spots and for holding every police officer accountable for everything so there can be no passing the buck and no excuses for failure. Hammer's attempt to introduce a new department shield with the New York motto *Courtesy, Professionalism, and Respect,* or CPR, is met with groans and boos, and gibes about getting hand-me-down NYPD uniforms too. Attempts to add "accountability" to the set of three results in acronyms like CRAP. Cornwell hilariously details Hammer's "occupation of Richmond" and the Richmond police force's rebellion against anything "Yankee" and anything out of the "turncoat" city of Charlotte. Inevitably, the plan proves disastrous. The Richmond cops are "unfriendly" and "unappreciative," and their ways are not northern (nor North Carolina) ways. Ultimately, southern solidarity defeats the aggressive northern assault and sends the outsiders seeking more familiar territory in which to practice their questionable professionalism.

Another theme is failures of communication. Such failures include the inability of parents to communicate with their children, children to communicate with adults, teachers to communicate with students, lovers to communicate with each other, administrators, managers, and employers to communicate with employees, inhabitants of different cities to communicate with each other, and so on. The breakdowns in communication occur across barriers of age, class, gender, race, and region. Oftentimes, such breakdowns are based on erroneous assumptions about the actions, motivations, reactions, and reasoning of others, or on fears taken for truths, or on truths too damning to be faced. Other times the breakdown is born of indifference or pride, snobbery or alienation.

Young Weed sends what he thinks is a clear computer warning to the police about where to find Smoke and his gang's hideout (a screensaver with roving fish homing in on Smoke's territory), but the police mistake it for a sophisticated criminal infiltration of their computer system and are on the alert for a high-level terrorist hacker. The *Richmond Times-Dispatch* police reporter, in turn, is certain that "fish spill" (the covert phrase for the computer fish) is police code for "big trouble" and seeks the big story behind the scenes. Likewise, spurred to an act of defacement by Smoke, Weed paints Richmond's prized statue of Confederate president Jefferson Davis to look like Weed's much beloved, dead brother as a call for help; however, doing so only gets the city up in arms about what citizens think is a racial attack made against the city government, the Confederacy, and whites in general. Mr. Pretty, Weed's Western Civilization teacher, has no idea how to communicate with his youthful charges about his subject or about themselves, while the art teacher, Mrs. Grannis does know how to communicate with them about art but not how to get them to open up to her about the problems and conflicts in their private lives. She can motivate Weed to artistic endeavors but she can not get him to explain how his paintings reflect his inner conflicts, his troubled family life, and the threats from dangerous older students like Smoke. She can touch his heart but not open it to examination. When he refuses to deliver a report he has worked on diligently for weeks, she accepts his failure to perform as a sign of his laziness rather than as a sign that something is truly amiss in his life. Deputy Chief West hides her fear of rejection behind curses and orders and blunt statements of discontent, distancing herself from her former lover when all he and she want is to be in each other's arms. He, in turn, is blind to West's need for him and actively works to increase her jealousy when, in fact, it is

jealousy that keeps them apart. Bubba's mechanic tries to convey to Bubba the need to distrust his former school chum, Smudge, who sells him a car that is a lemon (it has been previously wrecked) and takes advantage of him in a number of ways, but Bubba can not see past the illusion of friendship to the reality of exploitation. The police officer who pulls Bubba over can not see past the Southern Cross on Bubba's fender and the whiteness of his face, and reads racism where none is intended, just as Bubba misunderstands the black police officer's fears and imagines he is purposefully mocking his name, as so many former classmates did. On every level, among every group in the novel, characters fail to communicate in both minor and significant ways.

Other minor themes include the inevitable conflicts that result from factions with competing interests in the workplace and in the political realm, the conflict between tradition and modernity in city councils, the vulnerability of the elderly to urban crime, and the inadequacy of schools to deal with youths with easy access to drugs, alcohol, weapons, and information.

◆ CHARACTERS ◆

Southern Cross's characters are varied and distinct but at times seem painted superficially. Police Chief Judy Hammer, whose husband has recently died and who is purposefully breaking her ties with the past, is driven by a vision of proper police organization, but her closest companion is a bug-eyed Boston Terrier named Popeye (she talks to him about all her difficulties). Her deputy chief Virginia West is irritable, unhappy, and unbearably lonely; she has had an affair with a younger officer and feels inadequate, old, and unattractive. She expects infidelity so she finds it (though in fact it is nonexistent). She pushes Andy Brazil away when in reality she wants to hold him close. She too is dominated by a pet, a remarkably intelligent Abyssinian cat named Niles, who seems to intuitively make the computer work in his master's best interest. The private lives of both women repeatedly interfere with their public endeavors, and their pets seem to have more realistic and balanced visions of their owners' reality than do the owners themselves.

The love interest of the story, Andy Brazil, is a tall, handsome, blond with striking, chiseled features. Virginia West glares at him with anger at his defection and longs for his return. Brazil's father died when he was ten, and his mother was a miserable drunk who saw her son as simply an extension of her own sorrow. He is cocky and competent, a computer whiz. He relates easily to troubled youths like Weed, is kind to his nosy elderly landlady (whose calls to his office he has used to make West jealous), is adored by animals (both Popeye and Niles snuggle up to him), and is the only officer in the novel who comes close to understanding what is going on in the community. However, he has all the frailties of youth and is unable to decipher the complex mix of emotions that drives West.

The high school teachers and students make up another set of characters, with the teachers barely making an impact and with Weed and Smoke the two dominant figures in opposition. Weed is a decent youth with artistic talent, a love for his older brother who died, and a healthy sense of danger. He gets involved with Smoke against his will, intimidated and harassed into being initiated into a club he wants no part of, but he does not trust adults enough to share his fears with them. However, when he gets taken into police custody and understands the depths of Smoke's violence, he willingly testifies against him, and, in doing so, helps prevent a massacre. Smoke, in contrast, looks like every parent's dream but, in fact, is every parent's nightmare. He has learned to manipulate the system, his parents, his teachers, and his classmates to attain his ends. He is clever and bloodthirsty and takes sexual delight in sadism, but he fails to consider the long-term repercussions of his acts. After the fact, the police learn that he has manipulated his school records, faked his identity, and done his best to avoid the usual links by which the authorities could trace his whereabouts and tie him to particular school activities.

Still another set of characters circle around Bubba Fluck. These include his erstwhile friends (like Smudge), mechanics, employers, and fellow employees, all local Richmond types. Cornwell stereotypes them to a large degree as working-class Southern males with "good ol' boy" values, men who appreciate hunting and fishing more than anything else in life, who talk dogs, cars, cigars, and fish flies, and who have known each other—for good or ill—since childhood. Fluck, for example, has striven hard to overcome his name; he is an odd mixture of knowledgeability and incompetence, of efficiency and inefficiency, and the reports of his activities are both wonderfully comic and sadly pathetic.

Readers never truly enter the hearts of these characters though Cornwell does take time to humanize them to some degree as a counter to the stereotypes various characters have of each other: white stereotypes of blacks, black stereotypes of whites, outsider stereotypes of Southerners, Southern stereotypes of northerners, and so on. However, the authorial voice distances them from the readers and keeps them more figures of amusement and satiric targets than three-dimensional characters to whom readers can relate.

◆ TECHNIQUES ◆

Cornwell's approach in *Southern Cross* is at odds with that of her other detective novels. In this story, the key crime investigators, Chief Judy Hammer, Deputy Chief Virginia West, and Officer Andy Brazil, all three formerly from Charlotte, North Carolina, are out of their depth and out of their territory in Richmond, Virginia, and their "northern" take on crime, efficiency, and methodology are totally at odds with the sleepier patterns of their Virginia colleagues. The clash between investigative forces weakens the detective pattern and makes it vulnerable to digressions. Instead of the usual straight line from crime to detection, Cornwell leaves her investigators misdirected and misinformed. Hammer hears a muddled conversation that breaks in over her cell phone and leaps to the erroneous conclusion that a commonplace discussion of hunting and hound dogs is two rednecks planning a racially motivated hate crime, a homicide involving robbery. The "cold nose" of the dog she takes to be slang for a snub-nosed revolver and the dog's name "blue" she assumes to mean a blue steel gun (as opposed to a stainless steel or nickel-plated one). Thus, she chases down a non-existent conspiracy and never knows anything about the real threat to her new city. Communication breaks down between West and Brazil (she thinks he has a new lover; he thinks she used him and then rejected him because of his youth), and only Brazil's accidental contact with some of the city's young people (at one point they try to steal his car) connects him with the ongoing crime spree and final attempted massacre. The Richmond police mock their new supervisors and revel in their mistakes.

Consequently, instead of a tight focus on crime, investigation, and the processes of justice, this novel employs the strategies of satire, with many of its many characters and with organizational politics bearing the brunt of Cornwell's attack. One level of Cornwell's satiric attack occurs at the verbal level, such as calling the Civil War "the war that was not forgotten," naming a rural character Butner Fluck IV (whose cruel childhood classmates have variously called him "Fluck-head," "Mother-But-Flucker," and so on), or setting up parallel series that end in deflation: "Thomas Jefferson designed Monticello, the Capitol, and the state penitentiary" and he "founded the University of Virginia, drafted the Declaration of Independence, and was accused of fathering mulatto children." A teenaged black youth mispronounces "mead" and "pact" in his Western Civilization class and defines them as follows: "*Med* is what you feel when someone disses you. And *paced* is what you use in art class." The humor and the tragedy is that he is not trying to make a joke; he is earnestly striving for a right answer.

Another satiric method Cornwell employs is the sight gag. In one instance, the gag centers around the statue of Jefferson Davis, the symbol of the South and for Richmonders, a reminder of past glories lost. Forced by Smoke to vandalize and desecrate the statue of Jefferson Davis in the local cemetery park, Weed chooses disposable water-based paints that will wash off in the first rain over more permanent paints whose defacement would be longer lasting. However, no one knows this, and the city fathers believe they are stuck with a real embarrassment. Weed, in tribute to his dead brother who was a successful basketball player, has transformed the only president of the ill-fated Confederacy into a black basketball player, wearing the red-and-white uniform of the University of Richmond Spiders; his footwear has been painted as Nikes, the hat Davis holds in his left hand has been made to resemble a basketball, and the marble base that supports him has become day-glow orange.

Cornwell includes traditional satiric figures like the malaprop and the rustic. Her bubbleheaded Lelia Ehrhart, a vocal community spokesperson originally from Yugoslavia, repeatedly mispronounces and confuses words and grammar to create a tangle of nonsense. She adds "s's" to verbs where none are needed, transposes word order, mixes pronoun references, speaks of "a front to our unalien rights," "cold-bloody juvenile delinquents" that "descegraded everyone sitting in their room'" and calls Hammer a "Jack Footed Thung" who does not give a "hoo" about crime prevention. Cornwell's rustic, Bubba Fluck, is unlike other "fearless men devoted to pickup trucks, guns, topless bars, and the Southern Cross" because, as the son of a theologian with a deaf ear to the possibilities of his son's name, he has had to strive hard to fit in as a redneck hick for whom hunting, cars, dogs, and weapons are the most important part of his life. Cornwell makes fun of his excesses (a garage full of lovingly cared for weapons capable of terrible destruction) and his vulnerability to being ripped off by his supposed friends, but at the novel's end she locates him in the right place at the right time to give the police a hand with the real evil. In effect, Cornwell suggests that, to outsiders like her detective team, Bubba is the stereotypical Southern bigot and potential criminal, when, in fact, he is a decent, law-abiding citizen with grander dreams than he can attain, while the real villain is an assimilated urbanite, handsome, smooth-talking, and seemingly presentable but wicked to his core. Her metaphors about Bubba Fluck carry a satiric edge, as when she describes his intolerance for tailgaters resulting from his being "a cowboy herding cattle on the open prairie of motoring life." Her descriptions of everything associated with him are tinged with comedy. Typical are several pages devoted to a running conversation with his mechanic about his failures at home car repairs, getting turn signals on backwards, setting the trouble light to come on inside the car trunk so the battery dies, forgetting the cotter pin so the wheels drop

off—details not comic in themselves but comic in mass.

In keeping with her customary reliance on contrast, Cornwell alternates between sets of characters: Bubba, his family, and friends; Smoke and his gang, sometimes including Weed; Weed and his desperate attempts to escape Smoke's control; Hammer, West, and Brazil; and the Richmond police. These characters meet and interact in surprising ways. For example, Smoke visits a car repair shop and meets Bubba, whose chatter with his friendly mechanic yields information about a Sears remote control for Bubba's garage, where he keeps not only expensive machinery but also an impressive collection of weaponry. Smoke's theft of these weapons brings the police back to Bubba as a murder suspect. The accidental interruption of Hammer's cellular phone call by Bubba's conversation with his friend Smudge sends Hammer searching for racist killers but makes Bubba think he has a mandate from heaven to protect Hammer. Thus, throughout the novel, Cornwell interlocks the lives and actions of her characters through odd nexuses.

◆ LITERARY PRECEDENTS ◆

In *Southern Cross*, Cornwell moves into the territory of the Southern Gothic and of the satiric. Her literary precedents are Flannery O'Connor, as in the short story "A Good Man is Hard to Find," and John Kennedy O'Toole, as in the novel *A Confederacy of Dunces*. These are stories which depict Southern regional types with a satiric edge and which capture the differences between their world view and mainstream views. O'Connor captures the religious obsessions and metaphysical speculations that produce a cold-blooded existential killer, a rural misfit striking out at the emptiness and meaninglessness of the universe; O'Toole, in turn, spoofs Southern ways (in this case, South Louisiana ways) of thinking and acting, and paints hilarious portraits of eccentric behavior and Southern urban oddities.

In general, detective fiction lends itself easily to satire as a means by which to attack human frailties and the limitations of human institutions. The infusion of satire into the detective fiction medium is a means of breaking with formula and of adding further dimensions to a form usually characterized by clear-cut conventions. Sometimes such satire has been aimed at the detective genre itself, as in E. C. Bentley's parody of the contemporary detective in *Trent's Last Case* (1913) or in Agatha Christie's spoof on mystery writers in *Cards on the Table* (1936). Michael Innes's archly-written classical mystery spoofs are almost as abstract, convoluted, and obscure as stories by Jorge Borges. *Death at the President's Lodging,* (1989), for example, involves a puzzle-like mystery solved by a socially and intellectually superior detective who is quite at home in the elevated milieu of an Oxbridge college and who is as snobbish as those with whom he must deal. The third-person objective narrator stands above the lowly beings whose voices he records. Cornwell's affectionate but mocking portraits of her Charlotte detectives in Richmond are very much in this literary tradition, but are much more concrete and personal. The snobbish overtones of the third-person objective narrator are there, but so is a concrete delineation of the specifics that merit such snobbery.

However, in addition to spoofing the genre, Cornwell is also satiric about the region and the city in which her action takes place. A number of detective stories have mocked the pretensions of the types their characters portray. These include literary snobs, aristocratic twits, and artistic dabblers. Robert Barnard's *Death of an Old Goat* (1974) is a devastatingly humorous depiction of the smug hypocrites of Australian academia, while the Emma Lathen series of Wall Street mysteries expose the deviousness, greed, and falsity of the business world. Even the stories of Dashiell Hammett have a tinge of satire in their portraits of urban corruption and sleazy politicians. Cornwell, in this tradition, lays bare a city, its problems, its dreams, its pretensions, and its interior conflicts.

◆ RELATED TITLES ◆

The satiric detective story is rare in modern publishing, but does, occasionally, appear. However, it is more often a British than an American form. Robert Barnard's *The Bad Samaritan* (1997) is a good example of the genre, with its seamlessly plotted whodunit tale and yet its droll humor at the expense of small town gossips and tattletales. Therein, a pastor's wife who has lost her faith takes a seaside outing to rethink how her new mind-set changes her marital role. At her seaside hotel, she befriends a young Bosnian employee, whose wife and daughter remain in his beleaguered homeland, but when he follows her to her husband's parish, enlists her aid in his search for employment, and ends up a suspect in a murder case, she begins to see her village and her relationship to it in a new, less agreeable light. Barnard's *The Corpse at Haworth Tandoori* (1999) is closer in its satiric method to Cornwell's, for it features a black detective constable, Charlie Peace, whose skin coloring marks him as an oddity in the small English villages where he seeks answers to questions about murder, and its suspects are a small, eccentric set of people quite different from those normally experienced by the investigating detectives—an artist's colony consisting of a famous but irascible, aged painter, his haughty wife, their truculent son and daughter, a part-time cook with regional characteristics, and a number of oddballs living in the little cottages edging the great man's quarters. The offbeat characters and bizarre yet ultimately credible scenario make this British study of region, character, and eccentricity very much in the same vein as *Southern Cross*.

Cornwell's *Hornet's Nest* (1997), a prequel to *Southern Cross* set in Charlotte, North Carolina, is also a satire about crime and police but is somewhat less zany than *Southern Cross*.

◆ IDEAS FOR GROUP DISCUSSIONS ◆

Because *Southern Cross* departs widely from Cornwell's usual detective pattern, it is worth considering how and why. How does adding an element of satire to the traditional format change the detective genre and the reader's reaction to it? Certainly, where normally the narrative voice is distant or "transparent," the detectives are competent, and the suspect deserves investigation, in the satiric detective novel certainties and verities are missing. In this case, police actions are bungled; their complex computer systems are defeated by a well-meaning and ill-educated youth; and regional antagonisms dominate their responses. Cornwell emphasizes the clumsiness of her detectives, their preconceptions and prejudices, their difficulty adjusting to a new social environment, and the personal motives that affect their performance. At the same time she shows the humanity behind the "redneck" country-boy suspect: the superficial behavior and characteristics that arouse police suspicions and black-white antagonisms but that are really harmless patterns of a class and a region. The fact that her villain would seem, to all outward appearances, the best of youngsters from the high school crowd confirms her overriding theme of the deceptive nature of appearances.

1. As a satire, this novel is intentionally critical. List Cornwell's satiric targets. Comment briefly on each.

2. What is the function of Weed in the story? Why is he included? How is he set in contrast to Smoke and why? What makes him sympathetic? How does he further the plot?

3. What is the significance of the episode with the statue of Jefferson Davis?

4. Bubba is a stereotypical redneck, and yet he rises above this limiting role. Explain.

5. Cornwell always builds her novels around contrasts in characters. What particular contrasts dominate *Southern Cross*? Why are these contrasts important?

6. This article discusses some breakdowns in communication in the story. Find three additional examples of such breakdowns and explain how they affect the action.

7. What traditional elements of detective fiction remain in this novel? What is traditional about the ending?

8. How are the traditional elements changed by the satire?

Gina Macdonald
Nicholls State University, Thibodaux, LA

THE THANATOS SYNDROME

Novel

1987

Author: Walker Percy

◆━━━━━━━━━━━

◆ SOCIAL CONCERNS ◆

In 1961, at the ripe old age of forty-five, Walker Percy began his somewhat untypical but nonetheless illustrious career as a novelist with the publication of a slim novel set in New Orleans, *The Moviegoer*. The book was warmly received by the critics, edging past even Joseph Heller's smashingly popular and universally acclaimed *Catch-22* to capture the National Book Award, and finding a spot in the hearts of so many readers that it has never been out of print. Twenty-six years and six books later, two of them highly readable and thought-provoking volumes of nonfiction, Percy published what proved to be the last novel before his death, *The Thanatos Syndrome*. In a way, it was perhaps a fitting culmination of his belletristic career (in 1991 a posthumous collection of his nonfiction essays appeared in print under the title of *Signposts in a Strange Land*), inasmuch as it bolted within two weeks into the top ten of national best-seller lists, becoming a dual main selection of the Book-of-the-Month Club and rapidly selling out the first printing of 75,000 copies. Looking back at *The Moviegoer* in a 1984 interview, the author summed up his first novel in these words: "Yes, it's probably a good novel to teach; it's open to being taught because academics, after all, are interested

in ideas, and this is a novel of ideas as well as, I hope, a good novel in its own right." A novel of ideas as well as a good novel in its own right: no other words could serve as a better introduction to *The Thanatos Syndrome*.

Percy's near-future yarn reintroduces Tom More, a protagonist-psychiatrist who this time investigates the mysterious and, as he discovers, sinister conspiracy involving the diversion of heavy sodium coolant from a local nuclear reactor, a covert sociomedical experiment on the populace at large, an organized ring of sexual abusers and pedophiles, and perhaps worst of all, doctoring the human psyche in ways that lead to the loss of the "self." More's namesake is, of course, Sir Thomas More, the esteemed writer, scholar, philosopher, diplomat and statesman under Henry VIII, author of that famous social tract and literary trailblazer, *Utopia,* and a Catholic martyr who chose beheading at the order of his monarch rather than forswear the Catholic orthodoxy which forbade divorce and remarriage. More's manifold intellectual and moral endowments, brought to the untimely end in the wake of his steadfast refusal to accede to Henry's breakaway from Rome and the establishment of the Anglican church, earned him in the modern era the reputation of a man of integrity and enlightenment as well as the nickname of "a man for all seasons" in a celebrated movie of the same title. Appropriately enough, in the *Newsday* review of *The Thanatos Syndrome*, the creator of the fictional Tom More had been dubbed as a writer for all seasons and, one should hasten to add, for all readers.

Just like his previous novels, many of them at once serious and comic, profound and popular, erudite and accessible, *The Thanatos Syndrome* offers that and more, adding to the writer's already formidable reputation. In less than 400 pages Percy takes the reader through a mosaic of literary styles, themes and genres which would have buried a lesser writer. His last novel is all at once a brilliant medical thriller, surely one of the best in this demanding subgenre; a superbly nuanced and comically underplayed Southern novel of manners; a taut crime drama, with all the requisite elements of detection and suspense developed with a quirkiness and unpredictability that have become the author's hallmarks; and finally a moving and disturbing philosophical *roman*, demanding to be weighed and pondered long after the last peal of laughter has died.

There are many aspects of society and its management that Percy takes to task in his novel; after all, as he admitted with no qualms to Ashley Brown, "A good deal of my energy as a novelist comes from malice, the desire to attack things in our culture, both North and South." Yet underneath the variety of targets that draw his fire there is a common stem—what the novelist sees as a disturbing analogy between the cultural and medical practices of Weimar Germany and present-day America. In the world of *The Thanatos Syndrome*, removed into a familiar and only marginally different future, he gives vent to his fears by imagining a landmark Supreme Court decision which establishes a morally perilous precedent. The fictional *Doe v. Dade* case, which links

the advent of personhood in children to their acquisition of language, thus fixing it at about 1.5 years of age, allows for the termination of the life of children younger than one and a half who for various reasons— genetic, medical, intellectual—are deemed unfit to develop in society. Through the practice of such "pedeuthanasia" Percy naturally alludes to the famous pro-choice decision reached by the real-life Supreme Court in the case of *Roe v. Wade*, ruling that state laws banning abortion during the first six months of pregnancy are unconstitutional because they violate the "right to privacy" arising from the Fourteenth Amendment. As a staunchly Catholic writer (a convert to the Roman creed as an adult, following his prolonged and near-fatal fight with tuberculosis), Percy is at pains to suggest a parallel between fictional pedeuthanasia and the real-life practice of clinical abortion in medically and socially warranted situations, the latter, of course, severely condemned by all papal decrees.

Whether one agrees with Percy's orthodox Roman Catholic view of the moral and medical justification of permitting access to abortion, it remains an indisputable fact that, as Tom More would say, he is on to something. Couched in various ideological or medical cloaks, frequently derived from misguided ethnocentric or racial "theories," there have been numerous instances of eugenetic intervention in modern societies, their programs of betterment quickly becoming tantamount to partial or even total elimination of undesired individuals (the former through various forms of sterilization, the latter through outright killing). The most publicized (at least in its later stages) and systematic campaign of this kind remains, of course, Nazi Germany's planned extermination of the Jewish race; still, Percy is careful to point out that, if truth be known, it was actually a pre-Nazi German medical establishment— in some cases involving some of the most prestigious and humanitarian doctors and scientists—that initiated a eugenetic program for the purification of the Aryan stock. Such amelioration of the German nation through the "(ex)termination" of the unfit, i.e., the retarded, the autistic, the chronically ill, the genetically "inferior" (and later, inevitably, the politically subversive), has been instituted on a scale encompassing thousands of people, all in the name of . . . What? asks Percy, leaving us in no doubt that he perceives little value in the empty slogans of nation, patriotism, purer genetic stock, nothing that would transcend in value even a single human life. A society of Alfas that elects to get rid of its "inferior" Gammas, to use the shorthand nomenclature invented by Aldous Huxley for his *Brave New World*, is not a society worth living in.

Yet Percy's concern is even more wide-reaching, going beyond the scientific community and his accusatory portrayal of them as akin to pre-Nazi doctors ("So far," as he grimly reported in 1988, "the doctors haven't picked up on it"). The author's concern about the medical sanction of fictional pedeuthanasia and nonfiction abortion by no means indicates an opposition to or an indictment of science, to which he has always professed a strong allegiance. "I don't have any quarrel with science," is how Percy dismissed such patent misapprehensions of his concerns in the interview which appeared in the month of his death (May 1990). In an earlier novel which featured Tom More, *Love in the Ruins* (1971), the author goes as far as to make his protagonist openly profess his faith in science, its laws, its rationality, and its ability to contribute to society. Instead it is those who dictate policies of national "salvation," no matter which side of the political spectrum they come from, that fill the author with foreboding. Unopposed, often sanctioned, and sometimes even encouraged by the rest of us, they often look for scapegoats for their own failures, being ever ready to

impose technological all-or-nothing solutions precisely in social situations which require patience and humane vision. "Does anyone imagine that we are not capable of doing what the Germans did, or what the Stalinist Russians did given the proper circumstances?" The writer's bitter nonfictional warning is more than appropriate; it is true. In the book it is echoed in Father Rinaldo's confession about his visit to Germany in the 1930s, and in his simple admission of adulation for a dashing Hitler Jugend cousin destined for the SS: "If I had been German not American, I would have joined him."

Ultimately, Percy is concerned about our civil rights and access to information, including information about scientific experiments which may impinge on the population at large. This is not paranoia: after the hydrogen-bombing of the Bikini atoll and the innocent people living there, after the programs to covertly infect army soldiers with syphilis for the sake of monitoring the progress of the disease, after experiments with radiation exposure, hallucinogens, pathogens like nerve gases and the like, there is a great deal of nervousness and distrust of grand social projects for the betterment of society. It is true that in the novel it is a renegade group of doctors and scientists who administer heavy sodium ions to about 100,000 people of West Feliciana through the water supply system. Yet the fact that they do it without the knowledge or approval from the FDA or any other legitimate agency does not mean that such rogue actions are just a figment of the writer's imagination. As the Watergate and Iran-gate scandals of our recent past prove, it is possible for a few conspirators to penetrate even the highest echelons of policy-making and operate for a long time without detection (and, at least for the majority of the culprits, with subsequent impunity).

The picture is not, of course, as one-sided as this brief account might suggest. Percy is far too skilful a writer and *The Thanatos Syndrome* far too accomplished a book to reduce such complex issues to an imaginary standoff between the forces of good, represented by the nice and innocent citizenry, and unmitigated evil, incarnated in the sinister group of technocrats. The actions of the Fedville clique, spearheaded by Dr. Bob Comeaux and under the scientific tutelage of John Van Dorn, are motivated by a very real and mounting concern for the decline of the quality of life in America. This time, however, it cuts deeper than a concern for material affluence or this or that tenet of isolationist Cold War ideology. As Van Dorn puts it, the country is rent asunder by three plagues of almost biblical proportions: "One: crime. We can't go out in our own streets. . . . Two: teenage suicide and drug abuse, the number-one-and-two killers of our youth. Number three: AIDS." There are, of course, horrendous statistics to back him up, and the fact that the Fedville doctors attempt to cure the symptoms rather than the underlying causes only adds to the feeling of catastrophe enacted daily in the inner cities around the United States.

◆ THEMES ◆

The most frequent among the infrequent criticisms levelled at Percy's novels is the charge of repetitiveness in plot and theme. Although *The Thanatos Syndrome* is in many ways radically different from anything he had written previously, there is indeed a great deal of overlap in theme with his earlier novels. This fact, however, has nothing to do with lack of inspiration or even a monomaniacal attachment to a given range of experience. It is simply a testimony to the novelist's heartfelt belief in the importance of highlighting certain problems and issues, and to his belief that their continued presence in our lives demand continued fictional (and nonfictional) scrutiny.

As behooves an ex-scientist with thorough medical and pathological training, Percy himself coined a name which encapsulates his particular brand of the philosophical *roman:* the diagnostic novel. With the term's clear emphasis on the cognitive and moral content, there is nevertheless an additional connotation stemming from the fact that *The Thanatos Syndrome* is also a medical thriller. As such, it is almost inevitable that the author returns in it to the theme which had appeared on numerous occasions in his other works: the paradoxical relation between the ostensibly "abnormal" and the rest of the nominally healthy and sane society. The recovery of the real through the ordeal of pain, suffering, or illness forms, indeed, the bedrock of almost every Percy novel. It is rooted in his conviction, *pace* Carl Jung, that at least some of our neuroses, psychoses, anxieties or depressions may be more than just symptoms; they may be resources for learning something about our inner "selves," which may be trying to tell us things of value in these strange and sometimes pathological ways.

In the novel the relationship between the sane and the abnormal seems to be curiously reversed, almost like in Saul Bellow's *Herzog* (it may be worth noting that the author himself described his fictional design as combining Bellow's depth of character and Vonnegut's outrageousness and satire). In fact, this relation is not unlike the medieval or Renaissance courts, in which the royal "fool" would often usurp the role of an "idiot savant," a jester whose position granted him a special dispensation to speak truths that would be punishable in the mouths of others. In *The Thanatos Syndrome* the words of apocalyptic warning come thus from the mouth of Father Rinaldo Smith, an aging, decrepit and cranky priest given to seizures, catatonia and bouts of peculiar behaviour. Hardly a prepossessing subject for an oracle of profound social insight, he is, however, a typical Percy creation meant to make us question who really deserves to be branded as crazy.

Are the people routinely condemned as insane, unfit and abnormal (in a clear allusion to eugeneticists making decisions based on racial and intellectual attributes) to be disposed of in mental asylums, prisons, or even through painless and humane euthanasia? Or are they perhaps blessed with a clearer vision, a vision so penetrating in fact, that it blinds the rest of us to its sense? For the fact is that the paragons of the Feliciana community—John Van Dorn, scientist *sans pareil,* and Bob Comeaux, the super-physician—turn out after all to be ruthless and immoral techno-wizards, happy to turn the entire region into unwitting guinea pigs (or even more aptly, into laboratory chimps). On the other hand, the same Father Smith who during his sermon outrages, bewilders and alienates his parishioners, does so because he admonishes them that pedeuthanasia practised even for the most humanitarian reasons can all too easily degenerate into eugenetic murder. "Tenderness leads to the gas chamber," pontificates Father Smith in front of his gasping church audience, like Herzog becoming the madman who dares utter things that no normal person would, partly out of fear of being regarded as abnormal. "No one doubts the malevolence abroad in the world," argued Percy in a post-publication interview. "But the world is also deranged. What interests me as a novelist is not the malevolence of man, so what else is new? but his looniness."

Another important theme, if one can put it so succinctly, is the spiritual dimension of God's grace. Almost all of Percy's books are a form of fictional protest against complacent and secularized society in which the high numbers of self-professed believers attest only to their superficial identification with a given church rather than to the extent of their spirituality. This is not to im-

ply, of course, that the writer is in any way a religious dogmatist. While leaving no doubt that his allegiance is forever with the Roman Catholic doctrine, Walker Percy is more interested in spiritual communion with God than in any sectarian creed. If Tom More remains a Catholic, albeit lapsed and openly confessing the uncertainty of his beliefs and a general lack of interest in religion, his wife whom he loves dearly is a Presbyterian-turned-Episcopalian who, as Percy laughed in one of the subsequent interviews, donates their money to Jimmy Swaggart. Clearly the search for salvation and grace is more important than a cosy dogmatic acceptance of any superficial form of worship without substance.

Any discussion of Percy's themes would be incomplete without a brief mention of his treatment of science, always at the forefront of his life as well as his creative efforts, especially in the context of the often bandied "opposition" between science and religion. To what already has been said on this subject in the preceding section we can add that *The Thanatos Syndrome* dispels any facile binary oppositions that some critics are so fond of unearthing. While Percy is keenly aware of both the perils and limitations of the scientific enterprise in a way inextricably tied to his Christian view of the human condition, there is nothing in his science-imbued novel to suggest an anti-technological bias so characteristic of other Christian writers of the twentieth century. The truth is that his last novel, much as all those that preceded it, is thoroughly informed by and sympathetic to both Western science, with its theoretical-empirical apparatus and methodology, and to Christianity, especially but not exclusively in its Roman Catholic incarnation. Casting a scientist in the role of a protagonist—despite the fact that the latter's affiliation with the "science" of Dr. Freud must raise an eyebrow in the light of so much evidence against both the theoretical foundations and empirical efficacy of psychoanalysis—Percy gives an appreciative consideration to the scientific viewpoint even as he investigates the inherent limitations and potential abuses of science and its technological fruits.

◆ CHARACTERS ◆

In a 1986 *Paris Review* interview, subsequently republished in *Writers at Work*, the novelist had some warm words to say about the namesake and model of his hero from *The Thanatos Syndrome*: "My ideal is Thomas More, an English Catholic . . . who wore his faith with grace, merriment, and a certain wryness. Incidentally, I reincarnated him again in my new novel and I'm sorry to say he has fallen upon hard times; he is a far cry from the saint, drinks too much, and watches reruns of *M*A*S*H* on TV." Tom More is indeed the indisputable hero of *The Thanatos Syndrome,* even though the novel introduces him fresh after a two-year stint in a minimum security prison for peddling amphetamines to truckers. Although More plays the role of a Philip Marlowe in the ensuing investigation into the behavioural irregularities in West Feliciana, he is hardly the type of the lone, and even less hard-boiled detective we are used to from the movies. Tall and well built, Percy's protagonist is wholly a man of peace, shunning confrontations both verbal and physical, to the point of instructing Uncle Bob Hugh to aim for the ear when the use of firearms becomes unavoidable. This unusual shoot-out, in which one member of the pedophile gang at Belle Ame gets a bullet through his earlobe and another gets the seat of his pants literally shot off, occurs at the end of the novel when More, Uncle Bob and Vergil Bon confront the child abusers and gather evidence of their malfeasance. The only person who is missing from this scouting party is Dr. Lucy Lipscomb, an attractive and much younger cousin of More's who,

in the course of the novel, plays Watson to his Sherlock, or, perhaps more accurately, Della Street to his Perry Mason, given that they end up in bed during the night when they make the breakthrough discovery of the vector (pattern) in the syndrome plaguing the community.

On the other side of justice, so to speak, are a couple of ostensible pillars of the community who unite their not inconsiderable forces for the Blue Boy project. Bob Comeaux, the chief physician at the Fedville clinical complex, and John Van Dorn, a *Time*-cover renowned scientist employed at the nuclear reactor, divert heavy sodium from the reactor's coolant system into the water intake of a vast number of local residents, effecting dramatic changes in their behaviour. These can range from an attrition of their normal linguistic capabilities, so that the subjects lapse into chimp talk ("Mickey like—Donna want touch me") and generally communicate on the level of four- to five-year-olds; through a stunning and chillingly computer-like total recall of facts and data; a twenty-percent increase in IQ and computational abilities; a greater casualness in their sexual demeanor; to the factor that chills More the most: a kind of shedding of their old selves, including old fears, terrors, worries and anxieties. These are replaced by a sort of good natured animal vacancy, especially in those who, like his patients (Mickey LaFaye, Donna S——, or Ella Murdoch Smith), imbibe greater dosages. But the handsome, intelligent, prominent and respectable perpetrators of the Blue Boy experiment go much further, administering doses which begin to monkey with the evolution by pushing the female menstrual cycle into chimp-like estrus, in this way robbing the residents of sexual drive and "curing" the concurrent problems of teenage pregnancies, venereal diseases or AIDS. Another dimension of the program, this time racist and patronizing, leaps out in the scene when Comeaux gloats over rows of "darkies" who, chemically altered by the Na-24 ions, willingly and happily work the fields of the local jail, just like in the good ol' days of plantation prosperity.

The sad part of this setup is that otherwise respectable and well-meaning doctors, like Max Gottlieb, More's old friend and colleague from *Love in the Ruins*, become part of the program, convinced that it bears the stamp of approval from the federal medical authorities. The temptation to cure all social ills in one fell swoop must indeed be overwhelming if this kind Jewish doctor forgets the legacy of the social "betterment" programs of Nazi Germany, Mao's China or the Khmer Rouge's Cambodia. This aspect of the novel brings us to one of its most important and complex, even if enigmatic, characters, Father Rinaldo Smith. A priest who "looks like an old Ricardo Montalban," he removes himself permanently to a remote fire tower in which, living on Campbell soup and Jello, he lives out his weird sort of penance, looking for signs of fire and God's grace. Just like the protagonist, he is a lapsed Catholic, on top of being a lapsed priest and, as he fears, a lapsed human being with a great burden on his soul. As he reveals to More in the confession scene which forms the philosophical centrepiece of the novel, he is harrowed by the recollection of his infatuation as an adolescent visitor to Nazi Germany with the Hitler-inspired movement, as well as paralyzed by what he perceives as the evacuation of meaning from and the devaluation of human life. Yet, just like Graham Greene's tortured but ultimately noble figure of a "whiskey priest," Father Smith is Percy's spokesman of truths anguished enough to deserve such an anguished preacher. One can only marvel at the subtlety and restraint of the writer, akin to Thomas More's own narrative position vis-a-vis *Utopia*, who professes what is dear to him by means of a character of such peculiar, perhaps even doubtful credentials.

The most remarkable thing about *The Thanatos Syndrome* is the consummate skill with which Percy wove many disparate genres into a story of great erudition, profundity, and old-fashioned page-turning suspense. Although the first-person narrative and the sympathetic figure of Dr. More are conducive to an easy identification and immersion in the action, at various points in the book Percy punctures the flow of the narrative by experimenting with the form of case histories, a confessional monologue, a highly impressionistic sequence of short disjointed paragraphs during More and Lucy's nighttime lovemaking, and the rhythmic and emphatic sermon section at the end, with its imitation of a rolling free-verse chant. Setting the novel in the very near future (before the end of the century), and alternating the narration between the past and present tense, the action flashes forward on occasion, or back in order to fill in the background (recognizable to readers of *Love in the Ruins*). All this is held together by an almost classical closure, with the last scene of the novel, in which Mickey LaFaye delves into her recurrent dream in order to learn something about her life and herself, harking back to their encounter in More's office in the first pages. "Well well well," are the last words of the story, summarizing the hopefulness of the ending in which, paradoxically, the troubled patient could be better off than the anxiety-free but somehow diminished person she was under the influence of heavy sodium.

The positive, upbeat ending sits well with the rest of the book, inasmuch as it clearly follows the structural pattern of classical comedy, notwithstanding its grim and unsettling theme, visible in the title of *The Thanatos Syndrome* (from the Greek thanatos: death). After all, even though the novel deals with horrific issues such as sexual abuse of children and an unauthorized altering of people's psychological makeup with chemicals, and does so within the framework of a tense and clandestine investigation, round-the-clock surveillance of More, his eventual imprisonment and the final shoot-out, everything ends peacefully and without a loss of a single life. Retribution is indeed exacted, as requisite in a comic form, but in a restorative and integrative manner, rather than in an explosion of violence or vendetta-type punishment. More and his wife are happily reunited, Lucy's husband returns home, the culprits embrace their punishment/penance in the form of hospice work with genuine zeal, the Blue Boy project is dismantled and its ringleader, Comeaux, peaceably persuaded to convert Father Smith's ailing hospice into a refuge for patients formerly destined for euthanasia or pedeuthanasia. In a triumph of the comic spirit, the other primal mover of the sodium conspiracy, Van Dorn, recedes to the level of a primate, having been pressured by More to ingest a heavy dose of molar Na-24. Incarcerated in a cage with Eve, a female gorilla, this unlikely human Adam frolics with her until his return to his former self, only to become a celebrity as an author of *My Life and Love with Eve*. These are just some of the examples of a general movement towards reintegration which dominates the denouement of the book, as the author moves from character to character telling the reader how their lives were resolved in the aftermath of the disappearance of the syndrome.

On another level *The Thanatos Syndrome* is an exhilarating adaptation of the popular suspense novel, combining elements of a detective story such as the unearthing of clues, the investigation, or the apprehension of the culprits by the intuiting hero, and of an action thriller, with its conspiracy, surveillance, phone tapping, encounters with the police, and a cliff-hanging race to beat the clock in the rescue of the children of Belle Ame. This is of course not an

accident: Percy admitted to patterning his novel after *The Invasion of the Body Snatchers*, a classic horror/thriller hit in which the pursued hero must also investigate the nature of eerie changes in the local people. In fact, just like in the movie, early in the book More is suspected of delusion and paranoia in, as Percy writes, "imagining a conspiracy, a stealing of people's lives, an invasion of body snatchers." Entirely consistent with this popular tone and appeal is the imagery and characterization, the latter suffused with references to popular icons of American public life and cinema. Percy has a knack for introducing his characters with a well-chosen phrase, often evoking such household names as John Wayne, George Hamilton, Tom Selleck, Harold Lloyd, Clint Eastwood, Maximilian Schell, Walter Cronkite or Howard Cosell to contextualize his fictional personae for the reader. Why such an effort to cloak what is, after all, one of the most penetrating and thoughtful philosophical-cum-religious novels of the last two decades in a mantle of a fast-paced, popular thriller? "There is nothing wrong with the adjectives 'philosophical' and 'religious,' but when you apply them to a novel, it is enough to make the novelist turn pale," explains Percy. People would rather read a novel than a "serious" nonfictional article, on top of the fact that the novelist's first and most important task is to tell a gripping tale.

◆ RELATED TITLES ◆

If the presence of some of the same characters, many of the same concerns, most of the same themes, and the same linguistic virtuosity indicates a literary sequel, then *The Thanatos Syndrome* is undoubtedly a sequel to *Love in the Ruins*, quite apart from sharing with it much of the same comic flavour, and the same—albeit more sober (in both senses)—protagonist. In 1971, when the earlier Tom More novel was published,

Walker Percy had no inkling he would ever return to the same narrative setup and the same hero because *Love in the Ruins* was quite a departure from his up-till-then contemporary mode. While no less philosophical and thought-provoking, *Love in the Ruins* is removed into the unspecified future, although set as it is after the Auto Age—with vines sprouting in Manhattan, wolves roaming downtown Cleveland, old political parties defunct, and everyone watching stereo-V (among many other differences from our times)—it is a future a little further removed than the comparison with *The Thanatos Syndrome* (set after the events of the earlier novel but before the end of this century) would warrant.

Moved to write such a sweeping work—even if confined narratively to the first four days in July—by the approaching bicentennial of the United States, Percy takes as his additional subject a matter of no less grandeur than the state of the country: the psychic state of Man in the latter days of the second millennium after Christ. Given the epic, and at times openly mythical scope of his design, it is no wonder that More becomes the inventor of a decidedly futuristic contraption, called the ontological lapsometer. With this portable device, and with the hilarious even if ultimately ruinous help of the Devil himself (appearing as Art Immelman, a most peculiar foundation bureaucrat), More attempts to diagnose the ills plaguing society, all across the spectrum from angelism (total pseudo-intellectualized abstraction) to bestialism (total mindless hedonism).

Love in the Ruins was certainly, as *The New York Times* put it, Percy's biggest novel to date, and it remains the comic, epic and philosophical gem in his entire oeuvre. None of the book's concerns, including the more topical ones, such as the race riots of 1968 alluded to by the Bantu riots and upheavals in the novel's Feliciana, lost any pertinence for the contemporary reader (witness the L.A. revolt of the 1990s), and its language—rich, lusty and quirky like Tom More himself—remains one of the greatest achievements in American letters. The novel represents Walker Percy at his best: a writer who continues to thrill readers the world over (with a particularly esteemed status in France, where *The Moviegoer* has become part of national school curricula) by the sheer power and inventiveness of his story-telling, albeit always at the service of a more philosophical Muse.

◆ ADAPTATIONS ◆

The Thanatos Syndrome was adapted as an audiocassette, narrated by David Hilder, on Blackstone Audio Books, 1995.

◆ IDEAS FOR GROUP DISCUSSIONS ◆

The Thanatos Syndrome is surely one of the more unusual novels among the contemporary crop of minimalist, anti-narrative, self-centred literary offerings. It is ambitious in theme, profound in reference, topical in relevance, spine-tingling in thrills, and written in Percy's typically resonant and erudite prose. In your discussion of this action-driven, yet profound novel, you may wish to consider the following questions:

1. Did you find that the use of the crime-thriller genre detracted from the philosophical dimension of the book? Did you find that the philosophical dimension detracted from the enjoyment of the suspense and mystery of the thriller?

2. What points of similarity do you see between Sir Thomas More and Percy's Tom More? Between *Utopia* and *The Thanatos Syndrome*?

3. Given his many failings and a checkered past, did you find the hero a likeable character? Why?

4. In what ways do More and Lucy Lipscomb conform to the detective-sidekick model familiar from the classics of detective fiction?

5. Why would the author assign one of the more important statements in the novel to the sermon delivered by a rambling, senile and generally oddball priest, Father Smith?

6. Is *The Thanatos Syndrome* an existential novel? If so, in what sense? Can you identify a clear allusion to Camus' *The Plague* in the first pages of Percy's book?

7. Do you agree with Percy's uncompromising view that abortion amounts to killing?

8. Despite its grimness and profound philosophical implications, this is in many ways a funny and even comical novel. What elements make it so?

9. Can you detect any parts of the book that would identify Percy as a linguist and semiotician?

10. On the whole, did you find that Percy was involved in science-bashing in *The Thanatos Syndrome*?

Peter Swirski
Comparative Literature, University of
Alberta

THOSE BONES ARE NOT MY CHILD

Novel

1999

Author: Toni Cade Bambara

◆

◆ SOCIAL CONCERNS ◆

Because Toni Cade Bambara's *Those Bones Are Not My Child* is based upon the Atlanta child murders of the late 1970s and early '80s, her novel is a curious blend of fiction and nonfiction—what she identifies, in an interview for the American Audio Prose Library in 1982, as "the contradictory pull of the documentary impulse and the fictional impulse." The product of twelve years of research, Bambara's novel focuses on the political and social climate of those decades. But the novel is not merely documentary, for "The City Too Busy To Hate" is richly rendered as an Atlanta intimate to the author. With Bambara's insights as a member of its African American community at the time, the novel becomes an exploration of the emotions of that community. Through Bambara's focus on the struggles of a fictive black family, the Spencers, devastated by the abduction of their oldest son, Sonny, the story illustrates the community's tale of loss, desperation, hope, and rejuvenation.

While the narrative takes place between 1980 and 1982, its location in time appears fluid. Individual sections are marked by a specificity of day, month, and year, sometimes lapsing days and, at others, entire months. Although each moment is important to the Spencers who first notice the disappearance of their eldest son in the first year, and then discover the truth behind his abduction in the last, this ephemeral sense of time is telling for all of its characters, and the setting. In this world, the Atlanta of the early 1980s, there is a sense of hope and progress in the city's technological advances; it is "The City Too Busy to Hate." But there is another Atlanta in the novel, haunted by the ghosts of past wars, embodied in the Vietnam veterans who are alienated from the community at large and each other. And many members of the black community in Atlanta fail to reap the rewards of the budding economy and must struggle to make ends meet. Locating the story within the black community, Bambara tells us about this other Atlanta.

The African American community is in trouble—Atlanta's young are disappearing in frightening numbers. The government is stalling—Atlanta's authorities fail to alert the community of these abductions and murders. Despite the prosperity in Atlanta, parents struggle to keep food on the table, watchful eyes over their children, and their own lives intact. And, once they learn of the abductions and murders, families begin to live in fear. The government drags its heels and fails to publish a list of the "Missing and Murdered," denying any connection between the individual cases. And the black community itself is torn, some hopeful for the government's assistance while others are angered by its indifference. The Atlanta of Bambara's novel is one with multiple fissures; individuals attempt to come together to locate the lost children, but often become lost in a maze of unanswered questions and new complications.

In simple terms, *Those Bones Are Not My Child* is a story about a black community under siege. The community is threatened by the abductions and murders as well as the government's indifference. But it goes even further than that, for this community is one that has been suffering. While the immediacy of the Atlanta child murders threatens the bedrock of the community, the community itself is already in crisis. Families are divided, neighbors distanced. Spence, the father of the missing Sonny and a vet who is still shell-shocked from two tours in Vietnam, is the focus of much of the narrative. He is estranged from his family and any sense of community: "over a million and a half Black people in the city, two and a half million Black vets active and organized in the Southeast region, twenty-five of his thirty-one years on earth spent in Atlanta, and he could think of no one to drop in on and say, 'Hey, man, I'm hurtin'.'" As we learn of Spence's plight, we feel the alienation experienced during this period.

In response to these feelings of alienation, individuals fight to find new ways of raising their voices, banding together and making change. As Marzala Spencer, a mother driven to find her child, reflects on the indifference of her city and its people, she illustrates that she must find another way to tell her story, for even the newspapers fail to express it: "Children had been bludgeoned, shot, stabbed, and strangled, and nothing had stopped. Conventions came to town. Save the Fox Theatre luncheons were served at fifty dollars a plate. Newspaper and magazine articles put asterisks alongside the Fortune 500 branches in Atlanta. Suits were pressed, briefcases polished. And nothing stopped." In response to the indifference around them, Spence and Marzala attempt to find meaning in their world, beginning with an examination of their own community.

In the novel, issues of race, class, and gender conflate to tell a story that is specifically rooted in the problems of this African American community. As Marzala wonders, "Had the children been killed because they were Black, or should she say because the murderers were white? Had the authorities marginalized Dettlinger because he was white, because the high command was Black? Had the memo writers' warnings been trivialized because they were females, their supervisors male?" she illustrates the dangers at the center of this story—misunderstandings and misreadings of the "other." While most of the novel's narration consists of an omniscient narrator's exploration of and free indirect discourse with Marzala and Spence, both characters continually question how the white community is reading them. When Marzala is questioned about Sonny's disappearance, she wonders if she is suspected of neglect or violence. Each character, including the members of the Committee to Stop Children's Murders (STOP), children, clergy, psychics, and community members, wonder why little or no action is taken in response to the cases, leading to numerous allegations, racial conflict and division.

And often it appears that divisions are drawn along the lines of race, for, despite the fact that STOP explores the idea that the KKK is responsible for the crimes, authorities deny these links: "'Paranoia,' said the media to Blacks pointing out connections. 'No connection,' the FBI said in response to

Black organizations all over the country." When Wayne Williams is brought to trial, the community is not surprised that he is black, for they knew that it was far more "safe" in the eyes of the city's authorities to point the finger at a member of the black community and contain the threat, dividing the community in the process. Within this African American community, men become alienated from women, parents from children, neighbor from neighbor, and the reader is left to wonder if the community will survive.

Ultimately, the scope of *Those Bones Are Not My Child* transcends the historicity of the Atlanta child murders; the immediate threat of the murders becomes the setting for Bambara's exploration of the future of the African American community. While the novel's focus is the Atlanta of Bambara's experience, it symbolizes a larger world inscribed with fissures resulting from individual fears, insecurities, and needs. As a precarious balance of fiction and reality, Bambara's Atlanta reflects the horrors and atrocities of the time—the violation of children and the community at large. Detailing the historicity of that Atlanta, Bambara includes the key players and the events of the time, but she invents characters that allow her to explore the community's reactions to these events. As the medium for the community's forgotten story, Bambara is able to examine what community is and bear witness to its potential to overcome such tragedies.

◆ THEMES ◆

Those Bones Are Not My Child illustrates Bambara's attempt to tell her community's story. Locating the novel in the historical moment of the Atlanta child murders, Bambara examines its black community, voicing the stories overlooked by the journalists and authorities at the time. As Bambara states in the aforementioned interview, "We've gotten the media story, or the media version, the police version, but we've yet to get the domestic version or the community story." Although its focus is the abductions and murders of forty children, it presents a larger picture; perhaps most importantly, the novel seeks to redefine the African American community.

This is a community desperately in need of healing. Steeped with racial tension, Atlanta is divided between parents and policy-makers, the community-run STOP organization and the government-appointed Task Force, activism and indifference. Ostensibly, the community has only itself when all other avenues fail to assist, or even to lend a listening ear to individual suffering. Bambara continually reasserts the need for community; her character Marzala repeatedly voices concerns about the community's indifference and need for activism, for they must save themselves. The African American community is isolated, Bambara tells us, and she drives this point home in an exchange with a journalist who tells Marzala, "'Blacks just aren't news anymore, Mrs. Spencer. . . . The news of the moment is Iran, when it's not the election or stories about international terrorism . . . the Atlanta story lacks scope.'" But rather than become despondent and hopeless, Marzala continues the fight, searching for her son and a new sense of community.

Viewing Bambara's work in its entirety (as, sadly, her death in 1995 prematurely brought her career to a close), one notices the theme of community throughout—a concern for the welfare of children and women, as seen in her earlier works, the collections of short stories *Gorilla, My Love* and *The Sea Birds Are Still Alive*, as well as her novel, *The Salt Eaters*. But in *Those Bones Are Not My Child*, Bambara widens her gaze to take in all that is Atlanta—her immediate world, her black community (as Bambara had relocated herself there years before her death)—to recognize its limitations and potential. Without positing a solution, for the story is rooted in nonfiction and the case remains officially "closed," Bambara tests the limits of community. Even Marzala, STOP's driving force for much of the novel, retreats into the familial realm—the embrace of her mother and sister—after they find Sonny. Fearing the possibility of losing him again, Marzala turns away from Atlanta and the African American community there, reluctant to return.

But Bambara's solution is not one achieved by severing ties, for Marzala must return. And she cannot keep Sonny safe at home, for he must be able to go out into the community. Marzala and Spence force themselves to unearth the truth behind his disappearance, and, in doing so, realize the importance of community. In her speech to the congregation in one of the last scenes of the novel, Marzala implores that they question authority and raise their voices together. As a symbol of feminism and activism, Marzala leads the community to act, a message delivered throughout Bambara's earlier works, but now defined on a larger scale in *Those Bones Are Not My Child*. And members of the community respond to Marzala's speech with acceptance, "Say it again, sister," encouraging her to voice their story, while naming her their "sister." Ultimately, through the act of connecting with the congregation, encouraging their action and reaction to the events in Atlanta, Marzala's speech illustrates hope for the future of the black community. With the community's support and their activism, Marzala and Spence are finally able to lead Sonny to reveal the truth.

Although Bambara suggests this reformed notion of community, the case is not easily resolved, and a new theme emerges, one alluded to at the novel's beginning. The role of the storyteller, the writer herself, becomes important as Bambara seeks closure to the story that defies neat resolution. While we witness that the writer is the voice of the community, the Marzala, like Bambara, who speaks to and for them in that last address, the closing of a story that is so much fact and so much fiction proves complicated. After Sonny's truth is revealed and his case is "closed," we are reminded that these are fictitious characters placed in real circumstances, for Sonny's abductor is revealed as a fictional character (Bambara neatly distinguishes the fictitious from the real in her "Acknowledgments").

In the "Epilogue," Bambara invokes the figure of the writer compiling the facts and the story itself to illustrate this tension between reality and fiction for a story that has so much of both. In it, she dismisses the "official accounts" posited in FBI records, reports, and newspaper articles to raise new questions. As her writer-character assembles reports for a friend who asks about events in Atlanta, we are left to weed through what she finds, clarifying and yet complicating the writer's role.

But the writer becomes a familiar figure, for it is "You," the writer first rendered in the "Prologue." Now, rather than frantically searching for your daughter, only reading your notes when she is safely accounted for, under your watchful eye, you are finishing the story. You see the television, and its images: " . . . the man being turned into a matinee idol. In addition to arming the thug Savimbi to topple Angola, Oliver North also organized the invasion of Grenada." With this juxtaposition of the writing in hand, the story of Atlanta's child murders, and the images on screen, you begin to question everything proposed as "fact" and "fiction."

But we leave that world with many questions, and many ideas about who that writer is—the familiar purveyor of fact and creator of fiction. And while the use of fact and fiction is important for understanding Bambara's project, and the novel itself, we return, in the last moments, to the central theme, the community. You, the writer, leave your apartment with your daughter. As you walk into the street, it's "1981 all over again until you two reach the sidewalk heading for the post office." The chaos in the street leads you to worry about the present, for "People are shooting off guns still and flinging firecrackers all over the street." But there is hope, because the image is transformed into one of unity, for "they must have foreseen that you two would need an extension of the Independence Day celebrations." And you are not alone, for you are part of "two" and the two join the larger community. While this notion of community is not fully defined, it is a symbol of a new beginning: potential.

◆ CHARACTERS ◆

Bambara's cast of characters are intriguing, as some are fictional creations while others are public figures whose words Bambara documents from public records. As expressed in the aforementioned interview, Bambara explains that the "fictional characters allow me to pursue the various theories, for example, about the murders and allow me to lift up the community voice without hustling anyone." And her description of the process of writing this book, contained in the "Acknowledgments," illuminates the fictional characters that are clearly developed in the context of the novel, and the real people that are only represented by their names in the work. While B. J. Greaves is a character Bambara describes as "originally devised solely to enable me to tell the reader about actual police officers," and Mason, Vernon, and Lafayette characters that "enabled me to tip my hat to the numerous vets and community workers who were on the case," the Spencer family is clearly defined for their roles in the tragedy, and the amazing changes that they undergo.

Bambara's creation of the family unit, their struggles to find their missing son, and their attempts at reunion and unification lies at the heart of the novel. In addition to her role as the first character introduced to the reader, Marzala Rawls Spencer occupies the central position throughout the novel. Although she is a young mother at only twenty-seven years of age, she first appears distraught, "worried," with "Smudged mascara from the day before. . . . She looked feverish, her lips cracked and peeling, salt streaked across her breastbone." From her first appearance, she is out of control, angered at her twelve year old son who has failed to return home. She even appears alienated from her younger children, eight year old Kofi and seven year old Kenti, who complain that all of her stomping around the house awakens them. Marzala, or Zala, as she is called throughout the novel, is distracted and distraught. And she is tired, working two jobs as a manicurist at the barbershop and a teacher at the art center. She is estranged from her husband, as we learn at Kofi's question, "You call Dad?" and Kenti's thought, "But Daddy wasn't coming by so much no more." But once Marzala realizes that it isn't just a matter of Sonny disobeying her rules to go on a camping trip, she begins to change. Initially "dragg[ing] herself behind Officer Hall," and pleading, "Would somebody help me please?", Marzala remains a passive victim of a system that does not regard her case seriously; boys that age were prone to run away from home, they assure her. But, gradually, Marzala begins to "Question Authority," as her T-shirt reads at the end of the novel, at the community meeting where she finds her voice and encourages activism from her community. Quoting from Gwendolyn Brooks, Marzala begins, "'We are all each other's harvest, we are each other's business,'" and ends her speech with the words, "' . . . coerced silence is terrorism.'"

Marzala's estranged husband, Nathaniel Spencer, "Spence," is alienated from his family and his community. Hearing of his son's disappearance, he must travel a long way home to discover what happened. And his life is one of disillusionment, for we learn that "ten years ago, Spence had still been serious about becoming a community organizer." But he did not become one, and can no longer seem to find the passion he once had, "and now he was hurting . . . " As we learn of his history, Spence emerges as a character who fought to live his life under ideals, for he had "' . . . gone in the army, fled in fact, still using the Black Power salute to repair the damage, . . . hanging 'militant' posters over his bed. . . . Dogged, brave, noble, right on." But he had entered the war too late, and saw little action, so he returned disillusioned. He is in pain, and alone, for "he could think of no one to drop in on and say, 'Hey, man, I'm hurtin.'" But, like Marzala, Spence undergoes a change. As he continually searches for Sonny and possible leads alongside Marzala, he is inadvertently brought home. Restored to the family, he changes, realizing as he holds Kenti, "that he wanted Sonny to be there not so much to complete the family portrait as to give him the opportunity to alter it and his own relationship to it. 'My family,' he said aloud, to see what it felt like to say it now. . . . 'Family,' he said again." When Sonny is also restored to the family, roles are again redefined, but this time nothing is transient, and they all learn to grow together—a new community, a new family.

As the source of the emotional turmoil experienced by the Spencers, Sundiata, "Sonny," Spencer is a complex character. There are two Sonnys that emerge from the text—the one that everyone describes and fantasizes about returning, and the one that

does come home. At the novel's beginning, Marzala frets about Sonny's whereabouts, angry at him for worrying her: "Twelve years old and out all night long. . . . She mouthed all the things she would say to him, all the things she'd been lashing together to flay him with since the day before when Kofi had shrugged and said 'Went.' . . . He was asking for it, and he would get it this time." Even his siblings think that he is one to get away with everything, as Kofi complains, "'He always do what he wants.'" But once the Spencers realize that something has happened to Sonny, that he has been abducted, he becomes transformed into a symbol of all the lost innocence in the world: "Sacrificial children. Little Lamb, they'd called their firstborn long before he was Sundiata, Sundi, Sunday, Sonny. Who didn't call their babies little lambs?" And yet when he is found, returned to the Spencers, he is a stranger to them all. At first, he is "The John Doe Jr. in observation in Pediatrics, found wandering in a daze on the highway, barefoot, in khaki shorts and a ragged child's undershirt four sizes too small, . . . so badly battered . . . " At her family's home, away from Atlanta, ready for the healing to start, Zala still cannot claim her son:

> "That is not my boy," she had told them. . . . "Those bones are not my child." Brushing Spence's words away from her ear, she told them it was fruitless to try and palm the damaged boy off as their son. But Spence kept saying things to bring her around, to take a good look, to concentrate.

But once they start the process of healing, as a family, and learn to accept Sonny into the family again, to realize that he has changed, the family is able to piece together what happened. Sonny's abduction and return lie at the center of the story, for the family must redefine what they are, and ask that the community do the same, in the face of tragedy.

Those Bones Are Not My Child

Kofi Spencer is the eight-year-old younger brother of Sonny, and a boy that must renegotiate his role in the family once his brother is abducted. From the onset of the novel, he is sullen, unruly, and envious of his brother, complaining that his mother is too easy on Sonny: "'You don't never say nothing to him. You jump on me all the time, though.'" At first, Kofi believes that Sonny has gone on the camping trip, and envisions all the fun that he was missing. Kofi resents the way that Sonny treats him: "Bestor Brooks always spoke up and looked out for his younger brothers, but Sonny only sometimes . . . " Once Kofi realizes that Sonny is gone, he tries to step into the role of the older brother, almost becoming Sonny, as he asks his mother, "'Since Sonny ain't here . . . can I sleep on top and Kenti can take my bed?'" Then he goes to the closet and takes out a pair of cowboy boots, asking, "'Can I have these boots? I mean, can I wear them till I get new shoes?'" Wanting to literally step into Sonny's shoes, Kofi proclaims, "'Well, Sonny ain't here. . . . He ain't here.'" But, eventually, Kofi becomes protective of his older brother, once Sonny returns, weakened and fearful. As he holds his brother, Kofi assures him, "'I got you. It's all right. Ain't nobody gonna mess with you. . . . Don't cry. Awww, don't cry, Sonny. . . . It's okay. . . . I got him, Dad. Let go, ya'll. I got him.'" And Kofi does not let go.

Kenti Spencer is the youngest of the three Spencer children, and vacillates from extreme skepticism to idealism. She watches her mother with a critical eye, thinking, "If Daddy came by he would get on her about that." But only eight years old, she easily falls back into the role of the little girl, and curls up under the covers with her Baby Crawler. While waiting for her father one day after Sonny's disappearance, Kenti prays that she will be able to go to church, and declares that she would " . . . pray for Sonny to come home and put on his birthday bathrobe and get everybody to act right."

Despite her belief that " . . . house praying wasn't as strong as church praying," Kenti holds her Baby Crawler tightly and continues to pray. But Kenti's role is intriguing, for she has insight that many of the adults lack; she is the first to learn the lesson that the adult members of the community fail to realize: " . . . the lesson was that people who struggled in the dark and got scared should keep on with the struggling and then they'll be blessed and can change . . . " And she is a storyteller, like Bambara herself, for, at the end of the novel, Kenti stages a play for the young people while the adults discuss the state of the community; it is Kenti who attempts to write a "good last scene" as the novel spins to a close. And she is an activist, and will not sit by and wait for such a change, for " . . . she had her own work to do," while her mother stands before the group to speak.

Beyond the immediate family is the extended family, compiled mostly of a community of women. Paulette, "Aunty Lette," is a nurse, a healer by nature, and Zala's best friend and neighbor. When Zala falls apart, Paulette is there to clean her up, and her house, taking care of the Spencer children and inciting Zala into action. And it is Paulette's marriage at the end of the novel that brings hope to the Spencer family, for they are able to move on, and move out, into Paulette's vacated home. With more space to live, and a new commitment to each other, the family thrives as a result of Paulette's growth, symbolized by her wedding. And there are more women healers in the novel—Marzala comes from a family of healers. When Sonny is returned home, he is brought to Marzala's family, her mother, Mama Lovey, and her sister, Gerry. There, the family opens their arms to the Spencers, encouraging healing. But all must find ways of coming together, for Gerry only knows her own work in Africa and must try to help the Spencers from her experience; Gerry is able to help them understand Sonny's silence, while offering them all that she has: "'I hope I'm making sense. It's the only context I know.'" And the environment differs from Atlanta, for things heal here, as Mama Lovey takes medical students on a tour of her grounds explaining the medicinal plants, "'Just one more instance of that law of life, time. Right now, it's poison. In a few days, good medicine.'" And here, in this magical place, Sonny can heal, for evening primrose blooms in September, to everyone's surprise—under the right hands. It is finally Mama Lovey who tells Sonny that he must tell the truth, as she tells him, "' . . . you'll be called upon real soon to do something big that requires the kind of straight-up courage you've let strangers trash somewhere.'" He tries to lie to her, pretending he does not intend on running away, but she leads him to his truth. Out of love for her daughter, Lovey tells the boy that she will make certain he doesn't leave, for Marzala's sake: "'You can mend. But my girl, you see, I don't think she could take your going off, and she's my child.'" And, with that truth, Sonny surrenders himself to Lovey's embrace, to begin the healing, and the telling.

◆ TECHNIQUES ◆

As a contemporary work of fiction (written after 1945), *Those Bones Are Not My Child* illustrates concerns about the individual's role in the society, concerns best revealed through narration. The novel's narration is always located in the third person, and yet, with a modern sweep, in a technique experimented with by James Joyce and, later, Virginia Woolf, plays with free indirect discourse, where the boundaries between narrator and character disappear although the third person voice does not. Experimenting

with narration, Bambara is able to vacillate between her two main characters, Marzala and Spence, without impeding the pace of the novel, itself a frenzied search to find Sonny. In the aforementioned interview, Bambara explains her use of the narrator as a medium, or force, a magnet through which other people tell their stories. Such a narrator, she explains, is different from what she classifies as the narrator contained in Euro-American letters, the omniscient narrator that she finds "arrogant," imposing. And it is this type of unique narration that we find in the "Prologue" and "Epilogue," a type of narration that marks a significant departure from the "traditional" novel, as it is written in the second-person, invoking "You" at the first lines. Inviting the reader into the world through direct invocation illustrates the play with form that Bambara so readily executes within the novel.

Written after two world wars, and numerous others, the contemporary novel focuses on the plight of the individual living with knowledge of the wars, Depression, and a general disillusionment about their world. Bambara's characters fit this model, for the Vietnam vets appear shell-shocked, detached and haunted by nightmares day and night. Atlanta itself seems disillusioned, despite its seeming progress. The African American community feels its reality slipping, as they become sleepwalkers, hustling from job to job, or wandering in search of employment. *Those Bones Are Not My Child* reflects fears about the stability of family and the security of well-being.

Along with this sense of disjointedness experienced by the characters is a sense of longing for completion. And yet characters remain fragmented, alienated from others and their own fulfillment. Distinct from the modern novel, the postmodern novel explores these issues of fragmentation, a questioning of meaning now that the old orders have disappeared. In the postmodern novel, the classical unities of place and time are disrupted. Physical location(Atlanta) remains a constant, but we are often placed within the characters' minds. Time is dislocated, nonsensical, for days pass between brief sections while hundreds of pages mark the progress of a day. And yet *Those Bones Are Not My Child* retains elements of the modern novel as well, in which religion and romance are not banished, but return in new forms. At the novel's end, the church is transformed into a political forum where Marzala, replacing the clergyman, advocates action. Combining the communal spirit and a call for activism, the church is invigorated through a new metaphor.

Most distinctly, *Those Bones Are Not My Child* is part of the literary genre of African American fiction, for which the field of study is continually growing. Asked if her work should be classified as "black literature" in the aforementioned interview, Bambara responds, "There is a distinct black literature with very particular kinds of traditions . . . " She defines her work against works of Euro-American literature, stating that all that happens in Ernest Hemingway's and Nathaniel Hawthorne's novels could take place in Europe, while " . . . the literature in this country that confronts what is particular and peculiar about this country is black literature." And as a work of African American fiction, Bambara's novel is the child of a rich literary tradition. Drawing on oral storytelling, many African American writers transfer this orality to the written page. Bambara's novel, at times, sings with a lyricism rivaled only by poetry. While the novel contains less of the sheer translucency of language found in *The Salt Eaters*, in the moments when Marzala returns home to help Sonny get well, the language reaches such heights. And, thematically, the novel's concerns with the fate of the African American community, the raising of its voice, marks it as representative of this genre.

Those Bones Are Not My Child is part of a distinct tradition of contemporary African American literature. It should not be surprising that connections between Bambara's work and another prominent African American woman writer, Toni Morrison, exist, for the latter was Bambara's editor at Random House for years, and the two became close friends, and admirers of each other's work. As Bambara expresses in the aforementioned interview, " . . . we're friends . . . very much interested in each other's work, as women, as members of the same community. . . . "

Morrison's *Beloved* (1987) focuses on issues of community, the need for understanding the past for an active future. Both Bambara's and Morrison's novels focus on the loss of the children of the community, though in Morrison's work the death occurs at the hands of the mother, in desperation. But, perhaps more significantly, the source of Morrison's *Beloved* is an article that the author found, detailing a woman's murder of her child. Both Bambara and Morrison draw on fact and spin their fictional worlds around it, creating worlds familiar to them, locating the stories close to home.

And like *Beloved*, Morrison's *Paradise* (1997) focuses on the community, though this time it is a community of women cast outside the town of Ruby. Similarly, Gloria Naylor's *The Women of Brewster Place* (1980) focuses on the African American community struggling in Brewster Place, a hopeless place where dreams seem to die. But, in each of these works, like in Bambara's novel, hope is found through a shared vision—raised voices. But while Bambara's *The Salt Eaters* (1981) seems to resonate more with this theme with its focus on a community of women, Marzala's interactions with her mother and sister prove no less telling. And yet *Those Bones Are Not My Child* is filled with cries for activism, a redefined community achieved through action. Bambara's emerging feminist protagonist Marzala reminds us of Alice Walker's *Meridian* (1976), both novel and title character that explore, and take part in, the civil rights movement.

Beyond its connections to other works by African American women writers, *Those Bones Are Not My Child* is a portrait of the Atlanta child murders and one family's experiences, mixing elements of nonfiction with fiction. And Bambara's novel is connected to nonfictional accounts of the murders, specifically, Chet Dettlinger and Jeff Prugh's *The List*, now out of print, and James Baldwin's *Evidence of Things Not Seen* (1986), both referred to in Bambara's "Epilogue," that question the "official version." And while Bambara's novel is based on the Atlanta child murders, the fictitious Spencers' search for their son reads as a thriller, connecting it with yet another genre. The suspense with which the reader awaits the discovery of Sonny, and his abductor, at times, reminds the reader of the breathless anticipation with which he reads the contemporary thrillers of John Grisham. Despite the apparent differences between the *Those Bones Are Not My Child* and Grisham's *The Pelican Brief* (1992), the latter's focus on the discovery of a conspiracy behind the assassination of two Supreme Court justices leads the female protagonist through a labyrinth of political cover-ups and deception, much like Marzala Spencer's struggle to find her son and piece together the story.

◆ RELATED TITLES ◆

In *Race, Gender, and Desire*, Elliott Butler-Evans draws a connection between Bambara and Walter Benjamin's definition of a storyteller, "a person 'always rooted in the people'" through whom "the story becomes a medium through which groups of people

are unified, values sustained, and a shared world view sedimented." But where her earlier works, collections of stories, *Gorilla, My Love* (1960) and *The Sea Birds Are Still Alive* (1974), and the novel, *The Salt Eaters* (1981), focus upon segments of the African American community—young girls and women—*Those Bones Are Not My Child* extends its definition of community.

Bambara's "A Sort of Preface" to the first collection, *Gorilla, My Love,* provides an interesting lens for comparison between the works, as she writes, "So I deal in straight-up fiction myself, cause I value my family and friends, and mostly cause I lie a lot anyway," for even in response to her early works critics comment on her stories' connections to her own life, her own causes. So when Bambara states in the aforementioned interview that her role as a writer is to " . . . transform actual experiences you have been through . . . in order to make usable whatever lesson it is you've extracted from that experience that you want to lift up and share with other people," we are able to see how this theory applies to each of her works. *Those Bones Are Not My Child* marks a redefinition of Bambara's work, one in which the call for activism is sounded as a result of the real horrors of her Atlanta.

In her last work, all members of the community, men and women, are soldiers in a struggle, but are each alienated from the other, as families and individuals. The shell-shocked war veterans are haunted by solitude, and single mothers fight to keep their children safe as they leave home for their third jobs. This final novel, published posthumously, reflects a larger scope, a sweeping portrait of the black community. In *Deep Sightings and Rescue Missions: Fiction, Essays, and Conversations* (1996), Bambara articulates her visions. Writing about the role of the storyteller, Bambara discusses her interest in stories about resistance. *Those Bones Are Not My Child* is one such story.

Facing internal tension and external pressure, the community in *Those Bones Are Not My Child* is disjointed. But, through the positioning of Marzala and Spence, the parents of the missing child, Sonny, the narrative returns us to the family, and the possibilities of unification for the community at large. While *The Salt Eaters* illustrates how the faith healer Minnie Ransom is able to lead Velma Henry to life after an attempted suicide, the vision behind *Those Bones Are Not My Child* extends further. Marzala Spencer is healed by her community of women, at home, but must return to Atlanta to advocate change for her entire community, men, women, and children, all.

◆ IDEAS FOR GROUP DISCUSSIONS ◆

As Bambara's intent was to tell the community's story, issues of narration are extremely significant. From the "Prologue's" invitation for the reader to join the story, to the vacillation between Marzala and Spence's perspectives, to the reader's revised role in the "Epilogue," the shifts in narration provide an intriguing model for exploring the role of the writer. The reader is invited into the novel so that the community's story will be heard; Marzala's and Spence's words become the medium through which the silence is broken. Ultimately, *Those Bones Are Not My Child* represents one family's struggle to find their son, and, in the process, unify the entire community. The Atlanta of Bambara's novel is one steeped in racial conflict and division, tension that threatens the future of the African American community. Struggling in silence, the members of the community have no recourse and suffer until they are able to recognize their commonality and fight against a system guided by prejudice, blindness, and injustice.

1. Woven throughout the novel are numerous characters, some "real" people and others literary creations. Whose story is *Those Bones Are Not My Child*? Which perspective(s) does the reader feel most closely aligned with? Why?

2. In the "Prologue," the reader is addressed as "You." Why does Bambara begin here? What is the function of the "Prologue"?

3. How does Bambara's coupling of fiction and documentary depart from your expectations of the "traditional" novel? Why does she rely on both to tell this story?

4. Whose Atlanta is depicted in the story? Is there only one? What are the different depictions of Atlanta and why are they all contained in the story?

5. Identify the protagonist(s) and antagonist(s) of the novel. Considering the number of characters within the novel, how many fit into each category? What are the conflicts between these characters?

6. Critical commentators often focus on Bambara's depiction of the state of the African American community, as well as her visions of its future. How does the community function within this novel? Is Bambara advocating change? Of what kind?

7. The novel consists of multiple settings, most predominantly a focus on the political and familial realms. How are the two connected in the novel, and why are they woven together?

8. Many critical commentators have discussed the portrayal of the African American man in works by African American women writers. How does the representation of gender differ in the story?

9. Bambara's novel, taking place after the Korean and Vietnam wars, focuses on the role of the "vet" in Atlanta. How

does his role illuminate the position of the individual in this society?

10. The title, "Those Bones Are Not My Child," has many meanings. What is the significance of the title in the context of the novel? Who is the "child"? How might it be both a literal quote and a metaphor?

Lisa K. Perdigao
Northeastern University

TIMELINE

Novel

1999

Author: Michael Crichton

◆

◆ SOCIAL CONCERNS ◆

In *Timeline,* Michael Crichton dramatizes the contemporary distrust of corporate funding of cultural and academic projects. In today's society where new mega-mergers are common headlines in the daily newspapers, sports stadiums are named after banks and large corporations purchase their own news networks, the business world often seems to overshadow the other aspects of our lives. *Timeline* begins with the cover-up of the death of an employee of International Technology Corporation (ITC), which means that from the very beginning its president, Robert Doniger, is pegged as an unscrupulous villain. As the story unfolds, the reader learns that the brilliant but unstable physicist has unlocked the secret of quantum travel. Doniger started ITC to investigate the possibility of building a quantum computer capable of transporting people and objects from the present to the past, and back again. He hides his research from both the cutthroat scientific community, and from journalists like Louise Delvert, whose attitude that "Capitalism is bad, all corporations are evil" impedes his path to fame and fortune at whatever the cost. Doniger wants to corner the market on time travel once the technology is perfected. His business plans include marketing "real live history" events to the general public, and building a perfectly accurate historic theme park in the Dordogne region of France based on research done with quantum travel. It sounds like an admirable task, but Doniger's true interest comes out when his researchers present him with video recordings of Abraham Lincoln delivering the Gettysburg address and George Washington crossing the Delaware. The images prove to be too realistic for Doniger, and he explodes: "I don't care about reality. I want something intriguing, something sexy. You're showing me a walking corpse and a drowned rat." He refuses to accept history as it is and decides to use only still photographs of Lincoln to avoid revealing his squeaky voice, and to use Photoshop to erase the wrinkles from Lincoln's face. Profit is more important than honesty. Profit is also more important than human life. Doniger puts lives in danger with unperfected technology, and he wants to change the past to make it more cinematic. This warping of the truth and lack of compassion in the name of money and fame strikes at America's fears of large monopolies trampling the individual and perverting culture and art. Doniger embodies all of the negative attributes of unchecked capitalism.

On the other hand, the characters that represent scholarship and culture get their share of criticism as well. Professor Johnston and his students are conducting an archeological dig in Dordogne. Their work, it turns out, is fully funded by ITC. Because Delvert stirs up suspicion in Professor Johnston, he visits ITC's headquarters in Arizona and demands to know the truth. Doniger, seeking to quell any further information leaks, tries to placate Johnston by allowing him to try quantum travel, but does not warn him of the dangers and Johnston ends up trapped in the past. Doniger then brings in Johnston's students, Andre Marek, Chris Hughes, Kate Erickson and David Stern, to go back to the past and rescue him. The historians, Andre, Chris and Kate, naively trust Doniger's claims that the technology is safe, but the scientist, David, is wary and chooses to stay behind. It all suggests that humanities scholars are too detached from reality to protect themselves from corporate scientists like Doniger, and Stern, who is a blend of both research scientist and historian, is the one who ultimately finds a way to bring them all back.

The common attitude of the public toward scholars is further explored in *Timeline* as well. Chris finds himself unsatisfied with Kate's stockbroker friends because, " . . . like many successful business people, they tended to treat academics as if they were slightly retarded, unable to function in the real world, to play the real games." In a society where money buys all, choosing to be a historian is, in a sense, choosing not to make millions of dollars. The stockbroker's attitude hits home with Chris because he is not able to function in the real world at this point. Marek, on the other hand, is comfortable with his place as an academic and more critical of Kate's friends: "He had a term for people like this: temporal provincials—people who were ignorant of the past and proud of it . . . convinced that the present was the only time that mat-

tered, and that anything that had occurred earlier could be safely ignored."

Crichton's characters act out the rivalry between scholars and entrepreneurs. It is a battle waged on every university campus as funds are generally given to those disciplines that bring fame and more importantly, fortune, to the university at large and corporate donations often come with obligations to the donor. Thus, Johnston and his students are in a unique situation because their expedition is fully funded, and there is no piece of equipment that they cannot have. This is also why the minister of antiquities, Francios Bellin, and the journalist, Louise Delvert, are suspicious of Doniger. They cannot conceive of an American scientist and entrepreneur donating massive amounts of money to humanities research.

Although ultimately Doniger receives a fitting punishment for his cold-heartedness, and the historians return to the present unharmed, the novel closes with an image of foreboding: " . . . the rain had entirely stopped, but the clouds remained dark and heavy, hanging low over the distant hills." The immediate problem is solved, but the complex dangers of quantum travel remain on the horizon.

◆ THEMES ◆

Two themes dominate *Timeline*: history and technology. History is a large concern in the novel as well. Both the historians and Doniger recognize the past as the root of contemporary culture. Johnston's comment on temporal provincials is that "if you didn't know history, you didn't know anything. You were a leaf that didn't know it was part of a tree." Crichton maintains the importance of knowing the past throughout the novel: "Yet the truth was that the modern world was invented in the Middle Ages. Everything from the legal system, to nation-states, to reliance on technology, to the concept of romantic love had first been established in medieval times." Even Doniger seems to recognize its importance at some level. He predicts that people will want to pay to experience the past. He may also be right in thinking that people do not want to see the truth behind our romanticized ideals about history. The past may not be glamorous or exciting at some times, but its importance is undeniable to any of the characters.

The danger of technology is a common theme in modern writing, and this is no exception in *Timeline*. Crichton creates his most frightening image in the cat Wellsey, who was used to test early quantum travel machines. The invisible transcription errors of a few trips have lead to " . . . a third eye, smaller and only partially formed. And beneath that eye was a patch of flesh, and then a protruding bit of jaw that stuck out like a tumor from the side of the face" after many trips. That one word, tumor, recalls nightmares of nuclear radiation poisoning and chemically polluted water—all the dangers we have experienced with our current technology. Crichton warns us that new technologies will bring similar, initially unnoticeable effects.

◆ CHARACTERS ◆

Chris Hughes is the *bildungsroman* hero of the story. In the beginning, he is a pampered and sheltered American intellectual, in a sense a victim of a leisure-oriented society, who is conservative and most often described as being "anxious" about the situations he finds himself in—in other words, afflicted by a postmodern anxiety of influence and malaise. He is naïve and underdeveloped as a person because of the loss of his parents, and because he has spent all of his time with books, studies the history of experience rather than experiencing life for himself. When caught in bewil-

dering situations in medieval France, Chris slowly starts to realize his condition: "Such theoretical posturing turned history into a clever intellectual game. Chris was good at the game, but playing it, he had somehow lost track of a more straightforward reality—that the old texts recounted horrific stories and violent episodes that were all too often true." As he spends more time trapped in the Middle Ages, Chris continues his contemplation of modern life:

> For some reason, he found himself thinking of . . . the arguments among the graduate students. . . . It was no wonder they argued. The issues were pure abstractions, consisting of nothing but thin air—and hot air. Their empty debates could never be resolved; the questions could never be answered. Yet there had been so much intensity, so much passion in those debates. Where had it come from? Who cared? He couldn't quite remember now why it had been so important.

For Chris, the disorienting culture shock and the pain from the inadvertent jousting match with Sir Guy reunites him with the physical reality of life. His transformation is somewhat abrupt, but he gradually becomes less whiny and more manly until he is able to step into Marek's chivalric role and become Kate's protector. Ultimately the reader is led to identify with Chris as he rescues Kate from the knight at the Green Chapel and returns from his journey with a better understanding of not only the past, but the present as well.

Andre Marek is the scholar who does not study the past from a distance, but lives it even before experiencing quantum travel. He takes broadsword lessons and teaches archery because he believes in the romantic chivalric ideals. It is interesting to note that he is not an American as he speaks with " . . . just a trace of a Dutch accent," suggesting that Americans are too caught up in the pursuit of money and technological advancements to appreciate the value of history. The idea of Europe and its citizens as a cultural/historical artifact occurs again later in a discussion between the minister of antiquities of France and Professor Johnston: "You know there is a sentiment here that Americans destroy all culture, having none of their own." Marek, then, represents the culture itself as well as a way of incorporating the past into the present. Marek's decision to remain in the fourteenth century surprises no one. When Professor Johnston and the others find the location of Marek and Claire's tombs in the present, they discover that Marek's dying words were, "I have chosen a good life," indicating his satisfaction with his decision to stay. The Americans cannot quite accept this, however, and they invent a sadness for Marek that does not exist in the evidence given. When asked if he thought Marek was happy, Johnston replies affirmatively, but thinks to himself that " ... however much Marek loved it, it could never be his world. Not really. He must always have felt a foreigner there, a person separated from his surroundings, because he had come from somewhere else." Johnston can be seen as displacing his own feelings of exclusion from the rich cultural heritage of Europe.

Robert Doniger's personality is best described by his own words. When John Gordon reminds him that one of his employees has just died, suggesting that ITC is responsible, he gets the following response: "'That's true,' Doniger said coldly. 'And you know what? There's fuck all I can do about it. . . . Just handle it, okay?'" People do not matter to Doniger, and in that respect, he is "no different than other aggressive young entrepreneurs". All that concerns him is the pursuit of profit-generating knowledge. In many ways, Doniger is a caricature of Silicone Valley start-up entrepreneurs like Steve Jobs. His employees have nicknamed him "Dead March Doniger," but continue to work for him because he is nearly always

right in his criticisms, and he is undoubtedly a brilliant physicist.

Kate Erickson is the main female character of the novel, and as such modern feminist readers will particularly scrutinize her. At first glance, Kate seems to be an empowered woman character; she is not described physically, except as "ash-blond, blue-eyed and darkly tanned" but is instead characterized through her actions. Her rock-climbing ability makes her an active character early in the novel, and even allows her to rescue Andre and Chris from the tower in Castelguard. Her high-altitude action scene with Robert De Kere demonstrates her courage and wit. But in the end Kate's physically abilities and fearless nature fade into the background, and she becomes a woman in need of rescue at the Green Chapel. It is not surprising then, that she is seven months pregnant by the end of the book, incapable of rock climbing and seemingly resigned to a back-seat role of complaining about the air temperature.

The Lady Claire d'Eltham is a far better candidate for the empowered modern woman, except for the fact that she is a native of the fourteenth century. The reader is never privileged with Claire's thoughts, but she is always in the center of the action. Chris is the first to meet her, disguised as a boy. It turns out that she often cross-dresses in order to move freely in a society where women's roles are restricted. Claire seeks stability through marriage, and when she is discovered in an uncompromising position in the monastery, she defends her sexual exploits to Chris by saying, "How dare you judge me? I am a gentle woman, alone in a foreign part, with no one to champion me, to protect or guide me." Claire needs a husband whose physical strength and political power will shield her from rape and war, but she is not waiting for her prince to come, as the stereotypical medieval princess might, but instead has her first husband killed, directs Sir Guy (her next intended husband) in a charade of antagonism to allay the suspicion of the public about her husband's death, and grants the Abbot sexual favors in the hopes of gaining the secret of La Roque, displaying her political ambition. In the end, Claire's machinations pay off and she finds the husband and protector she desires in Marek.

◆ TECHNIQUES ◆

Crichton's background in science and medicine (he has a degree from Harvard medical school and worked as a medical researcher) has influenced his writing style to a great degree. His action and suspense novels are always based in scientific and technologic possibilities, earning him the title of master of the technothriller. He included a bibliography of his research in his first novel, *The Andromeda Strain*, as well as various graphics, charts and maps to aid the reader in understanding the medical jargon and setting the precedent for his future publications. By relying on research and facts to drive the narrative, Crichton avoids being criticized for his flat characters and generally uninteresting writing style. What he excels at is writing plots that combine action and pedantry to create exciting realism. He repeats this formula for success in *Timeline*. The reader knows only as much about the characters as is necessary to make their actions believable, but is given a crash course in quantum physics and medieval history.

Many of Crichton's novels are technothrillers, novels set in the present or near future, the plots of which revolve around scientific or technological advances. The decision by Crichton's publicists to call his novels technothrillers in the book jackets was probably also influenced by a desire to avoid the stigma attached to the term science fiction. Of course, any novel involv-

ing time travel also falls into that category and so it is useful to compare *Timeline* to other science fiction novels. Authors often use the genre as a way to avoid censorship or to allegorize their vision. Often, readers who are blind to certain aspects of their own culture when presented with them directly will be able to recognize them in an unfamiliar or futuristic setting. Thus, one aspect of H.G. Wells' *The War of the Worlds* (1898) is a commentary on England's fear of unchecked immigration, and Yevgeny Zamyatin's *We* (1921) is a direct criticism of communist Russia, but neither novel mentions their respective subjects directly. Crichton takes advantage of this aspect of science fiction and uses *Timeline* in part to criticize American corporate culture today without directly attacking it.

As in *Jurassic Park*, Crichton bases his vision of the future on his personal research on the subject. In the case of *Timeline*, he familiarized himself with a number of popular and scholarly publications on quantum physics and is therefore able to describe time travel in plausible language, avoiding the common science fiction writer's syndrome of employing meaningless pseudo-scientific terms that fool none but the most naïve of readers. Crichton makes the reader believe that if scientists have not yet been able to master time travel, they soon will. His research on fourteenth century France is even more extensive (compare the seventy-one history related citations to the ten scientific ones), and Chris, Kate and Marek's experiences in the past will satisfy both the general public and the historian. Readers must beware, however, of taking Crichton's footnoted citations in the novel seriously. Although Alistair I. M. Rae's "Quantum Physics: Illusion or Reality?" is listed in a footnote to the introduction, and the "typical episode of private warfare" account is similarly footnoted, he does not credit either author in the bibliography. Even more notably, "quotations" from Robert Doniger and Professor Johnston are mixed in with a quotation from Winston Churchill on the first page, blurring the line between research and fiction. Since Johnston and Doniger have net yet been introduced as characters, it is easy to mistake them for actual sources.

◆ LITERARY PRECEDENTS ◆

Timeline marks a turn away from modern and postmodern novels of discontent and disorganization, and a return to classical Romanticism. The medieval European setting facilitates a return to the epic tale and the chivalric romance. Traditionally, the hero of the epic slays the enemy and dies valiantly, as in *Beowulf* and *Sir Gawain and the Green Knight*. The return to equilibrium is not quite complete because Marek stays behind and there are notes of regret as well as satisfaction with his decision to do so. The plot follows the typical disturbance of equilibrium at the beginning (Professor Johnston gets lost in the past), a chronicle of the struggle (Chris, Kate and Marek enter the past to retrieve Johnston), and finally a return to balance that concludes the novel (everyone returns to their proper time periods). Although ITC still exists and will still pursue research in quantum travel, *Timeline* closes with the positive view that now that ITC is under capable management no further dangerous mistakes will occur.

Crichton's knight of the Green Chapel section is a clear nod to the medieval tale of *Sir Gawain and the Green Knight* (ca. 1390). Crichton's Green Chapel is defended by "a huge man, nearly seven feet tall, and his armor . . . smeared with green mold . . . ," basically a literal interpretation of the Green Knight. The original *Gawain* is an Arthurian romance which, according to prominent scholars in the field, focuses on the hero's personal growth in self-awareness as he journeys to meet and fight the Green Knight. In *Gawain*, the Green Knight issues his challenge to King Arthur, but Gawain accepts the challenge in his place. Similarly, Marek is the leader of the small group of twentieth century scholars, and the one with the most battle experience, but Chris is the one who fights the knight at the Green Chapel because the novel is about *his* journey to self-awareness.

Other time-travel narratives are worth examining in conjunction with *Timeline*, such as Tim Power's *The Anubis Gates* (1983), which has a very similar premise to *Timeline*. Brendan Doyle is a Samuel Taylor Coleridge scholar hired by a mysterious businessman, J. Cochran Darrow, to partake in a trial run of a new program his company has developed. Doyle is sent back to Victorian London for the unique opportunity of hearing Coleridge lecture in person. All goes well until he gets separated from the group and misses his chance to return. Like Professor Johnston and the others, Doyle must fend for himself. The idea of sending historians or other scholars back in time to do hands on research is not new then. Powers falls back on ancient Egyptian magic to enable his characters to travel in time, and although quantum physics is mentioned in trying to explain how it works, he on the whole avoids the technological specifics.

◆ RELATED TITLES ◆

In his 1990 *Jurassic Park*, Crichton brought dinosaurs to life in the present day. The goal of Dr. Alan Grant was to create a learning experience with his theme park, but he failed to foresee nature's adaptability and the dinosaurs learn to breed and escape. The message in *Jurassic Park* is that we cannot bring the past into the present for our enjoyment. *Timeline* takes up the converse of this idea: if we cannot bring the past alive in the present, then perhaps we can send ourselves into the past instead. The close of *Timeline* suggests that although this particular trip was disastrous (two dead, one missing), it might yet be possible to time travel safely. With Doniger out of the way, ITC is left to the levelheaded management of Stern and Gordon. *Eaters of the Dead* (1991) was renamed *The Thirteenth Warrior* after being made into a film in 1999. It relates to *Timeline* as it is a reworking of *Beowulf,* one of the oldest poems in English, and Crichton borrowed from medieval literary traditions in *Timeline* as well.

◆ ADAPTATIONS ◆

Timeline is available as a book on tape from USA Random House Audio Publishing, Inc. Read by John Bedford Lloyd. Producer Robert Kessler. 15 hours, 9 cassettes, unabridged. 1999. Also available abridged on cassette and compact disc and a Random House Large Print edition and hardcover from Alfred A. Knopf.

◆ IDEAS FOR GROUP DISCUSSIONS ◆

Timeline easily sparks many discussions about the role of technology and history in today's society. Science fiction writers always begin by asking the question, what if? What if time travel were possible in the future—what would the dangers be? What would the benefits be? Crichton's novel also asks readers to reevaluate their notions of what it means to be a scholar of history.

1. Robert Doniger makes the statement: ". . . it is an entirely benign and peaceful technology that will provide a great benefit to mankind." Discuss the accuracy of the statement. Is it possible for technology to be completely beneficial? You might consider the case of nuclear technology as well.

2. Notice that there is no mention of government intervention in Doniger's project. It is as if businesses operate in a world governed by separate rules. Does this make them a danger to the individual citizen? Discuss the dangers in corporate sponsorship of research and scholarly projects.

3. Discuss what Johnston means when he says that temporal provincials are like leaves that do not know they are part of a tree. Why is it so important to understand the past? How can it help us to foresee the future?

4. Crichton's characters are often criticized as being flat and having no interior personality. Discuss a) Chris Hughes' transition from pampered intellectual to man of action. Is it convincing? and b) compare Kate Erickson and Claire d'Eltham. Does Crichton portray them as convincing female characters?

Kara L. Andersen
Northeastern University

TO HAVE AND HAVE NOT

Novel

1937

Author: Ernest Hemingway

◆

◆ SOCIAL CONCERNS ◆

"*To Have and Have Not* is a stupid and foolish book, a disgrace to a good writer, a book which should never have been printed," wrote Delmore Schwartz a few months after it was published. Others reviewers concurred: "it is a book with neither poise nor integration, and with shocking lapses from professional skill." What is it about the story of Harry Morgan, ex-Miami cop, ex-gunrunner, ex-bootlegger turned fishing-boat charter captain, that could provoke such caustic reactions?

The 1930s were the decade of the Depression, hitting the nadir in 1932. In literature it was the decade of the proletarian novel, of the literary manifesto, and of the socially committed writer. How did Hemingway fit into this picture? Not at all. In the wake of his second marriage, he wallowed for the first time in luxury, going on expensive African safaris, fishing off his forty-foot oceangoing boat, and thumbing his nose at the Leftist press, which alternately wooed him or skewered him for his ostentatious disregard for the Cause. Worse for a writer, he had not published a novel since *A Farewell to Arms* (1929) and, if his commercial short fiction told a story, the supernova of his talent was burning itself out, settling into a dull glow. "Famous at twenty-five: thirty a master...," in Archibald MacLeish's well-known words, Hemingway in the 1930s was struggling for inspiration and artistic direction, while savagely resenting the critical success of writers like John Dos Passos, who in 1936 became the first of his generation to make the cover of *Time*. *To Have and Have Not* was thus the result of a prolonged artistic reinvention as well as a response to the Marxists who had pilloried Hemingway for his cult of the individual in the age of the masses.

In many ways *To Have and Have Not* is the most socially dedicated of all Papa's works. Perhaps not incidentally, it is also the sole novel he ever set in America, even if only in its rugged southern tip, the Florida Keys. Key West had become Hemingway's permanent residence in 1930, and this domestic setting likely intensified his domestic concerns, including the plight of World War One veterans employed by the government on highway construction on the Keys. On Labour Day, 1935—an irony that was not missed by the writer—a hurricane struck the Keys, destroying a Civilian Conservation Corps work camp in which several hundred Vets drowned. After rushing supplies to the survivors on his own boat, *Pilar*, an incensed Hemingway penned an article for the Marxist *New Masses*, calling it "Who Murdered the Vets." In it he demanded to know why the homeless and ill-paid veterans had been stranded in the camp despite advance hurricane warning, in effect accusing the Florida bureaucrats and the Roosevelt administration of manslaughter. It is obvious that these concerns carry over into the novel, both in its economic outlook, as well as into some of its last scenes in which the drunken, fractious veterans swap stories of Depression-era filth and decay. What is equally obvious is that the novel's social "message" is so intrusive and preachy that it fully justifies Schwartz's critical indictment. If Part One of this tripartite book is mostly devoid of ideological crudities and authorial commentary, Part Three is riddled with Hemingway's heavy-handed contrasts between the haves and have-nots. But it is actually in Part Two that a plaintive question from Harry's Negro deckhand, Wesley, nails down the ghost of 1930s economics. "Why they run liquor now?" whines Wesley, even as the two men bleed from gun wounds sustained in a botched smuggling run from Cuba. "Prohibition's over. Why they keep up a traffic like that? Why don't people be honest and decent and make a decent honest living?"

One answer is that honest work brings starvation wages. The 1930s meant breadlines, soup kitchens, twelve million unemployed, packing-box shanty towns (dubbed Hoovervilles), closed insolvent banks, boarded-up bankrupt stores, businesses frantically buying civil-order insurance at Lloyd's in London, nationwide garbage picking, and panhandling so widespread that the papers picked the popular song, "Brother, Can You Spare a Dime," as a new national anthem. If F. D. R. could say in his inaugural speech: "I see one-third of a nation ill-housed, ill-clad, ill-nourished," so could Captain Willie tell the two Florida bureaucrats who would later take away Harry's boat, and thus his livelihood: "Who the hell do you eat off of with people working here in Key West for the government for six dollars and a half a week?" This dark shadow is never far from the local Conchs who work for starvation wages, the whores harassed by new curfew regulations, and Harry who turns permanently to illicit hustling when the Depression puts charter-boat fishing on the bum.

Another answer is the economic twist on the "rags to riches" theme, as enshrined in the *American Mirage*. In this land of opportunity, anyone with a zest for entrepreneurship has an equal opportunity to pursue business or so goes the myth. Harry's post-Prohibition smuggling is a buccaneering form of civil disobedience, 100 percent American in spirit, directed at government interference through high taxes levied on alcohol. In his way Harry Morgan is no different from such figures as Joseph Kennedy, who made untold millions during the Prohibition bootlegging whisky from Montreal distilleries, becoming a symbol of economic success and the head of the country's top political clan. Like Kennedy, Hemingway's hero incarnates the spirit of laisser-faire, supply-demand economics. Unlike Kennedy, who was able to grease too many hands to fear the law, the lone-wolf, small-scale operator like Harry ends up in Part Three without his right arm or his boat, driven only by a gut conviction that "there ain't no law that you got to go hungry."

There are many ways in which *To Have and Have Not* labours to evoke a class- and society-conscious picture of the times. It shows us drunken and bestialized Vets who smash each other senseless just to prove they can take it, two generations of "sporting women" who trade in the only assets they have, Cuban revolutionaries who spit out political slogans about the tyranny in their native island, vindictive government officials, bristling with disdain for the working Joe, and the dissolute, corrupt, vacuous, millionaire haves. And yet, one cannot shake the feeling that in transcending his political indifference, Hemingway has not transcended his political ignorance. His criticism of the upper classes, for example, is developed in such naive and ridiculous terms (often degenerating into denunciations of sexual impotence, aberration, or promiscuity) that the reader wonders if the author misunderstood his own purpose. Likewise, his contrasts between the privileged haves and the underprivileged Harry (who owns a Florida house, good furniture, a piano, a car, several guns, a big boat with two engines, etc.) are so contrived that, as the *Nation* scorned, "nothing could be more inept here, more lacking in true insight."

This is harsh, but not unjust criticism. Yet even in this uneven book there are glimpses of the old Hemingway, subtle, hard-nosed and ironic, especially in his treatment of the Cuban revolution. Notwithstanding his deep involvement in the Spanish Civil War and his agitprop work for the Loyalists (e.g., on the 1937 film, *The Spanish Earth*), the novelist offers a more sophisticated attitude to the slogans about proletarian dictatorship, the brotherhood of working men, or the people's revolution in Cuba. Given the blistering irony which undermines the young Cuban's defense of Stalin-type terrorism, as well as Harry's curt verdict: "F—— his revolution," it is hard to believe that any Marxist faction could take *To Have and Have Not* as a piece of orthodox propaganda. That they did, thinking Hemingway a less discerning writer than he was, is clear from Edmund Wilson's 1939 exasperated report: "the Left . . . received his least credible piece of fiction as a delivery of a new revelation."

If Hemingway intended to create a fictional document of the surrounding social decay, his success must be measured not by the crude volleys he fires at the dissolute rich, but by more subtle scenes which, like his famous narrative iceberg, pack so much veracity that they freeze the spine. "When the fleet's in New York and you go ashore . . . there's old guys with long beards come down and you can piss in their beards for a dollar," gloats a smashed masochist veteran. This stark image of old men from the dregs of society inviting strangers to urinate on them says more about the poverty and despair which reduce human beings to such humiliating practices, than pages of righteous indignation. The feeling that for a dollar many people will embrace any indignity is as revealing as the realization that a supply of such abnormal services arises in response to the demand. Unflinching but understated, this image is vintage Hemingway telling us something about the decay of the American Dream.

◆ THEMES ◆

For a writer who once said that writing is architecture and not interior decoration, Hemingway's book betrays the haphazard story of its genesis. The many disparities between the three parts are only one sign of a midcourse switch from a hard-boiled and hard-hitting story of the decline of an individual, to an unfocused and watered-down novel about Harry Morgan and society. Still, enough remains of the initial design to make Harry's tragic downfall, played out with an almost classical relentlessness, a major theme. Like Oedipus Rex, whom we also encounter at the top of his station in life, Harry's efforts to outfox his fate are tinged with the premonition of doom. His fall is traced by the subtitles of the book's parts: Spring, Fall, and Winter, the last one a symbol of death. In Spring Harry suffers only a bite wound; in the Fall section he is shot and loses an arm; in Winter he loses his life. If in Spring he still appears in control of his destiny, refusing to smuggle Cuban revolutionaries, by Winter he is sufficiently ensnared in the web of his declining fortunes to do exactly what he had resisted before: taking them across to their island.

Harry's decline accelerates as he loses his fishing equipment, then his client, money, honour, contraband liquor, right arm, boat, shipmate, and finally his life. But even if his course in life is mapped by the economic forces around him, he never fully surrenders the helm. By not relieving Harry of the responsibility for his actions, Hemingway examines another theme: the limits of primitive individualism in the increasingly domesticated and bureaucratic America. Harry's uncompromising and lawless self-reliance is a living embodiment of the twin ideals to which so many literary intellectuals who read Emerson and Thoreau pay lip service. This is not to imply, of course, that Harry is a budding working-class agitator. His rebelliousness, just like his morality, is of a crassly pragmatic type ("what's moral is what you feel good after"), another theme in Papa's frequently hard-boiled but never amoral stories.

Harry is not interested in stirring up class consciousness in the oppressed Conchs, aiding the simmering Cuban revolt against the American-sponsored regime, or symbolically defying the Big Business government. His aims, like those of Walter Huff in James Cain's *Double Indemnity*, are much more selfish and nonprogrammatic. Hemingway's hero wants to beat the system designed more and more for government statistics and mass economics rather than for lone sea-cowboys. This is why he flatly refuses to help Cuban revolutionaries get to their island, unceremoniously robs Chinese poor of the passage which they had paid for, or guns down four militants in order to steal the cash set aside for the revolution. The author touches here on one of the great American themes: the cult of the romanticized nonconformist and maverick in, para-

doxically, a country of mass production, mass culture and mass culture-produced beliefs such as, for example, the belief in the value of maverick nonconformism.

Another theme which unites Hemingway's writings is the continuous presence of, and the need for response to, aggression and violence. Although focusing so often on the value of human relationships or the importance of the individual's conduct in society, Hemingway is sometimes stigmatized as an aficionado of machismo brutality. The waterfront milieu is, of course, in many ways like a city jungle, with its tough guys, hard no-nonsense attitudes, coarse talk, dark bars and crooked deals, guns, liquor, and the violent echoes of revolt in Cuba. It is a hard environment in a hard book in which thirteen men die a violent and at times naturalistically graphic death. But it is not half as hard as the picture of the world at war that so often emerges from Hemingway's novels. It is a harsh, indifferent world, with little hope for the lot of man. It is a place, it would seem, into which people are brought only to take a beating from life. What saves them, in the end, even while they lick their wounds, is their code of conduct: the saving grace of those doomed to suffer may be the style with which they go down.

In this light, Harry's famous last words, "No matter how a man alone ain't got no bloody fucking chance," seem a betrayal of the code, a breach of unwritten contract with the harsh but never valueless natural world, and a denial of all that he had been in his life. In truth, they read like a banner headline inserted by the author for the sake of giving a moral to the story—and for this reason they ring false. Some critics have taken these parting words as Hemingway's call to solidarity among the oppressed working poor. Such an interpretation may have been intended by the author; still, it seems false when considered in the context of

Harry's every thought and action prior to this miraculous proletarian conversion.

If we are to interpret the novel in terms of famous last words, we should remember that the last statement belongs not to Harry, but to his wife. For readers familiar with *Ulysses*, it may be hard to shake the feeling that Marie's soliloquy is patterned on Molly Bloom's free association from the end of Joyce's novel. The connection between the two novelists is not as farfetched as it might appear: in 1922 Hemingway went around Paris collecting subscriptions for Joyce's new novel and eventually even devised a plan to smuggle forty copies into the U.S. (his own copy, however, has pages cut only in the first half and in the final soliloquy). In a theme that weaves in and out of Hemingway's best fiction, Marie, in her muted outpouring of grief, seems not that different from Frederic Henry in *A Farewell to Arms*, who sees people's lives mirrored in the behaviour of frantic and meaningless ants on a burning log, forever scrambling to nonexistent safety. Yet akin to Molly's life-affirming "Yes," from underneath Marie's despair emerges a kind of resigned acceptance that life must indeed go on, with or without the people we care for. The sun also rises, teaches the Ecclesiastes, in a part of Nature's code with which Hemingway's characters always struggle to be in harmony.

◆ CHARACTERS ◆

As much as Hemingway may have wanted his protagonist to function as an individual, Harry Morgan is little more than a type of a rogue individualist with the Gulf as the last frontier for his masculine way of life. "Don't be so tough so early in the morning. I'm sure you've cut plenty people's throats. I haven't even had my coffee yet," replies the hero to a veiled threat on the third page, sounding for all the world like Hammett's or Chandler's tough hero. There are more ways in which Harry corresponds to the image of an independent hard-boiled operator from the pages of 1930s detective fiction. He hires out for a fixed amount a day plus expenses, talks in a tough mono-syllabic vernacular, and takes the law into his own hands when he kills unsavoury characters like Mr. Sing or the four trigger-happy bank robbers. This checks with his being an ex-cop from Miami who still keeps his Smith & Wesson .38 police special, is used to violence, thinks like a detective, and is an efficient killer, bare-handed or not.

Even in physical appearance he seems to be a Sam Spade look-alike: tall, hulking, strong, muscular, blond, with a broken nose in a formidable-looking face. Needless to say, women find him extremely attractive, perhaps because there is something piratical about him. This is hardly an accident: Harry's model, Henry Morgan, was a famed buccaneer who, prior to his being knighted, used to terrorize the Caribbean, even capturing the city of Panama. Another real-life precursor may have been Joe Russell, a boat captain in Key West who ran rum during Prohibition. On the literary front, there is also Hemingway's anonymous hero of a 1932 short story, "After the Storm," another tough-minded and hard-fisted Key West captain of a seagoing boat.

There are notable differences, of course, between the Marlowe-type detective-romantic and Hemingway's protagonist. For one, Harry is happily married to Marie, a big, heavyset, bleached-blonde ex-hooker with whom he has three daughters. He is also completely ruthless, expediently contemplating killing Eddie, the first of his three deckhands (the others are Wesley and a local Key-islander, Albert). A loner with no pity for himself or others, he acts (and kills) for his own selfish ends. In a 1943 letter to Howard Hawks, Hemingway tried to gloss it over, painting Harry as "a man who tried to buck this world single handed and found that it couldn't be done and that men had to stick together to win." But Morgan is a cold-blooded, venal, criminal manipulator not above unscrupulously ditching hapless Chinks so they don't smell up the boat, consenting to an armed bank robbery, or playing on Albert's emotions to secure a mate for a rite of mass murder. The implicit defense of Harry—that he only exterminates robbers of people, Mr. Sing and the four Cuban militants who kill Albert for no reason—leaves out too much to be persuasive. The questions remain: what would happen if people like Harry stuck together to win in society? And who exactly is Hemingway trying to make us sympathize with? All other characters of note are introduced in the longest Part Three, in which Harry gradually yields the center stage to the two groups which typecast the economic contrast between America's haves and have-nots. The first are the rowdy bar patrons: Vets, drunks, labour organizers; the second are mainly the owners of luxury yachts moored alongside the finger piers of Key West. Among them are a rich playboy and his homosexual companion, an old grain broker pursued by the "Internal Revenue Bureau," a nymphomaniacal Hollywood starlet and, in a contrast, the happy family of a business tycoon who earned his wealth by honest industry—all introduced in the single, albeit longest Chapter 24. Other members of this elite group are the sexually estranged couple, Tommy and Helène Bradley, as well as the latter's lover, Richard Gordon, a prominent writer of proletarian novels, on whom Hemingway pours most of his scorn. Hemingway insisted in a *Paris Review* interview with Philip Young: "The most essential gift for a good writer is a built-in, shock-proof, shit detector."

One wonders if it stood the author in good stead during the writing of *To Have and Have Not,* inasmuch as Richard Gordon is little more than a caricature of the type of a proletarian writer, and a vicious slander of John Dos Passos, the author of the brilliant epic *U.S.A.* (1930–1936). Ironically Gordon—who employs stock characters, errs in sizing up people, is given to cliches, and is despised by real labourites who tell him his novels are shit—specializes in the kind of fiction that his creator tried to write. Hemingway has allowed personal animosity to drain Gordon of any narrative distinction so that, like the distasteful lawyer, Bee-lips Simmons, the Marxist writer becomes no more than another cardboard type. The book's cast also includes his wife, Helen, who, dissatisfied with Richard in and out of bed, takes up with the quirky but amiable Professor MacWalsey.

◆ TECHNIQUES ◆

In many ways the first three quarters of *To Have and Have Not* are a gripping adventure story with many elements straight out of an action movie: violent shoot-outs, ruthless assassinations, big-game fishing, immigrant smuggling, rum running, boat stealing, bank robbery, cold-blooded murder. The action moves swiftly between boat decks and the back of Freddy's bar, peppered with shady deals hammered out in hard-boiled street talk. Hemingway's real-life model for the bar was an establishment on Key West run by Sloppy Joe in which, prior to the book's publication, he repeatedly boasted that it would be a blockbuster. True to his word, it went through four printings in the first two months, stayed on the best-sellers list from October to December 1937, sold 36,000 copies in the first five months, and earned him his first appearance on the cover of *Time.* How could anyone be so sure of success? It is likely that Hemingway's conviction had something to do with the popularity of the hard-boiled genre which he knew would sell well with the public. In fact, several years later he would describe *To Have and Have Not* tongue-in-cheek as a "frail volume . . . devoted to adultery, sodomy, masturbation, rape, mayhem, mass murder, frigidity, alcoholism, prostitution, impotency, anarchy, rum-running, chink-smuggling, nymphomania and abortion." In other words, a chart burner. True enough, the book has a ten-minute-egg equivalent of a hard-boiled hero with a hard-boiled attitude, copious amounts of murder and violence, and several sex scenes. Moreover, it is written mostly in the hard-boiled style, with terse and simple diction, repetitive and colloquial sentence structure, plenty of slang, little passive voice, an understated and unsentimental point of view, and on occasion a direct address to the reader. Among the welter of slapdash prose, pseudo-modernistic passages in italics, and comic-book contrasts between the floundering haves and the virile have-nots, the Third (and weakest) Part stylistically approaches at times the stream of consciousness.

Short chapters, minimum exposition, and few discursive passages (except at the end) coincide with a largely episodic structure, which reflects perhaps the book's piecemeal origin. During the summer of 1936 Hemingway wrote only Part Three—i.e., about sixty-five percent, inserting as the first two parts previously published stories: "One Trip Across" (*Cosmopolitan*, 1934) and "The Tradesman's Return" (*Esquire*, 1936). The lack of coherence, which led some critics to murmur that the book's only unity was in the binding, was not news to the author who admitted: "It came out as a new novel, but it was short stories, and there is a hell of a lot of difference." In 1937 he thus lobbied the publisher to issue the book in an omnibus volume together with previous short-story hits, "The Short Happy Life of Francis Macomber," "The Snows of Kilimanjaro," and "The Capital of the World." In another brainstorm, he pushed for an anthology (to be titled *To Have and Have Not, The Various Arms, or Return to the Wars*) which was to contain the novel, the three

stories, the *New Masses* article, one of his news dispatches from Madrid, and the speech he gave in New York at the Writers' Congress. In the end, on advice from his friend and editor, Max Perkins, the book was published as we know it. On further advice from Arnold Gingrich, Hemingway dropped large sections of material which libeled some of his erstwhile friends, notably Dos Passos. As Gingrich records, Hemingway simply mutilated the second half of the book "without any sort of replacements for the deleted elements. I thought the least he might have done would have been to change the title, because, as the book appeared, the title applied about like the 'fifty-fifty' recipe for hamburger: one horse, one rabbit. It was a little disillusioning."

To Have and Have Not experiments, sometimes more and sometimes less nimbly, with the point of view. Part One is entirely in Harry's first-person narration; Part Two employs a third-person narrator with a focus on Harry; Part Three is a melange of Albert's first-person narration, Harry's internal monologue in a stream of thought more cogent than a typical stream of consciousness, and an omniscient narrator who goes in and out of characters' minds. The imagery, metaphors and similes are often urban or military in origin, like a gigantic marlin described in terms of an aeroplane, submarine or a depth bomb, or the two icons of the lawless Prohibition, the Thompson gun and sawed-off shotgun, which make an appearance in gangster-style shoot-outs. While the book's irony is usually overdone, the symbolism is often subtle and poignant. Swindled by Mr. Johnson of a great deal of money, Harry is reduced, in his own words, to peddling his *cojones* in an effort to make a living. In an evocative parallel, Chapter 24 begins by introducing Henry Carpenter who, as a lover and hanger-on of Mr. Wallace Johnson, also peddles his *cojones* to the rich. In general, however, Hemingway's book is not convincing either as a socioeconomic study, nor as a study of the poor, a satire of the rich, a critique of the ineptitude of the government, a hero study, or even as a novel in the first place. Despite some fine writing in the sections involving Harry, there is little overall integration of the plot, much uninspired prose towards the end, a contrived feeling in the modernistic devices, all culminating in the portrayal of the rich which has the social and intellectual subtlety of a brilliant adolescent.

◆ RELATED TITLES ◆

It is difficult to talk about *To Have and Have Not* outside the context of hard-boiled fiction, a new and exciting subgenre that emerged in America in the first years of the century. The interest in and production of crime fiction grew so fast that almost overnight the detective story became a separate category in the magazine industry, getting its own heading in *The Reader's Guide to Periodical Literature* as early as 1905. By the 1930s there had been a virtual explosion of hard-boiled fiction on newsstands, as witnessed in the proliferation of pulp magazines such as *Action Detective, Clues,* and *Black Mask.* Although Hemingway disliked the hard-boiled school, on more than one occasion he acknowledged his admiration for Raymond Chandler, unquestionably the most renowned practitioner of the genre. Published in 1937, *To Have and Have Not* came of course before Chandler's first novel, *The Big Sleep* (1939), but several years after Chandler's contributions had begun to appear in *Black Mask* and other magazines.

A more immediate literary precedent may be John Steinbeck's little-known first novel, *Cup of Gold* (1929), a fictional account of the life of the historical Henry Morgan, the pirate. Even though there seems to be not a single passing reference to Steinbeck in the Hemingway canon, the subject matter alone suggests that Papa may have known of the earlier work, which begins with a young Henry Morgan who fancies going to sea and becoming a great adventurer. Betrayed and sold as an indentured servant, he shrewdly bides his time, eventually organizing a seaworthy band of pirates. After countless conquests he crowns his bloody reign with the capture of both Panama and the fabled Caribbean beauty known as La Santa Roja. Yet Morgan does not stick together with his brothers-in-arms, selling out for his own selfish ends. He deserts his companions and, granted a full pardon and knighthood from the British monarch, settles in Jamaica with a well-bred wife where he serves out his life as a Lieutenant-Governor. In the end, Steinbeck's protagonist isolates himself from his class and joins the ranks of the aristocratic "haves," proving, in his father's apt words, that just like Hemingway's Harry, "he can realize no thought, no reason, but his own."

◆ ADAPTATIONS ◆

In 1945 Hollywood released the first film adaptation of *To Have and Have Not.* With the screenplay developed by William Faulkner and Jules Furthman, and with very close directions from producer-director Howard Hawks, the film was essentially a screen version of Chapter 1 (of twenty-six) of the book. Although it bore the title of *To Have and Have Not,* thus capitalizing on Hemingway's marketability, Hawks agreed with the critics that the book was not worth much. It held little promise as movie material, he said, since it was too much of a proletarian novel of the '30s. For this reason the peacetime setting of the book's Key West is changed to the island of Martinique, the echoes of revolt in Cuba become the echoes of World War II, and the smuggled revolutionaries are replaced by a member of the French Resistance and his attractive wife. With Humphrey Bogart in the main role, and a local hotel as the backdrop, this all begins to sound suspiciously like Casablanca, and there is indeed plenty of indication that the studio intended *To Have and Have Not* to be another version of the film which won Warner Brothers the Best Picture Award for 1943. As a matter of fact, after the preview the studio chief sent out a memo to the staff: "Polish up the picks, shovels and pans for the gold mine on the way in Howard Hawks' production of Ernest Hemingway's *To Have and Have Not* ... which is not only a second Casablanca but two and a half times what Casablanca was."

The final product—a black-and-white film of 101 minutes, photographed by Sid Hickox, and co-starring the then-new starlet, Lauren Bacall, the incomparable Walter Brennan as Eddie, as well as Dolores Moran and Hoagy Carmichael—is a story of an American fishing-boat captain who gets involved with a young female drifter and some French freedom fighters pursued by the local Nazis. While Bogart and Bacall smoke cigarettes trading wisecracks and smouldering innuendos, the movie serves several musical numbers, lots of hard-boiled dialogue and the kind of Hollywood-cooked plot that makes it clear that the film was made as a vehicle for Bogart rather than out of any deference for the novel. In Jerry Wald-produced *Key Largo* (Warner Brothers, 1948), which also starred Bogey and Bacall, the director John Huston used another sliver of the book, the gunfight on the boat for the climax of the film. The second significant version of Hemingway's material is *The Breaking Point* (Warner Brothers, 1950), directed by Michael Curtiz (of *Casablanca* fame), produced again by Wald, written by Ranald MacDougall and starring John Garfield and Leona Charles. Key West has become Newport, California; there are no revolutionaries; in fact, in this '50s production there is nothing political at all. Harry is happily married, with two daughters (like in the book), and in another bow towards the original source, gets involved in smuggling Chinese for Mr. Sing whom he will kill in self-defense. Once again, this is roughly the subject of only the first part of Hemingway's novel; still, the author is on record as having sent notes to Wald and Garfield saying the movie suited him.

The last screen version of the novel, released in 1958 by Seven Arts Productions (which in the meantime acquired the rights from the Warner's) as *The Gun Runners*, had previously borne the working titles of *Rub My Back, One Trip Across* and *Ernest Hemingway's Gun Runners*. Despite the fact that the references in the last two titles were designed more for publicity than anything else, the movie is in some ways closer to the book than the previous versions. Produced by Clarence Green, directed by Don Siegel, with the script by Daniel Mainwaring, it introduces Sam Martin (played by Audie Murphy) and his sexy wife Lucy (Patricia Owens). Martin, who runs a charter-boat service, loses a valuable rod and reel when he takes a Mr. Peterson fishing and when he fails to settle the debt, takes up smuggling machine guns to Cuba with a shady operator named Hanagan. In the last fateful run Hanagan reveals himself to be a double-crosser and, while wounding the hero in the shoulder, is himself killed in the final onboard shoot-out.

◆ IDEAS FOR GROUP DISCUSSIONS ◆

Although the literary hard-boiled '20s and '30s are no longer with us, the persistent divisions between the haves and have-nots in society have only become more pronounced. With individuals effectively disfranchised by the political system, and with less than ten percent of the nation owning most of its wealth, Hemingway's protest novel strikes a surprisingly topical chord at the brink of the new millennium.

In forming your response to this novel you may wish to consider the following questions:

1. Does the book develop as a unified and seamless narrative or does it emerge as a collection of shorter pieces? How does it affect your appreciation of the story?

2. Is Hemingway's portrayal of Harry closer to that of a ruthless and self-centred killer or a solidarity-questing, working-class have-not?

3. How much of the criticism levelled at the proletarian writings of Richard Gordon applies to *To Have and Have Not?*

4. Can you ferret out all references and allusions to the Cuban Revolution? What role do the island and the revolution play in the novel?

5. Is Marie's final soliloquy a condemnation of the world and the social system, or an acceptance of life with all its tragedies and iniquities? Both? Neither?

6. Did you find the depiction of the novel's haves convincing? Why?

7. Given that the book uses so many points of view and styles of narration, what would be the author's reasons for such experimentation?

8. How much did you learn about America in the 1930s from reading this novel?

9. How do you interpret the book's closing image of a yacht and a tanker at sea?

10. Is *To Have and Have Not* a hard-boiled novel and, if so, in what respects?

Peter Swirski
Comparative Literature, University of
Alberta

TO SAY NOTHING OF THE DOG

Novel

1998

Author: Connie Willis

◆

T he primary social concern in *To Say Nothing of the Dog* focuses on our relation to the past. Many consider this a peculiarly American concern, a suspicion which seems to be shared by the narrator, Ned Henry. The novel, which takes place in England, shows early work on the time machine occurring at Oxford, suggesting that the English connection to the past is somehow more secure and accessible, even tangible, than elsewhere. It is also significant that Lady Schrapnell is American, not English. A certain amount of nationalism comes into play, as it is pointed out that Lady Schrapnell, who devises and coordinates the plan to rebuild Coventry Cathedral in Oxford, is American by birth, only having gained English nobility through marriage. Her desire to rebuild the cathedral arises from reading her great-great-great-great-grandmother's diary, where her ancestor records a life-changing visit to Coventry Cathedral where she saw the bishop's bird stump. The original cathedral, which had been partially destroyed in the Blitz in 1940 (ironically, destroyed by earlier renovations which had weakened the structure), had later been sold by the Church of England to a cult, been burned and restored, and eventually been turned into a shopping center. It takes an American to bring back what could be considered a national treasure, and most of the English characters do not seem grateful.

Judgments made by people of later periods almost always differ from the ideas of earlier eras. For instance, when Terence and Ned are on the river together, Ned admires the beautiful, unspoiled scenery, while Terence laments how industry has, to him, ruined the landscape. The architecture Ned and Verity admire, Mrs. Mering and her friends dismiss as "medieval," which, of course, it is, literally as well as figuratively. The artwork Mrs. Mering and her contemporaries admire, Ned and Verity and their peers dismiss as cluttered, sentimental, and, in essence, ugly. The reader is led to agree with the travelers from the future and Baine that Victorian artwork such as the bishop's bird stump is unattractive, because they are sympathetic and the reader agrees with other judgments they make. As a novelist cannot show his or her audience an object but must describe it, Willis does everything in her power to convey the message that the bishop's bird stump is bad art: the sympathetic characters criticize it while the unsympathetic characters rave about it; the description itself, highlighting its crowded nature and mixed themes, agrees with our usual notions of aesthetics; and even though the multiple scenes are meant to be representational, no one can agree on what a given scene is meant to portray.

This revulsion to the art of the time runs counter to the nostalgic appreciation of previous eras that people tend to begin with. It is easy to romanticize the past, but studying the real conditions that existed reveals that all times have their own problems. In the Victorian period, despite the elegant depiction suggested by the classical learning of Professor Peddick and Terence, and Terence's ability to quote poetry for all occasions, not all was in fact so utopian.

While Willis only lightly touches upon some of the problems brought about by the Industrial Revolution and increased urbanization, she does address sex-, nation-, and class-based inequities. For instance, the prejudice against educating women is central to the Tossie-Baine plot. Because of Tossie's annoying qualities and the fact that Terence, a generally likable character, predicts that Professor Peddick's niece Maud would be a bluestocking, overly educated for a woman, the reader may agree with the general attitude, excusing the misogyny as a product of its time. However, by the end of the novel, any doubts are resolved: Terence finds he prefers the well-educated Maud to the thoughtless Tossie; at the same time, Baine reveals that he thinks Tossie is petulant and spoiled not because she is naturally disagreeable but because her natural talents have never been encouraged. Once he begins educating her, she does not immediately become perfect, but her demeanor improves markedly.

Tossie's reformation is doubly significant as she overcomes the expectations she has acquired from her society for her sex and the prejudices taught her as a member of her class. Before her change, Tossie frequently reminds Baine that he is a servant. To Ned's non-contemporary eyes, the Merings' treatment of their butler is ridiculous. They treat him nearly as subhuman. They changed his name to suit their convenience, and never consider whether their demands of him are reasonable, often giving him multiple Herculean tasks to accomplish simultaneously. In fact, Baine, as a servant, is not even allowed to express his opinions without permission. Ned notes that this attitude is why Karl Marx wrote his Manifesto. Baine's curiosity about America and its opportunities for people of lower classes also serves as a challenge to the novel's earlier seeming Anglocentrism. When Baine and Tossie flee to America where their mismatched class status will not be objectionable, and Baine will be able to pursue a different career, America's advantages become obvious. (Humorously, Baine considers movie acting to be the best way to capitalize on his considerable intelligence and skills.) In another example, the Merings discourage Terence's infatuation with Tossie until Mrs. Mering discovers that he is from a titled and wealthy family. England's traditions and connection to the past turn out to be a potential burden as they inhibit change that could bring about beneficial, progressive transformation; America's comparative social openness allows greater personal freedom.

The high-handed attitude toward workers is not restricted to Victorian times, either. When Ned travels back in time to witness the building of the cathedral in the medieval period, he sees a woman (an ancestor of Mrs. Mering and Lady Schrapnell) behaving the same way. Interestingly, Ned, while feeling sympathetic for the workers and servants, and while he compares the dictatorial women to each other, does not typically compare himself to the other oppressed workers. Class is, however, still important in the future of this novel. Determined by money more than birth, class contributes largely to Lady Schrapnell's dominance. Her influence begins when she offers to buy equipment for Oxford they could not otherwise afford. Her role as benefactress is overshadowed by the tone of her commands: she treats the time travel workers with as little consideration as the Merings treat their servants. Because this is a comedy, her failure to comprehend the ridiculousness of her demands is treated humorously, but the potential for tragedy lurks behind her orders. Not only does she force the historians into exceeding the safe parameters for jump frequency, resulting in Ned and numerous other historians being severely time-lagged, but she sends historians to periods for which they are not properly trained. Lady Schrapnell's imperial tactics seriously undermine the potential benefits of her projects. Apparently, despite the initial contrast set up between England and America with England seeming more connected to a long history and America with the advantage of lack of tradition, the two countries are more similar than different: America cannot guarantee that its members value modern ideas of equality and fairness, and England is often oblivious to its history.

◆ THEMES ◆

The concept of time travel clearly invites social commentary and, as in her previous works, Connie Willis delivers, granting readers a humanistic vision of humanity whose central values, beliefs, and behaviors remain unchanged over time.

One of the central thematic issues at work, coinciding with the social concern of clarifying our relation to the past, is that of preservation. Willis examines several different facets of the question how, given limited resources, we decide what is worth preserving from the past. Lady Schrapnell decides Coventry Cathedral is worthy of being rebuilt and is willing to pour money into that project; however, at times it seems that Lady Schrapnell's abrasive personality undermines the value of what she is doing as an unsympathetic character who often functions almost as an antagonist. Lady Schrapnell does not seem like a character whose value judgments the reader can trust.

At the same time, other alternatives for the cathedral such as turning it into a shopping center make the project less objectionable, and showing the building's deep emotional value to different characters from the time of its building and throughout history reinforces the probability that Lady Schrapnell's goal is not inherently wrong.

Other issues of preservation are raised by the discussion of time travel. One of the "laws" of time travel is that nothing significant can be brought forward from the past— it is impossible to bring forward the Mona Lisa because it already exists once at present, and the same is true for other treasures. However, one time-traveler accidentally breaks part of the law, revealing a whole new corollary to this rule, and raising once again the question of "significance" and value.

Another theme that surfaces most noticeably in the interactions with Professor Peddick and his nemesis, Professor Overforce, is the question of what determines historical outcomes. The aptly named Overforce holds that natural forces acting on populations determine history; Peddick staunchly maintains the primacy of individuals. At the end, Overforce capitulates. Ironically, however, Ned and Verity discover that their actions have, to a great extent, been guided by the continuum, which itself is an impersonal natural force. The final word on the subject seems to be that details so small they are never noticed have the greatest effect, a thesis Willis develops in further detail in her earlier novel *Bellwether*.

◆ CHARACTERS ◆

As is often true in comedic works, the characters in *To Say Nothing of the Dog* are not very complex. The protagonists, Ned and Verity, are sympathetic and easy to identify with; the supporting characters are usually even less realistically rounded, although a single identifying characteristic makes them memorable, much in the style of Charles Dickens. For instance, Lady Schrapnell is bossy, Warder is rude, Finch is deferentially and politely helpful, Tossie is spoiled, Professor Peddick is equally obsessed with fish collecting and by the idea that individual actions determine the course of history, and so on.

Through their actions, Ned and Verity demonstrate the novel's important social concerns and themes. The two meet because Verity has chosen not to accept the dictum that historians cannot change history, and saves a cat from being drowned. Her impulsive nature, tender heart, and willingness to sacrifice general principles in specific cases (even though, as it turns out, her actions jeopardize all of history) are matched by Ned's, as he reassures Verity that he would have done the same thing. Both characters begin by prioritizing life: the life of the cat, the life of Professor Peddick, the life of Terence's dog, Cyril. But these choices, aside from the problem of affecting the continuum, are fairly simple as most people would agree that saving the life of another human or of a much loved animal companion is the proper moral choice. The fate of a building or object judged ugly by their own aesthetic standards is more difficult. Ned and Verity, like other characters, are less understanding of those goals. It appears, by the development of these characters' opinions, that wanting to change or destroy what one does not find attractive is a common, perhaps universal, human trait, but to want to preserve something for its historical value—which is an-

other way of saying that the object was valuable to other people, even if they are no longer present and their values have been abandoned, is a nobler and more difficult pursuit.

Characters remain fairly consistent throughout the book; growth and change are not primary in this comedy. Even so, many of the main characters do experience some growth: Ned and Verity come to understand Lady Schrapnell's obsession with rebuilding Coventry Cathedral; Terence St. Trewes learns that what appears to be the ideal of Victorian femininity is not as desirable as a well-educated, sympathetic soulmate; Tossie discovers that being the ideal of Victorian femininity is not as rewarding as making the most of her natural gifts; and even Lady Schrapnell, whom the protagonists spend most of their time fearing and avoiding, turns into a more sympathetic presence as she shows that she shares their horror at the aesthetic appearance of the bishop's bird stump. Lady Schrapnell, whose presence is only indirect and behind the scenes until the end of the book, is one of the more interesting characters. At first, she appears to be the antagonist, working against Ned and the other historians; then, as Ned and Verity gain an appreciation of her goal, if not of her methods, she seems to be simply the agonist, the force setting events in motion; but by the very end, it becomes apparent that her actions are directed by the same force that has been manipulating Ned and Verity. The continuum, aligned with the Victorian concept of a Grand Design, affected by time travelers from over six hundred years in the future, has been working to restore itself to prevent a breakdown that could destroy history. Once they understand this, Ned and Verity's opinion of Schrapnell changes, but the fact that this alteration is not actually a character change on Lady Schrapnell's part but a change in the major characters' perception of her is an interesting twist on traditional character development.

In *To Say Nothing of the Dog*, Willis combines a number of literary techniques effectively to create this unusual blend of science fiction, comedy, romance, and mystery, such as point of view, setting, characterization, narrative exposition, and comic techniques. The story is told from Ned Henry's first-person limited point of view. This choice is well suited to the story because it allows Willis to maximize the humorous and suspenseful aspects of the story at the same time. As an unprepared visitor from the future to the Victorian era, Ned's knowledge of the society and customs are necessarily limited, a fact which can and does place him in many awkward situations; his innocence and lack of understanding can be felt by the reader, who, unless well-versed in Victorian manners, may be as puzzled as Ned. Because the story is also a mystery, narrating it from Ned's point of view allows the author reasonably to withhold information or clues from the reader, who can only learn information when Ned does. Finally, the first-person limited viewpoint works well for Ned's romance with Verity, as the reader should be able to identify with Ned's situation, not knowing whether Verity reciprocates his affection, as this is how most romances begin.

The first-person point of view also works well as a mechanism for portraying the setting, especially the Victorian one, more actively than on the conventional third-person omniscient viewpoint. As Ned sees a new scene such as the river crowded with boats or the Merings' drawing room packed with furniture and bric-a-brac, the reader learns not only what the setting looks like but how Ned responds to it, which contributes to his characterization as well. Because

he is from a different era, Ned's surprise at certain scenes feels natural and, once again, helps the reader identify with the protagonist.

In an unusual twist, Willis also uses the first-person point of view as an interesting occasion for stylistic variation. As it turns out, one of the symptoms of severe time-lag is a tendency to maudlin sentimentality—a characteristic shared with the Victorians. Thus, when Ned waxes eloquent on, for example, the beauties of the river Thames, it sets the scene by describing the physical setting, reminds the reader of Ned's time-lagged state, and also corresponds with the prose style of the period. Fortunately, Ned's eloquence is only set off sporadically during the period when he is most time-lagged. Willis could, of course, have used this style throughout in third-person point of view, but the unfamiliar florid, wordy prose style would be difficult for most modern readers to tolerate in such large amounts.

Willis tends to utilize dialogue heavily in most of her writing, especially her comic writing, perhaps reflecting a certain Hollywood influence which she admits to elsewhere. *To Say Nothing of the Dog* is no exception. Examining each character's first line of dialogue reveals significant aspects of the characters almost instantly. Ned's—"'We came round Radford way,' I said, fairly sure the verger wouldn't have been out that direction. 'A milk lorry gave us a lift,'"—demonstrates that he is quick-witted enough to fabricate a plausible excuse in difficult circumstances. Finch, Mr. Dunworthy's secretary, factotum, and eventual Victorian butler extraordinaire, enters with "let me help you there, sir." Verity's first line, "I don't see why not," introduces her as a young woman who is an independent thinker not afraid of authority as she argues with Mr. Dunworthy; readers are immediately cued that she is not to be seen as strident by the qualifier that her voice "was sweet rather than stentorian." Terence, who has a mild habit of getting himself into difficult situations, enters the novel with "I'm late." Looking at Tossie's first two lines, one to Verity and the other ostensibly to Terence, is equally instructive: "Look, Cousin, it's Mr. St. Trewes. . . . I told you he would come!" emphasizes her unfounded confidence and faith in her own conclusions. "Did the dearie doggums come to see his Tossie? Did he know his Tossie missed her sweetums Cyril?" more or less speaks for itself as an indicator of her juvenile thought and appalling sentimentality.

Willis's expository technique, the means by which she reveals information she wants to convey to the reader, is fairly distinctive. As Ned attempts to solve the mystery of the disappearance of the bishop's bird stump and of the apparent time travel incongruities, he continually reviews the clues to himself in interior monologue, typically by quoting a key line from another character that seemed insignificant at the time but which has come to appear important. Sometimes he cannot identify its significance, which allows the reader an opportunity to analyze and put together the clues before Ned. In this way, Willis can introduce clues subtly, later highlight them as important in case the reader failed to note them the first time, and even return to them later. This, in addition to Ned's first-person descriptions, ensures that the reader can follow not only the story but the characters' journey along that path.

◆ LITERARY PRECEDENTS ◆

To Say Nothing of the Dog continues a long and rich tradition of time travel plots in science fiction from classics such as Edward Bellamy's *Looking Backward* and H. G. Wells's seminal *The Time Machine* to the more recent movie *Terminator*, James P. Hogan's *Thrice upon a Time*, Kage Baker's *In The Garden of Iden* and the rest of the Company

series, and a virtual host of other works exploring the often paradoxical nature of time travel.

In the novel Willis herself suggests other subgenres for comparison and a few specific works. For instance, much of the early part of the book is an extended tribute to Jerome K. Jerome's comic novel *Three Men in a Boat, To Say Nothing of the Dog*. Ned Henry draws attention to many of the shared attributes to that work, though most of the similarities are fairly superficial details either of setting or of plot. The plot on a larger scale shares more with romantic comedies and classic detective fiction, united most relevantly in Dorothy L. Sayers's Lord Peter Wimsey stories, especially *Strong Poison* and *Gaudy Night*. Agatha Christie mysteries in general and the Hercule Poirot novels in particular come in for a number of literary allusions as well. Ultimately, however, *To Say Nothing of the Dog* is a unique blend of genres and influences that owes most to Willis's own insights and humor.

◆ RELATED TITLES ◆

In addition to the science fiction time travel, romantic comedy, and classic detective novel traditions, *To Say Nothing of the Dog* is important within Willis's oeuvre. The most obvious connections to other Willis works are her award-winning *Doomsday Book* and "Fire Watch," both of which also feature Mr. Dunworthy as the professor in charge of Balliol College's time travel at Oxford University. In *To Say Nothing of the Dog* Willis continues to explore not only the physics of time travel, working out the "laws" and limitations, but a little more on the psychology of the historians doing the time travel. However, this novel is, in comparison, not so much driven by character as by the plot and solving the mystery of what happened to the bishop's bird stump; *Doomsday Book* and "Fire Watch" both focus to a much greater extent on the historian's adjusting to the ramifications of traveling backwards in time and understanding the historian's occasionally tragic inability to appreciably alter the lives of the people they meet or affect the outcome of historical events. Furthermore, because *To Say Nothing of the Dog* has a much lighter tone than the earlier works, it feels more closely related to Willis's other romantic comedies such as "Blued Moon," "Spice Pogrom," "At the Rialto," or even *Uncharted Territories*. In practice, perhaps it is closest to another Willis time-travel romantic comedy, "Time Out," although the settings and physics are quite different.

◆ IDEAS FOR GROUP DISCUSSIONS ◆

Because time travel almost automatically entails comparing two societies, it can be an excellent way of pointing out the good and the bad in our own society and in others. *To Say Nothing of the Dog* takes this one step further since the historians are not traveling from our own time but from the near future, encouraging the reader to consider what our society will be like in, say, a hundred years—whether it will be like the one Willis portrays or, if not, how it will differ, in addition to how it is like the past. Since no one can know what the future will be like, extrapolating probable futures from our present can be an entertaining exercise.

1. What period from the past would you most like to visit, and why?

2. If you could change one historical event, what would you change? How do you think that would affect our present society?

3. Do you agree with Willis's conclusion that history turns on events so insignificant that they cannot be identified?

4. Professor Peddick and Professor Overforce disagree over what determines the cause of history, individual actions or impersonal forces. At one point, Ned says that both are equally important, but at the end of the novel, Professor Overforce reportedly changes his mind to agree that individual actions are more important than impersonal forces. Which character do you agree with? Which character, if any, do you think voices the author's opinion?

5. Most communities have certain homes, buildings, or neighborhoods designated as of historical significance. What do you know about such areas in your town? What criteria would you use to determine what ought to be saved—the oldest, the most beautiful, the most famous, or something else?

6. Saving and rebuilding buildings costs money. A nurse in *To Say Nothing of the Dog* says, "Do you know what fifty billion pounds could do for medicine? . . . We could find a cure for Ebola II, we could vaccinate children all over the world against HIV, we could purchase some decent equipment. With what Lady Schrapnell is spending on the stained-glass windows alone, Radcliffe Infirmary could build an entire new facility with the latest in equipment." A protester asks, "Do you *know* how many trees we could have planted in Christ Church Meadow for the cost of that *building*?" Do you think Lady Schrapnell is immoral for spending so much money to rebuild a cathedral? What do you think the best, most moral, thing to do with so much money would be? Does the government have a responsibility to help preserve historic sites?

7. If you could go back in time and save either an extinct species such as the dodo or the passenger pigeon or rescue

a destroyed work of art such as a missing Shakespeare play or a missing Bach sonata, which would you do? Why?

8. Lady Schrapnell's bossy behavior is very effective. Are there ever times when it is appropriate for people to put their own priorities ahead of consideration for other people? What would some examples be?

Brian Forsyth

TRUE AT FIRST LIGHT

Novel

1999

Author: Ernest Hemingway

◆

◆ SOCIAL CONCERNS ◆

This novel (or fictional memoir, or non-fiction novel) is the product of posthumous editing of an unfinished manuscript that Ernest Hemingway wrote in the mid-1950s. Left unfinished and unpublished at Hemingway's death in 1961, the "African Book" (as scholars have long referred to it) was edited by the author's son Patrick Hemingway, provided with its current title (*True at First Light*), and published as capstone to the year-long celebrations of the Hemingway Centennial in 1999. Regardless of what may have been left out or insufficiently realized due to the incompleteness of the manuscript or the posthumous editing, certain key social concerns are clearly evident: 1) questions of racial and tribal identity and relationships in the waning hours of colonialism in Africa; 2) matters that fall under the ancient "man-and-nature" or, more properly, humankind-*in*-nature rubric, including numerous environmental issues and an examination of the ethics of hunting; 3) marriage complexities seen in the light of social and tribal intricacies; 4) codes of conduct—ethical, moral, religious—examined in the contexts of the sometimes jocular, sometimes serious "new religion" motif that is central to the book.

The narrator and the central character of the work is Ernest Hemingway. From his perspective as an acting game warden in Kenya, the narrator invites the reader to share in what has been called the "Africanization of Hemingway," to move beyond easy racial labels, and to inhabit truly the tribal complexities of Africa. During this process of Africanization, the narrator 1) criticizes many aspects of colonialism yet still grants integrity and dignity to certain British colonials; 2) treats ironically the rich European and American tourists who are the usual makers of safaris (safaris, we are given to understand, that have nothing in common with the narrator's big-game activities in Africa); 3) treats richly the racial and religious complexity of Kenyan Africa, the tribal and religious and Political identities (Masai, Kamba, Kikuyu, Mau Mau, Christian, Moslem, Sikh, Animist, etc.), as well as the place of Americans, Asians, and Europeans in Africa.

Hemingway's "Africanization" is grounded in his growing love for a *specific* part of Africa and Kenya, that terrain in the shadow of the Mountain-God Kilimanjaro; in his ever-deepening absorption into local tribal life, as hunter, friend and comrade, partner in "having fun" and in the "new religion" he founds with his tribal cohorts; in the delicate courtship of his tribal fiancee Debba; and in his sense of profound attachment to place, his love for the part of Africa that he never wants to leave. The essence of Hemingway's racial concerns here may be summed up as a dismissal of race as signifier of anything more than a kind of abstract categorization—what he really values is tribal brotherhood rooted in place and conduct. As Miss Mary (Hemingway's fourth wife), another major character, puts it: "One of the basic points of the faith as I gather it is that neither Papa nor I are white." Hemingway projects his racial identity as American Indian and African Kamba. Toward the end of the book, when Ngui, one of his tribal brothers and partners in the "new religion," asks what he prays for, Hemingway answers: "Africa for Africans. Kwisha Mau Mau. Kwisha all sickness. Rain good everywhere. Happy Hunting Grounds." The translation given for "kwisha" is "it is finished." Hemingway's prayer, then, calls for an end to colonialism, an end to terrorism, health and plenitude for all in the Africa he loves, the Africa in which he longs to stay.

Another social concern is addressed by Hemingway's brand of environmentalism, his presentation of the role of hunting and protecting big game and the land, thus seeking the proper relationship of humans and beasts, human settlements and the wild country. Early in the novel, Hemingway, who never hunted elephants and detested elephant-hunting, ponders the matter from the perspective of acting game warden:

> I was always depressed by this part of the forest. The elephants had to eat something and it was proper that they should eat trees rather than destroy the native farms. But the destruction was so great in proportion to the amount they ate from the trees they pulled down that it was depressing to see it. Elephants were the only animal that were increasing steadily throughout their present range in Africa. They increased until they became such a prob-

lem to the natives that they had to be slaughtered. Then they were killed off indiscriminately. . . . There had to be some sort of elephant control. But seeing this damage to the forest and the way the trees were pulled down and stripped and knowing what they could do in a native Shamba in a night, I started to think about the problems of control.

Then there is the quest for Miss Mary's lion, which drives the plot and action for much of the book. Hemingway, as game warden, has the duty to kill any marauding lion which destroys livestock and preys on human settlements, so he meditates on the "difference between a wild lion and a marauding lion and the type of lion tourists take pictures of in the National Parks. . . . Picture lions that are accustomed to being fed and photographed," lions that when they wander from protected areas where they have "learned not to fear human beings are easily killed by alleged sportsmen and their wives. But our problem," Hemingway concludes, "was not to criticize how other people had killed lions . . . [but to] find and kill an intelligent, destructive and much hunted lion in a way that had been defined if not by our religion [then] by certain ethical standards."

Indeed duty and ethics define most of the hunting that occurs. Here is another example of Hemingway's tonality regarding hunting-as-duty:

> That afternoon after lunch we did baboon control. We were supposed to keep the population of baboons down to protect the Shambas. . . . In order neither to sadden nor enrage baboon lovers I will give no details. We were not charged by the ferocious beasts and their formidable canine teeth by the time I reached them were stilled in death.

Hemingway sums up his hunting in this fashion: "The time of shooting beasts for trophies was long past with me. I still loved to shoot and to kill cleanly. But I was shooting for the meat we needed to eat and to back up Miss Mary and against beasts that had been outlawed for cause and for what is known as control of marauding animals, predators and vermin."

If duty and ethics define the game warden's responsibilities, the rest of the hunting may be summed up under the rubric meat-and-mystery. "It's wicked to kill things," Mary says. "But it's wonderful to have good meat in camp. When did meat get so important to everybody?" "It always has been," Hemingway says. "It's one of the oldest and most important things. Africa's starved for it. But if they killed the game the way the Dutch did in South Africa there wouldn't be any." And beyond the meat, there is the older mystery: "We were all hunters and it was the start of that wonderful thing, the hunt. There is much mystic nonsense written about hunting but it is something that is probably much older than religion. Some are hunters and some are not."

Other social concerns include the analysis of marriage projected through Hemingway's portrayal of his relationship with his wife Mary and his tribal fiancee Debba. Perhaps the cross-cultural contrasts of marriage would have received more development if Hemingway had finished the book. Nevertheless, even as it stands here, the portrait of Ernest and Mary's marriage, with all of its competition, cruelty, jealousy— what the narrator calls the "incalculable casualties of marriage"—balanced by their efforts to love each other well and truly, is the most complex treatment of marriage in Hemingway's work. Finally, the most resonant and comprehensive social concern, which covers all aspects of conduct—social, ethical, moral, religious—is centered in Hemingway's "new religion" leitmotif, which is best discussed under the heading of themes.

◆ THEMES ◆

The theme at the very heart of Hemingway's African pilgrimage centers on matters of religion. Religious motifs and images are so pervasive that the subject should be allotted much more than the brief space allowed here for such analysis. Statistical survey of key passages and allusions dealing with religion reveals at least 85 such occurrences. Likewise, references to the marijuana-effect Christmas Tree that Miss Mary quests for so assiduously amount to more than 30. And there are many references to the "Birthday of the Baby Jesus" and other formulations, some serious, some hilarious, involving the words "Baby Jesus"—e.g., when they go to dig up the magic Christmas Tree, Hemingway says they are "working for the Forestry Department of Our Lord, the Baby Jesus." There are dozens of such "Baby Jesus" references; and there are dozens of citations of the Mountain-God Kilimanjaro. As *Sports Illustrated* noted long ago, when it published portions of this manuscript in 1971–72, religion comes up "repeatedly, often in a humorous connotation; but at heart it [is] no laughing matter." Some Hemingway commentators have found that the weakest part of the book is Hemingway's new religious mythology, and dismissed it as humor, as comic play, that diminishes the effect of the work. But they have missed the point; as is always the case with Hemingway, religion is a serious matter. Hemingway did not go to Africa, and Pilgrims do not make pilgrimages, just for laughs.

In any case, there are, no doubt, dissertations, essays, and books already in progress on Hemingway's "New Religion" in *True at First Light*. Some of these studies will most likely see the "new religion" as a rejection of Christianity, or as Hemingway's farewell to Catholicism, which had informed his life and work since his conversion to Catholicism when he was a teenager. Other studies of the question may be sophisticated enough, it is to be hoped, to recognize that Hemingway's vision of Catholicism in relation to his African tribal religion is subsumptive, that beneath all the comic play with religion, there is a syncretic religious thesis at work, a syncretistic drive to reconcile, to localize and thus truly universalize his fundamental Catholic beliefs.

Under the rubric of syncretism *True at First Light* might seem to some students of Church history to be an adumbration of post-Vatican Two trends, and Hemingway might be seen as a kind of forerunner, a prophet of ecumenical inclusiveness and new modalities of worship. Here, for example, is Papa describing what Mary calls "Papa's religion": "We retain the best of various other sects and tribal law and customs. But we weld them into a whole that all can believe." All on one page "Papa's religion" is described as a "new religion," as a "frightfully old religion," as a religion that Papa makes "more complicated every day," and as a "revealed" religion rooted in Papa's "early visions." Whatever is serious, whatever is jocular, one theme remains constant: the syncretistic drive to reconcile the local and the universal.

Yet, in spite of all the syncretistic emphasis, Catholic themes familiar from Hemingway's earlier work persist—such as the rejection of certain aspects of Protestantism. For example, one rather unpleasant character who wants to convert to Hemingway's "new religion" is a Protestant, educated by Protestant missionaries. Hemingway notes that he has "strong black shoes to prove his Christianity." He tells Hemingway he is not Catholic. Hemingway replies: "I thought you were not of that faith from the shoes." The Protestant says: "We have many things in common with the Catholic faith but we do not worship images." "Too bad," Hemingway says. "There are many great images." When this character, renamed Peter by Hemingway, wants to convert, he will have to take off his Protestant shoes and learn to appreciate images. Later, when he tells Hemingway proudly that he never speaks "of the Baby Jesus except with contempt," Hemingway warns him: "We may need the Baby Jesus. Never speak of him with disrespect." And what else would Papa say, in a book that tends toward Christmas and the "Baby Jesus" on every other page?

There is much more in the religious design—throw in Gitchy Manitou, the Great Spirit, the Happy Hunting Grounds, add sacred trees and mountains and African religious ceremonies, animistic and Muslim references, meditations on the soul, pilgrimage allusions involving Rome, Mecca, and Santiago de Compostela, and the reader will have some notion of how rich the religious mix is. But readers who have not studied the omitted portions of the manuscript should tread cautiously before drawing firm conclusions about this serio-comic melange, and should remember also that Hemingway is always serious about religion, which is precisely why he jokes about it. Never preachy, *True at First Light* rides on the syntax of spirituality, moves in religious rhythms that alternate between mystical meditation and epiphanic moments and the self-deprecatory mockery of Papa, leader of the "new religion."

One striking example may be seen in the sequence of movements that begins with the death of Mary's lion. First, there is ceremonial drinking; then, Hemingway writes, "I drank and then lay down by the lion . . . and begged his pardon for us having killed him and while I lay beside him I felt for the wounds. . . . I drew a fish in front of him with my forefinger in the dirt and then rubbed it out with the palm of my hand." This Ichthus-ceremony (the fish as symbol of Christ) then flows directly into a meditation on the dark night of the soul and leads eventually to a quasi Eucharistic meal:

"It was wonderful to be eating the lion and have him in such close and final company and tasting so good." These incarnational moments of epiphanic communion with and in and through the body and blood of the lion are followed almost immediately by a sequence of self-mockery and mocking of religious cliches. Papa, paraphrasing the 18th-century Protestant hymn-writer Isaac Watts, tells his friend G.C. that "Satan will find work for idle hands to do." He asks—in inflated preacherly mode—if G.C. "will carry these principles into Life." Drinking a ceremonial beer (and beer drinking functions throughout the work as a ritual act of communion), G.C. says "Drink your beer, Billy Graham." If we read Hemingway accurately and well, such joking does not undercut but underlines the seriousness of religious matters. Beyond all irony, Hemingway's work *is* about carrying principles into action, and he is a kind of evangelist always teaching ethical and moral and spiritual codes of conduct, even in the very rhythms and syntax of his prose. As the Nobel Prize-winning poet Derek Walcott observed, the "sacred" is "even in the sound of Hemingway's prose" and in "the moral severity of his sentences." Walcott sees Hemingway's writing as "evangelical" in its hope for innocence and redemption; and he finds in Hemingway the "romance of the Protestant for the Catholic," "Franciscan tenderness towards animals," and "Bible-based moral conviction." While Walcott's observations refer to Hemingway's work in general, they are particularly apt for *True at First Light;* moreover, they confirm the view that Hemingway's narrativity, his story-telling and his style are profoundly religious, are (as Flannery O'Connor remarked) "God-haunted"; and Hemingway's ultimate subject (as Reynolds Price noted) is indeed "Saintliness." Hemingway's vocation does not take the same form as Billy Graham's; yet, at any given moment in Hemingway's fiction, it is always the Hour of Decision.

Students of *True at First Light* should be reluctant to make sweeping judgments regarding Hemingway and religion based on this published version, which might leave some readers with the feeling, for example, that Hemingway had actually become a true worshiper of the Mountain-God Kilimanjaro. Before reaching such a conclusion, careful consideration should be given to such omitted manuscript passages as this one: "We all worshiped the mountain with our borrowed and insecure religion . . . but she belonged to another people and we loved her but we knew that we were strangers and we looked at her as a boundary and a delight and a source of coolness and something to be enjoyed and loved. But she was another people's God." It should also be remembered that as he was writing his African pilgrimage, he was still praying at the Cathedrals of San Marco and Chartres and Burgos and Segovia, and still remaking segments of his old beloved Catholic pilgrimages of Santiago de Compostela and les Saintes-Maries-de-la-Mer.

Another major theme, already treated in part under "social concerns" (see above), involves the motifs and image-clusters that address matters of nature, hunting, and environmentalism. Much of what Hemingway has to say about hunting-as-ritual, about ethical standards of hunting, about his duty as a game warden, is precisely what we would expect from Hemingway. But there are some surprising variations in *True at First Light* on the theme of nature—e.g., Hemingway the Bird-watcher. He and Miss Mary study bird books and observe the extraordinary bird life very carefully, and Mary does so with greater precision. This leads Hemingway to write, after the lion quest is over: "by hunting one beast too hard and concentrating on him I had missed much in not observing the birds properly. . . . I had neglected them terribly. Reading the bird book I felt how stupid I had been and how much time I had wasted." He thinks of all the birds—their movements, colors, songs—that he loves to watch at home in Cuba and resolves to study African bird life with the same love and attention. Then he pronounces a touchstone value in his code for the well-lived life: "This looking and not seeing things was a great sin, I thought, and one that was easy to fall into. It was always the beginning of something bad and I thought that we did not deserve to live in the world if we did not see it."

Yet another primary theme, which resonates with the "social concerns" described above, and pervades the book as thematic focus, is the "Africanization of Hemingway." At the beginning, Hemingway states his love for Africa, then he narrows the range of that love to a specific part of Africa, Kenya, and then to the particular tribal part of Kenya that he most loves, that he wants "to know more about . . . than [he] had any right to know." He is there not as a tourist, not as just another rich and fashionable maker of safaris, but "to learn and to know about everything" and to do this not to serve some anthropo-missionary goal but in order to become increasingly a part of local tribal life. He stresses this intense localism throughout; he thinks "how lucky we were this time in Africa to be living long enough in one place so that we knew the individual animals and knew the snake holes and the snakes that lived in them. When I had first been in Africa we were always in a hurry to move from one place to another to hunt beasts for trophies." Although all white people are here called "Europeans," Hemingway emphatically asserts that he is "not a European," not "white"—he is an American and his American identity is proclaimed as Indian. That is to say, the primary mode of identity in this Hemingway work, as in most, is tribal and local. In this version of selective tribalism, nearly every chapter has some indication of Hem-

ingway's identification with, then his participation in, and finally his rootedness and membership in place and in the Kamba tribe.

Near the end of the book, Mary says that she wants "to go and really see something of Africa. . . . You don't have any ambition. You'd just as soon stay in one place." To which Ernest replies: "Have you ever been in a better place?" And again, more firmly: "I'd rather *live* in a *place* and have an *actual part in the life of it* than just see new strange things" (emphasis added). Of course, contrary to the popular view and the usual biocritical view, this has always been the fundamental Hemingway mode of being: in France, or Cuba, or Africa. He is never a tourist, always a local or in the process of being localized, or longing to be a member of a selected community, or *creating* a new tribe or community, rooted in place, in the best traditions of the best places.

Among secondary themes, the Mau Mau revolt and the weakening of British colonial power in Kenya is present mainly as a plot device, with the threat of a Mau Mau attack on the hunting camp serving to lend suspense and tension to the action of the first six chapters. Finally, what some readers may regard as a major theme of this work, the relationship of the author to his autobiographical material, the nature of the interplay of fact, fiction, and truth may best be treated below under the rubrics of "Techniques" and "Characters."

◆ CHARACTERS ◆

The central character and the omnipresent focal point of *True at First Light* is the narrator who is, in propria persona, Ernest Hemingway. Given this fact, the narrative's primary mode of being amounts to an ironic, humorous, and self-deprecating record of the interior meditative life of a writer set in juxtaposition against the life of action of a temporary game warden going about his duties. In the contemplative mode, there is much made here of the literary life, of the writer's relationship to readers, critics, biographers, and fellow writers. Literary allusions abound. For example, the passage which gives the work its current title (not Hemingway's title, but a good choice made by the editor) evokes both Virgil and Dante in a context dealing with art and truth: "We were all reading the *Georgics* then in the C. Day Lewis translation. We had two copies but they were always being lost or mislaid. . . . The only fault I could ever find with the Mantovan was that he made all normally intelligent people feel as though they too could write great poetry." Of course, Virgil's attention to husbandry, to divinity, to a religious attitude expressed in the mystery of sacrifice, as well as his sympathy with nature, animals and humankind make this allusion most apt for game warden Hemingway. The passage continues:

> Dante only made crazy people feel they could write great poetry. That was not true of course but then almost nothing was true and especially not in Africa. In Africa a thing is true at first light and a lie by noon and you have no more respect for it than for the lovely, perfect weed-fringed lake you see across the sun-baked salt plain. You have walked across that plain in the morning and you know that no such lake is there. But now it is there absolutely true, beautiful and believable.

The writer's job, then, the true vocation of the central character, part-time game warden and full-time writer Ernest Hemingway, is to make his Africa for the reader, to make it "absolutely true, beautiful and believable" at first, and last light. His success in doing so will be determined, for most readers, by how sympathetically they respond to the complex characterization of Hemingway presented here. Readers familiar with the Hemingway Legend, in thrall to the Papa Myth and the insistent biocritical

shadow of perhaps the world's most famous writer-as-celebrity, may have a hard time coming to terms with the actual character and his love song for Africa. First-time readers of Hemingway, with less cultural baggage, may have a better chance of doing justice to this complex character.

Other important characters include Mary Hemingway, Pop, G.C., Keiti, Arap Meina, Mthuka, Ngui, The Informer, and Debba. Significant minor characters include Willie, Charo, Mr. and Mrs. Singh. The portrait of Miss Mary is centered on her quest for the lion and how she conducts herself in that quest. All in all, she receives good marks on this score (except for marksmanship). Other aspects of her character are revealed tellingly in her relationship with her husband—her generosity in regard to Ernest's attraction to his African fiancee Debba, and her fierce jealousy and protectiveness of her husband when it comes to any female contenders for his affection from and within their "white tribe." Her impatience with Ernest's joking, and with his "new religion," provide important counterweight in the narrative. Her characterization is complex, and it is based rather closely on the actual relationship of Ernest and Mary Hemingway. But her character stands out as exemplary in her determination to follow Pop's code of the hunt.

Philip Percival, or Pop, or Mr. P, is the book's primary exemplar. Hemingway characterizes Percival as "my great friend and teacher . . . a very complicated man compounded of absolute courage, all the good human weaknesses and a strangely subtle and very critical understanding of people." He is "completely dedicated to his family and his home. . . . He loved his home and his wife and his children." (Here we note Hemingway's trademark repetition to emphasize a key value.) In the opening paragraph of the novel Hemingway identifies Percival as "a close friend of mine for many years. I respected him as I had never respected my father and he trusted me, which was more than I deserved. It was, however, something to try to merit." The real Philip Percival was, of course, one of the most famous of all white hunters in Africa; the consummate professional, he served as guide for Teddy Roosevelt and many other famous clients, and he appears in *True at First Light* in his own name and identity. While he is not physically present in the novel after the opening scenes, he remains very much in the narrator's mind and heart, and his presence dictates and enforces the ethical and moral codes of the hunt as conducted by Ernest and Mary as well as other native characters who had hunted with Pop. When Mary finally gets her lion and they have a celebratory meal, Ernest and Mary talk about Pop: "It was pleasant talking about Pop whom Mary and I both loved and whom I was fonder of than any man that I had ever known. . . . [It] was like having Pop there and I thought that even in his absence he could make things all right when they were difficult."

Another important character is the district game warden, G.C., also referred to as "Gin Crazed." His nickname notwithstanding, G.C. is an exemplary character who stands at the center of the inner circle of those who know "the values." Conversations between G.C. and the Hemingways reveal many variations on the novel's code of values. Ernest and Mary are always very happy when G.C. is in their camp "because we had become a family and we always missed each other when we were apart." A dedicated game warden, G.C. "loved his job and believed in it and its importance almost fanatically. He loved the game and wanted to care for it and protect it and that was about all he believed in, I think, except a very stern and complicated system of ethics." Since G.C. is, as Hemingway writes, "a little younger than my oldest son," he serves as the exemplary son-figure in the

narrator's conduct-based tribal family, in much the same fashion as Pop serves as the father-figure.

Included in the narrator's family are many African characters, all of whom are vivid "round" characters, very much alive on the page and very important in the novel's action, thematic motifs, and scheme of values. There are no "flat" characters among them, no mere caricatures as the reader might expect to find in a book written by a "white" author depicting life in colonial Africa. At the head of the list is Debba, who holds the role of Hemingway's African fiancee. Although some reviewers have dismissed her as a mere tacked-on "love-interest," she is a character of great presence and dignity, who is central to the process known as the "Africanization of Hemingway." From the beginning, Debba's relationship with the narrator is based in "a great delicacy of courtship." Since her tribal custom permits it, Debba wants to marry Hemingway "by your tribe or by hers. . . . [If] Memsahib [Mary] will accept her." She understands that Mary is "the principal wife," but Debba wants to be "a useful wife," not just "a play wife or a wife to leave." While the Debba courtship plot-line may be one of the novel's aspects that suffered from the fact that the work remained unfinished at Hemingway's death, and the reader might safely assume that Hemingway would have developed the matter and brought more clarity and resolution to the courtship/second bride motif, it is nevertheless, even in its unfinished state, the most important sub-plot and sub-text. And Debba is, as the editor insists, a very powerful character and prime evidence against those "politically correct" readers who fault Hemingway's depiction of women in his fiction. "Whatever the reader's opinions," Patrick Hemingway concludes in his useful character index, "he or she should pay attention to Debba."

Hemingway ranks his degrees of brotherhood with the Africans in his camp: his "closest friend and associate after Ngui and Mthuka" is Arap Meina. Ngui is Hemingway's tracker and gun bearer, a term that really means "native guide." No true hunter would let his rifle be carried by his so-called gun bearer; "A gun bearer," Patrick Hemingway observes, "was expected to have all the skills that General Baden-Powell and Ernest Thompson Seton thought a Boy Scout should. He had to know the animals and their habits, the useful properties of wild plants, how to track, especially how to follow a blood spoor, and how to look after himself and others in the African bush, in short, a Leather-Stocking or Crocodile Dundee." And Ngui has all these exemplary skills and heroic qualities.

Then there is Mthuka, who serves as Hemingway's driver. Like most of the characters in this fact-based novel, Mthuka is a real person in name and identity. Mthuka had been a driver for Philip Percival before he joined Hemingway's crew. One of Hemingway's "very close friends for a long time," he is depicted as an admirable character who would "never do a careless or irresponsible thing." He has "the best and quickest eyes," he is "ascetic, thin and intelligent"; he loves to hunt and he is "a beautiful driver." Third among Hemingway's closest African friends is Arap Meina. Hemingway regards him, as family, and Arap Meina tells people that Hemingway is his father and they have made the Pilgrimage to Mecca together. Arap Meina has a "great talent for affection" and he worships Miss Mary. Hemingway sees him as a fine man and wishes "that I had known him all my life and that we had spent our lives together."

Outside the circle of "close friends" two of the more interesting characters are Keiti and the man known as The Informer. Keiti is an elder exemplary figure, a long-time associate of Philip Percival, and the senior authority figure of the safari crew. As the editor notes, Keiti's "Edwardian opinions as to what was appropriate behavior on the part of Europeans differed little from those of the butler in the movie many readers may have seen: *The Remains of the Day.*" The Informer is exactly what he is called; he serves as the "Game Department Informer." He also serves as Hemingway's go-between in the Debba courtship. Far from an exemplary character, he is not well-liked by the other African characters. But Hemingway depicts him sympathetically—"a tall dignified man" with a "distinguished" face who speaks "accurate English"—and The Informer is an engaging and very effective character.

In sum, the cast of characters in *True at First Light* is large and memorable, even such minor characters as Willie, the white bush pilot, Charo, Miss Mary's gun bearer, and Mr. and Mrs. Singh. Willie is "handsome with fine merry eyes . . . shy without any awkwardness," and he is "the most natural and best-mannered person" Hemingway has ever known. Manners rate high in Hemingway's code of conduct, as does the fact that Willie has "all the sureness of a great pilot" yet he is "modest" and "he was doing what he loved in the country he loved." In short, he is another exemplar of Hemingway's scheme of values. The admirable Charo, "a truly devout Mohammedan," a wise and "very truthful" elder, illustrates clearly Hemingway's respect for and embrace of cultural diversity. Mr. and Mrs. Singh, who are Sikhs, are compelling minor characters who provide further evidence of Hemingway's delight in the cultural richness of Africa. Thus, whatever some critics, in the current fashion of "political correctness," may think of Hemingway's claims of African brotherhood and tribal identity, Hemingway invests all of his characters with their unique identities and individualities, and celebrates his love for all of them, his love of Africa.

The first caution when discussing techniques in *True at First Light* is this: the reader is dealing with an unfinished work, posthumously edited and severely cut in length without any direction from the writer. Whatever conclusions might be drawn concerning Hemingway's techniques may well need some revision when another version of the work appears, as it will in the future (a more complete edition is in the planning stages). That said, the reader may still confidently judge such matters as Hemingway's handling of point of view, especially with regard to the delicate relationship between autobiography and creative narration, or fact and fiction. All critical discussion must be premised on the recognition that this is not a mere "journal," a factual record of events. And it may be misleading to consider it a "fictionalized memoir," as it has also been called. The best description may be that of the editor who calls it "a fiction" and stresses that "ambiguous counter-point between fiction and truth lies at the heart of this memoir." Of course, this is probably true of all memoirs.

Readers familiar with Hemingway's earlier works (e.g., *In Our Time* and *The Sun Also Rises*) will recognize his deployment of familiar techniques: a modernist strategy of allusion, symbolic landscape, understatement (see Hemingway's well-known "iceberg theory" of writing and his "theory of omission"), skillful use of repetition, parallelism and counter-point, and variation and modulation of sentence rhythms according to principles that have more to do with poetry than with conventional prose. Allusions are abundant in *True at First Light*, especially literary allusions. Readers must do their homework to recognize unidentified literary quotations, and to understand the contextual implications of Hemingway's many allusions to such writers as Dante, D. H. and T. E. Lawrence, Orwell, and Virgil. Hemingway's use of landscape, or *paysage moralise*, terrain suffused with history and spirit, numinous landscape that points toward the deepest significations of the work, is crucial. The entire book takes place in the shadow of the Mountain-God Kilimanjaro, which is the *Deus Loci*, the Spirit of Place. Readers will want to refer to Hemingway's use of the mountain in "The Snows of Kilimanjaro," where the mountain is identified as the "House of God," the destination of the flight of the soul.

While Hemingway's techniques, devices, and style remain constant throughout his work, some readers will detect in *True at First Light*, a certain loosening of his severely disciplined style and his economy of narration. He is much more willing to talk explicitly and effusively about certain matters (e.g., religion) that were merely implied or extremely understated in his earlier work. Readers might thus conclude that he has abandoned his "iceberg theory," that he has decided to place everything on the textual surface rather than to allow key motifs and images to reverberate beneath the surface. Yet it could be argued that this entire book is grounded in and conditioned by Hemingway's long-standing principle of omission of crucial facts; in this case, the two well-known plane crashes that almost killed Hemingway a few weeks after the chronological moment when *True at First Light* ends. Those crashes are foreshadowed unobtrusively in the text, and that near-death experience that is not narrated conditions everything that transpires in the novel.

◆ LITERARY PRECEDENTS ◆

The history of the book—memoir or fiction—written about Africa by Americans and Europeans has a rich tradition. Asked about literary precedents in this mode, Hemingway's son Patrick noted that the tradition "started with Olive Schreiner in the

19th century, who wrote a book called *The Story of an African Farm* which was very popular. . . . Wonderful book." Schreiner, a South African, was the first colonial African writer to receive widespread recognition for her evocations of the African people and landscape in her fiction, as well as for her role as a champion of women's rights and advocate for the freedom and dignity of Africans suffering under colonialism. Another important writer in this vein is Isak Dinesen (pen name of Karen Blixen), a native of Denmark who lived in Kenya and wrote the widely praised *Out of Africa* (1937). Hemingway knew the Blixens (he used her husband Baron von Blixen in his writing) and he admired *Out of Africa*. Patrick Hemingway also cites Doris Lessing and the "so-called Martha Quest novels" as a literary precedent for his father's work. Lessing, especially in her early novels, deals with white-black relations and colonialism in Africa. Hemingway probably knew this work (*The Grass is Singing* (1950) and the first two Martha Quest novels, *Martha Quest* (1952) and *A Proper Marriage* (1954)). Patrick Hemingway asserts that his father knew the work of all three of these extraordinary women writers on Africa, and that their writing on Africa "made it extremely difficult for him to write this book. He had them all in mind."

Readers searching for literary precedents and influences should also bear in mind such works as Teddy Roosevelt's *African Game Trails*. From boyhood, Hemingway was an admirer of Teddy Roosevelt and he certainly knew *African Game Trails*. The reader will recall that Hemingway's primary exemplar in his African books, Philip Percival, had served as Roosevelt's guide in Africa. Hemingway also knew and admired Beryl Markham's 1942 memoir *West With the Night*, praising it as "really a bloody wonderful book." It is surely more than coincidental that one of Hemingway's closest friends in *True at First Light*, Arap Meina,

has the same name as the African guide who took Beryl Markham hunting in *West With the Night*. Hemingway then, knew well his predecessors in the mode of the African memoir and novel. Hemingway always did his homework—a voracious reader, he acquired deep and scholarly knowledge of any subject that interested him—and his best readers will do their homework, too, if they wish truly to understand Hemingway's work.

◆ RELATED TITLES ◆

The most important related title is *Green Hills of Africa* (1935), Hemingway's first fact-based "fiction" about Africa. This work is now considered one of the first of its kind, a prototype for the "non-fiction novel." In the foreword to *Green Hills of Africa* Hemingway wrote: "Unlike many novels, none of the characters or incidents in this book is imaginary. Any one not finding sufficient love interest is at liberty, while reading it, to insert whatever love interest he or she may have at the time. The writer has attempted to write an absolutely true book to see whether the shape of a country and the pattern of a month's action can, if truly presented, compete with a work of the imagination." *True at First Light* revisits this mode, as it revisits familiar characters from the earlier African book (Hemingway, Philip Percival, Charo), and many themes and techniques that the two books share can be profitably compared and contrasted. Given Hemingway's wry remark about "love interest" in his foreword, the reader will note that he has supplied that element—with the Debba courtship—in his second African book. Yet the deepest "love interest" remains constant in both works—his profound love for Africa.

Other related titles include the two classic African stories, "The Short Happy Life of Francis Macomber" and "The Snows of

Kilimanjaro." Another text that resonates with *True at First Light* is the African section of *The Garden of Eden,* another unfinished and posthumously edited novel that Hemingway was working on during the 1950s.

◆ IDEAS FOR GROUP DISCUSSIONS ◆

Discussions might usefully begin with comparison of other works that contain some of the same elements: memoir or fact-based fiction; the human and writerly problems inherent in a work written by a "foreigner" or "outsider" who loves, and wants to celebrate, a place and culture in which the writer was not born and raised; themes of hunting and quest; religious motifs and the desire to make religion more inclusive; the legacies of colonialism; the nature of human solidarity in a multicultural and multiethnic society.

1. How can *True at First Light* be understood as "fiction"? If the characters are real people, if the events really took place, where does the creative imagination enter into the process?

2. Do some background reading and discussion, e.g., one or more of the works that influenced Hemingway in writing about Africa (see Literary Precedents). Compare and contrast the way other authors treated similar matters: the African landscape, the legacy of colonialism, black-white relationships, etc.

3. Compare and contrast Hemingway's treatment of Africa and Africans in his other works dealing with Africa (see Related Titles).

4. Why does Hemingway love and admire Pop (Philip Percival)? List Pop's attributes, the specific values he em-

bodies. (You may wish to compare the earlier portrait of Pop in *Green Hills of Africa.*)

5. There are numerous exemplars in *True at First Light;* identify at least four of them. Do they all exemplify the same positive values, the same code of conduct? What, specifically, does this "code" tell us about how to behave, how to live our lives?

6. Analyze Miss Mary's quest for the lion. Why must she hunt it in a certain way? More generally, consider the reasons for hunting presented in the book. Given the evidence of this novel, should hunting be banned? Why? Why not?

7. Analyze the specific tenets of Hemingway's "new religion." How serious is Hemingway about this "new religion"? What does he think of Protestantism, Catholicism, Islam?

8. Discuss Hemingway's treatment of landscape and sense of place. Why does he feel so attached to and moved by the African landscape? What is the importance of Mount Kilimanjaro in this landscape?

9. Discuss aspects of Hemingway's style and technique: a) identify the quotations he employs in the text; b) learn something about the authors and the works to which Hemingway alludes and tell how such extratextual knowledge deepens understanding of the passage in which the allusion occurs; c) analyze some element of his style— syntax, sentence rhythm, repetition, metaphor, dialogue, etc.—and describe its effect.

10. Learn some facts about Hemingway's life, especially as he lived it in Africa. Compare and contrast his actual life with the depicted life of the book's

narrator. What conclusions do you draw regarding the relationship between autobiographical fact and fiction?

H. R. Stoneback
State University of New York at New Paltz

THE WAY WE LIVE NOW

Short Story

1986

Author: Susan Sontag

────────────────◆────────────────

◆ SOCIAL CONCERNS ◆

Susan Sontag's "The Way We Live Now" first appeared in the *New Yorker* in 1986. Narrated almost exclusively through dialogue, it tells of an unnamed man's struggle with AIDS through the reactions of his large circle of friends.

Sontag began writing the story on the night she learned that a close friend had been diagnosed with AIDS. Very upset and unable to sleep, she took a bath; it was there that the story began to take shape. "It was given to me, ready to be born. I got out of the bathtub and started to write very quickly standing up. I wrote the story very quickly, in two days, drawing on experiences of my own cancer and a friend's stroke," she told Kenny Fries of the *San Francisco Bay Times*. Selected for the collection *The Best American Short Stories of 1987* and also included in *The Best American Short Stories of the Eighties*, "The Way We Live Now" was written at the time that the impact of the AIDS epidemic was felt throughout America and the rest of the world. As such, critics maintain that it truly represents the spirit of its time. The characters reflect on the sudden omnipresence of death in their community and dissect their own changing attitudes about morality and mortality.

The story takes place in the mid-1980s, after AIDS had begun to decimate the gay population of Manhattan and other large urban centers. The lifestyle referred to in the title of the story stands in implicit contrast to "the way we used to live" before the AIDS epidemic. Sontag is careful to include characters of every sexual orientation, but gay history is a particularly pertinent context for her story.

In 1969, the Stonewall riots occurred to protest police harassment of a bar in the New York neighborhood of Greenwich Village. Many gay men and women were inspired by the solidarity exhibited at the uprising, and several historians point to that moment as a defining one in the burgeoning gay rights movement.

The free, often promiscuous sexual attitudes of gay liberation were in some ways an outgrowth of the more widespread and mainstream sexual revolution of the 1960s, which resulted from women's access to abortion and birth control. Yet sexual freedom had special meaning to homosexuals, who, before their "liberation," had lived either without a community or in a highly secretive one, and who often regarded their own sexuality as a sickness, sin, or shame. (It was not until 1973 that the American Psychiatric Association removed homosexuality from its list of mental illnesses.)

After Stonewall brought pride and attention to the homosexual community, gay men regarded promiscuity as a celebration of the unhampered male libido. While there were always people who saw this behavior as sordid and immoral, those who participated in the lifestyle viewed it as the reflection of a positive, optimistic, and even innocent time.

In 1981 reports of a mysterious and deadly disease affecting homosexual men first hit the mainstream press. By 1983 it was acknowledged as an epidemic. That year the Assistant Secretary of Health announced that AIDS was the country's number one health priority. Haitians, hemophiliacs, and intravenous drug users were also identified as populations at high risk for AIDS, but it was still widely perceived as a "gay disease." There was public hysteria and a backlash against gay people in the face of false reports that casual contact might spread AIDS. This is the attitude Yvonne refers to when she calls the man in the story with AIDS "fortunate" because "no one's afraid to hug him or kiss him lightly on the mouth."

There was no medical explanation for the disease and no clear understanding of how it was spread until 1984, when French and American teams of doctors simultaneously discovered Human Immunodeficiency Virus (HIV) as the most likely cause of AIDS. As it became clear that AIDS was spread by intimate sexual contact or blood, there was further hostility and moral judgment directed toward gay culture. The gay community itself responded with grief, shock, and denial.

Because sexual freedom was so closely associated with political liberation for this generation of gay men, many initially refused to change their risky behaviors. In the story Kate remembers asking the central character if he is being "careful, honey, you

know what I mean," one night at a disco before he gets sick. He responds by saying, "No, I'm not, listen, I can't, I just can't, sex is too important to me." Safe sex guidelines were not initially effective, but as the AIDS crisis wore on, and gay men became more involved in organized AIDS prevention, safe sex became a community standard.

In the early and mid-1980s AIDS was concentrated in a few urban gay communities, with New York and San Francisco particularly hard hit. In 1984 more than a third of all reported cases were in New York City. By 1987, one in 25 gay men in Greenwich Village had AIDS. Shops in that neighborhood started to close earlier and pedestrian traffic was down forty percent. The disease had profoundly transformed what once had been the wild and thriving center of gay liberation.

"The Way We Live Now" is also viewed as a dramatic rendering of some of Sontag's most important ideas on attitudes about sickness, as discussed in her essays *Illness as Metaphor* and *AIDS and Its Metaphors*.

◆ THEMES ◆

The title of the story, "The Way We Live Now," refers to the lifestyle of a group of friends and of a wider community of people like them who have made a fundamental change in their attitudes and worldviews in light of the AIDS epidemic. The characters reflect on their growing intimacy with death, as their friend's health declines and other friends fall ill from the disease. It is significant that Sontag chooses to end the story with the words "he's still alive," countering expectations that a story about a man with AIDS will end with his death. Sontag does not imply that the man will not die— which would be historically inaccurate given the treatments available at the time when the story is set—but makes a point of closing the story while his battle with the disease is still underway. This underscores her point that AIDS had become a way of *life,* not only for those who contracted it, but for the community at large.

In the story, Sontag suggests that there is a connection between language and survival. The AIDS patient begins to keep a diary after he becomes ill; in addition, Quentin speculates that writing is a way of "slyly staking out his claim to a future time." The story closes with Ursula's observation that the difference between a story and a photograph is language's ability to move beyond the present tense: "In a story you can write, He's still alive. But in a painting or a photo you can't show 'still.'"

Sontag again connects the use of language to survival when Paolo and Stephen discuss the sick man's use of the word *AIDS.* They see it as a good sign when he begins to name his illness freely and casually, which is ironic, given that the word *AIDS* never appears in the story. The fact that the disease is left unnamed suggests that "the way we live now" is not healthy or honest. In her book *AIDS and Its Metaphors* Sontag seeks to demystify the disease by revealing the cultural myths that attach themselves to the medical condition, obfuscating its reality. In "The Way We Live Now" she shows such mythologizing at work among the patient's closest friends.

The relationships the patient has with his friends are also used to illustrate the way friendship grows and changes in the face of a crisis. The AIDS epidemic is represented through its impact on a group of friends that forms a collective identity when one of them is diagnosed with the disease. Moreover, the story shows how AIDS brings not only death, but changes in life. Yvonne describes the circuit of communication and caring that springs up around the AIDS patient as a "utopia of friendship," which Kate modifies as a "pathetic utopia," as if to remind her of limits to how much their friendship can help him.

Closely linked to the theme of friendship is the theme of sexuality. It is a crucial element in the connection that holds the group of friends together. In the course of the story, they assume a group identity in caring for the man with AIDS; yet previously they had all been part of a circle of friends and lovers. Several of the characters—both male and female—are named as ex-lovers of the man with AIDS. He is bisexual, indicating a link between gay and straight worlds. Several members of the group have had affairs with one another, creating further links of love and risk between men and women, gay and straight.

In the words of one character, "everyone is at risk, everyone who has a sexual life, because sexuality is a chain that links each of us to many others, unknown others, and now the great chain of being has become a chain of death as well." The freedom to view sexuality as safe and positive is something that has been destroyed by the onslaught of AIDS. While homosexuality is closely associated with this phase of the AIDS crisis, Sontag is deliberate in representing sexuality *in general* as an important aspect of the disease and its impact.

◆ CHARACTERS ◆

"The Way We Live Now" comprises a series of conversations as a large network of friends share information and express concern about one of their friends, an anonymous character who is showing symptoms of an unnamed disease. The story opens with several characters describing these symptoms. They also point out that he must be frightened because he has quit smoking and put off a doctor's appointment. They discuss the panic that has spread among their circle of sophisticated gay, straight, and bisexual Manhattanites about the spreading AIDS epidemic. Although the struggle of this unnamed patient is the focus of the story, his experiences and struggle are narrated exclusively through their observations and descriptions. He remains nameless through the course of the story, only described as a sophisticated urbanite, a collector who lives in the penthouse of a pretentious apartment building in Manhattan. He lived a "risky" lifestyle before his illness—smoking, using drugs, and having unprotected sex with men and women. His circle of friends becomes a "family he's founded without meaning to."

As his friends visit him in the hospital, where he has been diagnosed with AIDS, they reflect on how the man's illness has changed their own lives and relationships to one another. Although his friends are named in the story, they are not defined clearly as characters. Instead, they are identified in relation to their connection with the patient. In a symbolic way, they represent the spectrum of society and its responses to the disease. There are twenty-six characters in all, besides the patient, and each one begins with a distinctive letter of the alphabet.

As the patient moves back home from the hospital, the focus of his friends' conversation turns to other things. They compare the conditions of living with AIDS to what it was a few years earlier, when less was known about the disease and there was more prejudice and hysteria. A friend from out of town says that the "utopia of friendship" that they have formed around the man in his illness is "rather beautiful." Another friend comments, "We are the family he's founded, without meaning to." A third objects to this collective identity, and they all discuss the differences between the man's responses to various visitors.

The man improves and informs the friend staying with him that he no longer needs his help. The friends hear about two other acquaintances that have been stricken with AIDS. They think it is best to keep the news from him. They talk about how life has changed for all of them, how none of them do the same things or take life for granted since the spread of AIDS. Soon after, another member of their immediate social circle is diagnosed, a fact that they also withhold from him.

The man's health appears relatively stable. Tensions and competition among his friends increase. The man takes their attention for granted. He begins to have fewer visitors. The man has a relapse. Facing death, he talks about his feelings of fear and exaltation. One of his friends comes up with the idea of a "visiting book" with a schedule for visitors, limiting the number to two at a time. The tension between the friends eases up in the face of the man's latest brush with death. His condition stabilizes and he is out of danger of not recovering from this particular downturn. Friends observe that he has become more detached. His death from the disease seems inevitable, but as the story ends he is still alive.

◆ TECHNIQUES ◆

The story's point of view is the most striking stylistic element of Sontag's story. It is told in the third person, through the voices of a large group of friends as they share information about a friend who has AIDS. No one character's perspective dominates the narration and the large number of characters creates a kaleidoscope effect. Within a single sentence, the perspective often shifts several times. The characters frequently disagree with each other and one of them, Quentin, objects to the constant references to the group as "we."

However, the experience forges a collective identity. The many individual voices that make up the group create a constantly shifting point of view, but the collective identity that they share lends the multiple points of view a certain unity. The fact that the friends are speaking to each other is more important than which particular friend is talking to another. Thus the story is narrated almost entirely through dialogue, with nearly all information expressed through the spoken words of the characters to one another. Sontag's use of dialogue is unusual not only because it plays such a large role in her telling of the story, but because it is presented in an idiosyncratic format, which means that she does not use the conventional paragraph breaks and quotation marks to distinguish between different speakers. Instead, she runs the dialogue of different speakers together, often using extremely long sentences to capture the flow of conversation. The very first sentence runs eleven lines and includes the comments of four different people. This has the effect of melding the identities of the different speakers and suggests the merging of their identities, as well as the urgency of their communication with each other.

Although she uses language in a mostly realistic manner in "The Way We Live Now," many of the conversations that make up the narration mimic the natural intonations and patterns of speech. The story represents a real situation and offers concrete historical details. Yet it can also be viewed as an allegory, where the characters and events represent larger ideas about the AIDS crisis. The story's symbolic quality is most clearly illustrated in Sontag's use of naming: she uses names in a manner that is intentionally unnatural, calling attention to the fact that the story is an artistic construct. The AIDS patient is never named and neither is his illness. While the way the characters talk is largely naturalistic, it is highly unlikely that real people would fail to mention the man's name in the course of their many conversations about him. The omission is symbolic of the absence of his perspective in the story, and his underlying isolation from the friends that surround him.

The rest of the twenty-six characters are given distinctive first names, each beginning with a different letter of the alphabet. These friends, as represented by the alphabet, suggest the universal scope of the disease. The characters themselves are all part of a narrow sector of society—well-educated, liberal, urban sophisticates—but their alphabetical naming suggests that AIDS touches every kind of person, from A to Z. However, it also suggests that the man who has AIDS is left out of the collective experience. Sontag's use of naming suggests that he is not one of the "we" that react in response to the illness, but one of the "them" who becomes irrevocably "other" when he contracts it.

◆ LITERARY PRECEDENTS ◆

AIDS is a relatively new disease and only recently has there been a focus on the plight of its victims and their families. In the past however, other pervasive illnesses have inspired numerous fictional works, including *The Plague* (1913), a classic novel by French existentialist Albert Camus, that offers an account of an Algerian town leveled by the bubonic plague. It explores the themes of death and illness from a psychological and philosophical approach. In the late twentieth-century, several works explored the struggle with AIDS as well as offering an account of the gay lifestyle in general. Included in this category are such works as *Borrowed Time: An AIDS Memoir* (1988), Paul Monette's moving memoir of his lover's two-year struggle with AIDS. It offers an intimate glimpse into the author's confrontations with love and loss. Also of interest might be David Leavitt's *The Lost Language of Cranes* (1986), which portrays the life of a young gay man living in New York.

Known both as a writer and theoretician, Sontag has held positions at various universities. She began publishing essays and book reviews in the early 1960s, making a name for herself as a prolific intellectual. Her works, which borrow heavily from a Western European tradition and take up broad modernist themes, range from philosophy and politics to art and cultural criticism. Her best known works of nonfiction, the novels *Against Interpretation* and *Styles of Radical Will,* provoked both controversy and renown.

In the late 1970s, after a successful fight against her own cancer, Sontag used her own experiences to write *Illness as Metaphor,* in which she explores the cultural myths surrounding disease. She similarly drew on these experiences while writing "The Way We Live Now." The story has often been viewed as a dramatic rendering of some of Sontag's most important ideas about attitudes about sickness, as discussed in her famous essays *Illness as Metaphor* and *AIDS and Its Metaphors.*

In 1992 Sontag achieved great commercial success with the publication of her novel, *The Volcano Lover.*

1. Why do you think that Sontag chose to tell the story from the perspective of the AIDS patient's many friends? How would the story be different if it were narrated from the perspective of only one friend or of the man with AIDS himself? Write your own version from another point of view.

2. One of the characters, Stephen, states that "to utter the name [of the disease] is a sign of health, a sign that one has accepted being who one is, mortal, vulnerable, not an exception after all, it's a sign that one is willing, truly willing, to fight for one's life." In the story, Sontag never names the disease. Why do you think that she never writes the word *AIDS*?

3. Research the Stonewall uprising of 1969 and the gay liberation movement that followed it. How does this historical context enhance your understanding of the story?

4. Sontag is known as a theoretician as well as a fiction writer. How are the main concerns of her essay *AIDS and Its Metaphors* reflected in the story? Take one of the main ideas from *AIDS and Its Metaphors* and explain how Sontag explores it in "The Way We Live Now."

WHITE OLEANDER

Novel

1999

Author: Janet Fitch

◆ SOCIAL CONCERNS ◆

Told through the eyes of young Astrid Magnussen, who is twelve years old at the beginning of the story, this novel is a coming-of-age narrative. Striving for autonomy, any young adult must find a fine balance between separating from and loving his or her mother. Astrid, however, has been separated from her mother prematurely after her mother kills her lover for being unfaithful. Even as a younger child, surrounded by her mother's own self-absorption, Astrid assumes more responsibility than her mother did. Fitch convincingly depicts the additional conflict and turmoil in the lives of children of jailed parents who have committed violent acts.

In addition, Fitch addresses the need to find adequate foster care, as we see Astrid passed from one poor choice of a foster family to another. Repeatedly she is victimized by being ignored, used, or abused. Fitch's character development of the foster care placement staff indicates the inconsistencies and ineptness of even well-intentioned bureaucratic interventions. The caseworker who places her with Amelia is so impressed by the lovely house and hospitable welcome of the hostess that she overlooks the underlying abuse of the system, wherein a foster parent might financially benefit from taking in foster children while the children suffer. Although the next social worker rescues Astrid from the situation and recognizes Astrid's talents, she overlooks the reasons that Claire and Ron choose to look for an foster child who is older than most. Once again Astrid arrives in another unstable environment in which she must assume the maturer role.

Not only does Fitch document the psychological scars that a young girl develops in the foster care system, she also documents the physical ones. Astrid's physical relationship with Ray ends in the tragedy of her being shot by her foster mother Starr. The jarring reaction of others to the ugliness of her wounds affects her relationship to everyone. As she becomes more of a loner, Astrid's psychological state worsens. Her luck, too, does not change and the dogs attack her. The scars that Astrid accumulates include not only the gunshot wounds and dog bites, but also those left by her mother. She writes, "Yes, I was tattooed, just as she'd said. Every inch of my skin was penetrated and stained. I was the original painted lady. . . . Hold me up to the light, read my bright wounds." Astrid recognizes that through her mother's selfish needs and impulsive reactions her own life has been permanently altered.

Fitch also develops a characterization pattern that suggests that a woman's relationship with men can be greatly affected by her own mother's relationship with men, particularly when the mother continually attempts to be the center of attention. Astrid knows little about her father because of her mother's refusal to discuss him. The men whom she encounters as her mother's lovers remain focused on her mother's need for constant attention. Attracted as much to the feminine power that she wields over them, much like her mother's, Astrid develops sexual relationships with Ray and Sergio to further discover her own strengths. Ironically, when she first meets Paul Astrid avoids any sense of sexuality, even though she enjoys his company. His caricature of Astrid when they first part will later blossom into a loving relationship of mutual respect.

◆ THEMES ◆

Astrid's conflicting hatred and love for her mother remain the central focus of this first-person narration. Because of her varied responses to her mother, Astrid's own sense of self is continually thrown off balance. Astrid distrusts language's ability to depict emotions accurately. In an early conversation with Paul Trout she muses, "That was the thing about words, they were clear and specific—*chair, eye, stone*—but when you talked about feelings, words were stiff, they were this and not that, they couldn't include all the meanings. In defining, they always left something out." As much as Astrid resists her mother's success with language as a poet, Astrid develops an affinity for lyrical language, as the narrative reveals. For example, her choice of imagery of the oleander flower that represents the poison that lurks beneath the su-

perficial beauty of the object perfectly reflects the power that Ingrid holds over her daughter. Astrid's nostalgic longings for the Santa Ana winds suggest her conflicting feelings for her mother will always be with her because they are forever bound together by their past. By the end, however, Astrid is strong enough to resist the lure of her mother's destructive presence.

As Astrid attempts to discover her own identity while moving from one foster family to another, her exploration of her past with her mother uncovers many missing pieces, including not only her father's identity but also that of her extended family. As Claire shares the family heirloom jewelry, Astrid muses, "In comparison to this, my past was smoke, a story my mother once told me and then denied. No onyxes for me, no aquamarines memorializing the lives of my ancestors. I had only their eyes, their hands, the shape of their nose, a nostalgia for snowfall and carved wood."

Her mother's faithful followers, who even seek out Astrid and become surrogate daughters to Ingrid, bewilder Astrid. In response to one of her mother's letters that twist the truth with its craftily stated words, Astrid responds in thought:

> Nobody took me away, Mother. My hand never slipped from your grasp. That wasn't how it went down. I was more like a car you'd parked while drunk, then couldn't remember where you'd left it. You looked away for seventeen years and when you looked back, I was a woman you didn't recognize. So now I was supposed to feel pity. . . . Save your poet's sympathy and find some better believer. Just because a poet said something didn't mean it was true, only that it sounded good.

Astrid ably takes her mother's words and reforms them by cutting and pasting them into a poem that indicates that she can clearly think for herself and knows that the truth remains somewhere other than what her mother chooses to portray.

Astrid's discovering herself is mixed up with determining who her mother is and what alliances she will accept with her. These angry words she imagines, directed to her mother, indicate her awareness of her mother's needs:

> You could judge her [pregnant Yvonne] as you judged everything else, inferior, but you could never see her. Things weren't real to you. They were just raw material for you to reshape to tell a story you liked better. You could never just listen to a boy play a guitar, you'd have to turn it into a poem, make it all about you.

Ultimately, after a number of harrowing and abusive experiences, Astrid separates her mother's words from her own definition of self.

Although Astrid has mixed feelings about Barry Kolker, her mother's murdered lover, she feels the guilt of not having warned him of her mother's emotional needs. Michael, their neighbor at the time, is the most stable male presence Astrid encounters until her relationship with Paul; however, the murder and her subsequent removal prevent a continued relationship with him. Once again, Astrid takes on the guilt, calling herself "the snake in the grass" when she and Ray become lovers and later feeling her body's need to consummate a relationship with Sergio. These relationships reflect her need to recognize the power of her own physicality outside the overshadowing presence of her mother.

None of the foster parents provide a stable role model that sincerely put Astrid's needs first. For one reason or another, they all could use an extra hand around the house to help look after kids or provide extra income or emotionally stabilize the parent.

Starr, her first foster parent, believes herself to be a born again Christian; however, Astrid soon recognizes her hypocritical ways. A recovering alcoholic, Starr reverts to alcohol when she suspects that her boyfriend Ray has been unfaithful to her with Astrid. By this point, Ray, having been Astrid's first lover, has become her obsession, and she continues to obsess about him after being removed from the situation until she finds a successor in her next placement. Astrid seems to displace her obsessive love and loss of her mother's presence onto an adult in each of her foster experiences.

Marvel and Ed Turlock were Astrid's "first real family," but she feels stifled by the conversation and demands to help Marvel. Attracted to the neighbor Olivia Johnstone's lifestyle of being a single woman living well by prostitution, Astrid next becomes obsessed with this new role model, whom Marvel despises. Unable to accept Astrid's needs to relate to a black prostitute, Marvel releases her without a good-bye.

Although she next finds herself in a lovely home in Hollywood rather than the poorer, working class suburbs, her next foster mother uses a number of foster children to maintain the gorgeous appearance of her home. The perfectly dressed Amelia insists the girls work to the point of exhaustion and starvation. Although Astrid is favored at first, when Amelia discovers that Astrid has been requesting a new placement, life becomes rough.

Although her next caseworker recognizes her intelligence and has her tested, Astrid is nervous about adoption. She states, "I handled the word adoption in my mind like it was radioactive. Saw my mother's face, pulpy and blind in sunken-cheeked fury."

With Claire Richards Astrid begins to love life again, until her husband Ron reappears and then she realizes that Claire, like her mother, thrives only in a man's presence. Finally, Astrid has someone interested in getting to know her as a person.

She states, "My mother had no idea what my favorite food was, where I'd live if I could live anywhere in the world. Claire was the one who discovered me." She both resents and recognizes the need for Ron's presence to uphold Claire's sanity. Astrid begins to realize, after Ron's extended trips, that he and Claire have requested an older foster child who might take on the responsibility of looking after Claire and her depression. Unaware, Astrid discovers Claire's suicide. Although angry at Ron for putting in her in such a position, Astrid also feels the guilt for not having been a worthy enough child to prevent Claire from killing herself.

In being an active participant in her next foster match, Astrid encounters the perfect Christian couple who has successfully helped raise a number of foster children. She rejects the salvation that they would provide, however, as if she would be rejecting a part of herself. Astrid realizes: "Without my wounds, who was I? My scars were my face, my past was my life.

It wasn't like I didn't know where all this remembering got you, all that hunger for beauty and astonishing cruelty and ever-present loss." Astrid continues,

> But I knew one more thing. That people who denied who they were or where they had been were in the greatest danger. They were blind sleepwalkers on tightropes, fingers scoring thin air. So I let them go ... knowing I'd given up something I could never get back. Not Ann and Bill Greenway, but some illusion I'd had, that I could be saved, start again.

With a new clarity about her life, Astrid recognizes her new foster mother, Rena Grushenka. At Rena's Astrid develops a relationship with the young pregnant Yvonne. Because of her forced wisdom from experience, Astrid has made few friends with peers. Yvonne and others are able to rely on her strengths.

After Claire's death, as Astrid recovers in a group home, Paul Trout befriends her. She states about his reassignment to another home that:

> I was sorry when he got his placement. . . . He was the first kid I'd really enjoyed spending time with since my days with Davey, the first one who could remotely understand what I had been through. We were just getting to know each other, and now he was gone. I had to get used to that. Everybody left you eventually.

After she makes her decision not to return to her mother, even after parole, then she can move on with her life. Paul Trout becomes her stable boyfriend and they move to Berlin. She notes:

> In Berlin, you had to wrestle with the past, you had to build on the ruins, inside them. It wasn't like America, where we scraped the earth clean, thinking we could start again every time. We hadn't learned yet, that there was no such thing as an empty canvas.

Astrid's ability to recognize her need to accept her past and build from it allows her to mature into a young woman with a bright future.

◆ TECHNIQUES ◆

The first person narrative effectively depicts the turmoil and conflicting emotions of an adolescent girl trying to make sense of the world in which even her parents let her down.

Astrid's memories of her mother are full of visual, auditory and olfactory sensations, mostly because of her mother's exaggerated need to be surrounded by such strong impressions. The first chapter begins with the sleepless nights during the Santa Ana winds immediately after her mother has poisoned her lover. Astrid awakens to find her mother on the rooftop where, "She held up her large hand and spread the fingers, let the desert dryness lick through. My mother was not herself in the time of the Santa Anas. I was twelve years old and I was afraid for her." As she moves closer to her mother, she recalls the scent of violets. This intimate moment is broken by the presence of the rest of the world: "Down below us in the streets of Hollywood, sirens whined and sawed along my nerves." Astrid knows it is only a matter of time before the world outside separates the two of them.

Continually Astrid recalls these Santa Ana winds and the fires that ignite, and so she dreams of herself as an ash girl, who is the charred manifestation of the fire's remains. This fire imagery reappears throughout the novel when Astrid thinks of her mother. Near the end, when Ingrid finally shares the secrets of her father with Astrid, that she discovers how her father unintentionally almost killed her with his neglected painter's turpentine, a smell that she strongly recalls.

Even though Astrid claims the visual arts to be her creative expressive outlet, the lyrical poetics indicate another skill she has inherited from her mother. One of her first literary analogies involves how she feels as the caseworkers escort her away from the life she knew with her mother:

How it was that the earth could open up under you and swallow you whole, close above you as if you never were. Like Persephone snatched by the god. The ground opened up and out he came, sweeping her into the black chariot. Then down they plunged under the ground, into the darkness, and the earth closed over her head, and she was gone, as if she had never been.

Astrid continues to remember the time of her mother's trial, when she should have testified, but could find no voice.

The whole truth and nothing but the truth. I wanted to lie, but the words deserted me. She was the one who always spoke for us.

She was the goddess who threw out the golden apples. . . . I had nothing to protect her with. . . . I had condemned her by my silence, condemned us both.

Unable to escape, Astrid inherits her mother's penchant for literary allusions. Once Astrid rediscovers her voice she begins her reassimilation with the rest of society, but it will be through words and drawings on paper that she most clearly expresses herself.

The letters to Astrid that her mother writes from jail are long-winded and self-absorbed manifestations. When she does address her daughter's needs, she tells her about her failures and mistakes and provides advice. Always, she demands superior thinking to that of the small-minded foster parents who threaten her hold over Astrid.

After a number of poor foster care experiences and time to sort out her feelings, Astrid can articulate how she differs from her mother. One of many examples is her analogy to distinguish between her and her mother: "my eyes aren't ice blue, tinted with your [Ingrid's] peculiar mix of beauty and cruelty. They are as dark as bruises on the inside of an arm, they never smile."

◆ LITERARY PRECEDENTS ◆

Relationships between mother and daughter have appeared in literature repeatedly. The guilt and crimes of Sethe, the mother in Toni Morrison's *Beloved*, are different from Ingrid's. Whereas Sethe's decisions are largely dictated by the unhappy historical circumstance of having a child while escaping slavery, Ingrid's choices are totally self-centered. Both Astrid and Denver, however, find it necessary to find coping strategies to survive their mother's unstable mental states. Their coming-of-age is forced upon them by their circumstances. In Amy Tan's

The Kitchen God's Wife, Winnie shows her daughter Pearl how to claim the present and future, regardless of the past. Astrid, on the other hand, must figure out how to do that on her own.

Having acknowledged her admiration of Joyce Carol Oates' work, Fitch would be familiar with the many coming of age stories that Oates has written over the years. Unlike Fitch, however, most of Oates' characters grow from a distant relationship with their mother. In *Man Crazy,* Oates presents the character Ingrid, who also learns to live with an unstable, self-absorbed mother. Abandoned by her father, whom she adored, Ingrid faces countless men who befriend her mother and eventually she enters an unhealthy relationship of her own. Oates' young woman descends further into a wrecked emotional state than Astrid before she recovers.

◆ RELATED TITLES ◆

Fitch's well-received first novel parallels the success of other contemporary titles dealing with mother/daughter relationships. Mona Simpson's *Anywhere But Here* has received a high profile because of its movie adaptation. Another child wiser than her parent, Ann is dragged along from Wisconsin to Los Angeles by her mother, Adele, who continually lives in a fantasy world of her own making. Sharon Creech's *Walk Two Moons,* the Newbery winner for young adult literature, also depicts a child picking up the pieces of her life that is dictated by her mother's self-centered, whimsical ways. Rebecca Wells provides another view of mother-daughter relationships in a wealthy Southern family in *Divine Secrets of the Ya-Ya Sisterhood.* Sidda and Vivi, daughter and mother, also discover that the truth of their past is somewhere between what the two of them recall and portray for others.

◆ ADAPTATIONS ◆

Selecting *White Oleander* for her book discussion prompted Oprah Winfrey to narrate an abridged reading of the novel, produced by Maja Thomas and released by Time Warner Audio Books. The unabridged version, read by Alyssa Breshahan, was released by Recorded Books.

◆ IDEAS FOR GROUP DISCUSSIONS ◆

First-person narration allows the reader to intimately observe the complicated and often conflicting workings of another's mind, particularly effective when developing characterization of a young adult determining her self identity. Relationships between mother and daughter can affect the daughter's self image as well as future relationships.

1. Why is the title fitting?

2. What is Astrid's greatest success?

3. How is Astrid like her mother?

4. Astrid's creative outlet is her drawing. Do you think this is her natural talent or what she was driven to because of her mother's success with words?

5. What functions do the letters from her mother play?

6. What character was Astrid's greatest support?

7. Is Astrid doomed in her future relationships?

8. How important is the setting of Los Angeles to the story?

Barbara Jaindl

THE WOMEN OF BREWSTER PLACE

Novel

1982

Author: Gloria Naylor

◆

*T*he *Women of Brewster Place,* which won an American Book Award, introduces and reaffirms its social concerns and themes with italicized sections entitled "Dawn" and "Dusk." In this prologue and epilogue, Gloria Naylor figures the neighborhood of four tenement buildings as a living entity, "the bastard child" of a corrupt city politician and racketeering realtor. "Dawn" goes on to show that however dubious Brewster Place's beginnings, however much it is marginalized and impoverished by white patriarchal society, it lives a life through the communities it houses; the first being World War I veterans and their young families, who move on quickly to better places and opportunities. By the time Brewster Place is literally walled off from mainstream society, it is already segregated because of its predominantly immigrant population. By the end of the Second World War, the Mediterranean children of Brewster Place claim places for themselves among the upwardly mobile, and Brewster Place becomes home to the descendants of America's slaves. Naylor writes that it "rejoiced in these multi-colored 'Afric' children of its old age," and that "Brewster Place became especially fond of its colored daughters as they milled

like determined spirits among its decay, trying to make it a home." Thus, "Dawn" figures African American women as the poorest and most marginal of the communities that have made Brewster Place their home, and they are the final community set apart in the crumbling tenement.

The final paragraph of "Dawn" shows these black women as a group and as individuals. They are differentiated by their various skin tones and ages, and by the ways in which they treat and are treated by their men; they are alike in the hopelessness of their situations. Where Brewster Place's former populations moved up and out into the world, these women were "unlike its other children, the few who would leave forever were to be the exception rather than the rule, since they came because they had no choice and would remain for the same reason." Naylor ends the section by first unifying these black women: "They came, they went, grew up, and grew old beyond their years." The section goes on, however, to make clear the individuality of these women, for each is "an ebony phoenix, each in her own time and with her own season had a story." "Dawn" reflects the bitterness of their social reality but also indicates that each woman has a unique voice and set of personal and social concerns, and that it takes individuals to build a community.

The first chapter of the novel introduces and tells the story of Mattie Michael, an older woman with great integrity and strength of character, who plays a part in each of the stories. Naylor says, in an interview with Michelle C. Loris in *The Critical Response to Gloria Naylor*, "I think that literature is politics; I think that life is politics." The political concerns in Mattie's life center on the treatment of black women by black men, and on the workings of the American legal system. While the issue of relationships between black women and black men forms a central thematic concern throughout the novel, Mattie's story introduces the theme, and illustrates it as complex and multidimensional. In terms of the legal system, this chapter illustrates the vexed relationship between poor, black Americans and American justice. While Mattie's son, Basil, is to blame for the criminal charges he faces, and for the abysmal way that he treats his mother, his terror in facing the justice system is understandable. The guarantees made by the criminal lawyer that Basil will receive probation seem hollow against a system that has different sets of rules for whites and blacks. When Basil breaks his bail bond and she loses her house and savings, Mattie reacts as she did when forced to leave her father's house. She calmly and bravely sets about making a new life for herself and becoming part of her new community.

At the same time that Mattie is forced onto Brewster Place, Kiswana Browne purposefully moves there, to work from within the community to change the social and political systems that oppress it. Kiswana recognizes that in this world of grinding poverty and seeming hopelessness, "practically every apartment contained a family, a Bible, and a dream that one day enough could be scraped from those meager Friday night paychecks to make Brewster Place a distant memory." She leaves her parents' home in affluent Linden Hills to live with "her people," to immerse herself in what she sees as black culture, and she spends her time organizing her neighbors to take legal and political steps to improve their living conditions. The block party of the last chapter comes about as part of Kiswana's plans to raise money needed to instigate change. Although her ideas and feelings burn with revolutionary fervor, Kiswana plays according to the rules of the white patriarchal system, and Naylor's strategy of irony seems to highlight the need for change, no matter how it may come about. Kiswana has a confrontation with her mother that highlights the irony of her youthful strategies and the need for black Americans to consider both revolutionary and mainstream plans for change. Furthermore, these plans are devolved along the lines of black feminism—or womanism, which is a term Naylor uses in interviews and speeches, although she does not apply labels to any of the social concerns or movements in this novel—as Kiswana and her mother before her claim the place of black women in the "Movement" for equal civil rights for African Americans. While, Kiswana is critical of her mother's membership in the NAACP, calling it a "middle-of-the-road, Uncle Tom dumping ground for black Republicans," she is willing to consider her mother's criticism of black nationalism. Mrs. Browne makes her influence felt as she points out that Kiswana was named Melanie after her grandmother, "a woman who bore nine children and educated them all, who held off six white men with a shotgun when they tried to drag one of her sons to jail for 'not knowing his place.'" While Mrs. Browne centers her criticism on the fact that Kiswana/ Melanie "needed to reach into an African dictionary" to find a name she could be proud of, her argument lies in recognizing one's own social reality. She describes the failure of black nationalism as having goals not grounded in reality, "when the smoke had cleared, you found yourself with a fistful of new federal laws and a country still full of obstacles for black people to fight their way over." Mrs. Browne argues that the system must be changed from within and concludes that she has raised her daughter to be strong enough to do just that, a point Kiswana takes as she plans the block association and the party, and returns to university.

Mrs. Browne and Kiswana delineate the legal and political systems as places to begin change, and they highlight the importance of education in furthering the goals of black women, a social concern drawn more clearly in the chapter on Cora Lee. Cora Lee is introduced through the depiction of her as a young girl, receiving a new baby doll every Christmas. Naylor draws Cora Lee as a complex person, whose emotional growth seems somewhat fixed in her obsession with babies. When her parents refuse to give her any more dolls, the adolescent Cora Lee discovers where babies come from and goes about getting real babies of her own. On Brewster Place she is the unwed mother of seven children by five different fathers, taking exquisite care of each baby, but neglecting her children. Cora Lee's story exposes the conventional myth of the welfare mother by presenting an individual who ends up in a stereotypical circumstance. Furthermore, her story shifts accusations of laziness and relentless reproduction away from the welfare mothers to the systems that create them: the education systems that fail them, the advertising industry that presents them with an unreachable maternal fantasy, and the social workers who compromise their autonomy.

Kiswana's intervention in Cora Lee's life comes about when she badgers Cora Lee to bring her children to a black production of *A Midsummer Night's Dream*. While there is irony in Naylor's suggestion that a little bit of education will fix what is wrong with Cora's life or that one evening's exposure to Shakespeare will right the ills of her children, and while the play itself is posited as a dream and a blanket of hope that Cora Lee will wrap around herself, her preparations to take her children to the play suggest that possibility and promise has entered the family dynamic. Cora Lee does not just clean and groom her children, and mend their clothes, she cleans her home to match the immaculate area where the baby sleeps. Moreover, she envisions a future for her children that includes education, careers, and possibilities that existed for her previously only on soap operas. Her new activity, her move towards a work ethic that will see her children cared and provided for, also forges for them and for herself a solid place within her community. Rather than viewing Brewster Place as a grimy playpen for her badly behaved children, Cora Lee begins to take her place in it as a community of women who can support her as she nurtures her children.

The necessity of community for women to thrive is made both a feminist issue and a wider social concern in the story of Lorraine and Theresa. As a lesbian couple, "The Two" move to Brewster not because of financial constraints, but because they must separate themselves from mainstream society in order for Lorraine, a schoolteacher, to stay in the closet and keep her job. That they are quickly found out and ostracized by some other women on Brewster Place speaks volumes about how wider social intolerance permeates even the furthest corners. The irony lies in Lorraine's desire to be part of this community of women, in her recognition that community is necessary if women are to gain any power and autonomy. As the marginalized and oppressed women of Brewster Place ostracize and vilify Lorraine, they give presence to the lesbian stereotyping that exposes society's fear of women's independence of men. When Lorraine is gang-raped, the phallic power of the rapists becomes a metaphor for both the phallic power present in the traditional nuclear family, and the power the women of Brewster Place take away from themselves and give to their men. The necessity for women to forge communal and individual power through feminist strategies becomes clear as the women and girls of Brewster Place are haunted and united in their dreams by the rape of Lorraine.

◆ THEMES ◆

Gloria Naylor has stated in interviews that one of the factors motivating her to write *The Women of Brewster Place* while she finished her Bachelor of Arts in English at Brooklyn College (1981) was her study of feminism and her own conclusions about it. Thus, the novel is overtly feminist and overtly literary, and these influences evoke and enhance the novel's main theme of women in community. Furthermore, for a first novel, the complexity and multiplicity of meaning with which Naylor imbues her theme seems quite remarkable. That this is a feminist novel is clear and that it sides with novels by Toni Morrison and Alice Walker in placing black men in a particularly bad light is equally clear. However, whether African American women writers are unduly harsh on black males is as much a political and social issue as it is a literary one. Furthermore, while there are many men in this novel that treat women badly, Naylor does not let all the blame rest with them. While she explicitly rests blame for their behavior on the men themselves, she implicitly shows the culpability of patriarchal white society. More interestingly, she makes clear that until black women stop allowing undue power to rest with their men, they are also responsible for the bad treatment they receive.

Naylor first forges this feminist ethic of responsibility with Mattie. While the reader must be moved by the treatment Mattie receives at the hands of three men, he or she must also acknowledge Mattie's culpability in how each treats her. The dichotomous aspects of each relationship are made clear as Mattie flirts with Butch Fuller and knowingly enters into a tryst with him, as she refuses to tell her father who made her pregnant, and as she spoils her son until he is emotionally stunted and unable to take responsibility for his actions. However, Mattie's actions do not justify that Butch does not acknowledge or support his son, that her father beats her severely, or that she loses her home and security because of her weak son.

That Naylor valorizes the sort of tough-minded womanism made evident by minor characters like Miss Eva or Mrs. Browne is clear in Mattie's story and in that of Etta Mae. Her narrative depicts her as strong and rebellious in her youth, but "America wasn't ready for her yet—not in 1937." So Etta "took her talents to the street," where she learned "to hook herself to any promising rising black star, and when he burnt out, she found another." Instead of making her own way like Billie Holiday or lesser talents, Etta sets her path according to that of a man, until "if someone had bothered to stop and tell her that the universe had expanded for her, just an inch, she wouldn't have known how to shine alone." She returns to Mattie and Brewster Place, weary, starting to feel her age, and thinking about settling down. Conditioned as she is to rely on men, Etta thinks of marrying well, rather than making her own way in the world, the way Mattie did and does. She allows herself to be seduced by Reverend Moreland T. Woods because she sees him as a retirement plan and does not realize he sees her as a mere one night stand. At the same time, Etta's story hints at ways in which she is and will be nurtured, redeemed and strengthened by other women. She returns with her Billie Holiday albums "clutched in front of her chest like cardboard armor," she finds acceptance among the women of Brewster Place, and in her relationship with Mattie she comes home to "the light and the love and the comfort that awaited her."

It seems clear in *The Women of Brewster Place* that Naylor's theme of black feminism is ultimately centered in the necessity for black women to enter into community with each other for the strength needed to make their way. Naylor reasserts the voice of the African American matriarch as a strategy of survival. Her move to center strength in the female-headed household, such as that of Mattie and Etta Mae, is a move to the flourishing of women in community. In the chapter "Lucielia Louise Turner," Ciel has been abandoned by her husband shortly after having their daughter. As her story begins, Serena is now a toddler, Ciel has recuperated from childbirth, illness, and being abandoned, and is getting along fine as head of her household, with emotional support from Mattie and the community. When Eugene returns, however, Ciel takes him back, and she privileges her love for him over love for herself as she allows him to persuade her to abort their second child, and over her love for Serena. While Ciel desperately pleads with Eugene to stay as he prepares to leave her once again, the child is left alone. Just as she begins to see him "as he really was—a tall, skinny black man with arrogance and selfishness," her daughter sticks a fork into an electrical outlet and is electrocuted. By the time of Serena's funeral, Ciel has stopped eating, drinking or caring for herself. She has willed herself to die, because "she was simply tired of hurting." Mattie alone recognizes Ciel's intention and forces the girl's reintegration into life and her community. Ciel's gradual reattachment to life is signaled by an elaborate bathing ritual in which Mattie rocks and cleanses her back from despair and isolation. Naylor thus creates

the sense of community and solidarity among these women, whose sense of responsibility for the welfare of each other binds them together. Furthermore, while their marginalization keeps the community they create nonthreatening to the outside world, these seemingly powerless women become sources of power for themselves and each other. Mattie nurtures Etta and Ciel, enabling them to get on with their lives; Kiswana encourages Cora Lee to become the active head of her household. The necessity of community is emphasized in "The Two" with its story about a lesbian couple trying to take their part within it. While only a few of the women openly reject the couple, none of the women stands up for them, including Mattie and Kiswana. Therefore the ostracization of Lorraine and Theresa can be seen as communal, and it creates a chain of events that leads to the brutalization of Lorraine, the death of Ben, and the haunted dreams of every female on Brewster Place.

Naylor's conscious and consistent use of dreams in a variety of literary devices situates her concerns with women's and black liberation within the theme of community. She opens *The Women of Brewster Place* with Langston Hughes's poem "Harlem" (1951), which asks "What happens to a dream deferred?" The poem goes on to posit that dreams deferred die in some way and then suggest that "Maybe it just sags / like a heavy load. / Or does it explode?" The conventional explication of Hughes's poem concludes that dreams deferred are life-defying. Naylor rethinks the poem by examining the many ways in which dreams are deferred, with both positive and negative implications. As Mattie is introduced, she smells a scent that reminds her of sugarcane and a Tennessee summer and lapses into a daydream that gives the details about how she conceived her son, and lost her family and home to have and keep him. Near the end of Mattie's reminiscing daydream, she has a symbolic awakening, when Basil calls her to come and get him out of jail. The irony lies in the fact that Mattie does not actually defer her dream until she shakes off the daydream and stands in the cold reality of Brewster Place. Similarly, Etta does not waken from her dream of an affluent marriage, from "weaving his tailored suit and the smell of his expensive cologne into a custom-made future for herself" until "it took his last floundering thrusts into her body to bring her back to reality." Most tellingly, the dreams of these two women depend upon men to make them come true.

However, in the narrative of Cora Lee, the thematic use of dreams is not predicated on men and becomes much more complex. The chapter opens with an epigraph from *A Midsummer Night's Dream*, the play to which Cora will take her children. The epigraph warns that dreams "are the children of an idle brain / and begot of nothing but vain fantasy." After Kiswana invites Cora to bring her family to the play, she remembers a line from *The Tempest* that points out the necessity of dreams: "We are such stuff as dreams are made of, and our little life is rounded with a sleep." Naylor thus complicates the idea of dreams as both necessary and as dangerous. In Cora's story the play awakens her poverty-deadened imagination and she dreams for the first time of her children as adults, flourishing in lives far removed from Brewster Place. Critical attention to the novel points out that Cora did not change all that much; by the time of the block party she is pregnant again, and her children are still unruly. However, from the moment Cora drags from her memory the line from *The Tempest*, she becomes newly active, cleaning, mending, and caring for her children's physical needs. It seems obvious that she has also become active in caring for their emotional and psychological needs. Near the end of "Cora Lee," the last lines of the play are

included, "And this weak and idle theme, / No more yielding but a dream," and herein lies the crux of Naylor's use of dreams. Neither plays nor dreams can change lives, but they can influence the course of lives. Just as the players awake from their fairy-induced dreaming and alter their paths, newly awakened imagination and hope may help Cora alter the paths of her children.

The final dream in the novel, Mattie's dream of the block party, is an inspirational, metaphoric foreshadowing of the possibilities for these women's lives. While "The Block Party" has been read as a false ending, a disappointment that precludes any real change in the reality of Brewster Place, the riot that occurs when the women tear down the wall suggests that with unity and activity power and autonomy may be claimed. Therefore, when Mattie wakes up to a sunny day, there is an inherent suggestion that the block party will be neither demonic nor apocalyptic, but if these women each arrived in Brewster Place because she had nowhere else to go, Mattie's dream suggests that new orders can be forged through unification. In Brewster Place there are no magic transformations, only gradual ones brought about by patience and hard work. And it is this hard work, the art of living, that remains a dream within the children of Brewster Place long after they leave. The novel ends with an epilogue, "Dusk," as the final part of the frame that began with "Dawn." In the same dreamlike language of "Dawn," Naylor describes Brewster Place as empty and condemned. But, like the half-light of dusk itself, Brewster Place is not dead. It continues in the dreams of its colored daughters, who "pin those dreams to wet laundry hung out to dry, they're mixed with a pinch of salt and thrown into pots of soup, and they're diapered around babies." Naylor has said that her subject is always the lives of African American women and her use of women's realities and women's dreams makes this subject immediate and important as she forges the theme of women in community.

◆ CHARACTERS ◆

In her interview with Loris, Naylor says that her work presents "a community of people who are both saints and sinners, who have beauty and blemishes. I don't glorify the African American and say we're all perfect. We are all human beings and that means complexity, that means light and shadow." Her characters are emphatically not perfect, but she makes each realistic and appealing in his or her imperfection. The depiction of Mattie as a young woman, largely obedient but rebellious and stubborn over things that mattered to her, makes the Mattie who spoils her child more understandable. Sadly, Mattie's strength and love does not humanize Basil, but causes him to be shiftless, selfish, and weak. However, in her mature years on Brewster Place, Mattie has become a calm, unifying force. Having disregarded most of Eva's advice about raising a child, she has lived and learned. And as she gives understated advice to Etta, Ciel, and Cora, she fully expects them to ignore and go their own way, which they do. At the same time, Mattie's very presence becomes their inspiration; she has gone through very difficult times of her own and survived. "Mattie Michael" figures as Naylor's exemplum for black women; she has lost everything and lives on, rebuilding her life, finding love and joy.

Mattie's self-reliance contrasts sharply with Etta, who relies on men. Etta's appeal to the reader lies in her resemblance to those often-wronged black women blues artists, like Billie Holiday, Big Mama Thornton, or Bessie Smith. Her hard living escapades are funny and entertaining, her dialogue is sassy and witty, and the frequent quotations from the songs of Billie Holiday add an artistic poignancy to her story. When Etta's interlude with Reverend Woods is signaled by lyrics from black spirituals, the link between slavery, gospel music and the blues is complete. But after her exploitation at the hands of a black minister, Etta, tired and defeated, returns to Brewster Place where Mattie waits up for her, playing Holiday's "loose-life music" and waiting to comfort her. In the light of Mattie's friendship, Etta rejuvenates and shows her usual spark through the rest of the novel.

Where Etta is described as being born before her time, as having no outlet for her fiery, independent spirit, Kiswana is figured as a woman of her time. Her education and affluent upbringing are apparent in her dialogue and thought patterns. Her integrity and commitment to her people is thorough and exciting. At the same time, Kiswana's youth and ingenuousness are apparent in her own generalized views of "her people" and how she can help them. The passionate speech of Mrs. Browne gives both the reader and Kiswana insight into how disparate a group any race is, and the folly inherent in generalization and stereotype. Mrs. Browne articulates for Kiswana a truth that the mature black women in Brewster Place live by: "I am alive because of the blood of proud people who never scraped or begged or apologized for what they were. They lived asking only one thing of this world—to be allowed to be. And I learned through the blood of these people that black isn't beautiful and it isn't ugly—black is!" Mrs. Browne's influence is clear as Kiswana continues to work to improve the neighborhood; she does not judge nor condemn Ben, or Cora. She stands up for Lorraine to C. C. Baker and his gang, and she shows patience and tolerance for those deserving of it.

As the young women identified most closely with motherhood, both Cora and Ciel evolve through several changes in the novel. Their characters move past being the stereotyped welfare mother, one an indiscriminate breeder, the other a fool for an unworthy husband, to claiming some control over their lives. Cora starts to mother all her children, not just the infant, and she begins to link her own childhood and dreams to possibilities for her children. As she reexamines her own childhood and dreams and begins to think her way into motherhood, Cora becomes a more fully rounded character. Mattie's dream, which must indicate Ciel's reality, shows Ciel getting on with her life, moving away, working, and beginning a new family with a decent man.

For the characters of Theresa and Lorraine the novel leaves them in much less promising circumstances, and Naylor has come under critical fire for "punishing" the lesbian pair. At the same time, every woman in the novel suffers for things she caused and for things she did not. Neither of the lesbian pair presents an entirely healthy way of life: Theresa rejects mainstream society and associates only with the homosexual community; Lorraine remains firmly in the closet and denies her sexuality so that she may be part of the larger community. Through these two characters, Naylor suggests that until society begins to adjust its thinking and its intolerance, there are no ideal options available for homosexual women. At the same time, the love and humor shown by this couple when alone makes them as accessible as any average heterosexual couple. Just as Lorraine and Theresa begin to adjust to Brewster, to make their way as individuals and as a couple, the ostracization they receive from the frustrated and unhappy Sophie and her ilk drives them into the circumstances that ruin both their lives. Lorraine is raped by C. C. Baker's gang and murders Ben, the only person on Brewster to accept her, in shock-induced insanity, and Theresa leaves their home to be haunted by the events on Brewster for the rest of her life.

As the only fully realized male character in the novel, Ben may be seen as both scapegoat and to blame for the sorts of misfortunes these women suffer. Naylor went on to publish *The Men of Brewster Place* in 1998, and in it she redeems some of the men from this novel and punishes others. She brings Ben back as a Greek chorus figure, one who knows and understands both the men and women of Brewster Place. In *The Women of Brewster Place,* Ben's understanding of himself and others causes him to drink himself into oblivion on a daily basis. Afraid to stop the landowner's weekly rape of his daughter and thus lose his sharecrop, Ben's cowardice ends up costing him everything and he is consumed by guilt. His kindness to Lorraine is endearing and the general regard for him by the women of the community makes Mattie's dream of tearing down the wall more poignant, for Ben's blood mingles with Lorraine's on the bricks. And while Ben has no culpability in the savaging of Lorraine, his death becomes a symbolic atonement for all the black women who suffer at the hands of their men, because of neglect as much as abuse.

◆ TECHNIQUES ◆

For a first novel, *The Women of Brewster Place* shows a sophistication in both formal and stylistic technique. Recently, the short story cycle has been touted as a vehicle for the development of ethnic fiction, because it combines the brief, teaching story form of traditional oral narrative, and because it tends to connect people through their place and history. Using an omniscient narrative speaker, Naylor explores this technique fully. She connects the women throughout the stories as they impact on each other's lives, through where they come from and Brewster Place, where they live now.

The content of each story links the women through shared suffering and common understanding. While the formal, physical isolation of Brewster Place makes clear that they carry the weight of the African American double consciousness—articulated by W. E. B. Du Bois, in *The Souls of Black Folk* (1903), as the sense of psychic two-ness resulting from the ongoing tensions between the black and American identities—as these women are marginalized by race. But through their linked stories, they are also isolated by commonalites of gender: the absence of husband and father figures, motherhood, sexual victimization. By using the form of the short story cycle, Naylor has room to integrate the social concerns of African American women and to satisfy both post-colonial and black feminist agendas.

◆ LITERARY PRECEDENTS ◆

Given Naylor's scholarly pursuits in literature, one would expect a number of literary allusions in *The Women of Brewster Place,* and she skillfully forges connections to classic literary figures, to other female writers, to other American writers, and to other African American writers. While she went on to link *Linden Hills* (1985) to Dante's *The Inferno,* and *Bailey's Café* (1992) to Chaucer's *The Canterbury Tales,* like *Mama Day* (1988), *The Women of Brewster Place* draws its canonical allusions from Shakespeare, and its contemporary references from African American writers. Aside from quoting directly from *A Midsummer Night's Dream* and *The Tempest,* the novel draws on the dream symbol and imagery used in both, on the wall in the former. As Cora Lee watches the play, she sees the wall give way to all walks of people mingling on the stage, which in turn foreshadows Mattie's dream of tearing down the wall. Both combine to suggest that walls may be figuratively torn down to enrich the lives of the women of Brewster Place.

Naylor also draws liberating devices from contemporary literature. Characters in the novel bear striking similarities to Ralph Ellison's *The Invisible Man* (1952) and Richard Wright's "The Man Who Lived Underground." Like Jean Toomer's *Cane* (1927), *The Women of Brewster Place* articulates the concept of black women as "everlasting songs," and Toomer also used an experimental form. Described as a composite novel, *Cane* consists of short stories, songs and poems. More important are the literary precedents written by African American women. While there are general similarities in characterization, poetic narrative style, and earthy dialogue between Naylor's writing and that of her contemporaries Toni Morrison and Alice Walker, *The Women of Brewster Place* seems more firmly connected to Anne Petry's *The Street* (1946). Both end with a terrible death that contributes to the meaning, a death symbolic of an end to the lack of action when action is desperately needed. In addition, both have a protagonist failed by three generations of men in her family, Petry's Lutie and Naylor's Mattie. Naylor also draws from the writing of novelist/playwright Ana Ata Aidoo, who uses similar framing devices in *No Sweetness Here* (1970), and both women pay only perfunctory attention to the role of white colonizers. Like Lorraine Hansberry's play, *A Raisin in the Sun* (1959), Naylor draws on Langston Hughes's poem "Harlem," which features a vexed mother-daughter relationship, and valorizes the mother. Additionally, the idea of black women supporting each other and the necessity of community for survival is also evident in Zora Neale Hurston's *Their Eyes Were Watching God* (1937) and Toni Morrison's *Sula* (1972)

◆ RELATED TITLES ◆

While the works of Hurston, Morrison, and Walker may provide readers with further understanding of the issues raised in *The Women of Brewster Place*, Naylor's later works are the most clearly related titles. After her first novel, she went on to rework its themes and some of its characters in three other novels to form the Linden Hills quartet. *The Women of Brewster Place* set forth a vision of unity furthered and enhanced by the continuum of narrative in the quartet. Kiswana Browne is a recurring figure, and the rich black neighborhood of Linden Hills also figures in *Linden Hills* (1985), *Mama Day* (1988), and *Bailey's Café* (1992). Naylor completes the quartet by repeating the same narrative frame in the first and last volumes. *Bailey's Café* also features a series of short stories set within a specific place. In 1998, Naylor returns to her original setting with *The Men of Brewster Place*, which complicates, completes, and enriches the stories told in her first novel.

◆ ADAPTATIONS ◆

In 1989, largely through the instigation of talk show host Oprah Winfrey, *The Women of Brewster Place* aired as a movie shown in two parts by the American Broadcasting Corporation. Winfrey served as the executive producer of the show and starred as Mattie Michael. Reviewers of the movie tended to dismiss it as yet another depiction of a novel written by a black women with an unflattering view of black men, or they complained that it was a black soap opera and a formulaic melodrama. On the other hand, audience response was hugely positive. The show earned a 23.5/36 Nielsen share the first night and 24.5/38 the second. Indications were that people who normally do not watch network televison made a point of watching Naylor's novel brought to television. That the miniseries was rerun on prime time within a year of its original broadcast also attests to positive viewer response. The movie was directed by a woman, Donna Deitch, and became the first of several with black, female ensemble casts. Aside from Winfrey as Mattie, the show featured Oscar winner Cicely Tyson as Etta Mae, and rising star Robin Givens as Kiswana. Other members of the cast included Jackee Kelly, Paula Kelly, Olivia Cole, Lonette McKee, and Jackee. The show is currently widely available on videotape.

◆ IDEAS FOR GROUP DISCUSSIONS ◆

The difficulties faced by the women of Brewster Place are symptomatic of wider social concerns and problems. Furthermore, as the feminist and womanist movements make clear, for every marginalized and oppressed group, the women of that group are even more deprived and victimized. Naylor suggests that responsibility for the problems with black women's lives must be taken by the women themselves, by the men in their homes and communities, and by society as a whole. At the same time, she allows these women the dignity that comes from action and autonomy, and the power that comes from community.

1. Consider the novel's minor characters, Miss Eva, Sophie, Elvira, Mrs. Browne. How are they both necessary plot devices, and yet more than just the function of their role? For example, Sophie is a bigot and she begins the chain of events that leads to Lorraine's tragedy, but how is she made more than these acts?

2. In an interview with Michelle Loris Gloria Naylor points out that she "would like someday for someone to look at the importance of naming, the whole act of naming, names themselves within my work because that's real conscious when I play certain games with that." How

are names significant in *The Women of Brewster Place,* and what games does Naylor play with them in the novel?

3. Aside from her musical prose, Naylor includes poetry and song lyrics throughout the novel. While the chapter on Etta Mae links black experience to the blues and to gospel music, where else do music and poetry figure in the novel? How are they used to delineate significant moments and enrich meaning?

4. In the Loris interview, Naylor points out the importance of the form of her work: "I would like for people to see how I played with structure and how often the form of the work has been either influenced by the content, or either the content demanded the form of the work." Imagine this novel in a more traditional form. Would it work equally as well? How does the short story form enhance the content, if it does?

5. The television adaptation of *The Women of Brewster Place* has been criticized for being a melodrama. Is there emotional exaggeration in the novel? Does it rely on stereotype or cliche for emotional richness? Is it merely sentimental?

6. Ben has been posited as an atonement figure, the sacrifice needed to make up for the injustices of his race and gender. Does this work? How else can Ben be understood? Can he be seen as a tragic figure? Discuss Ben's cowardice and guilt against the strength and courage of some of the women.

7. Given that Naylor privileges community as the way to autonomy and empowerment for black women, what can we make of the emptying of Brewster Place at the end of the novel. How will this community be reconfigured? By drawing evidence from each story, and especially from "The Block Party," suggest possible outcomes for the seven women, within the wider society and within their own communities.

Roxanne Harde
Queen's University

APPENDIX: TITLES GROUPED BY SOCIAL CONCERNS AND THEMES

VOLUME 14

◆

Abandonment/Desertion

Back Roads (Tawni O'Dell)
Before I Say Good-bye (Mary Higgins Clark)
The Blood Latitudes (William Harrison)
Hot Six (Janet Evanovich)
The Human Stain (Philip Roth)
Jack Maggs (Peter Carey)
Little Kingdoms (Steven Millhauser)
The Mambo Kings Play Songs of Love (Oscar Hijuelos)
On Mystic Lake (Kristin Hannah)
Rabbit Is Rich (John Updike)
Rabbit, Run (John Updike)
Timeline (Michael Crichton)
White Oleander (Janet Fitch)
The Women of Brewster Place (Gloria Naylor)

Abortion

Jack Maggs (Peter Carey)

Absurdity

Back Roads (Tawni O'Dell)
"The Birds" (Daphne du Maurier)
"The Bride Comes to Yellow Sky" (Stephen Crane)
Fierce Invalids Home from Hot Climates (Tom Robbins)
For the Relief of Unbearable Urges (Nathan Englander)
The Human Stain (Philip Roth)
To Say Nothing of the Dog (Connie Willis)

Abuse

Ashes to Ashes (Tami Hoag)
Back Roads (Tawni O'Dell)
Bastard out of Carolina (Dorothy Allison)
False Memory (Dean Koontz)
For the Relief of Unbearable Urges (Nathan Englander)
The Human Stain (Philip Roth)
Less Than Zero (Bret Easton Ellis)
The Mambo Kings Play Songs of Love (Oscar Hijuelos)
On Mystic Lake (Kristin Hannah)
Southern Cross (Patricia Cornwell)
To Say Nothing of the Dog (Connie Willis)
White Oleander (Janet Fitch)
The Women of Brewster Place (Gloria Naylor)

Acceptance and Belonging

Blood and Chocolate (Annette Curtis Klause)
"The Bride Comes to Yellow Sky" (Stephen Crane)
The Bride Price (Buchi Emecheta)
Empire of the Sun (J. G. Ballard)
Empress of the Splendid Season (Oscar Hijuelos)
For the Relief of Unbearable Urges (Nathan Englander)
The Human Stain (Philip Roth)
The Mambo Kings Play Songs of Love (Oscar Hijuelos)
On Mystic Lake (Kristin Hannah)

Out of Africa (Isak Dinesan)
Southern Cross (Patricia Cornwell)
True at First Light (Ernest Hemingway)
"The Way We Live Now" (Susan Sontag)
The Women of Brewster Place
    (Gloria Naylor)

Activity and Passivity
Ashes to Ashes (Tami Hoag)
Bastard out of Carolina (Dorothy Allison)
"The Birds" (Daphne du Maurier)
The Blood Latitudes (William Harrison)
Cradle and All (James Patterson)
False Memory (Dean Koontz)
For the Relief of Unbearable Urges (Nathan
    Englander)
A Gathering of Old Men (Ernest J. Gaines)
Hot Six (Janet Evanovich)
How the Dead Live (Will Self)
In the Time of the Butterflies (Julia Alvarez)
"The Knife Thrower" (Steven Millhauser)
Less Than Zero (Bret Easton Ellis)
On Mystic Lake (Kristin Hannah)
The Perfect Storm (Sebastian Junger)
The Pilot's Wife (Anita Shreve)
The Reader (Bernhard Schlink)
Southern Cross (Patricia Cornwell)
Those Bones Are Not My Child (Toni Cade
    Bambara)
The Women of Brewster Place
    (Gloria Naylor)

Adolescence and Youth
Ashes to Ashes (Tami Hoag)
Back Roads (Tawni O'Dell)
Bastard out of Carolina (Dorothy Allison)
Blood and Chocolate (Annette Curtis
    Klause)
The Blood Latitudes (William Harrison)
The Bride Price (Buchi Emecheta)
Southern Cross (Patricia Cornwell)
Those Bones Are Not My Child (Toni Cade
    Bambara)
White Oleander (Janet Fitch)

Adultery
Easy Prey (John Sandford)

Flaubert's Parrot (Julian Barnes)
Gertrude and Claudius (John Updike)
In the Time of the Butterflies (Julia Alvarez)
Jack Maggs (Peter Carey)
The Mambo Kings Play Songs of Love
    (Oscar Hijuelos)
O Is for Outlaw (Sue Grafton)
On Mystic Lake (Kristin Hannah)
The Pilot's Wife (Anita Shreve)
Rabbit Is Rich (John Updike)
Rabbit, Run (John Updike)

Adulthood
The Blood Latitudes (William Harrison)
The Bride Price (Buchi Emecheta)
Rabbit Is Rich (John Updike)
White Oleander (Janet Fitch)

Adventure
Blood and Chocolate (Annette Curtis
    Klause)
Empire of the Sun (J. G. Ballard)
Fierce Invalids Home from Hot Climates
    (Tom Robbins)
Out of Africa (Isak Dinesan)
The Perfect Storm (Sebastian Junger)
Timeline (Michael Crichton)
To Have and Have Not (Ernest
    Hemingway)
To Say Nothing of the Dog (Connie Willis)
True at First Light (Ernest Hemingway)

African Life and Thought
The Blood Latitudes (William Harrison)
The Bride Price (Buchi Emecheta)
Out of Africa (Isak Dinesan)
True at First Light (Ernest Hemingway)

African-American Life and
Thought
A Gathering of Old Men (Ernest J. Gaines)
Hugger Mugger (Robert B. Parker)
The Human Stain (Philip Roth)
Those Bones Are Not My Child (Toni Cade
    Bambara)

Appendix: Titles Grouped by Social Concerns and Themes

The Women of Brewster Place
(Gloria Naylor)

Aging
Fierce Invalids Home from Hot Climates
(Tom Robbins)
A Gathering of Old Men (Ernest J. Gaines)
How the Dead Live (Will Self)
The Human Stain (Philip Roth)
The Mambo Kings Play Songs of Love
(Oscar Hijuelos)
Rabbit Is Rich (John Updike)

Agriculture
Out of Africa (Isak Dinesan)

AIDS/HIV
"The Way We Live Now" (Susan Sontag)

Alcoholism and Addiction
Blood and Chocolate (Annette Curtis
Klause)
The Brethren (John Grisham)
Easy Prey (John Sandford)
Empress of the Splendid Season (Oscar
Hijuelos)
How the Dead Live (Will Self)
Less Than Zero (Bret Easton Ellis)
The Mambo Kings Play Songs of Love
(Oscar Hijuelos)
On Mystic Lake (Kristin Hannah)
Rabbit, Run (John Updike)
Southern Cross (Patricia Cornwell)

Alienation
Ashes to Ashes (Tami Hoag)
Back Roads (Tawni O'Dell)
Bastard out of Carolina (Dorothy Allison)
Black Notice (Patricia Cornwell)
Blood and Chocolate (Annette Curtis
Klause)
The Blood Latitudes (William Harrison)
The Bride Price (Buchi Emecheta)
Cradle and All (James Patterson)
For the Relief of Unbearable Urges (Nathan
Englander)

A Gathering of Old Men (Ernest J. Gaines)
Gertrude and Claudius (John Updike)
How the Dead Live (Will Self)
The Human Stain (Philip Roth)
Jack Maggs (Peter Carey)
The Mambo Kings Play Songs of Love
(Oscar Hijuelos)
O Is for Outlaw (Sue Grafton)
The Pilot's Wife (Anita Shreve)
The Reader (Bernhard Schlink)
Southern Cross (Patricia Cornwell)
Those Bones Are Not My Child (Toni Cade
Bambara)
"The Way We Live Now" (Susan Sontag)
White Oleander (Janet Fitch)
The Women of Brewster Place
(Gloria Naylor)

Alternative Societies
Blood and Chocolate (Annette Curtis
Klause)
The Blood Latitudes (William Harrison)
The Bride Price (Buchi Emecheta)
Fierce Invalids Home from Hot Climates
(Tom Robbins)
Gertrude and Claudius (John Updike)
Out of Africa (Isak Dinesan)
To Say Nothing of the Dog (Connie Willis)
True at First Light (Ernest Hemingway)

Alternative History
Timeline (Michael Crichton)

Altruism
Ashes to Ashes (Tami Hoag)
Back Roads (Tawni O'Dell)
Before I Say Good-bye (Mary
Higgins Clark)
Black Notice (Patricia Cornwell)
Cradle and All (James Patterson)
For the Relief of Unbearable Urges (Nathan
Englander)
A Gathering of Old Men (Ernest J. Gaines)
Hugger Mugger (Robert B. Parker)
Little Kingdoms (Steven Millhauser)
On Mystic Lake (Kristin Hannah)

Ambiguity

Ashes to Ashes (Tami Hoag)
"The Birds" (Daphne du Maurier)
Black Notice (Patricia Cornwell)
Blood and Chocolate (Annette Curtis
    Klause)
"The Bride Comes to Yellow Sky"
    (Stephen Crane)
Cradle and All (James Patterson)
Empire of the Sun (J. G. Ballard)
Fierce Invalids Home from Hot Climates
    (Tom Robbins)
Flaubert's Parrot (Julian Barnes)
A Gathering of Old Men (Ernest J. Gaines)
Hot Six (Janet Evanovich)
"The Knife Thrower" (Steven Millhauser)
Little Kingdoms (Steven Millhauser)
O Is for Outlaw (Sue Grafton)
On Mystic Lake (Kristin Hannah)
The Pilot's Wife (Anita Shreve)
Rabbit Is Rich (John Updike)
The Reader (Bernhard Schlink)
Those Bones Are Not My Child (Toni Cade
    Bambara)
Timeline (Michael Crichton)
To Say Nothing of the Dog (Connie Willis)
True at First Light (Ernest Hemingway)
White Oleander (Janet Fitch)

Ambition

Ashes to Ashes (Tami Hoag)
Before I Say Good-bye (Mary
    Higgins Clark)
Black Notice (Patricia Cornwell)
The Brethren (John Grisham)
The Bride Price (Buchi Emecheta)
Easy Prey (John Sandford)
Empress of the Splendid Season (Oscar
    Hijuelos)
False Memory (Dean Koontz)
Gertrude and Claudius (John Updike)
The Human Stain (Philip Roth)
The Mambo Kings Play Songs of Love
    (Oscar Hijuelos)
O Is for Outlaw (Sue Grafton)
Rabbit Is Rich (John Updike)
Timeline (Michael Crichton)

To Say Nothing of the Dog (Connie Willis)

American Dream

Ashes to Ashes (Tami Hoag)
Before I Say Good-bye (Mary
    Higgins Clark)
Easy Prey (John Sandford)
Empress of the Splendid Season (Oscar
    Hijuelos)
Hot Six (Janet Evanovich)
The Human Stain (Philip Roth)
The Mambo Kings Play Songs of Love
    (Oscar Hijuelos)
Rabbit Is Rich (John Updike)
Rabbit, Run (John Updike)
To Say Nothing of the Dog (Connie Willis)

American East

Before I Say Good-bye (Mary
    Higgins Clark)
Easy Prey (John Sandford)
Empress of the Splendid Season (Oscar
    Hijuelos)
Hot Six (Janet Evanovich)
The Human Stain (Philip Roth)
"The Way We Live Now" (Susan Sontag)

American Midwest

Rabbit Is Rich (John Updike)

American North

The Human Stain (Philip Roth)

American South

Bastard out of Carolina (Dorothy Allison)
Blood and Chocolate (Annette Curtis
    Klause)
A Gathering of Old Men (Ernest J. Gaines)
Hugger Mugger (Robert B. Parker)
Rabbit, Run (John Updike)
Southern Cross (Patricia Cornwell)
Those Bones Are Not My Child (Toni Cade
    Bambara)
To Have and Have Not (Ernest
    Hemingway)

American West

"The Bride Comes to Yellow Sky"
(Stephen Crane)
On Mystic Lake (Kristin Hannah)

Anarchism

O Is for Outlaw (Sue Grafton)

Anger

Back Roads (Tawni O'Dell)
Bastard out of Carolina (Dorothy Allison)
Black Notice (Patricia Cornwell)
Blood and Chocolate (Annette Curtis
Klause)
The Blood Latitudes (William Harrison)
A Gathering of Old Men (Ernest J. Gaines)
Gertrude and Claudius (John Updike)
The Human Stain (Philip Roth)
In the Time of the Butterflies (Julia Alvarez)
The Pilot's Wife (Anita Shreve)
Rabbit Is Rich (John Updike)
Rabbit, Run (John Updike)
The Reader (Bernhard Schlink)
Those Bones Are Not My Child (Toni Cade
Bambara)
Timeline (Michael Crichton)
The Women of Brewster Place
(Gloria Naylor)

Angry Young Men

Back Roads (Tawni O'Dell)
Blood and Chocolate (Annette Curtis
Klause)
The Blood Latitudes (William Harrison)
Gertrude and Claudius (John Updike)
Rabbit Is Rich (John Updike)

Angry Young Women

Bastard out of Carolina (Dorothy Allison)
Black Notice (Patricia Cornwell)
Blood and Chocolate (Annette Curtis
Klause)
The Bride Price (Buchi Emecheta)
In the Time of the Butterflies (Julia Alvarez)
O Is for Outlaw (Sue Grafton)

White Oleander (Janet Fitch)

Animals/Beasts

Back Roads (Tawni O'Dell)
"The Birds" (Daphne du Maurier)
Blood and Chocolate (Annette Curtis
Klause)
Hot Six (Janet Evanovich)
Hugger Mugger (Robert B. Parker)
The Perfect Storm (Sebastian Junger)
True at First Light (Ernest Hemingway)

Anthropomorphism

"The Birds" (Daphne du Maurier)
Blood and Chocolate (Annette Curtis
Klause)

Anti-Semitism

For the Relief of Unbearable Urges (Nathan
Englander)
How the Dead Live (Will Self)
The Reader (Bernhard Schlink)

Anticulture

Ashes to Ashes (Tami Hoag)
Back Roads (Tawni O'Dell)
Bastard out of Carolina (Dorothy Allison)
"The Birds" (Daphne du Maurier)
The Blood Latitudes (William Harrison)
The Brethren (John Grisham)
"The Bride Comes to Yellow Sky"
(Stephen Crane)
Easy Prey (John Sandford)
False Memory (Dean Koontz)
Fierce Invalids Home from Hot Climates
(Tom Robbins)
Hot Six (Janet Evanovich)
How the Dead Live (Will Self)
Hugger Mugger (Robert B. Parker)
The Human Stain (Philip Roth)
Jack Maggs (Peter Carey)
Less Than Zero (Bret Easton Ellis)
O Is for Outlaw (Sue Grafton)
The Reader (Bernhard Schlink)
Southern Cross (Patricia Cornwell)
Those Bones Are Not My Child (Toni Cade
Bambara)

The Women of Brewster Place
(Gloria Naylor)

Antiwar Protest
The Blood Latitudes (William Harrison)

Anxiety
Ashes to Ashes (Tami Hoag)
Back Roads (Tawni O'Dell)
"The Birds" (Daphne du Maurier)
Black Notice (Patricia Cornwell)
Blood and Chocolate (Annette Curtis
    Klause)
The Blood Latitudes (William Harrison)
"The Bride Comes to Yellow Sky"
    (Stephen Crane)
Cradle and All (James Patterson)
A Gathering of Old Men (Ernest J. Gaines)
Gertrude and Claudius (John Updike)
O Is for Outlaw (Sue Grafton)
The Perfect Storm (Sebastian Junger)
Rabbit Is Rich (John Updike)
Those Bones Are Not My Child (Toni Cade
    Bambara)
Timeline (Michael Crichton)
True at First Light (Ernest Hemingway)
"The Way We Live Now" (Susan Sontag)
White Oleander (Janet Fitch)

Apathy
Less Than Zero (Bret Easton Ellis)
Those Bones Are Not My Child (Toni Cade
    Bambara)

Apocalypse
Cradle and All (James Patterson)
Fierce Invalids Home from Hot Climates
    (Tom Robbins)

Appearance vs. Reality
Back Roads (Tawni O'Dell)
Before I Say Good-bye (Mary
    Higgins Clark)
Black Notice (Patricia Cornwell)
Blood and Chocolate (Annette Curtis
    Klause)
The Brethren (John Grisham)

Cradle and All (James Patterson)
Empress of the Splendid Season (Oscar
    Hijuelos)
False Memory (Dean Koontz)
Flaubert's Parrot (Julian Barnes)
A Gathering of Old Men (Ernest J. Gaines)
Gertrude and Claudius (John Updike)
Hot Six (Janet Evanovich)
How the Dead Live (Will Self)
Hugger Mugger (Robert B. Parker)
The Human Stain (Philip Roth)
O Is for Outlaw (Sue Grafton)
The Pilot's Wife (Anita Shreve)
The Reader (Bernhard Schlink)
Southern Cross (Patricia Cornwell)
Timeline (Michael Crichton)

Apprenticeship
Hot Six (Janet Evanovich)

Architecture
Before I Say Good-bye (Mary
    Higgins Clark)
To Say Nothing of the Dog (Connie Willis)
The Women of Brewster Place
    (Gloria Naylor)

Aristocracy
To Say Nothing of the Dog (Connie Willis)

Artificiality
Before I Say Good-bye (Mary
    Higgins Clark)
Easy Prey (John Sandford)
Empress of the Splendid Season (Oscar
    Hijuelos)
Gertrude and Claudius (John Updike)
Hugger Mugger (Robert B. Parker)
White Oleander (Janet Fitch)

Artists
Easy Prey (John Sandford)
Jack Maggs (Peter Carey)
Little Kingdoms (Steven Millhauser)
The Mambo Kings Play Songs of Love
    (Oscar Hijuelos)

Artists and Society
Little Kingdoms (Steven Millhauser)

Arts
Fierce Invalids Home from Hot Climates (Tom Robbins)
Flaubert's Parrot (Julian Barnes)
Little Kingdoms (Steven Millhauser)
To Say Nothing of the Dog (Connie Willis)

Assimilation and Acculturation
Blood and Chocolate (Annette Curtis Klause)
Empress of the Splendid Season (Oscar Hijuelos)
For the Relief of Unbearable Urges (Nathan Englander)
Hot Six (Janet Evanovich)
The Mambo Kings Play Songs of Love (Oscar Hijuelos)
True at First Light (Ernest Hemingway)

Atonement and Redemption
Black Notice (Patricia Cornwell)
Blood and Chocolate (Annette Curtis Klause)
Rabbit Is Rich (John Updike)
Rabbit, Run (John Updike)
True at First Light (Ernest Hemingway)

Australian Life and Thought
Jack Maggs (Peter Carey)

Authority
Ashes to Ashes (Tami Hoag)
Back Roads (Tawni O'Dell)
Black Notice (Patricia Cornwell)
The Brethren (John Grisham)
"The Bride Comes to Yellow Sky" (Stephen Crane)
The Bride Price (Buchi Emecheta)
Cradle and All (James Patterson)
Empire of the Sun (J. G. Ballard)
For the Relief of Unbearable Urges (Nathan Englander)
A Gathering of Old Men (Ernest J. Gaines)

Gertrude and Claudius (John Updike)
In the Time of the Butterflies (Julia Alvarez)
O Is for Outlaw (Sue Grafton)
The Reader (Bernhard Schlink)
Southern Cross (Patricia Cornwell)
Those Bones Are Not My Child (Toni Cade Bambara)
To Say Nothing of the Dog (Connie Willis)

Beauty and Aesthetics
Easy Prey (John Sandford)
Empire of the Sun (J. G. Ballard)
Fierce Invalids Home from Hot Climates (Tom Robbins)
Flaubert's Parrot (Julian Barnes)
For the Relief of Unbearable Urges (Nathan Englander)
Little Kingdoms (Steven Millhauser)
To Say Nothing of the Dog (Connie Willis)

Betrayal
Before I Say Good-bye (Mary Higgins Clark)
Black Notice (Patricia Cornwell)
Blood and Chocolate (Annette Curtis Klause)
Cradle and All (James Patterson)
Gertrude and Claudius (John Updike)
On Mystic Lake (Kristin Hannah)
The Pilot's Wife (Anita Shreve)
Playback (Raymond Chandler)
Rabbit, Run (John Updike)
Timeline (Michael Crichton)
White Oleander (Janet Fitch)

Birth
The Bride Price (Buchi Emecheta)
Cradle and All (James Patterson)
How the Dead Live (Will Self)
On Mystic Lake (Kristin Hannah)
Rabbit Is Rich (John Updike)
Rabbit, Run (John Updike)

Black Identity
The Blood Latitudes (William Harrison)
The Bride Price (Buchi Emecheta)
A Gathering of Old Men (Ernest J. Gaines)

Hugger Mugger (Robert B. Parker)
The Human Stain (Philip Roth)
Those Bones Are Not My Child (Toni Cade
   Bambara)
The Women of Brewster Place
   (Gloria Naylor)

Blasphemy and Heresy
Cradle and All (James Patterson)
Gertrude and Claudius (John Updike)

Bohemianism
Less Than Zero (Bret Easton Ellis)

Bourgeois Life
Jack Maggs (Peter Carey)

Bravery
Before I Say Good-bye (Mary
   Higgins Clark)
"The Knife Thrower" (Steven Millhauser)
The Perfect Storm (Sebastian Junger)
True at First Light (Ernest Hemingway)

Brotherhood
Fierce Invalids Home from Hot Climates
   (Tom Robbins)
A Gathering of Old Men (Ernest J. Gaines)
Out of Africa (Isak Dinesan)

Brutality
Ashes to Ashes (Tami Hoag)
Back Roads (Tawni O'Dell)
Bastard out of Carolina (Dorothy Allison)
Black Notice (Patricia Cornwell)
Blood and Chocolate (Annette Curtis
   Klause)
The Blood Latitudes (William Harrison)
Empire of the Sun (J. G. Ballard)
For the Relief of Unbearable Urges (Nathan
   Englander)
In the Time of the Butterflies (Julia Alvarez)
Less Than Zero (Bret Easton Ellis)
Playback (Raymond Chandler)
Southern Cross (Patricia Cornwell)

Those Bones Are Not My Child (Toni Cade
   Bambara)
The Women of Brewster Place
   (Gloria Naylor)

Bureaucracy
Black Notice (Patricia Cornwell)
How the Dead Live (Will Self)
Those Bones Are Not My Child (Toni Cade
   Bambara)

Business and Business Life
Before I Say Good-bye (Mary
   Higgins Clark)
Easy Prey (John Sandford)
Hot Six (Janet Evanovich)
The Mambo Kings Play Songs of Love
   (Oscar Hijuelos)
O Is for Outlaw (Sue Grafton)
Rabbit Is Rich (John Updike)
Timeline (Michael Crichton)

Capitalism
Rabbit Is Rich (John Updike)
Timeline (Michael Crichton)

Caribbean Life and Thought
In the Time of the Butterflies (Julia Alvarez)
The Mambo Kings Play Songs of Love
   (Oscar Hijuelos)

Carpe Diem
Fierce Invalids Home from Hot Climates
   (Tom Robbins)
Timeline (Michael Crichton)

Catastrophe
Before I Say Good-bye (Mary
   Higgins Clark)
"The Birds" (Daphne du Maurier)
The Bride Price (Buchi Emecheta)
For the Relief of Unbearable Urges (Nathan
   Englander)
The Human Stain (Philip Roth)
Jack Maggs (Peter Carey)
"The Knife Thrower" (Steven Millhauser)

Little Kingdoms (Steven Millhauser)
On Mystic Lake (Kristin Hannah)
Out of Africa (Isak Dinesan)
The Perfect Storm (Sebastian Junger)
The Pilot's Wife (Anita Shreve)
Rabbit, Run (John Updike)
Southern Cross (Patricia Cornwell)
Those Bones Are Not My Child (Toni Cade Bambara)
"The Way We Live Now" (Susan Sontag)

Catharsis
Black Notice (Patricia Cornwell)
"The Knife Thrower" (Steven Millhauser)

Catholicism (Roman)
Cradle and All (James Patterson)
Empress of the Splendid Season (Oscar Hijuelos)
Fierce Invalids Home from Hot Climates (Tom Robbins)
In the Time of the Butterflies (Julia Alvarez)
The Pilot's Wife (Anita Shreve)

Celebration
Little Kingdoms (Steven Millhauser)
The Perfect Storm (Sebastian Junger)

Censorship
For the Relief of Unbearable Urges (Nathan Englander)

Ceremonies and Rituals
"The Bride Comes to Yellow Sky" (Stephen Crane)
The Bride Price (Buchi Emecheta)
Empire of the Sun (J. G. Ballard)
Fierce Invalids Home from Hot Climates (Tom Robbins)
True at First Light (Ernest Hemingway)

Change and Transformation
Black Notice (Patricia Cornwell)
Blood and Chocolate (Annette Curtis Klause)

"The Bride Comes to Yellow Sky" (Stephen Crane)
Fierce Invalids Home from Hot Climates (Tom Robbins)
Gertrude and Claudius (John Updike)
How the Dead Live (Will Self)
To Say Nothing of the Dog (Connie Willis)

Chaos and Order
"The Birds" (Daphne du Maurier)
Black Notice (Patricia Cornwell)
The Blood Latitudes (William Harrison)
"The Bride Comes to Yellow Sky" (Stephen Crane)
Cradle and All (James Patterson)
Empire of the Sun (J. G. Ballard)
O Is for Outlaw (Sue Grafton)

Childhood
Bastard out of Carolina (Dorothy Allison)
Empire of the Sun (J. G. Ballard)
On Mystic Lake (Kristin Hannah)
White Oleander (Janet Fitch)

Christianity
Bastard out of Carolina (Dorothy Allison)
Cradle and All (James Patterson)
Fierce Invalids Home from Hot Climates (Tom Robbins)
Gertrude and Claudius (John Updike)
In the Time of the Butterflies (Julia Alvarez)
Rabbit, Run (John Updike)
True at First Light (Ernest Hemingway)

City Life
Back Roads (Tawni O'Dell)
Before I Say Good-bye (Mary Higgins Clark)
Easy Prey (John Sandford)
Empress of the Splendid Season (Oscar Hijuelos)
Hot Six (Janet Evanovich)
How the Dead Live (Will Self)
Jack Maggs (Peter Carey)
Southern Cross (Patricia Cornwell)
Those Bones Are Not My Child (Toni Cade Bambara)

"The Way We Live Now" (Susan Sontag)
The Women of Brewster Place
(Gloria Naylor)

Civil Rights

Bastard out of Carolina (Dorothy Allison)
The Bride Price (Buchi Emecheta)
A Gathering of Old Men (Ernest J. Gaines)
In the Time of the Butterflies (Julia Alvarez)
The Thanatos Syndrome (Walker Percy)
Those Bones Are Not My Child (Toni Cade
Bambara)
To Say Nothing of the Dog (Connie Willis)
The Women of Brewster Place
(Gloria Naylor)

Civilization

The Blood Latitudes (William Harrison)

Class Conflict

Back Roads (Tawni O'Dell)
Bastard out of Carolina (Dorothy Allison)
Before I Say Good-bye (Mary
Higgins Clark)
Black Notice (Patricia Cornwell)
"The Bride Comes to Yellow Sky"
(Stephen Crane)
The Bride Price (Buchi Emecheta)
A Gathering of Old Men (Ernest J. Gaines)
In the Time of the Butterflies (Julia Alvarez)
Jack Maggs (Peter Carey)
Playback (Raymond Chandler)
Southern Cross (Patricia Cornwell)
Those Bones Are Not My Child (Toni Cade
Bambara)
To Have and Have Not (Ernest
Hemingway)
To Say Nothing of the Dog (Connie Willis)

Class Structure

Back Roads (Tawni O'Dell)
Bastard out of Carolina (Dorothy Allison)
Before I Say Good-bye (Mary
Higgins Clark)
Black Notice (Patricia Cornwell)

"The Bride Comes to Yellow Sky"
(Stephen Crane)
The Bride Price (Buchi Emecheta)
Empress of the Splendid Season (Oscar
Hijuelos)
A Gathering of Old Men (Ernest J. Gaines)
Hugger Mugger (Robert B. Parker)
In the Time of the Butterflies (Julia Alvarez)
Jack Maggs (Peter Carey)
Out of Africa (Isak Dinesan)
The Reader (Bernhard Schlink)
Southern Cross (Patricia Cornwell)
Those Bones Are Not My Child (Toni Cade
Bambara)
To Say Nothing of the Dog (Connie Willis)

Clothing and Fashion

Bastard out of Carolina (Dorothy Allison)
Empress of the Splendid Season (Oscar
Hijuelos)

Cold War

"The Birds" (Daphne du Maurier)
In the Time of the Butterflies (Julia Alvarez)

Colonialism

The Blood Latitudes (William Harrison)
Jack Maggs (Peter Carey)
Out of Africa (Isak Dinesan)
True at First Light (Ernest Hemingway)

Comedy Of Life

"The Bride Comes to Yellow Sky"
(Stephen Crane)
Easy Prey (John Sandford)
Fierce Invalids Home from Hot Climates
(Tom Robbins)
For the Relief of Unbearable Urges (Nathan
Englander)
Hot Six (Janet Evanovich)
To Say Nothing of the Dog (Connie Willis)

Coming Of Age

Back Roads (Tawni O'Dell)
The Bride Price (Buchi Emecheta)

White Oleander (Janet Fitch)

Commercialism
Little Kingdoms (Steven Millhauser)
Rabbit Is Rich (John Updike)

Common Man/Common Woman
Back Roads (Tawni O'Dell)
Bastard out of Carolina (Dorothy Allison)
The Bride Price (Buchi Emecheta)
Empress of the Splendid Season (Oscar Hijuelos)
For the Relief of Unbearable Urges (Nathan Englander)
A Gathering of Old Men (Ernest J. Gaines)
In the Time of the Butterflies (Julia Alvarez)
Jack Maggs (Peter Carey)
The Perfect Storm (Sebastian Junger)
The Reader (Bernhard Schlink)
Those Bones Are Not My Child (Toni Cade Bambara)
To Have and Have Not (Ernest Hemingway)

Communism
For the Relief of Unbearable Urges (Nathan Englander)
In the Time of the Butterflies (Julia Alvarez)

Complacency
Less Than Zero (Bret Easton Ellis)
Southern Cross (Patricia Cornwell)
Those Bones Are Not My Child (Toni Cade Bambara)

Conformity
Before I Say Good-bye (Mary Higgins Clark)
Blood and Chocolate (Annette Curtis Klause)
"The Bride Comes to Yellow Sky" (Stephen Crane)
The Bride Price (Buchi Emecheta)
For the Relief of Unbearable Urges (Nathan Englander)
A Gathering of Old Men (Ernest J. Gaines)

Hugger Mugger (Robert B. Parker)
Less Than Zero (Bret Easton Ellis)
On Mystic Lake (Kristin Hannah)
The Reader (Bernhard Schlink)
Southern Cross (Patricia Cornwell)

Confusion
"The Birds" (Daphne du Maurier)
Black Notice (Patricia Cornwell)
Cradle and All (James Patterson)
For the Relief of Unbearable Urges (Nathan Englander)
On Mystic Lake (Kristin Hannah)
The Perfect Storm (Sebastian Junger)
The Pilot's Wife (Anita Shreve)
The Reader (Bernhard Schlink)
Those Bones Are Not My Child (Toni Cade Bambara)
Timeline (Michael Crichton)
White Oleander (Janet Fitch)

Conscience
Ashes to Ashes (Tami Hoag)
Back Roads (Tawni O'Dell)
Bastard out of Carolina (Dorothy Allison)
Black Notice (Patricia Cornwell)
Blood and Chocolate (Annette Curtis Klause)
"The Bride Comes to Yellow Sky" (Stephen Crane)
Cradle and All (James Patterson)
Fierce Invalids Home from Hot Climates (Tom Robbins)
For the Relief of Unbearable Urges (Nathan Englander)
A Gathering of Old Men (Ernest J. Gaines)
Hot Six (Janet Evanovich)
Hugger Mugger (Robert B. Parker)
In the Time of the Butterflies (Julia Alvarez)
The Mambo Kings Play Songs of Love (Oscar Hijuelos)
Rabbit Is Rich (John Updike)
Rabbit, Run (John Updike)
The Reader (Bernhard Schlink)
Southern Cross (Patricia Cornwell)
To Say Nothing of the Dog (Connie Willis)
True at First Light (Ernest Hemingway)

Consolation and Comfort

Black Notice (Patricia Cornwell)
For the Relief of Unbearable Urges (Nathan Englander)
The Mambo Kings Play Songs of Love (Oscar Hijuelos)
On Mystic Lake (Kristin Hannah)
Rabbit Is Rich (John Updike)
Rabbit, Run (John Updike)
"The Way We Live Now" (Susan Sontag)

Conspiracy

The Brethren (John Grisham)
The Pilot's Wife (Anita Shreve)
The Thanatos Syndrome (Walker Percy)

Construction

Before I Say Good-bye (Mary Higgins Clark)
Empire of the Sun (J. G. Ballard)
To Say Nothing of the Dog (Connie Willis)

Corruption

Ashes to Ashes (Tami Hoag)
Before I Say Good-bye (Mary Higgins Clark)
Black Notice (Patricia Cornwell)
The Blood Latitudes (William Harrison)
The Brethren (John Grisham)
Easy Prey (John Sandford)
False Memory (Dean Koontz)
For the Relief of Unbearable Urges (Nathan Englander)
A Gathering of Old Men (Ernest J. Gaines)
Gertrude and Claudius (John Updike)
Hot Six (Janet Evanovich)
Hugger Mugger (Robert B. Parker)
In the Time of the Butterflies (Julia Alvarez)
The Mambo Kings Play Songs of Love (Oscar Hijuelos)
Playback (Raymond Chandler)
O Is for Outlaw (Sue Grafton)
Timeline (Michael Crichton)
To Have and Have Not (Ernest Hemingway)

Country Life

A Gathering of Old Men (Ernest J. Gaines)
Hugger Mugger (Robert B. Parker)
Out of Africa (Isak Dinesan)

Courage

Ashes to Ashes (Tami Hoag)
"The Birds" (Daphne du Maurier)
Black Notice (Patricia Cornwell)
Blood and Chocolate (Annette Curtis Klause)
The Blood Latitudes (William Harrison)
Empire of the Sun (J. G. Ballard)
For the Relief of Unbearable Urges (Nathan Englander)
A Gathering of Old Men (Ernest J. Gaines)
In the Time of the Butterflies (Julia Alvarez)
Out of Africa (Isak Dinesan)
The Perfect Storm (Sebastian Junger)
Timeline (Michael Crichton)
True at First Light (Ernest Hemingway)

Courtly Love

Before I Say Good-bye (Mary Higgins Clark)
Blood and Chocolate (Annette Curtis Klause)
The Bride Price (Buchi Emecheta)
Gertrude and Claudius (John Updike)

Covenant

Blood and Chocolate (Annette Curtis Klause)
The Bride Price (Buchi Emecheta)
Cradle and All (James Patterson)
Fierce Invalids Home from Hot Climates (Tom Robbins)
For the Relief of Unbearable Urges (Nathan Englander)
Rabbit, Run (John Updike)
The Women of Brewster Place (Gloria Naylor)

Creative Process

Easy Prey (John Sandford)
Flaubert's Parrot (Julian Barnes)

For the Relief of Unbearable Urges (Nathan
  Englander)
Jack Maggs (Peter Carey)
Little Kingdoms (Steven Millhauser)
The Mambo Kings Play Songs of Love
  (Oscar Hijuelos)
Those Bones Are Not My Child (Toni Cade
  Bambara)
White Oleander (Janet Fitch)

Crime and Criminals
Ashes to Ashes (Tami Hoag)
Before I Say Good-bye (Mary
  Higgins Clark)
Black Notice (Patricia Cornwell)
The Blood Latitudes (William Harrison)
The Brethren (John Grisham)
Easy Prey (John Sandford)
False Memory (Dean Koontz)
A Gathering of Old Men (Ernest J. Gaines)
Hot Six (Janet Evanovich)
Hugger Mugger (Robert B. Parker)
Jack Maggs (Peter Carey)
The Mambo Kings Play Songs of Love
  (Oscar Hijuelos)
O Is for Outlaw (Sue Grafton)
The Pilot's Wife (Anita Shreve)
Playback (Raymond Chandler)
The Reader (Bernhard Schlink)
Southern Cross (Patricia Cornwell)
The Thanatos Syndrome (Walker Percy)
Those Bones Are Not My Child (Toni Cade
  Bambara)
Timeline (Michael Crichton)

Cruelty
Ashes to Ashes (Tami Hoag)
Back Roads (Tawni O'Dell)
Bastard out of Carolina (Dorothy Allison)
Black Notice (Patricia Cornwell)
Blood and Chocolate (Annette Curtis
  Klause)
The Blood Latitudes (William Harrison)
The Bride Price (Buchi Emecheta)
Easy Prey (John Sandford)
Empire of the Sun (J. G. Ballard)
False Memory (Dean Koontz)

For the Relief of Unbearable Urges (Nathan
  Englander)
A Gathering of Old Men (Ernest J. Gaines)
Hugger Mugger (Robert B. Parker)
The Human Stain (Philip Roth)
In the Time of the Butterflies (Julia Alvarez)
Less Than Zero (Bret Easton Ellis)
The Mambo Kings Play Songs of Love
  (Oscar Hijuelos)
Rabbit, Run (John Updike)
The Reader (Bernhard Schlink)
Southern Cross (Patricia Cornwell)
Timeline (Michael Crichton)
White Oleander (Janet Fitch)
The Women of Brewster Place
  (Gloria Naylor)

Cultural Differences
The Blood Latitudes (William Harrison)
Empire of the Sun (J. G. Ballard)
Empress of the Splendid Season (Oscar
  Hijuelos)
Fierce Invalids Home from Hot Climates
  (Tom Robbins)
For the Relief of Unbearable Urges (Nathan
  Englander)
The Mambo Kings Play Songs of Love
  (Oscar Hijuelos)
Out of Africa (Isak Dinesan)
True at First Light (Ernest Hemingway)

Culture Clash
The Blood Latitudes (William Harrison)
The Bride Price (Buchi Emecheta)
For the Relief of Unbearable Urges (Nathan
  Englander)
The Mambo Kings Play Songs of Love
  (Oscar Hijuelos)
True at First Light (Ernest Hemingway)

Curiosity
Empire of the Sun (J. G. Ballard)
Fierce Invalids Home from Hot Climates
  (Tom Robbins)
Flaubert's Parrot (Julian Barnes)
Timeline (Michael Crichton)

Customs and Traditions

The Blood Latitudes (William Harrison)
"The Bride Comes to Yellow Sky"
  (Stephen Crane)
The Bride Price (Buchi Emecheta)
Empire of the Sun (J. G. Ballard)
Empress of the Splendid Season (Oscar
  Hijuelos)
Fierce Invalids Home from Hot Climates
  (Tom Robbins)
For the Relief of Unbearable Urges (Nathan
  Englander)
Gertrude and Claudius (John Updike)
Hot Six (Janet Evanovich)
Hugger Mugger (Robert B. Parker)
To Say Nothing of the Dog (Connie Willis)
True at First Light (Ernest Hemingway)

Cynicism

Ashes to Ashes (Tami Hoag)
Back Roads (Tawni O'Dell)
Black Notice (Patricia Cornwell)
The Brethren (John Grisham)
How the Dead Live (Will Self)
Hugger Mugger (Robert B. Parker)
Less Than Zero (Bret Easton Ellis)

Danger

Ashes to Ashes (Tami Hoag)
Back Roads (Tawni O'Dell)
Bastard out of Carolina (Dorothy Allison)
Before I Say Good-bye (Mary
  Higgins Clark)
"The Birds" (Daphne du Maurier)
Black Notice (Patricia Cornwell)
Blood and Chocolate (Annette Curtis
  Klause)
The Blood Latitudes (William Harrison)
"The Bride Comes to Yellow Sky"
  (Stephen Crane)
The Bride Price (Buchi Emecheta)
Cradle and All (James Patterson)
Easy Prey (John Sandford)
Empire of the Sun (J. G. Ballard)
False Memory (Dean Koontz)
For the Relief of Unbearable Urges (Nathan
  Englander)

A Gathering of Old Men (Ernest J. Gaines)
Gertrude and Claudius (John Updike)
Hot Six (Janet Evanovich)
Hugger Mugger (Robert B. Parker)
The Human Stain (Philip Roth)
In the Time of the Butterflies (Julia Alvarez)
Jack Maggs (Peter Carey)
"The Knife Thrower" (Steven Millhauser)
Less Than Zero (Bret Easton Ellis)
The Mambo Kings Play Songs of Love
  (Oscar Hijuelos)
O Is for Outlaw (Sue Grafton)
The Perfect Storm (Sebastian Junger)
Playback (Raymond Chandler)
Southern Cross (Patricia Cornwell)
Those Bones Are Not My Child (Toni Cade
  Bambara)
Timeline (Michael Crichton)
To Say Nothing of the Dog (Connie Willis)
True at First Light (Ernest Hemingway)
"The Way We Live Now" (Susan Sontag)
The Women of Brewster Place
  (Gloria Naylor)

Death and Dying

Ashes to Ashes (Tami Hoag)
Before I Say Good-bye (Mary
  Higgins Clark)
Black Notice (Patricia Cornwell)
Blood and Chocolate (Annette Curtis
  Klause)
The Blood Latitudes (William Harrison)
The Bride Price (Buchi Emecheta)
Cradle and All (James Patterson)
Easy Prey (John Sandford)
Empire of the Sun (J. G. Ballard)
Empress of the Splendid Season (Oscar
  Hijuelos)
False Memory (Dean Koontz)
For the Relief of Unbearable Urges (Nathan
  Englander)
A Gathering of Old Men (Ernest J. Gaines)
Gertrude and Claudius (John Updike)
Hot Six (Janet Evanovich)
How the Dead Live (Will Self)
The Human Stain (Philip Roth)
In the Time of the Butterflies (Julia Alvarez)

Appendix: Titles Grouped by Social Concerns and Themes

Jack Maggs (Peter Carey)
The Mambo Kings Play Songs of Love (Oscar Hijuelos)
On Mystic Lake (Kristin Hannah)
Out of Africa (Isak Dinesan)
The Perfect Storm (Sebastian Junger)
The Pilot's Wife (Anita Shreve)
Rabbit, Run (John Updike)
Southern Cross (Patricia Cornwell)
The Thanatos Syndrome (Walker Percy)
Those Bones Are Not My Child (Toni Cade Bambara)
Timeline (Michael Crichton)
True at First Light (Ernest Hemingway)
"The Way We Live Now" (Susan Sontag)
The Women of Brewster Place (Gloria Naylor)

Death of Parent
The Blood Latitudes (William Harrison)
The Bride Price (Buchi Emecheta)
Empress of the Splendid Season (Oscar Hijuelos)
False Memory (Dean Koontz)
Gertrude and Claudius (John Updike)
On Mystic Lake (Kristin Hannah)
The Pilot's Wife (Anita Shreve)

Decadence
Black Notice (Patricia Cornwell)
Easy Prey (John Sandford)
Hugger Mugger (Robert B. Parker)
In the Time of the Butterflies (Julia Alvarez)
Less Than Zero (Bret Easton Ellis)
Southern Cross (Patricia Cornwell)
White Oleander (Janet Fitch)

Decay
Black Notice (Patricia Cornwell)
The Blood Latitudes (William Harrison)
The Brethren (John Grisham)
Easy Prey (John Sandford)
Less Than Zero (Bret Easton Ellis)
Those Bones Are Not My Child (Toni Cade Bambara)
The Women of Brewster Place (Gloria Naylor)

Deception and Delusion
Before I Say Good-bye (Mary Higgins Clark)
Black Notice (Patricia Cornwell)
Blood and Chocolate (Annette Curtis Klause)
The Brethren (John Grisham)
Cradle and All (James Patterson)
False Memory (Dean Koontz)
For the Relief of Unbearable Urges (Nathan Englander)
A Gathering of Old Men (Ernest J. Gaines)
Gertrude and Claudius (John Updike)
The Human Stain (Philip Roth)
Jack Maggs (Peter Carey)
The Pilot's Wife (Anita Shreve)
Playback (Raymond Chandler)
The Reader (Bernhard Schlink)
Southern Cross (Patricia Cornwell)
Timeline (Michael Crichton)

Dehumanization
Black Notice (Patricia Cornwell)
How the Dead Live (Will Self)
Less Than Zero (Bret Easton Ellis)
The Thanatos Syndrome (Walker Percy)
To Say Nothing of the Dog (Connie Willis)

Democracy
The Brethren (John Grisham)

Denial
A Gathering of Old Men (Ernest J. Gaines)
The Human Stain (Philip Roth)
Rabbit, Run (John Updike)
The Reader (Bernhard Schlink)
To Say Nothing of the Dog (Connie Willis)
White Oleander (Janet Fitch)

Dependence
Back Roads (Tawni O'Dell)
The Bride Price (Buchi Emecheta)
How the Dead Live (Will Self)

Despair
Bastard out of Carolina (Dorothy Allison)

"The Birds" (Daphne du Maurier)
Black Notice (Patricia Cornwell)
The Mambo Kings Play Songs of Love
   (Oscar Hijuelos)
The Perfect Storm (Sebastian Junger)
The Pilot's Wife (Anita Shreve)
Those Bones Are Not My Child (Toni Cade
   Bambara)
The Women of Brewster Place
   (Gloria Naylor)

Destruction

Black Notice (Patricia Cornwell)
Blood and Chocolate (Annette Curtis
   Klause)
The Blood Latitudes (William Harrison)
The Brethren (John Grisham)
Cradle and All (James Patterson)
False Memory (Dean Koontz)
For the Relief of Unbearable Urges (Nathan
   Englander)
Out of Africa (Isak Dinesan)
The Perfect Storm (Sebastian Junger)
The Pilot's Wife (Anita Shreve)
Southern Cross (Patricia Cornwell)
Those Bones Are Not My Child (Toni Cade
   Bambara)
To Say Nothing of the Dog (Connie Willis)
True at First Light (Ernest Hemingway)
The Women of Brewster Place
   (Gloria Naylor)

Detectives and Detection

Ashes to Ashes (Tami Hoag)
Before I Say Good-bye (Mary
   Higgins Clark)
Black Notice (Patricia Cornwell)
Cradle and All (James Patterson)
Easy Prey (John Sandford)
A Gathering of Old Men (Ernest J. Gaines)
Hot Six (Janet Evanovich)
O Is for Outlaw (Sue Grafton)
The Pilot's Wife (Anita Shreve)
Playback (Raymond Chandler)
Those Bones Are Not My Child (Toni Cade
   Bambara)

Devil

Cradle and All (James Patterson)

Diary Writing

Flaubert's Parrot (Julian Barnes)
Jack Maggs (Peter Carey)
Out of Africa (Isak Dinesan)

Dignity

Empress of the Splendid Season (Oscar
   Hijuelos)
For the Relief of Unbearable Urges (Nathan
   Englander)
A Gathering of Old Men (Ernest J. Gaines)

Disappointment

Gertrude and Claudius (John Updike)
The Mambo Kings Play Songs of Love
   (Oscar Hijuelos)
Timeline (Michael Crichton)
White Oleander (Janet Fitch)

Discipline

For the Relief of Unbearable Urges (Nathan
   Englander)
The Perfect Storm (Sebastian Junger)

Discrimination

Bastard out of Carolina (Dorothy Allison)
"The Bride Comes to Yellow Sky"
   (Stephen Crane)
The Bride Price (Buchi Emecheta)
For the Relief of Unbearable Urges (Nathan
   Englander)
A Gathering of Old Men (Ernest J. Gaines)
Those Bones Are Not My Child (Toni Cade
   Bambara)

Disease

Cradle and All (James Patterson)

Disillusionment

The Mambo Kings Play Songs of Love
   (Oscar Hijuelos)

On Mystic Lake (Kristin Hannah)
The Pilot's Wife (Anita Shreve)
The Reader (Bernhard Schlink)

Divorce

How the Dead Live (Will Self)
Little Kingdoms (Steven Millhauser)
On Mystic Lake (Kristin Hannah)
The Perfect Storm (Sebastian Junger)

Domesticity

Ashes to Ashes (Tami Hoag)
The Bride Price (Buchi Emecheta)
Empress of the Splendid Season (Oscar Hijuelos)
How the Dead Live (Will Self)
In the Time of the Butterflies (Julia Alvarez)
The Mambo Kings Play Songs of Love (Oscar Hijuelos)
On Mystic Lake (Kristin Hannah)
The Pilot's Wife (Anita Shreve)
Rabbit Is Rich (John Updike)
Rabbit, Run (John Updike)
The Women of Brewster Place (Gloria Naylor)

Doubt and Self-Doubt

Ashes to Ashes (Tami Hoag)
Bastard out of Carolina (Dorothy Allison)
Black Notice (Patricia Cornwell)
Blood and Chocolate (Annette Curtis Klause)
"The Bride Comes to Yellow Sky" (Stephen Crane)
Fierce Invalids Home from Hot Climates (Tom Robbins)
For the Relief of Unbearable Urges (Nathan Englander)
Gertrude and Claudius (John Updike)
The Mambo Kings Play Songs of Love (Oscar Hijuelos)
On Mystic Lake (Kristin Hannah)
The Pilot's Wife (Anita Shreve)
Rabbit Is Rich (John Updike)
Rabbit, Run (John Updike)
The Reader (Bernhard Schlink)
True at First Light (Ernest Hemingway)

Drifters and Nomads

Blood and Chocolate (Annette Curtis Klause)
Fierce Invalids Home from Hot Climates (Tom Robbins)
Jack Maggs (Peter Carey)
The Mambo Kings Play Songs of Love (Oscar Hijuelos)

Drugs/Drug Culture

Blood and Chocolate (Annette Curtis Klause)
Easy Prey (John Sandford)
False Memory (Dean Koontz)
Fierce Invalids Home from Hot Climates (Tom Robbins)
How the Dead Live (Will Self)
Less Than Zero (Bret Easton Ellis)
The Mambo Kings Play Songs of Love (Oscar Hijuelos)
Southern Cross (Patricia Cornwell)

Dualism

The Blood Latitudes (William Harrison)
Fierce Invalids Home from Hot Climates (Tom Robbins)
The Human Stain (Philip Roth)
Jack Maggs (Peter Carey)
The Pilot's Wife (Anita Shreve)

Duty and Responsibility

Ashes to Ashes (Tami Hoag)
Back Roads (Tawni O'Dell)
Before I Say Good-bye (Mary Higgins Clark)
Black Notice (Patricia Cornwell)
The Brethren (John Grisham)
"The Bride Comes to Yellow Sky" (Stephen Crane)
The Bride Price (Buchi Emecheta)
Cradle and All (James Patterson)
False Memory (Dean Koontz)
A Gathering of Old Men (Ernest J. Gaines)
Gertrude and Claudius (John Updike)
Hot Six (Janet Evanovich)
Hugger Mugger (Robert B. Parker)

On Mystic Lake (Kristin Hannah)
Out of Africa (Isak Dinesan)
The Perfect Storm (Sebastian Junger)
Rabbit Is Rich (John Updike)
The Reader (Bernhard Schlink)
Those Bones Are Not My Child (Toni Cade
    Bambara)
True at First Light (Ernest Hemingway)
White Oleander (Janet Fitch)
The Women of Brewster Place
    (Gloria Naylor)

Dystopia and Dystopian Ideas
Ashes to Ashes (Tami Hoag)
Blood and Chocolate (Annette Curtis
    Klause)
The Blood Latitudes (William Harrison)
The Brethren (John Grisham)
The Bride Price (Buchi Emecheta)
Easy Prey (John Sandford)
For the Relief of Unbearable Urges (Nathan
    Englander)
A Gathering of Old Men (Ernest J. Gaines)
Hot Six (Janet Evanovich)
The Human Stain (Philip Roth)
In the Time of the Butterflies (Julia Alvarez)
Less Than Zero (Bret Easton Ellis)

Eastern Traditions
Empire of the Sun (J. G. Ballard)

Ecology
True at First Light (Ernest Hemingway)

Economics
Hot Six (Janet Evanovich)
The Perfect Storm (Sebastian Junger)
Rabbit Is Rich (John Updike)

Education
Bastard out of Carolina (Dorothy Allison)
False Memory (Dean Koontz)
Gertrude and Claudius (John Updike)
Southern Cross (Patricia Cornwell)
To Say Nothing of the Dog (Connie Willis)

Egotism
Black Notice (Patricia Cornwell)
The Brethren (John Grisham)
False Memory (Dean Koontz)
The Human Stain (Philip Roth)
Southern Cross (Patricia Cornwell)
Timeline (Michael Crichton)

Eighties
How the Dead Live (Will Self)
Less Than Zero (Bret Easton Ellis)
Those Bones Are Not My Child (Toni Cade
    Bambara)

Emasculation
The Mambo Kings Play Songs of Love
    (Oscar Hijuelos)

Empathy
A Gathering of Old Men (Ernest J. Gaines)
Out of Africa (Isak Dinesan)
Those Bones Are Not My Child (Toni Cade
    Bambara)
To Say Nothing of the Dog (Connie Willis)
"The Way We Live Now" (Susan Sontag)

English Life and Thought
Jack Maggs (Peter Carey)
The Pilot's Wife (Anita Shreve)
To Say Nothing of the Dog (Connie Willis)

Enlightenment
Fierce Invalids Home from Hot Climates
    (Tom Robbins)

Ennui
Ashes to Ashes (Tami Hoag)
Less Than Zero (Bret Easton Ellis)
The Reader (Bernhard Schlink)

Enthusiasm
The Brethren (John Grisham)
Flaubert's Parrot (Julian Barnes)
Little Kingdoms (Steven Millhauser)
Timeline (Michael Crichton)

Environmental Issues

"The Birds" (Daphne du Maurier)
True at First Light (Ernest Hemingway)

Epiphany

Fierce Invalids Home from Hot Climates
   (Tom Robbins)

Equality

To Say Nothing of the Dog (Connie Willis)

Eroticism

Bastard out of Carolina (Dorothy Allison)
The Bride Price (Buchi Emecheta)
Easy Prey (John Sandford)
False Memory (Dean Koontz)
Fierce Invalids Home from Hot Climates
   (Tom Robbins)
The Human Stain (Philip Roth)
Less Than Zero (Bret Easton Ellis)
The Mambo Kings Play Songs of Love
   (Oscar Hijuelos)
Rabbit Is Rich (John Updike)
Rabbit, Run (John Updike)
The Reader (Bernhard Schlink)
White Oleander (Janet Fitch)

Escapism

Before I Say Good-bye (Mary
   Higgins Clark)
To Say Nothing of the Dog (Connie Willis)

Essay Writing

Flaubert's Parrot (Julian Barnes)

Establishment

Ashes to Ashes (Tami Hoag)
Back Roads (Tawni O'Dell)
Before I Say Good-bye (Mary
   Higgins Clark)
Black Notice (Patricia Cornwell)
The Brethren (John Grisham)
"The Bride Comes to Yellow Sky"
   (Stephen Crane)
The Human Stain (Philip Roth)
Southern Cross (Patricia Cornwell)

Those Bones Are Not My Child (Toni Cade
   Bambara)
To Say Nothing of the Dog (Connie Willis)

Ethics and Values

Ashes to Ashes (Tami Hoag)
Black Notice (Patricia Cornwell)
Blood and Chocolate (Annette Curtis
   Klause)
The Brethren (John Grisham)
"The Bride Comes to Yellow Sky"
   (Stephen Crane)
Cradle and All (James Patterson)
Fierce Invalids Home from Hot Climates
   (Tom Robbins)
A Gathering of Old Men (Ernest J. Gaines)
Gertrude and Claudius (John Updike)
Hot Six (Janet Evanovich)
Hugger Mugger (Robert B. Parker)
The Human Stain
In the Time of the ButterfliesJack Maggs
   (Peter Carey)
Rabbit Is Rich (John Updike)
The Reader (Bernhard Schlink)
Southern Cross (Patricia Cornwell)
Timeline (Michael Crichton)
To Say Nothing of the Dog (Connie Willis)
True at First Light (Ernest Hemingway)
"The Way We Live Now" (Susan Sontag)

Evil

Ashes to Ashes (Tami Hoag)
Bastard out of Carolina (Dorothy Allison)
Before I Say Good-bye (Mary
   Higgins Clark)
Black Notice (Patricia Cornwell)
Blood and Chocolate (Annette Curtis
   Klause)
The Blood Latitudes (William Harrison)
The Brethren (John Grisham)
Cradle and All (James Patterson)
False Memory (Dean Koontz)
For the Relief of Unbearable Urges (Nathan
   Englander)
A Gathering of Old Men (Ernest J. Gaines)
Hot Six (Janet Evanovich)
The Human Stain (Philip Roth)

In the Time of the Butterflies (Julia Alvarez)
Less Than Zero (Bret Easton Ellis)
O Is for Outlaw (Sue Grafton)
The Pilot's Wife (Anita Shreve)
Playback (Raymond Chandler)
The Reader (Bernhard Schlink)
Southern Cross (Patricia Cornwell)
Those Bones Are Not My Child (Toni Cade
  Bambara)
Timeline (Michael Crichton)
The Women of Brewster Place
  (Gloria Naylor)

Execution
The Blood Latitudes (William Harrison)
In the Time of the Butterflies (Julia Alvarez)

Exile
The Human Stain (Philip Roth)
Jack Maggs (Peter Carey)

Expatriatism
Empire of the Sun (J. G. Ballard)
Out of Africa (Isak Dinesan)
True at First Light (Ernest Hemingway)

Exploitation and Manipulation
Back Roads (Tawni O'Dell)
The Blood Latitudes (William Harrison)
The Brethren (John Grisham)
The Bride Price (Buchi Emecheta)
Easy Prey (John Sandford)
Empire of the Sun (J. G. Ballard)
False Memory (Dean Koontz)
Less Than Zero (Bret Easton Ellis)
Southern Cross (Patricia Cornwell)
White Oleander (Janet Fitch)

Failure and Success
The Brethren (John Grisham)
Little Kingdoms (Steven Millhauser)
Rabbit Is Rich (John Updike)

Faith
Cradle and All (James Patterson)

Empress of the Splendid Season (Oscar
  Hijuelos)
Fierce Invalids Home from Hot Climates
  (Tom Robbins)
For the Relief of Unbearable Urges (Nathan
  Englander)
Gertrude and Claudius (John Updike)
In the Time of the Butterflies (Julia Alvarez)
Rabbit, Run (John Updike)

Fall of Man
The Brethren (John Grisham)
The Human Stain (Philip Roth)
Rabbit, Run (John Updike)

Fame
Easy Prey (John Sandford)
False Memory (Dean Koontz)

Family Honor
The Bride Price (Buchi Emecheta)

Family Life
Ashes to Ashes (Tami Hoag)
Back Roads (Tawni O'Dell)
Bastard out of Carolina (Dorothy Allison)
The Blood Latitudes (William Harrison)
The Bride Price (Buchi Emecheta)
Empress of the Splendid Season (Oscar
  Hijuelos)
False Memory (Dean Koontz)
Hot Six (Janet Evanovich)
How the Dead Live (Will Self)
Hugger Mugger (Robert B. Parker)
In the Time of the Butterflies (Julia Alvarez)
The Mambo Kings Play Songs of Love
  (Oscar Hijuelos)
On Mystic Lake (Kristin Hannah)
The Pilot's Wife (Anita Shreve)
Rabbit Is Rich (John Updike)
Rabbit, Run (John Updike)
Southern Cross (Patricia Cornwell)
Those Bones Are Not My Child (Toni Cade
  Bambara)
The Women of Brewster Place
  (Gloria Naylor)

Family Values

Ashes to Ashes (Tami Hoag)
Empress of the Splendid Season (Oscar Hijuelos)
A Gathering of Old Men (Ernest J. Gaines)
Hot Six (Janet Evanovich)
How the Dead Live (Will Self)
In the Time of the Butterflies (Julia Alvarez)
On Mystic Lake (Kristin Hannah)
The Pilot's Wife (Anita Shreve)
Rabbit Is Rich (John Updike)
Those Bones Are Not My Child (Toni Cade Bambara)

Fanaticism

The Blood Latitudes (William Harrison)
The Brethren (John Grisham)
The Pilot's Wife (Anita Shreve)

Fantasy

"The Birds" (Daphne du Maurier)
Blood and Chocolate (Annette Curtis Klause)
Cradle and All (James Patterson)
Fierce Invalids Home from Hot Climates (Tom Robbins)
How the Dead Live (Will Self)
Little Kingdoms (Steven Millhauser)
Timeline (Michael Crichton)
To Say Nothing of the Dog (Connie Willis)

Fantasy Life

Back Roads (Tawni O'Dell)
Bastard out of Carolina (Dorothy Allison)
Easy Prey (John Sandford)
Empire of the Sun (J. G. Ballard)
Empress of the Splendid Season (Oscar Hijuelos)
Fierce Invalids Home from Hot Climates (Tom Robbins)
For the Relief of Unbearable Urges (Nathan Englander)
Little Kingdoms (Steven Millhauser)
On Mystic Lake (Kristin Hannah)
Rabbit Is Rich (John Updike)

The Women of Brewster Place (Gloria Naylor)

Far East

Empire of the Sun (J. G. Ballard)

Fascism

For the Relief of Unbearable Urges (Nathan Englander)
The Reader (Bernhard Schlink)

Fate and Chance

For the Relief of Unbearable Urges (Nathan Englander)
The Perfect Storm (Sebastian Junger)
The Reader (Bernhard Schlink)

Fatherhood

Bastard out of Carolina (Dorothy Allison)
The Blood Latitudes (William Harrison)
The Bride Price (Buchi Emecheta)
Empress of the Splendid Season (Oscar Hijuelos)
Gertrude and Claudius (John Updike)
The Human Stain (Philip Roth)
In the Time of the Butterflies (Julia Alvarez)
Little Kingdoms (Steven Millhauser)
The Pilot's Wife (Anita Shreve)
Rabbit Is Rich (John Updike)
Rabbit, Run (John Updike)
The Women of Brewster Place (Gloria Naylor)

Fear and Terror

Ashes to Ashes (Tami Hoag)
Bastard out of Carolina (Dorothy Allison)
Before I Say Good-bye (Mary Higgins Clark)
"The Birds" (Daphne du Maurier)
Black Notice (Patricia Cornwell)
Blood and Chocolate (Annette Curtis Klause)
The Blood Latitudes (William Harrison)
Cradle and All (James Patterson)
False Memory (Dean Koontz)
For the Relief of Unbearable Urges (Nathan Englander)

In the Time of the Butterflies (Julia Alvarez)
The Perfect Storm (Sebastian Junger)
Southern Cross (Patricia Cornwell)
Those Bones Are Not My Child (Toni Cade
    Bambara)
True at First Light (Ernest Hemingway)

Feminism
Ashes to Ashes (Tami Hoag)
Bastard out of Carolina (Dorothy Allison)
Before I Say Good-bye (Mary
    Higgins Clark)
The Bride Price (Buchi Emecheta)
In the Time of the Butterflies (Julia Alvarez)
O Is for Outlaw (Sue Grafton)
To Say Nothing of the Dog (Connie Willis)
The Women of Brewster Place
    (Gloria Naylor)

Femme Fatale
Blood and Chocolate (Annette Curtis
    Klause)
"The Bride Comes to Yellow Sky"
    (Stephen Crane)
Gertrude and Claudius (John Updike)
Hugger Mugger (Robert B. Parker)
The Human Stain (Philip Roth)
The Pilot's Wife (Anita Shreve)
The Reader (Bernhard Schlink)
White Oleander (Janet Fitch)

Fertility
The Bride Price (Buchi Emecheta)
Cradle and All (James Patterson)

Fidelity and Infidelity
The Blood Latitudes (William Harrison)
Flaubert's Parrot (Julian Barnes)
Gertrude and Claudius (John Updike)
Jack Maggs (Peter Carey)
The Mambo Kings Play Songs of Love
    (Oscar Hijuelos)
O Is for Outlaw (Sue Grafton)
On Mystic Lake (Kristin Hannah)
The Pilot's Wife (Anita Shreve)
Rabbit Is Rich (John Updike)
Rabbit, Run (John Updike)

White Oleander (Janet Fitch)

Fifties
Bastard out of Carolina (Dorothy Allison)
How the Dead Live (Will Self)
Rabbit, Run (John Updike)

Filth and Squalor
Jack Maggs (Peter Carey)

Fin de Siecle
Little Kingdoms (Steven Millhauser)

First Love
The Bride Price (Buchi Emecheta)
The Reader (Bernhard Schlink)

Flesh vs. Spirit
Blood and Chocolate (Annette Curtis
    Klause)
Cradle and All (James Patterson)

Flight
Blood and Chocolate (Annette Curtis
    Klause)
The Blood Latitudes (William Harrison)
For the Relief of Unbearable Urges (Nathan
    Englander)
The Human Stain (Philip Roth)
Rabbit, Run (John Updike)
To Say Nothing of the Dog (Connie Willis)

Food
Blood and Chocolate (Annette Curtis
    Klause)
The Mambo Kings Play Songs of Love
    (Oscar Hijuelos)
True at First Light (Ernest Hemingway)

Forensic Science
Black Notice (Patricia Cornwell)

Forgiveness
Black Notice (Patricia Cornwell)

Appendix: Titles Grouped by Social Concerns and Themes

Free Will vs. Determinism

The Bride Price (Buchi Emecheta)
False Memory (Dean Koontz)

Freedom

In the Time of the Butterflies (Julia Alvarez)
Out of Africa (Isak Dinesan)

Friendship

Black Notice (Patricia Cornwell)
Blood and Chocolate (Annette Curtis
    Klause)
Empire of the Sun (J. G. Ballard)
Empress of the Splendid Season (Oscar
    Hijuelos)
False Memory (Dean Koontz)
A Gathering of Old Men (Ernest J. Gaines)
Hot Six (Janet Evanovich)
Less Than Zero (Bret Easton Ellis)
On Mystic Lake (Kristin Hannah)
Out of Africa (Isak Dinesan)
Rabbit Is Rich (John Updike)
To Say Nothing of the Dog (Connie Willis)
"The Way We Live Now" (Susan Sontag)
The Women of Brewster Place
    (Gloria Naylor)

Frontier

True at First Light (Ernest Hemingway)

Frustration

Ashes to Ashes (Tami Hoag)
Gertrude and Claudius (John Updike)
The Mambo Kings Play Songs of Love
    (Oscar Hijuelos)
Southern Cross (Patricia Cornwell)
Those Bones Are Not My Child (Toni Cade
    Bambara)

Futility

Ashes to Ashes (Tami Hoag)
"The Birds" (Daphne du Maurier)
The Mambo Kings Play Songs of Love
    (Oscar Hijuelos)
Southern Cross (Patricia Cornwell)

Futurism

The Thanatos Syndrome (Walker Percy)
Timeline (Michael Crichton)
To Say Nothing of the Dog (Connie Willis)

Gender Warfare

Bastard out of Carolina (Dorothy Allison)
Before I Say Good-bye (Mary
    Higgins Clark)
The Bride Price (Buchi Emecheta)
Gertrude and Claudius (John Updike)
The Mambo Kings Play Songs of Love
    (Oscar Hijuelos)
O Is for Outlaw (Sue Grafton)
On Mystic Lake (Kristin Hannah)
Those Bones Are Not My Child (Toni Cade
    Bambara)
To Say Nothing of the Dog (Connie Willis)
The Women of Brewster Place
    (Gloria Naylor)

Generation Gap

Ashes to Ashes (Tami Hoag)
Back Roads (Tawni O'Dell)
The Bride Price (Buchi Emecheta)
Empress of the Splendid Season (Oscar
    Hijuelos)
Gertrude and Claudius (John Updike)
Hot Six (Janet Evanovich)
Rabbit Is Rich (John Updike)
The Reader (Bernhard Schlink)
Southern Cross (Patricia Cornwell)

Genius

Flaubert's Parrot (Julian Barnes)
Little Kingdoms (Steven Millhauser)
Timeline (Michael Crichton)

German Life and Thought

The Reader (Bernhard Schlink)

God

Bastard out of Carolina (Dorothy Allison)
Cradle and All (James Patterson)
Fierce Invalids Home from Hot Climates
    (Tom Robbins)

For the Relief of Unbearable Urges (Nathan Englander)

Good

Cradle and All (James Patterson)
A Gathering of Old Men (Ernest J. Gaines)
In the Time of the Butterflies (Julia Alvarez)

Good vs. Evil

Ashes to Ashes (Tami Hoag)
Before I Say Good-bye (Mary Higgins Clark)
Black Notice (Patricia Cornwell)
Blood and Chocolate (Annette Curtis Klause)
The Blood Latitudes (William Harrison)
Cradle and All (James Patterson)
Fierce Invalids Home from Hot Climates (Tom Robbins)
A Gathering of Old Men (Ernest J. Gaines)
In the Time of the Butterflies (Julia Alvarez)
O Is for Outlaw (Sue Grafton)
Those Bones Are Not My Child (Toni Cade Bambara)

Gossip

Black Notice (Patricia Cornwell)
"The Way We Live Now" (Susan Sontag)

Grandparents

Before I Say Good-bye (Mary Higgins Clark)
Rabbit Is Rich (John Updike)

Great Chain of Being

How the Dead Live (Will Self)
True at First Light (Ernest Hemingway)

Greed

Before I Say Good-bye (Mary Higgins Clark)
Black Notice (Patricia Cornwell)
The Brethren (John Grisham)
Hot Six (Janet Evanovich)
Playback (Raymond Chandler)
Rabbit Is Rich (John Updike)

Timeline (Michael Crichton)

Grief and Sorrow

Before I Say Good-bye (Mary Higgins Clark)
Black Notice (Patricia Cornwell)
The Blood Latitudes (William Harrison)
The Bride Price (Buchi Emecheta)
Cradle and All (James Patterson)
A Gathering of Old Men (Ernest J. Gaines)
Gertrude and Claudius (John Updike)
The Human Stain (Philip Roth)
Jack Maggs (Peter Carey)
On Mystic Lake (Kristin Hannah)
Out of Africa (Isak Dinesan)
The Perfect Storm (Sebastian Junger)
The Pilot's Wife (Anita Shreve)
Rabbit, Run (John Updike)
Those Bones Are Not My Child (Toni Cade Bambara)
The Women of Brewster Place (Gloria Naylor)

Growing Up

Back Roads (Tawni O'Dell)
Bastard out of Carolina (Dorothy Allison)
Blood and Chocolate (Annette Curtis Klause)
White Oleander (Janet Fitch)

Growth and Development

Back Roads (Tawni O'Dell)
Before I Say Good-bye (Mary Higgins Clark)
Blood and Chocolate (Annette Curtis Klause)
The Blood Latitudes (William Harrison)
The Bride Price (Buchi Emecheta)
Empire of the Sun (J. G. Ballard)
Fierce Invalids Home from Hot Climates (Tom Robbins)
Hot Six (Janet Evanovich)
On Mystic Lake (Kristin Hannah)
Rabbit Is Rich (John Updike)
Rabbit, Run (John Updike)
The Reader (Bernhard Schlink)
True at First Light (Ernest Hemingway)

Appendix: Titles Grouped by Social Concerns and Themes

White Oleander (Janet Fitch)

Guilt

Bastard out of Carolina (Dorothy Allison)
Black Notice (Patricia Cornwell)
Blood and Chocolate (Annette Curtis Klause)
"The Bride Comes to Yellow Sky" (Stephen Crane)
A Gathering of Old Men (Ernest J. Gaines)
Gertrude and Claudius (John Updike)
How the Dead Live (Will Self)
Rabbit Is Rich (John Updike)
Rabbit, Run (John Updike)
The Reader (Bernhard Schlink)
Timeline (Michael Crichton)

Hallucinations

Cradle and All (James Patterson)
On Mystic Lake (Kristin Hannah)

Happiness and Gaiety

Empress of the Splendid Season (Oscar Hijuelos)
Rabbit Is Rich (John Updike)

Hatred

Blood and Chocolate (Annette Curtis Klause)
The Blood Latitudes (William Harrison)
For the Relief of Unbearable Urges (Nathan Englander)
A Gathering of Old Men (Ernest J. Gaines)
The Human Stain (Philip Roth)
In the Time of the Butterflies (Julia Alvarez)
Jack Maggs (Peter Carey)
The Pilot's Wife (Anita Shreve)
The Reader (Bernhard Schlink)
Southern Cross (Patricia Cornwell)
Those Bones Are Not My Child (Toni Cade Bambara)
The Women of Brewster Place (Gloria Naylor)

Hedonism

Bastard out of Carolina (Dorothy Allison)

Easy Prey (John Sandford)
Hugger Mugger (Robert B. Parker)
Less Than Zero (Bret Easton Ellis)
The Mambo Kings Play Songs of Love (Oscar Hijuelos)
White Oleander (Janet Fitch)

Heredity

False Memory (Dean Koontz)
The Pilot's Wife (Anita Shreve)
Southern Cross (Patricia Cornwell)

Heritage and Ancestry

Before I Say Good-bye (Mary Higgins Clark)
Blood and Chocolate (Annette Curtis Klause)
The Blood Latitudes (William Harrison)
The Bride Price (Buchi Emecheta)
For the Relief of Unbearable Urges (Nathan Englander)
A Gathering of Old Men (Ernest J. Gaines)
Gertrude and Claudius (John Updike)
Hot Six (Janet Evanovich)
How the Dead Live (Will Self)
Hugger Mugger (Robert B. Parker)
The Human Stain (Philip Roth)
Little Kingdoms (Steven Millhauser)
The Mambo Kings Play Songs of Love (Oscar Hijuelos)
The Reader (Bernhard Schlink)
To Say Nothing of the Dog (Connie Willis)
The Women of Brewster Place (Gloria Naylor)

Heroes and Heroism

Before I Say Good-bye (Mary Higgins Clark)
"The Birds" (Daphne du Maurier)
Black Notice (Patricia Cornwell)
The Blood Latitudes (William Harrison)
Cradle and All (James Patterson)
For the Relief of Unbearable Urges (Nathan Englander)
A Gathering of Old Men (Ernest J. Gaines)
In the Time of the Butterflies (Julia Alvarez)
The Perfect Storm (Sebastian Junger)

High Society

Before I Say Good-bye (Mary Higgins Clark)
Hugger Mugger (Robert B. Parker)
Jack Maggs (Peter Carey)
Less Than Zero (Bret Easton Ellis)
To Say Nothing of the Dog (Connie Willis)

Hispanic-American Life and Thought

Empress of the Splendid Season (Oscar Hijuelos)
The Mambo Kings Play Songs of Love (Oscar Hijuelos)

History

Bastard out of Carolina (Dorothy Allison)
The Blood Latitudes (William Harrison)
Empire of the Sun (J. G. Ballard)
Empress of the Splendid Season (Oscar Hijuelos)
Flaubert's Parrot (Julian Barnes)
For the Relief of Unbearable Urges (Nathan Englander)
A Gathering of Old Men (Ernest J. Gaines)
Gertrude and Claudius (John Updike)
Hot Six (Janet Evanovich)
How the Dead Live (Will Self)
In the Time of the Butterflies (Julia Alvarez)
Jack Maggs (Peter Carey)
The Mambo Kings Play Songs of Love (Oscar Hijuelos)
Out of Africa (Isak Dinesan)
Rabbit Is Rich (John Updike)
The Reader (Bernhard Schlink)
Those Bones Are Not My Child (Toni Cade Bambara)
Timeline (Michael Crichton)
To Say Nothing of the Dog (Connie Willis)
"The Way We Live Now" (Susan Sontag)
The Women of Brewster Place (Gloria Naylor)

Holocaust

For the Relief of Unbearable Urges (Nathan Englander)

The Reader (Bernhard Schlink)

Home

Ashes to Ashes (Tami Hoag)
Back Roads (Tawni O'Dell)
Bastard out of Carolina (Dorothy Allison)
"The Birds" (Daphne du Maurier)
Black Notice (Patricia Cornwell)
The Bride Price (Buchi Emecheta)
Empress of the Splendid Season (Oscar Hijuelos)
False Memory (Dean Koontz)
For the Relief of Unbearable Urges (Nathan Englander)
A Gathering of Old Men (Ernest J. Gaines)
Hot Six (Janet Evanovich)
How the Dead Live (Will Self)
Hugger Mugger (Robert B. Parker)
In the Time of the Butterflies (Julia Alvarez)
Jack Maggs (Peter Carey)
Little Kingdoms (Steven Millhauser)
The Mambo Kings Play Songs of Love (Oscar Hijuelos)
On Mystic Lake (Kristin Hannah)
Out of Africa (Isak Dinesan)
The Perfect Storm (Sebastian Junger)
The Pilot's Wife (Anita Shreve)
Rabbit Is Rich (John Updike)
Rabbit, Run (John Updike)
Southern Cross (Patricia Cornwell)
Those Bones Are Not My Child (Toni Cade Bambara)
To Say Nothing of the Dog (Connie Willis)
True at First Light (Ernest Hemingway)
White Oleander (Janet Fitch)
The Women of Brewster Place (Gloria Naylor)

Homelessness

Blood and Chocolate (Annette Curtis Klause)
Fierce Invalids Home from Hot Climates (Tom Robbins)
Jack Maggs (Peter Carey)
Less Than Zero (Bret Easton Ellis)
White Oleander (Janet Fitch)

Homosexuality

Bastard out of Carolina (Dorothy Allison)
Black Notice (Patricia Cornwell)
Easy Prey (John Sandford)
Hugger Mugger (Robert B. Parker)
"The Way We Live Now" (Susan Sontag)

Honor and Integrity

Ashes to Ashes (Tami Hoag)
Black Notice (Patricia Cornwell)
The Blood Latitudes (William Harrison)
The Brethren (John Grisham)
"The Bride Comes to Yellow Sky"
    (Stephen Crane)
The Bride Price (Buchi Emecheta)
A Gathering of Old Men (Ernest J. Gaines)
Hugger Mugger (Robert B. Parker)

Hope

Empress of the Splendid Season (Oscar
    Hijuelos)
Those Bones Are Not My Child (Toni Cade
    Bambara)
To Say Nothing of the Dog (Connie Willis)

Hospitalization

How the Dead Live (Will Self)
Rabbit, Run (John Updike)

Human Body

Bastard out of Carolina (Dorothy Allison)
Easy Prey (John Sandford)
How the Dead Live (Will Self)
The Mambo Kings Play Songs of Love
    (Oscar Hijuelos)

Human Condition

Back Roads (Tawni O'Dell)
Bastard out of Carolina (Dorothy Allison)
The Blood Latitudes (William Harrison)
"The Bride Comes to Yellow Sky"
    (Stephen Crane)
The Bride Price (Buchi Emecheta)
Cradle and All (James Patterson)
Empire of the Sun (J. G. Ballard)

Empress of the Splendid Season (Oscar
    Hijuelos)
Fierce Invalids Home from Hot Climates
    (Tom Robbins)
For the Relief of Unbearable Urges (Nathan
    Englander)
Rabbit Is Rich (John Updike)

Human Nature

Ashes to Ashes (Tami Hoag)
"The Birds" (Daphne du Maurier)
Blood and Chocolate (Annette Curtis
    Klause)
The Blood Latitudes (William Harrison)
The Brethren (John Grisham)
Fierce Invalids Home from Hot Climates
    (Tom Robbins)
Hugger Mugger (Robert B. Parker)
"The Knife Thrower" (Steven Millhauser)
The Perfect Storm (Sebastian Junger)

Humanism

Little Kingdoms (Steven Millhauser)
To Say Nothing of the Dog (Connie Willis)

Humiliation and Degradation

Ashes to Ashes (Tami Hoag)
Back Roads (Tawni O'Dell)
Bastard out of Carolina (Dorothy Allison)
The Bride Price (Buchi Emecheta)
Easy Prey (John Sandford)
False Memory (Dean Koontz)
The Human Stain (Philip Roth)
In the Time of the Butterflies (Julia Alvarez)
Jack Maggs (Peter Carey)
Less Than Zero (Bret Easton Ellis)
The Mambo Kings Play Songs of Love
    (Oscar Hijuelos)
Southern Cross (Patricia Cornwell)
The Women of Brewster Place
    (Gloria Naylor)

Humility

"The Bride Comes to Yellow Sky"
    (Stephen Crane)
For the Relief of Unbearable Urges (Nathan
    Englander)

Hunger

Empire of the Sun (J. G. Ballard)

Hypocrisy

Black Notice (Patricia Cornwell)
A Gathering of Old Men (Ernest J. Gaines)
Jack Maggs (Peter Carey)
Rabbit, Run (John Updike)
The Reader (Bernhard Schlink)
Southern Cross (Patricia Cornwell)
Those Bones Are Not My Child (Toni Cade Bambara)

Idealism

Cradle and All (James Patterson)
Empire of the Sun (J. G. Ballard)
Empress of the Splendid Season (Oscar Hijuelos)
Fierce Invalids Home from Hot Climates (Tom Robbins)
Flaubert's Parrot (Julian Barnes)
For the Relief of Unbearable Urges (Nathan Englander)
A Gathering of Old Men (Ernest J. Gaines)
In the Time of the Butterflies (Julia Alvarez)
Little Kingdoms (Steven Millhauser)
The Mambo Kings Play Songs of Love (Oscar Hijuelos)
Out of Africa (Isak Dinesan)
Rabbit Is Rich (John Updike)
To Say Nothing of the Dog (Connie Willis)
True at First Light (Ernest Hemingway)

Ignorance

Back Roads (Tawni O'Dell)
Bastard out of Carolina (Dorothy Allison)
For the Relief of Unbearable Urges (Nathan Englander)
Less Than Zero (Bret Easton Ellis)
The Pilot's Wife (Anita Shreve)
The Reader (Bernhard Schlink)
Timeline (Michael Crichton)
To Say Nothing of the Dog (Connie Willis)

Illegitimacy

Cradle and All (James Patterson)

White Oleander (Janet Fitch)

Illusion vs. Reality

Back Roads (Tawni O'Dell)
Before I Say Good-bye (Mary Higgins Clark)
Black Notice (Patricia Cornwell)
Blood and Chocolate (Annette Curtis Klause)
The Brethren (John Grisham)
Cradle and All (James Patterson)
Empress of the Splendid Season (Oscar Hijuelos)
False Memory (Dean Koontz)
Hot Six (Janet Evanovich)
Hugger Mugger (Robert B. Parker)
O Is for Outlaw (Sue Grafton)
The Pilot's Wife (Anita Shreve)
The Reader (Bernhard Schlink)
Southern Cross (Patricia Cornwell)
Timeline (Michael Crichton)

Imagination

Back Roads (Tawni O'Dell)
Empire of the Sun (J. G. Ballard)
Empress of the Splendid Season (Oscar Hijuelos)
False Memory (Dean Koontz)
Fierce Invalids Home from Hot Climates (Tom Robbins)
Flaubert's Parrot (Julian Barnes)
For the Relief of Unbearable Urges (Nathan Englander)
Little Kingdoms (Steven Millhauser)
White Oleander (Janet Fitch)

Imitation

To Say Nothing of the Dog (Connie Willis)

Immigrants

Empress of the Splendid Season (Oscar Hijuelos)
The Mambo Kings Play Songs of Love (Oscar Hijuelos)

Immortality

How the Dead Live (Will Self)

Incest

Easy Prey (John Sandford)
Hugger Mugger (Robert B. Parker)

Individual and Society

Ashes to Ashes (Tami Hoag)
Back Roads (Tawni O'Dell)
Black Notice (Patricia Cornwell)
The Blood Latitudes (William Harrison)
The Brethren (John Grisham)
"The Bride Comes to Yellow Sky"
   (Stephen Crane)
The Bride Price (Buchi Emecheta)
Empress of the Splendid Season (Oscar
   Hijuelos)
For the Relief of Unbearable Urges (Nathan
   Englander)
A Gathering of Old Men (Ernest J. Gaines)
How the Dead Live (Will Self)
The Human Stain (Philip Roth)
In the Time of the Butterflies (Julia Alvarez)
Jack Maggs (Peter Carey)
Less Than Zero (Bret Easton Ellis)
The Mambo Kings Play Songs of Love
   (Oscar Hijuelos)
The Reader (Bernhard Schlink)
Southern Cross (Patricia Cornwell)
Those Bones Are Not My Child (Toni Cade
   Bambara)
To Say Nothing of the Dog (Connie Willis)

Individualism

Blood and Chocolate (Annette Curtis
   Klause)
The Blood Latitudes (William Harrison)
The Bride Price (Buchi Emecheta)
Empire of the Sun (J. G. Ballard)
Fierce Invalids Home from Hot Climates
   (Tom Robbins)
For the Relief of Unbearable Urges (Nathan
   Englander)
To Have and Have Not (Ernest
   Hemingway)

Industrial Revolution

To Say Nothing of the Dog (Connie Willis)

Industry and Labor

The Bride Price (Buchi Emecheta)

Inner Conflict

Back Roads (Tawni O'Dell)
Bastard out of Carolina (Dorothy Allison)
Black Notice (Patricia Cornwell)
Blood and Chocolate (Annette Curtis
   Klause)
The Blood Latitudes (William Harrison)
"The Bride Comes to Yellow Sky"
   (Stephen Crane)
Cradle and All (James Patterson)
Fierce Invalids Home from Hot Climates
   (Tom Robbins)
On Mystic Lake (Kristin Hannah)
The Pilot's Wife (Anita Shreve)
Rabbit Is Rich (John Updike)
Rabbit, Run (John Updike)
The Reader (Bernhard Schlink)
True at First Light (Ernest Hemingway)

Innocence and Experience

Back Roads (Tawni O'Dell)
Before I Say Good-bye (Mary
   Higgins Clark)
Blood and Chocolate (Annette Curtis
   Klause)
The Brethren (John Grisham)
Cradle and All (James Patterson)
Empire of the Sun (J. G. Ballard)
For the Relief of Unbearable Urges (Nathan
   Englander)
Jack Maggs (Peter Carey)
The Mambo Kings Play Songs of Love
   (Oscar Hijuelos)
Out of Africa (Isak Dinesan)
The Pilot's Wife (Anita Shreve)
The Reader (Bernhard Schlink)
Southern Cross (Patricia Cornwell)
Those Bones Are Not My Child (Toni Cade
   Bambara)
Timeline (Michael Crichton)
To Say Nothing of the Dog (Connie Willis)
True at First Light (Ernest Hemingway)
"The Way We Live Now" (Susan Sontag)

Insecurity

Before I Say Good-bye (Mary
    Higgins Clark)
Blood and Chocolate (Annette Curtis
    Klause)
"The Bride Comes to Yellow Sky"
    (Stephen Crane)
Gertrude and Claudius (John Updike)
Jack Maggs (Peter Carey)
On Mystic Lake (Kristin Hannah)
The Pilot's Wife (Anita Shreve)
Rabbit Is Rich (John Updike)
Those Bones Are Not My Child (Toni Cade
    Bambara)
Timeline (Michael Crichton)
True at First Light (Ernest Hemingway)
"The Way We Live Now" (Susan Sontag)
The Women of Brewster Place
    (Gloria Naylor)

Intellectuals and Intellectualism

The Blood Latitudes (William Harrison)
False Memory (Dean Koontz)
Flaubert's Parrot (Julian Barnes)
For the Relief of Unbearable Urges (Nathan
    Englander)
The Human Stain (Philip Roth)
Jack Maggs (Peter Carey)
The Reader (Bernhard Schlink)
Timeline (Michael Crichton)

Interracial Relationships

A Gathering of Old Men (Ernest J. Gaines)
How the Dead Live (Will Self)
The Human Stain (Philip Roth)
True at First Light (Ernest Hemingway)

Intoxication

Blood and Chocolate (Annette Curtis
    Klause)
The Brethren (John Grisham)
Easy Prey (John Sandford)
Hot Six (Janet Evanovich)
How the Dead Live (Will Self)
Less Than Zero (Bret Easton Ellis)

The Mambo Kings Play Songs of Love
    (Oscar Hijuelos)
On Mystic Lake (Kristin Hannah)
Rabbit, Run (John Updike)
Southern Cross (Patricia Cornwell)

Irish Republican Army

The Pilot's Wife (Anita Shreve)

Islam

True at First Light (Ernest Hemingway)

Isolation

Out of Africa (Isak Dinesan)
The Perfect Storm (Sebastian Junger)
Those Bones Are Not My Child (Toni Cade
    Bambara)

Jealousy

Black Notice (Patricia Cornwell)
The Human Stain (Philip Roth)
White Oleander (Janet Fitch)

Jewish Life and Thought

For the Relief of Unbearable Urges (Nathan
    Englander)
How the Dead Live (Will Self)
The Human Stain (Philip Roth)

Journey

Empire of the Sun (J. G. Ballard)
Fierce Invalids Home from Hot Climates
    (Tom Robbins)
The Pilot's Wife (Anita Shreve)

Justice and Injustice

Ashes to Ashes (Tami Hoag)
Black Notice (Patricia Cornwell)
The Brethren (John Grisham)
For the Relief of Unbearable Urges (Nathan
    Englander)
A Gathering of Old Men (Ernest J. Gaines)
Hot Six (Janet Evanovich)
The Human Stain (Philip Roth)
O Is for Outlaw (Sue Grafton)
The Reader (Bernhard Schlink)

Appendix: Titles Grouped by Social Concerns and Themes

Southern Cross (Patricia Cornwell)
Those Bones Are Not My Child (Toni Cade
  Bambara)

Justice/Court System

Ashes to Ashes (Tami Hoag)
Back Roads (Tawni O'Dell)
Black Notice (Patricia Cornwell)
The Brethren (John Grisham)
The Reader (Bernhard Schlink)
Those Bones Are Not My Child (Toni Cade
  Bambara)

Kindness

Empress of the Splendid Season (Oscar
  Hijuelos)
Fierce Invalids Home from Hot Climates
  (Tom Robbins)
On Mystic Lake (Kristin Hannah)
Out of Africa (Isak Dinesan)
Rabbit Is Rich (John Updike)
The Reader (Bernhard Schlink)
To Say Nothing of the Dog (Connie Willis)

Knowledge

Blood and Chocolate (Annette Curtis
  Klause)
Fierce Invalids Home from Hot Climates
  (Tom Robbins)
Flaubert's Parrot (Julian Barnes)
The Human Stain (Philip Roth)
Jack Maggs (Peter Carey)
The Pilot's Wife (Anita Shreve)
The Reader (Bernhard Schlink)
Timeline (Michael Crichton)
To Say Nothing of the Dog (Connie Willis)

Language and Meaning

Fierce Invalids Home from Hot Climates
  (Tom Robbins)
Flaubert's Parrot (Julian Barnes)
For the Relief of Unbearable Urges (Nathan
  Englander)
Hot Six (Janet Evanovich)
The Human Stain (Philip Roth)
Jack Maggs (Peter Carey)
White Oleander (Janet Fitch)

Law and Order

Ashes to Ashes (Tami Hoag)
Black Notice (Patricia Cornwell)
The Brethren (John Grisham)
A Gathering of Old Men (Ernest J. Gaines)
Playback (Raymond Chandler)
Those Bones Are Not My Child (Toni Cade
  Bambara)
True at First Light (Ernest Hemingway)

Leaders

The Blood Latitudes (William Harrison)
The Brethren (John Grisham)
The Bride Price (Buchi Emecheta)
For the Relief of Unbearable Urges (Nathan
  Englander)
A Gathering of Old Men (Ernest J. Gaines)
Gertrude and Claudius (John Updike)
Hot Six (Janet Evanovich)
In the Time of the Butterflies (Julia Alvarez)
O Is for Outlaw (Sue Grafton)
The Perfect Storm (Sebastian Junger)
Southern Cross (Patricia Cornwell)
The Women of Brewster Place
  (Gloria Naylor)

Leadership

The Brethren (John Grisham)
The Women of Brewster Place
  (Gloria Naylor)

Liberation

Before I Say Good-bye (Mary
  Higgins Clark)
In the Time of the Butterflies (Julia Alvarez)
O Is for Outlaw (Sue Grafton)
To Say Nothing of the Dog (Connie Willis)

Life Cycle

Gertrude and Claudius (John Updike)
How the Dead Live (Will Self)
Out of Africa (Isak Dinesan)
Rabbit Is Rich (John Updike)
True at First Light (Ernest Hemingway)
The Women of Brewster Place
  (Gloria Naylor)

Literature

Flaubert's Parrot (Julian Barnes)
For the Relief of Unbearable Urges (Nathan Englander)
Gertrude and Claudius (John Updike)
Jack Maggs (Peter Carey)

Logic

Black Notice (Patricia Cornwell)
Those Bones Are Not My Child (Toni Cade Bambara)

Loneliness

The Mambo Kings Play Songs of Love (Oscar Hijuelos)
White Oleander (Janet Fitch)

Loss

Ashes to Ashes (Tami Hoag)
Back Roads (Tawni O'Dell)
Bastard out of Carolina (Dorothy Allison)
Black Notice (Patricia Cornwell)
Blood and Chocolate (Annette Curtis Klause)
The Blood Latitudes (William Harrison)
The Bride Price (Buchi Emecheta)
Cradle and All (James Patterson)
For the Relief of Unbearable Urges (Nathan Englander)
Gertrude and Claudius (John Updike)
How the Dead Live (Will Self)
The Human Stain (Philip Roth)
In the Time of the Butterflies (Julia Alvarez)
Jack Maggs (Peter Carey)
The Mambo Kings Play Songs of Love (Oscar Hijuelos)
On Mystic Lake (Kristin Hannah)
Out of Africa (Isak Dinesan)
The Pilot's Wife (Anita Shreve)
Rabbit, Run (John Updike)
Southern Cross (Patricia Cornwell)
Those Bones Are Not My Child (Toni Cade Bambara)
The Women of Brewster Place (Gloria Naylor)

Love and Passion

Before I Say Good-bye (Mary Higgins Clark)
Blood and Chocolate (Annette Curtis Klause)
The Blood Latitudes (William Harrison)
The Bride Price (Buchi Emecheta)
Flaubert's Parrot (Julian Barnes)
Gertrude and Claudius (John Updike)
The Human Stain (Philip Roth)
The Mambo Kings Play Songs of Love (Oscar Hijuelos)
Out of Africa (Isak Dinesan)
The Pilot's Wife (Anita Shreve)
Rabbit Is Rich (John Updike)
The Reader (Bernhard Schlink)
To Say Nothing of the Dog (Connie Willis)
The Women of Brewster Place (Gloria Naylor)

Loyalty

Back Roads (Tawni O'Dell)
Blood and Chocolate (Annette Curtis Klause)
The Blood Latitudes (William Harrison)
Cradle and All (James Patterson)
A Gathering of Old Men (Ernest J. Gaines)
Timeline (Michael Crichton)

Lust

Bastard out of Carolina (Dorothy Allison)
The Blood Latitudes (William Harrison)
Easy Prey (John Sandford)
Fierce Invalids Home from Hot Climates (Tom Robbins)
Gertrude and Claudius (John Updike)
Hugger Mugger (Robert B. Parker)
The Human Stain (Philip Roth)
Jack Maggs (Peter Carey)
Less Than Zero (Bret Easton Ellis)
The Mambo Kings Play Songs of Love (Oscar Hijuelos)
The Pilot's Wife (Anita Shreve)
Rabbit Is Rich (John Updike)
Rabbit, Run (John Updike)
The Reader (Bernhard Schlink)
White Oleander (Janet Fitch)

Machismo

Bastard out of Carolina (Dorothy Allison)
The Mambo Kings Play Songs of Love
   (Oscar Hijuelos)
To Have and Have Not (Ernest
   Hemingway)
The Women of Brewster Place

Madness and Insanity

Ashes to Ashes (Tami Hoag)
Black Notice (Patricia Cornwell)
False Memory (Dean Koontz)
The Human Stain (Philip Roth)

Magic

Blood and Chocolate (Annette Curtis
   Klause)
The Bride Price (Buchi Emecheta)
Hot Six (Janet Evanovich)

Manhood

The Blood Latitudes (William Harrison)
Rabbit Is Rich (John Updike)

Man vs. Machine

Empire of the Sun (J. G. Ballard)
Timeline (Michael Crichton)

Man vs. Nature

"The Birds" (Daphne du Maurier)
Blood and Chocolate (Annette Curtis
   Klause)
Out of Africa (Isak Dinesan)
The Perfect Storm (Sebastian Junger)
To Say Nothing of the Dog (Connie Willis)
True at First Light (Ernest Hemingway)

Man vs. Universe

Back Roads (Tawni O'Dell)
Blood and Chocolate (Annette Curtis
   Klause)
Cradle and All (James Patterson)
Fierce Invalids Home from Hot Climates
   (Tom Robbins)
How the Dead Live (Will Self)

The Human Stain (Philip Roth)

Manipulation

Before I Say Good-bye (Mary
   Higgins Clark)
Black Notice (Patricia Cornwell)
Cradle and All (James Patterson)
False Memory (Dean Koontz)
Hugger Mugger (Robert B. Parker)
The Pilot's Wife (Anita Shreve)
Southern Cross (Patricia Cornwell)
Timeline (Michael Crichton)
White Oleander (Janet Fitch)

Manners

Before I Say Good-bye (Mary
   Higgins Clark)
"The Bride Comes to Yellow Sky"
   (Stephen Crane)
The Bride Price (Buchi Emecheta)
Easy Prey (John Sandford)
Empress of the Splendid Season (Oscar
   Hijuelos)
For the Relief of Unbearable Urges (Nathan
   Englander)
A Gathering of Old Men (Ernest J. Gaines)
Gertrude and Claudius (John Updike)
Hot Six (Janet Evanovich)
Hugger Mugger (Robert B. Parker)
The Human Stain (Philip Roth)
Jack Maggs (Peter Carey)
"The Knife Thrower" (Steven Millhauser)
The Mambo Kings Play Songs of Love
   (Oscar Hijuelos)
O Is for Outlaw (Sue Grafton)
On Mystic Lake (Kristin Hannah)
Out of Africa (Isak Dinesan)
The Pilot's Wife (Anita Shreve)
Rabbit Is Rich (John Updike)
Rabbit, Run (John Updike)
The Reader (Bernhard Schlink)
Southern Cross (Patricia Cornwell)
Those Bones Are Not My Child (Toni Cade
   Bambara)
To Say Nothing of the Dog (Connie Willis)
True at First Light (Ernest Hemingway)
"The Way We Live Now" (Susan Sontag)

White Oleander (Janet Fitch)
The Women of Brewster Place
    (Gloria Naylor)

Marriage and Courtship

Bastard out of Carolina (Dorothy Allison)
Before I Say Good-bye (Mary
    Higgins Clark)
"The Bride Comes to Yellow Sky"
    (Stephen Crane)
The Bride Price (Buchi Emecheta)
Empress of the Splendid Season (Oscar
    Hijuelos)
For the Relief of Unbearable Urges (Nathan
    Englander)
Gertrude and Claudius (John Updike)
How the Dead Live (Will Self)
The Human Stain (Philip Roth)
The Mambo Kings Play Songs of Love
    (Oscar Hijuelos)
On Mystic Lake (Kristin Hannah)
Rabbit Is Rich (John Updike)
Rabbit, Run (John Updike)
To Say Nothing of the Dog (Connie Willis)
The Women of Brewster Place
    (Gloria Naylor)

Marital Conflict

Bastard out of Carolina (Dorothy Allison)
The Brethren (John Grisham)
Gertrude and Claudius (John Updike)
Little Kingdoms (Steven Millhauser)
The Mambo Kings Play Songs of Love
    (Oscar Hijuelos)
On Mystic Lake (Kristin Hannah)
Rabbit, Run (John Updike)
True at First Light (Ernest Hemingway)
The Women of Brewster Place
    (Gloria Naylor)

Marital Relations

Bastard out of Carolina (Dorothy Allison)
The Blood Latitudes (William Harrison)
The Bride Price (Buchi Emecheta)
Empress of the Splendid Season (Oscar
    Hijuelos)
False Memory (Dean Koontz)

Flaubert's Parrot (Julian Barnes)
Gertrude and Claudius (John Updike)
How the Dead Live (Will Self)
The Human Stain (Philip Roth)
Jack Maggs (Peter Carey)
The Mambo Kings Play Songs of Love
    (Oscar Hijuelos)
On Mystic Lake (Kristin Hannah)
The Pilot's Wife (Anita Shreve)
Rabbit Is Rich (John Updike)
Rabbit, Run (John Updike)

Mass Murder

The Blood Latitudes (William Harrison)
For the Relief of Unbearable Urges (Nathan
    Englander)
The Pilot's Wife (Anita Shreve)
The Reader (Bernhard Schlink)
Southern Cross (Patricia Cornwell)

Materialism

Before I Say Good-bye (Mary
    Higgins Clark)
Empress of the Splendid Season (Oscar
    Hijuelos)
Hot Six (Janet Evanovich)
Hugger Mugger (Robert B. Parker)
Less Than Zero (Bret Easton Ellis)
Rabbit Is Rich (John Updike)
Timeline (Michael Crichton)

Meaning of Life

Fierce Invalids Home from Hot Climates
    (Tom Robbins)
How the Dead Live (Will Self)

Media

Easy Prey (John Sandford)
The Mambo Kings Play Songs of Love
    (Oscar Hijuelos)
Those Bones Are Not My Child (Toni Cade
    Bambara)

Medicine

How the Dead Live (Will Self)

Memory and Reminiscence

Black Notice (Patricia Cornwell)
Empire of the Sun (J. G. Ballard)
Flaubert's Parrot (Julian Barnes)
How the Dead Live (Will Self)
Less Than Zero (Bret Easton Ellis)
The Mambo Kings Play Songs of Love
   (Oscar Hijuelos)
O Is for Outlaw (Sue Grafton)
Out of Africa (Isak Dinesan)
The Pilot's Wife (Anita Shreve)
Rabbit Is Rich (John Updike)
The Reader (Bernhard Schlink)
Those Bones Are Not My Child (Toni Cade
   Bambara)
To Say Nothing of the Dog (Connie Willis)
True at First Light (Ernest Hemingway)
"The Way We Live Now" (Susan Sontag)
White Oleander (Janet Fitch)

Mental Instability

Ashes to Ashes (Tami Hoag)
Back Roads (Tawni O'Dell)
Black Notice (Patricia Cornwell)
False Memory (Dean Koontz)
The Human Stain (Philip Roth)
Southern Cross (Patricia Cornwell)

Mentors

The Brethren (John Grisham)
Fierce Invalids Home from Hot Climates
   (Tom Robbins)
Hot Six (Janet Evanovich)
The Women of Brewster Place
   (Gloria Naylor)

Merchants and Trade

Black Notice (Patricia Cornwell)
Rabbit Is Rich (John Updike)

Messianism

Cradle and All (James Patterson)

Metamorphosis

Blood and Chocolate (Annette Curtis
   Klause)

Metaphysics

Cradle and All (James Patterson)
Fierce Invalids Home from Hot Climates
   (Tom Robbins)
For the Relief of Unbearable Urges (Nathan
   Englander)
Gertrude and Claudius (John Updike)
How the Dead Live (Will Self)
Little Kingdoms (Steven Millhauser)
Rabbit Is Rich (John Updike)
Rabbit, Run (John Updike)
True at First Light (Ernest Hemingway)

Middle Ages

Gertrude and Claudius (John Updike)
To Say Nothing of the Dog (Connie Willis)

Middle Class

Hot Six (Janet Evanovich)
Rabbit Is Rich (John Updike)
The Reader (Bernhard Schlink)

Military and Soldier Life

Empire of the Sun (J. G. Ballard)
The Reader (Bernhard Schlink)

Miracles

For the Relief of Unbearable Urges (Nathan
   Englander)

Misanthropy

Ashes to Ashes (Tami Hoag)
Back Roads (Tawni O'Dell)
Bastard out of Carolina (Dorothy Allison)
Black Notice (Patricia Cornwell)
Blood and Chocolate (Annette Curtis
   Klause)
The Blood Latitudes (William Harrison)
The Brethren (John Grisham)
Easy Prey (John Sandford)
Less Than Zero (Bret Easton Ellis)
The Reader (Bernhard Schlink)

Misfortune

Back Roads (Tawni O'Dell)

For the Relief of Unbearable Urges (Nathan Englander)
The Perfect Storm (Sebastian Junger)
Rabbit, Run (John Updike)
"The Way We Live Now" (Susan Sontag)
White Oleander (Janet Fitch)

Misogyny

Ashes to Ashes (Tami Hoag)
Bastard out of Carolina (Dorothy Allison)
The Mambo Kings Play Songs of Love (Oscar Hijuelos)
To Say Nothing of the Dog (Connie Willis)

Modern Times

Ashes to Ashes (Tami Hoag)
Back Roads (Tawni O'Dell)
Black Notice (Patricia Cornwell)
The Blood Latitudes (William Harrison)
The Brethren (John Grisham)

Money

Back Roads (Tawni O'Dell)
Before I Say Good-bye (Mary Higgins Clark)
The Brethren (John Grisham)
The Bride Price (Buchi Emecheta)
Easy Prey (John Sandford)
Empress of the Splendid Season (Oscar Hijuelos)
Hot Six (Janet Evanovich)
Hugger Mugger (Robert B. Parker)
Less Than Zero (Bret Easton Ellis)
The Mambo Kings Play Songs of Love (Oscar Hijuelos)
The Perfect Storm (Sebastian Junger)
Rabbit Is Rich (John Updike)
Timeline (Michael Crichton)
To Have and Have Not (Ernest Hemingway)
To Say Nothing of the Dog (Connie Willis)

Monsters and Dragons

Blood and Chocolate (Annette Curtis Klause)

Moral Confusion

Back Roads (Tawni O'Dell)
Black Notice (Patricia Cornwell)
Blood and Chocolate (Annette Curtis Klause)
"The Bride Comes to Yellow Sky" (Stephen Crane)
Cradle and All (James Patterson)
A Gathering of Old Men (Ernest J. Gaines)
Gertrude and Claudius (John Updike)
Hot Six (Janet Evanovich)
The Human Stain (Philip Roth)
Jack Maggs (Peter Carey)
The Mambo Kings Play Songs of Love (Oscar Hijuelos)
O Is for Outlaw (Sue Grafton)
Rabbit, Run (John Updike)
The Reader (Bernhard Schlink)
White Oleander (Janet Fitch)

Moral Corruption and Decline

Ashes to Ashes (Tami Hoag)
Back Roads (Tawni O'Dell)
Bastard out of Carolina (Dorothy Allison)
Black Notice (Patricia Cornwell)
The Blood Latitudes (William Harrison)
The Brethren (John Grisham)
Cradle and All (James Patterson)
Easy Prey (John Sandford)
False Memory (Dean Koontz)
For the Relief of Unbearable Urges (Nathan Englander)
A Gathering of Old Men (Ernest J. Gaines)
Gertrude and Claudius (John Updike)
Hot Six (Janet Evanovich)
Hugger Mugger (Robert B. Parker)
The Human Stain (Philip Roth)
In the Time of the Butterflies (Julia Alvarez)
Jack Maggs (Peter Carey)
Less Than Zero (Bret Easton Ellis)
The Mambo Kings Play Songs of Love (Oscar Hijuelos)
O Is for Outlaw (Sue Grafton)
The Pilot's Wife (Anita Shreve)
Playback (Raymond Chandler)
The Reader (Bernhard Schlink)
Southern Cross (Patricia Cornwell)

Those Bones Are Not My Child (Toni Cade
    Bambara)
Timeline (Michael Crichton)
White Oleander (Janet Fitch)
The Women of Brewster Place
    (Gloria Naylor)

Morals and Morality

Back Roads (Tawni O'Dell)
Black Notice (Patricia Cornwell)
Blood and Chocolate (Annette Curtis
    Klause)
The Blood Latitudes (William Harrison)
Cradle and All (James Patterson)
Fierce Invalids Home from Hot Climates
    (Tom Robbins)
Gertrude and Claudius (John Updike)
Hugger Mugger (Robert B. Parker)
The Human Stain (Philip Roth)
In the Time of the Butterflies (Julia Alvarez)
Jack Maggs (Peter Carey)
The Mambo Kings Play Songs of Love
    (Oscar Hijuelos)
Rabbit, Run (John Updike)
The Reader (Bernhard Schlink)
The Thanatos Syndrome (Walker Percy)
True at First Light (Ernest Hemingway)
"The Way We Live Now" (Susan Sontag)

Morbidity

Ashes to Ashes (Tami Hoag)
Before I Say Good-bye (Mary
    Higgins Clark)
"The Birds" (Daphne du Maurier)
Black Notice (Patricia Cornwell)
Blood and Chocolate (Annette Curtis
    Klause)
The Blood Latitudes (William Harrison)
The Bride Price (Buchi Emecheta)
Cradle and All (James Patterson)
Easy Prey (John Sandford)
Empire of the Sun (J. G. Ballard)
False Memory (Dean Koontz)
For the Relief of Unbearable Urges (Nathan
    Englander)
A Gathering of Old Men (Ernest J. Gaines)
Gertrude and Claudius (John Updike)

Hot Six (Janet Evanovich)
How the Dead Live (Will Self)
The Human Stain (Philip Roth)
In the Time of the Butterflies (Julia Alvarez)
Jack Maggs (Peter Carey)
"The Knife Thrower" (Steven Millhauser)
Little Kingdoms (Steven Millhauser)
The Mambo Kings Play Songs of Love
    (Oscar Hijuelos)
On Mystic Lake (Kristin Hannah)
Out of Africa (Isak Dinesan)
The Perfect Storm (Sebastian Junger)
The Pilot's Wife (Anita Shreve)
Rabbit, Run (John Updike)
The Reader (Bernhard Schlink)
Southern Cross (Patricia Cornwell)
Those Bones Are Not My Child (Toni Cade
    Bambara)
Timeline (Michael Crichton)
True at First Light (Ernest Hemingway)
"The Way We Live Now" (Susan Sontag)
The Women of Brewster Place
    (Gloria Naylor)

Motherhood

Ashes to Ashes (Tami Hoag)
Bastard out of Carolina (Dorothy Allison)
Black Notice (Patricia Cornwell)
The Bride Price (Buchi Emecheta)
Cradle and All (James Patterson)
Empress of the Splendid Season (Oscar
    Hijuelos)
False Memory (Dean Koontz)
Gertrude and Claudius (John Updike)
Hot Six (Janet Evanovich)
How the Dead Live (Will Self)
In the Time of the Butterflies (Julia Alvarez)
On Mystic Lake (Kristin Hannah)
The Pilot's Wife (Anita Shreve)
Rabbit Is Rich (John Updike)
Rabbit, Run (John Updike)
Southern Cross (Patricia Cornwell)
Those Bones Are Not My Child (Toni Cade
    Bambara)
White Oleander (Janet Fitch)
The Women of Brewster Place
    (Gloria Naylor)

Murder

Ashes to Ashes (Tami Hoag)
Before I Say Good-bye (Mary Higgins Clark)
Black Notice (Patricia Cornwell)
Blood and Chocolate (Annette Curtis Klause)
The Blood Latitudes (William Harrison)
Easy Prey (John Sandford)
False Memory (Dean Koontz)
For the Relief of Unbearable Urges (Nathan Englander)
A Gathering of Old Men (Ernest J. Gaines)
Gertrude and Claudius (John Updike)
Hot Six (Janet Evanovich)
The Human Stain (Philip Roth)
In the Time of the Butterflies (Julia Alvarez)
The Pilot's Wife (Anita Shreve)
Playback (Raymond Chandler)
Rabbit, Run (John Updike)
The Reader (Bernhard Schlink)
Southern Cross (Patricia Cornwell)
Those Bones Are Not My Child (Toni Cade Bambara)
To Have and Have Not (Ernest Hemingway)
The Women of Brewster Place (Gloria Naylor)

Music

Less Than Zero (Bret Easton Ellis)
The Mambo Kings Play Songs of Love (Oscar Hijuelos)

Mutilation

Ashes to Ashes (Tami Hoag)
Black Notice (Patricia Cornwell)
The Blood Latitudes (William Harrison)
False Memory (Dean Koontz)
Southern Cross (Patricia Cornwell)

Mystery and Intrigue

Ashes to Ashes (Tami Hoag)
Before I Say Good-bye (Mary Higgins Clark)

Black Notice (Patricia Cornwell)
The Brethren (John Grisham)
Cradle and All (James Patterson)
Easy Prey (John Sandford)
False Memory (Dean Koontz)
A Gathering of Old Men (Ernest J. Gaines)
Gertrude and Claudius (John Updike)
Hot Six (Janet Evanovich)
Hugger Mugger (Robert B. Parker)
O Is for Outlaw (Sue Grafton)
The Pilot's Wife (Anita Shreve)
Playback (Raymond Chandler)
Those Bones Are Not My Child (Toni Cade Bambara)
Timeline (Michael Crichton)

Mysticism

Blood and Chocolate (Annette Curtis Klause)
The Bride Price (Buchi Emecheta)
Cradle and All (James Patterson)
Fierce Invalids Home from Hot Climates (Tom Robbins)
For the Relief of Unbearable Urges (Nathan Englander)
How the Dead Live (Will Self)
Little Kingdoms (Steven Millhauser)
True at First Light (Ernest Hemingway)

Myths and Legends

Blood and Chocolate (Annette Curtis Klause)

Narcissism

Less Than Zero (Bret Easton Ellis)
Southern Cross (Patricia Cornwell)

Nationalism and Patriotism

The Brethren (John Grisham)
Empire of the Sun (J. G. Ballard)
Gertrude and Claudius (John Updike)
The Reader (Bernhard Schlink)
To Say Nothing of the Dog (Connie Willis)
True at First Light (Ernest Hemingway)

Native-South American Life and Thought
Fierce Invalids Home from Hot Climates (Tom Robbins)

Natural Disasters
"The Birds" (Daphne du Maurier)
The Perfect Storm (Sebastian Junger)

Natural Law
Blood and Chocolate (Annette Curtis Klause)
Gertrude and Claudius (John Updike)
Out of Africa (Isak Dinesan)
True at First Light (Ernest Hemingway)

Naturalism
Ashes to Ashes (Tami Hoag)
Bastard out of Carolina (Dorothy Allison)
The Blood Latitudes (William Harrison)
Flaubert's Parrot (Julian Barnes)
Southern Cross (Patricia Cornwell)

Nature
"The Birds" (Daphne du Maurier)
Out of Africa (Isak Dinesan)
The Perfect Storm (Sebastian Junger)
To Say Nothing of the Dog (Connie Willis)
True at First Light (Ernest Hemingway)

Nature, Return to
True at First Light (Ernest Hemingway)

Nazism
For the Relief of Unbearable Urges (Nathan Englander)
The Reader (Bernhard Schlink)

New England
The Human Stain (Philip Roth)

Nihilism
Ashes to Ashes (Tami Hoag)
Blood and Chocolate (Annette Curtis Klause)
The Blood Latitudes (William Harrison)

The Brethren (John Grisham)
Easy Prey (John Sandford)
False Memory (Dean Koontz)
Less Than Zero (Bret Easton Ellis)
Southern Cross (Patricia Cornwell)
White Oleander (Janet Fitch)

Nineties
How the Dead Live (Will Self)

Nonconformity
Back Roads (Tawni O'Dell)
Blood and Chocolate (Annette Curtis Klause)
"The Bride Comes to Yellow Sky" (Stephen Crane)
The Bride Price (Buchi Emecheta)
Cradle and All (James Patterson)
Empire of the Sun (J. G. Ballard)
False Memory (Dean Koontz)
Fierce Invalids Home from Hot Climates (Tom Robbins)
For the Relief of Unbearable Urges (Nathan Englander)
A Gathering of Old Men (Ernest J. Gaines)
Hot Six (Janet Evanovich)
"The Knife Thrower" (Steven Millhauser)
Little Kingdoms (Steven Millhauser)
Rabbit, Run (John Updike)
Those Bones Are Not My Child (Toni Cade Bambara)
To Have and Have Not (Ernest Hemingway)
True at First Light (Ernest Hemingway)
The Women of Brewster Place (Gloria Naylor)

Nostalgia
The Blood Latitudes (William Harrison)
The Mambo Kings Play Songs of Love (Oscar Hijuelos)
To Say Nothing of the Dog (Connie Willis)

Nouveau Riche
Before I Say Good-bye (Mary Higgins Clark)
Jack Maggs (Peter Carey)

Novel Writing

Jack Maggs (Peter Carey)
Those Bones Are Not My Child (Toni Cade
  Bambara)

Obedience and Submission

Bastard out of Carolina (Dorothy Allison)
The Bride Price (Buchi Emecheta)
False Memory (Dean Koontz)
For the Relief of Unbearable Urges (Nathan
  Englander)
Gertrude and Claudius (John Updike)
The Mambo Kings Play Songs of Love
  (Oscar Hijuelos)
The Reader (Bernhard Schlink)
Southern Cross (Patricia Cornwell)
To Say Nothing of the Dog (Connie Willis)

Obsession

Black Notice (Patricia Cornwell)
Little Kingdoms (Steven Millhauser)
Those Bones Are Not My Child (Toni Cade
  Bambara)

Occult

Before I Say Good-bye (Mary
  Higgins Clark)
The Bride Price (Buchi Emecheta)
Cradle and All (James Patterson)
Fierce Invalids Home from Hot Climates
  (Tom Robbins)
Hot Six (Janet Evanovich)

Opportunism

The Brethren (John Grisham)
Jack Maggs (Peter Carey)
Timeline (Michael Crichton)
To Say Nothing of the Dog (Connie Willis)

Oppression

Back Roads (Tawni O'Dell)
The Blood Latitudes (William Harrison)
The Brethren (John Grisham)
The Bride Price (Buchi Emecheta)
For the Relief of Unbearable Urges (Nathan
  Englander)

A Gathering of Old Men (Ernest J. Gaines)
Gertrude and Claudius (John Updike)
In the Time of the Butterflies (Julia Alvarez)
Those Bones Are Not My Child (Toni Cade
  Bambara)
To Say Nothing of the Dog (Connie Willis)
The Women of Brewster Place
  (Gloria Naylor)

Optimism and Pessimism

Empress of the Splendid Season (Oscar
  Hijuelos)
Hugger Mugger (Robert B. Parker)
Rabbit Is Rich (John Updike)
Those Bones Are Not My Child (Toni Cade
  Bambara)

Oral Tradition

Fierce Invalids Home from Hot Climates
  (Tom Robbins)
The Reader (Bernhard Schlink)

Outsider

Bastard out of Carolina (Dorothy Allison)
Before I Say Good-bye (Mary
  Higgins Clark)
Blood and Chocolate (Annette Curtis
  Klause)
The Blood Latitudes (William Harrison)
"The Bride Comes to Yellow Sky"
  (Stephen Crane)
The Bride Price (Buchi Emecheta)
Empire of the Sun (J. G. Ballard)
Empress of the Splendid Season (Oscar
  Hijuelos)
Fierce Invalids Home from Hot Climates
  (Tom Robbins)
For the Relief of Unbearable Urges (Nathan
  Englander)
Jack Maggs (Peter Carey)
The Mambo Kings Play Songs of Love
  (Oscar Hijuelos)
Out of Africa (Isak Dinesan)
The Pilot's Wife (Anita Shreve)
To Say Nothing of the Dog (Connie Willis)
True at First Light (Ernest Hemingway)

Pain and Suffering

Ashes to Ashes (Tami Hoag)
Back Roads (Tawni O'Dell)
Bastard out of Carolina (Dorothy Allison)
Black Notice (Patricia Cornwell)
The Blood Latitudes (William Harrison)
Cradle and All (James Patterson)
Empire of the Sun (J. G. Ballard)
False Memory (Dean Koontz)
For the Relief of Unbearable Urges (Nathan Englander)
How the Dead Live (Will Self)
The Human Stain (Philip Roth)
In the Time of the Butterflies (Julia Alvarez)
Less Than Zero (Bret Easton Ellis)
On Mystic Lake (Kristin Hannah)
The Pilot's Wife (Anita Shreve)
Rabbit, Run (John Updike)
The Reader (Bernhard Schlink)
Southern Cross (Patricia Cornwell)
Those Bones Are Not My Child (Toni Cade Bambara)
"The Way We Live Now" (Susan Sontag)
White Oleander (Janet Fitch)
The Women of Brewster Place (Gloria Naylor)

Paradise

Out of Africa (Isak Dinesan)
True at First Light (Ernest Hemingway)

Paradise Lost

"The Birds" (Daphne du Maurier)
Black Notice (Patricia Cornwell)
Blood and Chocolate (Annette Curtis Klause)
The Blood Latitudes (William Harrison)
The Brethren (John Grisham)
"The Bride Comes to Yellow Sky" (Stephen Crane)
Cradle and All (James Patterson)
For the Relief of Unbearable Urges (Nathan Englander)
Jack Maggs (Peter Carey)
Less Than Zero (Bret Easton Ellis)
The Mambo Kings Play Songs of Love (Oscar Hijuelos)

Out of Africa (Isak Dinesan)
The Pilot's Wife (Anita Shreve)
Rabbit, Run (John Updike)
The Reader (Bernhard Schlink)
"The Way We Live Now" (Susan Sontag)

Paradise Regained

Rabbit Is Rich (John Updike)

Paranoia

Black Notice (Patricia Cornwell)
"The Bride Comes to Yellow Sky" (Stephen Crane)
Those Bones Are Not My Child (Toni Cade Bambara)

Parent-Teen Relationship

Ashes to Ashes (Tami Hoag)
Bastard out of Carolina (Dorothy Allison)
Empress of the Splendid Season (Oscar Hijuelos)
False Memory (Dean Koontz)
The Pilot's Wife (Anita Shreve)
Southern Cross (Patricia Cornwell)
The Women of Brewster Place (Gloria Naylor)

Passion vs. Reason

The Blood Latitudes (William Harrison)
"The Bride Comes to Yellow Sky" (Stephen Crane)
Easy Prey (John Sandford)
Rabbit, Run (John Updike)

Peer Pressure

Less Than Zero (Bret Easton Ellis)
The Mambo Kings Play Songs of Love (Oscar Hijuelos)
The Reader (Bernhard Schlink)
Southern Cross (Patricia Cornwell)
The Women of Brewster Place (Gloria Naylor)

Perfection and Perfectionism

On Mystic Lake (Kristin Hannah)

Performing Arts

"The Knife Thrower" (Steven Millhauser)
The Mambo Kings Play Songs of Love
(Oscar Hijuelos)

Persecution

Blood and Chocolate (Annette Curtis Klause)
The Bride Price (Buchi Emecheta)
For the Relief of Unbearable Urges (Nathan Englander)
A Gathering of Old Men (Ernest J. Gaines)
The Human Stain (Philip Roth)
The Reader (Bernhard Schlink)
The Women of Brewster Place
(Gloria Naylor)

Philosophical Ideas

Fierce Invalids Home from Hot Climates
(Tom Robbins)
Flaubert's Parrot (Julian Barnes)
For the Relief of Unbearable Urges (Nathan Englander)
Gertrude and Claudius (John Updike)
Little Kingdoms (Steven Millhauser)
Rabbit Is Rich (John Updike)
Rabbit, Run (John Updike)
The Reader (Bernhard Schlink)
True at First Light (Ernest Hemingway)

Physical Appearance

Bastard out of Carolina (Dorothy Allison)
Blood and Chocolate (Annette Curtis Klause)
Easy Prey (John Sandford)
Empress of the Splendid Season (Oscar Hijuelos)
Fierce Invalids Home from Hot Climates
(Tom Robbins)
The Human Stain (Philip Roth)
The Mambo Kings Play Songs of Love
(Oscar Hijuelos)
Southern Cross (Patricia Cornwell)
The Women of Brewster Place
(Gloria Naylor)

Physical Disability

Fierce Invalids Home from Hot Climates
(Tom Robbins)

Pioneers

Out of Africa (Isak Dinesan)

Poetry Writing

White Oleander (Janet Fitch)

Political Activism

Before I Say Good-bye (Mary Higgins Clark)
The Brethren (John Grisham)
For the Relief of Unbearable Urges (Nathan Englander)
In the Time of the Butterflies (Julia Alvarez)
The Pilot's Wife (Anita Shreve)

Politics and Society

Ashes to Ashes (Tami Hoag)
Black Notice (Patricia Cornwell)
The Brethren (John Grisham)
For the Relief of Unbearable Urges (Nathan Englander)
The Pilot's Wife (Anita Shreve)
The Reader (Bernhard Schlink)

Pornography

Easy Prey (John Sandford)
Less Than Zero (Bret Easton Ellis)

Postcolonialism

The Blood Latitudes (William Harrison)
In the Time of the Butterflies (Julia Alvarez)

Postmodernism

Fierce Invalids Home from Hot Climates
(Tom Robbins)

Poverty

Back Roads (Tawni O'Dell)
Bastard out of Carolina (Dorothy Allison)
Empress of the Splendid Season (Oscar Hijuelos)
A Gathering of Old Men (Ernest J. Gaines)

Appendix: Titles Grouped by Social Concerns and Themes

Jack Maggs (Peter Carey)
The Mambo Kings Play Songs of Love
    (Oscar Hijuelos)
Those Bones Are Not My Child (Toni Cade
    Bambara)
The Women of Brewster Place
    (Gloria Naylor)

Power

Black Notice (Patricia Cornwell)
The Blood Latitudes (William Harrison)
The Brethren (John Grisham)
False Memory (Dean Koontz)
Gertrude and Claudius (John Updike)
Hot Six (Janet Evanovich)
Hugger Mugger (Robert B. Parker)
In the Time of the Butterflies (Julia Alvarez)
Jack Maggs (Peter Carey)
Southern Cross (Patricia Cornwell)
Those Bones Are Not My Child (Toni Cade
    Bambara)
Timeline (Michael Crichton)

Pragmatism

Little Kingdoms (Steven Millhauser)
Out of Africa (Isak Dinesan)
The Perfect Storm (Sebastian Junger)
Rabbit Is Rich (John Updike)

Preachers and Prophets

Cradle and All (James Patterson)

Prejudice

"The Bride Comes to Yellow Sky"
    (Stephen Crane)
The Bride Price (Buchi Emecheta)
Cradle and All (James Patterson)
For the Relief of Unbearable Urges (Nathan
    Englander)
A Gathering of Old Men (Ernest J. Gaines)
How the Dead Live (Will Self)
Hugger Mugger (Robert B. Parker)
The Human Stain (Philip Roth)
Jack Maggs (Peter Carey)
The Reader (Bernhard Schlink)
To Say Nothing of the Dog (Connie Willis)

Pride

Empress of the Splendid Season (Oscar
    Hijuelos)
The Mambo Kings Play Songs of Love
    (Oscar Hijuelos)

Primitivism

The Bride Price (Buchi Emecheta)
True at First Light (Ernest Hemingway)

Prisons and Confinement

Back Roads (Tawni O'Dell)
The Brethren (John Grisham)
Empire of the Sun (J. G. Ballard)
For the Relief of Unbearable Urges (Nathan
    Englander)
Hot Six (Janet Evanovich)
In the Time of the Butterflies (Julia Alvarez)
The Reader (Bernhard Schlink)

Progress

The Bride Price (Buchi Emecheta)
Out of Africa (Isak Dinesan)
The Perfect Storm (Sebastian Junger)
Rabbit Is Rich (John Updike)
Timeline (Michael Crichton)
To Say Nothing of the Dog (Connie Willis)

Prophecy

Cradle and All (James Patterson)
Fierce Invalids Home from Hot Climates
    (Tom Robbins)

Prostitution

Ashes to Ashes (Tami Hoag)
Hugger Mugger (Robert B. Parker)
Jack Maggs (Peter Carey)
Less Than Zero (Bret Easton Ellis)

Psychology and the Human Mind

Ashes to Ashes (Tami Hoag)
Back Roads (Tawni O'Dell)
False Memory (Dean Koontz)
On Mystic Lake (Kristin Hannah)

Punishment

Back Roads (Tawni O'Dell)
Bastard out of Carolina (Dorothy Allison)
The Brethren (John Grisham)
Easy Prey (John Sandford)
Empire of the Sun (J. G. Ballard)
For the Relief of Unbearable Urges (Nathan Englander)
Hot Six (Janet Evanovich)
In the Time of the Butterflies (Julia Alvarez)
Jack Maggs (Peter Carey)
O Is for Outlaw (Sue Grafton)
The Reader (Bernhard Schlink)
Southern Cross (Patricia Cornwell)
Timeline (Michael Crichton)

Quest

Cradle and All (James Patterson)
Fierce Invalids Home from Hot Climates (Tom Robbins)
Flaubert's Parrot (Julian Barnes)
The Pilot's Wife (Anita Shreve)
Those Bones Are Not My Child (Toni Cade Bambara)
Timeline (Michael Crichton)

Race Relations

A Gathering of Old Men (Ernest J. Gaines)
How the Dead Live (Will Self)
Hugger Mugger (Robert B. Parker)
The Human Stain (Philip Roth)
Out of Africa (Isak Dinesan)
Those Bones Are Not My Child (Toni Cade Bambara)
True at First Light (Ernest Hemingway)

Racism and Racial Conflict

The Blood Latitudes (William Harrison)
A Gathering of Old Men (Ernest J. Gaines)
How the Dead Live (Will Self)
Hugger Mugger (Robert B. Parker)
The Human Stain (Philip Roth)
Out of Africa (Isak Dinesan)
Southern Cross (Patricia Cornwell)
Those Bones Are Not My Child (Toni Cade Bambara)

Rape

Ashes to Ashes (Tami Hoag)
The Bride Price (Buchi Emecheta)
False Memory (Dean Koontz)
Gertrude and Claudius (John Updike)
Less Than Zero (Bret Easton Ellis)
The Women of Brewster Place (Gloria Naylor)

Rebellion against Parents

Ashes to Ashes (Tami Hoag)
The Bride Price (Buchi Emecheta)
Empress of the Splendid Season (Oscar Hijuelos)
False Memory (Dean Koontz)
Gertrude and Claudius (John Updike)
Hot Six (Janet Evanovich)
Rabbit Is Rich (John Updike)
White Oleander (Janet Fitch)

Rebirth

How the Dead Live (Will Self)

Reconciliation

A Gathering of Old Men (Ernest J. Gaines)
On Mystic Lake (Kristin Hannah)
Rabbit, Run (John Updike)

Redemption

Cradle and All (James Patterson)
Fierce Invalids Home from Hot Climates (Tom Robbins)
Rabbit Is Rich (John Updike)
Rabbit, Run (John Updike)

Reform

Gertrude and Claudius (John Updike)
To Say Nothing of the Dog (Connie Willis)
True at First Light (Ernest Hemingway)
The Women of Brewster Place (Gloria Naylor)

Refugees

For the Relief of Unbearable Urges (Nathan Englander)

To Say Nothing of the Dog (Connie Willis)

Regression
Black Notice (Patricia Cornwell)
The Blood Latitudes (William Harrison)
The Human Stain (Philip Roth)
Rabbit, Run (John Updike)

Reincarnation
How the Dead Live (Will Self)

Rejection
Blood and Chocolate (Annette Curtis
    Klause)
The Bride Price (Buchi Emecheta)
Little Kingdoms (Steven Millhauser)
The Mambo Kings Play Songs of Love
    (Oscar Hijuelos)
The Reader (Bernhard Schlink)
To Say Nothing of the Dog (Connie Willis)
White Oleander (Janet Fitch)

Religion and Religious Thought
Bastard out of Carolina (Dorothy Allison)
Cradle and All (James Patterson)
Empress of the Splendid Season (Oscar
    Hijuelos)
Fierce Invalids Home from Hot Climates
    (Tom Robbins)
For the Relief of Unbearable Urges (Nathan
    Englander)
Gertrude and Claudius (John Updike)
In the Time of the Butterflies (Julia Alvarez)
The Pilot's Wife (Anita Shreve)
Rabbit, Run (John Updike)
True at First Light (Ernest Hemingway)

Remorse and Regret
Black Notice (Patricia Cornwell)
"The Bride Comes to Yellow Sky"
    (Stephen Crane)
The Mambo Kings Play Songs of Love
    (Oscar Hijuelos)
The Pilot's Wife (Anita Shreve)
Rabbit, Run (John Updike)
True at First Light (Ernest Hemingway)

Repression
Bastard out of Carolina (Dorothy Allison)
Rabbit Is Rich (John Updike)
Rabbit, Run (John Updike)
To Say Nothing of the Dog (Connie Willis)

Revenge
Black Notice (Patricia Cornwell)
The Bride Price (Buchi Emecheta)
Easy Prey (John Sandford)
False Memory (Dean Koontz)
A Gathering of Old Men (Ernest J. Gaines)
Gertrude and Claudius (John Updike)
The Human Stain (Philip Roth)

Rites of Passage
"The Knife Thrower" (Steven Millhauser)

Rivalry
Black Notice (Patricia Cornwell)
"The Bride Comes to Yellow Sky"
    (Stephen Crane)
False Memory (Dean Koontz)
Gertrude and Claudius (John Updike)
To Say Nothing of the Dog (Connie Willis)

Romanticism
"The Bride Comes to Yellow Sky"
    (Stephen Crane)
To Say Nothing of the Dog (Connie Willis)

Romantic Love
Before I Say Good-bye (Mary
    Higgins Clark)
Blood and Chocolate (Annette Curtis
    Klause)
"The Bride Comes to Yellow Sky"
    (Stephen Crane)
The Bride Price (Buchi Emecheta)
Empress of the Splendid Season (Oscar
    Hijuelos)
For the Relief of Unbearable Urges (Nathan
    Englander)
Gertrude and Claudius (John Updike)
The Human Stain (Philip Roth)

The Mambo Kings Play Songs of Love
  (Oscar Hijuelos)
Out of Africa (Isak Dinesan)
The Pilot's Wife (Anita Shreve)
Rabbit Is Rich (John Updike)
Rabbit, Run (John Updike)
The Reader (Bernhard Schlink)
To Say Nothing of the Dog (Connie Willis)
True at First Light (Ernest Hemingway)
White Oleander (Janet Fitch)

Royalty
Gertrude and Claudius (John Updike)

Rural Life
A Gathering of Old Men (Ernest J. Gaines)

Sacrifice
Empire of the Sun (J. G. Ballard)
For the Relief of Unbearable Urges (Nathan
  Englander)
A Gathering of Old Men (Ernest J. Gaines)
In the Time of the Butterflies (Julia Alvarez)
Rabbit Is Rich (John Updike)
The Women of Brewster Place
  (Gloria Naylor)

Sadism and Masochism
Ashes to Ashes (Tami Hoag)
Bastard out of Carolina (Dorothy Allison)
Black Notice (Patricia Cornwell)
Less Than Zero (Bret Easton Ellis)

Salvation
Cradle and All (James Patterson)
Fierce Invalids Home from Hot Climates
  (Tom Robbins)
Rabbit, Run (John Updike)

Sanity
Black Notice (Patricia Cornwell)

Savagery
Ashes to Ashes (Tami Hoag)
Bastard out of Carolina (Dorothy Allison)
"The Birds" (Daphne du Maurier)

The Blood Latitudes (William Harrison)
False Memory (Dean Koontz)
Southern Cross (Patricia Cornwell)

Scandal
The Brethren (John Grisham)
"The Bride Comes to Yellow Sky"
  (Stephen Crane)
Cradle and All (James Patterson)
Easy Prey (John Sandford)
False Memory (Dean Koontz)
Gertrude and Claudius (John Updike)
How the Dead Live (Will Self)
Hugger Mugger (Robert B. Parker)
The Human Stain (Philip Roth)
O Is for Outlaw (Sue Grafton)
Southern Cross (Patricia Cornwell)

School Life
Less Than Zero (Bret Easton Ellis)
Southern Cross (Patricia Cornwell)

Science and Technology
The Perfect Storm (Sebastian Junger)
The Thanatos Syndrome (Walker Percy)
Timeline (Michael Crichton)

Sea and Sea Adventures
The Perfect Storm (Sebastian Junger)

Self and Self-Discovery
Before I Say Good-bye (Mary
  Higgins Clark)
Black Notice (Patricia Cornwell)
Fierce Invalids Home from Hot Climates
  (Tom Robbins)
For the Relief of Unbearable Urges (Nathan
  Englander)
How the Dead Live (Will Self)
Little Kingdoms (Steven Millhauser)
The Mambo Kings Play Songs of Love
  (Oscar Hijuelos)
On Mystic Lake (Kristin Hannah)
Out of Africa (Isak Dinesan)
The Pilot's Wife (Anita Shreve)

Rabbit Is Rich (John Updike)
Rabbit, Run (John Updike)
Those Bones Are Not My Child (Toni Cade Bambara)
To Say Nothing of the Dog (Connie Willis)
True at First Light (Ernest Hemingway)
White Oleander (Janet Fitch)

Self-Destruction

Ashes to Ashes (Tami Hoag)
Bastard out of Carolina (Dorothy Allison)
Before I Say Good-bye (Mary Higgins Clark)
Black Notice (Patricia Cornwell)
Blood and Chocolate (Annette Curtis Klause)
"The Bride Comes to Yellow Sky" (Stephen Crane)
Easy Prey (John Sandford)
False Memory (Dean Koontz)
Gertrude and Claudius (John Updike)
How the Dead Live (Will Self)
Hugger Mugger (Robert B. Parker)
The Human Stain (Philip Roth)
Less Than Zero (Bret Easton Ellis)
Little Kingdoms (Steven Millhauser)
The Mambo Kings Play Songs of Love (Oscar Hijuelos)
The Pilot's Wife (Anita Shreve)
Rabbit, Run (John Updike)
Southern Cross (Patricia Cornwell)
"The Way We Live Now" (Susan Sontag)
The Women of Brewster Place (Gloria Naylor)

Self-Expression

Empire of the Sun (J. G. Ballard)
Fierce Invalids Home from Hot Climates (Tom Robbins)
Flaubert's Parrot (Julian Barnes)
For the Relief of Unbearable Urges (Nathan Englander)
Jack Maggs (Peter Carey)
Little Kingdoms (Steven Millhauser)
The Mambo Kings Play Songs of Love (Oscar Hijuelos)
White Oleander (Janet Fitch)

Self-Image

Back Roads (Tawni O'Dell)
Bastard out of Carolina (Dorothy Allison)
Black Notice (Patricia Cornwell)
"The Bride Comes to Yellow Sky" (Stephen Crane)
Empress of the Splendid Season (Oscar Hijuelos)
Fierce Invalids Home from Hot Climates (Tom Robbins)
For the Relief of Unbearable Urges (Nathan Englander)
A Gathering of Old Men (Ernest J. Gaines)
How the Dead Live (Will Self)
The Human Stain (Philip Roth)
Jack Maggs (Peter Carey)
On Mystic Lake (Kristin Hannah)
Out of Africa (Isak Dinesan)
The Pilot's Wife (Anita Shreve)
Rabbit, Run (John Updike)
The Reader (Bernhard Schlink)
Southern Cross (Patricia Cornwell)
To Say Nothing of the Dog (Connie Willis)
True at First Light (Ernest Hemingway)
White Oleander (Janet Fitch)
The Women of Brewster Place (Gloria Naylor)

Self-Pity

Bastard out of Carolina (Dorothy Allison)
Black Notice (Patricia Cornwell)
Gertrude and Claudius (John Updike)
The Mambo Kings Play Songs of Love (Oscar Hijuelos)
O Is for Outlaw (Sue Grafton)
The Pilot's Wife (Anita Shreve)
Rabbit, Run (John Updike)
The Women of Brewster Place (Gloria Naylor)

Self-Preservation

Back Roads (Tawni O'Dell)
Black Notice (Patricia Cornwell)
The Brethren (John Grisham)
The Bride Price (Buchi Emecheta)
Empire of the Sun (J. G. Ballard)
False Memory (Dean Koontz)

For the Relief of Unbearable Urges (Nathan Englander)
Hot Six (Janet Evanovich)
The Reader (Bernhard Schlink)
Timeline (Michael Crichton)
White Oleander (Janet Fitch)

Self-Reliance

Ashes to Ashes (Tami Hoag)
Back Roads (Tawni O'Dell)
Black Notice (Patricia Cornwell)
The Blood Latitudes (William Harrison)
Cradle and All (James Patterson)
Empire of the Sun (J. G. Ballard)
Hot Six (Janet Evanovich)
Out of Africa (Isak Dinesan)
Those Bones Are Not My Child (Toni Cade Bambara)
To Have and Have Not (Ernest Hemingway)
White Oleander (Janet Fitch)

Selfishness

Before I Say Good-bye (Mary Higgins Clark)
Black Notice (Patricia Cornwell)
"The Bride Comes to Yellow Sky" (Stephen Crane)
Easy Prey (John Sandford)
False Memory (Dean Koontz)
Gertrude and Claudius (John Updike)
Hugger Mugger (Robert B. Parker)
Less Than Zero (Bret Easton Ellis)
O Is for Outlaw (Sue Grafton)
Rabbit Is Rich (John Updike)
Rabbit, Run (John Updike)
Southern Cross (Patricia Cornwell)
Timeline (Michael Crichton)
White Oleander (Janet Fitch)
The Women of Brewster Place (Gloria Naylor)

Sense Perception

Fierce Invalids Home from Hot Climates (Tom Robbins)
How the Dead Live (Will Self)
Little Kingdoms (Steven Millhauser)

To Say Nothing of the Dog (Connie Willis)
True at First Light (Ernest Hemingway)

Sensuality

The Bride Price (Buchi Emecheta)
Easy Prey (John Sandford)
Fierce Invalids Home from Hot Climates (Tom Robbins)
The Human Stain (Philip Roth)
Rabbit Is Rich (John Updike)
Rabbit, Run (John Updike)
The Reader (Bernhard Schlink)
White Oleander (Janet Fitch)

Sentimentality

Empress of the Splendid Season (Oscar Hijuelos)
For the Relief of Unbearable Urges (Nathan Englander)
How the Dead Live (Will Self)
Little Kingdoms (Steven Millhauser)
The Mambo Kings Play Songs of Love (Oscar Hijuelos)
On Mystic Lake (Kristin Hannah)
Out of Africa (Isak Dinesan)
Rabbit Is Rich (John Updike)
True at First Light (Ernest Hemingway)
"The Way We Live Now" (Susan Sontag)

Separation and Estrangement

Ashes to Ashes (Tami Hoag)
Back Roads (Tawni O'Dell)
Before I Say Good-bye (Mary Higgins Clark)
Black Notice (Patricia Cornwell)
Blood and Chocolate (Annette Curtis Klause)
Empire of the Sun (J. G. Ballard)
False Memory (Dean Koontz)
Hot Six (Janet Evanovich)
The Human Stain (Philip Roth)
Jack Maggs (Peter Carey)
Less Than Zero (Bret Easton Ellis)
Little Kingdoms (Steven Millhauser)
The Mambo Kings Play Songs of Love (Oscar Hijuelos)
On Mystic Lake (Kristin Hannah)

Rabbit Is Rich (John Updike)
Rabbit, Run (John Updike)
The Reader (Bernhard Schlink)
"The Way We Live Now" (Susan Sontag)
White Oleander (Janet Fitch)
The Women of Brewster Place
   (Gloria Naylor)

Separatism

Blood and Chocolate (Annette Curtis
   Klause)
A Gathering of Old Men (Ernest J. Gaines)
The Human Stain (Philip Roth)
The Women of Brewster Place
   (Gloria Naylor)

Serial Killers/Serial Killing

Ashes to Ashes (Tami Hoag)
Black Notice (Patricia Cornwell)
False Memory (Dean Koontz)
Those Bones Are Not My Child (Toni Cade
   Bambara)

Seventies

How the Dead Live (Will Self)
Rabbit Is Rich (John Updike)
Those Bones Are Not My Child (Toni Cade
   Bambara)

Sex and Sexuality

Bastard out of Carolina (Dorothy Allison)
The Bride Price (Buchi Emecheta)
Easy Prey (John Sandford)
False Memory (Dean Koontz)
Fierce Invalids Home from Hot Climates
   (Tom Robbins)
Gertrude and Claudius (John Updike)
Hot Six (Janet Evanovich)
Hugger Mugger (Robert B. Parker)
The Human Stain (Philip Roth)
Jack Maggs (Peter Carey)
Less Than Zero (Bret Easton Ellis)
The Mambo Kings Play Songs of Love
   (Oscar Hijuelos)
The Pilot's Wife (Anita Shreve)
Rabbit Is Rich (John Updike)
Rabbit, Run (John Updike)

The Reader (Bernhard Schlink)
"The Way We Live Now" (Susan Sontag)
White Oleander (Janet Fitch)

Sex Roles

Bastard out of Carolina (Dorothy Allison)
Before I Say Good-bye (Mary
   Higgins Clark)
The Bride Price (Buchi Emecheta)
False Memory (Dean Koontz)
Flaubert's Parrot (Julian Barnes)
Gertrude and Claudius (John Updike)
Hot Six (Janet Evanovich)
How the Dead Live (Will Self)
Hugger Mugger (Robert B. Parker)
In the Time of the Butterflies (Julia Alvarez)
Jack Maggs (Peter Carey)
The Mambo Kings Play Songs of Love
   (Oscar Hijuelos)
O Is for Outlaw (Sue Grafton)
On Mystic Lake (Kristin Hannah)
Rabbit Is Rich (John Updike)
Rabbit, Run (John Updike)
The Reader (Bernhard Schlink)
To Say Nothing of the Dog (Connie Willis)
White Oleander (Janet Fitch)
The Women of Brewster Place
   (Gloria Naylor)

Sexual Abuse

Bastard out of Carolina (Dorothy Allison)
False Memory (Dean Koontz)
Hugger Mugger (Robert B. Parker)
The Human Stain (Philip Roth)
Less Than Zero (Bret Easton Ellis)

Sexual Equality

To Say Nothing of the Dog (Connie Willis)

Sibling Relationships

Back Roads (Tawni O'Dell)
The Bride Price (Buchi Emecheta)
Easy Prey (John Sandford)
Empress of the Splendid Season (Oscar
   Hijuelos)
False Memory (Dean Koontz)

Fierce Invalids Home from Hot Climates
(Tom Robbins)
Hugger Mugger (Robert B. Parker)
In the Time of the Butterflies (Julia Alvarez)

Sickness and Health
The Bride Price (Buchi Emecheta)
Cradle and All (James Patterson)
How the Dead Live (Will Self)
Jack Maggs (Peter Carey)
The Reader (Bernhard Schlink)
"The Way We Live Now" (Susan Sontag)

Silence
Bastard out of Carolina (Dorothy Allison)
For the Relief of Unbearable Urges (Nathan Englander)
A Gathering of Old Men (Ernest J. Gaines)
Less Than Zero (Bret Easton Ellis)

Simple Life
Little Kingdoms (Steven Millhauser)

Sin and Sinners
Cradle and All (James Patterson)
Rabbit, Run (John Updike)

Single Life
Ashes to Ashes (Tami Hoag)
Black Notice (Patricia Cornwell)
Hot Six (Janet Evanovich)
The Mambo Kings Play Songs of Love (Oscar Hijuelos)
Out of Africa (Isak Dinesan)

Sixties
How the Dead Live (Will Self)

Skepticism
Gertrude and Claudius (John Updike)

Snobs and Snobbery
Before I Say Good-bye (Mary Higgins Clark)
False Memory (Dean Koontz)
Jack Maggs (Peter Carey)

Less Than Zero (Bret Easton Ellis)
Southern Cross (Patricia Cornwell)

Social Responsibility
Before I Say Good-bye (Mary Higgins Clark)
Black Notice (Patricia Cornwell)
The Brethren (John Grisham)
"The Bride Comes to Yellow Sky" (Stephen Crane)
Cradle and All (James Patterson)
Out of Africa (Isak Dinesan)
The Pilot's Wife (Anita Shreve)
The Reader (Bernhard Schlink)
Southern Cross (Patricia Cornwell)
Those Bones Are Not My Child (Toni Cade Bambara)
To Say Nothing of the Dog (Connie Willis)
True at First Light (Ernest Hemingway)
"The Way We Live Now" (Susan Sontag)
The Women of Brewster Place (Gloria Naylor)

Social Protest
Ashes to Ashes (Tami Hoag)
Back Roads (Tawni O'Dell)
Bastard out of Carolina (Dorothy Allison)
"The Birds" (Daphne du Maurier)
Black Notice (Patricia Cornwell)
The Blood Latitudes (William Harrison)
The Brethren (John Grisham)
The Bride Price (Buchi Emecheta)
False Memory (Dean Koontz)
For the Relief of Unbearable Urges (Nathan Englander)
A Gathering of Old Men (Ernest J. Gaines)
Hot Six (Janet Evanovich)
Hugger Mugger (Robert B. Parker)
The Human Stain (Philip Roth)
Jack Maggs (Peter Carey)
Less Than Zero (Bret Easton Ellis)
O Is for Outlaw (Sue Grafton)
The Pilot's Wife (Anita Shreve)
The Reader (Bernhard Schlink)
Southern Cross (Patricia Cornwell)
Those Bones Are Not My Child (Toni Cade Bambara)

Appendix: Titles Grouped by Social Concerns and Themes

To Have and Have Not (Ernest Hemingway)
The Women of Brewster Place (Gloria Naylor)

Solidarity

Blood and Chocolate (Annette Curtis Klause)
For the Relief of Unbearable Urges (Nathan Englander)
A Gathering of Old Men (Ernest J. Gaines)
Those Bones Are Not My Child (Toni Cade Bambara)
"The Way We Live Now" (Susan Sontag)
The Women of Brewster Place (Gloria Naylor)

Solitude

True at First Light (Ernest Hemingway)

Soul

Cradle and All (James Patterson)
Fierce Invalids Home from Hot Climates (Tom Robbins)
How the Dead Live (Will Self)

Spirits

On Mystic Lake (Kristin Hannah)

Spirituality

Cradle and All (James Patterson)
Empress of the Splendid Season (Oscar Hijuelos)
Fierce Invalids Home from Hot Climates (Tom Robbins)
For the Relief of Unbearable Urges (Nathan Englander)
How the Dead Live (Will Self)
Rabbit Is Rich (John Updike)
Rabbit, Run (John Updike)
The Thanatos Syndrome (Walker Percy)
True at First Light (Ernest Hemingway)

Spiritual Quest

Cradle and All (James Patterson)

Fierce Invalids Home from Hot Climates (Tom Robbins)
Rabbit, Run (John Updike)

Spirit World

How the Dead Live (Will Self)

Stalinism

For the Relief of Unbearable Urges (Nathan Englander)

Stalking

The Human Stain (Philip Roth)

Strength and Endurance

Empire of the Sun (J. G. Ballard)
Out of Africa (Isak Dinesan)
The Perfect Storm (Sebastian Junger)

Struggle and Conflict

Back Roads (Tawni O'Dell)
"The Birds" (Daphne du Maurier)
Black Notice (Patricia Cornwell)
The Blood Latitudes (William Harrison)
Cradle and All (James Patterson)
The Perfect Storm (Sebastian Junger)
Those Bones Are Not My Child (Toni Cade Bambara)

Sublime

"The Bride Comes to Yellow Sky" (Stephen Crane)
Empire of the Sun (J. G. Ballard)
Fierce Invalids Home from Hot Climates (Tom Robbins)
Flaubert's Parrot (Julian Barnes)
For the Relief of Unbearable Urges (Nathan Englander)
Little Kingdoms (Steven Millhauser)
Rabbit Is Rich (John Updike)
Rabbit, Run (John Updike)
To Say Nothing of the Dog (Connie Willis)
True at First Light (Ernest Hemingway)

Suicide

False Memory (Dean Koontz)

On Mystic Lake (Kristin Hannah)
The Pilot's Wife (Anita Shreve)

Superstition
Before I Say Good-bye (Mary Higgins Clark)
Blood and Chocolate (Annette Curtis Klause)
The Bride Price (Buchi Emecheta)
Hot Six (Janet Evanovich)
True at First Light (Ernest Hemingway)

Survival
Back Roads (Tawni O'Dell)
Bastard out of Carolina (Dorothy Allison)
"The Birds" (Daphne du Maurier)
The Blood Latitudes (William Harrison)
Empire of the Sun (J. G. Ballard)
Empress of the Splendid Season (Oscar Hijuelos)
For the Relief of Unbearable Urges (Nathan Englander)
The Perfect Storm (Sebastian Junger)
Timeline (Michael Crichton)
True at First Light (Ernest Hemingway)

Survival in the Wilderness
True at First Light (Ernest Hemingway)

Sympathy and Compassion
Blood and Chocolate (Annette Curtis Klause)
Fierce Invalids Home from Hot Climates (Tom Robbins)
The Mambo Kings Play Songs of Love (Oscar Hijuelos)
On Mystic Lake (Kristin Hannah)
Out of Africa (Isak Dinesan)
Rabbit Is Rich (John Updike)
To Say Nothing of the Dog (Connie Willis)
True at First Light (Ernest Hemingway)
"The Way We Live Now" (Susan Sontag)

Temperance
The Brethren (John Grisham)

Temptation
Blood and Chocolate (Annette Curtis Klause)
The Brethren (John Grisham)
Hugger Mugger (Robert B. Parker)
Rabbit Is Rich (John Updike)

Terrorism
The Blood Latitudes (William Harrison)
For the Relief of Unbearable Urges (Nathan Englander)
The Pilot's Wife (Anita Shreve)
True at First Light (Ernest Hemingway)

The Theater
Gertrude and Claudius (John Updike)
"The Knife Thrower" (Steven Millhauser)

Thinkers and Thinking
The Brethren (John Grisham)
Cradle and All (James Patterson)
Flaubert's Parrot (Julian Barnes)
For the Relief of Unbearable Urges (Nathan Englander)
The Human Stain (Philip Roth)
Jack Maggs (Peter Carey)
Rabbit Is Rich (John Updike)
The Reader (Bernhard Schlink)
Those Bones Are Not My Child (Toni Cade Bambara)
Timeline (Michael Crichton)

Time Travel
Timeline (Michael Crichton)
To Say Nothing of the Dog (Connie Willis)

Tolerance
To Say Nothing of the Dog (Connie Willis)
True at First Light (Ernest Hemingway)
"The Way We Live Now" (Susan Sontag)

Tradition
The Bride Price (Buchi Emecheta)
For the Relief of Unbearable Urges (Nathan Englander)
Gertrude and Claudius (John Updike)

Hot Six (Janet Evanovich)
The Mambo Kings Play Songs of Love (Oscar Hijuelos)
The Perfect Storm (Sebastian Junger)
To Say Nothing of the Dog (Connie Willis)
True at First Light (Ernest Hemingway)

Transportation
For the Relief of Unbearable Urges (Nathan Englander)
The Perfect Storm (Sebastian Junger)
The Pilot's Wife (Anita Shreve)
Rabbit Is Rich (John Updike)
Rabbit, Run (John Updike)
Timeline (Michael Crichton)
To Say Nothing of the Dog (Connie Willis)

Travel
For the Relief of Unbearable Urges (Nathan Englander)
Rabbit Is Rich (John Updike)
Timeline (Michael Crichton)
To Say Nothing of the Dog (Connie Willis)

Treachery
Before I Say Good-bye (Mary Higgins Clark)
Black Notice (Patricia Cornwell)
The Brethren (John Grisham)
For the Relief of Unbearable Urges (Nathan Englander)
Gertrude and Claudius (John Updike)
Hugger Mugger (Robert B. Parker)
The Human Stain (Philip Roth)
The Pilot's Wife (Anita Shreve)
Playback (Raymond Chandler)
Timeline (Michael Crichton)

Truth
Black Notice (Patricia Cornwell)
Blood and Chocolate (Annette Curtis Klause)
Cradle and All (James Patterson)
Fierce Invalids Home from Hot Climates (Tom Robbins)
Flaubert's Parrot (Julian Barnes)

A Gathering of Old Men (Ernest J. Gaines)
The Human Stain (Philip Roth)
The Pilot's Wife (Anita Shreve)
The Reader (Bernhard Schlink)
Those Bones Are Not My Child (Toni Cade Bambara)
Timeline (Michael Crichton)

Tyranny and Authoritarianism
The Blood Latitudes (William Harrison)
Empire of the Sun (J. G. Ballard)
For the Relief of Unbearable Urges (Nathan Englander)
Gertrude and Claudius (John Updike)
In the Time of the Butterflies (Julia Alvarez)
The Reader (Bernhard Schlink)

Underclass
Back Roads (Tawni O'Dell)
Bastard out of Carolina (Dorothy Allison)
"The Bride Comes to Yellow Sky" (Stephen Crane)
The Bride Price (Buchi Emecheta)
Empress of the Splendid Season (Oscar Hijuelos)
A Gathering of Old Men (Ernest J. Gaines)
Hot Six (Janet Evanovich)
Jack Maggs (Peter Carey)
Less Than Zero (Bret Easton Ellis)
The Reader (Bernhard Schlink)
Those Bones Are Not My Child (Toni Cade Bambara)
To Have and Have Not (Ernest Hemingway)
To Say Nothing of the Dog (Connie Willis)
The Women of Brewster Place (Gloria Naylor)

Universe
Fierce Invalids Home from Hot Climates (Tom Robbins)

Unrequited Love
Blood and Chocolate (Annette Curtis Klause)
Rabbit Is Rich (John Updike)

Upper Class

Before I Say Good-bye (Mary Higgins Clark)
False Memory (Dean Koontz)
Jack Maggs (Peter Carey)
Less Than Zero (Bret Easton Ellis)
Out of Africa (Isak Dinesan)
Southern Cross (Patricia Cornwell)
To Say Nothing of the Dog (Connie Willis)

Upper Middle Class

Jack Maggs (Peter Carey)
The Pilot's Wife (Anita Shreve)

Urban Blight

Hot Six (Janet Evanovich)
Jack Maggs (Peter Carey)
Playback (Raymond Chandler)
Those Bones Are Not My Child (Toni Cade Bambara)

Vanity

Empress of the Splendid Season (Oscar Hijuelos)
False Memory (Dean Koontz)
The Human Stain (Philip Roth)
White Oleander (Janet Fitch)

Vice and Virtue

Black Notice (Patricia Cornwell)
The Brethren (John Grisham)
Cradle and All (James Patterson)
Easy Prey (John Sandford)
Gertrude and Claudius (John Updike)
Hot Six (Janet Evanovich)
Hugger Mugger (Robert B. Parker)
Jack Maggs (Peter Carey)
Less Than Zero (Bret Easton Ellis)
The Mambo Kings Play Songs of Love (Oscar Hijuelos)
O Is for Outlaw (Sue Grafton)
Playback (Raymond Chandler)
Rabbit, Run (John Updike)
"The Way We Live Now" (Susan Sontag)
White Oleander (Janet Fitch)

Victim and Victimization

Ashes to Ashes (Tami Hoag)
Back Roads (Tawni O'Dell)
Bastard out of Carolina (Dorothy Allison)
"The Birds" (Daphne du Maurier)
Black Notice (Patricia Cornwell)
Blood and Chocolate (Annette Curtis Klause)
The Blood Latitudes (William Harrison)
The Brethren (John Grisham)
The Bride Price (Buchi Emecheta)
Cradle and All (James Patterson)
Easy Prey (John Sandford)
Empire of the Sun (J. G. Ballard)
False Memory (Dean Koontz)
For the Relief of Unbearable Urges (Nathan Englander)
A Gathering of Old Men (Ernest J. Gaines)
Gertrude and Claudius (John Updike)
The Human Stain (Philip Roth)
In the Time of the Butterflies (Julia Alvarez)
Jack Maggs (Peter Carey)
Less Than Zero (Bret Easton Ellis)
The Pilot's Wife (Anita Shreve)
Rabbit, Run (John Updike)
The Reader (Bernhard Schlink)
Southern Cross (Patricia Cornwell)
Those Bones Are Not My Child (Toni Cade Bambara)
Timeline (Michael Crichton)
White Oleander (Janet Fitch)
The Women of Brewster Place (Gloria Naylor)

Victorian Age

Jack Maggs (Peter Carey)
To Say Nothing of the Dog (Connie Willis)

Victory and Defeat

The Brethren (John Grisham)
"The Bride Comes to Yellow Sky" (Stephen Crane)
Cradle and All (James Patterson)

Vietnam War

O Is for Outlaw (Sue Grafton)

Vigilantes and Outlaws

The Blood Latitudes (William Harrison)
Hot Six (Janet Evanovich)

Villains, Rakes, and Rogues

Ashes to Ashes (Tami Hoag)
Bastard out of Carolina (Dorothy Allison)
Before I Say Good-bye (Mary
    Higgins Clark)
Black Notice (Patricia Cornwell)
Blood and Chocolate (Annette Curtis
    Klause)
The Blood Latitudes (William Harrison)
The Brethren (John Grisham)
"The Bride Comes to Yellow Sky"
    (Stephen Crane)
False Memory (Dean Koontz)
Fierce Invalids Home from Hot Climates
    (Tom Robbins)
A Gathering of Old Men (Ernest J. Gaines)
Gertrude and Claudius (John Updike)
Hot Six (Janet Evanovich)
The Human Stain (Philip Roth)
In the Time of the Butterflies (Julia Alvarez)
Less Than Zero (Bret Easton Ellis)
O Is for Outlaw (Sue Grafton)
The Pilot's Wife (Anita Shreve)
The Reader (Bernhard Schlink)
Southern Cross (Patricia Cornwell)
Those Bones Are Not My Child (Toni Cade
    Bambara)
Timeline (Michael Crichton)
White Oleander (Janet Fitch)
The Women of Brewster Place
    (Gloria Naylor)

Villainy

Ashes to Ashes (Tami Hoag)
Back Roads (Tawni O'Dell)
Bastard out of Carolina (Dorothy Allison)
Before I Say Good-bye (Mary
    Higgins Clark)
Black Notice (Patricia Cornwell)
The Blood Latitudes (William Harrison)
The Brethren (John Grisham)
Easy Prey (John Sandford)

False Memory (Dean Koontz)
A Gathering of Old Men (Ernest J. Gaines)
Gertrude and Claudius (John Updike)
Hot Six (Janet Evanovich)
The Human Stain (Philip Roth)
In the Time of the Butterflies (Julia Alvarez)
Less Than Zero (Bret Easton Ellis)
The Pilot's Wife (Anita Shreve)
Playback (Raymond Chandler)
Southern Cross (Patricia Cornwell)
Those Bones Are Not My Child (Toni Cade
    Bambara)
Timeline (Michael Crichton)

Violence

Ashes to Ashes (Tami Hoag)
Back Roads (Tawni O'Dell)
Bastard out of Carolina (Dorothy Allison)
Before I Say Good-bye (Mary
    Higgins Clark)
"The Birds" (Daphne du Maurier)
Black Notice (Patricia Cornwell)
Blood and Chocolate (Annette Curtis
    Klause)
The Blood Latitudes (William Harrison)
Easy Prey (John Sandford)
Empire of the Sun (J. G. Ballard)
False Memory (Dean Koontz)
For the Relief of Unbearable Urges (Nathan
    Englander)
A Gathering of Old Men (Ernest J. Gaines)
Hot Six (Janet Evanovich)
How the Dead Live (Will Self)
The Human Stain (Philip Roth)
In the Time of the Butterflies (Julia Alvarez)
"The Knife Thrower" (Steven Millhauser)
On Mystic Lake (Kristin Hannah)
The Perfect Storm (Sebastian Junger)
The Pilot's Wife (Anita Shreve)
Playback (Raymond Chandler)
Southern Cross (Patricia Cornwell)
Those Bones Are Not My Child (Toni Cade
    Bambara)
To Have and Have Not (Ernest
    Hemingway)
True at First Light (Ernest Hemingway)
White Oleander (Janet Fitch)

The Women of Brewster Place
(Gloria Naylor)

Virginity and Chastity
The Bride Price (Buchi Emecheta)
Cradle and All (James Patterson)
Gertrude and Claudius (John Updike)
The Pilot's Wife (Anita Shreve)

Vitality
Blood and Chocolate (Annette Curtis Klause)
Fierce Invalids Home from Hot Climates (Tom Robbins)
The Human Stain (Philip Roth)
True at First Light (Ernest Hemingway)

Vulgarity
Ashes to Ashes (Tami Hoag)
Bastard out of Carolina (Dorothy Allison)
The Blood Latitudes (William Harrison)
Easy Prey (John Sandford)
Less Than Zero (Bret Easton Ellis)
Southern Cross (Patricia Cornwell)

War
The Blood Latitudes (William Harrison)
Empire of the Sun (J. G. Ballard)
For the Relief of Unbearable Urges (Nathan Englander)
Gertrude and Claudius (John Updike)
The Reader (Bernhard Schlink)

Weather
The Perfect Storm (Sebastian Junger)

Western Civilization
Gertrude and Claudius (John Updike)

Wisdom
Fierce Invalids Home from Hot Climates (Tom Robbins)

Witchcraft and Magic
Blood and Chocolate (Annette Curtis Klause)

The Bride Price (Buchi Emecheta)
Hot Six (Janet Evanovich)

Womanhood
Bastard out of Carolina (Dorothy Allison)
The Bride Price (Buchi Emecheta)
To Say Nothing of the Dog (Connie Willis)
White Oleander (Janet Fitch)

Women's Rights
Bastard out of Carolina (Dorothy Allison)
Before I Say Good-bye (Mary Higgins Clark)
Black Notice (Patricia Cornwell)
The Bride Price (Buchi Emecheta)
Gertrude and Claudius (John Updike)
In the Time of the Butterflies (Julia Alvarez)
The Mambo Kings Play Songs of Love (Oscar Hijuelos)
O Is for Outlaw (Sue Grafton)
On Mystic Lake (Kristin Hannah)
Those Bones Are Not My Child (Toni Cade Bambara)
To Say Nothing of the Dog (Connie Willis)
The Women of Brewster Place (Gloria Naylor)

Work and Play
Easy Prey (John Sandford)
Empress of the Splendid Season (Oscar Hijuelos)
Fierce Invalids Home from Hot Climates (Tom Robbins)
For the Relief of Unbearable Urges (Nathan Englander)
Gertrude and Claudius (John Updike)
Hot Six (Janet Evanovich)
Little Kingdoms (Steven Millhauser)
The Mambo Kings Play Songs of Love (Oscar Hijuelos)
On Mystic Lake (Kristin Hannah)
Out of Africa (Isak Dinesan)
The Perfect Storm (Sebastian Junger)
Rabbit Is Rich (John Updike)
To Say Nothing of the Dog (Connie Willis)
True at First Light (Ernest Hemingway)

Working Class

Back Roads (Tawni O'Dell)
Bastard out of Carolina (Dorothy Allison)
The Bride Price (Buchi Emecheta)
Empress of the Splendid Season (Oscar
  Hijuelos)
The Perfect Storm (Sebastian Junger)
The Reader (Bernhard Schlink)
Those Bones Are Not My Child (Toni Cade
  Bambara)
To Have and Have Not (Ernest
  Hemingway)
To Say Nothing of the Dog (Connie Willis)

World War II

Empire of the Sun (J. G. Ballard)
For the Relief of Unbearable Urges (Nathan
  Englander)
The Reader (Bernhard Schlink)

Yearning

Blood and Chocolate (Annette Curtis
  Klause)

Empress of the Splendid Season (Oscar
  Hijuelos)
Rabbit, Run (John Updike)

Zeitgeist

Ashes to Ashes (Tami Hoag)
Back Roads (Tawni O'Dell)
Black Notice (Patricia Cornwell)
The Blood Latitudes (William Harrison)
The Brethren (John Grisham)
Empire of the Sun (J. G. Ballard)
A Gathering of Old Men (Ernest J. Gaines)
In the Time of the Butterflies (Julia Alvarez)
Less Than Zero (Bret Easton Ellis)
Out of Africa (Isak Dinesan)
Rabbit Is Rich (John Updike)
Southern Cross (Patricia Cornwell)
Those Bones Are Not My Child (Toni Cade
  Bambara)

Zionism

For the Relief of Unbearable Urges (Nathan
  Englander)

CUMULATIVE INDEX TO
AUTHORS WITH ANALYZED TITLES

VOLUMES 1–14

◆

Achebe, Chinua, 1:1 (Bio, v. 1)
Anthills of the Savannah, 1:173
Arrow of God, 1:203
Man of the People, A, 10:6019
No Longer at Ease, 7:4186
Things Fall Apart, 7:4180

Adams, Alice
Caroline's Daughters, 9:5248
Medicine Men, 10:6069
Superior Women, 11:6454

Adams, Richard, 1:15 (Bio, v. 1)
Maia, 7:3807
Plague Dogs, The, 8:4549
Shardik, 7:3805
Watership Down, 8:4547

Alcott, Louisa May, 1:19 (Bio, v. 1)
Behind a Mask: or, A Woman's Power, 1:313
Inheritance, The, 10:5721
Little Women, 4:2444
Little Women series, 4:2452
Work: A Story of Experience, 11:6717

Alexander, Lloyd, 1:27 (Bio, v. 1)
Black Cauldron, The, 1:389
Book of Three, The, 1:485
Castle of Llyr, 1:390
High King, The, 1:391
Taran Wanderer, 1:391

Algren, Nelson, 1:30 (Bio, v. 1)
Man with the Golden Arm, The, 5:2637

Neon Wilderness, The, 5:2924

Allende, Isabel
House of the Spirits, The, 12:157

Allison, Dorothy
Bastard out of Carolina, 14:21

Alther, Lisa, 1:34 (Bio, v. 1)
Bedrock, 1:295
Five Minutes in Heaven, 3:1460
Kinflicks, 4:2282
Other Women, 4:2283

Alvarez, Julia
How the Garcia Girls Lost Their Accents, 13:203
In the Time of the Butterflies, 14:237

Amis, Kingsley, 1:38 (Bio, v. 1)
Difficulties with Girls, 2:1104
Folks That Live on the Hill, The, 3:1484
Lucky Jim, 5:2578

Anderson, Poul, 1:43 (Bio, v. 1)
Game of Empire, The, 3:1617
Harvest of Stars, 10:5646
Queen of Air and Darkness, The, 6:3409
Trader to the Stars, 7:4329

Anderson, Poul and Karen Anderson
Roma Mater, 11:6297
Avatar, The, 9:5120

Anderson, Sherwood, 1:48 (Bio, v. 1)
Dark Laughter, 2:988
Winesburg, Ohio, 8:4681

Angelou, Maya, 1:53 (Bio, v. 1)
All God's Children Need Traveling Shoes, 1:94
I Know Why the Caged Bird Sings, 4:2059

Archer, Jeffrey, 1:59 (Bio, v. 1)
Kane and Abel, 4:2241
Prodigal Daughter, The, 4:2243

Arnow, Harriette, 1:62 (Bio, v. 1)
Dollmaker, The, 2:1145
Hunter's Horn, 2:1149
Mountain Path, 2:1149

Asimov, Isaac, 1:67 (Bio, v. 1)
Forward the Foundation, 3:1509
Foundation Trilogy, The, 3:1522
I, Robot, 4:2063

Atwood, Margaret, 1:74 (Bio, v. 1)
Alias Grace, 9:5047
Bodily Harm, 4:1843
Cat's Eye, 2:687
Dancing Girls and Other Stories, 4:2319
Edible Woman, The, 9:5423
Handmaid's Tale, The, 4:1838
Lady Oracle, 4:2316
Robber Bride, The, 6:3612
Surfacing, 11:6462
Wilderness Tips, 11:6688

Auel, Jean, 1:83 (Bio, v. 1)
Clan of the Cave Bear, The, 2:821
Mammoth Hunters, The, 5:2626
Plains of Passage, The, 6:3275

Austen, Jane
Emma, 12:91
Pride and Prejudice, 12:335

Bach, Richard, 1:87 (Bio, v. 1)
Jonathan Livingston Seagull, 4:2203

Bachman, Richard (see King, Stephen)

Baldwin, Alex (Griffin, W. E. B.)
Last Heroes, The, 10:5830

Baldwin, James, 1:89 (Bio, v. 1)
Another Country, 3:1696
Go Tell It on the Mountain, 3:1692

Ballard, J. G.
Empire of the Sun, 14:115

Bambara, Toni Cade
Those Bones Are Not My Child, 14:385

Barnes, Julian
Flaubert's Parrot, 14:155

Barker, Clive, 1:94 (Bio, v. 1)
Clive Barker's Books of Blood, 2:840
Damnation Game, The, 2:985

Barth, John, 1:97 (Bio, v. 1)
Floating Opera, The, 3:1472
Giles Goat-Boy, 3:1673
Sabbatical, 7:4244
Sot-Weed Factor, The, 7:3968
Tidewater Tales, The, 7:4238

Barthelme, Donald, 1:107 (Bio, v. 1)
Dead Father, The, 2:1016
Paradise, 6:3195
Snow White, 7:3915

Baum, L. Frank
Marvelous Land of Oz, The, 12:253

Beagle, Peter, 1:111 (Bio, v. 1)
Fine and Private Place, A, 3:1422
Folk of the Air, The, 3:1481
Innkeeper's Song, The, 4:2368
Last Unicorn, The, 4:2366, 10:5842

Bear, Greg, 1:114 (Bio, v. 1)
Blood Music, 1:421
Eon, 3:1255
Moving Mars, 5:2825

Beattie, Ann, 1:118 (Bio, v. 1)
Chilly Scenes of Winter, 2:748
Falling in Place, 6:3256
"Janus," 13:223
Picturing Will, 6:3251, 8:4574
What Was Mine, 8:4570
Where You'll Find Me, 6:3256

Beauvoir, Simone de, 1:129 (Bio, v. 1)
All Men Are Mortal, 8:4700
Blood of Others, The, 8:4699
Les Belles Images, 1:332
Mandarins, The, 5:2651
Second Sex, The, 8:4700
She Came to Stay, 8:4699
Woman Destroyed, A, 8:4698

Bell, Madison Smartt, 1:135 (Bio, v. 1)
Save Me, Joe Louis, 6:3707
Waiting for the End of the World, 8:4485
Washington Square Ensemble, The, 8:4526

Bellow, Saul, 1:138 (Bio, v. 1)
Adventures of Augie March, The, 1:13
Herzog, 4:1903
Humboldt's Gift, 4:2034
More Die of Heartbreak, 10:6092
Seize the Day, 13:325

Benchley, Peter, 1:144 (Bio, v. 1)
Beast, 9:5157
Girl of the Sea Cortez, The, 4:2189
Jaws, 4:2187
Q Clearance, 6:3405
White Shark, 8:4654

Benford, Gregory, 1:148 (Bio, v. 1)
Furious Gulf, 3:1597
Great Sky River, 3:1791
In the Ocean of Night, 4:2113
Timescape, 11:6574

Berger, Thomas, 1:151 (Bio, v. 1)
Being Invisible, 9:5171
Houseguest, The, 10:5671
Little Big Man, 4:2431
Meeting Evil, 5:2703

Neighbors, 10:6103
Reinhart's Women, 6:3525
Return of Little Big Man, The, 12:345

Bester, Alfred, 1:159 (Bio, v. 1)
"Adam and Eve," 7:4017
Demolished Man, The, 2:1076
"Oddly and Id," 7:4017
Stars My Destination, The, 7:4014

Binchy, Maeve, 1:165 (Bio, v. 1)
Circle of Friends, 2:790
Copper Beech, The, 2:912
Evening Class , 9:5451
Glass Lake, The, 9:5579
This Year It Will Be Different: And Other Stories, 11:6552

Blasco Ibáñez, Vincente, 1:168 (Bio, v. 1)
Blood and Sand, 1:418
Four Horsemen of the Apocalypse, The, 3:1529
Torrent, The, 7:4320

Blatty, William Peter
Exorcist, The, 9:5472
Legion, 10:5870
Ninth Configuration, The, 10:6117

Blish, James, 1:172 (Bio, v. 1)
Black Easter, 2:650
Case of Conscience, A, 2:647
Cities in Flight series, 2:799
    Earthman Come Home, 2:799
    Life for the Stars, A, 2:799
    They Shall Have Stars, 2:799
    Triumph of Time, The, 2:799
Day After Judgment, The, 2:651
Mirabilis, 2:650

Block, Lawrence, 1:177 (Bio, v. 1)
Burglar Who Studied Spinoza, The, 1:559
Eight Million Ways to Die, 9:5429
Even the Wicked, 9:5445
Out on the Cutting Edge, 7:4231
Thief Who Couldn't Sleep, The, 7:4172
Ticket to the Boneyard, A, 7:4230

Böll, Heinrich, 1:181 (Bio, v. 1)
Clown, The, 2:856
Group Portrait with Lady, 3:1817

Borges, Jorge Luis, 1:185 (Bio, v. 1)
Doctor Brodie's Report, 2:1120
"Garden of Forking Paths, The," 13:157
Labyrinths: Selected Stories and Other Writings, 4:2304

Boyle, T. Coraghessan, 1:189 (Bio, v. 1)
Road to Wellville, The, 6:3607
Water Music, 8:4542
World's End, 8:4725

Bradbury, Ray, 1:193 (Bio, v. 1)
Graveyard For Lunatics, A, 3:1762
Fahrenheit 451, 3:1313
Martian Chronicles, The, 5:2676
Quicker Than the Eye, 10:6236
Something Wicked This Way Comes, 7:3935

Bradley, Marion Zimmer, 1:201
(Bio, v. 1)
City of Sorcery, 2:817
Firebrand, The, 9:5516
Forest House, The, 3:1494
Heirs of Hammerfell, The, 4:1888
Heritage of Hastur, 10:5661
Lady of Avalon, 10:5808
Lady of the Trillium, 4:2311
Thendara House, 11:6516

Bradshaw, Gillian, 1:206 (Bio, v. 1)
Beacon at Alexandria, The, 1:274
Bearkeeper's Daughter, The, 1:284
Hawk of May, 4:1872
In Winter's Shadow, 4:1875
Kingdom of Summer, 4:1874

Brand, Max, 1:208 (Bio, v. 1)
Destry Rides Again, 2:1083
Montana Rides Again, 5:2792
Singing Guns, 7:3876

Braun, Lilian Jackson, 1:219 (Bio, v. 1)
Cat Who Blew the Whistle, The, 2:668

Cat Who Saw Red, The, 9:5254
Cat Who Turned On and Off, The, 2:667

Brautigan, Richard, 1:222 (Bio, v. 1)
Confederate General from Big Sur, 2:898
Trout Fishing in America, 8:4359

Brontë, Charlotte
Shirley, 11:6354
Villette, 11:6651
Jane Eyre, 10:5753

Brontë, Emily, 1:228 (Bio, v. 1)
Wuthering Heights, 8:4733

Brown, Rita Mae, 1:234 (Bio, v. 1)
Bingo, 1:380
Dolley, 2:1140
Rubyfruit Jungle, 6:3650
Six of One, 1:382, 6:3652
Venus Envy, 11:6634

Buck, Pearl, 1:239 (Bio, v. 1)
Dragon Seed, 3:1197
House of Earth trilogy, 4:2020
    Good Earth, The, 4:2020
    House Divided, A, 4:2020
    Sons, 4:2020

Buckley, William F., 1:244 (Bio, v. 1)
High Jinx, 6:3719
Marco Polo, If You Can, 6:3718
Mongoose R.I.P., 5:2789
Saving the Queen, 6:3715
See You Later Alligator, 6:3719
Story of Henri Tod, 6:3719
Who's on First, 6:3718

Buechner, Frederick, 1:248 (Bio, v. 1)
Alphabet of Grace, The, 3:1715
Book of Bebb, The, 1:475
    Lion Country, 1:475
    Love Feast, 1:475
    Open Heart, 1:475
    Treasure Hunt, 1:475
Godric, 3:1713
Peculiar Treasures, 3:1714
Sacred Journey, The, 3:1715

Telling the Truth, 3:1715
Wishful Thinking, 3:1714

Buffett, Jimmy, 1:253 (Bio, v. 1)
Tales from Margaritaville, 8:4608
Where Is Joe Merchant?, 8:4611

Bulgakov, Mikhail, 1:256 (Bio, v. 1)
Master and Margarita, The, 5:2684

Burns, Olive Ann, 1:261 (Bio, v. 1)
Cold Sassy Tree, 2:867
Leaving Cold Sassy, 2:871

Burroughs, Edgar Rice, 1:265 (Bio, v. 1)
Land That Time Forgot, The, 4:2329
Princess of Mars, A, 6:3369
Tarzan of the Apes, 7:4120

Burroughs, William S., 1:271 (Bio, v. 1)
Naked Lunch, 5:2903
Nova Express, 5:2998
Western Lands, The, 8:4557

Butler, Jack, 1:279 (Bio, v. 1)
Dreamer, 9:5401
Jujitsu for Christ, 4:2215
*Living in Little Rock with Miss Little
    Rock*, 5:2463
Nightshade, 5:2955

Butler, Octavia E., 1:283 (Bio, v. 1)
Kindred, 4:2278
Parable of the Sower, 6:3191
Wild Seed, 8:4663

Butler, Robert Olen, 1:287 (Bio, v. 1)
Alleys of Eden, The, 1:119
Deuce, The, 9:5391
*Good Scent from a Strange Mountain,
    A* 1746
On Distant Ground, 10:6139
Tabloid Dreams, 11:6470
They Whisper, 7:4166

Byatt, A. S., 1:293 (Bio, v. 1)
Angels & Insects, 1:142

Babel Tower, 9:5127
Possession, 1:145, 6:3315
Virgin in the Garden, The, 8:4472

Cain, James M., 1:296 (Bio, v. 1)
Double Indemnity, 2:1185
Postman Always Rings Twice, The, 6:3321

Caldwell, Erskine, 1:301 (Bio, v. 1)
God's Little Acre, 3:1717
Journeyman, 3:1721
Tobacco Road, 3:1725

Caldwell, Taylor, 1:307 (Bio, v. 1)
Captains and the Kings, 2:631
Dear and Glorious Physician, 2:1025

Camus, Albert, 1:309 (Bio, v. 1)
Fall, The, 3:1324
Plague, The, 6:3272
Stranger, The, 7:4059

Čapek, Karel
War with the Newts, 13:411

Capote, Truman, 1:314 (Bio, v. 1)
Breakfast at Tiffany's, 9:5199
Grass Harp, The, 9:5621
In Cold Blood, 4:2092
Other Voices, Other Rooms, 10:6165

Card, Orson Scott, 1:321 (Bio, v. 1)
Ender's Game, 3:1242
Lost Boys, 5:2536
Seventh Son, 7:3787

Carey, Peter
Jack Maggs, 14:245

Carré, John (see Le Carré, John)

Carver, Raymond, 1:329 (Bio, v. 1)
Cathedral, 2:708
*What We Talk About When We Talk About
    Love*, 8:4576
Where I'm Calling From, 8:4608

Cather, Willa, 1:337 (Bio, v. 1)
My Ántonia, 5:2859
O Pioneers!, 5:3007

Chandler, Raymond, 1:343 (Bio, v. 1)
Big Sleep, The, 1:366
Farewell, My Lovely, 3:1361
Playback, 14:327

Charnas, Suzy McKee, 1:352 (Bio, v. 1)
Dorothea Dreams, 2:1177
Furies, The, 3:1593
Motherlines, 8:4507
Walk to the End of the World, 8:4506

Cheever, John, 1:355 (Bio, v. 1)
Cheever: John Cheever's Short Stories, 2:733
Falconer, 3:1322
Stories of John Cheever, The, 2:733
Wapshot Chronicle, The, 8:4509
Wapshot Scandal, The, 8:4511

Cherryh, C. J., 1:360 (Bio, v. 1)
Cyteen, 2:973
Faded Sun trilogy, The, 3:1305
   Faded Sun: Kesrith,The, 3:1305
   Faded Sun: Kutath, The, 3:1305
   Faded Sun: Shon'jir,The, 3:1305
Foreigner, The, 2:975
Inheritor, 2:976

Chopin, Kate
Awakening, The, 13:19

Christie, Agatha, 1:365 (Bio, v. 1)
Murder of Roger Ackroyd, The, 5:2842
Moving Finger, The, 5:2842
Ten Little Indians, 13:367

Cisneros, Sandra
House on Mango Street, The, 12:169
"Woman Hollering Creek," 13:445

Clancy, Tom, 1:371 (Bio, v. 1)
Cardinal of the Kremlin, The, 4:2040, 9:5243
Clear and Present Danger, 2:824
Debt of Honor, 4:2041

Executive Orders, 9:5459
Hunt for Red October, The, 4:2036
Patriot Games, 10:6206
Red Storm Rising, 6:3514
Sum of All Fears, The, 4:2041

Clark, Mary Higgins, 1:375 (Bio, v. 1)
Before I Say Good-bye, 14:29
Crime of Passion, A, 9:5337
Let Me Call You Sweetheart, 10:5881
*They All Ran After the President's
   Wife,* 11:6531
We'll Meet Again, 13:421
Where Are the Children?, 8:4600

Clarke, Arthur C., 1:381 (Bio, v. 1)
Childhood's End, 9:5286
City and the Stars, 8:4394
Cradle, 2:936
Ghost from the Grand Banks, The, 9:5563
Hammer of God, The, 4:1831
Imperial Earth, 8:4394
Rendezvous with Rama, 8:4394
2001: A Space Odyssey, 8:4392
2010: Odyssey Two, 8:4394
2061: Odyssey Three, 11:6601
3001: The Final Odyssey, 11:6558

Clarke, Arthur C. and Gentry Lee
Garden of Rama, The, 9:5543

Clavell, James, 1:388 (Bio, v. 1)
King Rat, 4:2295
Noble House, 7:3855
Shogun, 7:3853
Taipan, 7:3855
Whirlwind, 8:4622

Cleage, Pearl
*What Looks Like Crazy on an Ordinary
   Day,* 13:431

Clemens, Samuel Langhorne (see
   Twain, Mark)

Colette, 1:391 (Bio, v. 1)
Chéri, 2:736

Gigi, 3:1669
Last of Chéri, The, 2:736
Vagabond, The, 8:4437

Collins, Jackie, 1:398 (Bio, v. 1)
Hollywood Husbands, 4:1941
Hollywood Kids, 10:5666
Hollywood Wives, 4:1945
Love Killers, The, 5:2552
Rock Star, 6:3632

Conan Doyle, Arthur, 1:401 (Bio, v. 1)
"Adventure of the Speckled Band,
    The," 1:8
Hound of the Baskervilles, The, 4:1986
Land of Mist, The, 5:2542
Lost World, The, 5:2540
"Lot No. 249," 13:259
Poison Belt, The, 5:2542
Professor Challenger Stories, The, 5:2542

Condon, Richard, 1:407 (Bio, v. 1)
Emperor of America, 3:1237
Manchurian Candidate, The, 5:2648
Prizzi's Honor, 6:3389

Conrad, Joseph, 1:410 (Bio, v. 1)
Chance, 2:720
Heart of Darkness, 4:1883
"Il Conde," 10:5696
Lord Jim, 10:5954
Nostromo, 5:2990
"Outpost of Progress," 10:6186
Secret Agent, The, 11:6346
"Secret Sharer, The," 7:3756
Typhoon, 11:6606
Victory, 11:6640
"Youth," 11:6734 , 4:1866

Conroy, Pat, 1:420 (Bio, v. 1)
Beach Music, 1:265
Great Santini, The, 3:1782, 6:3363
Prince of Tides, The, 6:3356
Water Is Wide, The, 8:4535

Constantine, J. C., 1:424 (Bio, v. 1)
Always a Body Trade, 8:4431

Blank Page, The, 8:4430
Fix Like This, A, 8:4431
Joey's Case, 4:2198
Man Who Liked to Look at Himself,
    The, 8:4430
Man Who Liked Slow Tomatoes, The, 8:4431
Rocksburg Railroad Murders, The, 8:4430
Upon Some Midnights Clear, 8:4426

Cook, Robin, 1:428 (Bio, v. 1)
Coma, 2:886
Godplayer, 2:888
Harmful Intent, 4:1847
Mortal Fear, 4:1848
Mutation, 5:2857
Outbreak, 2:888

Cooper, James Fenimore, 1:432 (Bio, v. 1)
Deerslayer, The, 2:1061
Leatherstocking Tales, The, 6:3202
Pathfinder, The, 6:3202

Coover, Robert, 1:436 (Bio, v. 1)
Gerald's Party, 3:1659
Origin of the Brunists, The, 6:3130
Public Burning, The, 6:3401
Universal Baseball Association, The, 8:4412

Cormier, Robert
Tenderness, 11:6491

Cornwell, Patricia Daniels, 1:443
    (Bio, v. 1)
All That Remains, 1:457
Black Notice, 14:45
Body Farm, The, 1:451
Body of Evidence, 1:461
From Potter's Field, 1:458
Postmortem, 6:3325
Southern Cross, 14:365
Time for Remembering, A, 6:3331
Unnatural Exposure, 11:6613

Cortázar, Julio, 1:449 (Bio, v. 1)
"Axolotl," 13:27
Hopscotch, 4:1972
Manual for Manuel, A, 5:2671

Cozzens, James Gould, 1:454 (Bio, v. 1)
By Love Possessed, 2:574
Guard of Honor, 2:577

Crane, Stephen, 1:457 (Bio, v. 1)
"Blue Hotel, The," 9:5187
"Bride Comes to Yellow Sky, The," 14:79
Maggie: A Girl of the Street's, 10:5998
"Open Boat, The," 10:6157
Red Badge of Courage, The, 6:3475
"Veteran, The," 6:3479

Crews, Harry, 1:464 (Bio, v. 1)
Feast of Snakes, A, 3:1392
Knockout Artist, The, 4:2300
Naked in Garden Hills, 5:2899

Crichton, Michael, 1:468 (Bio, v. 1)
Airframe, 9:5031
Andromeda Strain, The, 9:5082
Jurassic Park, 4:2230
Lost World, The, 10:5962
Sphere, 7:3978
Timeline, 14:397

Cronin, A. J., 1:480 (Bio, v. 1)
Citadel, The, 4:2257
Hatter's Castle, 4:2258
Keys of the Kingdom, The, 4:2255

Cross, Amanda, 1:482 (Bio, v. 1)
Death in a Tenured Position, 2:1031
Imperfect Spy, An, 4:2087
In the Last Analysis, 10:5709
No Word From Winifred, 5:2983
Players Come Again, The, 6:3282

Crowley, John, 1:486 (Bio, v. 1)
Aegypt, 1:33
Little, Big, 4:2427
Love & Sleep, 1:35, 5:2562
Novelty, 5:3004

Dahl, Roald, 1:489 (Bio, v. 1)
*Ah, Sweet Mystery of Life: The Country
    Stories of Roald Dahl*, 13:11
Charlie and the Chocolate Factory, 2:727

"Lamb to the Slaughter," 4:2326
My Uncle Oswald, 5:2885

Danticat, Edwidge
Breath, Eyes, Memory, 13:55
"Children of the Sea," 13:73

Davies, Robertson, 1:495 (Bio, v. 1)
Fifth Business, 3:1409
Mixture of Frailties, A, 5:2770
What's Bred in the Bone, 8:4579

De Beauvoir, Simone (see Beauvoir,
    Simone de)

De Camp, L. Sprague, 1:500 (Bio, v. 1)
Goblin Tower, The, 3:1698
Honorable Barbarian, The, 4:1968
Lest Darkness Fall, 4:2397
Rogue Queen, 11:6292
"Satanic Illusion, The," 11:6339

**De Camp, L. Sprague and Catherine
    Crook**
Stones of Nomuru, The, 11:6442

Deighton, Len, 1:505 (Bio, v. 1)
Faith, 7:3993
Funeral in Berlin, 3:1584
Hope, 7:3993
Ipcress File, The, 4:2153
Spy Line, 7:3989

Delany, Samuel R., 1:510 (Bio, v. 1)
Babel-17, 2:1102
Bridge of Lost Desire, The, 1:521
Dhalgren, 2:1098
Einstein Intersection, The, 2:1102
Triton, 2:1102

DeLillo, Don, 1:515 (Bio, v. 1)
Endzone, 3:1248
Great Jones Street, 3:1779
Running Dog, 3:1250
Underworld, 12:445
White Noise, 8:4651

Derleth, August, 1:520 (Bio, v. 1)
Lonesome Places, 5:2494
No Future for Luana, 5:2974
Wind Over Wisconsin, 8:4668

Dick, Philip K., 1:524 (Bio, v. 1)
"Faith of Our Fathers," 5:2635
Man in the High Castle, The, 5:2633
Martian Time-Slip, 5:2679
Three Stigmas of Palmer Eldritch, The, 5:2676

Dickey, James, 1:532 (Bio, v. 1)
Alnilam, 1:124
Deliverance, 2:1071
To The White Sea, 7:4294

Didion, Joan
Democracy, 13:99

Dinesen, Isak
Out of Africa, 14:301

Disch, Thomas M., 1:537 (Bio, v. 1)
Silver Pillow, The, 3868
Businessman: A Tale of Terror, The, 9:5223
Genocides, The, 3:1644
M.D.: A Horror Story, The 10:5991
On Wings of Song, 5:3072

Doctorow, E. L., 1:541 (Bio, v. 1)
Billy Bathgate, 1:376
City of God, 13:81
Lives of the Poets, 8:4553
Ragtime, 6:3431, 13:303
Waterworks, The, 8:4551
World's Fair, 11:6730

Donaldson, Stephen R., 1:545 (Bio, v. 1)
Chronicles of Thomas Covenant Unbeliever, The, 2:780
   Lord Foul's Bane, 2:780
   Illearth War, The, 2:780
   Power That Preserves, The, 2:780

Donleavy, J. P., 1:548 (Bio, v. 1)
Fairy Tale of New York, A, 3:1317

Ginger Man, The, 3:1676
Lady Who Liked Clean Restrooms, The, 10:5816

Dos Passos, John, 1:553 (Bio, v. 1)
Adventures of a Young Man, 9:5021
Big Money, The, 1:353
Manhattan Transfer, 5:2658
Midcentury, 5:2741
Nineteen, Nineteen, 1:353

Dostoevsky, Fyodor
Brothers Karamazov, The, 9:5206
Crime and Punishment, 9:5327
Possessed, The, 10:6212

Doyle, Arthur Conan (see Conan Doyle, Arthur)

Dresser, Davis (see Halliday, Brett)

du Maurier, Daphne, 1:561 (Bio, v. 1)
"Birds, The," 14:37
"Don't Look Now," 13:109
My Cousin Rachel, 5:2870
Rebecca, 6:3458

Duras, Marguerite, 1:565 (Bio, v. 1)
Lover, The, 6:3730
Moderato Cantabile, 5:2781
Sea Wall, The, 6:3730
Square, The, 7:3999
War, 8:4513

Durrell, Lawrence, 1:569 (Bio, v. 1)
Alexandria Quartet, The, 1:80
   Balthazar, 1:80
   Clea, 1:80
   Justine, 1:80
   Mountolive, 1:80
Avignon Quintet, The, 1:247
   Constance: Or Solitary Practices, 1:247
   Livia: Or Buried Alive, 1:247
   Monsieur, 1:247
   Quinx: Or The Ripper's Tale, 1:247
   Sebastian: Or Ruling Passions, 1:247
Revolt of Aphrodite, The, 6:3539
   Nunquam, 6:3539
   Tunc, 6:3539

Eco, Umberto, 1:576 (Bio, v. 1)
Foucault's Pendulum, 3:1516
Island of the Day Before, The, 4:2179
Name of The Rose, The, 5:2911

Elkin, Stanley, 1:578 (Bio, v. 1)
Bad Man, A, 1:254
George Mills, 3:1653
Stanley Elkin's The Magic Kingdom, 7:4006

Ellis, Bret Easton
Less Than Zero, 14:261

Ellison, Harlan, 1:585 (Bio, v. 1)
Adrift Just Off the Islets of Langerhans,
"I Have No Mouth and I Must
    Scream," 4:2050
Memos from Purgatory, 6:3654
Rumble, 6:3654

Ellison, Ralph, 1:592 (Bio, v. 1)
Flying Home and Other Stories, 9:5522
Invisible Man, 4:2143
Juneteenth, 12:211

Emecheta, Buchi
Bride Price, The, 14:95

Englander, Nathan
For the Relief of Unbearable Urges, 14:163

Erdrich, Louise, 1:599 (Bio, v. 1)
Antelope Wife, The, 12:17
Beet Queen, The, 1:301
Bingo Palace, The, 1:384
Love Medicine, 5:2555
Tales of Burning Love, 5:2560, 11:6482
Tracks, 7:4326

Esquivel, Laura
Law of Love, The, 10:5850
Like Water for Chocolate, 10:5917

Evanovich, Janet
Hot Six, 14:197

Exley, Frederick, 1:603 (Bio, v. 1)
Fan's Notes, A, 3:1349
Last Notes from Home, 4:2351
Night of Light, 10:6111
Pages from a Cold Island, 6:3176

Farmer, Philip Jóse, 1:606 (Bio, v. 1)
Alley God, The, 5:2576
Feast Unknown, A, 5:2576
Lovers, The, 5:2573
Riders of the Purple Wage, 6:3568
Riverworld Series, 6:3590
Strange Relations, 5:2576
Tarzan Alive, 7:4113

Farrell, James T., 1:612 (Bio, v. 1)
Studs Lonigan Trilogy, The, 7:4072
    Judgment Day, 7:4072
    Young Lonigan, 7:4072
    Young Manhood of Studs Lonigan,
        The, 7:4072

Fast, Howard, 1:616 (Bio, v. 1)
Immigrant's Daughter, The, 4:2082
Immigrants, The, 4:2078
Legacy, The, 4:2081
Second Generation, 4:2081
Spartacus, 7:3974

Faulkner, William, 1:624 (Bio, v. 1)
As I Lay Dying, 12:27
"Barn Burning," 12:37
Bear, The, 1:277
Faulkner's Short Fiction, 3:1378
    Collected Stories of William
        Faulkner, 3:1378
    Knight's Gambit, 3:1378
    Uncollected Stories of William
        Faulkner, 3:1378
Light in August, 12:225
"Red Leaves," 12:37
Reivers, The, 6:3528
Sanctuary, 11:6328, 6:3691
Sound and the Fury, The, 12:379
"That Evening Sun," 12:37
Unvanquished, The, 11:6622

Finney, Jack, 1:637 (Bio, v. 1)
Bodysnatchers, The, 1:467
I Love Galesburg in the Springtime, 7:4256
Time and Again, 7:4254
Woodrow Wilson Dime, The, 7:4256

Fitch, Janet
White Oleander, 14:443

Fitzgerald, F. Scott, 1:639 (Bio, v. 1)
Beautiful and Damned, The, 1:287
Great Gatsby, The, 3:1773
Last Tycoon, The, 4:2363
Tender Is the Night, 7:4145
This Side of Paradise, 7:4197
Fitzgerald's Short Fiction, 3:1450
 "Absolution," 3:1453
 "Babylon Revisited," 3:1452
 "Ice Palace, The," 3:1450
 "May Day," 3:1451

Flagg, Fannie
Fried Green Tomatoes at the Whistle Stop Cafe, 13:141

Fleming, Ian, 1:648 (Bio, v. 1)
Goldfinger, 3:1730
Thunderball, 7:4222

Follett, Ken, 2:654 (Bio, v. 1)
Eye of the Needle, 3:1299
Key to Rebecca, The, 10:5790
On Wings of Eagles, 5:3069

Ford, Richard
Independence Day, 10:5714
Sportswriter, The, 10:5719, 13:349

Forster, E. M.
Howards End, 10:5685
Maurice, 10:6045
Passage to India, A, 10:6193

Fowles, John, 1:657 (Bio, v. 1)
French Lieutenant's Woman, The, 3:1564
Magus, The, 5:2606

Francis, Dick, 1:665 (Bio, v. 1)
Banker, 7:4058
Come to Grief, 12:77
Straight, 7:4048
To the Hilt, 11:6584
Whip Hand, 7:4051

Frazier, Charles
Cold Mountain, 9:5300

French, Marilyn, 1:669 (Bio, v. 1)
Her Mother's Daughter, 4:1894
Our Father, 6:3151
Women's Room, The, 8:4706, 4:1897

Fuentes, Carlos, 1:672 (Bio, v. 1)
Campaign, The, 2:600
Death of Artemio Cruz, The, 9:5375
Old Gringo, The, 5:3035
Where the Air Is Clear, 8:4593

Gaddis, William, 1:680 (Bio, v. 1)
Carpenter's Gothic, 2:635
J R, 6:3467
Recognitions, The, 6:3465

Gaines, Ernest J., 2:683 (Bio, v. 2)
Autobiography of Miss Jane Pittman, The 236
Bloodline, 1:241
Gathering of Old Men, A, 3:1640, 14:171
In My Father's House, 4:2109
Lesson before Dying, A, 13:249
Of Love and Dust, 1:241

Gann, Ernest K., 2:691 (Bio, v. 2)
Antagonists, The 169
High and the Mighty, The, 4:1910

Garcia Marquez, Gabriel, 2:694
 (Bio, v. 2)
Chronicle of a Death Foretold, 2:773
"Handsomest Drowned Man in the World, The," 12:133
Love in the Time of Cholera, 5:2549
One Hundred Years of Solitude, 6:3097

"Very Old Man with Enormous Wings, A," 13:385

Gardner, Erle Stanley, 2:700 (Bio, v. 2)
Bats Fly at Dusk, 1:261
Case of the Grinning Gorilla, The, 653

Gardner, John, 2:707 (Bio, v. 2)
Grendel, 3:1808
Mickelsson's Ghosts, 5:2736
Shadows, 7:3796

Garrett, George, 2:712 (Bio, v. 2)
Death of the Fox, 2:1041
Entered from the Sun, 2:1051
Succession, The, 2:1050

Garrett, Randall, 2:720 (Bio, v. 2)
Too Many Magicians, 7:4310
Unwise Child, 8:4421

Gibbons, Kaye
Ellen Foster, 13:127
Virtuous Woman, A, 13:395

Gibson, William, 2:722 (Bio, v. 2)
Mona Lisa Overdrive, 5:2784
Neuromancer, 5:2927
Virtual Light, 8:4480

Gilchrist, Ellen, 2:727 (Bio, v. 2)
In the Land of Dreamy Dreams, 4:2106
*Light Can Be Both Wave and
    Particle,* 4:2415
Victory Over Japan, 4:2106

Godden, Rumer, 2:730 (Bio, v. 2)
Candle for St. Jude, A, 6:3216
Coromandel Sea Change, 2:916
Five for Sorrow, Ten for Joy, 3:1456
Greengage Summer, The, 3:1798
Peacock Spring, The, 6:3214
Thursday's Children, 6:3216

Godwin, Gail, 2:733 (Bio, v. 2)
Dream Children, 13:117
Father Melancholy's Daughter, 3:1372

Good Husband, The, 3:1741
Mother and Two Daughters, A, 5:2818
Southern Family, A, 11:6420

Golden, Arthur
Memoirs of a Geisha, 13:287

Golding, William, 2:737 (Bio, v. 2)
Inheritors, The, 5:2517
Lord of the Flies, 5:2514
Rites of Passage Sea Triology, 6:3585
    Close Quarters, 6:3585
    Fire Down Below, 6:3585
    Rites of Passage, 6:3585
Spire, The, 7:3981

Goldman, William, 2:743 (Bio, v. 2)
Princess Bride, The, 6:3365
Silent Gondoliers, The, 6:3366

Gordimer, Nadine
July's People, 13:229

Gordon, Mary, 2:745 (Bio, v. 2)
Final Payments, 3:1418
Men and Angels, 5:2715
Other Side, The, 6:3143

Grafton, Sue
O Is for Outlaw, 14:285

Grass, Günter, 2:750 (Bio, v. 2)
Cat and Mouse, 7:4278
Dog Years, 2:1136
Flounder, The, 2:1138
Local Anesthetic, 2:1138
Meeting at Telgte, The, 2:1139
Rat, The, 6:3448
Tin Drum, The, 7:4276

Graves, Robert, 2:754 (Bio, v. 2)
Count Belisarius, 2:926
I, Claudius, 4:2046
"Shout, The," 7:3857

Greeley, Andrew M., 2:758 (Bio, v. 2)
Ascent into Hell, 7:4227

Cardinal Virtues, The, 3:1330
Fall From Grace, 3:1327
Lord of the Dance, 7:4228
Patience of A Saint, The, 6:3208
Summer at the Lake, 11:6447
Thy Brother's Wife, 7:4225

Greene, Graham, 2:764 (Bio, v. 2)
Brighton Rock, 6:3338
Captain and the Enemy, The, 2:617
End of the Affair, The, 13:137
Monsignor Quiote, 6:3338
Power and the Glory, The, 6:3334
Quiet American, The, 6:3419

Grey, Zane, 2:771 (Bio, v. 2)
Heritage of the Desert, The, 6:3566
Riders of the Purple Sage, 6:3562

Griffin, W. E. B., 2:776 (Bio, v. 2)
Aviators, The, 1:243
Blood and Honor, 9:5182
Last Heroes, The (As Alex Baldwin)
Men in Blue, 5:2722
Semper Fi, 7:3762

Grimes, Martha, 2:779 (Bio, v. 2)
Horse You Came In On, The, 4:1976
Man with a Load of Mischief, The, 5:2642
Old Contemptibles, The, 5:3027

Grisham, John, 2:781 (Bio, v. 2)
Brethren, The, 14:73
Chamber, The, 6:3445, 7:4272
Client, The, 2:831
Firm, The, 3:1431
Rainmaker, The, 6:3438
Runaway Jury, The, 11:6312
Time to Kill, A, 7:4265

Guest, Judith
Ordinary People, 12:287

Guterson, David
Snow Falling on Cedars, 11:6379

Hailey, Arthur, 2:789 (Bio, v. 2)
Airport, 1:55
Evening News, The, 3:1281
Strong Medicine, 7:4069

Haley, Alex, 2:792 (Bio, v. 2)
Different Kind of Christmas, A, 6:3637
Roots, 6:3635

Halliday, Brett, 2:797 (Bio, v. 2)
"Deadly Visions," 2:1019
Private Practice of Michael Shayne,
    The, 6:3381
Taste for Violence, A, 6:3382

Hamill, Pete
Flesh and Blood, 12:103
Loving Women: A Novel of the
    Fifties, 10:5983
Snow in August, 11:6398

Hammett, Dashiell, 2:800 (Bio, v. 2)
Dain Curse, The, 6:3495
Maltese Falcon, The, 5:2621
Red Harvest, 6:3491
Thin Man, The, 5:2624

Hannah, Barry, 2:805 (Bio, v. 2)
Airships, 1:58
Boomerang, 1:488
Hey Jack!, 4:1906
Ray, 6:3452

Hannah, Kristin
On Mystic Lake, 14:295

Hansen, Joseph, 2:811 (Bio, v. 2)
Death Claims, and Nightwork, 2:1028

Hardy, Thomas
Mayor of Casterbridge, The, 10:6054
Jude the Obscure, 10:5761
Return of the Native, The, 12:355
Tess of the D'Urbervilles: A Pure
    Woman, 11:6496

Harington, Donald, 2:815 (Bio, v. 2)
Architecture of the Arkansas Ozarks,
The 194
Choiring of the Trees, The, 2:756
Cockroaches of Stay More, The, 1:199
Let Us Build Us a City, 1:199
Lightning Bug, 10:5909

Harris, Thomas, 2:821 (Bio, v. 2)
Black Sunday, 1:401
Hannibal, 12:141
Red Dragon, 6:3487
Silence of the Lambs, The, 7:3864

Harrison, William
Blood Latitudes, The, 14:63

Hawkes, John, 2:823 (Bio, v. 2)
Lime Twig, The, 4:2418
Second Skin, 4:2421
Whistlejacket, 8:4625

Hawthorne, Nathaniel, 2:829 (Bio, v. 2)
House of the Seven Gables, The, 4:2029
"My Kinsman, Major Molineux," 5:2873
Scarlet Letter, The, 6:3725
"Young Goodman Brown," 8:4746

Haycox, Ernest, 2:839 (Bio, v. 2)
Bugles in the Afternoon, 1:551
Earthbreakers, The, 1:553

Hegi, Ursula
Stones from the River, 13:353

Heinlein, Robert A., 2:842 (Bio, v. 2)
Have Space Suit—Will Travel, 4:1862
Stranger in a Strange Land, 7:4062
To Sail Beyond the Sunset, 7:4289

Heller, Joseph, 2:846 (Bio, v. 2)
Catch-22, 2:695, 2:849
Closing Time, 2:845
God Knows, 9:5586
Good as Gold, 9:5616
Picture This, 6:3245
Something Happened, 7:3921

Hemingway, Ernest, 2:856 (Bio, v. 2)
The Complete Short Stories of Ernest Hem-
ingway, 4:1891
Farewell to Arms, A, 3:1364
For Whom the Bell Tolls, 3:1490
Garden of Eden, The, 3:1631
Nick Adams Stories, The, 4:2121
In Our Time, 4:2116
Old Man and the Sea, The, 5:3041
Sun Also Rises, The, 7:4081
To Have and Have Not, 14:405
True at First Light, 14:423

Herbert, Frank, 2:863 (Bio, v. 2)
Dosadi Experiment, The, 8:4620
Dragon in the Sea, The, 2:1194
Dune, 3:1216
Dune Messiah, 3:1219
Whipping Star, 8:4619

Herriot, James, 2:866 (Bio, v. 2)
All Creatures Great and Small, 1:89
Every Living Thing, 3:1284
James Herriot's Cat Stories, 4:2183

Hersey, John, 2:870 (Bio, v. 2)
Antonietta, 1:182
Bell for Adano, A, 1:320
Call, The, 590
Single Pebble, A, 2:593
Wall, The, 11:6658

Hesse, Herman, 2:877 (Bio, v. 2)
Demian, 12:85
Magister Ludi, 2:1125
Siddhartha, 7:3860
Steppenwolf, 12:391

Higgins, George V., 2:882 (Bio, v. 2)
Defending Billy Ryan, 2:1068
Friends of Eddie Coyle, The, 3:1574
Trust, 8:4367
Victories, 8:4367
Wonderful Years, Wonderful Years, 11:6712

Highwater, Jamake, 2:885 (Bio, v. 2)
Anpao: An American Indian Odyssey, 1:162

Ceremony of Innocence, The, 2:713
Ghost Horse Cycle, The, 4:2264
Kill Hole, 4:2264
I Wear the Morning Star, 2:717
Legend Days, 2:714, 4:2382

Hijuelos, Oscar
Empress of the Splendid Season, 14:125
Mambo Kings Play Songs of Love,
   The, 14:275

Hillerman, Tony, 2:891 (Bio, v. 2)
Coyote Waits, 2:932
Fallen Man, 9:5482
Finding Moon, 9:5501
Hunting Badger, 13:213
Sacred Clowns, 6:3668
Skinwalkers, 7:3889
Talking God, 7:4102

Himes, Chester, 2:896 (Bio, v. 2)
Blind Man with a Pistol, 2:924
Cotton Comes to Harlem, 2:921
Pinktoes, 6:3261

Hinton, S. E., 2:900 (Bio, v. 2)
Outsiders, The, 6:3170
Taming the Star Runner, 7:4105
Tex, 7:4158

Hoag, Tami
Ashes to Ashes, 14:1

Hoban, Russell, 2:903 (Bio, v. 2)
Riddley Walker, 6:3558

Hobson, Laura Z., 2:906 (Bio, v. 2)
Consenting Adult, 3:1648
Gentleman's Agreement, 3:1647

Holt, Victoria, 2:908 (Bio, v. 2)
Daughter of Deceit, 2:996
Mistress of Mellyn, 5:2764
Seven for a Secret, 7:3780

Horgan, Paul, 2:912 (Bio, v. 2)
Distant Trumpet, A, 2:1114

Whitewater, 8:4658

Howard, Robert E., 2:915 (Bio, v. 2)
Hour of the Dragon, The, 4:2002
Red Nails, 6:3497

Hughes, Langston
"Blues I'm Playing, The," 12:51
"Slave on the Block," 13:333

Hugo, Victor
Les Miserables, 13:239

Hunter, Evan/Ed McBain, 2:918
   (Bio, v. 2)
Blackboard Jungle, The, 1:409
Fuzz, 3:1602
Nocturne, 10:6127 (As Ed McBain)
There Was a Little Girl, 7:4161

Hutchinson, A. S. M., 2:925 (Bio, v. 2)
If Winter Comes, 4:2074
This Freedom, 4:2077

Huxley, Aldous Leonard, 2:927 (Bio, v. 2)
Brave New World, 1:495

Ibáñez, Vicente Blasco (see BlascoIbáñez,
   Vicente)

Irving, John, 2:934 (Bio, v. 2)
Cider House Rules, The, 2:786
Hotel New Hampshire, The, 4:1982
Prayer for Owen Meany, A, 6:3340
Son of the Circus, A, 7:3945
World According to Garp, The, 11:6725

Isaacs, Susan, 2:940 (Bio, v. 2)
After All These Years, 1:37
Compromising Positions, 2:890
Lily White, 10:5930
Magic Hour, 10:6006
Shining Through, 7:3834

Ishiguro, Kazuo, 2:944 (Bio, v. 2)
Artist of the Floating World, An, 1:212
Pale View of Hills, A, 6:3188

Remains of the Day, The, 6:3532

Jackson, Shirley, 2:947 (Bio, v. 2)
Haunting of Hill House, The, 4:1859
Lottery, The, 5:2546

Jakes, John, 2:952 (Bio, v. 2)
American Dreams, 12:1
Kent Chronicles, 4:2249
   Bastard, The 4:2249
   Rebels, The 4:2249
   Seekers, The, 4:2249
Homeland, 4:1951

James, Henry, 2:956 (Bio, v. 2)
Daisy Miller, 2:977
Portrait of a Lady, The, 6:3299
Turn of the Screw, The, 8:4375

James, P. D., 2:962 (Bio, v. 2)
Black Tower, The, 2:1039
Death of an Expert Witness, 2:1037
Devices and Desires, 2:1087
Innocent Blood, 4:2133
Shroud for a Nightingale, 2:1039
Taste for Death, A, 2:1090, 7:4128
Unnatural Causes, 2:1039

Jenkins, Dan, 2:965 (Bio, v. 2)
Baja Oklahoma, 1:259
Semi-Tough, 7:3759

Johnson, Diane, 2:967 (Bio, v. 2)
Burning, 1:562
Le Divorce, 10:5860
Shadow Knows, The, 7:3790

Jones, James, 2:970 (Bio, v. 2)
From Here to Eternity, 3:1579
Thin Red Line, The, 3:1581
Whistle, 3:1582

Jong, Erica, 2:975 (Bio, v. 2)
Fanny, 3:1353
Fear of Flying, 3:1389
Inventing Memory, 10:5735
Serenissima: A Novel of Venice, 3:1355

Junger, Sebastian
Perfect Storm, The, 14:309

Kafka, Franz, 2:979 (Bio, v. 2)
Castle, The, 2:664
Metamorphosis, The, 5:2726
Trial, The, 7:4344

Karon, Jan
At Home in Mitford, 9:5104
Light in the Window, A, 10:5899
These High, Green Hills, 11:6520

Kazantzakis, Nikos, 2:986 (Bio, v. 2)
Freedom or Death, 8:4757
Last Temptation of Christ, The, 4:2360
Zorba the Greek, 8:4755

Keillor, Garrison, 2:989 (Bio, v. 2)
Lake Wobegon Days, 4:2322
We Are Still Married, 8:4554

Kemelman, Harry, 2:992 (Bio, v. 2)
Saturday the Rabbi Went Hungry, 6:3702

Keneally, Thomas
Schindler's List, 13:313

Kennedy, William, 2:995 (Bio, v. 2)
Billy Phelan's Greatest Game, 4:2170
Flaming Corsage, The, 4:2170
Inktruck, The, 4:2170
Ironweed, 4:2166
Legs, 4:2388
Quinn's Book, 10:6244
Very Old Bones, 8:4456

Kerouac, Jack, 2:1002 (Bio, v. 2)
Dharma Bums, The, 5:3067
On the Road, 5:3065

Kesey, Ken, 2:1006 (Bio, v. 2)
One Flew Over the Cuckoo's Nest, 5:3088
Last Go Round, 4:2346
Sailor Song, 11:6323
Sometimes a Great Notion, 7:3939

Kincaid, Jamaica
"Girl," 12:109
"What I Have Been Doing
    Lately," 12:463

King, Stephen, 2:1017 (Bio, v. 2)
Dark Tower Series, The, 2:991
    Drawing of the Three, The, 2:991
    Gunslinger, The, 2:991
Desperation, 9:5381
Dolores Claiborne, 2:1151
Eyes of the Dragon, The, 3:1302
Gerald's Game, 9:5558
Girl Who Loved Tom Gordon, The, 13:171
Green Mile, The, 9:5630
Misery, 5:2754
Pet Sematary, 6:3227
Regulators, The, (as Richard
    Bachman), 11:6277
Shining, The, 7:3829

Kingsolver, Barbara
Animal Dreams, 12:11
Bean Trees, The, 12:45
Poisonwood Bible, The, 12:327

Kingston, Maxine Hong, 2:1030
    (Bio, v. 2)
China Men, 2:753
Tripmaster Monkey: His Fake Book, 7:4348
The Woman Warrior, 8:4702

Kinsella, W. P., 2:1034 (Bio, v. 2)
Fencepost Chronicles, The, 3:1406
Iowa Baseball Confederacy, The, 7:3851
Moccasin Telegraph, The, 5:2778
Shoeless Joe, 7:3849

Klause, Annette Curtis
Blood and Chocolate, 14:55

Klein, Norma, 2:1037 (Bio, v. 2)
No More Saturday Nights, 5:2977
Older Men, 5:3046

Knowles, John, 2:1040 (Bio, v. 2)
Separate Peace, A, 7:3771

Koontz, Dean
False Memory, 14:133

Kogawa, Joy
Obasan, 12:277

Kosinski, Jerzy, 2:1043 (Bio, v. 2)
Blind Date, 7:4038
Devil Tree, The, 7:4038
Hermit of 69th Street, The, 4:1899
Painted Bird, The, 6:3179
Steps, 7:4035

Kotzwinkle, William, 2:1051 (Bio, v. 2)
Bear Went Over the Mountain, The, 9:5147
Exile, The, 9:5467
Fan Man, The, 3:1345
Game of Thirty, The, 3:1624
Hot Jazz Trio, The, 4:1979
Midnight Examiner, The, 10:6078

Krantz, Judith, 2:1054 (Bio, v. 2)
I'll Take Manhattan, 4:2066
Mistral's Daughter, 5:2761
Princess Daisy, 10:6221
Till We Meet Again, 7:4249

Kundera, Milan, 2:1056 (Bio, v. 2)
Art of the Novel, The, 4:2085
Book of Laughter and Forgetting, The, 1:481
Immortality, 4:2083
Unbearable Lightness of Being, The, 8:4397

Kurtz, Katherine, 2:1061 (Bio, v. 2)
Camber of Culdi, 9:5237
Harrowing of Gwynedd, The, 4:1850
King Javan's Year, 4:2286
Lammas Night, 5:2477
Lodge of the Lynx, The, 5:2472
Quest for Saint Camber, The, 4:2289

L'Amour, Louis, 2:1069 (Bio, v. 2)
Hondo, 4:1965
Jubal Sackett, 4:2211
Shadow Riders, The, 7:3793

L'Engle, Madeleine, 2:1110 (Bio, v. 2)
Arm of the Starfish, The, 8:4731
Dragons in the Water, 8:4731
Swiftly Tilting Planet, A, 8:4731
Wrinkle in Time, A, 8:4729

Lackey, Mercedes, 2:1065 (Bio, v. 2)
By the Sword, 2:580
Children of the Night, 2:743
Firebird, The, 9:5508
Sacred Ground, 6:3672

Lardner, Ring, 2:1075 (Bio, v. 2)
Big Town, The, 1:374
You Know Me Al, 8:4743

Lathen, Emma, 2:1080 (Bio, v. 2)
By Hook or By Crook, 7:3929
Death Shall Overcome, 2:1053
Green Grows the Dollars, 7:3929
Murder Against the Grain, 5:2839
Right on the Money, 6:3573
Something in the Air, 7:3927

Lawrence, D. H., 2:1084 (Bio, v. 2)
Lady Chatterley's Lover, 4:2307
Rainbow, The, 7:3957, 10:6252
Sons and Lovers, 11:6405
Women in Love, 7:3960

Le Carré, John, 2:1094 (Bio, v. 2)
Little Drummer Girl, The, 4:2439
Russia House, The, 6:3658
Secret Pilgrim, The, 7:3750
Spy Who Came in from the Cold,
  The, 7:3996
Tinker, Tailor, Soldier, Spy, 11:6578

Le Guin, Ursula, 2:1101 (Bio, v. 2)
Always Coming Home, 1:128
Dispossessed, The, 2:1111
Left Hand of Darkness, The, 4:2376

Lee, Harper, 2:1098 (Bio, v. 2)
To Kill a Mockingbird, 7:4280

Leiber, Fritz, 2:1105 (Bio, v. 2)
Big Time, The, 1:370
Conjure Wife, 2:905
Fafyrd and Grey Mouser Stories, The, 1309

Lem, Stanislaw
Chain of Chance, The, 9:5267
Fiasco, 9:5491
Invincible, The, 10:5745

Leonard, Elmore, 2:1113 (Bio, v. 2)
Freaky Deaky, 3:1554
Glitz, 3:1689
Hombre, 4:1948
Killshot, 10:5799
La Brava, 10:5804
Maximum Bob, 5:2692
Out of Sight, 10:6174
Pronto, 6:3392

Lessing, Doris
Golden Notebook, The, 13:181
Love, Again, 13:269
Summer before the Dark, The, 13:361

Lewis, C. S., 2:1118 (Bio, v. 2)
Narnia series, 4:2425
  Horse and His Boy, The, 4:2425
  Lion, the Witch, and the Wardrobe,
    The, 4:2423
  Magician's Nephew, The, 4:2426
  Prince Caspian, 4:2425
  Silver Chair, The, 4:2425
  Voyage of the Dawn Treader, 4:2425
Out of the Silent Planet, 6:3158
That Hideous Strength, 6:3161
Till We Have Faces, 7:4246

Lewis, Sinclair, 2:1122 (Bio, v. 2)
Babbitt, 1:251
Main Street, 5:2613

Lindbergh, Anne Morrow, 2:1127
  (Bio, v. 2)
Gift from the Sea, 3:1666
Steep Ascent, 7:4032

Lively, Penelope, 2:1132 (Bio, v. 2)
City of the Mind, 2:811
Judgment Day, 6:3605
Moon Tiger, 5:2801
Road to Lichfield, The, 6:3600

London, Jack, 2:1138 (Bio, v. 2)
Call of the Wild, The, 2:596
Sea-Wolf, The, 7:3735
White Fang, 8:4639

Lord, Bette Bao, 2:1144 (Bio, v. 2)
Eighth Moon, 3:1232
Middle Heart, The, 7:3987
Legacies: A Chinese Mosaic, 4:2378
Spring Moon, 7:3983

Lovecraft, H. P., 2:1148 (Bio, v. 2)
The Case of Charles Dexter Ward, 2:642
The Dream-Quest of Unknown
  Kadath, 3:1211
"Dunwich Horror, The," 3:1222

Lowry, Malcolm, 2:1154 (Bio, v. 2)
The Forest Path to the Spring, 3:1502
October Ferry to Gabriola, 3:1502
Under the Volcano, 8:4405

Ludlum, Robert, 2:1162 (Bio, v. 2)
Aquitaine Progression, The, 4:1935
Bourne Ultimatum, The, 1:491
Cry of the Halidon, The, 9:5343
Holcroft Covenant, The, 4:1932
Icarus Agenda, The, 4:2069

Lurie, Alison, 2:1164 (Bio, v. 2)
Foreign Affairs, 8:4373
Only Children, 10:6148
Truth about Lorin Jones, The, 8:4371
War Between the Tates, The, 8:4373

MacDonald, John D., 2:1167 (Bio, v. 2)
Empty Coppper Sea, The, 5:2488
Lonely Silver Rain, The, 5:2485
One More Sunday, 6:3105
Pale Gray for Guilt, 5:2488

Macdonald, Ross, 2:1170 (Bio, v. 2)
Blue City, 1:438
Doomsters, The, 2:1168
Sleeping Beauty, 7:3901

MacInnes, Helen, 2:1176 (Bio, v. 2)
North from Rome, 6:3689
Salzburg Connection, The, 6:3687

Mahfouz, Naguib
"Half a Day," 12:127

Mailer, Norman, 2:1179 (Bio, v. 2)
Advertisements for Myself, 1:28
Executioner's Song, The, 3:1294
Marilyn, 1:30
Naked and the Dead, The, 5:2895
Tough Guys Don't Dance, 7:4323

Malamud, Bernard, 2:1185 (Bio, v. 2)
Fixer, The, 3:1465
God's Grace , 9:5592
Natural, The, 5:2920
Stories of Bernard Malamud, The, 5:2616

Malraux, André, 2:1189 (Bio, v. 2)
Man's Fate, 5:2668

Mann, Thomas, 2:1193 (Bio, v. 2)
Death in Venice, 2:1034
Doctor Faustus, 2:1123
Magic Mountain, The, 5:2594
Magister Ludi, 2:1125

Mansfield, Katherine, 2:1198 (Bio, v. 2)
"At the Bay," 6:3334
"Bliss," 1:414
"Garden-Party, The," 3:1638
"Je ne parle pas français," 4:2192
"Little Governess, The," 1:416
"Prelude," 6:3344

Marquand, John Phillips, 2:1203
  (Bio, v. 2)
Late George Apley, The, 4:2370
Melville Goodwin, USA, 6:3292
Point of No Return, 6:3290

Marquez, Gabriel Garcia (see Garcia Marquez, Gabriel)

Marshall, Catherine, 2:1206 (Bio, v. 2)
Christy, 2:768
Julie, 4:2223

Marshall, Paule, 2:1209 (Bio, v. 2)
Brown Girl, Brownstones, 1:541
Chosen Place, the Timeless People, The, 1:542
Praisesong for the Widow, 1:543

Mason, Perry series, 2:653

Mason, Bobbie Ann, 2:1212 (Bio, v. 2)
Feather Crowns, 3:1395
In Country, 4:2099
Shiloh and Other Stories, 7:3825

Matthiessen, Peter, 2:1216 (Bio, v. 2)
At Play in the Fields of the Lord, 1:218
Far Tortuga, 3:1357
Killing Mister Watson, 4:2274

Maugham, W. Somerset, 2:1222 (Bio, v. 2)
Cakes and Ale: Or The Skeleton in the Cupboard, 9:5229
Moon and Sixpence, The, 10:6083
Of Human Bondage, 5:3021
"Rain," 6:3435
Razor's Edge, The, 6:3455
"Red," 10:6272

McBain, Ed (also see Hunter, Evan/ EdMcBain)
Nocturne, 10:6127

McCaffrey, Anne, 2:1226 (Bio, v. 2)
Dolphins of Pern, The, 2:1157
Dragonflight Trilogy, 3:1200
Dragonquest, 3:1202
Dragonsdawn, 3:1206
Killashandra, 10:5795
Rowan, The, 6:3644

McCarthy, Cormac, 2:1232 (Bio, v. 2)
All the Pretty Horses, 1:114
Crossing, The, 2:951
Outer Dark, 6:3162
Suttree, 7:4087

McCarthy, Mary, 2:1235 (Bio, v. 2)
Cannibals and Missionaries, 2:610
Group, The, 3:1812

McCullers, Carson, 2:1241 (Bio, v. 2)
Ballad of the Sad Cafe, The, 4:1880
Heart Is a Lonely Hunter, The, 4:1878
Member of the Wedding, The, 4:1881

McCullough, Colleen, 2:1245 (Bio, v. 2)
First Man in Rome, The, 3:1443
Fortune's Favorites, 3:1505
Indecent Obsession, An, 7:4202
Thorn Birds, The, 7:4200

McGuane, Thomas, 2:1250 (Bio, v. 2)
Bushwhacked Piano, The, 1:565
Keep the Change, 4:2245
Ninety-Two in the Shade, 5:2966
Nothing But Blue Skies, 5:2993
Something to Be Desired, 4:2247

McInerney, Jay, 2:1254 (Bio, v. 2)
Bright Lights, Big City, 1:533
Brightness Falls, 1:537
Story of My Life, 1:535, 7:4045

McKillip, Patricia Anne, 2:1257 (Bio, v. 2)
Changeling Sea, The, 2:723
Forgotten Beasts of Eld, The, 6:3555
Harpist in the Wind, 6:3554
Heir of Sea and Fire, 6:3554
Riddle-Master of Hed, The, 6:3553

McMillan, Terry, 2:1260 (Bio, v. 2)
How Stella Got Her Groove Back, 10:5677
Waiting to Exhale, 8:4494

McMurtry, Larry, 2:1265 (Bio, v. 2)
Comanche Moon, 9:5314

Last Picture Show, The, 10:5836
Lonesome Dove, 10:5948, 5:2491
Some Can Whistle, 7:4149
Terms of Endearment, 7:4148

Metalious, Grace, 2:1269 (Bio, v. 2)
No Adam in Eden, 5:2970
Peyton Place, 6:3231
Return to Peyton Place, 6:3234
Tight White Collar, 11:6570

Michener, James, 2:1275 (Bio, v. 2)
Alaska, 1:66
Drifters, The, 9:5411
Hawaii, 4:1865
Mexico, 5:2730
Tales of the South Pacific, 7:4097

Miller, Henry, 2:1280 (Bio, v. 2)
Tropic of Cancer, 7:4353
Tropic of Capricorn, 7:4356
Rosy Crucifixion, The, 6:3640
   Sexus, 6:3640
   Nexus, 6:3640
   Plexus, 6:3640

Miller, Jr., Walter M., 2:1287 (Bio, v. 2)
Canticle for Leibowitz, A, 2:613

Millhauser, Steven,
"Knife Thrower, The," 14:255
Little Kingdoms, 14:269

Mishima, Yukio, 2:1289 (Bio, v. 2)
Confessions of a Mask, 7:4193
Forbidden Colors, 7:4194
Thirst for Love, 7:4192

Mitchell, Margaret, 2:1293 (Bio, v. 2)
Gone With the Wind, 3:1734
Scarlett, 3:1739

Momaday, N. Scott, 2:1299 (Bio, v. 2)
Ancient Child, The, 1:134
House Made of Dawn, 4:2015
In the Presence of the Sun, 4:2127
Way to Rainy Mountain, The, 4:2018

Monsarrat, Nicholas, 2:1305 (Bio, v. 2)
Cruel Sea, The, 2:956

Morrison, Toni, 2:1308 (Bio, v. 2)
Beloved, 1:335
Bluest Eye, The, 1:442
Jazz, 12:195
Paradise, 12:295
Song of Solomon, 7:3949

Morse, L. A., 2:1317 (Bio, v. 2)
Big Enchilada, The, 1:349
Old Dick, The, 5:3031

Mosley, Walter, 2:1320 (Bio, v. 2)
Always Outnumbered, Always
   Outgunned, 9:5069
Black Betty, 8:4636
Devil in a Blue Dress, 2:1092 , 8:4636
Gone Fishin', 9:5606
Little Yellow Dog, A, 10:5939
Red Death, A, 6:3481 , 8:4636
White Butterfly, 8:4632

Munro, Alice, 2:1324 (Bio, v. 2)
"Albanian Virgin, The,"73
Beggar Maid: Stories of Flo and Rose [Who
   Do You Think You Are?], The, 1:305
Lives of Girls and Women, 4:2455
Who Do You Think You Are? (see The
   Beggar Maid), 1:305

Nabokov, Vladimir, 2:1331 (Bio, v. 2)
Despair, 5:2483
Enchanter, The, 5:2483
Lolita, 5:2480
Pale Fire, 6:3185

Naipaul, V. S., 2:1339 (Bio, v. 2)
Guerrillas, 3:1820
House for Mr Biswas, A, 4:2012
Miguel Street, 5:2894
Mystic Masseur, The, 5:2892

Narayan, R. K., 2:1344 (Bio, v. 2)
Financial Expert, The, 3:1824
Guide, The, 3:1822

Man-Eater of Malgudi, The, 5:2656

Naylor, Gloria
Mama Day, 13:279
Women of Brewster Place, The, 14:449

Nin, Anaïs, 2:1349 (Bio, v. 2)
Cities of the Interior, 2:804
    Children of the Albatross, 2:807
    Four Chambered Heart, The, 807
    Ladders to Fire, 2:807
    Solar Barque, 2:807
    Spy in the House of Love, A, 2:807

Niven, Larry, 2:1355 (Bio, v. 2)
Integral Trees, The, 4:2136
Ringworld, 6:3582
World of Ptavvs, 8:4722

Norman, John, 2:1359 (Bio, v. 2)
Captive of Gor, 5:2604
Magicians of Gor, 5:2597
Tarnsman of Gor, 5:2603

Norris, Frank, 2:1362 (Bio, v. 2)
McTeague, 5:2697
Octopus, The, 5:3014

Norton, Andre, 2:1366 (Bio, v. 2)
Catseye, 9:5260
Key Out of Time, 10:5784
Star Gate, 7:4011
Witch World, 11:6697

O. Henry, 3:1395 (Bio, v. 3)
Four Million, The, 3:1532
Trimmed Lamp, The, 3:1534

O'Brian, Patrick
Commodore, The, 9:5320

O'Connor, Flannery, 3:1379 (Bio, v. 3)
Complete Stories of Flannery O'Connor,
    The, 5:3011
Wise Blood, 8:4687, 13:437

O'Dell, Scott, 3:1387 (Bio, v. 3)
Island of the Blue Dolphins, 4:2172

Sing Down the Moon, 4:2176, 3871
Streams to the River, 4:2176
Thunder Rolling in the Mountains, 7:4218
Zia, 4:2176

O'Dell, Tawni
Back Roads, 14:11

O'Hara, John, 3:1391 (Bio, v. 3)
Appointment in Samarra, 1:187
Sermons and Soda-Water, 7:3777
Ten North Frederick, 7:4142

Oates, Joyce Carol, 2:1373 (Bio, v. 2)
Assassins: A Book of Hours, The, 1:215
Because It Is Bitter, and Because It Is My
    Heart, 1:291
Bellefleur, 1:329
Marya: A Life, 5:2681
Snake Eyes, 7:3908
them, 11:6512
We Were the Mulvaneys, 11:6670
What I Lived For, 11:6676

Ondaatje, Michael
English Patient, The, 9:5436

Orwell, George, 3:1400 (Bio, v. 3)
Animal Farm, 1:154
Nineteen Eighty-Four, 5:2963

Parker, Dorothy
"Here We Are," 10:5657
"Lovely Leave, The," 10:5979
Small Vices, 11:6371
"Waltz, The," 11:6665

Parker, Robert B., 3:1407 (Bio, v. 3)
All Our Yesterdays, 1:97
Chance, 9:5277
Godwulf Manuscript, The, 3:1722
Hugger Mugger, 14:215
Hush Money, 12:179
Sudden Mischief, 12:397
Thin Air, 7:4175

Passos, John Dos (see Dos Passos, John)

Pasternak, Boris, 3:1412 (Bio, v. 3)
Doctor Zhivago, 2:1127

Paton, Alan, 3:1416 (Bio, v. 3)
Cry, the Beloved Country, 2:960
Too Late the Phalarope, 7:4299

Patterson, James
Cradle and All, 14:103

Percy, Walker, 3:1420 (Bio, v. 3)
Moviegoer, The, 5:2821
Second Coming, The, 7:3741
Thanatos Syndrome, The, 14:375

Perelman, S. J., 3:1425 (Bio, v. 3)
Acres and Pains, 1:5

Petry, Ann, 3:1431 (Bio, v. 3)
Country Place, 7:4067
Narrows, The, 7:4066
Street, The, 7:4065

Phillips, Jayne Anne, 3:1436 (Bio, v. 3)
Black Tickets, 1:405
Fast Lanes, 1:408, 3:1367
Machine Dreams, 5:2588
Shelter, 5:2591, 7:3813

Piercy, Marge, 3:1439 (Bio, v. 3)
Fly Away Home, 3:1477
Longings of Women, The, 5:2498
Vida, 8:4465

Plath, Sylvia, 3:1444 (Bio, v. 3)
Bell Jar, The, 1:325

Poe, Edgar Allan, 3:1449 (Bio, v. 3)
"Fall of the House of Usher, The," 3:1332
"Gold Bug, The," 5:2854
"Ligeia," 10:5889
"Murders in the Rue Morgue," 5:2852
"Mystery of Marie Roget, The," 5:2854
"Pit and the Pendulum, The," 6:3264
"Purloined Letter, The," 5:2854

"Tell-Tale Heart, The," 7:4132

Porter, Gene Stratton, 3:1457 (Bio, v. 3)
Daughter of the Land, A, 2:1002
Freckles, 3:1558
Girl of the Limberlost, A, 3:1685
Harvester, The, 3:1687

Porter, Katherine Anne, 3:1460 (Bio, v. 3)
"Flowering Judas," 4:1930
Noon Wine, 5:2987
Ship of Fools, 7:3838

Portis, Charles, 3:1464 (Bio, v. 3)
True Grit, 8:4362

Potok, Chaim, 3:1467 (Bio, v. 3)
Chosen, The, 2:763
Davita's Harp, 2:1005
Gift of Asher Lev, The, 5:2877
In the Beginning, 2:766
My Name Is Asher Lev, 5:2876
Promise, The, 2:766

Powers, Richard, 3:1471 (Bio, v. 3)
*Three Farmers on Their Way to a
    Dance*, 7:4214
Galatea 2.2, 3:1609
Gold Bug Variations, The, 9:5602
Operation Wandering Soul, 6:3113
Prisoner's Dilemma, 10:6225

Pratchett, Terry, 3:1475 (Bio, v. 3)
Colour of Magic, The, 2:882
Equal Rites, 3:1261
Hogfather, 13:197
Interesting Times, 10:5729
Small Gods, 7:3904

Pritchett, V. S., 3:1478 (Bio, v. 3)
Complete Collected Stories, 6:3372

Proulx, E. Annie, 3:1484 (Bio, v. 3)
Accordion Crimes, 7:3846
Postcards, 7:3846
Shipping News, The, 7:3841

Proust, Marcel, 3:1488 (Bio, v. 3)
Remembrance of Things Past, 7:4094
Swann's Way, 7:4091

Puig, Manuel, 3:1492 (Bio, v. 3)
Betrayed by Rita Hayworth, 1:345
Blood of Requited Love, 1:427
Kiss of the Spider Woman, 4:2297
Pubis Angelical, 10:6230

Puzo, Mario, 3:1496 (Bio, v. 3)
Godfather, The, 3:1707
Last Don, The, 3:1711
Sicilian, The, 3:1711

Pym, Barbara, 3:1499 (Bio, v. 3)
Crampton Hodnet, 3:1293
Excellent Women, 3:1288
Few Green Leaves, A, 3:1292
Glass of Blessings, A, 3:1289
Jane and Prudence, 3:1292
Less Than Angels, 3:1291
No Fond Return of Love, 3:1292
Quartet in Autumn, 3:1292
Some Tame Gazelle, 3:1291
Sweet Dove Died, The, 3:1290

Pynchon, Thomas, 3:1502 (Bio, v. 3)
Crying of Lot 49, The, 2:969
Gravity's Rainbow, 3:1767
Mason & Dixon, 10:6036
V., 8:4432
Vineland, 8:4468

Queen, Ellery, 3:1509 (Bio, v. 3)
French Powder Mystery, The, 3:1568
Last Woman in His Life, The, 5:2850
Murderer Is a Fox, The, 5:2847

Rampling, Anne (see Rice, Anne)

Rand, Ayn, 3:1515 (Bio, v. 3)
Atlas Shrugged, 1:222
Fountainhead, The, 3:1526

Rawlings, Marjorie Kinnan, 3:1518
   (Bio, v. 3)
Cross Creek, 2:948
South Moon Under, 7:3971
Yearling, The, 8:4738

Reed, Ishmael, 3:1521 (Bio, v. 3)
Free-Lance Pallbearers, The, 3:1561
Mumbo Jumbo, 5:2835
Reckless Eyeballing, 6:3461

Remarque, Erich Maria, 3:1526 (Bio, v. 3)
All Quiet on the Western Front, 1:102
Arch of Triumph, 1:190
Road Back, The, 1:104, 6:3597
Shadows in Paradise, 1:192

Renault, Mary, 3:1531 (Bio, v. 3)
Fire from Heaven, 4:2358
King Must Die, The, 4:2357
Last of the Wine, The, 4:2355

Rendell, Ruth, 3:1534 (Bio, v. 3)
Bridesmaid, The, 8:4453
Gallowglass, 3:1614
House of Stairs, The, 8:4454
Veiled One, The, 8:4451

Rice, Anne, 3:1538 (Bio, v. 3)
Interview with the Vampire, 4:2139
Queen of the Damned, The, 6:3412
Servant of the Bones, 12:375
Vampire Lestat, The, 4:2142, 8:4447
Witching Hour, The, 8:4693

Rinehart, Mary Roberts, 3:1542
   (Bio, v. 3)
Circular Staircase, The, 2:795
K., 4:2239

Robbe-Grillet, Alain, 3:1547 (Bio, v. 3)
Djinn, 2:1117
Erasers, The, 3:1265
Regicide, A, 2:1119

Robbins, Harold, 3:1551 (Bio, v. 3)
Carpetbaggers, The, 2:638

Dream Merchants, The, 2:640
Inheritors, The, 2:640
Never Love a Stranger, 7:4043
Stone for Danny Fisher, A, 7:4040

Robbins, Tom, 3:1555 (Bio, v. 3)
Another Roadside Attraction, 1:158
Even Cowgirls Get the Blues, 3:1277
*Fierce Invalids Home from Hot
    Climates*, 14:143
Half Asleep in Frog Pajamas, 3:1826
Skinny Legs and All, 7:3886

Rolvaag, O. E.
Giants in the Earth, 13:163

Roquelaure, A. N. (see Rice, Anne)

Rossner, Judith, 3:1558 (Bio, v. 3)
Attachments , 9:5115
August, 1:226
His Little Women, 4:1916
Looking for Mr. Goodbar, 5:2507
Olivia, 5:3052

Roth, Philip, 3:1561 (Bio, v. 3)
Breast, The, 1:503
Counterlife, The, 2:929
Human Stain, The, 14:225
Operation Shylock, 6:3108
Portnoy's Complaint, 6:3296
Professor of Desire, The, 1:504

Ruark, Robert, 3:1567 (Bio, v. 3)
Something of Value, 7:3931
Uhuru, 7:3934

Rushdie, Salman, 3:1570 (Bio, v. 3)
Ground Beneath Her Feet, The, 12:115
Midnight's Children, 5:2746
Moor's Last Sigh, The, 12:267
Satanic Verses, The, 6:3697
Shame, 7:3799

Russ, Joanna, 3:1576 (Bio, v. 3)
And Chaos Died, 1:139
Female Man, The, 3:1403

Two of Them, The, 8:4385
"*When It Changed*," 8:4589

Sabatini, Rafael, 3:1580 (Bio, v. 3)
Captain Blood: His Odyssey, 2:620
Scaramouche, 6:3722

**Saint-Exupéry, Antoine-Marie-Roger de,
    3:1586** (Bio, v. 3)
Little Prince, The, 4:2441
Night Flight, 5:2937
Wind, Sand and Stars, 8:4673

Salinger, J. D., 3:1589 (Bio, v. 3)
Catcher in the Rye, The, 2:703
Franny and Zooey, 9:5536
Hapworth 16, 1:1924, 10:5639

Sanders, Lawrence, 3:1595 (Bio, v. 3)
Burglar in the Library, The, 9:5217
Fourth Deadly Sin, The, 3:1536
Sixth Commandment, The, 11:6359

Sandford, John
Easy Prey, 14:109

Sarraute, Nathalie, 3:1598 (Bio, v. 3)
Planetarium, The, 6:3278
Tropisms, 6:3280

Sayers, Dorothy L., 3:1602 (Bio, v. 3)
Busman's Honeymoon, 2:569
Clouds of Witness, 2:851
Five Red Herrings, 2:854
Gaudy Night, 2:571
Have His Carcase, 2:571
Murder Must Advertise, 2:854
Striding Folly, 2:572
Strong Position, 2:570
Unnatural Death, 2:854
Whose Body, 2:853

Schaefer, Jack, 3:1608 (Bio, v. 3)
Shane, 7:3802

Schlink, Bernhard
Reader, The, 14:357

Schmitz, James H., 3:1611 (Bio, v. 3)
Demon Breed, The, 2:1080
Lion Game, The, 8:4419
Telzey Toy, The, 8:4419
Universe Against Her, The, 8:4417
Witches of Karres, The, 8:4691

Schulberg, Budd, 3:1613 (Bio, v. 3)
What Makes Sammy Run?, 8:4564

Scott, Sir Walter
Bride of Lammermoor, The, 12:59
Heart of Midlothian, The, 12:149
Ivanhoe, 12:187

Segal, Erich, 3:1618 (Bio, v. 3)
Love Story, 5:2567
Man, Woman and Child, 5:2571
Oliver's Story, 5:2570

Self, Will
How the Dead Live, 14:207

Settle, Mary Lee, 3:1621 (Bio, v. 3)
Blood Tie, 1:431
Celebration, 2:711

Shaara, Michael, 3:1625 (Bio, v. 3)
Gods and Generals, 4:2272(by Jeff Shaara)
Killer Angels, The, 4:2270
Soldier Boy, 7:3918

Shatner, William
Man O' War, 12:247

Shaw, Irwin, 3:1628 (Bio, v. 3)
Beggarman, Thief, 6:3550
Rich Man, Poor Man, 6:3548
Shaw: Short Stories, 7:3808
Young Lions, The, 8:4750

Sheldon, Sidney, 3:1633 (Bio, v. 3)
Bloodline, 1:434
Doomsday Conspiracy, The, 2:1163
Other Side of Midnight, The, 6:3148
Stars Shine Down, The, 7:4019

Shellabarger, Samuel, 3:1637 (Bio, v. 3)
Captain from Castile, 2:624
Lord Vanity, 2:629
Prince of Foxes, 2:627

Shelley, Mary, 3:1640 (Bio, v. 3)
*Frankenstein: or, The Modern
    Prometheus,* 3:1547

Shields, Carol
Larry's Party, 10:5824
Republic of Love, The, 11:6287
Stone Diaries, The, 11:6433

Shreve, Anita
Pilot's Wife, The, 14:319

Shute, Nevil, 3:1646 (Bio, v. 3)
On the Beach, 5:3059

Silko, Leslie Marmon
Ceremony, 12:67
"Yellow Woman," 12:469

Silverberg, Robert, 3:1650 (Bio, v. 3)
Book of Skulls, The, 9:5194
Letters from Atlantis, 4:2404
Lord Valentine's Castle, 5:2533
Nightfall, 5:2942
Star of Gypsies, 11:6427

Simenon, Georges, 3:1655 (Bio, v. 3)
Act of Passion, 5:2612
Burgomaster of Furnes, 5:2612
Maigret Meets a Milord, 5:2609
Pedigree, 5:2611

Sinclair, Upton, 3:1659 (Bio, v. 3)
Jungle, The, 4:2226
King Coal, 4:2229

Singer, Isaac Bashevis, 3:1662 (Bio, v. 3)
Enemies: A Love Story, 3:1252
Gimpel the Fool and Other Stories, 9:5571
King of the Fields, The, 4:2291
Slave, The, 11:6363

Sjöwal, Maj and Per Wahlöö, 3:1667
(Bio, v. 3)
Laughing Policeman, The, 7:4156
Terrorists, The, 7:4151

Smiley, Jane, 3:1671 (Bio, v. 3)
At Paradise Gate, 7:4211
Barn Blind, 7:4211
Duplicate Keys, 7:4212
Good Will, 7:4212
Greenlanders, The, 3:1803
MOO, 5:2796
Thousand Acres, A, 7:4208

Smith, Martin Cruz, 3:1677 (Bio, v. 3)
Gorky Park, 3:1753
Nightwing, 7:4005
Polar Star, 6:3512
Red Square, 6:3509
Stallion Gate, 7:4002

Smith, Rosamond (see Oates, Joyce
Carol)

Smith, Thorne, 3:1679 (Bio, v. 3)
Topper, 7:4316
Turnabout, 7:4318

Smith, Betty, 3:1674 (Bio, v. 3)
Joy in the Morning, 7:4342
Maggie Now, 7:4342
Tomorrow Will Be Better, 7:4342
Tree Grows in Brooklyn, A, 7:4339

Solzhenitsyn, Aleksandr, 3:1682
(Bio, v. 3)
August 1914, 1:231
Candle in the Wind, 3:1441
First Circle, The, 3:1439
*One Day in the Life of Ivan
Denisovich*, 5:3083

Sontag, Susan
"Way We Live Now, The," 14:437

Southern, Terry, 3:1688 (Bio, v. 3)
Blue Movie, 2:608

Candy, 2:606

Spark, Muriel
Ballad of Peckham Rye, The, 13:35

Spillane, Mickey, 3:1691 (Bio, v. 3)
Day of the Guns, 2:1008
Erection Set, The, 3:1268
I, the Jury, 4:2052

Spinrad, Norman, 3:1696 (Bio, v. 3)
Bug Jack Barron, 1:546
Iron Dream, The, 4:2160
World Between, A, 8:4709

Steel, Danielle, 3:1700 (Bio, v. 3)
Novels of Danielle Steel, The, 7:4023
Changes, 7:4026
Crossings, 7:4025
Days of Shame, 7:4029
Family Album, 7:4023, 7:4026
Five Days in Paris, 7:4029
Full Circle, 7:4028
Lightning, 7:4029
Loving, 7:4024

Stegner, Wallace, 3:1703 (Bio, v. 3)
Angle of Repose, 1:146
Big Rock Candy Mountain, The, 1:361
Genesis, 9:5553

Steinbeck, John, 3:1709 (Bio, v. 3)
Grapes of Wrath, The, 3:1757
In Dubious Battle, 4:2103
Of Mice and Men, 5:3024
Red Pony, The, 6:3505

Stevenson, Robert Louis, 3:1716
(Bio, v. 3)
Kidnapped, 4:2260
Master of Ballantrae, The, 5:2688
*Strange Case of Dr. Jekyll and Mr. Hyde,
The*, 7:4055
Treasure Island, 7:4335

Stewart, Mary, 3:1723 (Bio, v. 3)
Hollow Hills, The, 4:1937
My Brother Michael, 5:2867

Thornyhold, 7:4204
Wicked Day, The, 11:6682

Stoker, Bram, 3:1726 (Bio, v. 3)
Dracula, 2:1188

Stone, Irving, 3:1731 (Bio, v. 3)
Agony and the Ecstasy, The, 1:52
Lust for Life, 5:2580
Origin, The, 6:3127

Stone, Robert, 3:1736 (Bio, v. 3)
Bear and His Daughter, 9:5138
Children of Light, 2:740
Dog Soldiers, 2:1132
Flag for Sunrise, A, 3:1469
Outerbridge Reach, 6:3165

Stout, Rex, 3:1741 (Bio, v. 3)
Black Mountain, The, 1:396
Doorbell Rang, The, 2:1172
Too Many Cooks, 7:4305

Stowe, Harriet Beecher
Uncle Tom's Cabin, 13:375

Straub, Peter, 3:1744 (Bio, v. 3)
Ghost Story, 3:1662

Strugatsky, Arkady, and Boris Strugatsky
Hard to Be a God, 13:187

Sturgeon, Theodore, 3:1746 (Bio, v. 3)
E Pluribus Unicorn, 3:1228
Godbody, 3:1704
More Than Human, 10:6098
Sturgeon Is Alive and Well, 3:1228

Styron, William, 3:1750 (Bio, v. 3)
Confessions of Nat Turner, The, 2:901
Lie Down in Darkness, 4:2411
Sophie's Choice, 7:3962
Tidewater Morning, A, 7:4233

Susann, Jacqueline, 3:1761 (Bio, v. 3)
Once Is Not Enough, 5:3080

Valley of the Dolls, 8:4442

Süskind, Patrick, 3:1766 (Bio, v. 3)
Double Bass, The, 2:1180
Mr. Summer's Story, 2:1182
Perfume, 6:3222
Pigeon, The, 6:3258

Tan, Amy, 3:1772 (Bio, v. 3)
Hundred Secret Senses, The, 4:2210
Joy Luck Club, The, 4:2208
Kitchen God's Wife, The, 4:2210
"Two Kinds," 12:439

Tarkington, Booth, 3:1776 (Bio, v. 3)
Alice Adams, 1:85
Gentleman from Indiana, The, 3:1650
Magnificent Ambersons, The, 10:6011
Penrod, 6:3219

Tarr, Judith, 3:1780 (Bio, v. 3)
Alamut, 1:61
Hounds of God, The, 4:1997
Lord of the Two Lands, 5:2528

Taylor, Peter, 3:1783 (Bio, v. 3)
In the Miro District, 7:4079
Old Forest, The, 7:4079
"Spinster's Tale, A," 13:341
Summons to Memphis, A, 7:4078

Theroux, Paul, 3:1786 (Bio, v. 3)
Half Moon Street, 5:2812
Mosquito Coast, The, 5:2808
My Secret History, 5:2881
Saint Jack, 5:2812

Thomas, D. M., 3:1790 (Bio, v. 3)
White Hotel, The, 8:4642

Thompson, Hunter S., 3:1793 (Bio, v. 3)
Fear and Loathing in Las Vegas, 3:1385

Thompson, Jim, 3:1796 (Bio, v. 3)
After Dark, My Sweet, 1:42
Criminal, The, 2:942
Recoil, 6:3469

Thurber, James, 3:1803 (Bio, v. 3)
"American Romance, An," 1:132
"Night the Bed Fell, The," 5:2940
"Secret Life of Walter Mitty, The," 7:3744

Tolkien, J. R. R., 3:1809 (Bio, v. 3)
Hobbit, The, 4:1924
Lord of the Rings, The, 5:2521
Silmarillion, The, 5:2523

Toomer, Jean
Cane, 13:63

Toole, John Kennedy, 3:1817 (Bio, v. 3)
Confederacy of Dunces, A, 2:895

Trevor, William
"After Rain," 13:1

Tryon, Thomas, 3:1819 (Bio, v. 3)
Harvest Home, 4:1856
Other, The, 6:3139

Turow, Scott, 3:1822 (Bio, v. 3)
Burden of Proof, The, 1:555
One L, 6:3101
Personal Injuries, 13:293
Pleading Guilty, 6:3286
Presumed Innocent, 1:557, 6:3352

Twain, Mark, 3:1826 (Bio, v. 3)
Adventures of Tom Sawyer, The, 1:23
Adventures of Huckleberry Finn, The, 1:16

Tyler, Anne, 3:1839 (Bio, v. 3)
Accidental Tourist, The, 1:1
Breathing Lessons, 1:507
Dinner at the Homesick Restaurant,
    1:509, 2:1108
Saint Maybe, 6:3683

Updike, John, 3:1844 (Bio, v. 3)
Buchanan Dying, 5:2713
Gertrude and Claudius, 14:181
In the Beauty of the Lilies, 10:5702
Memories of the Ford Administration, 5:2711
Rabbit at Rest, 6:3423

Rabbit Is Rich, 14:337
Rabbit Redux, 6:3427
Rabbit, Run, 14:347
S., 6:3664
Toward the End of Time, 12:421
Witches of Eastwick, The, 11:6704

Uris, Leon, 3:1849 (Bio, v. 3)
Exodus, 3:1296

Van Vogt, A. E., 3:1855 (Bio, v. 3)
Quest for the Future, 6:3416
Slan, 7:3892
World of Null-A, The, 3219, 8:4717

Vanderhaeghe, Guy, 3:1852 (Bio, v. 3)
Homesick, 4:1962
Man Descending, 5:2629
My Present Age, 5:2879

Vargas Llosa, Mario, 3:1859 (Bio, v. 3)
Captain Pantoja and the Special Serv-
    ice, 2:911
Conversation in the Cathedral, 2:908
Green House, The, 3:1795
In Praise of the Stepmother, 4:2123
Time of the Hero, 2:910

Varley, John, 3:1863 (Bio, v. 3)
Ophiuchi Hotline, The, 6:3118
"Press Enter," 6:3348
Tango Charlie and Foxtrot Romeo, 7:4108

Verne, Jules
Around the World in Eighty Days, 9:5089
Begum's Fortune, The, 9:5163
Twenty Thousand Leagues Under the
    Sea, 11:6593

Vidal, Gore, 3:1865 (Bio, v. 3)
City and the Pillar, The, 2:808
Myra Breckinridge, 5:2889
Myron, 5:2890
Two Sisters, 8:4389

Vine, Barbara (see Rendell, Ruth)

Vinge, Joan D., 3:1869 (Bio, v. 3)
Catspaw, 6:3400
Dreamfall, 6:3400
Mother and Child, 5:2814
Phoenix in the Ashes, 6:3242
Psion, 6:3397
Snow Queen, The, 7:3911
Summer Queen, 7:3913
World's End, 7:3913

Vonnegut, Kurt, 3:1873 (Bio, v. 3)
Breakfast of Champions, 1:500
Cat's Cradle, 2:685
Deadeye Dick, 9:5379
Hocus Pocus, 4:1929
Slaughterhouse-Five, 7:3898

Wahlöö, Per (see Maj Sjöwal)

Walker, Alice, 3:1878 (Bio, v. 3)
Color Purple, The, 2:874
Possessing the Secret of Joy, 6:3309
Temple of My Familiar, The, 7:4136
Third Life of Grange Copeland, The, 11:6538

Wallace, Irving, 3:1889 (Bio, v. 3)
Fan Club, The, 3:1340
Miracle, The, 5:2750
Prize, The, 6:3385
Word, The, 5:2752

Waller, Robert, 3:1893 (Bio, v. 3)
Bridges of Madison County, The, 1:524

Wambaugh, Jr., Joseph, 3:1898 (Bio, v. 3)
Black Marble, The, 1:393
Blue Knight, The, 5:2936
Choirboys, The, 5:2936
Finnegan's Week, 3:1425
Golden Orange, The, 3:1727
New Centurions, The, 5:2934
Onion Field, The, 1:395

Warren, Robert Penn, 3:1901 (Bio, v. 3)
All the King's Men, 1:107

At Heaven's Gate, 9:5097
"Blackberry Winter," 9:5176
Circus in the Attic, 9:5292
Place to Come To, A, 6:3269
World Enough and Time, 8:4714

Waugh, Evelyn, 3:1910 (Bio, v. 3)
Brideshead Revisited, 1:518
Decline and Fall, 2:1058
Men at Arms, 5:2719
Unconditional Surrender, 5:2721

Wells, H. G., 3:1915 (Bio, v. 3)
Invisible Man, The, 4:2148
Time Machine, The, 7:4257
War of the Worlds, The, 8:4521

Welty, Eudora, 3:1923 (Bio, v. 3)
Delta Wedding, 6:3126
Losing Battles, 8:4662
Optimist's Daughter, The, 6:3122
Ponder Heart, The, 6:3293
Robber Bridegroom, The, 6:3629
"Why I Live at the P.O.," 8:4661

West, Morris, 3:1931 (Bio, v. 3)
Cassidy, 2:659
Clowns of God, The, 4:2374
Lazarus, 4:2372
Navigator, The, 2:660
Proteus, 2:662
Salamander, The, 2:662
Shoes of the Fisherman, The, 4:2374

West, Nathanael, 3:1934 (Bio, v. 3)
Day of the Locust, The, 2:1013
Miss Lonelyhearts, 5:2758

West, Rebecca, 3:1938 (Bio, v. 3)
Return of the Soldier, The, 6:3536
Thinking Reed, The, 7:4189

Wharton, Edith, 3:1949 (Bio, v. 3)
Age of Innocence, The, 1:48
Custom of the Country, The, 9:5355
Ethan Frome, 3:1273
House of Mirth, The, 4:2025

Reef, The, 6:3519

White, T. H., 3:1955 (Bio, v. 3)
Once and Future King, The, 5:3075

Wideman, John Edgar, 3:1958 (Bio, v. 3)
Lynchers, The, 5:2583
Philadelphia Fire, 6:3237
Sent For You Yesterday, 7:3765

Wiesel, Elie
Accident, The, 9:5013
Dawn, 9:5362
Forgotten, The, 9:5530

Willis, Connie
To Say Nothing of the Dog, 14:415

Wister, Owen, 3:1961 (Bio, v. 3)
The Jimmy-John Boss, 4:2195
The Virginian, 8:4476

Wolfe, Thomas, 3:1964 (Bio, v. 3)
Look Homeward, Angel, 5:2501
Of Time and the River, 5:2501

Wolfe, Tom, 3:1968 (Bio, v. 3)
Bonfire of the Vanities, The, 1:471
Man in Full, A, 12:237
Right Stuff, The, 6:3579

Woolf, Virginia, 3:1974 (Bio, v. 3)
"Duchess and the Jeweller, The," 9:5416
"Kew Gardens," 10:5777
"Mark on the Wall, The," 10:6028
Mrs. Dalloway, 5:2832
Orlando, 6:3134
Room of One's Own, A, 6:3135
Three Guineas, 6:3135
To the Lighthouse, 7:4286

Wouk, Herman, 3:1985 (Bio, v. 3)
Caine Mutiny, The, 2:586

War and Remembrance, 8:4517
Winds of War, The, 8:4677

Wright, Harold Bell, 3:1989 (Bio, v. 3)
Calling of Dan Matthews, 7:3823
God and the Groceryman, 7:3823
Shepherd of the Hills, The, 7:3821
When a Man's a Man, 8:4686
Winning of Barbara Worth, The, 8:4684

Wright, Richard, 3:1993 (Bio, v. 3)
Black Boy, 13:45
Native Son, 5:2916
Uncle Tom's Children, 8:4401

Yarbro, Chelsea Quinn, 3:1999 (Bio, v. 3)
False Dawn, 3:1337
Firecode, 3:1338
Saint-Germain Series, 6:3678
  Flame in Byzantium, A, 6:3678
  Crusader's Torch, 6:3678
  Candle for D'Artagnan, A, 6:3678
  Hotel Transylvania, 6:3678

Yerby, Frank G., 3:2003 (Bio, v. 3)
Benton's Row, 3:1546
Floodtide, 3:1545
Foxes of Harrow, The, 3:1540
Judas, My Brother, 3:1546
McKenzie's Hundred, 3:1545
Serpent and the Staff, The, 3:1546

Yolen, Jane, 3:2008 (Bio, v. 3)
Briar Rose, 1:512
Sister Light, Sister Dark, 7:3880, 8:4649
White Jenna, 8:4646

Yourcenar, Marguerite, 3:2012 (Bio, v. 3)
Abyss, The, 5:2710
Coin in Nine Hands, A, 2:865
Memoirs of Hadrian, 5:2708

Zahn, Timothy, 3:2016 (Bio, v. 3)
Cobra, 2:860
Dark Force Rising, 4:2343

Deadman Switch, 2:1021
Last Command, The, 4:2340

Zelanzy, Roger, 3:2019 (Bio, v. 3)
Chronicles of Amber, The, 2:775
Lord of Light, 5:2518
Second Chronicles of Amber, The, 7:3738
Second Chronicles of Amber, The, 7:3738

CUMULATIVE MASTER INDEX

VOLUMES 1–14

◆

Black Mountain, The, 1:396
Black Notice, 14:45
Black Sunday, 1:401
Black Tickets, 1:405
Black Tower, The, 2:1039
"Blackberry Winter," 9:5176
Blackboard Jungle, The, 1:409
Blank Page, The, 8:4430
Blasco Ibáñez, Vicente, 1:168 (Bio, v. 1)
Blind Date, 7:4038
Blind Man with a Pistol, 2:924
Blish, James, 1:172 (Bio, v. 1)
"Bliss," 1:414
Block, Lawrence, 1:177 (Bio, v. 1)
Blood and Chocolate, 14:55
Blood and Honor, 9:5182
Blood and Sand, 1:418
Blood Latitudes, The, 14:63
Blood Meridian, 1:117
Blood Music, 1:421
Blood of Others, The, 8:4699
Blood of Requited Love, 1:427
Blood Tie, 1:431
Bloodline, 1:241 (Ernest J. Gaines)
Bloodline, 1:434 (Sidney Sheldon)
Blue City, 1:438
"Blue Hotel, The," 9:5187
Blue Knight, The, 5:2936
Blue Movie, 2:608
"Blues I'm Playing, The," 12:51
Bluest Eye, The, 1:442
Bodily Harm, 4:1843
Body Farm, The, 1:451, 11:6620
Body of Evidence, 1:461
Bodysnatchers, The, 1:467
Böll, Heinrich, 1:181 (Bio, v. 1)
Bonfire of the Vanities, The, 1:471
Book of Bebb, The, 1:475
Book of Laughter and Forgetting, The, 1:481
Book of Skulls, The, 9:5194
Book of Three, The, 1:485
Boomerang, 1:488
Borges, Jorge Luis, 1:185 (Bio, v. 1)
Bourne Ultimatum, The, 1:491
Boyle, T. Coraghessan, 1:189 (Bio, v. 1)
Bradbury, Ray, 1:193 (Bio, v. 1)
Bradley, Marion Zimmer, 1:201 (Bio, v. 1)
Bradshaw, Gillian, 1:206 (Bio, v. 1)
Brand, Max, 1:208 (Bio, v. 1)
Braun, Lilian Jackson, 1:219 (Bio, v. 1)
Brautigan, Richard, 1:222 (Bio, v. 1)
Brave New World, 1:495
Breakfast at Tiffany's, 9:5199
Breakfast of Champions, 1:500
Breast, The, 1:503
Breath, Eyes, Memory, 13:55

Breathing Lessons, 1:507
Brethren, The, 14:73
Briar Rose, 1:512
"Bride Comes to Yellow Sky, The," 9:5192,
    14:79
Bride of Lammermoor, The, 12:59
Bride Price, The, 14:95
Brideshead Revisited, 1:518
Bridesmaid, The, 8:4453
Bridge of Lost Desire, The, 1:521
Bridges of Madison County, The, 1:524
Bright Lights, Big City, 1:533
Brightness Falls, 1:537
Brighton Rock, 6:3338
Brontë, Emily, 1:228 (Bio, v. 1)
Brothers Karamazov, The, 9:5206
Brown Girl, Brownstones, 1:541
Brown, Rita Mae, 1:234 (Bio, v. 1)
Buchanan Dying, 5:2713
Buck, Pearl S., 1:239 (Bio, v. 1)
Buckley, Jr., William F., 1:244 (Bio, v. 1)
Buechner, Frederick, 1:248 (Bio, v. 1)
Buffett, Jimmy, 1:253 (Bio, v. 1)
Bug Jack Barron, 1:546
Bugles in the Afternoon, 1:551
Bulgakov, Mikhail, 1:256 (Bio, v. 1)
Burden of Proof, The, 1:555
Burglar in the Library, The, 9:5217
Burglar Who Studied Spinoza, The, 1:559
Burgomaster of Furnes, 5:2612
Burning, 1:562
Burns, Olive Ann, 1:261 (Bio, v. 1)
Burroughs, Edgar Rice, 1:265 (Bio, v. 1)
Burroughs, William S., 1:271 (Bio, v. 1)
Bushwhacked Piano, The, 1:565
Businessman: A Tale of Terror, The, 9:5223
Busman's Honeymoon, 2:569
Butler, Jack, 1:279 (Bio, v. 1)
Butler, Octavia E., 1:283 (Bio, v. 1)
Butler, Robert Olen, 1:287 (Bio, v. 1)
Butler, Walter (see Brand, Max), 1:208
    (Bio, v. 1)
By Hook or By Crook, 7:3929
By Love Possessed, 2:574
By the Sword, 2:580
Byatt, A. S., 1:293 (Bio, v. 1)

C
Cain, James M., 1:296 (Bio, v. 1)
Caine Mutiny, The, 2:586
Cakes and Ale: Or The Skeleton in the
    Cupboard, 9:5229
Caldwell, Erskine, 1:301 (Bio, v. 1)
Caldwell, Taylor, 1:307 (Bio, v. 1)
Call of the Wild, The, 2:596
Call, The, 2:590

Calling of Dan Matthews, 7:3823
Camber of Culdi, 9:5237
Campaign, The, 2:600
Camus, Albert, 1:309 (Bio, v. 1)
Candle for D'Artagnan, A, 6:3678
Candle for St. Jude, A, 6:3216
Candle in the Wind, 3:1441
Candy, 2:606
Cane, 13:63
Cannibals and Missionaries, 2:610
Cannon, Curt (see Hunter, Evan/Ed McBain), 2:918 (Bio, v. 2)
Canticle for Leibowitz, A, 2:613
Capote, Truman, 1:314 (Bio, v. 1)
Captain and the Enemy, The, 2:617
Captain Blood: His Odyssey, 2:620
Captain Blood Returns, 2:622
Captain from Castile, 2:624
Captain Pantoja and the Special Service, 2:911
Captains and the Kings, 2:631
Captive of Gor, 5:2604
Card, Orson Scott, 1:321 (Bio, v. 1)
Cardinal of the Kremlin, 9:5243
Cardinal Virtues, The, 3:1330
Caroline's Daughters, 9:5248
Carpenter's Gothic, 2:635
Carpetbaggers, The, 2:638
Carré, John (see Le Carré, John), 2:1094 (Bio, v. 2)
Carrie, 9:5387
Carter, Nick (see Smith, Martin Cruz), 3:1677 (Bio, v. 3)
Carver, Raymond, 1:329 (Bio, v. 1)
Case of Charles Dexter Ward, The, 2:642
Case of Conscience, A, 2:647
Case of the Grinning Gorilla, The, 2:653
Cassidy, 2:659
Castle of Llyr, 1:390
Castle, The, 2:664
Cat and Mouse, 7:4278
Cat Who Blew the Whistle, The, 2:668
Cat Who Saw Red, The, 9:5254
Cat Who Turned On and Off, The, 2:677
Cat's Cradle, 2:685
Cat's Eye, 2:687
Catch-22, 2:695
Catcher in the Rye, The, 2:703
Cathedral, 2:708
Cather, Willa, 1:337 (Bio, v. 1)
Catseye, 9:5260
Catspaw, 6:3400
Cause of Death,11:6620
Cave, The, 9:5102
Celebration, 2:711
Ceremony, 12:67
Ceremony of Innocence, The, 2:713

Chain of Chance, The, 9:5267
Challis, George (see Brand, Max), 1:208 (Bio, v. 1)
Chamber, The, 6:3445, 7:4272
Chance,720, 5277
Chandler, Raymond, 1:343 (Bio, v. 1)
Changeling Sea, The, 2:723
Changes, 7:4026
Charlie and the Chocolate Factory, 2:727
Charnas, Suzy McKee, 1:352 (Bio, v. 1)
Cheever, John, 1:355 (Bio, v. 1)
Cheever: Stories of John Cheever, The 733
Chéri, 2:736
Cherryh, C. J., 1:360 (Bio, v. 1)
Childhood's End, 9:5286
Children of Light, 2:740
"Children of the Corn," 9:5388
Children of the Night, 2:743
"Children of the Sea," 13:73
Children of the Albatross, 2:807
Chilly Scenes of Winter, 2:748
China Men, 2:753
Choirboys, The, 5:2936
Choiring of the Trees, The, 2:756
Chosen Place, the Timeless People, The, 1:542
Chosen, The, 2:763
Christie, Agatha, 1:365 (Bio, v. 1)
Christy, 2:768
Chronicle of a Death Foretold, 2:773
Chronicles of Amber, The, 2:775
Chronicles of Thomas Covenant the Unbeliever, The, 2:780
Cider House Rules, The, 2:786
Circle of Friends, 2:790
Circular Staircase, The, 2:795
Circus in the Attic, 9:5292
Citadel, The, 4:2257
Cities in Flight series, 2:799
Cities of the Interior, 2:804
City and the Stars, 8:4394
City and the Pillar, The, 2:808
City of God, 13:81
City of Sorcery, 2:817
City of the Mind, 2:811
Clan of the Cave Bear, The, 2:821
Clancy, Tom, 1:371 (Bio, v. 1)
Clark, Curt (see Westlake, Donald), 4:1944 (Bio, v. 3)
Clark, Mary Higgins, 1:375 (Bio, v. 1)
Clarke, Arthur C., 1:381 (Bio, v. 1)
Clavell, James, 1:388 (Bio, v. 1)
Clea, 1:80
Clear and Present Danger, 2:824, 4:2041, 9:5464
Clemens, Samuel Langhorne (see Twain, Mark), 3:1826 (Bio, v. 3)
Client, The, 2:831

Emma, 12:91
Emperor of America, 3:1237
Empire of the Sun, 14:115
Empress of the Splendid Season, 14:125
Empty Coppper Sea, The, 5:2488
Enchanter, The, 5:2483
End of the Affair, The, 13:137
Ender's Game, 3:1242
Endzone, 3:1248
Enemies: A Love Story, 3:1252
English Patient, The, 9:5436
Entered from the Sun, 2:1051
Eon, 3:1255
Equal Rites, 3:1261
Erasers, The, 3:1265
Erdrich, Louise, 1:599 (Bio, v. 1)
Erection Set, The, 3:1268
Esteven, John (see Shellabarger, Samuel), 3:1637 (Bio, v. 3)
Ethan Frome, 3:1273
Evans, Evan (see Brand, Max), 1:208 (Bio, v. 1)
Even Cowgirls Get the Blues, 3:1277
Even the Wicked, 9:5445
Evening Class, 9:5451
Evening News, The, 3:1281
Every Living Thing, 3:1284
Excellent Women, 3:1288
Executioner's Song, The, 3:1294
Executive Orders, 9:5459
Exile, The, 9:5467
Exley, Frederick, 1:603 (Bio, v. 1)
Exodus, 3:1296
Exorcist, The, 9:5472
Expensive People, 11:6514
Eye of the Needle, 3:1299
Eyes of the Dragon, The, 3:1302

F
Faded Sun: Kesrith, The, 3:1305
Faded Sun Trilogy, The, 3:1305
Fafyrd and Grey Mouser Stories, The, 3:1309
Fahrenheit 451, 3:1313
Fairy Tale of New York, A, 3:1317
Faith, 7:3993
"Faith of Our Fathers," 5:2635
Falconer, 3:1322
Fall From Grace, 3:1327
"Fall of the House of Usher, The," 3:1332
Fall, The, 3:1324
Fallen Man, 9:5482
Falling in Place, 6:3256
False Dawn, 3:1337
False Memory, 14:133
Family Album, 7:4023
Fan Club, The, 3:1340

Fan Man, The, 3:1345
Fan's Notes, A, 3:1349
Fanny, 3:1353
Far Tortuga, 3:1357
Farewell, My Lovely, 3:1361
Farewell to Arms, A, 3:1364
Farmer, Philip Jóse, 1:606 (Bio, v. 1)
Farrell, James T., 1:612 (Bio, v. 1)
Fast, Howard, 1:616 (Bio, v. 1)
Fast Lanes, 1:408, 3:1367
Fat Man, The, 9:5154
Father Melancholy's Daughter, 3:1372
Faulkner, William, 1:624 (Bio, v. 1)
Faulkner's (William) Short Fiction, 3:1378
Faust, Frederick (see Brand, Max), 1:208 (Bio, v. 1)
Fear and Loathing in Las Vegas, 3:1385
Fear of Flying, 3:1389
Feast of Snakes, A, 3:1392
Feast Unknown, A, 5:2576
Feather Crowns, 3:1395
Female Man, The, 3:1403
Fencepost Chronicles, The, 3:1406
Few Green Leaves, A, 3:1292
Fiasco, 9:5491
Fierce Invalids Home from Hot Climates, 14:143
Fifth Business, 3:1409
Final Payments, 3:1418
Financial Expert, The, 3:1824
Finding Moon, 9:5501
Fine and Private Place, A, 3:1422
Finnegan's Week, 3:1425
Finney, Jack, 1:637 (Bio, v. 1)
Fire Down Below, 6:3585
Fire from Heaven, 4:2358
Firebird, The, 9:5508
Firebrand, The, 9:5516
Firecode, 3:1338
Firm, The, 3:1431
First Circle, The, 3:1439
First Man in Rome, The, 3:1443
Fitzgerald, F. Scott, 1:639 (Bio, v. 1)
Fitzgerald's (F. Scott) Short Fiction, 3:1450
Five Days in Paris, 7:4029
Five for Sorrow, Ten for Joy, 3:1456
Five Minutes in Heaven, 3:1460
Five Red Herrings, 2:854
Fix Like This, A, 8:4431
Fixer, The, 3:1465
Flag for Sunrise, A, 3:1469
Flame in Byzantium, A, 6:3678
Flaming Corsage, The, 4:2170
Flaubert's Parrot, 14:155
Fleming, Ian, 1:648 (Bio, v. 1)
Flesh and Blood, 12:103

God's Grace, 5592
God's Little Acre, 3:1717
Godbody, 3:1704
Godden, Rumer, 2:730 (Bio, v. 2)
Godfather, The, 3:1707
Godplayer, 2:888
Godric, 3:1713
Gods and Generals, 4:2272 (by Jeff Shaara)
Godwin, Gail, 2:733 (Bio, v. 2)
Godwulf Manuscript, The, 3:1722
"Gold Bug, The," 5:2854
Gold Bug Variations, The, 9:5602
Golden Notebook, The, 13:181
Golden Orange, The, 3:1727
Goldfinger, 3:1730
Golding, William, 2:737 (Bio, v. 2)
Goldman, William, 2:743 (Bio, v. 2)
Gone Fishin', 9:5606
Gone With the Wind, 3:1734
Good as Gold, 9:5616
Good Bones and Simple Murders, 9:5066
Good Earth, The, 4:2020
Good Husband, The, 3:1741
Good Scent from a Strange Mountain, A, 3:1746
Good Will, 7:4212
Gordon, Mary, 2:745 (Bio, v. 2)
Gorky Park, 3:1753
Grapes of Wrath, The, 3:1757
Grass, Günter, 2:750 (Bio, v. 2)
Grass Harp, The, 9:5621
Graves, Robert, 2:754 (Bio, v. 2)
Graveyard For Lunatics, A, 3:1762
Gravity's Rainbow, 3:1767
Great Gatsby, The, 3:1773
Great Jones Street, 3:1779
Great Santini, The, 3:1782, 6:3363
Great Sky River, 3:1791
Greeley, Andrew M., 2:758 (Bio, v. 2)
Green Grows the Dollars, 7:3929
Green House, The, 3:1795
Green Mile, The, 9:5630
Greene, Graham, 2:764 (Bio, v. 2)
Greengage Summer, The, 3:1798
Greenlanders, The, 3:1803
Grendel, 3:1808
Grey, Zane, 2:771 (Bio, v. 2)
Griffin, W. E. B., 2:776 (Bio, v. 2)
Grimes, Martha, 2:779 (Bio, v. 2)
Grisham, John, 2:781 (Bio, v. 2)
Ground Beneath Her Feet, The, 12:115
Group Portrait with Lady, 3:1817
Group, The, 3:1812
Guard of Honor, 2:577
Guerrillas, 3:1820
Guide, The, 3:1822
"Gun for Dinosaur, A," 11:6344

Gunslinger, The, 2:991

H
Hailey, Arthur, 2:789 (Bio, v. 2)
Haley, Alex, 2:792 (Bio, v. 2)
"Half a Day," 12:127
Half Asleep in Frog Pajamas, 3:1826
Half Moon Street, 5:2812
Halliday, Brett, 2:797 (Bio, v. 2)
Hammer of God, The, 4:1831
Hammett, Dashiell, 2:800 (Bio, v. 2)
Handmaid's Tale, The, 4:1838
"Handsomest Drowned Man in the World,
    The," 12:133
Hannah, Barry, 2:805 (Bio, v. 2)
Hannibal, 12:141
Hansen, Joseph, 2:811 (Bio, v. 2)
Happenstance, 10:5828
Hapworth 16, 1:1924, 10:5639
Hard to Be a God, 13:187
Harington, Donald, 2:815 (Bio, v. 2)
Harmful Intent, 4:1847
Harpist in the Wind, 6:3554
Harris, Thomas, 2:821 (Bio, v. 2)
Harrowing of Gwynedd, The, 4:1850
Harvest Home, 4:1856
Harvest of Stars, 10:5646
Harvester, The, 3:1687
Hatter's Castle, 4:2258
Haunting of Hill House, The, 4:1859
Have His Carcase, 2:571
Have Space Suit—Will Travel, 4:1862
Hawaii, 4:1865
Hawk of May, 4:1872
Hawkes, John, 2:823 (Bio, v. 2)
Hawthorne, Nathaniel, 2:829 (Bio, v. 2)
Haycox, Ernest, 2:839 (Bio, v. 2)
Heart Is a Lonely Hunter, The, 4:1878
Heart of Darkness, 2:722, 4:1883
Heart of Midlothian, The, 12:149
Heilbrun, Carolyn G. (see Cross, Amanda,
    1:482, Bio, v. 1)
Heinlein, Robert A., 2:842 (Bio, v. 2)
Heir of Sea and Fire, 6:3554
Heirs of Hammerfell, The, 4:1888
Heller, Joseph, 2:846 (Bio, v. 2)
Hemingway (Ernest): Complete Short Stories of,
    The, 4:1891
Hemingway, Ernest, 2:856 (Bio, v. 2)
Henissart, Martha (see Lathen, Emma), 2:1080
    (Bio, v. 2)
Her Mother's Daughter, 4:1894
Herbert, Frank, 2:863 (Bio, v. 2)
Here to Stay: Stories in Human Tenacity, 11:6661
"Here We Are," 10:5657
Heritage of Hastur, 10:5661

Heritage of the Desert, The, 6:3566
Hermit of 69th Street, The, 4:1899
Herriot, James, 2:866 (Bio, v. 2)
Hersey, John, 2:870 (Bio, v. 2)
Herzog, 4:1903
Hesse, Hermann, 2:877 (Bio, v. 2)
Hey Jack!, 4:1906
Higgins, George V., 2:882 (Bio, v. 2)
High and the Mighty, The, 4:1910
High Deryni, 9:5240
High Jinx, 6:3719
High King, The, 1:391
Highwater, Jamake, 2:885 (Bio, v. 2)
Hillerman, Tony, 2:891 (Bio, v. 2)
Himes, Chester, 2:896 (Bio, v. 2)
Hinton, S. E., 2:900 (Bio, v. 2)
His Little Women, 4:1916
Hoban, Russell, 2:903 (Bio, v. 2)
Hobbit, The, 4:1924
Hobson, Laura Z., 2:906 (Bio, v. 2)
Hocus Pocus, 4:1929
Hogfather, 13:197
Holcroft Covenant, The, 4:1932
Hollow Hills, The, 4:1937
Hollywood Husbands, 4:1941
Hollywood Kids, 10:5666
Hollywood Wives, 4:1945
Holt, Victoria, 2:908 (Bio, v. 2)
Hombre, 4:1948
Homeland, 4:1951
Homesick, 4:1962
Hondo, 4:1965
Honorable Barbarian, The, 4:1968
Honorable Schoolboy, The, 11:6580
Hope, 7:3993
Hopscotch, 4:1972
Horgan, Paul, 2:912 (Bio, v. 2)
Hornet's Nest, 11:6620
Horse and His Boy, The, 4:2425
Horse You Came In On, The, 4:1976
Hot Jazz Trio, The, 4:1979
Hot Six, 14:197
Hotel New Hampshire, The, 2:788, 4:1982
Hotel Transylvania, 6:3678
Hound of the Baskervilles, The, 4:1986
Hounds of God, The, 4:1997
Hour of the Dragon, The, 4:2002
House Divided, A, 4:2020
House for Mr. Biswas, A, 4:2012
House Made of Dawn, 4:2015
House of Earth trilogy, 4:2020
House of Mirth, The, 4:2025
House of Stairs, The, 8:4454
House of the Seven Gables, The, 4:2029
House of the Spirits, The, 12:157
House on Mango Streeet, The, 12:169

Houseguest, The, 10:5671
How Stella Got Her Groove Back, 10:5677
How the Dead Live, 14:207
How the Garcia Girls Lost Their Accents, 13:203
Howard, Robert E., 2:915 (Bio, v. 2)
Howards End, 10:5685
Hugger Mugger, 14:215
Human Stain, The, 14:225
Humboldt's Gift, 4:2034
Hundred Secret Senses, The, 4:2210
Hunt for Red October, The, 4:2036
Hunter, Evan/Ed McBain, 2:918 (Bio, v. 2)
Hunter, The, 4:2043
Hunter's Horn, 2:1149
Hunting Badger, 13:213
Hush Money, 12:179
Hutchinson, A. S. M., 2:925 (Bio, v. 2)
Huxley, Aldous Leonard, 2:927 (Bio, v. 2)

I

I, Claudius, 4:2046
"I Have No Mouth and I Must
   Scream," 4:2050
I Know Why the Caged Bird Sings, 4:2059
I Love Galesburg in the Springtime, 7:4256
I, Robot, 4:2063
I, the Jury, 4:2052
I Wear the Morning Star, 2:717
I'll Take Manhattan, 4:2066
Ibáñez, Vicente Blasco (see Blasco
   Ibáñez,Vicente), 1:168 (Bio, v. 1)
Icarus Agenda, The, 4:2069
"Ice Palace, The," 3:1450
If Winter Comes, 4:2074
"Il Conde," 10:5696
Illearth War, The, 2:780
Immigrant's Daughter, The, 4:2082
Immigrants, The, 4:2078
Immortality, 4:2083
Imperfect Spy, An, 4:2087
Imperial Earth, 8:4394
In Cold Blood, 4:2092
In Country, 4:2099
In Dubious Battle, 4:2103
"In Love," 11:6415
In My Father's House, 4:2109
In Our Time, 4:2116
In Praise of the Stepmother, 4:2123
In the Beauty of the Lilies, 10:5702
In the Beginning, 2:766
In the Land of Dreamy Dreams, 4:2106
In the Last Analysis, 10:5709
In the Midst of Death, 9:5432
In the Miro District, 7:4079
In the Ocean of Night, 4:2113
In the Presence of the Sun, 4:2127

In the Time of the Butterflies, **14:237**
In Winter's Shadow, 4:1875
Indecent Obsession, An, 7:4202
Independence Day, 10:5714
Inheritance, The, 10:5721
Inheritors, The, 5:2517 (William Golding)
Inheritors, The, 2:640 (Harold Robbins)
Inktruck, The, 4:2170
Innkeeper's Song, The, 4:2368
Innocent Blood, 4:2133
Integral Trees, The, 4:2136
Interesting Times, 10:5729
Interview with the Vampire, 4:2139
Inventing Memory, 10:5735
Investigation, The, 9:5274
Invincible, The, 10:5745
Invisible Man, 4:2143 (Ralph Ellison)
Invisible Man, The, 4:2148 (H. G. Wells)
Iowa Baseball Confederacy, The, 7:3851
Ipcress File, The, 4:2153
Iron Dream, The, 4:2160
Ironweed, 4:2166
Irving, John, 2:934 (Bio, v. 2)
Isaacs, Susan, 2:940 (Bio, v. 2)
Ishiguro, Kazuo, 2:944 (Bio, v. 2)
Island of the Day Before, The, 4:2179
Island of the Blue Dolphins, 4:2172
Ivanhoe, 12:187

J
J R, 6:3467
Jack Maggs, 14:245
Jackson, Shirley, 2:947 (Bio, v. 2)
Jakes, John, 2:952 (Bio, v. 2)
James, Henry, 2:956 (Bio, v. 2)
James Herriot's Cat Stories, 4:2183
James, P. D., 2:962 (Bio, v. 2)
Jane and Prudence, 3:1292
Jane Eyre, 10:5753
"Janus," 13:223
Jaws, 4:2187, 9:5160
Jazz, 12:195
"Je ne parle pas français," 4:2192
Jenkins, Dan, 2:965 (Bio, v. 2)
Jimmy-John Boss, The, 4:2195
Joey's Case, 4:2198
Johnson, Diane, 2:967 (Bio, v. 2)
Jonathan Livingston Seagull, 4:2203
Jones, James, 2:970 (Bio, v. 2)
Jong, Erica, 2:975 (Bio, v. 2)
Journals of Susanna Moodie, The, 9:5066, 11:6467
Journeyman, 3:1721
Joy in the Morning, 7:4342
Joy Luck Club, The, 4:2208
Jubal Sackett, 4:2211
Judas, My Brother, 3:1546

Jude the Obscure, 10:5761
Judgment Day, 6:3605, 7:4072
Jujitsu for Christ, 4:2215
Julie, 4:2223
July's People, 13:229
Juneteenth, 12:211
Jungle, The, 4:2226
Jurassic Park, 4:2230, 10:5974
Justine, 1:80

K
K., 4:2239
Kafka, Franz, 2:979 (Bio, v. 2)
Kane and Abel, 4:2241
Kazantzakis, Nikos, 2:986 (Bio, v. 2)
Keep the Change, 4:2245
Keillor, Garrison, 2:989 (Bio, v. 2)
Kemelman, Harry, 2:992 (Bio, v. 2)
Kennedy, William, 2:995 (Bio, v. 2)
Kent Family Chronicles, 4:2249
Kenton, Maxwell (see Southern, Terry), 3:1688
   (Bio, v. 3)
Kerouac, Jack, 2:1002 (Bio, v. 2)
Kesey, Ken, 2:1006 (Bio, v. 2)
"Kew Gardens," 10:5777
Key Out of Time, 10:5784
Key to Rebecca, The, 10:5790
Keys of the Kingdom, The, 4:2255
Kidnapped, 4:2260
Kill Hole, 4:2264
Killashandra, 10:5795
Killer Angels, The, 4:2270
Killing Mister Watson, 4:2274
Killshot, 10:5799
Kindred, 4:2278
Kinflicks, 4:2282
King Coal, 4:2229
King Javan's Year, 4:2286
King Must Die, The, 4:2357
King of the Fields, The, 4:2291, 11:6368
King Rat, 4:2295
King, Stephen, 2:1017 (Bio, v. 2)
Kingdom of Summer, 4:1874
Kingston, Maxine Hong, 2:1030 (Bio, v. 2)
Kinsella, W. P., 2:1034 (Bio, v. 2)
Kiss of the Spider Woman, 4:2297
Kitchen God's Wife, The, 4:2210
Klein, Norma, 2:1037 (Bio, v. 2)
"Knife Thrower, The," 14:255
Knight's Gambit, 3:1378
Knockout Artist, The, 4:2300
Knowles, John, 2:1040 (Bio, v. 2)
Kosinski, Jerzy, 2:1043 (Bio, v. 2)
Kotzwinkle, William, 2:1051 (Bio, v. 2)
Krantz, Judith, 2:1054 (Bio, v. 2)
Kundera, Milan, 2:1056 (Bio, v. 2)

Kurtz, Katherine, 2:1061 (Bio, v. 2)

L

L'Amour, Louis, 2:1069 (Bio, v. 2)
L'Engle, Madeleine, 2:1110 (Bio, v. 2)
La Brava, 10:5804
Labyrinths: Selected Stories and Other Writings, 4:2304
Lackey, Mercedes, 2:1065 (Bio, v. 2)
Ladders to Fire, 2:807
Lady Chatterley's Lover, 4:2307
Lady of Avalon, 10:5808
Lady of the Trillium, 4:2311
Lady Oracle, 4:2316
Lady Who Liked Clean Restrooms, The, 10:5816
Lake Wobegon Days, 4:2322
"Lamb to the Slaughter," 4:2326
Lammas Night, 5:2477
Land of Mist, The, 5:2542
Land That Time Forgot, The, 4:2329
Lardner, Ring, 2:1075 (Bio, v. 2)
Larry's Party, 10:5824
Last Command, The, 4:2340
Last Don, The, 3:1711
Last Go Round, 4:2346
Last Heroes, The, (as Alex Baldwin), 10:5830
Last Notes from Home, 4:2351
Last of Chéri, The, 2:736
Last of the Wine, The, 4:2355
Last Picture Show, The, 10:5836
Last Temptation of Christ, The, 4:2360
Last Tycoon, The, 4:2363
Last Unicorn, The, 4:2366, 10:5842
Last Woman in His Life, The, 5:2850
Late George Apley, The, 4:2370
Lathen, Emma, 2:1080 (Bio, v. 2)
Latsis, Mary Jane (see Lathen, Emma), 2:1080 (Bio, v. 2)
Laughing Policeman, The, 7:4156
Law of Love, The, 10:5850
Lawrence, D. H., 2:1084 (Bio, v. 2)
Lazarus, 4:2372
Le Carré, John, 2:1094 (Bio, v. 2)
Le Divorce, 10:5860
Le Guin, Ursula, 2:1101 (Bio, v. 2)
Leatherstocking Tales, The, 6:3202
Leaving Cold Sassy, 2:871
Lee, Harper, 2:1098 (Bio, v. 2)
Left Hand of Darkness, The, 4:2376
Legacies: A Chinese Mosaic, 4:2378
Legacy, The, 4:2081
Legend Days, 2:714, 4:2382
Legion, 10:5870
Legs, 4:2388
Leiber, Fritz, 2:1105 (Bio, v. 2)
Leonard, Elmore, 2:1113 (Bio, v. 2)

Lepofsky, Manford (see Queen, Ellery), 3:1509 (Bio, v. 3)
Les Miserables, 13:239
Less Than Angels, 3:1291
Less Than Zero, 14:261
Lesson before Dying, A, 13:249
Lest Darkness Fall, 4:2397
Let Me Call You Sweetheart, 10:5881
Let Us Build Us a City, 1:199
Letters from Atlantis, 4:2404
Lewis, C. S., 2:1118 (Bio, v. 2)
Lewis, Sinclair, 2:1122 (Bio, v. 2)
"Library Policeman, The," 11:6283
Lie Down in Darkness, 4:2411
Life Before Man, 11:6466
Life for the Stars, A, 2:799
"Ligeia," 10:5889
Light Can Be Both Wave and Particle, 4:2415
Light in August, 12:225
Light in the Window, A, 10:5899
Lightning, 7:4029
Lightning Bug, 10:5909
Like Water for Chocolate, 10:5917
Lily White, 10:5930
Lime Twig, The, 4:2418
Lindbergh, Anne Morrow, 2:1127 (Bio, v. 2)
Lion Country, 1:475
Lion Game, The, 8:4419
Lion, the Witch, and the Wardrobe, The, 4:2423
Little, Big, 4:2427
Little Big Man, 4:2431
Little Drummer Girl, The, 4:2439
"Little Governess, The," 1:416
Little Kingdoms, 14:269
Little Prince, The, 4:2441
Little Women, 4:2444
Little Women series, 4:2452
Little Yellow Dog, A, 8:4637, 10:5939
Lively, Penelope, 2:1132 (Bio, v. 2)
Lives of Girls and Women, 4:2455
Lives of the Poets, 8:4553
Livia: Or Buried Alive, 1:247
Living in Little Rock with Miss Little Rock, 5:2463
Local Anesthetic, 2:1138
Lodge of the Lynx, The, 5:2472
Logan, Jake (see Smith, Martin Cruz), 3:1677 (Bio, v. 3)
Lolita, 5:2480
London, Jack, 2:1138 (Bio, v. 2)
Lonely Silver Rain, The, 5:2485
Lonesome Dove, 5:2491, 10:5948
Lonesome Places, 5:2494
Longings of Women, The, 5:2498
Look Homeward, Angel, 5:2501
Looking for Mr. Goodbar, 5:2507

Lord, Bette Bao, 2:1144 (Bio, v. 2)
Lord Foul's Bane, 2:780
Lord Jim, 10:5954
Lord of Light, 5:2518
Lord of the Dance, 7:4228
Lord of the Flies, 5:2514
Lord of the Rings, The, 5:2521
Lord of the Two Lands, 5:2528
Lord Valentine's Castle, 5:2533
Lord Vanity, 2:629
Losing Battles, 8:4662
Lost Boys, 5:2536
Lost World, The, 5:2540 (Conan Doyle)
Lost World, The, 4:2236, 10:5962 (Crichton)
"Lot No. 249," 13:259
Lottery, The, 5:2546
Love & Sleep, 5:2562
Love, Again, 13:269
Love Feast, 1:475
Love in the Time of Cholera, 5:2549
Love Killers, The, 5:2552
Love Medicine, 5:2555
Love Story, 5:2567
Lovecraft, H. P., 2:1148 (Bio, v. 2)
"Lovely Leave, The," 5979
Lover, The, 6:3730
Lovers, The, 5:2573
Loving, 7:4024
Loving Women: A Novel of the Fifties, 10:5983
Lowry, Malcolm, 2:1154 (Bio, v. 2)
Lucky Jim, 5:2578
Ludlum, Robert, 2:1162 (Bio, v. 2)
Lurie, Alison, 2:1164 (Bio, v. 2)
Lust for Life, 5:2580
Lynchers, The, 5:2583

M
M.D.: A Horror Story, The 10:5991
Macdonald, Ross, 2:1170 (Bio, v. 2)
MacDonald, John D., 2:1167 (Bio, v. 2)
Machine Dreams, 5:2588
MacInnes, Helen, 2:1176 (Bio, v. 2)
Maggie: A Girl of the Streets, 10:5998
Maggie Now, 7:4342
Magic Hour, 10:6006
Magic Mountain, The, 5:2594
Magician's Nephew, The, 4:2426
Magicians of Gor, 5:2597
Magister Ludi, 2:1125
Magnificent Ambersons, The, 10:6011
Magus, The, 5:2606
Maia, 7:3807
Maigret Meets a Milord, 5:2609
Mailer, Norman, 2:1179 (Bio, v. 2)
Main Street, 5:2613
Malamud, Bernard, 2:1185 (Bio, v. 2)

Malamud: Stories of Bernard Malamud,
  The, 5:2616
Malraux, André, 2:1189 (Bio, v. 2)
Maltese Falcon, The, 5:2621
Mama Day, 13:279
Mambo Kings Play Songs of Love, The, 14:275
Mammoth Hunters, The, 5:2626
Man Descending, 5:2629
Man in Full, A, 12:237
Man in the High Castle, The, 5:2633
Man O' War, 12:247
Man of the People, A, 10:6019
Man Who Liked to Look at Himself, The, 8:4430
Man Who Liked Slow Tomatoes, The, 8:4431
Man with a Load of Mischief, The, 5:2642
Man with the Golden Arm, The, 5:2637
Man, Woman and Child, 5:2571
Man's Fate, 5:2668
Man-Eater of Malgudi, The, 5:2656
Manchurian Candidate, The, 5:2648
Mandarins, The, 5:2651
Manhattan Transfer, 5:2658
Mann, Thomas, 2:1193 (Bio, v. 2)
Manning, David (see Brand, Max), 1:208
  (Bio, v. 1)
Mansfield, Katherine, 2:1216 (Bio, v. 2)
Manual for Manuel, A, 5:2671
Marco Polo, If You Can, 6:3718
Marilyn, 1:30
"Mark on the Wall, The," 10:6028
Marquand, John P., 2:1203 (Bio, v. 2)
Marquez, Gabriel Garcia (see Garcia Marquez,
  Gabriel), 2:694 (Bio, v.2)
Marshall, Catherine, 2:1206 (Bio, v. 2)
Marshall, Paule, 2:1209 (Bio, v. 2)
Marsten, Richard (see Hunter, Evan/Ed
  McBain), 2:918 (Bio, v. 2)
Martian Chronicles, The, 5:2676
Martian Time-Slip, 5:2679
Marvelous Land of Oz, The, 12:253
Marya: A Life, 5:2681
Mason & Dixon, 10:6036
Mason, Bobbie Ann, 2:1212 (Bio, v. 2)
Mason, Perry series, 2:653
Master and Margarita, The, 5:2684
Master of Ballantrae, The, 5:2688
Matthiessen, Peter, 2:1216 (Bio, v. 2)
Maugham, W. Somerset, 2:1222 (Bio, v. 2)
Maurice, 10:6045
Maximum Bob, 5:2692
"May Day," 3:1451
Mayor of Casterbridge, The, 10:6054
McBain, Ed (see Hunter, Evan/Ed McBain),
  2:918 (Bio, v. 2)
McCaffrey, Anne, 2:1226 (Bio, v. 2)
McCarthy, Cormac, 2:1232 (Bio, v. 2)

Natural, The, 5:2920
Navigator, The, 2:660
Neighbors, 10:6103
Neon Wilderness, The, 5:2924
Neuromancer, 5:2927
Never Love a Stranger, 7:4043
New Centurions, The, 5:2934
Nexus, 6:3640
Nick Adams Stories, The, 4:2121
Nigger of the Narcissus, The, 11:6738
Night, 9:5534, 9:5367
Night Flight, 5:2937
Night of Light, 10:6111
"Night the Bed Fell, The," 5:2940
Nightfall, 5:2942
Nightshade, 5:2955
Nightwing, 7:4005
Nightwork, 2:1028
Nin, Anaïs, 2:1349 (Bio, v. 2)
Nine Tailors, The, 2:854
Nineteen Eighty-Four, 5:2963
Nineteen, Nineteen, 1:353
Ninety-Two in the Shade, 5:2966
Ninth Configuration, The, 10:6117
Niven, Larry, 2:1355 (Bio, v. 2)
No Adam in Eden, 5:2970
No Fond Return of Love, 3:1292
No Future for Luana, 5:2974
No Longer at Ease, 1:209, 7:4186
No More Saturday Nights, 5:2977
No Word From Winifred, 5:2983
Noble House, 7:3855
Nocturne, 10:6127
Noon Wine, 5:2987
Norman, John, 2:1359 (Bio, v. 2)
Norris, Frank, 2:1362 (Bio, v. 2)
North from Rome, 6:3689
Norton, Andre, 2:1366 (Bio, v. 2)
Nostromo, 5:2990
Notes from the Underground, 9:5334
Nothing But Blue Skies, 5:2993
Nova Express, 5:2998
Novels of Danielle Steel, The, 7:4023
Novelty, 5:3004
Nunquam, 6:3539

O

O Is for Outlaw, 14:285
O Pioneers!, 5:3007
O. Henry, 3:1395 (Bio, v. 3)
O'Connor: Complete Stories of Flannery
    O'Connor, The,5:3011
O'Connor, Flannery, 3:1379 (Bio, v. 3)
O'Dell, Scott, 3:1387 (Bio, v. 3)
O'Hara, John, 3:1391 (Bio, v. 3)
Oates, Joyce Carol, 2:1373 (Bio, v. 2)

Oath, The, 9:5534
Obasan, 12:277
"Oblong Box, The," 10:5895
October Ferry to Gabriola, 3:1502
Octopus, The, 5:3014
"Oddly and Id," 7:4017
Of Human Bondage, 5:3021
Of Love and Dust, 1:241
Of Mice and Men, 5:3024
Of Time and the River, 5:2501
Old Contemptibles, The, 5:3027
Old Dick, The, 5:3031
Old Forest, The, 7:4079
Old Gringo, The, 5:3035
Old Man and the Sea, The, 5:3041
Older Men, 5:3046
Oliver's Story, 5:2570
Olivia, 5:3052
On Distant Ground, 10:6139
On Mystic Lake, 14:295
On the Beach, 5:3059
On the Road, 5:3065
On Wings of Eagles, 5:3069
On Wings of Song, 5:3072
Once and Future King, The, 5:3075
Once Is Not Enough, 5:3080
One Day in the Life of Ivan Denisovich, 5:3083
One Flew Over the Cuckoo's Nest, 5:3088
One Hundred Years of Solitude, 6:3097
One L, 6:3101
One More Sunday, 6:3105
Onion Field, The, 1:395
Only Children, 10:6148
"Open Boat, The," 10:6157
Open Heart, 1:475
Operation Shylock, 6:3108
Operation Wandering Soul, 6:3113
Ophiuchi Hotline, The, 6:3118
Optimist's Daughter, The, 6:3122
Ordinary People, 12:287
Origin, The, 6:3127
Origin of the Brunists, The, 6:3130
Orlando, 6:3134
Orwell, George, 3:1400 (Bio, v. 3)
Other, The, 6:3139
Other Side, The, 6:3143
Other Side of Midnight, The, 6:3148
Other Voices, Other Rooms, 10:6165
Other Women, 4:2283
Our Father, 6:3151
Out of Africa, 14:301
Out of Sight, 10:6174
Out of the Silent Planet, 6:3158
Out on the Cutting Edge, 7:4231
Outbreak, 2:888
Outer Dark, 6:3162

Outerbridge Reach, 6:3165
"Outpost of Progress," 10:6186
Outsiders, The, 6:3170

P

Pages from a Cold Island, 6:3176
Painted Bird, The, 6:3179
Pale Fire, 6:3185
Pale Gray for Guilt, 5:2488
Pale View of Hills, A, 6:3188
Parable of the Sower, 6:3191
Paradise, 6:3195
Paradise, 12:295
Parker, Robert B., 3:1407 (Bio, v. 3)
Partner, The, 11:6320
Passage to India, A, 10:6193
Passos, John Dos (see Dos Passos, John), 1:553
　(Bio, v. 1)
Pasternak, Boris, 3:1412 (Bio, v. 3)
Pathfinder, The, 6:3202
Patience of A Saint, The, 6:3208
Paton, Alan, 3:1416 (Bio, v. 3)
Patriot Games, 10:6206
Peacock Spring, The, 6:3214
Peculiar Treasures, 3:1714
Pedigree, 5:2611
Pelican Brief, The, 2:837
Penrod, 6:3219
Percy, Walker, 3:1420 (Bio, v. 3)
Perelman, S. J., 3:1425 (Bio, v. 3)
Perfect Storm, The, 14:309
Perfume, 6:3222
Perry Mason Series, 2:653
Personal Injuries, 13:293
Pet Sematary, 6:3227
Petry, Ann, 3:1431 (Bio, v. 3)
Peyton Place, 6:3231
Philadelphia Fire, 6:3237
Phillips, Jayne Anne, 3:1436 (Bio, v. 3)
Phoenix in the Ashes, 6:3242
Picture This, 6:3245
Picturing Will, 6:3251, 8:4574
Piercy, Marge, 3:1439 (Bio, v. 3)
Pigeon, The, 6:3258
Pilot's Wife, The, 14:319
Pinktoes, 6:3261
"Pit and the Pendulum, The," 6:3264
Place to Come To, A, 6:3269
Plague Dogs, The, 8:4549
Plague, The, 6:3272
Plains of Passage, The, 6:3275
Planetarium, The, 6:3278
Plath, Sylvia, 3:1444 (Bio, v. 3)
Playback, 14:327
Players Come Again, The, 6:3282
Pleading Guilty, 6:3286

Plexus, 6:3640
Poe, Edgar Allan, 3:1449 (Bio, v. 3)
Poetic Justice, 10:5712
Point of No Return, 6:3290
Poison Belt, The, 5:2542
Poisonwood Bible, The, 12:327
Polar Star, 6:3512
Ponder Heart, The, 6:3293
Porter, Gene Stratton, 3:1457 (Bio, v. 3)
Porter, Katherine Anne, 3:1460 (Bio, v. 3)
Porter, William Sydney (see O. Henry), 3:1395
　(Bio, v. 3)
Portis, Charles, 3:1464 (Bio, v. 3)
Portnoy's Complaint, 6:3296
Portrait of a Lady, The, 6:3299
Possessed, The, 10:6212
Possessing the Secret of Joy, 6:3309
Possession, 6:3315
Postcards, 7:3846
Postman Always Rings Twice, The, 6:3321
Postmortem, 6:3325
Potok, Chaim, 3:1467 (Bio, v. 3)
Power and the Glory, The, 6:3334
Power Politics, 9:5427
Power That Preserves, The, 2:780
Powers, Richard, 3:1471 (Bio, v. 3)
Praisesong for the Widow, 1:543
Pratchett, Terry, 3:1475 (Bio, v. 3)
Prayer for Owen Meany, A, 6:3340
"Prelude," 6:3344
"Press Enter," 6:3348
Presumed Innocent, 1:557, 6:3352
Pride and Prejudice, 12:335
Prince Caspian, 4:2425
Prince of Foxes, 2:627
Prince of Tides, The, 6:3356
Princess Bride, The, 6:3365
Princess Daisy, 10:6221
Princess of Mars, A, 6:3369
Prisoner's Dilemma, 10:6225
Pritchett (V. S.): Complete Collected Stories
　of, 6:3372
Pritchett, V. S., 3:1478 (Bio, v. 3)
Private Practice of Michael Shayne, The, 6:3381
Prize, The, 6:3385
Prizzi's Honor, 6:3389
Prodigal Daughter, The, 4:2243
Professor Challenger Stories, The, 5:2542
Professor of Desire, The, 1:504
Promise, The, 2:766
Pronto, 6:3392
Proteus, 2:662
Proulx, E. Annie, 3:1484 (Bio, v. 3)
Proust, Marcel, 3:1488 (Bio, v. 3)
Psion, 6:3397
Pubis Angelical, 10:6230

Public Burning, The, 6:3401
Puig, Manuel, 3:1492 (Bio, v. 3)
Puppies of Terra, The, 9:5226
"Purloined Letter, The," 5:2854
Puzo, Mario, 3:1496 (Bio, v. 3)
Pym, Barbara, 3:1499 (Bio, v. 3)
Pynchon, Thomas, 3:1502 (Bio, v. 3)

Q

Q Clearance, 6:3405
Quartet in Autumn, 3:1292
Queen, Ellery, 3:1509 (Bio, v. 3)
Queen of Air and Darkness, The, 6:3409
Queen of the Damned, The, 6:3412
Quest for Saint Camber, The, 4:2289
Quest for the Future, 6:3416
Quicker Than the Eye, 10:6236
Quiet American, The, 6:3419
Quinn, Martin (see Smith, Martin Cruz),
    3:1677 (Bio, v. 3)
Quinn, Simon (see Smith, Martin Cruz),
    3:1677 (Bio, v. 3)
Quinn's Book, 10:6244
Quinx: Or The Ripper's Tale, 1:247

R

Rabbit at Rest, 6:3423
Rabbit Is Rich, 14:337
Rabbit Redux, 6:3427
Rabbit, Run, 14:347
Ragtime, 6:3431, 13:303
"Rain," 6:3435
Rainbow, The, 7:3960, 10:6252
Rainmaker, The, 6:3438, 11:6320
"Raise High the Roof Beam,
    Carpenters," 10:5643
Rampling, Anne (see Rice, Anne), 3:1538
    (Bio, v. 3)
Rand, Ayn, 3:1515 (Bio, v. 3)
Rat, The, 6:3448
Rawlings, Marjorie Kinnan, 3:1518 (Bio, v. 3)
Ray, 6:3452
Razor's Edge, The, 6:3455
Reader, The, 14:357
Rebecca, 6:3458
Rebels, The 2249
Reckless Eyeballing, 6:3461
Recognitions, The, 6:3465
"Red," 10:6272
Recoil, 6:3469
Red Badge of Courage, The, 6:3475
Red Death, A, 6:3481, 8:4636, 9:5614, 10:5946
Red Dragon, 6:3487
Red Harvest, 6:3491
"Red Leaves," 12:37
Red Nails, 6:3497

Red Pony, The, 6:3505
Red Square, 6:3509
Red Storm Rising, 6:3514
Reed, Ishmael, 3:1521 (Bio, v. 3)
Reef, The, 6:3519
Regicide, A, 2:1119
Regulators, The, (as Richard Bachman), 11:6277
Reinhart's Women, 6:3525
Reivers, The, 6:3528
Remains of the Day, The, 6:3532
Remarque, Erich Maria, 3:1526 (Bio, v. 3)
Remembrance of Things Past, 7:4094
Renault, Mary, 3:1531 (Bio, v. 3)
Rendell, Ruth, 3:1534 (Bio, v. 3)
Rendezvous with Rama, 8:4394
Republic of Love, The, 11:6287
Requiem for a Nun, A, 11:6336
Return of Little Big Man, The, 12:345
Return of the Native, The, 12:355
Return of the Soldier, The, 6:3536
Return to Peyton Place, 6:3234
Revolt of Aphrodite, The, 6:3539
Rice, Anne, 3:1538 (Bio, v. 3)
Rich Man, Poor Man, 6:3548
Riddle-Master of Hed, The, 6:3553
Riddley Walker, 6:3558
Riders of the Purple Wage, 6:3568
Riders of the Purple Sage, 6:3562
Right on the Money, 6:3573
Right Stuff, The, 6:3579
Rinehart, Mary Roberts, 3:1542 (Bio, v. 3)
Ringworld, 6:3582
Rising Sun, 9:5043
Rites of Passage Sea Triology, 6:3585
Riverworld Series, 6:3590
Road Back, The, 1:104, 6:3597
Road to Lichfield, The, 6:3600
Road to Omaha, 9:5352
Road to Wellville, The, 6:3607
Robbe-Grillet, Alain, 3:1547 (Bio, v. 3)
Robber Bride, The, 6:3612
Robber Bridegroom, The, 6:3629
Robbins, Harold, 3:1551 (Bio, v. 3)
Robbins, Tom, 3:1555 (Bio, v. 3)
Rock Star, 6:3632
"Rocking Horse Winner, The," 11:6415
Rocksburg Railroad Murders, The, 8:4430
Rogue Queen, 11:6292
Roma Mater, 11:6297
Room of One's Own, A, 6:3135
Roots, 6:3635
Roquelaure, A. N. (see Rice, Anne), 3:1538
    (Bio, v. 3)
Ross, Barnaby (see Queen, Ellery), 3:1509
    (Bio, v. 3)
Rossner, Judith (Perelman), 3:1558 (Bio, v. 3)

Rosy Crucifixion, The, 6:3640
Roth, Philip, 3:1561 (Bio, v. 3)
Rowan, The, 6:3644
Ruark, Robert, 3:1567 (Bio, v. 3)
Rubyfruit Jungle, 6:3650
Rumble, 6:3654
Runaway Jury, The, 11:6312
Running Dog, 3:1250
Rushdie, Salman, 3:1570 (Bio, v. 3)
Russ, Joanna, 3:1576 (Bio, v. 3)
Russia House, The, 6:3658

S
S., 6:3664
Sabatini, Rafael, 3:1580 (Bio, v. 3)
Sabbatical, 7:4244
Sacred Clowns, 6:3668
Sacred Ground, 6:3672
Sacred Journey, The, 3:1715
Sailor Song, 11:6323
Saint-Exupéry, Antoine de, 3:1586 (Bio, v. 3)
Saint Jack, 5:2812
Saint Maybe, 6:3683
Saint-Germain series, 6:3678
Salamander, The, 2:662
Salinger, J. D., 3:1589 (Bio, v. 3)
Salzburg Connection, The, 6:3687
Sanctuary, 6:3691, 11:6328
Sanders, Lawrence, 3:1595 (Bio, v. 3)
Sarraute, Nathalie, 3:1598 (Bio, v. 3)
"Satanic Illusion, The," 11:6339
Satanic Verses, The, 6:3697
Saturday the Rabbi Went Hungry, 6:3702
Save Me, Joe Louis, 6:3707
Saving the Queen, 6:3715
Sayers, Dorothy L., 3:1602 (Bio, v. 3)
Scaramouche, 6:3722
Scarlet Letter, The, 6:3725
Scarlett, 3:1739
Schaefer, Jack, 3:1608 (Bio, v. 3)
Schmitz, James H., 3:1611 (Bio, v. 3)
Schulberg, Budd, 3:1613 (Bio, v. 3)
Schindler's List, 13:313
Sea Wall, The, 6:3730
Sea-Wolf, The, 7:3735
Search for Maggie Ward, 11:6453
Sebastian: Or Ruling Passions, 1:247
Second Chronicles of Amber, The, 7:3738
Second Coming, The, 7:3741
Second Generation, 4:2081
Second Sex, The, 8:4700
Second Skin, 4:2421
Secret Agent, The, 11:6346
"Secret Life of Walter Mitty, The," 7:3744
Secret Pilgrim, The, 7:3750

"Secret Sharer, The," 7:3756
See You Later Alligator, 6:3719
Seekers, The, 4:2249
Segal, Erich, 3:1618 (Bio, v. 3)
Seize the Day, 13:325
Semi-Tough, 7:3759
Semper Fi, 7:3762
Sent For You Yesterday, 7:3765
Separate Peace, A, 7:3771
Serenissima: A Novel of Venice, 3:1355
Sermons and Soda-Water, 7:3777
Serpent and the Staff, The, 3:1546
Servant of the Bones, 12:375
Settle, Mary Lee, 3:1621 (Bio, v. 3)
Seven for a Secret, 7:3780
Seventh Son, 7:3787
Sexus, 6:3640
Shaara, Michael, 3:1625 (Bio, v. 3)
Shadow Knows, The, 7:3790
Shadow Riders, The, 7:3793
Shadows, 7:3796
Shadows in Paradise, 1:192
Shame, 7:3799
Shane, 7:3802
Shardik, 7:3805
Shattered Chain, The, 10:5664
Shaw, Irwin, 3:1628 (Bio, v. 3)
Shaw: Irwin Shaw's Short Fiction, 7:3808
She Came to Stay, 8:4699
Sheldon, Sidney, 3:1633 (Bio, v. 3)
Shellabarger, Samuel, 3:1637 (Bio, v. 3)
Shelley, Mary, 3:1640 (Bio, v. 3)
Shelter, 5:2591, 7:3813
Shepherd of the Hills, The, 7:3821
Shiloh and Other Stories, 7:3825
Shining, The, 7:3829
Shining Through, 7:3834
Ship of Fools, 7:3838
Shipping News, The, 7:3841
Shirley, 11:6354
Shoeless Joe, 7:3849
Shoes of the Fisherman, The, 4:2374
Shogun, 7:3853
"Shout, The," 7:3857
Shroud for a Nightingale, 2:1039
Shute, Nevil, 3:1646 (Bio, v. 3)
Sicilian, The, 3:1711
Siddhartha, 7:3860
Silence of the Lambs, The, 7:3864
Silent Gondoliers, The, 6:3366
Silmarillion, The, 5:2523
Silver Chair, The, 4:2425
Silver Pillow, The, 7:3868
Silverbery, Robert, 3:1650 (Bio, v. 3)
Simenon, Georges, 3:1655 (Bio, v. 3)
Sinclair, Upton, 3:1659 (Bio, v. 3)

Sing Down the Moon, 4:2176, 7:3871
Singer, Isaac Bashevis, 3:1662 (Bio, v. 3)
Singing Guns, 7:3876
Single Pebble, A, 2:593
Sins of the Fathers, 9:5432
Sister Light, Sister Dark, 7:3880, 8:4649
Six of One, 1:382, 6:3652
Sixth Commandment, The, 11:6359
Sjöwal, Maj and Per Wahlöö, 3:1667 (Bio, v. 3)
Skinny Legs and All, 7:3886
Skinwalkers, 7:3889
Slan, 7:3892
Slaughterhouse-Five, 7:3898
Slave, The, 11:6363
"Slave on the Block," 13:333
Sleaze, 1:351
Sleeping Beauty, 7:3901
Slow Waltz in Cedar Bend, 1:530
Small Gods, 7:3904
Small Vice 11:6371
Smiley, Jane, 3:1671 (Bio, v. 3)
Smiley's People, 11:6580
Smith, Betty, 3:1674 (Bio, v. 3)
Smith, Martin Cruz, 3:1677 (Bio, v. 3)
Smith, Rosamond (see Oates, Joyce Carol),
    3:1373 (Bio, v. 3)
Smith, Thorne, 3:1679 (Bio, v. 3)
Snake Eyes, 7:3908
Snow Falling on Cedars, 11:6379
Snow in August, 11:6398
Snow Queen, The, 7:3911
Snow White, 7:3915
Solar Barque, 2:807
Soldier Boy, 7:3918
Solzhenitsyn, Aleksandr, 3:1682 (Bio, v. 3)
Some Can Whistle, 7:4149
Some Other Place. The Right Place., 10:5914
Some Tame Gazelle, 3:1291
Something Happened, 7:3921
Something in the Air, 7:3927
Something of Value, 7:3931
Something to Be Desired, 4:2247
Something Wicked This Way Comes, 7:3935
Sometimes a Great Notion, 7:3939
Son of the Circus, A, 7:3945
Song of Solomon, 7:3949
Sons, 4:2020
Sons and Lovers, 3957, 11:6405
Sophie's Choice, 7:3962
Sot-Weed Factor, The, 7:3968
Sound and the Fury, The, 12:379
South Moon Under, 7:3971
Southern Cross, 14:365
Southern Exposure, A, 10:6076, 11:6460
Southern Family, A, 11:6420
Southern, Terry, 3:1688 (Bio, v. 3)

Spartacus, 7:3974
Sphere, 7:3978
Spillane, Mickey, 3:1691 (Bio, v. 3)
Spinrad, Norman, 3:1696 (Bio, v. 3)
"Spinster's Tale, A," 13:341
Spire, The, 7:3981
Sportswriter, The, 10:5719, 13:349
Spring Moon, 7:3983
Spy in the House of Love, A, 2:807
Spy Line, 7:3989
Spy Who Came in from the Cold, The, 7:3996
Square, The, 7:3999
Stab in the Dark, A, 9:5432
Stallion Gate, 7:4002
Stanley Elkin's The Magic Kingdom, 7:4006
Star Gate, 7:4011
Star of Gypsies, 11:6427
Stark, Richard (see Westlake, Donald), 3:1944
    (Bio, v. 3)
Stars My Destination, The, 7:4014
Stars Shine Down, The, 7:4019
Steel, Danielle, 3:1700 (Bio, v. 3)
Steel: Novels of Danielle, The, 7:4023
Steep Ascent, 7:4032
Stegner, Wallace, 3:1703 (Bio, v. 3)
Steinbeck, John, 3:1709 (Bio, v. 3)
Steppenwolf, 12:391
Steps, 7:4035
Stevenson, Robert Louis, 3:1716 (Bio, v. 3)
Stewart, Mary, 3:1723 (Bio, v. 3)
Still Life, 9:5135
Stoker, Bram, 3:1726 (Bio, v. 3)
Stone Diaries, The, 11:6433
Stone for Danny Fisher, A, 7:4040
Stone, Irving, 3:1731 (Bio, v. 3)
Stone, Robert, 3:1736 (Bio, v. 3)
Stones from the River, 13:353
Stones of Nomuru, The, 11:6442
Stories of Bernard Malamud, The, 5:2616
Stories of John Cheever, The, 2:733
Story of Henri Tod, 6:3719
Story of My Life, 1:535, 7:4045
Stout, Rex, 3:1741 (Bio, v. 3)
Straight, 7:4048
Strange Case of Dr. Jekyll and Mr. Hyde, The,
4055
Strange Relations, 5:2576
Stranger in a Strange Land, 7:4062
Stranger, The, 7:4059
Straub, Peter, 3:1744 (Bio, v. 3)
Streams to the River, 4:2176
Street, The, 7:4065
Striding Folly, 2:572
Strong Medicine, 7:4069
Strong Position, 2:570
Studs Lonigan Trilogy, The, 7:4072

Summer before the Dark, The, 13:361
Sturgeon Is Alive and Well, 3:1228
Sturgeon, Theodore, 3:1746 (Bio, v. 3)
Styron, William, 3:1750 (Bio, v. 3)
Succession, The, 2:1050
Sudden Mischief, 12:397
Sum of All Fears, The, 4:2041
Summer at the Lake, 11:6447
Summer Queen, 7:3913
Summons to Memphis, A, 7:4078
Sun Also Rises, The, 7:4081
Sun He Dies, The, 1:167
Superior Women, 11:6454
Surfacing, 11:6462
Susann, Jacqueline, 3:1761 (Bio, v. 3)
Süskind, Patrick, 3:1766 (Bio, v. 3)
Suttree, 7:4087
Swann's Way, 7:4091
Sweet Dove Died, The, 3:1290
Swiftly Tilting Planet, A, 8:4731

T

Tabloid Dreams, 11:6470
Taipan, 7:3855
Tales from Margaritaville, 8:4615
Tales from Watership Down, 8:4549
Tales of Burning Love, 5:2560, 11:6482
Tales of the South Pacific, 7:4097
Talking God, 7:4102
Taming the Star Runner, 7:4105
Tan, Amy, 3:1772 (Bio, v. 3)
Tango Charlie and Foxtrot Romeo, 7:4108
Taran Wanderer, 1:391
Tarkington, Booth, 3:1776 (Bio, v. 3)
Tarnsman of Gor, 5:2603
Tarr, Judith, 3:1780 (Bio, v. 3)
Tarzan Alive, 7:4113
Tarzan of the Apes, 7:4120
Taste for Death, A, 2:1090, 7:4128
Taste for Violence, A, 6:3382
Taylor, Peter, 3:1783 (Bio, v. 3)
"Tell-Tale Heart, The," 7:4132
Telling the Truth, 3:1715
Telzey Toy, The, 8:4419
Temple of My Familiar, The, 7:4136
Ten Little Indians, 13:367
Ten North Frederick, 7:4142
Tender Is the Night, 7:4145
Tenderness, 11:6491
Terminal Man, The, 9:5086
Terms of Endearment, 7:4148
Terrorists, The, 7:4151
Tess of the D'Urbervilles: A Pure
    Woman, 11:6496
Tex, 7:4158

Texasville, 10:5840
Thanatos Syndrome, The, 14:375
That Hideous Strength, 6:3161
"That Evening Sun," 12:37
them, 11:6512
Thendara House, 11:6516
There Was a Little Girl, 7:4161
Theroux, Paul, 3:1786 (Bio, v. 3)
These High, Green Hills, 11:6520
They All Ran After the President's Wife, 11:6531
They Shall Have Stars, 2:799
They Whisper, 7:4166
Thief Who Couldn't Sleep, The, 7:4172
Thin Air, 7:4175
Thin Man, The, 5:2624
Thin Red Line, The, 3:1581
Things Fall Apart, 7:4180
Thinking Reed, The, 7:4189
Third Life of Grange Copeland, The, 11:6538
Thirst for Love, 7:4192
This Freedom, 4:2077
This Side of Paradise, 7:4197
This Year It Will Be Different: And Other
    Stories, 11:6552
Thomas, D. M., 3:1790 (Bio, v. 3)
Thompson, Hunter S., 3:1793 (Bio, v. 3)
Thompson, Jim, 3:1796 (Bio, v. 3)
Thompson Travel Agency, The, 9:5094
Thorn Birds, The, 7:4200
Thornyhold, 7:4204
Those Bones Are Not My Child, 14:385
Thousand Acres, A, 7:4208
3001: The Final Odyssey, 11:6558
Three Corvettes, 2:959
Three Farmers on Their Way to a Dance, 7:4214
Three Guineas, 6:3135
Three Stigmas of Palmer Eldritch, The, 5:2676
Thunder Rolling in the Mountains, 7:4218
Thunderball, 7:4222
Thurber, James, 3:1803 (Bio, v. 3)
Thursday's Children, 6:3216
Thy Brother's Wife, 7:4225
Ticket to the Boneyard, A, 7:4230
Tidewater Morning, A, 7:4233
Tidewater Tales, The, 7:4238
Tight White Collar, 11:6570
Till We Have Faces, 7:4246
Till We Meet Again, 7:4249
Time and Again, 7:4254
Time for Remembering, A, 6:3331
Time Machine, The, 7:4257
Time of the Hero, 2:910
Time to Kill, A, 7:4265
Time to Murder and Create, A, 9:5432
Timeline, 14:397
Timescape, 11:6574

Tin Drum, The, 7:4276
Tinker, Tailor, Soldier, Spy, 11:6578
To Have and Have Not, 14:405
To Kill a Mockingbird, 7:4280
To Sail Beyond the Sunset, 7:4289
To Say Nothing of the Dog, 14:415
To the Hilt, 11:6584
To the Lighthouse, 7:4286
To The White Sea, 7:4294
Tobacco Road, 3:1725
Tolkien, J. R. R., 3:1809 (Bio, v. 3)
Tomorrow Will Be Better, 7:4342
Too Late the Phalarope, 7:4299
Too Many Cooks, 7:4305
Too Many Magicians, 7:4310
Toole, John Kennedy, 3:1817 (Bio, v. 3)
Topper, 7:4316
Torrent, The, 7:4320
Tough Guys Don't Dance, 7:4323
Toward the End of Time, 12:421
Tracks, 7:4326
Trader to the Stars, 7:4329
Treasure Hunt, 1:475
Treasure Island, 7:4335
Tree Grows in Brooklyn, A, 7:4339
Trial of God, The, 9:5019
Trial, The, 7:4344
Trimmed Lamp, The, 3:1534
Tripmaster Monkey: His Fake Book, 7:4348
Triton, 2:1102
Triumph of Time, The, 2:799
Tropic of Cancer, 7:4353
Tropic of Capricorn, 7:4356
Tropisms, 6:3280
Trout Fishing in America, 8:4359
True at First Light, 14:423
True Grit, 8:4362
Trust, 8:4367
Truth about Lorin Jones, The, 8:4371
Tryon, Thomas, 3:1819 (Bio, v. 3)
Tunc, 6:3539
Turmoil, The, 10:6017
Turn of the Screw, The, 8:4375
Turnabout, 7:4318
Turow, Scott, 3:1822 (Bio, v. 3)
Twain, Mark, 3:1826 (Bio, v. 3)
Twenty Thousand Leagues Under the Sea, 11:6593
Twinkle, Twinkle, "Killer" Kane, 10:6124
"Two Kinds," 12:439
2001: A Space Odyssey, 8:4392
2010: Odyssey Two, 8:4394
2061: Odyssey Three, 11:6601
Two of Them, The, 8:4385
Two Sisters, 8:4389
Tyler, Anne, 3:1839 (Bio, v. 3)

Typhoon, 11:6606

U
Uhuru, 7:3934
Unbearable Lightness of Being, The, 8:4397
Uncle Tom's Cabin, 13:375
Uncle Tom's Children, 8:4401
Uncollected Stories of William Faulkner, 3:1378
Unconditional Surrender, 5:2721
Under the Volcano, 8:4405
Underworld, 12:445
Universal Baseball Association, The, 8:4412
Universe Against Her, The, 8:4417
Unnatural Causes, 2:1039
Unnatural Death, 2:854
Unnatural Exposure, 11:6613
Unsuitable Attachment, An, 3:1292
Unvanquished, The, 11:6622
Unwise Child, 8:4421
Updike, John, 3:1844 (Bio, v. 3)
Upon Some Midnights Clear, 8:4426
Uris, Leon, 3:1849 (Bio, v. 3)

V
V., 8:4432
Vagabond, The, 8:4437
Valley of the Dolls, 8:4442
Vampire Lestat, The, 4:2142, 8:4447
Van Vogt, A. E., 3:1855 (Bio, v. 3)
Vanderhaeghe, Guy, 3:1852 (Bio, v. 3)
Vargas Llosa, Mario, 3:1859 (Bio, v. 3)
Varley, John, 3:1863 (Bio, v. 3)
Veiled One, The, 8:4451
Venus Envy, 11:6634
Very Old Bones, 8:4456
"Very Old Man with Enormous Wings, A," 13:385
"Veteran, The," 6:3479
Victories, 8:4367
Victory, 11:6640
Victory Over Japan, 4:2106
Vida, 8:4465
Vidal, Gore, 3:1865 (Bio, v. 3)
Villette, 11:6651
Vine, Barbara (see Rendell, Ruth), 3:1534 (Bio, v. 3)
Vineland, 8:4468
Vinge, Joan D., 3:1869 (Bio, v. 3)
Violent Bear It Away, The, 8:4689
Virgin in the Garden, The, 8:4472
Virginian, The, 8:4476
Virtual Light, 8:4480
Virtuous Woman, A, 13:395
Vonnegut, Kurt, 3:1873 (Bio, v. 3)

Voyage of the Dawn Treader, 4:2425

W

Wahlöö, Per (see Maj Sjöwal), 3:1667
  (Bio, v. 3)
Waiting for the End of the World, 8:4485
Waiting to Exhale, 8:4494
Walk to the End of the World, 8:4506
Walker, Alice, 3:1878 (Bio, v. 3)
Wall, The, 11:6658
Wallace, Irving, 3:1889 (Bio, v. 3)
Waller, Robert, 3:1893 (Bio, v. 3)
"Waltz, The," 11:6665
Wambaugh, Jr., Joseph, 3:1898 (Bio, v. 3)
Wapshot Chronicle, The, 8:4509
Wapshot Scandal, The, 8:4511
War, 8:4513
War and Remembrance, 8:4517
War of the Worlds, The, 8:4521
War with the Newts, 13:411
Warren, Robert Penn, 3:1901 (Bio, v. 3)
Washington Square Ensemble, The, 8:4526
Water Is Wide, The, 8:4535
Water Music, 8:4542
Watership Down, 8:4547
Waterworks, The, 8:4551
Waugh, Evelyn, 3:1910 (Bio, v. 3)
Way to Rainy Mountain, The, 4:2018
"Way We Live Now, The," 14:437
We Are Still Married, 8:4554
We Were the Mulvaneys, 11:6670
We'll Meet Again, 13:421
Wells, H. G., 3:1915 (Bio, v. 3)
Welty, Eudora, 3:1923 (Bio, v. 3)
West, Morris, 3:1931 (Bio, v. 3)
West, Nathanael, 3:1934 (Bio, v. 3)
West, Rebecca, 3:1938 (Bio, v. 3)
Western Lands, The, 8:4557
Westlake, Donald E., 3:1944 (Bio, v. 3)
Wharton, Edith, 3:1949 (Bio, v. 3)
"What I Have Been Doing Lately," 12:463
What I Lived For, 11:6676
What Looks Like Crazy on an Ordinary
  Day, 13:431
What Makes Sammy Run?, 8:4564
What Was Mine, 8:4570
What We Talk About When We Talk About
  Love, 8:4576
What's Bred in the Bone, 8:4579
When a Man's a Man, 8:4686
"When It Changed," 8:4589
When the Sacred Ginmill Closes, 9:5433
Where Are the Children?, 8:4600
Where I'm Calling From, 8:4608
Where Is Joe Merchant?, 8:4611
Where the Air Is Clear, 8:4593

Where You'll Find Me, 6:3256
Whip Hand, 7:4051
Whipping Star, 8:4619
Whirlwind, 8:4622
Whistle, 3:1582
Whistlejacket, 8:4625
White Butterfly, 8:4632
White Fang, 8:4639
White Hotel, The, 8:4642
White Jenna, 8:4646
White Noise, 8:4651
White Oleander, 14:443
White Shark, 8:4654, 9:5160
White, T. H., 3:1955 (Bio, v. 3)
Whitewater, 8:4658
Who Do You Think You Are? (see *The Beggar*
  Maid), 1:305
Who's on First, 6:3718
Whose Body, 2:853
"Why I Live at the P.O.," 8:4661
Wicked Day, The, 11:6682
Wideman, John Edgar, 4:1958 (Bio, v. 3)
Wild Seed, 8:4663
Wilderness Tips, 11:6688
Wind Over Wisconsin, 8:4668
Wind, Sand and Stars, 8:4673
Winds of War, The, 8:4677
Winesburg, Ohio, 8:4681
Winning of Barbara Worth, The, 8:4684
Wise Blood, 8:4687, 13:437
Wishful Thinking, 3:1714
Wister, Owen, 3:1961 (Bio, v. 3)
Witch World, 11:6697
Witches of Eastwick, The, 11:6704
Witches of Karres, The, 8:4691
Witching Hour, The, 8:4693
Wolfe, Thomas, 3:1964 (Bio, v. 3)
Wolfe, Tom, 3:1968 (Bio, v. 3)
Woman Destroyed, A, 8:4698
"Woman Hollering Creek," 13:445
Woman Warrior, The, 8:4702
Women in Love, 7:3960
Women of Brewster Place, The, 14:449
Women's Room, The, 4:1897, 8:4706
Wonderful Years, Wonderful Years, 11:6712
Woodrow Wilson Dime, The, 7:4256
Woolf, Virginia, 3:1974 (Bio, v. 3)
Word, The, 5:2752
Work: A Story of Experience, 11:6717
World According to Garp, The, 11:6725
World Between, A, 8:4709
World Enough and Time, 8:4714
World of Null-A, The, 8:4717
World of Ptavvs, 8:4722
World's End, 7:3913 (Joan Vinge)
World's End, 8:4725 (T. C. Boyle)

World's Fair, 11:6730
Wouk, Herman, 3:1985 (Bio, v. 3)
Wright, Harold Bell, 3:1989 (Bio, v. 3)
Wright, Richard, 3:1993 (Bio, v. 3)
Wrinkle in Time, A, 8:4729
Wuthering Heights, 8:4733

Y

Yarbro, Chelsea Quinn, 3:1999 (Bio, v. 3)
Yearling, The, 8:4738
"Yellow Woman," 12:469
Yerby, Frank G., 3:2003 (Bio, v. 3)
Yolen, Jane, 3:2008 (Bio, v. 3)
You Know Me Al, 8:4743

You Must Remember This, 11:6679
"Young Goodman Brown," 8:4746
Young Lions, The, 8:4750
Young Lonigan, 7:4072
Young Manhood of Studs Lonigan, The 7:4072
Yourcenar, Marguerite, 3:2012 (Bio, v. 3)
"Youth," 4:1886, 11:6734

Z

Zahn, Timothy, 3:2016 (Bio, v. 3)
Zelanzy, Roger, 3:2019 (Bio, v. 3)
Zia, 4:2176
Zorba the Greek, 8:4755